EMERGING

CONTEMPORARY READINGS FOR WRITERS

EMERGING

CONTEMPORARY READINGS FOR WRITERS

SECOND EDITION

BARCLAY BARRIOS
Florida Atlantic University

BEDFORD/ST. MARTIN'S
Boston ◆ New York

For Bedford/St. Martin's

Senior Executive Editor: Leasa Burton
Executive Editor: John E. Sullivan III
Senior Production Editor: Gregory Erb
Senior Production Supervisor: Jennifer Peterson
Executive Marketing Manager: Molly Parke
Associate Editor: Alyssa Demirjian
Copy Editor: Jennifer S. Brett Greenstein
Photo Researcher: Susan Doheny
Permissions Manager: Kalina K. Ingham
Senior Art Director: Anna Palchik
Text Design: Jean Hammond
Cover Design: Marine Miller
Cover Photo: Cara Barer, *Carousel*, 2007
Composition: Achorn International, Inc.
Printing and Binding: RR Donnelley and Sons

President, Bedford/St. Martin's: Denise B. Wydra
Presidents, Macmillan Higher Education: Joan E. Feinberg and Tom Scotty
Editor in Chief: Karen S. Henry
Director of Marketing: Karen R. Soeltz
Production Director: Susan W. Brown
Associate Production Director: Elise S. Kaiser
Managing Editor: Elizabeth M. Schaaf

Manufactured in the United States of America.

7   6   5   4   3
f   e   d   c   b

For information, write: Bedford/St. Martin's, 75 Arlington Street, Boston, MA 02116
(617-399-4000)

ISBN 978–1–4576–0197–2

Acknowledgments

Arwa Aburawa, "Veiled Threat: The Guerrilla Graffiti of Princess Hijab," from bitchmedia.com is reprinted by permission of Bitch Media.

Acknowledgments and copyrights are continued at the back of the book on pages 593–97, which constitute an extension of the copyright page. It is a violation of the law to reproduce these selections by any means whatsoever without the written permission of the copyright holder.

PREFACE FOR INSTRUCTORS

Emerging/Thinking

One of the fundamental facts of teaching writing is that when students leave our class-rooms, they go back to their increasingly busy lives: They go to other classes, go to their jobs after school, go hang out with friends, go into their disciplines, go into their careers, go into the world. The challenge for us as instructors is to help students acquire the skills of critical reading, thinking, and writing that will allow them to succeed in these diverse contexts.

Emerging seeks to address this challenge. It offers sustained readings that present complex ideas in approachable language; it encourages critical thinking and writing skills by prompting students to make connections among readings; it draws from a broad cross section of themes and disciplines in order to present students with numer-ous points of entry and identification; and it introduces emerging problems — such as cultural conflict (in social and linguistic dimensions), the impact of technology (from Wikipedia to brain science), race and social rights (such as conflicts between individu-als and groups), and the dilemmas of ethics (concerns about genetic engineering, for instance, and the relations between religion and foreign politics) — that have not yet been solved and settled.

The readings are organized alphabetically to open up possibilities for connections. (Alternative tables of contents highlight thematic clusters and paired selections.) The table of contents includes both the readings in the text and the readings online as e-Pages. Because they consist of entire book chapters or complete articles, readings can stand on their own as originally intended. However, the readings in *Emerging* were cho-sen because they connect to each other in interesting and illuminating ways. The issues under discussion resonate across readings, genres, and disciplines, prompting students to think about each selection in multiple dimensions. These resonant connections are shown through "tags" indicating central concepts treated in the selections. About a half-dozen tags for each piece are listed in the table of contents, in each headnote, and for each assignment sequence — highlighting concepts such as "community," "diver-sity," "identity," "culture," and "technology." Thus one can see at a glance the possi-bilities for thematic connections among the readings. Connections are also highlighted through the assignment sequences (included at the back of the book; see p. 563). The assignment sequences suggest a succession of readings that are linked conceptually so that one assignment sequence provides the structure for an entire semester. (Sequences are further explained below.)

Emerging/Reading

Because students ultimately enter diverse disciplines, the readings are drawn from across fields of knowledge located both inside and outside the academy. Political sci-ence, sociology, journalism, anthropology, economics, advertising, and art are some of the disciplines one might expect to find in such a collection, but *Emerging* also includes readings from diplomacy, public health, psychology, business, philosophy, neurology, transportation, technology, and law. The author of each selection addresses his or her concerns to an audience outside the discipline—a useful model for students who eventually will need to communicate beyond the boundaries of their chosen fields. Many of the readings also represent cross-disciplinary work—an economist thinking about politics, an anthropologist thinking about education—since the walls between departments in academia are becoming increasingly permeable.

Yet despite this disciplinary grounding, the readings, though challenging, are accessible, written as they are with a general audience in mind. The readings thus demonstrate multiple ways in which complex ideas and issues can be presented in formal yet approachable language. The accessible nature of the essays also allows for many readings longer than those typically seen in first-year composition anthologies, because the level of writing makes them comprehensible to students. Yet even the briefer readings are substantive, providing greater opportunities for nuanced arguments.

Of course, in addition to referencing emerging issues, the title of this collection refers also to the students in first-year composition courses who themselves are emerging as readers, thinkers, and writers. By providing them with challenging texts along with the tools needed to decode, interpret, and deploy those texts, *Emerging* helps college readers to develop the skills they will need as they move into working with the difficult theoretical texts presented in their choice of majors—and ultimately into their twenty-first-century careers.

Emerging/Writing

One of the philosophical tenets supporting *Emerging* is that students need to be prepared to deal with emerging issues in their jobs and lives, and to do so, they not only require information about those issues (since such information will continually change) but also must possess an ability to think critically in relation to them. The editorial apparatus in *Emerging* includes the following features that will help students develop the skills needed to become fluid, reflective, and critically self-aware writers:

▶ **General Introduction.** The introduction presents key skills of academic success: the ability to read critically, argue, use evidence, and revise.

▶ **Assignment Sequences.** In order to stress the iterative processes of thinking and writing, nine assignment sequences are included in the back of the book, each of which uses multiple selections—both in print and in e-Pages—to engage students' thinking about a central theme, issue, or problem. Each sequence frames a project extensive enough for an entire semester's work and can be easily adapted for individual classes.

Additionally, apparatus accompanying each reading provides substantial help for students while featuring innovative approaches to understanding the essays and their relation to the world outside the classroom:

▶ **Headnotes.** A headnote preceding each reading selection provides biographical information about the author and describes the context of the larger work from which the reading has been taken.

▶ **Questions for Critical Reading.** These questions at the start of each reading direct students to central concepts, issues, and ideas from the essay in order to prompt a directed rereading of the text while providing a guide for the student's own interpretive moves.

▶ **Exploring Context.** In order to leverage students' existing literacies with digital technologies, these questions ask students to use the Web and other electronic sources to contextualize each reading further, using sites and tools such as Facebook and Twitter.

▶ **Questions for Connecting.** Because thinking across essays provides particular circumstances for critical thinking, these opportunities for writing ask students to make connections between essays and to apply and synthesize authors' ideas. Questions that connect selections in the print book to e-Pages online are marked "connecting to e-Pages."

▶ **Language Matters.** The Language Matters questions are a unique feature of this reader. These questions address issues of grammar and writing through the context of the essays, presenting language not as a set of rules to be memorized but as a system of meaning-making that can also be used as a tool for analysis.

▶ **Assignments for Writing.** Each reading has three Assignments for Writing questions that ask students to build on the work they've done in the other questions of the apparatus and create a piece of writing with a sustained argument supported by textual engagement.

What's New

New readings on a wider variety of topics. Nearly thirty selections are new, both in print and online in e-Pages, broadening the range of topics in *Emerging*. And in response to reviewer requests, these include a dozen brief, accessible selections, and new images. Authors of the readings include public intellectuals, many with familiar names. For instance, Elizabeth Dickinson examines the world's ability to feed its growing population in an infographic essay, "The Future of Food"; Daniel Gilbert looks at wealth and happiness in "Reporting Live from Tomorrow"; Malcolm Gladwell examines the weak ties promoted by social networking in "Small Change"; and Alexandra Samuel considers the ethics of online life in "'Plug In Better': A Manifesto" (in e-Pages). Additionally, new image portfolios add a visual perspective: Visual selections include paintings by Steve Mumford of American soldiers in Afghanistan and PostSecret postcards.

   e-Pages — online multimodal selections — present intriguing options. Videos, images, infographics, reportage, and text essays provide the kinds of selections possible only online, for a new generation of composition reader. Selections in e-Pages include a multimedia report on the dangerous Chinese factories where iPads are made, featuring text, video, photographs, and a graph; a video report on a video game the U.S. Army uses to train its soldiers; interesting and informative infographics; and more. For a complete list of e-Pages, see the table of contents. Instructors can also use the free tools accompanying the e-Pages to upload a syllabus, readings, and assignments to share with the class.

You and your students can access the e-Pages from a tab on the Student Site for *Emerging* at **bedfordstmartins.com/emerging/epages**. Students receive access automatically with the purchase of a new book. If the activation code printed on the inside front cover of the student edition has already been revealed and is expired, students can purchase access at the Student Site. Instructors receive access information in a separate e-mail and can also log in or request access information at the Student Site.

More help with academic writing and critical thinking. A revised introduction includes additional student writing samples, new coverage of visual analysis, and more on academic argument and citation. In order to help provide more context for students, prereading questions and gloss notes have been added throughout.

More options for ways to teach *Emerging*. Updated assignment sequences provide compelling ways to structure a course by modeling the practice of intellectual inquiry and open-ended synthesis. Sequences now have assignments marked "analyze," "connect," "synthesize," and "emerge" in order to show more clearly the kind of work that students are being asked to do. Alternative thematic tables of contents show connections between and among readings by pairs and by themes in order to offer additional ways to connect readings and plan a course.

You Get More Choices with *Emerging*

Emerging doesn't stop with a book. Online, you'll find both free and affordable premium resources to help students get even more out of the book and your course. You'll also find convenient instructor resources, such as downloadable sample syllabi, classroom activities, and even a nationwide community of teachers. To learn more about or order any of the products below, contact your sales representative, e-mail sales support (sales_support@bfwpub.com), or visit bedfordstmartins.com.

Student Site *for* Emerging

bedfordstmartins.com/emerging
Send students to free and open resources, choose flexible premium resources to supplement your print text, or upgrade to an expanding collection of innovative digital content. Access to e-Pages is also available from the student site.

Free and open resources for *Emerging* provide students with easy-to-access reference materials, visual tutorials, and support for working with sources.

- five free videos of real writers from *VideoCentral*
- three free tutorials from *ix visual exercises* by Cheryl Ball and Kristin Arola
- *TopLinks* and *AuthorLinks* with reliable online sources
- *Research and Documentation Online* by Diana Hacker
- *Bedford Bibliographer*: a tool for collecting source information and making a bibliography in MLA, APA, and *Chicago* styles

Re:Writing Plus gathers all of Bedford/St. Martin's premium digital content for composition into one online collection. It includes hundreds of model documents, the first-ever peer review game, and *VideoCentral* and i-cite: visualizing sources. *Re:Writing Plus* can be purchased separately or packaged with the print book at a significant discount. An activation code is required. To order *Re:Writing Plus* packaged with the print book, use ISBN 978-1-4576-0620-5. *ix visualizing composition 2.0* (available online) helps students put into practice key rhetorical and visual concepts. To order *ix visualizing composition* packaged with the print book, use ISBN 978-1-4576-0619-9. *i-claim: visualizing argument 2.0* (available online) offers a new way to see argument—with six tutorials, an illustrated glossary, and over seventy multimedia arguments. To order *i-claim: visualizing argument* packaged with the print book, use ISBN 978-1-4576-0621-2. *i-cite: visualizing sources* (available online as part of *Re:Writing Plus*) brings research to life through an animated introduction, four tutorials, and hands-on source practice. To order *i-cite: visualizing sources* packaged with the print book, use ISBN 978-1-4576-0611-3.

Packaging a handbook saves money for your students

Emerging can be combined with a Bedford/St. Martin's handbook for a 20% discount.

- *Easy Writer* use package ISBN 978-1-4576-4847-2.
- *Everyday Writer* use package ISBN 978-1-4576-4845-8.
- *A Pocket Style Manual* use package ISBN 978-1-4576-4848-9.
- *A Writer's Reference* use package ISBN 978-1-4576-4844-1.

You can also package *Emerging* with **Portfolio Keeping** at a 20% discount. Use package ISBN 978-1-4576-4846-5.

Instructor Resources

You have a lot to do in your course. Bedford/St. Martin's wants to make it easy for you to find the support you need—and to get it quickly.

The ***Instructor's Manual for* Emerging** is available as a PDF that can be downloaded from bedfordstmartins.com/emerging/catalog. In addition to selection overviews and teaching tips, the Instructor's Manual includes sample syllabi and suggestions for classroom activities.

Teaching Central (bedfordstmartins.com/teachingcentral) offers the entire list of Bedford/St. Martin's print and online professional resources in one place. You'll find landmark reference works, sourcebooks on pedagogical issues, award-winning collections, and practical advice for the classroom—all free for instructors.

Bits (bedfordbits.com) collects creative ideas for teaching a range of composition topics in an easily searchable blog. A community of teachers—including Barclay Barrios—leading scholars, authors, and editors—discuss revision, research, grammar and style, technology, peer review, and much more. Take, use, adapt, and pass the ideas around. Then come back to the site to comment or share your own suggestion.

Bedford Coursepacks allow you to easily integrate our most popular content into your own course management systems. For details, visit bedfordstmartins.com/coursepacks.

Acknowledgments

This collection itself has been a long time emerging, and I would be remiss not to thank the many people who contributed their time, energy, feedback, and support throughout the course of this project.

I would first like to acknowledge past and current colleagues who have played a role in developing this text. Richard E. Miller and Kurt Spellmeyer, both of Rutgers University, through their mentorship and guidance laid the foundations for my approach to composition as reflected in this reader. My department chairs during my time here at Florida Atlantic University, Andrew Furman and Wenying Xu, provided reassurance and support as I balanced the work of this text and the work of serving as Director of Writing Programs. The members of the Writing Committee for Florida Atlantic University's Department of English—Jeff Galin, Joanne Jasin, Jennifer Low, Julia Mason, Daniel Murtaugh, and Magdalena Ostas—generously allowed me to shape both this reader and the writing program. The dean's office of the Dorothy F. Schmidt College of Arts and Letters of Florida Atlantic University provided a Summer Teaching Development Award, which aided in the creation of the materials that form the core of the Instructor's Manual.

This second edition was made possible by the relentless work of a large group of teachers at Florida Atlantic University. I'd like to thank members of the "E-Beta Team": Amanda Dutton—for helping locate new readings—and Beau Ewan, Tiffany Frost, Erin Hobbie, Mary Ann Hogan, Michael Linder, Mary Long, Michelle Maher, Jeanette Moffa, Kimberly Pekala, Simone Puleo, and Emilija Stanic for finding new readings, class-testing them, and contributing assignments.

Nicole Oquendo, as my research assistant, worked long and hard under a tight deadline to finish the final manuscript. Michelle Hasler and Ashley Harrington were exceptionally helpful, going above and beyond all of my expectations by finding new readings, testing them, writing assignments, composing headnotes, and contributing to the Instructor's Manual. I could not have completed this project without them.

More than anyone else, though, I must thank my assistant Mike Shier, who helped with every facet of this edition, handled all the details that threatened to overwhelm me, and kept me sane all the while. He never said no when I asked him to take on extra work for the book and somehow managed to help me get everything done while completing his degree.

I am also grateful to the reviewers who examined the manuscript of the first edition and provided valuable feedback: Sonja Andrus, Collin County Community College; Susan Bailor, Front Range Community College; Barbara Booker, Pasco-Hernando Community College; Patricia Webb Boyd, Arizona State University; John Champagne, Penn State Erie, The Behrend College; Michael Cripps, York College/CUNY; Brock Dethier, Utah State University; Kimberly Harrison, Florida International University; Karen Head, The Georgia Institute of Technology; Virginia Scott Hendrickson, Missouri State University; Lindsay Lewan, Arapahoe Community College; April Lewandowski, Front Range Community College–Westminster; Gina Maranto, University of Miami; Erica Messenger, Bowling Green State University–Main Campus; Beverly Neiderman, Kent State University; Jill Onega, Calhoun Community College; Roberta Stagnaro, San Diego State University; and Melora G. Vandersluis, Azusa Pacific University.

I am grateful as well to the reviewers who helped shape the second edition: Lena Ampadu, Towson University; John Barbour, University of Kentucky; Aaron Barrell, Everett Community College; Bridgett Blaque, Truckee Meadows Community College; Barbara B. Booker, Pasco-Hernando Community College; Patricia Boyd, Arizona State University; Sonya C. Brown, Fayetteville State University; Sakina Bryant, Sonoma State University; Michael J. Cripps, University of New England; Sarah Duerden, Arizona State University; Rebecca Gerdes, Indiana University South Bend; Rachael Groner, Temple University; Barbara E. Hamilton, Montclair State University; Susanmarie Harrington, University of Vermont; D. Alexis Hart, Virginia Military Institute; Elaine Hays, College of the Holy Cross; Wendy Hinshaw, Florida Atlantic University; Charlotte Hogg, Texas Christian University; M. Kamel Igoudjil, American University; Thomas Irwin, University of Missouri, St. Louis; Carol M. Lane, California State University, Chico; Kerry K. Lawson, Indiana University South Bend; Amy Letter, Florida Atlantic University; Lindsay Lewan, Arapahoe Community College; Gina Maranto, University of Miami; Margaret McBride, University of Oregon; Alisea Williams McLeod, Indiana University South Bend; Julia Mendenhall, Temple University; Scott Orme, Spokane Community College; Nancy Paris, Indiana University; Susan Piqueira, Central Connecticut State University; Spencer Schaffner, University of Illinois; Allison D. Smith, Middle Tennessee State University; LuAnn Sorenson, University of Illinois–Urbana-Champaign; Brian Spears, Florida Atlantic University; Christopher L. Stockdale, Sonoma State University; Christopher Walters, Normandale Community College and Jeff Wheeler, Long Beach City College.

I cannot say enough about the support I have received from Bedford/St. Martin's. Joan Feinberg's enthusiasm for this project was always appreciated, as was that shown by Denise Wydra, Karen Henry, and Leasa Burton. And my editor John Sullivan patiently pushed me to make the best book possible and provided vital encouragement whenever my spirits drooped. Thanks, too, to Alyssa Demirjian for getting to me what I needed when I needed it. I am grateful to Margaret Gorenstein for clearing text permissions and to Susan Doheny for obtaining art and e-Pages permissions. Greg Erb expertly guided the manuscript through production, assisted by copy editor Jennifer Greenstein. I appreciate their help.

Finally, a special thanks to those who kept me centered and strong, most especially my partner, Joseph Tocio, who offered not only love and support but a compelling reason to be in Boston so that I could meet with the publisher. I offer this edition in loving memory of my mother, Elaine Montalbano Barrios.

CONTENTS

THE READINGS

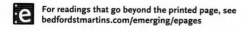 **For readings that go beyond the printed page, see**
bedfordstmartins.com/emerging/epages

bedfordstmartins.com/emerging/epages

girl they know rather than the most accomplished. "Women who've wanted to be perceived as powerful have long found it more efficient to identify with men than to try and elevate the entire female sex to their level."

▶ TAGS: *Female Chauvinist Pig, loophole woman, gender, girly-girl, feminism, Tomming*

bedfordstmartins.com/emerging/epages

ASSIGNMENT SEQUENCES

 bedfordstmartins.com/emerging/epages

Fire 🄴 • **Jayme Poisson**, Parents Keep Child's Gender Secret • **PostSecret**, Portfolio of Postcards • **Mara Hvistendahl**, Missing: 163 Million Women • **Ariel Levy**, Female Chauvinist Pigs

Assignments

Life is filled with rites of passage—attending college, for example. Many such rites—as is the case with the quinceañera—are located at the intersection of the personal and the social, the individual and the community. These assignments explore the role that such rites play in the political sphere by exploring their relationship to rights.

▶ TAGS: *kinship, family, change, rituals, tradition, religion, gender, community, anonymity, culture, identity*

- -

SEQUENCE 2 568

Cosmopolitanism: Ethical Conflict in a Global Economy

Kwame Anthony Appiah, Making Conversation *and* The Primacy of Practice • **Helen Epstein**, AIDS, Inc. • **Thomas L. Friedman**, The Dell Theory of Conflict Prevention • **Charles Duhigg and David Barboza**, In China, Human Costs Are Built Into an iPad 🄴 • **Malcolm Gladwell**, Small Change • **Patricia Churchland**, Networking: Genes, Brains, and Behavior • **Andrew Marantz**, My Summer at an Indian Call Center

Assignments

Living in a globalized world doesn't mean we all have to get along; it does mean, however, that we must learn how to mediate cultural differences in order to solve the problems we face in common with others. This sequence of

🄴 bedfordstmartins.com/emerging/epages

assignments examines authors' writing and thinking about an array of global problems. The essays and assignments suggest tools and concepts needed to advocate for change not only globally but locally as well.

▶ TAGS: *international policy, globalization, ethics, terrorism, community, social change*

We tend to think of science as the neutral search for truth, but as the readings in this sequence make clear, scientific endeavors are enmeshed in political and ethical concerns. This sequence explores the relationship between science and politics in order to foster conversations about the ethics of a broad spectrum of scientific and technological research.

▶ TAGS: *diplomacy, morality, biotechnology, knowledge and responsibility, human dignity, ethics, civil rights*

Assignments

Psychotherapy is called the "talking cure" since it allows people to talk through and resolve their inner conflicts with the help of a trained professional. But can conversation function more generally as a kind of social medicine? Can talking about things make them better? The authors in this sequence all explore the value of conversation in a variety of contexts. These assignments explore the potential for spoken exchanges to create personal and social change.

▶ TAGS: *conversation, social change, technology, surrogates*

. . . .

SEQUENCE 5   577

Art: Revelations, Displays, and Cultures

RACHEL KADISH, Who Is This Man, and Why Is He Screaming? • ARWA ABURAWA, Veiled Threat: The Guerrilla Graffiti of Princess Hijab • PORTFOLIO 🄴 • RICHARD RESTAK, Attention Deficit: The Brain Syndrome of Our Era • DAN SAVAGE AND URVASHI VAID, It Gets Better *and* Action Makes It Better • STEVE MUMFORD, The Things They Carry

Assignments

We often think of art as rarefied and separated from our lives—that which hangs on a wall in a museum. But this sequence asks us to think about the ways in which art, performance, and aesthetics have very real effects on our lives and on culture. These effects force us to ask questions about the limits of creative expression, the rights of individuals and of communities in relation to art, and the future of aesthetics itself.

▶ TAGS: *culture, art, performance, aesthetic boundaries, censorship, creativity, technology*

🄴 bedfordstmartins.com/emerging/epages

bedfordstmartins.com/emerging/epages

bedfordstmartins.com/emerging/epages

PAIRED READINGS

bedfordstmartins.com/emerging/epages

THEMATIC CONTENTS

TECHNOLOGY

WAR

WOMEN AND GENDER

EMERGING

CONTEMPORARY READINGS FOR WRITERS

INTRODUCTION
EMERGING AS A CRITICAL THINKER AND ACADEMIC WRITER

I N SOME CLASSES, such as biology, sociology, economics, or chemistry, what you learn and what you're tested on is content—a knowledge of terms and concepts. In contrast, what you need to learn in a composition class is a *process*—a process of reading and writing that you will practice with the essays in this book (in print and with e-Pages at bedfordstmartins.com/emerging/epages), in class discussions, and by responding to essay assignments. This class is not just about the readings in this book and online but also about what you can do with them. What you will do with them, of course, is write. And yet it's not entirely accurate to say you're here to learn how to write, either. After all, you already did a lot of writing in high school, and if you couldn't write, you wouldn't have gotten into college. But you will learn a particular *kind* of writing in this class, one which may be new to you: *academic writing*—joining a conversation by researching, weighing, and incorporating what others say into your own work in order to make a point of your own. It is the type of writing you'll be expected to do throughout your college career. The skills you learn in this class will also help you throughout your life. That's because academic writing involves *critical thinking*—the ability to evaluate, assess, apply, and generate ideas, an essential skill no matter what career you choose. Thriving in a career—any career—is never about how much you know but about what you can do with the knowledge you have. College will prepare you for your career by providing you with knowledge (your job here is part memorization), but college will also help

> **Whenever we solve problems or make decisions, we use critical thinking because we gather, evaluate, and apply knowledge to the situation at hand.**

you learn how to evaluate knowledge, how to apply it, and how to create it; these are the skills of critical thinking.

What's *Emerging?* The Readings, in Print and Online

Emerging: Contemporary Readings for Writers comes in two parts. The physical part, the book you hold, is only half of the project. The other part is made up of e-Pages—text, photos, video, and audio, online at bedfordstmartins.com/emerging/epages. The redemption code in the print book allows you to access the online selections. As new media forms change the way we think about literacy, working with these various genres will allow you to hone your critical thinking and multimodal literacy skills. The only constant in new media is change, and the multimodal nature of the readings in *Emerging* reflects this reality.

College is also, of course, a time for change. You're not just moving into your career—you're moving into a new phase of your life. In this sense, you might think of yourself as an emerging thinker and writer, one who builds on existing skills and expands them in an academic context. In some ways, emerging is also very much the theme of the readings. Each was chosen to give you an opportunity to practice critical thinking through academic writing. But each one also concerns an emerging issue in the world today, something you might have already encountered but also something you will have to deal with as you move on in your life.

Take, for example, Thomas Friedman's chapter "The Dell Theory of Conflict Prevention" (p. 166), taken from his best-selling book *The World Is Flat*. Friedman is an expert in foreign relations, but he writes not to academics or economists or political theorists but to people like you and me. At the same time, his argument—that worldwide business supply chains promote political stability—requires a lot of thinking. Comprehension is not so much the issue. Friedman lays out his argument logically and supports it with many kinds of evidence (as you will learn to do as well). But the ideas he proposes about the relationship between economics and geopolitics, as well as his ideas about war, peace, and terrorism, will require you to think about the implications of his argument, and that kind of work is the start of critical thinking. Figuring out what's in the text is challenging, but even more challenging is figuring out what's not in the text: the examples that would challenge Friedman's argument, or new areas where his ideas have value, or modifications of his argument based on your experience or on other things you have read. That's critical thinking. What follows will help you do that thinking.

Emerging as a Critical Reader

Each of the readings comes with a set of tools to help you develop your skills as a critical reader, thinker, and writer:

- **Tags.** If you look in the table of contents and at the end of each headnote, you'll find that each reading comes with a number of "tags." These tags give you a quick sense of the topics—such as gender or technology—covered in the reading.

- **Headnotes.** The headnotes that appear before each reading provide context. In addition to finding out about the author, you'll learn about the larger context of writing from which the reading is taken, so that you can have a sense of the author's overall project. Headnotes help you prepare for the reading by giving you a quick sense of what you're about to encounter.

- **Questions for Critical Reading.** As you read the headnotes, you may find that you are already developing questions about the selection you're about to read, questions that can serve as the basis of your critical thinking. Your own questions can be supplemented by the Questions for Critical Reading at the start of each selection, which are specifically designed to focus your reading and thinking in ways that will develop your critical thinking skills while helping you to produce the writing asked of you in this class.

- **Exploring Context.** The Exploring Context questions use technology to deepen your understanding of the essay and its context in the world. These questions also underscore the fact that the readings have a life outside of this text where their ideas are discussed, developed, refuted, and extended—a life that you will contribute to through your work in this class.

- **Questions for Connecting.** These questions prompt you to apply your critical reading and thinking skills by relating the current reading to other selections in the book. Connecting the ideas of one author to the ideas or examples of another author is a key skill in critical thinking. Many of the connecting questions link the readings in the print book with the e-Pages online at bedfordstmartins.com/emerging /epages.

- **Language Matters.** The Language Matters questions at the end of each reading will help you practice skills with language and grammar by asking you to look at how meaning is created in these readings. Thinking critically about the language used by these authors will help you think critically about the language you use in your writing as well, so that you can take these insights back to your own writing.

- **Assignments for Writing.** These questions provide opportunities to join the conversation of these essays. Your instructor may assign these to you or you may wish to use them more informally to help you develop a deeper understanding of the text.

- **Assignment Sequences.** There are also a series of assignment sequences in this text; your instructor may choose to use or adapt one for your class. They're termed "sequences" because each assignment builds on the one that came before. In this way, you'll get to see how your understanding of a reading changes as you work with it alongside other readings from the text. As you return to previous readings while developing a central theme of thinking through these assignments, you will refine your critical thinking skills by paying close attention not only to each text but also to the relationships among groups of texts.

Fortunately, just as you've entered class with many writing skills, so too do you enter with skills in critical thinking. Critical thinking, after all, involves processing information, and we live in an information-rich world. So chances are that many of the things you do every day involve some kind of critical thinking; this class will hone those skills and translate them into the academic realm.

For now, it might be helpful to focus on five skills you might already use that correspond to aspects of academic writing and that also will enable you to thrive in the world at large: the abilities to read critically, connect and synthesize, argue, support, and revise.

Reading Critically

We live in a world saturated with information—so much so that Richard Restak notes in "Attention Deficit: The Brain Syndrome of Our Era" (p. 411) that our brains are being rewired by the multiple and competing demands information makes on our attention. Mastering the ability to read critically is crucial to managing these demands, since doing so allows us to select just the information we're looking for. So crucial is this skill to our survival today that we don't even think about it anymore. Indeed, you probably read for information on the Web every day, and you probably find what you need, too.

Yet, while it seems intuitive, reading involves a kind of critical thinking. Though reading is a way to find information, you may find it difficult to find the information you need in these readings. They likely are not the kind of texts you've read previously in your life or educational career, and so they might feel very difficult. That's OK; they're supposed to be challenging, because dealing with difficulty is the best way to develop your skills with critical thinking. In other words, if you didn't have to think about what you read in this class, you wouldn't be doing any critical thinking at all.

Strategies for Reading Critically

There are a number of steps you can take to help you read these essays critically:

- **Acknowledge that the reading is hard.** The first step is to acknowledge any difficulty you're having—recognizing it forces you to activate your skills with critical thinking consciously.

- **Keep reading the essay.** The second step is to keep reading, even if you feel you don't understand what you're reading. Often, the opening of an essay might be confusing or disorienting, but as you continue to read, you start to see the argument emerge. Similarly, the author might repeat key points throughout the essay, and so by the time you complete the reading, what seemed impossible to understand begins to make sense.

- **Write down what you *did* understand.** After you've completed the reading, you might still feel confused. Write down what you *did* understand—no matter how little that might be and no matter how unsure you are of your understanding. Recognizing what you know is the best way to figure out what you need to learn.

- **Identify specific passages that confused you.** Identifying specific passages that you did not understand is an important strategy, too. In locating any points of confusion, you can focus your critical thinking skills on those passages in order to begin to decode them.

- **Make a list of specific questions.** Make a list of specific questions you have, and then bring those questions to class as a way of guiding the class's discussion to enhance your understanding of the reading.

- **Discuss the reading with peers.** The questions accompanying the reading will give you some help, but your peers are another valuable resource. Discussing the reading with them will allow you and your classmates to pool your comprehension—the section you didn't understand might be the one your peers did, and vice versa.

- **Reread the essay at least once, or more.** Finally, reread the essay. Reading, like writing, is a looping process. We read and reread, just as we write and revise, and each time, we get a little more out of it.

Annotating

While reading, one of the things you'll want to search for is the author's argument, the point he or she is trying to make in the selection. In addition, you'll want to search for concepts, terms, or ideas that are unique or central to the author's argument. Reading with a pen, highlighter, laptop, or sticky notes at hand will help you as you find this information. In academic terms, you will be *annotating* the text, adding questions, comments, and notes while highlighting material you feel is important in some way; annotation is the start of critical reading because it identifies the most important information in the essay, and that's exactly the information you need to think about.

You might think of annotation as keeping a running guide of your thoughts while reading. That way, when you return to work with the essay, you have the start of your critical thinking. There are a number of things you might want to pay attention to during this process:

- **Look for the author's argument.** What is the overall point the author wants to make? Consider this one of the central tasks of your reading and annotation, both because you will want to engage this argument and because it will model for you how *you* can make your own point about the issue.

- **Mark key terms, concepts, and ideas.** Pay special attention to any words or phrases in italics or quotation marks. Often this indicates that the author is introducing an idea and will then go on to define it. Critical thinking often involves ideas, so it's important for you to locate and identify the ideas of the essay.

- **Mark information you will need again.** For example, there may be certain quotations that strike you as important or as puzzling. By annotating these you will be able to find them quickly for class discussion or while you are writing your paper.

- **Mark words you don't understand.** Look them up in a dictionary. This process will enhance your comprehension of the essay.

- **Ask questions in response to the text.** Don't assume that the author's words are gospel truth. Your job as a critical thinker is to evaluate everything the author says based on your knowledge and experience. Whenever you locate a mismatch between what the author says and what you think, note it with a question about the essay.

- **Summarize key points in the margin.** Summarizing the key points will help you map the overall flow of the argument. This process will help you comprehend the essay better and, as with locating the argument, will help you see how to structure your own writing as well.

HOW TO ANNOTATE A READING

- Read with a pen, highlighter, or sticky notes at hand.
- Look for the author's argument.
- Mark key terms, concepts, and ideas.
- Mark information you will need again.
- Mark words you don't understand.
- Ask questions in reaction to the text.
- Summarize key points in the margin.

Let's look at an example, an annotated excerpt from "Authenticating" (p. 95), Brian Christian's essay about artificial intelligence, online communication, and what it means to be human:

> German philosopher Friedrich Nietzsche held the startling opinion that the most important part of "being oneself" was — in Brown University philosopher Bernard Reginster's words — "being *one* self, *any* self."
>
> Nietzsche spoke of this as "giving style to one's character," comparing people to works of art, which we often judge according to their "concinnity," the way their parts fit together to make a whole: "In the end, when the work is finished, it becomes evident how the constraint of a single taste governed and formed everything large and small." (p. 101)

Note to self: look this person up.

I'm not sure this is a fair comparison. Do I think of myself as a painting?

Important term!

Summary: Coherence is key to being human. Does this somehow connect to what he was saying about form and content?

Let's look at how these annotation strategies work in this passage. For example, in this passage you would want to note the definition of "concinnity," which is underlined in the passage above to lend it visual importance. The definition is highlighted to make it easy to spot and remember. You will also want to mark any terms you don't understand or names you're not familiar with, such as Friedrich Nietzsche. Another set of strategies, though, involves questions you have in reaction to the text, each of which can serve as a point for re-searching the text. Each question you ask during your initial reading of the text gives you a new direction for searching the text again — both for an answer to your question and for support for any alternative position you want to take.

Returning to the text and reading it again refines your reading, making it more critical. Rereading is not something we usually do if we're just reading for comprehension; generally we understand enough of what we read that we don't have to read it again. But in an academic context rereading is essential, because critical reading goes beyond comprehension to *evaluation* — determining the accuracy and applicability of the information and ideas of the text. And before we can evaluate, we have to know the key points that need evaluation. The Questions for Critical Reading located at the start of each selection will help you in this process by focusing your rereading on a significant point in the essay — a particular term, concept, or idea that will allow you to read and think critically. Rereading Christian's essay with these questions in mind might cause you to pay attention to those parts of the selection where he explains form, content, and the relation between the two. For example, Christian opens his essay by noting that when it comes to machines "we authenticate on *content*," but with humans "we authenticate on *form*" (p. 95). The difference may not make much sense when reading that section but might make more sense when you think about how humans are made of pieces that fit together to make a whole, their "concinnity."

Glossing the Text

Each of these texts is taking part in a larger conversation about a particular topic. You might find parts of a reading confusing because you are jumping into the middle of a conversation without knowing its complete history. At times, then, you will want to go beyond annotating the text by using a skill called *glossing*. A gloss is a quick explanation of a term or concept—think of it as a quick summary of the conversation that has come before what you are reading. You probably already know what a glossary is—a list of terms and their definitions. Some words have already been glossed for you. When you provide your own glosses for a text, you're building your own sort of glossary, filling in technical details you need to understand the text as a whole. There are a number of techniques you can use to gloss parts of the text while you read and annotate it:

- **Look at the context.** Oftentimes, you can determine a quick sense of a term or concept by looking at the surrounding context or the way the author uses it.

- **Use a dictionary.** Using a dictionary to look up a word or term can help you confirm what you learn from the context.

- **Use Wikipedia.** Wikipedia is a controversial tool in academia because it has no single source of authority. Instead, everyone writes it, everyone edits it, and anyone can change it. In fact, Marshall Poe explores the pros and cons of this technique for gathering knowledge in "The Hive" (p. 349). In most cases, you won't want to use Wikipedia as a source for your writing. For one thing, your writing is about critical thinking, which is about ideas, and Wikipedia is more centrally concerned with factual information. At the same time, because it contains so much knowledge, it's a useful source for glossing because it can give you a quick sense of not only a technical term's meaning but also its history.

- **Use a search engine.** Wikipedia is not the only source for information on the Web. Indeed, each of its entries includes links to other sites used in compiling the information on that page. Thus you can also do a Web search to find a quick gloss.

Let's look at an example of how you might gloss a text as you read and annotate it. Here's a short passage from Francis Fukuyama's "Human Dignity":

In the words of Nietzsche's Zarathustra, "One has one's little pleasure for the day and one's little pleasure for the night: But one has a regard for health. 'We have invented happiness,' say the last men, and they blink." Indeed, both the return of hierarchy and the egalitarian demand for health, safety, and relief of suffering might all go hand in hand if the rulers of the future could provide the masses with enough of the "little poisons" they demanded. (p. 190)

Nineteenth-century German philosopher who often challenged traditional values and morality. (Web search)

Philosophical novel where Nietzsche discusses his concept of the "Superman."

"A system of organization in which people or groups are ranked one above the other according to status or authority." (Dictionary definition)

"Of, relating to, or believing in the principle that all people are equal and deserve equal rights and opportunities."

The context of this quotation helps, too. Fukuyama is discussing how Nietzsche foresaw the implications of natural science for human dignity—specifically the possibility of a ranking or hierarchy of humans. These glosses can help you understand Fukuyama's larger argument about human dignity.

Reading Visuals

You may notice that many of the print readings contain visual elements such as images or graphs, and the online selections include color and video. Indeed, some of the readings are entirely visual. These, too, are opportunities for critical reading. After all, *every text is an image and every image is a text.*

Consider the page you are reading now. Though not readily apparent, it has a number of visual elements—the font selected for the text, the color of the print, the amount of empty or white space around the text and in the margins. Normally, we don't pay attention to the visual elements of printed texts. That's because printed texts are designed to minimize their visual elements. Since visual elements carry meaning, too, they are minimized so that you can focus on the meaning of the words on the page. But imagine how the meaning of these words would change if they were printed in **bold** or if they used a curly, informal font.

Visual texts often invert this relationship, bringing the visual elements into the foreground and letting words sit in the background or letting them work with or against the meaning suggested by the visual elements. The words and the images together make meaning, and like all of the texts you will read, this meaning is open to interpretation and analysis. In this sense, reading a visual text isn't all that different from reading any other kind of text, and you will want to use many of the same skills with critical reading that you would use with other selections in this book:

- **Identify the elements.** To begin reading a visual text, make note of each of its elements—not only any words it might contain but also each visual item included in the overall image. Think of each element as a sentence. Together, these elements express meaning just as the sentences of a paragraph do. When you identify each element, you are using your skills with annotation.

- **Identify the connections.** Once you've located the elements, think about the relationships between them. Do the visual and textual elements reinforce each other or do they work against each other? What meaning is the author trying to convey in each case?

- **Analyze and interpret the whole.** Just as you would with other readings in the book, you will want to analyze and interpret the visual image as a whole. This again involves critical thinking because you will need to think about not only the *explicit meanings*—what the image as a whole says—but also the *implicit meanings*—what the image as a whole implies.

Let's look at an example from PostSecret. PostSecret is an online project in which people are invited to reveal a secret about themselves on a postcard that is then shared on the Web (postsecret.com). Here is one such postcard:

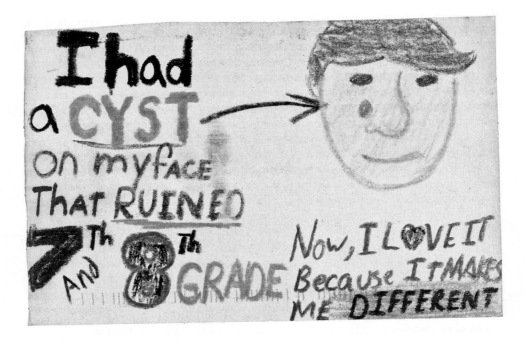

Some of the things you might note when "reading" this postcard include:

- The use of crayons to make it. How might that relate to an experience from seventh or eighth grade?

- The parts that are underlined ("cyst" and "ruined") and the part that is highlighted ("different"). How do these forms of emphasis relate?

- The use of a heart in "love." How does that create its own kind of emphasis for that word?

- The smile on the self-portrait as well as the cyst. How does it reinforce what the words say?

Connecting and Synthesizing

Once you've completed a critical reading, you're ready to do some thinking. One of the methods you can use in critical thinking is *connection*—the ability to draw relationships between ideas or examples from different essays or contexts. Each of the essays you will read here is already connected to the conversation taking place around that author's particular topic. When you read, you might be able to guess some of these connections, but as you think critically about these readings, you will make new connections of your own, which is essential to critical thinking. You'll start by connecting what you read to your own life, to what you know and think and how you feel. Your instructor might ask you to keep a reading journal or a blog where you can record these initial connections.

For example, here's a short response assignment I recently gave students in one of my classes before we started discussing Hal Herzog's "Animals Like Us" (p. 242):

What is the "troubled middle"? Does it offer a sufficient moral ground?

Here's how one student responded:

> The term "troubled middle" describes the "gray areas" of what is morally right concerning animal relations. Philosopher Strachan Donnelley refers to it as "murky ethical territory" (6). It is basically described as the conflict between brain and heart in terms of how we treat animals. The decisions these "middlers" make are not cut-and-dried like that of an animal activist would be. The so-called, "fence-sitters" may eat some meat but not a lot or maybe will not conduct experiments on animals, but will in fact use mice in searching for a cure for cancer. Although they do feel compassion for animals, they also believe that humans are on a different "moral plane" from that of other animals.
>
> Being a part of the "troubled middle" means you have a conscience, but does it necessarily offer a sufficient moral ground? I do not believe teeter-tottering about such ideas can be considered in that manner. Although it is difficult to come to a cut-and-dried decision concerning these issues, that is what needs to happen to establish a legitimate set of rules. If someone in the United States had a "troubled middle" opinion concerning an issue such as murder, it would not be tolerated.

These personal reactions will help you to think about the ideas of each essay. What will help you even more is connecting ideas *between* the essays. The strongest way to evaluate the information in an essay is to test it against other information, such as the ideas expressed in another essay. Connecting the readings might mean using a concept from one piece, such as Francis Fukuyama's idea of "Factor X," to explain another essay, such as the Dalai Lama's "Ethics and the New Genetics." But it might also mean using the ideas from one essay to modify the ideas in another: elaborating Michael Pollan's idea of the "holon" through Daniel Gilbert's concept of "super-replicators," for example. (See Figure 1.)

Connecting is a kind of critical thinking used by the authors of the essays in this book, too. We've already seen how Brian Christian connects the concept of "concinnity" to being human. In "AIDS, Inc." (p. 152), Helen Epstein does something similar in discussing HIV prevention programs in Africa:

> . . . Ugandans are more likely to know their neighbors and to live near members of their extended families. This in turn may have contributed to what sociologists call "social cohesion" — the tendency of people to talk openly with one another and form trusted relationships. Perhaps this may have facilitated more realistic and open discussion of AIDS, more compassionate attitudes toward infected people, and pragmatic behavior change. (p. 158)

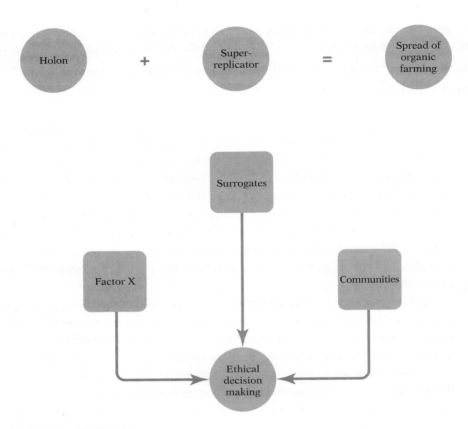

Figure 1 Clustering
Connecting and synthesizing are crucial ways of thinking critically about what you read.

Epstein, a molecular biologist and specialist in public health, connects a concept from sociology, "social cohesion," with HIV prevention in Uganda. In making that connection, she uses the idea to support her argument and to create a new idea about what an effective prevention program should look like. It's the connections between ideas that allow authors like Christian and Epstein—and *you*—to make an argument.

In working with these readings, you might feel like there simply are no connections between them, that the topic of each essay is unique. But keep in mind that a connection is not something you find; it's something you *make.* If the connections were already sitting there in the essays, then there wouldn't be much critical thinking involved, because there wouldn't be much thinking involved at all. The process of making connections between disparate ideas is part of critical thinking. Sociology and public health might not seem to have much in common, but when we make connections between them, we generate a new understanding of how to slow the spread of HIV.

Strategies for Making Connections

When making connections between the readings for this class, you might want to try a few different strategies:

- **Draw the connections.** Start by listing the important terms, concepts, and ideas from each essay on a sheet of paper. Once you've done that, you can literally draw lines between ideas that have some relation.

- **Use clustering.** You might also try a technique called clustering. Put the main concept of each essay in a circle on a sheet of paper. Draw other circles containing related or subsidiary ideas and connect them with lines to the circles containing the main ideas of the readings. When you find ways to connect the branches of these separate groups, you're locating relationships between the essays that you might want to pursue. Through figuring out exactly what these relationships are, you not only utilize critical thinking but also start the process of forming your own ideas, which you will express in your writing for this class.

- **Use the questions with the readings.** The Questions for Connecting at the end of each reading will also help in this process by asking you to think specifically about one essay in terms of another. These questions will direct you to think about both essays, giving you an opportunity to use each reading to test the concepts and ideas of the other.

- **Compare the tags.** The "tags" for each essay show key concepts, some of which overlap with the tags for other selections. Use the list of the essays' tags in the Table of Contents to help you see some of the connections between the readings.

Synthesizing

Connecting defines relationships. Synthesizing goes one step further by combining different sources of information to generate something new. Synthesis happens a lot in the real world. For example, a doctor might combine test results, a patient's medical history, and his or her own knowledge to reach a diagnosis; a businessperson might use a marketing report, recent sales figures, a demographic study, and data on the current economic outlook to craft a business strategy. Whenever you combine multiple sources of information to create new information or ideas, you're *synthesizing*. Synthesis always creates something new; because you'll be using it in this class to create new ideas and thus new knowledge, you'll use it to demonstrate your critical thinking.

All of the authors in this text use synthesis, because all of them are working from what's already been said and written about a subject to say and write something new. You'll do the same. After you've read a piece and connected its ideas to other contexts, you will synthesize the ideas into a new idea, your own idea. That idea will form the center of the writing you do in this class.

Strategies for Synthesizing

There are several techniques you can use to synthesize the ideas of these readings:

- **Combine ideas.** You might, for example, use ideas from two authors and combine them into a new concept that you use in your paper.

- **Apply ideas.** You might instead use a concept from one essay to show the limitations of another author's argument. In this case you would apply the first idea to the second and, in doing so, you'd produce something new, which would be the synthesis you create between the two.

- **Invent your own term.** You might even invent a term all your own, defining and deploying it through your analyses of the readings in the papers you will write. You can define the term using ideas that you pull from multiple readings, connecting and synthesizing them into a new understanding represented by your term.

- **Pay attention to similarities *and* differences.** When synthesizing, you want to ask yourself not simply how the two elements you're working with are alike but also how they're different. Paying attention to both similarities and differences allows you to discover how different ideas fit together in different ways.

Making an Argument

All the processes we've discussed so far take place before you actually start writing in response to an assignment. You need to read (and reread), connect, and synthesize in order to begin the process of critical thinking which forms the core of academic writing. Once you've done all that, it's time to form an argument. If you've ever joined a discussion online or kept a blog, then you're familiar with making an argument. In academic terms, *argument* involves joining a conversation, taking a stand, or making a point. When you write in this class, you'll be doing all of these things.

You may already be familiar with this academic sense of "argument," though you may have been introduced to it in different terms. In the grading criteria we use at my school, we make the meaning clear:

> When we use the term "argument" . . . we mean the central, problem-solving idea that drives the paper, a concept that many of us learned to think of as a "thesis." We might also think of this as a "position" or as a "project," all of which suggest that there is a central point the student is trying to make in the paper. The argument will usually show up in a thesis statement on the first page of the paper, but this is not the sole defining characteristic of an argument.
>
> The student should have a goal in a paper, something he or she is trying to accomplish, often defined by a specific, argumentative statement. But even when this statement is absent, the goal is often still apparent, whether as a summation in the conclusion or an underlying/recurring theme of the paper.
>
> An ideal argument will be spelled out in a clear thesis statement and will provide both a direction for the paper and a motivation for that direction (a problem to solve, a goal to accomplish, a position to defend, a project to complete, etc.).

Forming an argument can be really challenging, in part because the word itself can mean so many things—an argument between lovers is quite different from an argument in a courtroom, which is also different from a scientific argument. Rather than thinking of your argument as the position you defend, like an army protecting its territory, try thinking of it as the words you send out into the world, like a participant joining a conversation.

Strategies for Forming an Argument

Finding your argument is not as hard as it sounds, because you've already done a lot of the work necessary by the time you get to thinking about your argument. In forming an argument, you will probably want to draw from:

- **The assignment or prompt.** We'll talk more about these later in this introduction and offer some tips on how to decode the focus of an assignment, but for now, consider the assignment a foundation on which you can build your argument. It offers a central focus that you can use to organize your critical thinking and join the conversation.

- **Your annotations.** You will want to go back to your annotations of any selections connected to the assignment. Since you noted the important ideas and concepts in each essay and, most crucially, your own questions or concerns, these annotations will give you a preliminary sense of how you want to respond to each text.

- **Your connections and synthesis.** Many times strong arguments are built out of the connections you make between the texts. You may, for example, build an argument around the application of an idea from one essay to an example from another. In the process, you will offer a new insight into the essays, which represents your synthesis and your addition to the larger conversation of the texts.

From Argument to Draft

Once you have a good sense of your argument, you're in a good position to start drafting your paper. The first step in this process is to think about your argument as a map. That is, your argument should tell you exactly what you need to do in the paper and then should also tell your reader exactly how you will proceed in the paper.

Let's look at a student's argument from a class I taught recently:

> A new civil rights can be achieved by replacing idle conversations with meaningful discussions that aid the presence of our true selves through websites that offer a safe place for human interaction.

Given this argument, it's clear the first thing the author will need to discuss is the idea of a "new civil rights," a concept from Kenji Yoshino's essay (p. 552). In the next body paragraph, the author will need to discuss how "idle conversations" prevent these new civil rights and then how "meaningful discussions" can help create them. Then the author will need to argue that such discussions support our "true selves" (another concept from Yoshino) before looking at how all of this can take place on websites that "offer a safe place for human interaction." The argument, in essence, contains an outline of the whole paper.

Once you have a good sense of the shape and flow of your paper as suggested by the map of your argument, it's time to think about how you will support that argument.

Using Support

As you lay out your thinking, you'll need proof to *support*, or provide evidence for, your point, which in academic writing happens through working with quotations from the texts. When you use quotation in your writing, you support your words and ideas through the words and ideas of others. Quotation supports critical thinking in two ways. First, it provides evidence for your argument, thesis, or position, showing the reader how and why you thought that way and reached the conclusions that led to your argument. Second, integrating quotation into your text itself requires some critical thinking. That's the difference between "having" quotations in your paper and "using" them. It's not enough to drop in a quotation every now and then. You need to think about the function of every quotation you use, its purpose in your paper. Is it defining a term? Supporting an assertion? Connecting ideas? To make that function clear, you will want to explain each quotation you use. That doesn't mean you should summarize or reiterate each quotation; it means you should write about what that piece of text does for your overall project. Think of it as connecting that text to your own text. You might also analyze the quotation in this process. *Analyzing* a quotation means explaining what it says and what it means.

Here's a pattern you can use to incorporate quotation into your paragraphs in ways that show your critical thinking through connection. When I share this with my students, I call it "Barclay's Super-Secret Formula" (though I suppose it's not so secret anymore):

$$C_1 > I > Q_1 > E > T > Q_2 > C_e$$

This pattern for a paragraph is a great way to connect and synthesize quotations from two essays in support of your argument. Let's break this formula down:

1. "C_1" is your **claim**. Begin your paragraph with a sentence that contains the main idea you want to make or the connection you want to show between two essays. You might have learned to call this a topic sentence. Regardless, the key is to start with a sentence that lets the reader know exactly what the paragraph will be about. Your claim should be related to your argument and should offer the reader a clear sense of how this paragraph proves a part of the argument.

2. "I" is an **introduction**. After you state your claim for the paragraph, introduce the first quotation. Sometimes you will need a sentence to set up the quotation; other times you might just use an introductory phrase like "Friedman writes" or "According to Yoshino."

3. "Q_1" is your first **quotation**. After you introduce the quotation, provide it. You will want to make sure it's completely accurate, and, of course, you will want to provide proper citation (we'll discuss this more below).

4. "E" is an **explanation** of the quotation. After you provide the first quotation, add a sentence that explains that quotation. This can be particularly useful if the quotation contains an idea or concept. You may want to take another sentence or two to explain that idea even more so that your reader completely understands it.

5. "T" is a **transition** sentence. Before you move on to the next quotation, offer some sort of short transition sentence. This transition should provide a sense of the kind of connection you're trying to make in the paragraph as a whole. For example, you might have a sentence like "Friedman's concept is useful for explaining the spread of HIV in Africa."

6. "Q_2" is your **second quotation**, most likely from another essay. This second quotation needs only a brief introduction or signal phrase.

7. "C_e" is your **explanation of the connection**. Finally, add several sentences that explain the connection you see between the quotations and the way in which this connection supports your overall argument. This part of the formula is, in many ways, the most important part of the paragraph. These sentences should also explain how the relationship between the quotations supports your argument. These sentences record your critical thinking, allowing you to use the connection you've made between these two authors to support your project for the paper.

Here's an example of what this kind of paragraph looks like:

> For starters, as both Christian and Poe demonstrate, statelessness is increasingly changing what it means to be human by how we behave. In "Authenticating," Brian Christian explains the definition of being stateless in the following quote:, "state-less, that is, each reply depends only on the current query, without any knowledge of the history of the conversation required to formulate the reply" (Christian 35). Basically Christian is simply saying that being stateless is in a sense a robotic response, which, of course, can be linked with technology in our society. In another example, Christian states, "one of the classic stateless conversation types, it turns out, is verbal abuse," (Christian 36), which relates to in Michael Poe's "The Hive." The demonstration of verbal abuse is clearly exhibited in the classic edit war between the "Cunctator" and Sanger in "The Hive." As quoted from the book, "In an edit war, two or more parties cyclically cancel each other's work on an article with no attempt to find the NPOV. It's the wiki equivalent of No, *your* mother wears combat boots." (Poe 272). Statelessness is again presented in the robotic deletion between the "Cunctator" and Sanger during their edit war. The stateless presence in both Christian's "Authenticating," and Poe's "The Hive" further remarks on the changes technology has casted on humans today.

About Citation

It is absolutely essential that you acknowledge the words of others when you use them. In the real world, failure to do so can result in expensive lawsuits and ruined careers. In the academic world, failure to do so is considered plagiarism. Every time you use the words or ideas of another, you must provide a citation. Once you enter your major, you'll learn a specific system for providing that citation — every discipline has its own system. In this class, the system you will likely use is MLA citation, developed through the Modern Language Association, the governing body for the discipline of English. You will probably spend time in class learning the intricacies of this system, but for now remember the basics: Every time you use a quotation or paraphrase, include the author's name and the page number in parentheses at the end of the sentence, just before the period. That's true for visual images as well. Publication information for all of your sources should be listed at the end of your paper. Visual images require a special format. You will want to consult a grammar handbook, a citation guide, or a reliable Web source for specific information on how to cite these sources.

You'll no doubt notice that not every author you read in this collection uses citation. Why do you have to if they don't? The answer has a lot to do with *audience*. Whenever we write, we are addressing a particular audience — that's why it's useful to think about this process as joining a conversation. The audience you select determines a lot about how you will write — your tone, for example. It also determines the need for citation. *Academic writing always requires citation because it addresses an academic audience.* Addressing an academic audience doesn't mean using complicated sentences or fancy words. A lot of academic writing has a conversational tone, but it also always uses citation.

About Research

Research has a very specific meaning in the context of the academic world. When you generate new ideas in your writing for this class, you'll be doing a kind of research, but research also involves working with academic sources to support your points. For this class, those sources are largely provided for you by the essays in this book. If your argument needs support beyond that, you will need to find valid and reliable evidence, and that will involve more than what you can find through Google or Wikipedia. Academic research demands academic sources, the kind you will find through the library in books and journals across the disciplines. You will need to draw on your Web-searching skills to use the electronic interfaces that can help you find those sources. This is what we mean when we say that academic writing is an "iterative" process — you do it, and then you do it again.

Of course, you'll be researching these essays when you respond to the Exploring Context questions, which often ask you to use the Web to elaborate your understanding of the text. However, before you use any website in an academic setting, you will want to make sure you evaluate it. You begin that process by asking yourself how you want to use the site. Any site on the Web can be used as an example of your ideas or the ideas of any essay. But whenever you take ideas or evidence from websites, you need to be careful about which sites you use. Ask yourself questions such as:

- **Who wrote the material?** Is the site authored by an individual, an organization, a governmental agency?

- **How qualified is the source?** What makes this author an expert on this material? What are this author's qualifications? If the site doesn't contain information about the qualifications of the author, then you may want to reconsider using it.

- **When was the site last updated?** Often this information will be provided on each page of the site, usually at the bottom of the page. If the site doesn't include any update information, then you will want to ask yourself how current the material is.

- **How stable is the address or URL?** Websites come and go. Generally speaking, websites from established groups or organizations are more stable than websites with their own domain name, which in turn are more stable than websites hosted with a free service.

- **How do you want to use the site in your writing?** Any website can be used as an example, but only those websites that establish their authority should be used for ideas or evidence.

Revising, Editing, and Proofreading

So far, we've discussed all the stages of critical thinking you'll need to exercise in order to produce a draft of your paper. Each stage relates to a skill you might already use, and each, too, will have value in your future career. Once you've written a draft, making an argument that contributes to the larger conversation and supporting it by working with quotations, there is still more work to be done, because every good piece of writing goes through at least one revision. This is the tenth draft of this introduction, for example.

Often students think of revision as "fixing" their papers—just correcting all the errors. But that's only part of the process. Revision involves making changes and should produce something new. Again, when we produce something new in the realm of ideas, we're doing critical thinking; revision, then, is also a form of critical thinking. Instead of thinking about the readings of the class, though, revision asks you to think critically about—to evaluate, test, and assess—your own writing.

When we discussed connecting, we said that it's easier to evaluate ideas against something else. The same is true with revision. Often when we write, our initial draft looks fine to us; it seems like our best thinking. This is where connecting with others— in this case, through the process of peer revision—is again useful. As part of my job coordinating the writing classes at my university, I read the class evaluations for all of the writing courses, and one thing students say over and over again is that they don't value peer review because they believe that only the teacher has "the" answer and so only the teacher's comments count. On the contrary, I believe that *peer review is one of the most practical things you'll learn in this class*. In the rest of your life, you may not be asked to write papers, but you will be asked to work with others on committees or teams again and again. Learning to work well with others—to recognize valuable feedback and to give it in turn—is essential, since, as James Surowiecki shows in "Committees, Juries, and Teams: The *Columbia* Disaster and How Small Groups Can Be Made to Work" (p. 472), the failure of small groups can lead to disaster.

Peer review gives you practice in testing your ideas with actual readers. As noted above, every piece of writing has an audience, and your peers form part of that audience when it comes to the writing you will do for this class. Since the goal of each paper is to contribute to the conversation started in the texts, and since your classmates have also read and written about the texts, they are the interlocutors for your written conversation.

That process works in reverse, too. When you read your peers' writing, you will want to bring all your critical thinking skills to bear. You might be tempted to just write "Good job!" no matter what you think about the writing, for fear of being critical, but that shows no critical thinking. *Critical thinking is not the same as being critical.* When you offer valuable feedback, you're helping your classmates, no matter how strong that feedback is. Start by reading your peer's paper, using the same skills of critical reading that you used when you read the texts for this class. Annotate it just as you would one of the readings, marking what you think is important and asking questions in the margin when you are lost or confused. Then think critically about what your classmate is saying, using the skills you have with connection — connect what he or she says about the text to what you know about the text as well as to what you think and have written about the text. Then form your response as a way of joining the conversation.

Sample Student Paper

It might be useful for you to see how this all comes together in an actual student paper. Let's start with the assignment, taken from one of my recent classes:

Paper Two: Poe and Christian
In "The Hive," Marshall Poe looks at the humans and technologies behind the online knowledge repository known as Wikipedia, focusing on the ways in which collaboration works to generate and manage knowledge in this online encyclopedia. As with Brian Christian in "Authenticating," then, Poe is concerned with the relationship between humans and technology. **Using ideas from both Poe's and Christian's essays, write a paper in which you assess how technology has changed what it means to be human.**

Questions for Exploration:
Does a project like Wikipedia make us more human or less human? Does collaboration threaten being "one" self? How do form and content operate in Wikipedia? Are Wikipedia entries also the "ghosts" of real people? What role does statelessness have to play in Wikipedia? Does "openness" promote the human element in technological arenas? What roles do top-down or bottom-up systems play in being human and in computers? Does the NPOV remove the human element? Did the arguments between Cunc and Sanger involve statelessness? Should knowledge be collaborative?

You can apply the same critical thinking skills to the text of this assignment as you would to one of the readings in this book. For starters, critically reading the assignment will help you locate key information in writing your response, and you should annotate it as you would a reading. Notice, for example, that the middle section is in bold, highlighting the main task of the assignment: "Using ideas from both Poe's and Christian's essays, write a paper in which you assess how technology has changed what it means to be human." In annotating the assignment, you'd probably want to highlight that sentence so that you know where to focus your own critical thinking and response.

The questions that follow the assignment are not that different from the kinds of questions you might ask yourself when reading these two essays. Each one offers a jumping-off point for your own critical thinking, which can then lead to an argument you might use for your paper.

Here is one student's response to the assignment:

Technology has provided us with the resources that we need to expand our knowledge and be the best human that we can be. In the article "The Hive" by Marshall Poe, he uses the very popular Wikipedia as an example of technology. In the case of Wikipedia, technology has brought our individual knowledge together as a whole to form a central personal vision. In Brian Christian's book *The Most Human Human*, he introduces "concinnity", how individual pieces form together to make a whole, as a key point. In this sense, we can interpret how important concinnity has become in regards to technology and its relationship with humans. Technology has become a great accomplishment, allowing us as humans to exchange common knowledge in such a way that we end up with a neutral purée of conversation, thus making us more human.

Technology, through the collaborative efforts that humans have put forth, has progressed a great deal in such a short amount of time. When we think of all the search engines we have like Google and Yahoo we see the direct examples of the "collaborative knowledge" (Poe 349) technology brings to the table; however, technology would be meaningless if it wasn't for the concinnity and how each of the pieces of knowledge are intertwined. When Brian Christian talks about Nietzsche he tells us that "concinnity" is "the way their parts fit together to make a whole" (101). For example, while working with kids at a summer camp called St. Paul Lutheran, I had to find things to do in the classroom to keep me occupied while the kids were doing their own activities. In which I came across the brilliant idea of putting together a puzzle. I was so thrilled to finally find something to do just to open the box and see ten different puzzles combined into one box. The pieces were all there and intact but without them all being able to fit together, the box is full of useless junk. When talking about Wikipedia, Marshall Poe tells us that "Wikipedia has the potential to be the greatest effort in collaborative knowledge gathering the world has ever known, and it may well be the greatest effort in voluntary collaboration of any kind" (349). While this is true and accurate, collaborating knowledge of several human beings is not difficult by any means. Each and every conversation we have consists of two or more individuals collaborating their knowledge, but it is how their knowledge fits together to equal one final thought that leads us to concinnity. Although discussions with friends might not always lead to a final thought, Wikipedia, among other websites, does. We could all make a site that consists of all of our ideas and thoughts but without them fitting together we would have a whole bunch of insignificant pieces, just like the puzzle.

Along with the collaborative effort put into technology, comes the central personal vision that every subdivision must have. The central personal vision is pretty much equivalent to the main idea of a particular article or book. For you to be curious about something or to show interest in it, you must have a common personal vision as the author. Brian Christian, using the words of Nietzsche says, "Whether this taste was good or bad is less important than one might suppose, if only it was a single taste!" (101). What he is trying to say, using a Wikipedia article as an example, is that the article, consisting of different opinions from many different people, is not opinionated and is essentially a "neutral point of view" (Poe 355) in which the "single taste" being the single unbiased conclusion to the article. Due to the contributors telling us strictly facts about the topic and not adding how they really feel into it is what makes it easy for everyone to collaborate without stepping on each other's toes. This neutral point of view allows us as humans to relate to one another, thus making us a better human able to get along with others.

With the endless possibilities that technology has to offer, comes the possibility of conflict, especially when you're on a site that you have the ability to state your own opinion and block others. In regards to Wikipedia, the site gives "You, I, and any wired-up fool" (Poe 349) the ability to "add entries" (Poe 349).

Any site that does this is prone to have some sort of animosity. In the section "The Cunctator," Poe tells us about the "edit war" (356) going on between Cunc and Sanger. He explains to us that "In an edit war, two or more parties cyclically cancel each other's work on an article" (356). He also says that "It's the wiki equivalent of 'No, *your* mother wears combat boots'." (356) What he means by his statement "No, your mother wears combat boots" is that we let this "reflex" (Christian 108) kick in that pertains more "to the very last sentence of the conversation than it does with either the actual issue at hand or the person I'm talking to" (Christian 108). Afterwards, when have calmed down, we realize "the absurdity and ridiculousness of this kind of escalation" (Christian 108).

As humans, we feel that we have to express our opinions and let the whole world know how we feel, and although expressing ourselves is good and fine, "There's a sense in which verbal abuse is simply *less complex* than other forms of conversation" (Christian 107). This *"less complex"* form of conversation being kept out of sites such as Wikipedia is a tremendous accomplishment; however, keeping it out of sites such as Facebook would be limiting us as humans. Arguing is a childish form of behavior but unfortunately it is a characteristic that us as humans have. As humans, we will encounter many people that oppose the way that we feel so standing up for our beliefs does not necessarily make us any less of a human; it just goes to show that there is not a perfect human.

As we explore the different technologies that we have, such as surfing the web, we take into account the many different sites, some of which aren't contributors to making us more human. In Christian' site called Cleverbot. Christian tells us that Cleverbot is "the cobbling together of hundreds of thousands of prior conversations . . . Made of human parts, but less than a human sum" (100). When comparing technologies like Wikipedia and Cleverbot, we notice that they are both similar in that they are websites that consist of *"ghosts* of real people" (Christian 100); however, there is a major difference between how they are both used on the internet. Cleverbot is used somehow for the entertainment of its users with aimless conversation, while on the other hand Wikipedia is used to collect knowledge from average everyday people like you and me to form something great, an encyclopedia written by millions of people, each bringing something new and unique to the discussion. Technology is a terrific commodity to have, and even though it sometimes provides useless material, it just goes to show that every person is different. Some people enjoy learning for their entertainment, while others are amused by pointless conversation with a robot, both of which make us more human by making us individuals with diverse interests.

As we get older we see technology having more and more of an effect on majority of the population and sometimes that is a negative effect. We have become more prone to talking to a friend through Facebook or a text message than you are to meeting up with them face to face. However, technology has also made it possible to communicate with hundreds of people across the country and relate in some way to this person that you have never seen before. It is not the technology that makes us less of a human, but the human that makes us less of a human. We control the manner in which we use technology. When we take the approach to use technology the right way, we see that technology is not separating us further away from one another and that it is really bringing us together to create a whole.

Every paper needs an argument, the main point that the author is positing. The author of this paper makes that argument clear at the end of the introduction: "Technology has become a great accomplishment, allowing us as humans to exchange common knowledge in such a way that we end up with a neutral purée of conversation, thus making us more human." The argument addresses the prompt by suggesting that the way technology has changed what it means to be human is by making us *more* human. It's also clear that both Poe and Christian have a role to play in this argument, since Poe discusses "common knowledge" and Christian introduces the idea of a "neutral purée of conversation." This argument might have been more specific in order to provide readers with a better sense of just how the paper will proceed, but, overall, it offers a good start by staking out a position in relation to the texts and the prompt.

Throughout the paper, the author supports that argument by connecting Poe and Christian and synthesizing their ideas. Notice the point made in the second paragraph, for example: Poe celebrates the collaboration behind Wikipedia, but the author of the paper points out that such collaboration would be meaningless if the parts didn't fit together as a whole, an idea borrowed from Christian. By connecting these two essays, the author is able to begin supporting the larger argument that technology is making us more human.

As the paper proceeds, each paragraph makes the same moves—connecting the authors to form a synthesis that supports the argument. There are, of course, some stumbles along the way; this author is, after all, still emerging as an academic writer. You might notice, for example, that the paragraph about Cleverbot doesn't seem to fit in. It just feels out of place, given the overall argument. Similarly, there are grammatical and language issues that might distract us as readers, including sentence fragments. And while sometimes the author does a great job of using the texts to create a synthesis, there are certainly places where the text is used too much or not enough.

This is the second, revised draft of this paper and in many ways it is a success. By the conclusion, the author has managed to provide support and evidence for the argument. That should be your goal when you write in this class, too. Because despite its shortcomings, this paper does demonstrate critical thinking by presenting a clear argument supported with specific examples and quotations from the text. Your work in this class may look very different (in part, because the writing prompts you work with may look very different), but the skills will remain the same. And in the end, those skills are what matter—not just in this class and not just in college, but in your career and your life as well.

THE READINGS

ARWA ABURAWA

Arwa Aburawa is a freelance journalist and blogger whose articles have been published in *Islam Online*, *SISTERS* magazine, *Green Prophet*, and *Al Jazeera*. Aburawa's work focuses on the intersections between Islam, feminism, culture, and environmentalism. She runs a blog called *A World of Green Muslims* and is a contributor to Friends of Al Aqsa, an organization concerned with human rights issues in Palestine.

"Veiled Threat: The Guerrilla Graffiti of Princess Hijab" originally appeared in *Bitch* magazine in the Winter 2009 "Art/See" issue. *Bitch* magazine has been published by nonprofit Bitch Media since 1996 as a feminist alternative to traditional women's magazines. The "Art/See" issue focused on feminist issues in art, especially how art overlaps with the political. In addition to this selection, the issue included an article by Ellen Papazian about Yoko Ono and an interview with journalist and novelist Farai Chideya.

In "Veiled Threat," Aburawa describes the works of an anonymous graffiti artist known only as "Princess Hijab." Princess Hijab works in Paris, where she covers billboards and advertisements with stylized, paint-markered headscarves and burqas. Aburawa sorts through the varying reports on the anonymous artist, ultimately trying to uncover her motives, which have been interpreted both as a right-wing argument advocating modesty and as a left-wing critique of capitalism's objectification of women. Given France's recent ban on the wearing of burqas in public, is this gorilla street art a response to increasing Islamophobia, or is it something else entirely? Princess Hijab's manifesto provides some insight into her motives, but the interpretation of her art remains highly individualized.

▶ TAGS: *artistic jihad, provocation, culture jammers, community, aesthetic objects, art, religion*

Questions for Critical Reading

1. Is Princess Hijab's work art or graffiti? Define these two terms for yourself before you begin reading the essay. Then mark passages that support your position as you read.

2. Aburawa indicates that some people consider Princess Hijab's work radical while others believe it supports a conservative agenda. As you read, mark places in the essay that comment on her position. Which interpretation do you feel is correct? Support your response with passages from the text.

3. Princess Hijab suggests that her work is related to questions of identity. How does her own identity (and her relative anonymity) affect interpretations of her work? What is the relationship between identity, authorship, and reception? Find quotations from the text that support your position.

Veiled Threat: The Guerrilla Graffiti of Princess Hijab

Since 2006, the elusive guerrilla artist known as Princess Hijab* has been subverting Parisian billboards, to a mixed reception. Her anonymity irritates her critics, many of whom denounce her as extremist and antifeminist; when she recently conceded, in the pages of a German newspaper, that she wasn't a Muslim, it opened the floodgates to avid speculation in the blogosphere. If her claim of being a 21-year-old Muslim girl was only partially true, some wondered what the real message was behind her self-described "artistic jihad."

In her online manifesto, PH declares that she "acts upon her own free will" and is "not involved in any lobby or movement, be it political, religious, or to do with advertising." The Princess insists that, like the ape-masked Guerrilla Girls and Mexico's balaclava-clad Zapatistas, by being nobody, she is free to be anybody. But as liberating as this anonymity may seem, it does leave her work open to conflicting—and occasionally unflattering—interpretations. On the popular blog Art21 critic Paul Schmelzer points to Princess Hijab's work as an example of right-wing street art, surmising that her motivation is to cover the "shame of omnipresent (and often sexualized) ads." Another blogger, Evil Fionna, argues that if Princess Hijab were acting as a fundamentalist Christian, her work would be recognized as "religious extremis[m]" that demonizes women and makes them ashamed of their bodies. And a commentator on the anti-Islam site Infidel Bloggers accused the artist of urging women to submit to the "tyranny of Islam."

These observers also allude to the uncanny similarity between the work of Princess Hijab and that of conservative religious groups that have historically used less literal hijabizing to police the female form. In Saudi Arabia the 80-year-old government agency known as the Committee for the Promotion of Virtue and the Prevention of Vice is tasked with, among other things, blacking out bare skin wherever it shows up. In line with Sharia law, women in the pages of magazines, on billboards, and in other public images are painstakingly covered up: Katy Perry may be sporting high-waisted hot pants and a tiny top on her cd cover, but once the Committee gets through with it, she's garbed in a long-sleeved shirt with matching leggings. (The group, notorious for beating up men and women engaged in "immoral behavior," has also made headlines for banning Valentine's Day and restricting the sale of cats and dogs, lest they be used by men to attract women's attention.)

---

* Hijab: Head scarf worn by many Muslim women. The word can also refer to an extremely modest style of dress [Ed.].

And in the U.K. in 2005, the activists behind Muslims Against Advertising (MAAD) began daubing blobs of paint on the underdressed models in street ads for the likes of Dove and Wonderbra, and in some cases ripping down the posters altogether.

The ongoing conflict over hijabs in her home country does give Princess Hijab's work an inescapable political context, or what she calls a "shade of provocation." France's hijab debates first erupted in 1989 when three high-school girls were suspended after they refused to remove their Islamic headscarves at a school in a suburb of Paris. Successive years of controversy led to former President Jacques Chirac passing a bill in 2004 banning "religious symbols" in schools on the grounds that they clashed with France's cherished notions of secularization; more recently, President Nicolas Sarkozy upheld the ban on burqas and headscarves in public spaces, stating, "The burqa is not a religious symbol, it is a sign of the subjugation, of the submission of women. I want to say solemnly that it will not be welcome on the territory of the French Republic. We cannot accept women in cages, amputated of all dignity, on French soil."

"The burqa is not a religious symbol, it is a sign of the subjugation, of the submission of women."

But Princess Hijab insists that anyone confusing her work with that of either conservative culture-jammers or Muslims supporting freedom of religious expression is missing the mark. "My work supports right-wing radicalism like *Taxi Driver**

---

* *Taxi Driver*: Reference to the 1976 film starring Robert De Niro as a violent and unstable New York City cab driver [Ed.].

support[s] cabbies. I'm using the hijab for myself." And looking through her catalog of work, neither label seems right. If her goal really is to cover up the skin-flashing women in ads, then why leave slinky legs on display underneath the painted-on hijabs? And if she's aiming to make a statement about the dignity of Muslim women, why hijabize male models in Dolce & Gabbana briefs with shoulder-length chadors, leaving their tanned, oiled abs and legs even more preposterously exposed?

In fact, Princess Hijab asserts, her dressing up of billboards is a symbolic act of resistance meant to reassert a "physical and mental integrity" against what she calls the "visual terrorism" of advertising. Arguing that the human right of expression has been displaced by publicists, advertisers, and the machinery of capitalist, commodified culture, she offers that, "My work explores how something as intimate as the human body has become as distant as a message from your corporate sponsor."

"Like that poster of Farrah Fawcett," she continues, "with her teeth clenched in fear above her perfect polyester swimsuit. When she revealed her cancer, we had to see her and her body as something capable of tragedy. It's that sort of re-humanization that I aim for with hijabization." Princess Hijab later admitted that this example, and equating wearing the hijab with physical suffering, was a clumsy one, but wanted the point to stand: Her work attempts to remove the hijab from its gendered and religious context and convert it into a symbol of empowerment and re-embodiment.

Equally central to her work is the goal of social equality. She notes that, in France, "You're always being asked your origin, which religion you follow. It's something that is very French, actually; you don't see it in New York or Berlin." Hinting that she is a racial outsider in France, Princess Hijab states that she is never taken at face value, but

instead pushed into a homogeneous social group and then judged by a corresponding set of stereotypes. With stratification by gender, religion, place of origin, and sexuality, she asserts, comes groups that are closed off from one another's experiences. Even during her time at university, she recalls her modes of expression being explained away by her origins: "I would be told [that it was] 'natural,' given my background, that I would work on [one] topic and not on another. I felt trapped." But by highlighting everyone's potential "outsider" status by imposing the hijab on public figures, PH asserts that she is "trying to create a connection with and between people."

Back when Princess Hijab was believed to be a Muslim, blogger Ethar El-Katatney of Muslimah Media Watch noted, "I'd actually love it if it turns out she's not a Muslim, because it lends credibility to the idea that the dislike of being exposed to 'visual aggression'

10

> **It's work that owes much more to Adbusters or No Logo than to the Taliban.**

is not necessarily rooted in religious belief. Fed up with women being used to sell products, hijabizing ads could be a way to 'take back' women's rights to their bodies." Indeed, in Princess Hijab's marked-up art, the headscarf is an agent not of covering but of exposure — of the oppressive nature of the advertising industry, of the displacement and disempowerment of women who are repeatedly told that they are not good, skinny, beautiful, sexy, or rich enough. It's work that owes much more to Adbusters or No Logo than to the Taliban.

Though Princess Hijab's work has gained international notice, like much street art it still actively resists a simplistic reading. And that she uses such a contested icon to wreak artistic revenge on the dual constructs of advertising and social prejudice means her work is ultimately as much about the interpretation of others as it is about her own intent. "People are confused by me," admits PH. "Some say I am pro-feminist, some say I am antifeminist; some say I am pro-Islam, others that I am anti-Islam. It's all very interesting — but at the end of the day, I am above all an artist."

Exploring Context

1. Adbusters is a network of "culture jammers." Among other campaigns, they have produced a number of spoofed ads for various products. Visit the gallery for these advertisements at adbusters.org/spoofads. In what ways is Princess Hijab "culture jamming"? Does her art seem to have the same goals as Adbusters' spoofs?

2. Using Google or another search engine, look for images of Princess Hijab's work. Do these images suggest that her work is art or graffiti? Do they suggest that her work is radical or conservative? Incorporate your findings into your response for Question 2 of Questions for Critical Reading.

3. Explore the website for the Hijab Shop (thehijabshop.com). How do both the design and content of the site challenge the work of Princess Hijab? Is the hijab repressive? Is it commercialized?

Questions for Connecting

1. In "Faith and Diplomacy" (p. 35), Madeleine Albright suggests that we need to be sensitive to issues of faith in the realm of diplomacy. Is that true in other areas of culture such as art? Synthesize Albright's position and Aburawa's exploration of Princess Hijab's work. What role does faith play in art? Does Princess Hijab's work support or subvert international diplomacy? What role should art play in politics?

2. Rachel Kadish, in "Who Is This Man, and Why Is He Screaming?" (p. 256), discusses the appropriation and circulation of one particular image as well as the ways in which that image changes meaning in different contexts. Apply her discussion to Princess Hijab's work. How would shifting the context change its meaning? You might want to draw on your work in Question 1 of Questions for Critical Reading and Question 1 of Exploring Context.

3. How does Princess Hijab's work relate to stereotypes about Muslims? Use Jennifer Pozner's analysis of stereotypes in reality television in "Ghetto Bitches, China Dolls, and Cha Cha Divas" (p. 397) to determine whether Princess Hijab supports or subverts stereotypes.

4. **CONNECTING TO E-PAGES** Aburawa writes, "In fact, Princess Hijab asserts, her dressing up of billboards is a symbolic act of resistance meant to reassert a 'physical and mental integrity' against what she calls the 'visual terrorism' of advertising" (p. 30). What does she mean by "visual terrorism"? Could the infographics by Buckfire & Buckfire,

carinsurancecomparison.org, and Drake Martinet (bedfordstmartins.com/emerging/epages) be thought of as "visual terrorism"? Do they require "symbolic acts of resistance"? If not, how are they different from the materials that Princess Hijab alters?

Language Matters

1. Aburawa's essay contains a number of foreign words and phrases, such as *jihad* and, most prominently, *hijab*. Use a grammar handbook or other reference resource to review the rules for including words from other languages. How well does Aburawa conform to these rules? How should you demarcate foreign words in your own writing?

2. At times Aburawa refers to Princess Hijab as "PH." What grammatical rules govern this usage? Review material on acronyms and abbreviations in a grammar handbook or other reliable resource. How well does Aburawa follow these rules? Why might she choose to use "PH"? When should you use acronyms or abbreviations in your own writing? How should they be introduced?

3. Wordle (wordle.net) is a tool for generating "word clouds" — it transforms text into a visual representation. Use Wordle to create a word cloud for this essay by either typing key quotations or key terms. How does the visual representation enhance or change your understanding of the text?

Assignments for Writing

1. What is the role of art in social change? Write a paper in which you assess Princess Hijab's work in the context of social change, based on Aburawa's discussion. Does this art create change or does it merely create controversy? Can art produce change or is it relegated to a separate sphere? How does the very public nature of Princess Hijab's work affect its potential for creating change?

2. Aburawa titles her essay "Veiled Threat." Write a paper in which you interpret the meaning of that title in the context of her discussion of Princess Hijab's work. What is the "veiled threat" in this work?

3. At the end of the essay, Princess Hijab claims that she is neither pro- nor anti-feminist, neither pro- nor anti-Islam. Write a paper in which you evaluate her claims using Aburawa's discussion as support. Is it possible to remain neutral as an artist? Do variable interpretations of what art means allow Princess Hijab to be neither pro nor anti? Or can you argue that she is indeed one or the other?

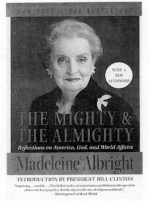

MADELEINE ALBRIGHT

Madeleine Albright is the Mortara Distinguished Professor of
Diplomacy at Georgetown University, but she is more widely
known for being the first woman to serve as U.S. secretary of
state, a position she held under President Bill Clinton from 1997
to 2001 and a role for which she was confirmed unanimously by
the Senate. She has also served as the U.S. ambassador to the
United Nations and as a member of the board of directors for
the Council on Foreign Relations, a nonpartisan foreign policy think tank. Albright attended
Wellesley College and Johns Hopkins University, and earned a Ph.D. in public law in government from Columbia University. She has written a number of books, including *The Mighty
and the Almighty: Reflections on America, God, and World Affairs* (2006), from which the
following chapter is taken; *Read My Pins: Stories from a Diplomat's Jewel Box* (2009); and,
most recently, *Prague Winter: A Personal Story of Remembrance and War, 1937–1948* (2012).

    The Mighty and the Almighty explores the role of religion in government affairs. As a
former government official and a person whose identity was shaped dramatically by religion
(she was raised Catholic but discovered her Jewish heritage when she was an adult), Albright
is able to offer a unique perspective on the power and place of religion in politics.

    In "Faith and Diplomacy," Albright suggests that religion's influence on world events is
inherent and persistent. Our government, she argues, must recognize this reality and adjust
its diplomatic strategy accordingly. Albright proposes concrete steps the government can
take to prepare itself for the religious dimensions of inter- and intranational disputes, but
she also advises that religiously informed diplomacy will not always solve the complicated
problems of a complicated world.

    Albright's aim, then, is to remind us that while dividing the religious from the political
has fostered peace and stability here at home, we must keep in mind that religion often plays
a much more central role in the affairs of nations abroad. Attending to that fact, Albright
shows us, should be central to U.S. foreign policy.

▶ TAGS: *religion, faith, conflict, community, diplomacy, diversity*

Questions for Critical Reading

1. Does religion help or hinder diplomacy? As you read Albright's text, search for quotations that support your interpretation.

2. Create a definition for the term *faith-based diplomacy*. What might such a term mean?
   How do you imagine it working, if at all? Compare your thoughts to Albright's arguments as you read the text.

3. Is faith-based diplomacy best pursued through the government or through private organizations? Read Albright's text, looking for passages that support your position.

Faith and Diplomacy

"This would be the best of all possible worlds if there were no religion in it!!" So wrote John Adams to Thomas Jefferson. The quotation, well known to proselytizing atheists, appears differently when placed in context. The full passage reads:

> Twenty times in the course of my late reading have I been on the point of breaking out, "This would be the best of all possible worlds if there were no religion in it!!" But in this exclamation I would have been . . . fanatical. . . . Without religion this world would be something not fit to be mentioned in polite company, I mean hell.

In his song "Imagine," John Lennon urged us to dream of a world free of religious doctrines. For many nonbelievers, religion is not the solution to anything. For centuries, they argue, people have been making each other miserable in the name of God. Studies indicate that wars with a religious component last longer and are fought more savagely than other conflicts. As the acerbic liberal columnist I. F. Stone observed, "Too many throats have been cut in God's name through the ages, and God has enlisted in too many wars. War for sport or plunder has never been as bad as war waged because one man's belief was theoretically 'irreconcilable' with another."

The fault in such logic is that, although we know what a globe plagued by religious strife is like, we do not know what it would be like to live in a world where religious faith is absent. We have, however, had clues from Lenin, Stalin, Mao Zedong,* and, I would also argue, the Nazis, who conjured up a soulless Christianity that denied and defamed the Jewish roots of that faith. It is easy to blame religion — or, more fairly, what some people do in the name of religion — for all our troubles, but that is too simple. Religion is a powerful force, but its impact depends entirely on what it inspires people to do. The challenge for policy-makers is to harness the unifying potential of faith, while containing its capacity to divide. This requires, at a minimum, that we see spiritual matters as a subject worth studying. Too often, as the Catholic theologian Bryan Hehir notes, "there is an assumption that you do not have to understand religion in order to understand the world. You need to understand politics, strategy, economics, and law, but

> **It is easy to blame religion . . . for all our troubles, but that is too simple.**

you do not need to understand religion. If you look at standard textbooks of international relations or the way we organize our foreign ministry, there's no place where a sophisticated understanding of religion as a public force in the world is dealt with."

To anticipate events rather than merely respond to them, American diplomats will need to take Hehir's advice and think more expansively about the role of religion in

---

* Lenin, Stalin, Mao Zedong: Vladimir Lenin (1870–1924) was a leading figure in the Russian revolution of 1917 (which led to the communist takeover); Lenin was the first head of the USSR. Joseph Stalin (1879–1953) was dictator of the Soviet Union after the death of Lenin and was responsible for the murder and enslavement of millions. Mao Zedong (1893–1976) was a communist leader and the founder of the People's Republic of China. All three promoted atheism as official government policy [Ed.].

foreign policy and about their own need for expertise. They should develop the ability to recognize where and how religious beliefs contribute to conflicts and when religious principles might be invoked to ease strife. They should also reorient our foreign policy institutions to take fully into account the immense power of religion to influence how people think, feel, and act. The signs of such influence are all around us in the lives of people of many different faiths. By way of illustration, I offer three stories.

In 1981, I visited Poland; it was during the second year of the uprising by the Solidarity movement against the communist government. I had long studied central and eastern Europe, where, for decades, very little had changed. Now the entire region was awakening, as from a deep slumber. A large part of the reason was that Pope John Paul II had earlier returned for the first time to Poland, his native land. Formerly Karol Wojtyla, a teacher, priest, and bishop of Kraków, the pope exemplified the pervasive role that religion had played in the history of Poland. While communist leaders in Warsaw dictated what Poles could do, parish priests in every corner of the country still spoke to what Poles believed. The government, alarmed by the prospect of the pope's pilgrimage, sent a memorandum to schoolteachers identifying John Paul II as "our enemy" and warning of the dangers posed by "his uncommon skills and great sense of humor." The authorities nevertheless made a tactical mistake by allowing church officials to organize the visit, giving them a chance to schedule a series of direct contacts between the "people's pope" and the pope's people.

One of the titles of the bishop of Rome is pontifex maximus, or "greatest bridge-builder." In Poland, John Paul II helped construct a bridge that would ultimately restore the connection between Europe's East and West. For bricks, he used words carefully chosen to expose the void at the heart of the communist system, arguing that if people were to fulfill their responsibility to live according to moral principles, they must first have the right to do so. He made plain his conviction that the totalitarian regime could not survive if Poles had the courage to withhold their cooperation. Above all, he urged his countrymen not to be afraid—a simple request with enormous impact. Slowly at first, but with gathering momentum, the pope's listeners drew strength from one another. No longer were they separated into small, controllable groups; the communists' obsession with isolating dangerous ideas had met its match. Standing amid huge crowds, the listeners recognized in each other once again the qualities that made them proud to be Polish—faith in God and a willingness to run risks for freedom. The pope's visits—for he made more than one—sparked a revolution of the spirit that liberated Poland, brought down the Berlin Wall, reunited Europe, and transformed the face of the world.

The pope helped the people of Poland to overcome their fear. Bob Seiple, who served with me in the State Department as the first American ambassador-at-large for international religious freedom, tells a second story, this one about overcoming hate. It concerns Mary, a young Lebanese woman he encountered while working as the head of World Vision, a Christian relief and development agency. In the 1980s, Lebanon had been the scene of a destructive and multisided civil war. Mary lived in a mostly Christian village; and when a Muslim militia invaded it, everyone fled. Mary tripped on a root, plunging face-first to the ground. As she scrambled to her knees, a young man of no more than twenty pressed the barrel of a pistol into the side of her head and demanded, "Renounce the cross or die." Mary did not flinch. "I was born a Christian," she said. "I will die a Christian." The pistol fired, propelling a bullet through Mary's neck and spine. Remorselessly, the militiaman carved a cross on her chest with his bayonet, then left her to die.

The following day, the militia returned and prepared to occupy the village. As they carted off the dead, a few of them came across Mary, still alive but unable to move; she was paralyzed. Instead of finishing her off, the militiamen improvised a stretcher out of wood and cloth and took her to a hospital. Seiple continues:

> And I'm talking to Mary, sitting across from her, and I said, "Mary, this makes absolutely no sense. These are people who tried to kill you. Why in the world would they take you to the hospital the next day?"
>
> She says, "You know, sometimes bad people are taught to do good things."
>
> And I said, "Mary, how do you feel about the person who pulled the trigger? Here you are, an Arab woman in a land twice occupied at that time—the Israelis in the south, the Syrians every place else—strapped to a wheelchair, held hostage by your own body, a ward of the state for the rest of your life. How do you feel about the guy who pulled the trigger?"
>
> She said, "I have forgiven him."
>
> "Mary, how in the world could you forgive him?"
>
> "Well, I forgave him because my God forgave me. It's as simple as that."

In Seiple's view, there are two lessons in this story. The first is that there are people who are willing to die—and kill—for their faith. This was true thousands of years ago and is no less true today. The second lesson is that religion at its best teaches forgiveness and reconciliation, not only when those acts are relatively easy but also when they are almost unbelievably difficult. (Mary, I need hardly add, is a more forgiving person than most—including me.)

The third story involves a boy with haunted eyes whom I met on a blisteringly hot   10 afternoon in December 1997 during my first trip to Africa as secretary of state. The youngster looked about five years old and spoke softly, in a voice drained of emotion. He told me that, two weeks earlier, the small village where his family lived had been attacked. His mother had thrown him to the ground, shielding him with her body. When it was quiet, he wriggled his way out from under her and looked. His mother was dead. The bodies of other women were nearby, more than a dozen, drenched in blood. The boy then heard an infant crying; it was his sister, lying among the corpses. He gathered the baby into his arms and started walking. For hours, as the youngster stumbled along over hills and rocks, the infant wailed. Eventually they came to a place where the boy knew from experience that they would be welcomed and kept safe.

That place was Gulu, a town in a remote part of northern Uganda. World Vision ran the camp and hospital there—a haven for local villagers, who were being terrorized by an outlaw militia group. During the previous decade, an estimated 8,000 children had been kidnapped; most were presumed dead. Boys who survived and did not escape were impressed into rebel units; girls were taken as servants or "wives."

Camp officials blamed rebel leaders who had twisted religion into something grotesque. The tragedy had begun in 1986, when a change in government threatened the privileges of a previously dominant tribe, the Acholi. Fear is a powerful motivator, and the Acholi feared retribution for the many abuses they had committed while in power. A potential savior arrived in the unlikely form of a thirty-year-old woman, Alice Auma, who said that she was able to commune with spirits—a rare but by no means unique claim in her culture. She told her companions that she had been possessed by a deceased Italian military officer who had instructed her to organize an army and retake Kampala, the Ugandan capital. Once victory was achieved, commanded the spirit, the Acholi should cleanse themselves by seeking forgiveness. Auma's sacred campaign was launched but lacked the military clout to match its supernatural inspiration. After some initial successes, the movement—armed only with sticks, stones, and voodoo dolls—was crushed. Auma, her mind no longer host to the Italian officer, found refuge across the border in Kenya.

That would have ended the story had not Joseph Kony, Auma's nephew, decided to take up the cause of holy war. Piecing together a small force from various rebel groups, he assembled what came to be known as the Lord's Resistance Army (LRA). From 1987 on, the LRA has attacked villagers throughout the region, also targeting local governments and aid workers. Because Kony finds adults hard to control and reluctant to enlist, he kidnaps children as a means of procuring troops. Once captured, the children are forced to obey or be put to death; and obedience demands a willingness to kill anyone, including one another. Discipline is administered in the form of beatings, lashings, and amputations predicated on their leader's reading of the Old Testament. The LRA's professed goal is to overthrow the Ugandan government and replace it with one based on the Ten Commandments—or actually ten plus one. The eleventh, added by Kony to restrict the movements of adversaries, is "Thou shalt not ride a bicycle."

Itself a product of fear, the LRA has survived twenty years by instilling fear in others. The Ugandan government has veered between efforts to make peace with the LRA and efforts to destroy it, but officials lack the resources to protect those living in the vicinity of the rebel force. That task has been left to World Vision and similar groups whose resources are also limited, as I saw during my tour of the camp in Gulu. The surroundings reminded me of pictures I had seen of the Crimean War. The camp hospital smelled of disinfectant and human waste. Ancient IVs dripped. Mosquitoes were buzzing everywhere. There were hundreds of patients, most of them children, many covered with welts and scars, some missing a limb. I met a group of teenage girls sitting on mattresses, braiding each other's hair. They looked as if they belonged in junior high school, yet several were already mothers, their babies sired by LRA rapists. "Even if you are a very young girl," said one, who was wearing a Mickey Mouse T-shirt, "you would be given to a man who was the age of my father."

As I started to leave, a young man came up to me holding an infant. "This is the girl that little boy brought to us, his little sister. Her name is Charity." As I cradled the tiny orphan, I was told that the girl had been named for one of the volunteers at the mission. There were many such volunteers. It was a place filled with terrible suffering but also a resilient joy. Patients and volunteers laughed, sang, played games, and cared for each other. The Italian doctor who ran the facility had been in Gulu for more than twenty years. What a contrast between the faith that manifests itself in such love and the twisted fantasies pursued by the LRA.*

One insight that is present in these stories and often in religious faith more generally is that we share a kinship with one another, however distant it may sometimes seem; we are all created in the image of God. This in turn places upon us a responsibility to our neighbors. That principle provides both a solid foundation for religion and a respectable basis for organizing the affairs of secular society. What complicates matters is that religion can be interpreted in ways that exclude large numbers of people from any claim to kinship. Those truly imbued with religious faith—such as Pope John Paul II, Bob Seiple's Mary, and the volunteers in Gulu—may affirm "We are all God's children"; but others may follow their convictions to a more argumentative conclusion—"I am right, you are wrong, go to hell!"

When I appeared on a panel with the Jewish writer and thinker Elie Wiesel, a survivor of the Holocaust, he recalled how a group of scholars had once been asked to name the unhappiest character in the Bible. Some said Job, because of the trials he endured. Some said Moses, because he was denied entry to the promised land. Some said the Virgin Mary, because she witnessed the death of her son. The best answer, Wiesel suggested, might in fact be God, because of the sorrow caused by people fighting, killing, and abusing each other in His name.

This is why so many practitioners of foreign policy—including me—have sought to separate religion from world politics, to liberate logic from beliefs that transcend logic. It is, after all, hard enough to divide land between two groups on the basis of legal or economic equity; it is far harder if one or both claim that the land in question was given to them by God. But religious motivations do not disappear simply because they are not mentioned; more often they lie dormant only to rise up again at the least convenient moment. As our experience in Iran reflected, the United States has not always understood this well enough. To lead internationally, American policy-makers must learn as much as possible about religion, and then incorporate that knowledge in their strategies. Bryan Hehir has compared this challenge to brain surgery—a necessary task, but fatal if not done well.

In any conflict, reconciliation becomes possible when the antagonists cease dehumanizing each other and begin instead to see a bit of themselves in their enemy. That is why it is a standard negotiating technique to ask each side to stand in the shoes of the other. Often this is not as difficult as it might seem. The very fact that adversaries have been fighting over the same issue or prize can furnish a common ground. For centuries, Protestants and Catholics competed for religious ascendancy in Europe. That was a point of similarity: wanting to be number one. For even longer, Christians, Muslims, and Jews have pursued rival claims in Jerusalem; that, too, is a point of similarity—wanting to occupy the same space. In parts of Asia and Africa, Christians and Muslims are fighting,

---

* In October 2005, the International Criminal Court issued arrest warrants for Joseph Kony and four other LRA leaders on the charge of crimes against humanity. The court does not, however, have any independent capacity to enforce those warrants.

but they share a desire to worship freely and without fear. When people are pursuing the same goal, each side should be able to understand what motivates the other. To settle their differences, they need only find a formula for sharing what both want—a tricky task, but one that can at least be addressed through an appeal to reason.

Not all conflicts lend themselves to this sort of negotiation. During World War II,   20 the Axis and the Allies* were fighting for two entirely different visions of the future. Today, Al Qaeda's lust for a war of vengeance fought with the tools of terror cannot be accommodated. Some differences are too great to be reconciled. In most situations, however, reconciliation will be eminently preferable to continued stalemate or war. But how is reconciliation achieved?

When participants in a conflict claim to be people of faith, a negotiator who has the credentials and the credibility to do so might wish to call their bluff. If the combatants argue the morality of their cause, how is that morality reflected in their actions? Are they allowing their religion to guide them or using it as a debating point to advance their interests? Has their faith instilled in them a sense of responsibility toward others or a sense of entitlement causing them to disregard the rights and views of everyone else?

Effective foreign policy requires that we comprehend why others act as they do.

If I were secretary of state today, I would not seek to mediate disputes on the basis of religious principles any more than I would try to negotiate alone the more intricate details of a trade agreement or a pact on arms control. In each case, I would ask people more expert than I to begin the process of identifying key issues, exploring the possibilities, and suggesting a course of action. It might well be that my involvement, or the president's, would be necessary to close a deal, but the outlines would be drawn by those who know every nuance of the issues at hand. When I was secretary of state, I had an entire bureau of economic experts I could turn to, and a cadre of experts on nonproliferation and arms control whose mastery of technical jargon earned them a nickname, "the priesthood." With the notable exception of Ambassador Seiple, I did not have similar expertise available for integrating religious principles into our efforts at diplomacy. Given the nature of today's world, knowledge of this type is essential.

If diplomacy is the art of persuading others to act as we would wish, effective foreign policy requires that we comprehend why others act as they do. Fortunately, the constitutional requirement that separates state from church in the United States does not also insist that the state be ignorant of the church, mosque, synagogue, pagoda, and temple. In the future, no American ambassador should be assigned to a country where religious feelings are strong unless he or she has a deep understanding of the faiths commonly practiced there. Ambassadors and their representatives, wherever they are assigned, should establish relationships with local religious leaders. The State Department should hire or train a core of specialists in religion to be deployed both in Washington and in key embassies overseas.

---

* Axis and the Allies: The Axis powers consisted primarily of Germany, Italy, and Japan. They were opposed by the Allied forces of France, Poland, the United Kingdom, Britain, Australia, New Zealand, Canada, and South Africa and, after 1941, the Soviet Union and the United States [Ed.].

In 1994, the Center for Strategic and International Studies published *Religion, the Missing Dimension of Statecraft*. The book makes a compelling case for recognizing the role of religion in affecting political behavior and for using spiritual tools to help resolve conflicts. Douglas Johnston, the book's coauthor, subsequently formed the International Center for Religion and Diplomacy (ICRD), which has continued to study what it calls "faith-based diplomacy" while also playing an important mediating role in Sudan and establishing useful relationships in Kashmir, Pakistan, and Iran. Johnston, a former naval officer and senior official in the Defense Department, believes that, ordinarily, everyone of influence in a given situation is not necessarily bad, and those who are bad aren't bad all the time. He argues that a faith-based mediator has means that a conventional diplomat lacks, including prayers, fasting, forgiveness, repentance, and the inspiration of scripture.

The ICRD is not alone in its efforts. After leaving the State Department, Bob Seiple founded the Institute for Global Engagement, which is working to improve the climate for religious liberty in such volatile nations as Uzbekistan and Laos. The institute's mantra is, "Know your faith at its deepest and richest best, and enough about your neighbor's faith to respect it."

While in office, I had occasion to work closely with the Community of Sant'Egidio, a lay movement that began in Rome in the 1960s, inspired by the Second Vatican Council of Pope John XXIII. Over a period of years, Sant'Egidio successfully brokered negotiations ending a long and bloody civil war in Mozambique. It has also played a constructive role in, among other places, Kosovo, Algeria, Burundi, and Congo. The community sees prayer, service to the poor, ecumenism, and dialogue as the building blocks of interreligious cooperation and problem solving.

Numerous other faith-based organizations, representing every major religion, are in operation. They are most effective when they function cooperatively, pooling their resources and finding areas in which to specialize. Some are most skilled at mediation; others are best at helping former combatants readjust to civilian life. Still others emphasize prevention, addressing a problem before it can explode into violence. Many are experts in economic development or building democracy, both insurance policies against war. Together, these activists have more resources, more skilled personnel, a longer attention span, more experience, more dedication, and more success in fostering reconciliation than any government.

The most famous example of faith-based peacemaking was orchestrated by President Jimmy Carter at Camp David in 1978. Most observers acknowledge that the peace agreement between Egypt and Israel would never have come about if not for Carter's ability to understand and appeal to the deep religious convictions of President Sadat and Prime Minister Begin. I recently asked the former president how policy-makers should think about religion as part of the foreign policy puzzle. He told me that it is not possible to separate what people feel and believe in the spiritual realm from what they will do as a matter of public policy. "This is an opportunity," he argued, "because the basic elements of the major religious faiths are so similar—humility, justice, and peace." He said that in the unofficial diplomacy he is often asked to conduct through the Carter Center, one of the first aspects he investigates is whether the parties to a dispute represent the same faith. He said it is often simpler to deal with people of completely different faiths than with those who share a religion but disagree about how it should be interpreted. As a moderate Baptist, Carter said he found it less complicated to have a conversation with a Catholic than with a Baptist fundamentalist; with the Catholic it was easier simply to accept the differences and not feel obliged to argue about them.

When I broached this same subject with Bill Clinton, he stressed two points. First, religious leaders can help to validate a peace process before, during, and after negotiations; through dialogue and public statements, they can make peace easier to achieve and sustain. Second, persuading people of different faiths to work cooperatively requires separating what is debatable in scripture from what is not. "If you're dealing with people who profess faith," he said, "they must believe there is a Creator; if they believe that, they should agree that God created everyone. This takes them from the specific to the universal. Once they acknowledge their common humanity, it becomes harder to kill each other; then compromise becomes easier because they've admitted that they are dealing with people like themselves, not some kind of Satan or subhuman species."

Faith-based diplomacy can be a useful tool of foreign policy. I am not arguing,   30
however, that it can replace traditional diplomacy. Often the protagonists in a political drama are immune to, or deeply suspicious of, appeals made on religious or moral grounds. But if we do not expect miracles, little is lost in making the attempt. The resurgence of religious feeling will continue to influence world events. American policymakers cannot afford to ignore this; on balance they should welcome it. Religion at its best can reinforce the core values necessary for people from different cultures to live in some degree of harmony; we should make the most of that possibility.

Exploring Context

1. Using Flickr (flickr.com), search for images that illustrate Albright's argument. Paste these images into a document to create a visual montage of this essay.

2. Visit the website for the U.S. Department of State at state.gov. Explore the site, reading it critically to determine the role that religion currently plays in U.S. foreign policy. Does this website support your response to Question 3 of Questions for Critical Reading?

3. The International Center for Religion and Diplomacy (icrd.org) is an organization that seems to pursue Albright's goals of considering religion in diplomacy. Search through the center's website for evidence that would support Albright's arguments. Does it reflect your vision of faith-inflected diplomacy from Question 2 of Questions for Critical Reading?

Questions for Connecting

1. How would the primacy of practice, as described by Kwame Anthony Appiah in "Making Conversation" and "The Primacy of Practice" (p. 67), complicate Albright's vision of diplomacy? Would Appiah's understanding of cosmopolitanism enhance a faith-based diplomacy, or do political practices resist the kinds of changes Albright suggests? How can you synthesize their positions to argue for an effective diplomacy?

2. Is Kenji Yoshino's vision of civil rights in "Preface" and "The New Civil Rights" (p. 552) compatible with Albright's call for taking religion into consideration in foreign policy? Is the diplomacy described by Albright akin to a liberty or equality paradigm? Synthesize the ideas of these two authors and support your argument with quotations from both texts.

3. Which author provides a better strategy for reaching peace, Albright or Thomas L. Friedman in "The Dell Theory of Conflict Prevention" (p. 166)? Are their proposals concerning religion and economics and the roles each plays in global politics compatible? Is it possible to synthesize their ideas?

4. **CONNECTING TO E-PAGES** What reaction do you think Albright might have to "Call of Duty: Afghanistan," the Wired.com report on the video game the U.S. Army produced in order to train soldiers (bedfordstmartins.com/emerging/epages)? How might viewing our enemies as video game characters influence the way we think of them? What is gained in such a view, and what is lost? Using quotations from Albright, explain your answer.

Language Matters

1. Varying your word choice adds interest for the reader, but it can be a particularly challenging task. Look back through Albright's essay. How does she vary her word choice to convey meaning? How many different words for "diplomacy" or "faith" does she use? How does she handle the implications of these terms? How might you vary your word choice in your own writing?

2. Select a key passage from Albright and replace all the verbs with blanks ("_____"). Working in small groups, fill in the blanks with verbs and then reflect on which verbs you chose and why. How does the context of each sentence determine which word to use? More important, how significant are verbs to the meaning of a sentence? Could you change Albright's entire argument by changing the verbs?

3. Constellations help us to make sense out of the stars — they give the stars meaning by grouping them into meaningful patterns. Examine how sentence structure does the same with words. Select a key quotation from Albright's essay and then create a map of its different parts. How did you choose to break up the sentence? What relationships can you find among the parts? Are some connections more important than others? That is, if you took out certain parts of the sentence, would it still have the same meaning?

Assignments for Writing

1. Albright's essay makes it clear that faith can both unite and divide people. Write a paper in which you argue for faith's potential to enable political unification. Draw on your work on the role of religion in diplomacy from Question 1 in Questions for Critical Reading as well as the current political climate — both domestic and international — in your discussion. The goal of this assignment is for you to synthesize your experiences and observations of faith's function in current political climates with Albright's arguments. Consider, for example, what Albright says about a world without political doctrine; also, pay close attention to the stories she shares and the examples she offers the reader.

2. Albright finds a shared sense of humanity through religion, but the idea of a common sense of humanity extends to other fields of knowledge and experience. Write a paper in which you identify another avenue through which humans might find commonalities. Extend Albright's insights to these other instances of shared humanity, synthesizing her arguments with your examples. You may wish to use your work with one of the authors from Questions for Connecting in formulating your argument. To begin thinking critically about this assignment, consider these questions: In the end, is religion the only thing that binds humans together? Is religion the only thing that separates humans from everything else in existence?

3. Albright stresses that ignorance must be overcome in order for all of us to find common political ground. Although her essay focuses specifically on religious ignorance, her position could be the foundation for a much more comprehensive conversation on the matter. Write an essay in which you examine the possibilities of overcoming ignorance in relation to diplomacy. Must we overcome ignorance—religious or otherwise—in order to achieve productive international relations? If so, how do we overcome this ignorance? You may wish to incorporate the work you did in Question 3 of Exploring Context.

JULIA ALVAREZ

Julia Alvarez was born in New York. Shortly afterward, her family returned to the Dominican Republic, where they lived under the infamous Trujillo dictatorship. Alvarez's father became involved with the underground resistance, and eventually the family was forced to flee the country and return to the United States, an experience that led Alvarez to write the 1994 novel *In the Time of the Butterflies*. She has written many other novels, including *How the García Girls Lost Their Accents* (1991), as well as essays, poetry, and children's literature. She earned her B.A. from Middlebury College and an M.A. in creative writing from Syracuse University. Alvarez has received numerous awards and honors, including the Latina Leader Award in Literature from the Congressional Hispanic Caucus Institute in 2007. Her nonfiction book *Once Upon a Quinceañera: Coming of Age in the USA*, from which the following selection is taken, was a 2007 finalist for a National Book Critics Circle Award.

In *Once Upon a Quinceañera,* Alvarez follows the female coming-of-age tradition known among Hispanic communities as quinceañera (or *quince*, for short). Throughout the book, Alvarez spends time with Monica, who is preparing for her quinceañera, as well as other teen girls and their families. Through her journey with these girls and their families, Alvarez is able to explore the history and evolution of the quince tradition in the context of immigration, culture, class, and gender. In addition, Alvarez looks to the influences of religion, cultural tradition, and American consumerism for reasons this ritual is able to thrive throughout generations. Overall, while the book closely examines the motions and traditions of quinces, Alvarez pushes readers and herself to interrogate cultural perceptions of gender, as well as rituals and rites of passage, and examine how these perceptions might be influenced when crossing cultural boundaries.

In the following selections, Alvarez touches on various aspects of the quinceañera. While some view the quince as the initiation of a young girl into a community of womanhood and culture of responsibility, Alvarez wonders if such arguments merely provide an illusion of female power within a traditionally patriarchal system. Though Alvarez is continually skeptical of the quince craze, she often finds herself caught up in the excitement. Moments such as these lead Alvarez to a new stage of investigation in which she explores the social, familial, and economic implications of the quince tradition. Perhaps as Isabella, founder of bellaquinceanera.com, suggests, quinceañeras in the twenty-first century are an opportunity to offer young Latina women a sense of empowerment and individual importance. In order to do this, the tradition must be redefined in a way that reflects and embodies the values and desires of women today. Alvarez addresses the idea of whether and how this redefining might occur by leading readers and herself to consider the meaning of tradition and gender as they are practiced today. How can traditions be redefined in the spirit of these changing values and desires? Is it possible to redefine traditions without losing the original ties to them? How is it possible for traditions to offer a means of crossing cultural and social boundaries? What role does gender play in the preservation of cultural traditions, and how might these traditions differ according to gender? In what ways has consumerism affected the importance of quinceañeras and other traditions?

▶ TAGS: *rites, culture, identity, tradition, race, gender*

Questions for Critical Reading

1. In this text, Alvarez introduces the term *retroculturation*. Before reading the essay, what would you have thought this term might mean? Reread Alvarez's text to locate passages that define the term. Can you think of additional examples? Do these examples support Alvarez's argument?

2. What do you think is the importance (if any) of coming-of-age rituals like the quince? As you read Alvarez's text, search for passages that reveal the author's stance on this issue.

3. What is the value of tradition? Find quotations from Alvarez that support your position. Are the economic costs of traditions like quinces worth their cultural value?

Selections from *Once Upon a Quinceañera*

Every Girl Should Have One

I wish I'd had Isabella Martínez Wall to call up and talk to back when I was a young teen in need of rescue and an infusion of self-esteem.

Based in Los Angeles, Isabella is the founder of a one-stop quinceañera Web site cum advice column, bellaquinceañera.com. She's also an actress, a former Miss Dominican Republic, a successful fashion model, and founder of Someone Cares International, a nonprofit that is described on her Web site as "benefiting needy children" in her native country. Speaking by phone with this passionate and inspirational woman, I feel the same unsettling mixture of amazement, caution, and yearning that I feel toward televangelists. Can somebody really believe this? And if so, why can't I?

I learned about Isabella from a Dominican contact at Disney World, whom I had called to find out more about the Disney quince package. She described Isabella as an "awesome, full-bodied Latina" who is doing amazing things for young Hispanic girls. According to my contact, Isabella had actually found that young girls who had quinceañeras didn't drop out of school, didn't get pregnant, didn't get in trouble.

"Really? I mean, statistically?" I shot back. Here you go, I thought, peppering these kids with questions. But a quinceañera panacea seemed too good to be true. I'd just barely surfaced from *The State of Hispanic Girls** with a sense of dread in my heart, which was also making me want to grab for a cure.

"I don't know," my contact said. "Talk to Isabella, she'll tell you."   5

Ah, my people, I thought. Statistics are for the gringos. We trust testimonials, what our hearts and telenovelas tell us. I had just attended a lecture by Dr. James Martin titled "The Meaning of the 21st Century." Solutions to world problems didn't have to be costly or complex, the information technology guru explained. In Mexico, a vanguard group of TV producers who understood the dangers of population explosion had started a campaign to bring down the birthrate by introducing female leads who practiced birth control into popular telenovelas. Initial results showed the campaign was working. Better than pamphlets or science classes or lectures like Dr. Martin's.

When I reached Isabella, after the initial honorifics, "So you're the author!" "So you're the beauty queen!" I asked her about this claim I'd heard that quinceañeras really turn girls around. Not that I wanted an analysis or anything academic, I added, thinking maybe I was sounding too much like a doubting-Thomas gringa. But with all those statistics still heavy in my heart, I wanted to hear why she thought quinceañeras were so effective. "Well, let me tell you." Isabella laughed right out. "There's nothing academic about a quinceañera!

"What I mean is there's no textbook about how you have to do a quinceañera," Isabella went on to explain. She hears from a lot of young ladies on her Web site, where she offers free advice, a kind of Ann Landers to Latina girls.

"They write me, and they ask, can I wear a short dress? Does it have to be white? Can I have a court with only my best friend and my sister? I tell them, listen, there are no rules. The most important thing is to make this celebration yours, totally yours. I try to educate them, I talk to them, the site is highly interactive. Quinceañeras are about creating strong women. Our girls need all the help we can give them."

> **The most important thing is to make this celebration yours, totally yours.**

It's funny how you are sure you are going to end up on the other side of an opin-   10
ion from someone, and it turns out you're in each other's court. Never would I have guessed that a former beauty queen promoting a princessy fantasy would turn out to be a crown-carrying feminist. But how on earth can this quasi beauty pageant cum mini wedding make an Amazon out of a stardust girl?

"I have seen it happen!" In fact, it happened to Isabella herself. As a teenager growing up in the Dominican Republic, she hit a wall. "I was smoking, drinking, I had body issues and identity problems." I'm dying to ask her to be specific, but she is on a roll. "When I turned fifteen, everybody started having quinceañeras. I mean everybody. Quinceañeras know no social or class boundaries. You might not have the money but you have a quinceañera for your daughter. The family is making that statement. We might not be rich but we value our daughter."

---

* A study published by the National Coalition of Hispanic Health and Human Services Organizations in 1999 that documented the high rates of teen pregnancy, substance abuse, school dropouts, and suicide attempts by young Latinas.

Isabella's quinceañera turned her around. "It made me feel so special." In fact, she credits it with leading her down the path to being crowned Miss Dominican Republic. "I've been there," Isabella says. "I had that moment. But how many women in the world get to feel like a queen? How many?"

Not this skinny, undersized Latina for sure, I have to agree.

"Well, that's the first reason to have a quinceañera," Isabella says. "To have that experience and not because you're marrying someone."

The second reason comes from her own experience. "Being fifteen, let's face it, it's a tough age. Your body is all over the map. You wonder who you are. Who your friends are. Where you're going. You can get lost for sure. What better time in your life to have your family, friends, community come together and create a support system for you for the rest of your life?"

Isn't that asking an awful lot of a quinceañera?

But Isabella dismisses my skepticism. "About two years ago, I realized that I had a mission: to promote this important ritual. And yes, I've seen it turn girls around. I don't have statistics, this is not academic, like I said, but girls who have quinces, think about it, they're spending a lot of time with their moms, shopping, talking about life. Their friends are coming over to do rehearsals. I mean, a room full of fifteen-year-olds learning dance steps right under your nose. Parents are always complaining they don't know what to do when their daughters hit puberty. *Hel*-lo?! Here's something to do. Give her a wishing well."

"Of course, we've got to take the quinceañera a step forward," Isabella adds. Before, the whole quinceañera thing was about a girl being of marriageable age, goods to be displayed. But now we can invest this old tradition with new meaning.

"We can create a support platform for that young lady that she can have to look back upon for the rest of her life. That moment when she stands dressed like a queen with her mom beside her looking in the mirror, for that moment, if only that moment, she knows she is all right just as she is. She is the queen of her life if she can hold on to that feeling."

In fact, Isabella thinks quinces are so special, the tradition should come out of its ethnic closet and become an American phenomenon. "I don't care what class or group you come from," Isabella claims. "Every girl should have one."

When I hang up I feel that uplifted feeling that must be why folks pick up the phone after watching a TV evangelist and put a donation on their charge card.

One-(Very Small)-Size-Fits-All Script

My first year at Abbot* did for me what Isabella Martínez Wall's year of going to quinceañeras and having her own quinceañera did for her. It gave me a new community to belong to, a narrative I could follow into adulthood. Instead of a family and community rallying around the quinceañera's transformation into a woman, planning and preparing sometimes for a year for that symbolic pageant marking her passage, I had a community of classmates and female teachers and coaches and housemothers honing

---

* Abbot Academy: A private boarding school for girls in Massachusetts. [Ed.]

my skills, encouraging my talents, preparing me for being what Isabella Martínez Wall would call "queen of my own life."

Incidentally, I was also turning from fourteen to fifteen, and, needless to say, away at a school where we were the only Latinas (the closest thing to us was a German girl whose parents lived in Guatemala and an American girl whose father was posted in Venezuela), I did not have a quinceañera. Nor was much made of my fifteenth birthday: a cake in the dorm, a phone call from my parents, a card with a check for twenty-five dollars. My older sister had already gotten my mother's ring, and away at school I could shave my legs and wear makeup without asking anyone for permission.

But although some psychological elements of the American quinceañera and my first Abbot year were the same—a community grooming a young lady for her entry into womanhood—the content of that grooming was significantly different. We Abbot girls were encouraged to develop our minds, not leave our brains parked at the door of our gender. In fact, the plaque at the front gate encouraged us to ENTER INTO UNDERSTANDING, SO YOU MAY GO FORTH TO NOBLER LIVING. Nobler living! True, many of my Abbot classmates would eventually marry and have children (this was, after all, the mid-sixties), but it was assumed we would all go to college first. (Out of a class of seventy-eight girls, only one, my roommate, did not go to college, but married her longtime boyfriend instead.) And since many of our teachers were unmarried women, making their own way in the world, the subliminal message was clear: We were to be smart, resourceful, independent women.

This new narrative of female possibility was groundbreaking and bracing even for my American classmates. "Although Columbus and Cabot never heard of Abbot," one of our school songs began. A good thing, too. Those old-world explorers would not have approved of young women taking over the helm of their journey through life and discovering their own new worlds.

In contrast, the typical quinceañera enacts a traditional narrative that is, let's face it, a one-(very small)-size-fits-all script corseting a full-bodied female life. The young Latina is dressed up in finery not unlike a bride, her father is changing her shoes, claiming that first waltz, then passing her on to a brother or uncle or grandfather, until finally she ends up in the arms of her escort to a round of applause. The quinceañera is like a rehearsal wedding without a groom, and it sends a clear message to the Latina girl: We expect you to get married, have children, devote yourself to your family. It's no wonder that girls end up getting pregnant soon after celebrating their quinces. Jaider Sánchez, a hairdresser and dance coach for quinceañeras in Denver, mentioned in a recent interview that out of seven quinceañeras he instructed in 2005, four have already invited him to their baby showers.

It's no wonder that girls end up getting pregnant soon after celebrating their quinces.

And so, although it gives her a momentary illusion of power (the princess rhetoric, the celebration of her sexual power, her youth, her beauty), in fact, the ritual enacts an old paradigm of the patriarchy increasingly (in the U.S.A.) pumped up by a greedy market. In a fascinating book titled *Emerging from the Chrysalis: Studies in Rituals of Women's Initiations*, Bruce Lincoln, who teaches at the University of Chicago Divinity School, amplifies Arnold van Gennep's classic theory about rites of passage as they

25

apply to females. According to van Gennep, who coined the term, rites of passage are ceremonies within cultures that enable an individual to pass from one well-defined role to another. Male initiation rites of passage involve the stripping, testing, and reintegration of the young man into the sociopolitical adult society.

But what Bruce Lincoln found was that female initiations follow a different pattern: The girl is decked in ceremonial finery, often layer on layer is piled on her, a magnification that confers on her cosmic status and participation in a mythic drama. "Rituals of women's initiation claim to transform a girl into a woman, [they] claim to renew society by providing it with a new productive member." During the ceremonies, the initiant is "regarded as having become a deity, a culture heroine, the link between past and future." So far so good, but Bruce Lincoln goes on to suggest that this mythic power is a substitution for actual power, a pie in the sky versus options and opportunities in the here and now:

> The strategy of women's initiation is to lead a woman's life . . . away from the sociopolitical arena, introducing her to the real or imagined splendors of the cosmos instead. To put it in different terms, women's initiation offers a religious compensation for a sociopolitical deprivation. Or to put it differently still, it is an opiate for an oppressed class. . . .
>
> Cosmic claims notwithstanding, the desired result of the ritual is to make a girl ready and willing to assume the traditional place of a woman as defined within a given culture. . . . The strategy is that of placing women on a pedestal, carried to its outermost possibilities: speak of her as a goddess to make of her a drudge.

Although the young quinceañera is being crowned queen, the ritual doesn't change anything. It merely casts its net of glittering meaning over what might be a dismal situation: "It is rare that a ritual can alter the basic ways in which a society is organized," Bruce Lincoln concludes. "Nor do rituals shape the way in which people live as much as they shape the way people understand the lives they would lead in any event."

Even if she is at the bottom of the American heap, if the young Latina girl can believe the fantasy — that her condition is temporary, that she is a Cinderella waiting for that fairy godmother or husband to endow her with their power — then she can bear the burden of her disadvantage. And as years go by, and the probability of her dream becoming true lessens, she can at least pass on the story to her daughter.

Maybe that is why I get tearful at quinceañeras. I'm watching the next generation 30 be tamed into a narrative my generation fought so hard to change. Why I feel like a snake in the garden, because here I sit in their living rooms or in their rented halls, eating their catered food, celebrating with la familia, and I am thinking, Why spend all this money enacting a fantasy that the hard numbers out there say is not going to come true?

Quinceañera Expo

At the Quinceañera Expo in the Airport Convention Center in San Antonio, little girls are walking around with tiaras in their hair, oohing and ahing at the fancy dresses, the pink balloons, the wedding-cake-size cakes, the last dolls encased in plastic, the fluffy pillows with straps for securing the heels in case the page trips as he bears them to the altar to be blessed by the priest.

At a cordoned-off area at the rear of the hall, Victoria Acosta, a fourteen-year-old local pop sensation, is singing into a microphone as she dances and gestures with her free hand. "Crazy, crazy, crazy, I think the world's gone crazy!" Her next song, "Once Upon a Time," is dedicated to "all of you out there who have had your hearts broken." "All of you out there" is a semicircle of pudgy preteens sitting on the floor, mesmerized by the slender, glamorous Victoria with her long mascara'd lashes, her glittery eye shadow, her slinky black outfit and sparkly silver tie. "You bet I'm going to have a quince," she tells me during a break between songs, although I don't see why. She seems to have already made her passage into womanhood quite successfully.

There isn't a male shopper in sight. In fact, the only men around are manning booths or working the floor:

- a couple of boy models, one in a white tuxedo with a pale pink vest, the other in a white suit with a yellow vest;
- a grown man in a military uniform, a popular escort outfit with some girls, he tells me;
- a dj in a cowboy hat who plays loud music while his sidekick, a skinny boy, hands out flyers;
- Seve, the clown (who come to think of it might be female under all that face paint and bulbous, attached nose);
- Dale of Awesome Ice Designs (for $350 you can have the "Fire & Ice Sculpture" with the quinceañera's picture embedded in a central medallion of ice);
- Ronny of VIP Chocolate Fountains, whose wife, Joanne, does most of the talking. (Did you know that you can run chili con queso through the fountains for a Mexican theme at your daughter's quinceañera? The young people still prefer chocolate, as you can imagine);
- and Tony Guerrero, the owner of Balloons Over San Antonio ("We Blow for u").

Add the two photographers at Tilde (Photography, Invitations, Videography), Mr. Acosta (Victoria's manager-dad), the guy with a Starbucks urn strapped to his back, and Manuel Villamil at the Primerica Financial Services booth—and that makes for just over a dozen men in a crowd of about three hundred women of all ages here to shop for some member of their family's quinceañera. The hall is so girl-packed that the discreetly curtained BABY CHANGING/NURSING booth seems extraneous. You could breast-feed your baby out in the open and still be within the strict bounds of modesty, like peeing without shutting your stall door in the ladies' room because everyone inside except the little toddler in Mommy's arms is female.

I feel as if I've wandered into the back room where the femaleness of the next generation of Latinas is being manufactured, displayed, and sold. A throwback vision, to be sure. Lots of pink-lacey-princessy-glittery-glitzy stuff. One little girl wheels a large última muñeca around while her mother follows, carting the baby sister, who has ceded her stroller to a doll bigger than she is. "How beautiful!" I bend down to admire the little girl's proud cargo. "Is that for your quince?" The little girl looks pleadingly toward her mom. "It's her cousin's," the mom says, gesturing with her head toward a chunky teenager carting a large shopping bag and lolling at Joanne and Ronny's

35

booth, scooping her toothpick of cake into the chocolate fountain. The little girl looks forlorn. "I'm sure you'll have a last doll, too, when you have your quince," I console her. She gives me a weak smile in return. Why on earth am I encouraging her?

Crazy, crazy, crazy, I think the world's gone crazy.

It's not that. It's that after an hour roaming up and down the aisles, I fall in with the spirit of the expo. There is a contagious, evangelical air to the whole thing that sweeps you up and makes you want to be part of the almost religious fervor that surrounds this celebration. I half expect to find Isabella Martínez Wall here, addressing a crowd of wide-eyed teens.

In fact, my guide, Priscilla Mora, reminds me of Isabella. Both women share a crusading enthusiasm for a tradition they believe is one of the best things going for Latina womanhood. Plump and pretty with the sunny face of someone perennially in a good mood, Priscilla has organized six of these expos, and even though some have not been as well attended as she would have liked, her faith is undimmed. When not organizing these expos, she is a quinceañera planner, an author of the *Quinceañera Guide and Handbook,* and most of all a passionate promoter of the tradition. She actually thought up this business at a workshop where participants had to write down their dreams on little pieces of paper. Then they all put their pieces of paper in a fire and let their dreams go up to God. This isn't just a business, Priscilla explains, it's a calling, part of God's plan for her.

It's from Priscilla that I first hear that when the quinceañera makes her vow in the church, "it's about chastity. You're promising God that you're not going to have sex till you're back at the altar, getting married. That's why it's important that these girls learn all about the meaning," Priscilla insists. Otherwise, the quinceañera "is nothing but a party."

Priscilla's missionary zeal seems to be shared by many of the providers, who tell inspirational stories of why they got involved in quinces. Take Tony Guerrero of Balloons Over San Antonio. Tony grew up real poor in a family of four boys and four girls. ("Are you kidding?" he replies when I ask if the girls had quinceañeras.) A few years ago, Tony gave up his office job to do this because "I just wanted the opportunity to give back something to my community." He loves seeing people having fun, being happy, and hey, if nothing else, "I got myself another entry once I go over to the other side." "Another" because he already has a great-aunt over there. "She promised me she was going to have a spot waiting for me." Ruby of Great Expectations (a photography studio) thinks it's "a privilege" to share this special day with a girl. "I love the idea of rededicating your life to the Lord." (Echoes of Priscilla.) Curiously, the nuns' booth next to Ruby's is empty. "They told me they were coming." Priscilla looks momentarily nonplussed. But her sunny personality bounces back. "Maybe they'll be by later after Mass." This is Sunday, after all. The sisters, it turns out, are the Missionary Catechists of Divine Providence, the first and only religious order of Mexican American women founded in the United States. Their focus on the quinceañera is part of their larger mission as "evangelizadoras del barrio and transmitters of a rich Mexican American faith to the universal Church."

The only heavy hitter at the expo is Sunita Trevino, who was born in Bombay but is married to a Hispanic. At her seminar on financing a quinceañera, Sunita gives us the opposite of the hard sell: the watch-your-financial-back-as-a-minority-woman talk that has me sitting at the edge of my chair. As she talks, Sunita paces up and down the raised platform stage like a lion trapped in a too-small cage.

Sunita works for Primerica Financial Services, but her training is in clinical psychology, which she ends up using a lot as she counsels families about their finances. "I'll tell you," she tells the audience of about a dozen, mostly grandmothers, as this is the only area of the whole hall where there are chairs to sit down, "quinceañeras are high-stress times." A lot of couples come to see her for extra sessions. But the majority of Sunita's clients are single women who are in financial trouble. They don't budget. They overspend. They get into debt. She knows women in their seventies still paying off second mortgages they took out for their daughter's quinceañera. She finds this devastating.

"Nobody sits down to talk to us women! We are playing a money game but no one taught us the rules!" Sunita's own mother came from Bombay to America, thinking her husband would always be there to take care of her, and then her parents separated, and her mother was lost. She had no idea how to take care of herself. Sunita doesn't want to see this happen to any woman. We women are sinking into a hole of debt and the quinceañera is often where we get in over our heads.

Her recommendation to all of us sitting in the audience: pay cash. "If you budget eighteen hundred dollars for flowers, and what you pick amounts to double that, don't do it. DON'T DO IT! Stay within your budget. A lot of women get in trouble at the last minute. They think, oh, I'll go ahead, just this once."

If you end up borrowing money, "please," Sunita pleads with us, "read the terms, read them carefully. What the big print giveth, the small print taketh away. Educate yourselves! Don't think banks and savings accounts are there to do you a favor. Okay, let's see, who can tell me what banks do with your money?" she asks.

None of us grown women in the audience would dare hazard a guess. But a young girl about eleven years old raises her hand and says proudly, "They save it for you."

Sunita shakes her head fondly. "Out of the mouths of babes." She sighs. Nobody laughs. Nobody seems to get the biblical reference that Sunita is misusing anyway. Out of the mouths of babes usually the truth comes. But this young girl is headed for that sinkhole of debt unless Sunita can steer her away from the dangers of borrowing. "No, honey, that's not what they do. They use your money to make money."

The girl sits back in her chair, a chastened, embarrassed expression on her face. Her tiara glints as Sunita explains to her that what she just said is what most people think. But that's why Sunita is here today. To tell us the truth no one else is going to tell us. To get us thinking about these things. "Two hundred fifty families declare bankruptcy every hour of every day in the U.S.A. I know a seventy-nine-year-old retired guy who is now bagging groceries. People don't plan to fail," Sunita explains. "They fail to plan. So, get mad. Get mad and learn the rules."

The girl squirms in her chair, as do the rest of us. After all, we came here in a party mood, not to feel that at the end of our adult lives we will end up as bag ladies, wishing we hadn't started down the road of debt with our own or our daughters' quinceañeras.

Throwing the House Out the Window

So, how much does a quinceañera cost? You ask any of the party planners and they'll   50
tell you the same thing—anywhere from a hundred bucks for a cookout in the backyard and a stereo booming music for the young lady and her friends to fifty grand and
up in a hall with a party planner, a limo, dinner for a hundred or more.

Everyone talks about this range, but after interviewing dozens of quinceañeras
and talking to as many party planners, events providers, choreographers, caterers, I
have to conclude that the cookout quinceañeras are becoming the exception. In the
past, perhaps they were the rule. In the old countries, of course. In small homogenous
pockets—a border town in Texas, a barrio composed solely of Central Americans; in
other words, a group still largely out of the mainstream loop, perhaps. But now, as one
quinceañera remarked, "If I had to be that cheap I just wouldn't have one. What for?"
It is in the nature of the beast to be a splurge, an extravaganza. More than one person
describing a recent quinceañera used the Spanish expression for an over-the-top expense: *throwing the house out the window.* They threw the house out the window for that
girl's quinceañera.

They threw the house out the window.
In a country where the rate of poverty is
growing (12.7 percent of U.S. citizens were
living below the poverty line in 2004, up
from 11.3 percent in 2000), with Latinos

> **They threw the house out
> the window for that girl's
> quinceañera.**

forming a sizeable portion of those impoverished numbers (21.9 percent of the Hispanic population was living below the poverty line in 2004 according to a U.S. census
survey). Sunita, it turns out, was not exaggerating.

They threw the house they probably didn't own out the window.

Monica's quinceañera was actually quite modest if her estimate of "maybe three
thousand dollars" is correct. Why don't I have an exact number? Let me just come right
out and say that talking to my people about money is not easy. Maybe if I were an
Americana reporter with a stenographic notebook and only a sprinkling of classroom
Spanish, I could get away with asking the parents how much they paid for the party.
But I'm a Latina. I know the rules. They know I know the rules. To ask my host for the
price tag of the fiesta would be una falta de vergüenza. And so, I learned any number of
discreet ways to approach the topic. Aproximadamente, how much does a quinceañera
cost in your experience? If someone were to throw a party not unlike this one, how
much would that quinceañera cost them?

The one person I could openly ask this question turned out to be the quinceañera   55
herself. But though fifteen-year-old girls are really good at knowing how much their
dress or makeup session cost, they're not so good at knowing the charges for halls,
or what it costs to have beef Wellington instead of Swedish meatballs for a hundred
people, or what additional charge was made for the linen napkins and tablecloths or
the chairs draped in white covers and tied with satin bows, which seem to be de rigueur
for anything but the cheapest quinceañera. Fifteen-year-old girls like to throw out
huge numbers to impress their friends, but they are not so good at addition—that is, if
they paid $250 for a dress, and $250 for the limo, and the hall with a catered meal was
$2,500 for one hundred people, not counting the cake made up of four cakes, which

was no less than $300, and let's throw in another $100 to $200 for sessions at the beauty parlor, and at least $300 for the photographer and pictures, and because things always come up at the last minute and Mami definitely needs a new dress herself and Papi will probably have to rent a tux and some family members will need help with travel costs, another $500 to $1,000 more—anyhow, I've gone way over the low-end figure of $3,000 that Monica Ramos with uncharacteristic teenage understatement calculated.

And her father was not working.

They threw the rented apartment out the window. Why not? It's not theirs to keep anyhow, just as this American dream isn't as easy to achieve as it seems, so why not live it up, give your little girl a party she won't forget, enjoy the only thing you really have, tonight's good time, before the bills start rolling in.

When Abuelita Is No Longer a Resource

Will Cain is president and founder of *Quince Girl*, a new national magazine targeting the more than four hundred thousand Latinas in the United States who turn fifteen every year. Early in 2006, the magazine sent out a survey asking its readers how much they had spent or were planning to spend on their quinces. The resulting average was $5,000.

I confess to Will that I find that average low given the figures events planners and quinceañeras and their families have been quoting me. I'm thinking of Idalia's quinceañera, which cost her affluent Dominican family $80,000, not surprising given a guest list of more than five hundred and a fully choreographed performance by her court of twenty-eight couples (double the usual number so as not to leave out any friends or cousins) with special effects to rival a Broadway show and mermaid dresses for the girls designed by Leonel Lirio, renowned for Miss Universe Amelia Vega's gown. Granted that's the top end of the Q-scale, but the low end is rising. In Miami, Sofía's dad apologetically confessed that he was "only" spending about $12,000 on his daughter's quince, though his wife corrected him by appending, "Twelve thousand dollars not counting all the food and goodies we fed twenty-eight kids for three months of rehearsals."

"You have to remember that $5,000 takes into account the full spectrum," Will Cain reminds me about the *Quince Girl* average. "It includes the girl who is spending $25,000 with the one who might spend $1,000. The point is that even working-class folks who don't have a whole lot of purchasing power are going to devote a significant portion of their resources to this one tradition. It cuts across a wide range of strata."

Will himself did the numbers before he decided to launch his magazine. The Latino population is exploding, and it is mostly a young population. "I don't have to tell you about the demographics," Will tells me. "One out of every five teens is Hispanic. And that population is growing at the rate of 30 percent, while the non-Hispanic population rate is just 8 percent."

I'm trying to follow what Will is saying, but the question that keeps tugging at my curiosity is not about Hispanic demographics but about Will himself. Will Cain does not sound even close to a Hispanic name. How did "your run-of-the-mill white boy," as he describes himself when I ask him about his background, end up founding a magazine for young Latinas celebrating their quinceañeras?

Will, who is all of thirty-one—just over twice a quinceañera's age—grew up in Texas surrounded by Mexican Americans and has always been interested in the Hispanic culture. He was also interested in media. So, he decided to put the two things together and came up with the idea of *Quince Girl*. Though it's a shrewd economic decision, Will believes he's also providing an important service for Hispanics in this country.

"The Hispanic community is this very fractured community," he explains. "You have your Mexican Americans and your Puerto Ricans and your Cuban Americans. And the only thing that ties all these separate nationalities together—no, it's not Spanish," he says, anticipating what I might think, "in fact, many in the second and third generation don't even speak Spanish. What ties them together, the one single tie that binds all these cultures . . ."

As he drumrolls toward his conclusion, I'm thinking that Will Cain learned some-   65
thing from growing up surrounded by a Hispanic community: a sense of drama.

". . . is this tradition celebrated across the whole diverse group: the quinceañera. I mean, it is big! And the rest of America is starting to pay attention to it."

"Amen," I say. I'm writing a whole book about it.

As if he can hear my mind thinking, Will adds, "We would not be having this conversation right now if this were not so."

What Will realized was that there was no magazine out there that these girls could consult about the tradition and trends and fashions. "Girls were in chat rooms asking each other about the ceremony, what to do. It used to be you could learn these things from your grandmother . . ." But with immigration and the amount of mobility in this country, la abuelita is not always a resource. Plus it's a different world from the one she grew up in. A different budget. Five thousand dollars is probably more than the grandparents earned in a year back in their home countries.

Does he think the tradition is becoming more popular here?   70

"Well." Will hesitates. He is rightly cautious about delivering opinions beyond what the numbers can tell him. "The quince tradition has always been important, but there's this retroculturation going on right now—"

"Retroculturation?" This is the first I've heard of the term.

"It's a pattern that's been happening with the Hispanic community," Will goes on to explain. "First generation comes to the United States, and they push to assimilate. They adopt the American culture and norms. Second generation, they want to be all-American. Many don't even speak Spanish. They aren't that familiar with the culture. By the third generation, they're born and bred here, but they have this special something that makes them unique, their Hispanic culture. They want to learn Spanish—many, in fact, speak more Spanish than the second generation. They make a concerted effort to hold on to their traditions, to establish cultural ties with their past."

Will quotes a study on Hispanic teens "just released today" by the Cheskin Group, an international consulting and marketing firm that has done a great deal of research on Hispanics. The study confirms Will's point that the up-and-coming generation of Hispanic teens is "predominantly bilingual and bicultural," celebrating its ethnic identity and combining it with mainstream teen culture. "They live on MySpace.com and shop at Abercrombie, but they listen to Spanish radio and embrace diversity," a summary of the study reads. Most important for businesses that are considering purchasing the full report with its $5,850 price tag—the cost of your average quinceañera—is that Hispanic teens are

> a bellwether for one of the most important trends shaping the future of the United States—the growth of the U.S. Hispanic population. Clearly, the future is theirs and they know it.

The future is ours and we know it. Meanwhile the present needs to be lived through and paid for. 75

The Difference between Boys and Girls

How did the quinceañera get to be so expensive? Even the *Quince Girl* average of five thousand dollars is a lot of money to blow on a birthday party.

Kern's Nectar, which has developed a niche market of "untraditional" juices (guava, papaya, mango) popular among Latinos, sponsors a yearly Dulce Quinceañera Sweepstakes: "Fifteen lucky Quinceañeras will be awarded $1,000 each plus a year's supply of Kern's Nectars; the grand prize winner selected at random from this group takes home $15,000."

Why did Kern's Nectar single out this one tradition? "Next to marriage, a quinceañera is perhaps the most meaningful moment in a young woman's life," the press announcement reads. Given such claims, perhaps five thousand dollars is not a lot to spend on a girl's coming-of-age.

I decide to ask the girls themselves about such claims.

In the wood-paneled faculty lounge at Lawrence High School I speak with a gath- 80 ering of a dozen girls who have volunteered to be interviewed about the tradition. Light streams down from a magnificent stained-glass window, giving the room the hallowed feel of a chapel. At first glance, the robed scholar portrayed in the window could be Aristotle or Plato, but on closer inspection it turns out to be a woman. With one hand clutching a book, the other lifted, palm out, she seems to be setting the example of telling the truth, the whole truth, and nothing but, which is precisely what I am after. Later I find out that this testifying woman is Emily Greene Weatherbee, the first female principal of the high school, in the 1880s.

A century and a quarter later, the room fills with the likes of students that Miss Emily could never have imagined. The young Latinas present are mostly of Dominican and Puerto Rican descent, though one junior varsity softball player in sweatpants and sweatshirt whom it's a stretch to imagine in the girly-girl getup of a quinceañera is of Ecuadorian parentage. Except for one girl who feels "really gypped" that she didn't have one (her mother said the expense was too high), the other eleven girls have all had or will be having quinceañeras before the year is out. A few days before my visit they were reminded to bring their albums along to school. They file in, lugging large pink or white wedding-type albums of what amounts to extensive photo shoots. A few of the empty-handed girls confess they left their albums at home so as not to have to haul such a heavy weight around all day.

After paging through several of these albums, I ask the girls if they consider their quinceañeras as important as their eventual marriages. "I mean if you get married," I add. I do not want to be pushing any assumptions on their life stories.

"That's the thing," Soraya pipes up. Hers is among the largest albums, borne in by her brother, who has carted it around all day for her. "You don't ever know if you're going to get married. I mean you hope you will, but that's not for sure. But you are going to turn fifteen no matter what." The other girls agree.

But if it's just about turning fifteen, boys turn fifteen, too. Why not give them a quinceañera?

"Boys don't need a quinceañera," Madeline, who left her heavy album at home,   85
explains. "Boys are born men but girls turn into women."

I have pondered that statement many times in the last year. The comment highlights that very deep, heavily guarded (at least traditionally) divide in a young Latina's life when she goes from niña to señorita and becomes sexualized. In her memoir, *Silent Dancing: A Partial Remembrance of a Puerto Rican Childhood*, Judith Ortiz Cofer describes how when she became una señorita, she was watched closely as if she "carried some kind of time-bomb in [my] body that might go off any minute . . . Somehow my body with its new contours and new biological powers had changed everything: Half the world had now become a threat, or felt threatened by its potential for disaster."

"We never touch the girls," more than one male photographer told me when I interviewed them about the very popular photo shoots in Miami. The full package features young quinceañeras in a variety of provocative poses and outfits, including teensy bikinis. "We tell the mothers, 'Mami, there's a little masita that needs tucking in.' We let the mothers do it." Why was I being assured of this sexual delicacy over and over? Girls hitherto blithely living inside children's bodies turn into women with sexy, enticing cuerpos, and suddenly, it's open season. Meanwhile, boys, born men, who have been taught since day one to prove themselves as healthy machos, are going to prey on them.

When I make these observations to the Lawrence group, the roomful of young girls erupts into excited giggles. Obviously, I'm onto something.

All the girls admit that once they started developing, their parents, especially their papis, were like, *Who are you going out with? Who was that that just called? Whose parents will be there?*

These girls are on the receiving end of the ill effects of machismo, no arguing with   90
that. But what of those poor boys having to perform from day one, if Madeline is to be believed? Often at quinceañeras, I'd spot some little tyke in a teensy tuxedo pushed and prodded to pick up some girl at a dance or given a shot of rum and encouraged to strut around. Contrary to how it's often described, machismo oppresses not just the girls but also the boys. And yet, understandably, would you want your pubescent daughter to be in the company of a grown version of this little macho, unsupervised?

"The quinceañera is the sanctioned way that a nice family says, okay, now my daughter may receive male attention," Gloria González, a Spanish professor at Middlebury College, explains to me about her experience growing up in Guadalajara, Mexico. "We are permitting this and we are monitoring it." That *is* a big moment. In fact, in his song "De Niña a Mujer," which is arguably *the* quinceañera anthem of all time, Julio Iglesias bewails how as a father he has been anticipating this moment when his little girl disappears forever inside a woman. The lament goes on for six pained stanzas. The song makes a daughter's growing up sound like something that's going to break her father's heart.

If so, then why celebrate this loss?

Enter the mothers.

If the father is losing his little girl, the mother is gaining a potential girlfriend. More than one girl in the Lawrence group mentions—and when she does the others agree—that planning their quinceañeras really brought them and their moms close together. "We were deciding about what dress and what decorations and addressing all the invitations. I'd say that I was spending most of my time when I wasn't in school with my mom," Soraya recalls about the months of preparations. "We were already close, but we got even closer."

Even if the ceremony itself focuses on the father-daughter transaction (he changes her flat shoes to heels, he dances her first grown-up dance in public with her), the months of preparations are intense mother-daughter time. Inevitably, this causes fights and disagreements, but even those moments offer opportunities for negotiation and bonding. And it's not just mothers and daughters, but the extended familia of tías, abuelitas, primas who often get involved. Sofía's mom in Miami, Consuelo, explained how in deciding each detail of her daughter's quinceañera her mother, her sisters, and Sofía's girl cousins would all vote. "We'd go into a store and try on dresses or pick out decorations and the whole gang would be giving their opinions." As her mom recounted how special it had been for her to share this experience with her only daughter, Sofía, who had been sitting quietly beside her, began to cry.

"Are you okay?" her father, who had come along for the interview, asked from the other end of the couch. "What's wrong?"

Consuelo, who had been distracted talking to me, turned to her daughter. In profile they were time-lapsed copies of each other. Consuelo understood. Tears filled her own eyes as she reached over and the two women joined hands like little girls who were going to be best friends for life.

Remote Control

Another factor that has upped the price tag of this traditional celebration is that tricky word "traditional."

Más católico que el Papa, goes a Dominican saying, more Catholic than the pope. Our exported tradiciones mix and combine with those of other Latin American and Caribbean countries stateside and become more elaborate, more expensive, more traditional than they ever were back home.

In fact, to have a full-blown traditional quinceañera in our Pan-Hispanic United States is to have adopted every other Latino group's little traditions and then some. So that now, Cuban quinceañeras in Miami are hiring Mexican mariachis to sing the traditional "Las Mañanitas." The full court of fourteen damas and chambelanes, "each couple representing a year of the quinceañera's life," a mostly Mexican practice, is now a traditional must. As is the changing of the shoes to heels, which seems to originally have been a Puerto Rican embellishment. From the Puerto Ricans as well, though some say from the Mexicans, came the tradition of la última muñeca, a "last doll" dressed exactly like the quinceañera, which the girl cradles to symbolize the "end of her childhood" or "the child that she herself will be having in the not-too-distant future" (both explanations given to me by different events planners). The quinceañera might keep this last doll as a keepsake or give it away to a younger member of the family. In one celebration, perhaps inspired by the wedding bouquet, the quinceañera threw her last doll over her shoulder to be caught by a screaming group of little girls, anticipating their own future quinceañeras.

This symbol of bygone childhood is also mirrored in a Central American or Puerto Rican custom (I've heard both) of having a very little girl dress up in a minuscule version of the quinceañera's dress and be "the symbol of innocence." Sometimes she is accompanied by a little escort, though the tradition has now been further elaborated so that "the symbol of innocence" as well as a little prince and princess (slightly older) are part of a full traditional court.

There is also always some sort of photo session to commemorate the event. This is not a custom exclusive to quinceañeras. In our old countries every important life event is marked by a photograph. Your First Communion photo, your quince photo, your graduation photo, your wedding photo. Even in my husband's old German-Nebraskan family, there were the formal portraits shot in a studio, the principals in dress clothes, hair combed and tamped down: a wedding, a christening, a son shipping off to war. Of course, now there are whole albums of the young lady in different outfits, in different locations, a practice that seems to have started with the Cuban community in Miami, where girls sometimes just have the photo shoot and forego the party. Many girls also have videos made, recounting their lives since birth, with still shots and footage of themselves at different ages and credits rolling as if this were a real movie with the quinceañera playing the lead and her parents starring as "padre" and "madre" and Julio Iglesias's "De Niña a Mujer" as the score, of course. Clearly, the old-country portrait tradition has arrived stateside and, as one Cuban friend put it, "taken steroids."

The tradition of crowning the young girl is often ascribed to the Mexicans, who seem to be the group that has most ritualized the ceremony. But here in America, every quinceañera gets her tiara. The bouquet the quinceañera carries to put at the Virgin Mary's statue at the Mass is also part of the Mexican and Central American tradition, as is the Mass, which our more hedonistic Caribbean party-cultures dispensed with back home. But now the Mass and the Virgin's bouquet have become part of our Dominican and Puerto Rican and Cuban "tradition" in the United States.

One economically sensible and emotionally gratifying tradition that has not been picked up by other Hispanic groups is the Mexican custom of sponsorships by madrinas and padrinos. In a Mexican quince, every aspect of the fiesta from the cake to the dj has a sponsor, which spreads the cost of the celebration around. It is also a touching symbol of the emotional, spiritual, as well as financial investment of a whole community in this young person. Why aren't others adopting this custom?

"It's a point of pride not to go begging for your party," my Cuban friend Carmel confided. But in fact, a lot of informal sponsorships are going on. The grandmother who buys the quinceañera's earrings and necklace, the brother who gives her the birthday gift of paying for the limo, the sister who contributes to the dress. Still, when the twenty or more names of sponsors are read out in a Mexican-American quinceañera, there is a sense of public participation that is not lost on the young lady. "Everybody I knew contributed something," Verónica Fajardo remembers about her quinceañera fifteen years ago. "I felt like I received so many bendiciones, my whole community made it happen!" In actual fact, Verónica's family is from Nicaragua, but she grew up in a Mexican

American neighborhood in Los Angeles, so though sponsorships were not part of the custom back home, by the time her quince came around, her family had adopted that tradition.

Sometimes these cultural borrowings are not even coming from fellow Latinos. The tradition of lighting and dedicating candles, for example, seems to have been lifted from the Bar and Bat Mitzvah. In fact many critics see the quinceañera as going the same route as the Jewish celebration. Rabbi Jeffrey Salkin, author of *Putting God on the Guest List: How to Reclaim the Spiritual Meaning of Your Child's Bar or Bat Mitzvah,* compares this moment in time for the Hispanic community to the early 1960s for the Jewish community, when the Bar and Bat Mitzvah ceremonies became increasingly secular and extravagant. "These rites of passage are a way for a minority group to demonstrate that they have succeeded in America."

But given the statistics, our Hispanic community cannot yet lay claim to such wholesale success. For many, the quinceañera becomes an extravaganza that, as Sunita warned, puts the family further into the hole. Marie Arana of the *Washington Post* shared with me stories of visiting migrant camps in the Maryland and Virginia countryside where families with almost nothing would put out hundreds of dollars to throw their girls' quinceañeras. Perhaps these are the cookout parties everybody talks about, the ones that are under the radar because they are taking place in segregated, often undocumented populations? If you do the numbers, several hundred dollars for a migrant worker with no citizenship or papers or cushion of savings might as well be several thousand for a working-class family that owns a car and has access to unemployment benefits and credit cards.

"Today, it's all about supersizing," Nina Diaz, the executive producer of *My Super Sweet 16,* told *U.S. News & World Report.* (The price tag for a recent quince party featured in one of the episodes was $180,000.) One quince site I happened upon in cruising the Web for Q-lore—just Google "quinceañera" and you will get 8,230,000 hits (if you put the tilde over the "n") or 4,220,000 hits (if you dispense with the tilde)—urged providers to register with their site. "The Hispanic population's buying power is expected to reach $300 billion by 2006. Timing is prime to begin your Sweet 16 and Quinceañera advertising campaign. The demand for more vendors that cater to Latinos is of epic proportions."

Epic proportions; the house out the window; 8,230,000 hits and rising.

"Upholding this coming of age celebration is definitely expensive," Kimberly Gar- 110 cía concluded in her 1999 article: "Sweet 15: A Financial Affair." In the seven years since her article was published in *Hispanic Magazine,* the trend is growing. Her shocking high-end figure of $15,000 for a celebration would not raise an eyebrow now. More likely, it would elicit an apology, as with Sofía's dad. "Hispanics are likely to make a big spending decision no matter their income level," Lisa Holton reported in an article about quinceañeras for the *Chicago Sun-Times.*

At Disneyland, Denny Nicholas, manager of corporate and wedding sales, says he has seen anything from a modest $5,000 to $50,000 for a quinceañera, the average nowadays being about $12,000 to $15,000. When I ask Denny if he doesn't find this *average* shocking given that the poverty threshold for a family of three is $15,277, he laughs. "By the time families come to me, they've already made the decision that this is what they want. All I do is provide the elements they need to make their dreams come to life." It's just a different world, Denny reminds me. "Kids are growing up expecting so much more." He chuckles, sounding a lot more cheerful about this than I obviously feel. "I joke with my two boys that when I was growing up, the remote control was me standing by the TV and my dad saying, 'Change it to such and such a channel'!"

Dinero vs. Money

The supersizing of the tradition might well be blamed on U.S. consumerism, but the spending of money now instead of mañana seems to be our very own bagaje.

"Hispanics tend to make immediate use of their money," writes Rose Carbonell in her article "Dinero vs. Money." As part of her graduate research in Hispanic Marketing Communication at Florida State University, Carbonell studied the different attitudes of Hispanics toward money. She found that "capital accumulation is not a characteristic of Hispanics, especially because being wealthy has a negative connotation . . . as the masses of Hispanics have endured slavery and endemic poverty over the past 500 years, the meaning of wealth has been associated with the experience of others, not oneself."

Initially, I dismissed this as a kind of cultural profiling we do to ourselves as it hath been done unto us, until I found this point curiously echoed by none other than Octavio Paz, the seminal writer on Mexican identity and thought and the 1990 winner of the Nobel Prize in Literature. "Our poverty can be measured by the frequency and luxuriousness of our holidays. Fiestas are our only luxury," Paz writes in *The Labyrinth of Solitude*. "Wasting money and expending energy affirms the community's wealth in both. When life is thrown away it increases. What is sought is potency, life, health. In this sense the fiesta . . . is one of the most ancient economic forms."

Another way of understanding this phenomenon is an interesting term I found ¹¹⁵ bandied about in academic articles: "cultural capital." The term, originally coined by French social theorist Pierre Bourdieu, describes other kinds of assets, not monetary, that are important for status in a community. A family's throwing its daughter a lavish quinceañera represents a kind of cultural statement that counts for a lot more than the dollar cost. Thinking only of "how much it cost" in dollar amount is to simplify a much more complex and layered transaction. Patricia Saldarriaga, a professor of Spanish at Middlebury College, turned fifteen in 1975 in the port city of Talara, Peru, where her father was mayor. Although she did not want one, she was obligated to have a big quince party because of her father's position.

"*Somos decentes* is a very important concept in our communities," Eduardo Béjar, also a Spanish professor at Middlebury, explains. Eduardo, who grew up in Cuba in the forties and fifties, recalls how fiestas de quince años were a family's way of maintaining status. "Ser una familia decente. You work hard, you do things for the welfare of your family. La quinceañera reflects that: a way of saying we are decentes."

But why not have both? After all, being Latina/o is about being a hybrid, a made-in-the-U.S.A. sancocho of all our different cultures and races and histories and nationalities. Why not be una familia decente that celebrates a daughter's quinceañera without going into debt? Throw a fiesta, not the house, out the window? Our cultural habits and traditions can be revised to work better for us in the new realities we are facing right now.

But whenever I've suggested restraint to quinceañera parents and events provid-ers, the refrain I often hear is, "We love to party!" That's the way we are.

This ethnic profiling persists both internally within our communities and with-out. It's a reductionist either/or way of thinking about ourselves that ill prepares us for this new millennium in which the world is shrinking and we are all becoming ever more permeable mixtures of traditions and cultures.

Mami, too, always maintained we couldn't have it both ways. We couldn't be both   120
girls from una familia decente and little Americanitas with minds (and bodies) of our own.

"Why not?" I would challenge. "'I resist anything better than my own diversity.'"

"Don't you answer me back!" she'd scold. "Don't you be fresh with me!"

"But that's Walt Whitman. We're reading him in English class."

That always made her stop.

"You live in this house, you respect our rules!" she'd grumble, more quietly now.   125
What monster had she created by sending her daughter to Abbot? "Who do you think you are?"

"'I am large, I contain multitudes.'" I was finding a new way to defend myself. Technically, it was not "answering back" if I was reciting poetry.

Exploring Context

1. *My Super Sweet 16* is a television show chronicling a coming-of-age ritual similar to the quinceañera. Explore the website for the series at mtv.com/shows/sweet_16/series .jhtml and connect what you find there to Alvarez's text. In what ways does the series reflect the issues and concerns about quinces that Alvarez explores? You might want to use your work on Alvarez's feelings about quinces from Question 2 of Questions for Critical Reading in making your response.

2. This selection opens with Alvarez's visit to Isabella Martínez Wall, who has her own website (isabellawall.com). How does the website, in its design and advertising, reflect the points that Alvarez wants to make about quinces and the kinds of women they produce? Does the website reflect Alvarez's arguments about quinces? How does the website support or complicate your response to Question 3 of Questions for Critical Reading about the value of tradition?

3. What coming-of-age rituals exist in other cultures? Use the Web to search for informa-tion on another ritual, perhaps one from your own cultural, national, ethnic, or religious background. How is it preserved today? Does it have the same economic implications as the quince? In what ways is it connected to quinceañeras?

Questions for Connecting

1. Daniel Gilbert's essay "Reporting Live from Tomorrow" (p. 211) is about predicting our future happiness. How can his ideas help explain the features of quinces that Alvarez explores? Is the quinceañera a super-replicator? Does it function as a kind of cultural surrogate for womanhood? Is it possible to synthesize Gilbert's concepts with Alvarez's examples?

2. Retroculturation seems to promote diversity. How might colleges and universities promote retroculturation on their campuses? Would such a strategy solve the problems with community and diversity that Rebekah Nathan notes in "Community and Diversity" (p. 314)? Draw on your definition of the term from Question 1 in Questions for Critical Reading.

3. Ariel Levy presents a very different view of womanhood in "Female Chauvinist Pigs" (p. 266). How might we reconcile raunch culture with a tradition like the quinceañera? What role does economics play in shaping the role of women, according to Levy and Alvarez? Incorporate your response from Question 3 of Questions for Critical Reading.

4. **CONNECTING TO E-PAGES** Sabrina Rubin Erdely's story of "Kiki Kannibal: The Girl Who Played with Fire" (bedfordstmartins.com/emerging/epages) is an account of a teenage girl for whom things go terribly wrong. How might Alvarez view Kiki's revelatory self-presentations? What social functions do they perform? To what end? What social rules might Alvarez say Kiki violated? Is there a relationship between the cultural performance in quinces and in Kiki's videos? Support your assertions with quotations from the selections.

Language Matters

1. Each discipline has a specific approach to evidence. Start by finding information on how research is done in your intended major or field. How would you pursue Alvarez's arguments through that field? How would that discipline make this argument?

2. In small groups, select a common grammatical error, such as sentence fragments or subject-verb agreement problems. Select a key quotation from Alvarez's text and then change it to represent the error. Share the original and altered quotations in small groups to create a list of error examples and corrections using this essay.

3. Spanish has a unique punctuation mark—an inverted question mark at the start of a question. In small groups, create your own punctuation marks and apply them to passages from Alvarez. What do you want your punctuation to do? What does any punctuation mark do?

Assignments for Writing

1. How do quinceañeras help define self-identity in the Hispanic community? Write a paper in which you define the relationship between these rituals and self-identity. In making your argument you may want to use the other rituals you explored in Question 3 of Exploring Context or some of the concepts you synthesized in Questions for Connecting, such as super-replicators or cultural performance. To help you begin your critical thinking on this assignment, consider these questions: How do traditions, both native and acquired, contribute to the development of identity? How does gender determine self-identity in the Hispanic community? Why do only girls receive quinceañeras? What part does retroculturation play in the establishing of self-identity? Is this rite of passage similar to or different from rites of passage in other cultures? Does the commercialization of the quinceañera affect its overall value in establishing a girl's self-worth and self-identity? If so, how?

2. Alvarez examines the expanding marketplace emerging around the quinceañera. What role does business play in developing ideas of femininity? Write an essay in which you explore the intersection of commercialism and gender. In making your argument, draw not only from Alvarez's text but also from your work on the value of tradition in Question 3 of Questions for Critical Reading or your responses to the questions in Exploring Context. The following questions might help you locate a focus for your response; use them to think critically about this assignment: Does the quinceañera lend itself to the promotion of a specific view of femininity? What function does the Quinceañera Expo play in manufacturing femininity? How does the media shape perceptions of femininity in the Hispanic community? Is there still a generational gap in determining the social position of women?

3. Quinceañeras have an important role to play not simply in the lives of individuals but also, as Alvarez makes clear, in the lives of families and communities. Using Alvarez's text and your response to Question 3 of Questions for Critical Reading on the value of tradition and/or Question 4 of Questions for Connecting on cultural performances, determine the function of social rituals like the quinceañera in the lives of communities. Write a paper in which you specify the role of social ritual in community life, using Alvarez as well as your own experiences. Consider: What is the role of the individual in a community effort? What is the effect on a community when cultural events absorb outside cultural influences? How does retroculturation revitalize communities?

KWAME ANTHONY APPIAH

Kwame Anthony Appiah was born in London, grew up in Ghana, and earned a Ph.D. at Cambridge University. He is the Laurance S. Rockefeller University Professor of Philosophy and a faculty member of the University Center for Human Values at Princeton University. He has also taught at Duke, Harvard, Yale, Cornell, Cambridge, and the University of Ghana. He serves as an editor for *Transition* magazine and has published numerous academic books and articles as well as three detective novels. In 2008, Appiah was recognized for his contributions to racial, ethnic, and religious relations when Brandeis University awarded him the first Joseph B. and Toby Gittler Prize.

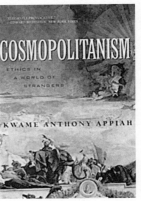

Appiah's *Cosmopolitanism: Ethics in a World of Strangers* (2006) was one of the first books published in Henry Louis Gates Jr.'s Issues of Our Time series, which aims to tackle the important concerns of the information age. In *Cosmopolitanism*, Appiah examines the imaginary boundaries that have separated people around the world and the ways we can redraw those boundaries. Appiah claims with the book's title that we are all citizens of the world. In the time of al Qaeda, we can no longer afford to draw significant lines between different groups and regions. Humanity has fundamental commonalities, Appiah suggests, and we should embrace them.

The following selections, "Making Conversation" and "The Primacy of Practice," appear in *Cosmopolitanism* as the introduction and one of the book's chapters. Appiah first defines "cosmopolitanism" and its problems but ultimately determines that practicing a citizenship of the world is not only helpful in a post-9/11 world, but necessary. There is no divide between "us" and "them," he suggests, only a basic moral obligation we have to each other. It is not necessary for people to agree to behave morally for the right reason, or the right god, or the right country or custom. It is only necessary that they agree to behave morally. Conversation, Appiah writes, is the best starting point.

It's tempting to reduce what follows to something as simple as "We should all just get along," but Appiah is also challenging us to think about how we can make that happen. How primal is practice in your own life? Is what you do more important than why you do it?

▶ TAGS: *community, identity, obligation, human dignity, conversation, globalization*

Questions for Critical Reading

1. As you read Appiah, use his text to create a definition of what he means by "cosmopolitanism," working with quotations from Appiah that support your interpretation. Then apply this definition to a current national or world situation. How does it show cosmopolitanism at work, or how might embracing this concept help resolve the situation?

2. According to Appiah, what are some crucial tools needed to enact his vision of cosmopolitanism? Reread his essay to locate quotations in which Appiah discusses these tools. How realistic is his vision? Based on the examples he offers, do you think these tools would be effective? Why or why not?

3. In order to make his argument, Appiah includes some stories from his own life. How does he use these stories? What sort of evidence do they provide? What other forms of evidence does he use? Support your answers by searching for specific examples from the text.

Making Conversation

Our ancestors have been human for a very long time. If a normal baby girl born forty thousand years ago were kidnapped by a time traveler and raised in a normal family in New York, she would be ready for college in eighteen years. She would learn English (along with—who knows?—Spanish or Chinese), understand trigonometry, follow baseball and pop music; she would probably want a pierced tongue and a couple of tattoos. And she would be unrecognizably different from the brothers and sisters she left behind. For most of human history, we were born into small societies of a few score people, bands of hunters and gatherers, and would see, on a typical day, only people we had known most of our lives. Everything our long-ago ancestors ate or wore, every tool they used, every shrine at which they worshipped, was made within that group. Their knowledge came from their ancestors or from their own experiences. That is the world that shaped us, the world in which our nature was formed.

Now, if I walk down New York's Fifth Avenue on an ordinary day, I will have within sight more human beings than most of those prehistoric hunter-gatherers saw in a lifetime. Between then and now some of our forebears settled down and learned agriculture; created villages, towns, and, in the end, cities; discovered the power of writing. But it was a slow process. The population of classical Athens when Socrates* died, at the end of the fifth century BC, could have lived in a few large skyscrapers. Alexander† set off from Macedon to conquer the world three-quarters of a century later with an army of between thirty and forty thousand, which is far fewer people than commute into Des Moines every Monday morning. When, in the first century, the population of Rome reached a million, it was the first city of its size. To keep it fed, the Romans had

---

* Socrates: Athenian Greek (469–399 BC); one of the founders of Western philosophy known chiefly through the writings of his students, notably Plato [Ed.].
† Alexander: Alexander the Great (356–323 BC) founded an empire that eventually covered about two million square miles [Ed.].

had to build an empire that brought home grain from Africa. By then, they had already worked out how to live cheek by jowl in societies where most of those who spoke your language and shared your laws and grew the food on your table were people you would never know. It is, I think, little short of miraculous that brains shaped by our long history could have been turned to this new way of life.

Even once we started to build these larger societies, most people knew little about the ways of other tribes, and could affect just a few local lives. Only in the past couple of centuries, as every human community has gradually been drawn into a single web of trade and a global network of information, have we come to a point where each of us can realistically imagine contacting any other of our six billion conspecifics and sending that person something worth having: a radio, an antibiotic, a good idea. Unfortunately, we could also send, through negligence as easily as malice, things that will cause harm: a virus, an airborne pollutant, a bad idea. And the possibilities of good and of ill are multiplied beyond all measure when it comes to policies carried out by governments in our name. Together, we can ruin poor farmers by dumping our subsidized grain into their markets, cripple industries by punitive tariffs, deliver weapons that will kill thousands upon thousands. Together, we can raise standards of living by adopting new policies on trade and aid, prevent or treat diseases with vaccines and pharmaceuticals, take measures against global climate change, encourage resistance to tyranny and a concern for the worth of each human life.

And, of course, the worldwide web of information—radio, television, telephones, the Internet—means not only that we can affect lives everywhere but that we can learn about life anywhere, too. Each person you know about and can affect is someone to whom you have responsibilities: To say this is just to affirm the very idea of morality. The challenge, then, is to take minds and hearts formed over the long millennia of living in local troops and equip them with ideas and institutions that will allow us to live together as the global tribe we have become.

Under what rubric to proceed? Not "globalization"—a term that once referred to a   5 marketing strategy, and then came to designate a macroeconomic thesis, and now can seem to encompass everything, and nothing. Not "multiculturalism," another shape shifter, which so often designates the disease it purports to cure. With some ambivalence, I have settled on "cosmopolitanism." Its meaning is equally disputed, and celebrations of the "cosmopolitan" can suggest an unpleasant posture of superiority toward the putative provincial. You imagine a Comme des Garçons–clad sophisticate with a platinum frequent-flyer card regarding, with kindly condescension, a ruddy-faced farmer in workman's overalls. And you wince.

Maybe, though, the term can be rescued. It has certainly proved a survivor. Cosmopolitanism dates at least to the Cynics* of the fourth century BC, who first coined the expression cosmopolitan, "citizen of the cosmos." The formulation was meant to be paradoxical, and reflected the general Cynic skepticism toward custom and tradition. A citizen—a *politēs*—belonged to a particular *polis*, a city to which he or she

---

* Cynics: Ancient school of Greek philosophy. Cynics advocated a simple life, free from material things, rejecting desires for fame and even health [Ed.].

owed loyalty. The cosmos referred to the world, not in the sense of the earth, but in the sense of the universe. Talk of cosmopolitanism originally signaled, then, a rejection of the conventional view that every civilized person belonged to a community among communities.

The creed was taken up and elaborated by the Stoics,* beginning in the third century BC, and that fact proved of critical importance in its subsequent intellectual history. For the Stoicism of the Romans—Cicero, Seneca, Epictetus, and the emperor Marcus Aurelius—proved congenial to many Christian intellectuals, once Christianity became the religion of the Roman Empire. It is profoundly ironic that, though Marcus Aurelius sought to suppress the new Christian sect, his extraordinarily personal *Meditations*, a philosophical diary written in the second century AD as he battled to save the Roman Empire from barbarian invaders, has attracted Christian readers for nearly two millennia. Part of its appeal, I think, has always been the way the Stoic emperor's cosmopolitan conviction of the oneness of humanity echoes Saint Paul's insistence that "there is neither Jew nor Greek, there is neither bond nor free, there is neither male nor female: for ye are all one in Christ Jesus."[1]

Cosmopolitanism's later career wasn't without distinction. It underwrote some of the great moral achievements of the Enlightenment, including the 1789 "Declaration of the Rights of Man" and Immanuel Kant's work proposing a "league of nations." In a 1788 essay in his journal *Teutscher Merkur,* Christoph Martin Wieland—once called the German Voltaire—wrote, in a characteristic expression of the ideal, "Cosmopolitans . . . regard all the peoples of the earth as so many branches of a single family, and the universe as a state, of which they, with innumerable other rational beings, are citizens, promoting together under the general laws of nature the perfection of the whole, while each in his own fashion is busy about his own well-being."[2] And Voltaire himself—whom nobody, alas, ever called the French Wieland—spoke eloquently of the obligation to understand those with whom we share the planet, linking that need explicitly with our global economic interdependence. "Fed by the products of their soil, dressed in their fabrics, amused by games they invented, instructed even by their ancient moral fables, why would we neglect to understand the mind of these nations, among whom our European traders have traveled ever since they could find a way to get to them?"[3]

So there are two strands that intertwine in the notion of cosmopolitanism. One is the idea that we have obligations to others, obligations that stretch beyond those to whom we are related by the ties of kith and kind, or even the more formal ties of a shared citizenship. The other is that we take seriously the value not just of human life but of particular human lives, which means taking an interest in the practices and beliefs that lend them significance. People are different, the cosmopolitan knows, and there is much to learn from our differences. Because there are so many human possibilities

> **Cosmopolitanism is the name not of the solution but of the challenge.**

---

* Stoics: School of philosophy influenced by the Cynics. Stoics held that destructive emotions should be controlled and that clear thinking would lead to reason [Ed.].

worth exploring, we neither expect nor desire that every person or every society should converge on a single mode of life. Whatever our obligations are to others (or theirs to us) they often have the right to go their own way. As we'll see, there will be times when these two ideals—universal concern and respect for legitimate difference—clash. There's a sense in which cosmopolitanism is the name not of the solution but of the challenge.

A citizen of the world: How far can we take that idea? Are you really supposed to abjure all local allegiances and partialities in the name of this vast abstraction, humanity? Some proponents of cosmopolitanism were pleased to think so; and they often made easy targets of ridicule. "Friend of men, and enemy of almost every man he had to do with," Thomas Carlyle* memorably said of the eighteenth-century physiocrat the Marquis de Mirabeau, who wrote the treatise *L'Ami des hommes* when he wasn't too busy jailing his own son. "A lover of his kind, but a hater of his kindred," Edmund Burke† said of Jean-Jacques Rousseau,° who handed each of the five children he fathered to an orphanage.

Yet the impartialist version of the cosmopolitan creed has continued to hold a steely fascination. Virginia Woolf‡ once exhorted "freedom from unreal loyalties"—to nation, sex, school, neighborhood, and on and on. Leo Tolstoy,§ in the same spirit, inveighed against the "stupidity" of patriotism. "To destroy war, destroy patriotism," he wrote in an 1896 essay—a couple of decades before the tsar was swept away by a revolution in the name of the international working class. Some contemporary philosophers have similarly urged that the boundaries of nations are morally irrelevant—accidents of history with no rightful claim on our conscience.

But if there are friends of cosmopolitanism who make me nervous, I am happy to be opposed to cosmopolitanism's noisiest foes. Both Hitler and Stalin—who agreed about little else, save that murder was the first instrument of politics—launched regular invectives against "rootless cosmopolitans"; and while, for both, anti-cosmopolitanism was often just a euphemism for anti-Semitism, they were right to see cosmopolitanism as their enemy. For they both required a kind of loyalty to one portion of humanity—a nation, a class—that ruled out loyalty to all of humanity. And the one thought that cosmopolitans share is that no local loyalty can ever justify forgetting that each human being has responsibilities to every other. Fortunately, we need take sides neither with the nationalist who abandons all foreigners nor with the hard-core cosmopolitan who regards her friends and fellow citizens with icy impartiality. The position worth defending might be called (in both senses) a partial cosmopolitanism.

There's a striking passage, to this point, in George Eliot's *Daniel Deronda*, published in 1876, which was, as it happens, the year when England's first—and, so far, last—Jewish prime minister, Benjamin Disraeli, was elevated to the peerage as Earl of Beaconsfield. Disraeli, though baptized and brought up in the Church of England,

———————————

* Thomas Carlyle: Scottish essayist and historian (1795–1881) [Ed.].
† Edmund Burke: Anglo-Irish politician and political philosopher (1729–1797) [Ed.].
° Jean-Jacques Rousseau: French political philosopher (1712–1778) [Ed.].
‡ Virginia Woolf: English novelist, critic, and essayist (1882–1941) [Ed.].
§ Leo Tolstoy: Russian writer best known for his novels, such as *War and Peace* (1828–1910) [Ed.].

always had a proud consciousness of his Jewish ancestry (given the family name, which his father spelled D'Israeli, it would have been hard to ignore). But Deronda, who has been raised in England as a Christian gentleman, discovers his Jewish ancestry only as an adult; and his response is to commit himself to the furtherance of his "hereditary people":

> It was as if he had found an added soul in finding his ancestry—his judgment no longer wandering in the mazes of impartial sympathy, but choosing, with the noble partiality which is man's best strength, the closer fellowship that makes sympathy practical—exchanging that bird's-eye reasonableness which soars to avoid preference and loses all sense of quality, for the generous reasonableness of drawing shoulder to shoulder with men of like inheritance.

Notice that in claiming a Jewish loyalty—an "added soul"—Deronda is not rejecting a human one. As he says to his mother, "I think it would have been right that I should have been brought up with the consciousness that I was a Jew, but it must always have been a good to me to have as wide an instruction and sympathy as possible." This is the same Deronda, after all, who has earlier explained his decision to study abroad in these eminently cosmopolitan terms: "I want to be an Englishman, but I want to understand other points of view. And I want to get rid of a merely English attitude in studies."[4] Loyalties and local allegiances determine more than what we want; they determine who we are. And Eliot's talk of the "closer fellowship that makes sympathy practical" echoes Cicero's claim that "society and human fellowship will be best served if we confer the most kindness on those with whom we are most closely associated."[5] A creed that disdains the partialities of kinfolk and community may have a past, but it has no future.

In the final message my father left for me and my sisters, he wrote, "Remember you are citizens of the world." But as a leader of the independence movement in what was then the Gold Coast, he never saw a conflict between local partialities and a universal morality—between being part of the place you were and a part of a broader human community. Raised with this father and an English mother, who was both deeply connected to our family in England and fully rooted in Ghana, where she has now lived for half a century, I always had a sense of family and tribe that was multiple and overlapping: Nothing could have seemed more commonplace.

Surely nothing *is* more commonplace. In geological terms, it has been a blink of an eye since human beings first left Africa, and there are few spots where we have not found habitation. The urge to migrate is no less "natural" than the urge to settle. At the same time, most of those who have learned the languages and customs of other places haven't done so out of mere curiosity. A few were looking for food for thought; most were looking for food. Thoroughgoing ignorance about the ways of others is largely a privilege of the powerful. The well-traveled polyglot is as likely to be among the worst off as among the best off—as likely to be found in a shantytown as at the Sorbonne. So cosmopolitanism shouldn't be seen as some exalted attainment: It begins with the simple idea that in the human community, as in national communities, we need to develop habits of coexistence: conversation in its older meaning, of living together, association.

And conversation in its modern sense, too. The town of Kumasi, where I grew up, is the capital of Ghana's Asante region, and, when I was a child, its main commercial thoroughfare was called Kingsway Street. In the 1950s, if you wandered down it toward the railway yards at the center of town, you'd first pass by Baboo's Bazaar, which sold imported foods and was run by the eponymous Mr. Baboo—a charming and courteous Indian—with the help of his growing family. Mr. Baboo was active in the Rotary and could always be counted on to make a contribution to the various charitable projects that are among the diversions of Kumasi's middle class, but the truth is that I remember Mr. Baboo mostly because he always had a good stock of candies and because he was always smiling. I can't reconstruct the tour down the rest of the street, for not every store had bonbons to anchor my memories. Still, I remember that we got rice from Irani Brothers; and that we often stopped in on various Lebanese and Syrian families, Muslim and Maronite, and even a philosophical Druze, named Mr. Hanni, who sold imported cloth and who was always ready, as I grew older, for a conversation about the troubles of his native Lebanon. There were other "strangers" among us, too: In the military barracks in the middle of town, you could find many northerners among the "other ranks," privates and NCOs,* their faces etched in distinctive patterns of ethnic scarification. And then there was the occasional European—the Greek architect, the Hungarian artist, the Irish doctor, the Scots engineer, some English barristers and judges, and a wildly international assortment of professors at the university, many of whom, unlike the colonial officials, remained after independence. I never thought to wonder, as a child, why these people traveled so far to live and work in my hometown; still, I was glad they did. Conversations across boundaries can be fraught, all the more so as the world grows smaller and the stakes grow larger. It's therefore worth remembering that they can also be a pleasure. What academics sometimes dub "cultural otherness" should prompt neither piety nor consternation.

Cosmopolitanism is an adventure and an ideal: But you can't have any respect for human diversity and expect everyone to become cosmopolitan. The obligations of those who wish to exercise their legitimate freedom to associate with their own kind—to keep the rest of the world away as the Amish do in the United States—are only the same as the basic obligations we all have: to do for others what morality requires. Still, a world in which communities are neatly hived off from one another seems no longer a serious option, if it ever was. And the way of segregation and seclusion has always been anomalous in our perpetually voyaging species. Cosmopolitanism isn't hard work; repudiating it is.

In the wake of 9/11, there has been a lot of fretful discussion about the divide between "us" and "them." What's often taken for granted is a picture of a world in which conflicts arise, ultimately, from conflicts between values. This is what we take to be good; that is what they take to be good. That picture of the world has deep philosophical roots; it is thoughtful, well worked out, plausible. And, I think, wrong.

I should be clear: This book [Appiah's *Cosmopolitanism*] is not a book about policy, nor is it a contribution to the debates about the true face of globalization. I'm a philosopher by trade, and philosophers rarely write really useful books. All the same, I hope to persuade you that there are interesting conceptual questions that lie beneath

---

* NCOs: Noncommissioned officers [Ed.].

the facts of globalization. The cluster of questions I want to take up can seem pretty abstract. How real are values? What do we talk about when we talk about difference? Is any form of relativism right? When do morals and manners clash? Can culture be "owned"? What do we owe strangers by virtue of our shared humanity? But the way these questions play out in our lives isn't so very abstract. By the end, I hope to have made it harder to think of the world as divided between the West and the Rest; between locals and moderns; between a bloodless ethic of profit and a bloody ethic of identity; between "us" and "them." The foreignness of foreigners, the strangeness of strangers: These things are real enough. It's just that we've been encouraged, not least by well-meaning intellectuals, to exaggerate their significance by an order of magnitude.

As I'll be arguing, it is an error—to which we dwellers in a scientific age are pe- 20 culiarly prone—to resist talk of "objective" values. In the absence of a natural science of right and wrong, someone whose model of knowledge is physics or biology will be inclined to conclude that values are not real; or, at any rate, not real like atoms and nebulae. In the face of this temptation, I want to hold on to at least one important aspect of the objectivity of values: that there are some values that are, and should be, universal, just as there are lots of values that are, and must be, local. We can't hope to reach a final consensus on how to rank and order such values. That's why the model I'll be returning to is that of conversation—and, in particular, conversation between people from different ways of life. The world is getting more crowded: In the next half a century the population of our once foraging species will approach nine billion. Depending on the circumstances, conversations across boundaries can be delightful, or just vexing: What they mainly are, though, is inevitable.

The Primacy of Practice

Local Agreements

Among the Asante,* you will be glad to hear, incest between brothers and sisters and parents and children is shunned as *akyiwadeε*. You can agree with an Asante that it's wrong, even if you don't accept his explanation of why. If my interest is in discouraging theft, I needn't worry that one person might refrain from theft because she believes in the Golden Rule; another because of her conception of personal integrity; a third because she thinks God frowns on it. I've said that value language helps shape common responses of thought, action, and feeling. But when the issue is what to do, differences in what we think and feel can fall away. We know from our own family lives that conversation doesn't start with agreement on principles. Who but someone in the grip of a terrible theory would want to insist on an agreement on principles before discussing which movie to go to, what to have for dinner, when to go to bed?

Indeed, our political coexistence, as subjects or citizens, depends on being able to agree about practices while disagreeing about their justification. For many long

---

* Asante: A people living primarily in Ghana and the Ivory Coast [Ed.].

years, in medieval Spain under the Moors and later in the Ottoman Near East, Jews and Christians of various denominations lived under Muslim rule. This modus vivendi* was possible only because the various communities did not have to agree on a set of universal values. In seventeenth-century Holland, starting roughly in the time of Rembrandt, the Sephardic Jewish community began to be increasingly well integrated into Dutch society, and there was a great deal of intellectual as well as social exchange between Christian and Jewish communities. Christian toleration of Jews did not depend on express agreement on fundamental values. Indeed, these historical examples of religious toleration — you might even call them early experiments in multiculturalism — should remind us of the most obvious fact about our own society.

Americans share a willingness to be governed by the system set out in the U.S. Constitution. But that does not require anyone to agree to any particular claims or values. The Bill of Rights tells us, "Congress shall make no law respecting an establishment of religion, or prohibiting the free exercise thereof. . . ." Yet we don't need to agree on what values underlie our acceptance of the First Amendment's treatment of religion. Is it religious toleration as an end in itself? Or is it a Protestant commitment to the sovereignty of the individual conscience? Is it prudence, which recognizes that trying to force religious conformity on people only leads to civil discord? Or is it skepticism that any religion has it right? Is it to protect the government from religion? Or religion from the government? Or is it some combination of these, or other, aims?

Cass Sunstein, the American legal scholar, has written eloquently that our understanding of Constitutional law is a set of what he calls "incompletely theorized agreements."[6] People mostly agree that it would be wrong for the Congress to pass laws prohibiting the building of mosques, for example, without agreeing exactly as to why. Many of us would, no doubt, mention the First Amendment (even though we don't agree about what values it embodies). But others would ground their judgment not in any particular law but in a conception, say, of democracy or in the equal citizenship of Muslims, neither of which is explicitly mentioned in the Constitution. There is no agreed-upon answer — and the point is there doesn't need to be. We can live together without agreeing on what the values are that make it good to live together; we can agree about what to do in most cases, without agreeing about why it is right.

I don't want to overstate the claim. No doubt there are widely shared values that help Americans live together in amity. But they certainly don't live together successfully because they have a shared theory of value or a shared story as to how to bring "their" values to bear in each case. They each have a pattern of life that they are used to; and neighbors who are, by and large, used to them. So long as this settled pattern is not seriously disrupted, they do not worry over-much about whether their fellow citizens agree with them or their theories about how to live. Americans tend to have, in sum, a broadly liberal reaction when they *do* hear about their fellow citizens' doing something that they would not do themselves: They mostly think it is not their business and not the government's business either. And, as a general rule, their shared Americanness matters to them, although many of their fellow Americans are remark-

25

---

* Modus vivendi: Latin phrase meaning mode (or way) of living that accommodates divergent points of view; agreeing to disagree [Ed.].

ably unlike themselves. It's just that what they do share can be less substantial than we're inclined to suppose.

Changing Our Minds

It's not surprising, then, that what makes conversation across boundaries worthwhile isn't that we're likely to come to a reasoned agreement about values. I don't say that we can't change minds, but the reasons we exchange in our conversations will seldom do much to persuade others who do not share our fundamental evaluative judgments already. (Remember: The same goes, mutatis mutandis,* for factual judgments.)

When we offer judgments, after all, it's rarely because we have applied well-thought-out principles to a set of facts and deduced an answer. Our efforts to justify what we have done—or what we plan to do—are typically made up after the event, rationalizations of what we have decided intuitively. And a good deal of what we intuitively take to be right, we take to be right just because it is what we are used to. If you live in a society where children are spanked, you will probably spank your children. You will believe that it is a good way to teach them right from wrong and that, despite the temporary suffering caused by a beating, they will end up better off for it. You will point to the wayward child and say, sotto voce,† that his parents do not know how to discipline him; you will mean that they do not beat him enough. You will also, no doubt, recognize that there are people who beat their children too hard or too often. So you will recognize that beating a child can sometimes be cruel.

Much the same can be said about the practice of female genital cutting. . . . If you've grown up taking it for granted as the normal thing to do, you will probably respond at first with surprise to someone who thinks it is wrong. You will offer reasons for doing it—that unmodified sexual organs are unaesthetic; that the ritual gives young people the opportunity to display courage in their transition to adulthood; that you can see their excitement as they go to their ceremony, their pride when they return. You will say that it is very strange that someone who has not been through it should presume to know whether or not sex is pleasurable for you. And, if someone should try to force you to stop from the outside, you may decide to defend the practice as an expression of your cultural identity. But this is likely to be as much a rationalization as are the arguments of your critics. They say it is mutilation, but is that any more than a reflex response to an unfamiliar practice? They exaggerate the medical risks. They say that female circumcision demeans women, but do not seem to think that male circumcision demeans men.

I am not endorsing these claims, or celebrating the argumentative impasse, or, indeed, the poverty of reason in much discussion within and across cultures. But let's recognize this simple fact: A large part of what we do we do because it *is* just what we do. You get up in the morning at eight-thirty. Why *that* time? You have coffee and cereal. Why not porridge? You send the kids to school. Why not teach them at home? You have to work. Why that job, though? Reasoning—by which I mean the public act

---

* Mutatis mutandis: "With the necessary modifications" (Latin) [Ed.].
† Sotto voce: Italian for "under the breath"; a dramatic lowering of volume for emphasis [Ed.].

of exchanging stated justifications—comes in not when we are going on in the usual way, but when we are thinking about change. And when it comes to change, what moves people is often not an argument from a principle, not a long discussion about values, but just a gradually acquired new way of seeing things.

My father, for example, came from a society in which neither women nor men were   30 traditionally circumcised. Indeed, circumcision was *akyiwadeɛ*; and since chiefs were supposed to be unblemished, circumcision was a barrier to holding royal office. Nevertheless, as he tells us in his autobiography, he decided as a teenager to have himself circumcised.

> As was the custom in those happy days, the young girls of Adum would gather together in a playing field nearby on moonlight nights to regale themselves by singing traditional songs and dancing from about 7 PM until midnight each day of the week.
>
> . . . On one such night, these girls suddenly started a new song that completely bowled us over: Not only were the words profane in the extreme, but they also constituted the most daring challenge to our manhood and courage ever flung at us. More than that, we were being invited to violate an age-old tradition of our ancestors, long respected among our people, namely the taboo on circumcision. Literally translated the words were:
>
> "An uncircumcised penis is detestable, and those who are uncircumcised should come for money from us so that they can get circumcised. We shall never marry the uncircumcised."[7]

To begin with, my father and his friends thought the girls would relent. But they were wrong. And so, after consultation with his mates, my father found himself a *wansam*—a Muslim circumcision specialist—and had the operation performed. (It was, he said, the most painful experience of his life and, if he'd had it to do again, he would have refrained. He did not, of course, have the advantage of the preparation, the companionship of boys of his own age, and the prestige of suffering bravely that would have come if the practice had been an Akan tradition.)

My father offered a reason for this decision: He and his friends conceded that "as our future sweethearts and wives, they were entitled to be heard in their plea in favor of male circumcision, even though they were not prepared to go in for female circumcision, which was also a taboo among our people." This explanation invites a question, however. Why did these young women, in the heart of Asante, decide to urge the young men of Adum to do what was not just untraditional but taboo? One possibility is that circumcision somehow became identified in their minds with being modern. If that was the point, my father would have been sympathetic. He was traditional in some ways; but like many people in Kumasi in the early twentieth century, he was also excited by a modern world that was bringing new music, new technology, new possibilities. To volunteer for circumcision in his society he surely had not just to hear the plea of the young women of Adum but to understand—and agree with—the impulse behind it. And, as I say, it may have been exactly the fact that it was untraditional that made it appealing. Circumcision—especially because it carried with it exclusion from the possibilities of traditional political office—became a way of casting his lot with modernity.

This new fashion among the young people of Adum was analogous to, if more substantial than, the change in taste that has produced a generation of Americans with piercings and tattoos. And that change was not simply the result of argument and debate, either (even though, as anyone who has argued with a teenager about a pierced belly button will attest, people on both sides can come up with a whole slew of arguments). There's some social-psychological truth in the old Flanders & Swann song "The Reluctant Cannibal," about a young "savage" who pushes away from the table and declares, "I won't eat people. Eating people is wrong." His father has all the arguments, such as they are. ("But people have always eaten people, / What else is there to eat? / If the Juju had meant us not to eat people, / He wouldn't have made us of meat!") The son, though, just repeats his newfound conviction: Eating people is wrong. He's just sure of it, he'll say so again and again, and he'll win the day by declamation.

Or take the practice of foot-binding* in China, which persisted for a thousand years—and was largely eradicated within a generation. The anti-foot-binding campaign, in the 1910s and 1920s, did circulate facts about the disadvantages of bound feet, but those couldn't have come as news to most people. Perhaps more effective was the campaign's emphasis that no other country went in for the practice; in the world at large, then, China was "losing face" because of it. Natural-foot societies were formed, with members forswearing the practice and further pledging that their sons would not marry women with bound feet. As the movement took hold, scorn was heaped on older women with bound feet, and they were forced to endure the agonies of unbinding. What had been beautiful became ugly; ornamentation became disfigurement. (The success of the anti-foot-binding campaign was undoubtedly a salutary development, but it was not without its victims. Think of some of the last women whose feet were bound, who had to struggle to find husbands.) The appeal to reason alone can explain neither the custom nor its abolition.

So, too, with other social trends. Just a couple of generations ago, in most of the industrialized world, most people thought that middle-class women would ideally be housewives and mothers. If they had time on their hands, they could engage in charitable work or entertain one another; a few of them might engage in the arts, writing novels, painting, performing in music, theater, and dance. But there was little place for them in the "learned professions"—as lawyers or doctors, priests or rabbis; and if they were to be academics, they would teach young women and probably remain unmarried. They were not likely to make their way in politics, except perhaps at the local level. And they were not made welcome in science. How much of the shift away from these assumptions is the result of arguments? Isn't a significant part of it just the consequence of

> **Reasoning . . . comes in not when we are going on in the usual way, but when we are thinking about change.**

our getting used to new ways of doing things? The arguments that kept the old pattern in place were not—to put it mildly—terribly good. If the *reasons* for the old sexist way of doing things had been the problem, the women's movement could have been done

35

---

* Foot-binding: Ancient Chinese practice of wrapping female feet in order to keep them from growing more than about three inches long, resulting in terrible pain and deformity [Ed.].

with in a couple of weeks. There are still people, I know, who think that the ideal life for any woman is making and managing a home. There are more who think that it is an honorable option. Still, the vast majority of Westerners would be appalled at the idea of trying to force women back into these roles. Arguments mattered for the women who made the women's movement and the men who responded to them. This I do not mean to deny. But their greatest achievement has been to change our habits. In the 1950s, if a college-educated woman wanted to go to law or business school, the natural response was "Why?" Now the natural response is "Why not?"

Or consider another example: In much of Europe and North America, in places where a generation ago homosexuals were social outcasts and homosexual acts were illegal, lesbian and gay couples are increasingly being recognized by their families, by society, and by the law. This is true despite the continued opposition of major religious groups and a significant and persisting undercurrent of social disapproval. Both sides make arguments, some good, most bad, if you apply a philosophical standard of reasoning. But if you ask the social scientists what has produced this change, they will rightly not start with a story about reasons. They will give you a historical account that concludes with a sort of perspectival shift. The increasing presence of "openly gay" people in social life and in the media has changed our habits. Over the last thirty or so years, instead of thinking about the private activity of gay *sex*, many Americans started thinking about the public category of gay *people*. Even those who continue to think of the sex with disgust now find it harder to deny these people their respect and concern (and some of them have learned, as we all did with our own parents, that it's better not to think too much about other people's sex lives anyway).

Now, I don't deny that all the time, at every stage, people were talking, giving each other reasons to do things: accept their children, stop treating homosexuality as a medical disorder, disagree with their churches, come out. Still, the short version of the story is basically this: People got used to lesbians and gay people. I am urging that we should learn about people in other places, take an interest in their civilizations, their arguments, their errors, their achievements, not because that will bring us to agreement, but because it will help us get used to one another. If that is the aim, then the fact that we have all these opportunities for disagreement about values need not put us off. Understanding one another may be hard; it can certainly be interesting. But it doesn't require that we come to agreement.

Fighting for the Good

I've said we can live in harmony without agreeing on underlying values (except, perhaps, the cosmopolitan value of living together). It works the other way, too: We can find ourselves in conflict when we do agree on values. Warring parties are seldom at odds because they have clashing conceptions of "the good." On the contrary, conflict arises most often when two peoples have identified the same thing as good. The fact that both Palestinians and Israelis—in particular, that both observant Muslims and observant Jews—have a special relation to Jerusalem, to the Temple Mount, has been a reliable source of trouble. The problem isn't that they disagree about the importance of Jerusalem: The problem is exactly that they both care for it deeply and, in part, for the same reasons. Muhammad, in the first years of Islam, urged his followers to turn toward Jerusalem in prayer because he had learned the story of Jerusalem from the Jews among whom he lived in Mecca. Nor is it an accident that the West's fiercest adversaries among other societies tend to come from among the most Westernized of the group. *Mon semblable mon frère?** Only if the *frère* you have in mind is Cain.† We all know now that the foot soldiers of al Qaeda who committed the mass murders at the Twin Towers and the Pentagon were not Bedouins from the desert; not unlettered fellahin.°

Indeed, there's a wider pattern here. Who in Ghana excoriated the British and built the movement for independence? Not the farmers and the peasants. Not the chiefs. It was the Western-educated bourgeoisie. And when in the 1950s Kwame Nkrumah—who went to college in Pennsylvania and lived in London—created a nationalist mass movement, at its core were soldiers who had returned from fighting a war in the British army, urban market women who traded Dutch prints, trade unionists who worked in industries created by colonialism, and the so-called veranda boys, who had been to colonial secondary schools, learned English, studied history and geography in textbooks written in England. Who led the resistance to the British Raj?‡ An Indian-born South African lawyer, trained in the British courts, whose name was Gandhi; an Indian named Nehru who wore Savile Row suits and sent his daughter to an English boarding school; and Muhammad Ali Jinnah, founder of Pakistan, who joined Lincoln's Inn in London and became a barrister at the age of nineteen.

In Shakespeare's *Tempest,* Caliban, the original inhabitant of an island commandeered by Prospero, roars at his domineering colonizer, "You taught me language and my profit on't / Is, I know how to curse." It is no surprise that Prospero's "abhorred slave" has been a figure of colonial resistance for literary nationalists all around the world. And in borrowing from Caliban, they have also borrowed from Shakespeare. Prospero has told Caliban, 40

> When thou didst not, savage,
> Know thine own meaning, but wouldst gabble like
> A thing most brutish, I endowed thy purposes
> With words that made them known.

Of course, one of the effects of colonialism was not only to give many of the natives a European language, but also to help shape their purposes. The independence movements of the post-1945 world that led to the end of Europe's African and Asian empires were driven by the rhetoric that had guided the Allies' own struggle against Germany and Japan: democracy, freedom, equality. This wasn't a conflict between values. It was a conflict of interests couched in terms of the same values.

The point applies as much within the West as elsewhere. Americans disagree about abortion, many vehemently. They couch this conflict in a language of conflicting values: They are pro-life or pro-choice. But this is a dispute that makes sense only because each side recognizes the very values the other insists upon. The disagreement is about their significance. Both sides respect something like the sanctity of human life. They disagree about such things as why human life is so precious and where it begins.

---

* *Mon semblable mon frère?:* French for "My likeness my brother?" [Ed.].
† Cain: Biblical son of Adam and Eve who murdered his brother Abel (see Genesis 4:1–8) [Ed.].
° Fellahin: Middle Eastern peasant or farmer [Ed.].
‡ British Raj: Term for British rule in India from 1858 to 1947 [Ed.].

Whatever you want to call those disagreements, it's just a mistake to think that either side doesn't recognize the value at stake here. And the same is true about choice: Americans are not divided about whether it's important to allow people, women and men, to make the major medical choices about their own bodies. They are divided about such questions as whether an abortion involves two people—both fetus and mother—or three people, adding in the father, or only one. Furthermore, no sane person on either side thinks that saving human lives or allowing people medical autonomy is the only thing that matters.

Some people will point to disputes about homosexuality and say that there, at least, there really is a conflict between people who do and people who don't regard homosexuality as a perversion. Isn't that a conflict of values? Well, no. Most Americans, on both sides, have the concept of perversion: of sexual acts that are wrong because their objects are inappropriate objects of sexual desire. But not everyone thinks that the fact that an act involves two women or two men makes it perverted. Not everyone who thinks these acts are perverse thinks they should be illegal. Not everyone who thinks they should be illegal thinks that gay and lesbian people should be ostracized. What is at stake, once more, is a battle about the meaning of perversion, about its status as a value, and about how to apply it. It is a reflection of the essentially contestable character of perversion as a term of value. When one turns from the issue of criminalization of gay sex—which is, at least for the moment, unconstitutional in the United States—to the question of gay marriage, all sides of the debate take seriously issues of sexual autonomy, the value of the intimate lives of couples, the meaning of family, and, by way of discussions of perversion, the proper uses of sex.

What makes these conflicts so intense is that they are battles over the meaning of the *same* values, not that they oppose one value, held exclusively by one side, with another, held exclusively by their antagonists. It is, in part, because we have shared horizons of meaning, because these are debates between people who share so many other values and so much else in the way of belief and of habit, that they are as sharp and as painful as they are.

Winners and Losers

But the disputes about abortion and gay marriage divide Americans bitterly most of all because they share a society and a government. They are neighbors and fellow citizens. And it is laws governing all of them that are in dispute. What's at stake are their bodies or those of their mothers, their aunts, their sisters, their daughters, their wives, and their friends; those dead fetuses could have been their children or their children's friends.

We should remember this when we think about international human rights treaties. Treaties are law, even when they are weaker than national law. When we seek to embody our concern for strangers in human rights law and when we urge our government to enforce it, we are seeking to change the world of law in every nation on the planet. We have outlawed slavery not just domestically but in international law. And in so doing we have committed ourselves, at a minimum, to the desirability of its eradication everywhere. This is no longer controversial in the capitals of the world. No one defends enslavement. But international treaties define slavery in ways that arguably include debt bondage; and debt bondage is a significant economic institution in parts of South Asia. I hold no brief for debt bondage. Still, we shouldn't be surprised if people whose income and whose style of life depend upon it are angry. Given that we have neighbors—even if only a few—who think that the fact that abortion is permitted in the United States turns the killing of the doctors who perform them into an act of heroism, we should not be surprised that there are strangers—even if only a few—whose anger turns them to violence against us.

I do not fully understand the popularity among Islamist movements in Egypt, Algeria, Iran, and Pakistan of a high-octane anti-Western rhetoric. But I do know one of its roots. It is, to use suitably old-fashioned language, "the woman question." There are Muslims, many of them young men, who feel that forces from outside their society—forces that they might think of as Western or, in a different moment, American—are pressuring them to reshape relations between men and women. Part of that pressure, they feel, comes from our media. Our films and our television programs are crammed with indescribable indecency. Our fashion magazines show women without modesty, women whose presence on many streets in the Muslim world would be a provocation, they think, presenting an almost irresistible temptation to men. Those magazines influence publications in their own countries, pulling them inevitably in the same direction. We permit women to swim almost naked with strange men, which is our business; but it is hard to keep the news of these acts of immodesty from Muslim women and children or to protect Muslim men from the temptations they inevitably create. As the Internet spreads, it will get even harder, and their children, especially their girls, will be tempted to ask for these freedoms too. Worse, they say, we are now trying to force our conception of how women and men should behave upon them. We speak of women's rights. We make treaties enshrining these rights. And then we want their governments to enforce them.[8]

Like many people in every nation, I support those treaties, of course; I believe that women, like men, should have the vote, should be entitled to work outside their homes, should be protected from the physical abuse of men, including their fathers, brothers, and husbands. But I also know that the changes that these freedoms would bring will change the balance of power between men and women in everyday life. How do I know this? Because I have lived most of my adult life in the West as it has gone through the latter phases of just such a transition, and I know that the process is not yet complete.

The recent history of America does show that a society can radically change its attitudes—and more importantly, perhaps, its habits—about these issues over a single generation. But it also suggests that some people will stay with the old attitudes, and the whole process will take time. The relations between men and women are not abstractions: They are part of the intimate texture of our everyday lives. We have strong feelings about them, and we have inherited many received ideas. Above all, we have deep *habits* about gender. A man and a woman go out on a date. Our habit is that, even if the woman offers, the man pays. A man and a woman approach an elevator door. The man steps back. A man and a woman kiss in a movie theater. No one takes a second look. Two men walk hand in hand in the high street.* People are embarrassed. They hope their children don't see. They don't know how to explain it to them.

---

* The high street: Term used in the United Kingdom for what Americans call main street [Ed.].

Most Americans are against gay marriage, conflicted about abortion, and amazed 50
(and appalled) that a Saudi woman can't get a driver's license. But my guess is that
they're not as opposed to gay marriage as they were twenty years ago. Indeed, twenty
years ago, most Americans would probably just have thought the whole idea ridiculous. On the other hand, those Americans who are in favor of recognizing gay marriages probably don't have a simple set of reasons why. It just seems right to them,
probably, in the way that it just seems wrong to those who disagree. (And probably
they're thinking not about couples in the abstract but about Jim and John or Jean and
Jane.) The younger they are, the more likely it is that they think that gay marriage is
fine. And if they don't, it will often be because they have had religious objections reinforced regularly through life in church, mosque, or temple.

    I am a philosopher. I believe in reason. But I have learned in a life of university
teaching and research that even the cleverest people are not easily shifted by reason
alone—and that can be true even in the most cerebral of realms. One of the great
savants of the postwar era, John von Neumann, liked to say, mischievously, that "in
mathematics you don't understand things, you just get used to them." In the larger
world, outside the academy, people don't always even care whether they *seem* reasonable. Conversation, as I've said, is hardly guaranteed to lead to agreement about what
to think and feel. Yet we go wrong if we think the point of conversation is to persuade,
and imagine it proceeding as a debate, in which points are scored for the Proposition
and the Opposition. Often enough, as Faust said, in the beginning is the deed: Practices
and not principles are what enable us to live together in peace. Conversations across
boundaries of identity—whether national, religious, or something else—begin with
the sort of imaginative engagement you get when you read a novel or watch a movie or
attend to a work of art that speaks from some place other than your own. So I'm using
the word "conversation" not only for literal talk but also as a metaphor for engagement
with the experience and the ideas of others. And I stress the role of the imagination
here because the encounters, properly conducted, are valuable in themselves. Conversation doesn't have to lead to consensus about anything, especially not values; it's
enough that it helps people get used to one another.

NOTES

1. Galatians 3:28. In quoting the Bible, I have used the King James version, except for the
   Pentateuch, where I have used Robert Alter's powerful modern translation, *The Five
   Books of Moses* (New York: Norton, 2004).
2. Christoph Martin Wieland. "Das Geheimniß des Kosmopolitenordens," *Teutscher
   Merkur*, August 1788, p. 107. (Where I give a reference only to a source that is not in
   English, the translation is mine.)
3. *Essai sur les mœurs et l'esprit des nations*, vol. 16 of *Oeuvres complètes de Voltaire* (Paris:
   L'Imprimerie de la Société Litteraire-Typographique, 1784), p. 241. Voltaire is speaking specifically here of "the Orient," and especially of China and India, but he would
   surely not have denied its more general application.
4. George Eliot, *Daniel Deronda* (London: Penguin, 1995), pp. 745, 661–62, 183.
5. Cicero, *De officiis* 1.50.
6. Cass R. Sunstein, "Incompletely Theorized Agreements," *Harvard Law Review* 108
   (1995): 1733–72.

7. Joseph Appiah, *Joe Appiah: The Autobiography of an African Patriot* (New York: Praeger, 1990), p. 22.
8. I have put this complaint in the mouth of a Muslim. But the truth is you could hear it from non-Muslims in many places as well. It is less likely to be heard in non-Muslim Africa, because there, by and large (as Amartya Sen has pointed out), women have a less unequal place in public life. See Jean Drèze and Amartya Sen, *Hunger and Public Action* (Oxford: Clarendon Press, 1989).

Exploring Context

1. Appiah uses the term *cosmopolitanism* to describe an ability to get along with others in a globalized and deeply connected world, an ability he relates to having conversation. Locate a website that you think represents Appiah's understanding of *cosmopolitan*. What makes it so? What kinds of conversations happen on this site? Locate passages from Appiah's text that support your interpretation of the website as an example of cosmopolitanism. Does the site fit the definition you created in Question 1 of Questions for Critical Reading?

2. Appiah looks at a number of culturally specific practices, including foot-binding in China and circumcision in African nations. Select one of Appiah's examples and use information from the Web to prepare a short report on how the practice has changed in its home culture. Are the reasons for these changes consistent with Appiah's arguments?

3. Visit a social networking site such as Twitter (twitter.com) or Facebook (facebook.com). If you don't currently have a profile on either site, create one. Explore the site and consider the role it might play in Appiah's vision of cosmopolitanism. Does it promote that ideal? What sorts of conversations does the site allow? Is it the kind of tool you described in Question 2 of Questions for Critical Reading?

Questions for Connecting

1. How do Appiah's insights about conversation confirm Helen Epstein's findings in "AIDS, Inc." (p. 152)? How can AIDS prevention be further promoted in Africa despite differences in values and practices? Synthesize the ideas of these authors to suggest strategies for halting the spread of HIV.

2. In "Community and Diversity" (p. 314), Rebekah Nathan explores the idea and the reality of community and diversity on college campuses. Can Appiah's ideas about cosmopolitanism be applied to educational settings to redress the problems that Nathan sees? Use your work on Appiah's concepts from Questions for Critical Reading or your findings from Exploring Context in composing your response.

3. Could cosmopolitanism have a genetic basis? Consider Patricia Churchland's arguments in "Networking: Genes, Brains, and Behavior" (p. 113). What role might biology play in the evolution and change of values and practices?

4. **CONNECTING TO E-PAGES** What sorts of values are at play in the manufacturing of consumer electronics, as described in Charles Duhigg and David Barboza's essay "In China, Human Costs Are Built Into an iPad" (bedfordstmartins.com/emerging/epages)? Do these practices reflect cosmopolitanism or more local values?

Language Matters

1. Transition words or phrases help readers move from one idea or unit in an essay to another. In order to practice using transitions, locate a passage in Appiah that you found difficult or confusing. To clarify the thinking of your selected passage, write a short paragraph that could precede your selection, using transitions to ease the difficulty of the passage from Appiah. Think about what Appiah is trying to do in that part of his essay and then clarify that purpose with transition words or phrases. How might the paragraph you write work as a transitional paragraph for Appiah's ideas? How can you more effectively use transitions in your own writing?

2. As an exercise in being concise, summarize Appiah's argument in a haiku, a Japanese form of nonrhyming poetry that has three lines, with five syllables in the first line, seven syllables in the second line, and five in the third. For example:

Language matters much.
Working on a haiku can
Clarify this text.

Use the haiku to express Appiah's argument in just a few words.

3. If you are not familiar with simple sentences — sentences with just a subject and verb — locate information on them in a grammar handbook or other reference resource. Then choose one of Appiah's key sentences and transform it into a simple sentence or into a series of simple sentences. Does breaking down Appiah's sentence into simple sentences make his ideas easier to understand? When are simple sentences useful? Why didn't Appiah write this whole essay in simple sentences? When should you use these in your own writing? What makes them useful?

Assignments for Writing

1. For Appiah, cosmopolitanism is as much a challenge as a solution to the problems of a globalized world. Using Appiah's sense of the term *cosmopolitanism*, locate the challenges presented by the examples he uses to illustrate his arguments. Then write a paper in which you propose the best strategies for overcoming the challenges presented by cosmopolitanism. In what way does Appiah offer a solution to facing these challenges in an increasingly diverse world? Is the solution Appiah finds in cosmopolitanism adequate in addressing these challenges in a way that respects the diversity of local populations? Use your work in Exploring Context to offer specific examples of successful strategies.

2. Appiah discusses his choice of cosmopolitanism as a rubric for moving forward. At the same time, he discusses the problems of realizing social change. Based on his discussion of the primacy of practice, how can we advocate for change in social practices? Write a paper in which you identify the best tools for achieving social change. In constructing and supporting your argument, you may wish to build on the cultural practice you explored in Question 2 of Exploring Context.

3. Appiah is invested in conversation as an engagement with others, but has this engagement been constructive in the ideological conflicts Appiah discusses? Using one of the examples Appiah describes in the sections "Changing Our Minds" (p. 75) and "Fighting for the Good" (p. 78), write a paper in which you determine whether conversation has helped to resolve the conflict Appiah describes, and if so, how.

NAMIT ARORA

Namit Arora, a graduate of the Indian Institute of Technology, is the creator of Shunya, a website devoted to his writing and photography, which has operated since 2000. His writings have been published in the *Philosopher*, the *Kyoto Journal*, and *Philosophy Now*. Arora is also a prolific photographer whose works have been licensed by over one hundred organizations, including over twenty-five academic institutions. He is a regular contributor to *3 Quarks Daily*, a blog that presents "interesting items from around the Web on a daily basis, in the areas of science, design, literature, current affairs, art, and anything else [the editors] deem inherently fascinating," and is the winner of the 3 Quarks Daily 2011 Arts & Literature Prize for his book review of Omprakash Valmiki's *Joothan: A Dalit's Life*.

Arora's "What Do We Deserve?" was published in the *Humanist*, the journal of the American Humanist Association, an organization that advocates a secular, compassionate, and human-based system of ethics. The May/June 2011 issue in which "What Do We Deserve?" was first published also featured articles by Steven Surman, David Niose, and biologist PZ Myers, dealing with morality issues from a distinctly liberal and secular point of view. The articles included in the issue cover topics as diverse as secularism in the military, corporatism, and a critique of "family values" politics, but they are all united through their commitment to a humanist outlook.

In "What Do We Deserve?" Arora examines three forms of economic systems: the libertarian model, the meritocratic model, and the egalitarian model. Arora briefly evaluates each model, ultimately questioning the idea that both the rich and the impoverished "deserve" or have somehow earned their economic positions.

▶ TAGS: *ethics, libertarian model, meritocratic model, egalitarian model, difference principle, social justice, economics*

Questions for Critical Reading

1. As you read, make note of the three different models of economic justice that Arora discusses. Which of these do you feel is the most just? Find quotations from Arora that support your position.

2. What is the "Difference Principle"? Define this term as you read the essay and consider what role it plays in our current economic system.

3. What role do media and culture play in our understanding of "what we deserve"? Use Arora's essay to form your response.

What Do We Deserve?

I often think of the good life I have. By most common measures—say, type of work, income, health, leisure, and social status—I'm doing well. Despite the adage, "call no man happy until he is dead," I wonder no less often: How much of my good life do I really deserve? Why me and not so many others?

The dominant narrative has it that I was a bright student, worked harder than most, and competed fairly to gain admission to an Indian Institute of Technology, where my promise was recognized with financial aid from a U.S. university. When I took a chance after graduate school and came to Silicon Valley, I was justly rewarded for my knowledge and labor with a measure of financial security and social status. While many happily accept this narrative, my problem is that I don't buy it. I believe that much of my socioeconomic station in life was not realized by my own doing, but was accidental or due to my being in the right place at the right time.

A pivotal question in market-based societies is "What do we deserve?" In other words, for our learning, natural talents, and labor, what rewards and entitlements are just? How much of what we bring home is fair or unfair, and why? To chase these questions is to be drawn into the thickets of political philosophy and theories of justice. American political philosopher Michael Sandel's 2009 book *Justice: What's the Right Thing to Do?* proves valuable here in synthesizing a few thoughts on the matter, including a review of the three major approaches to distributive economic justice: libertarian, meritocratic, and egalitarian, undermining en route the dominant narrative on my own well-being.

The *libertarian model* of distributive justice favors a free market with well-defined rules that apply to all. "Citizens are assured equal basic liberties, and the distribution of income and wealth is determined by the free market," says Sandel. This model offers a formal equality of opportunity—making it a clear advance over feudal or caste arrangements—so anyone can, in theory, strive to compete and win. But in practice, people don't have real equality of opportunity due to various disadvantages, for example, of family income, social class, gender, race, caste, etc. So while the racetrack may look nice and shiny, the runners don't begin at the same starting point. What does it mean to say that the first to cross the finish line deserves his or her victory? Isn't the contest rigged from the start, based on factors that are arbitrary and derive from accidents of birth?

Take my own example. I was born into the upper-caste, riding on eons of unearned privilege over 80 percent of my fellow Indians. I was also a boy raised in a society that lavished far more attention on male students. My parents fell closer to the upper-middle class, had university degrees, and valued education and success—both my grandfathers had risen up to claim senior state government posts. I lived in a kid-friendly neighborhood with parks, playgrounds, and a staff clubhouse. I had role models and access to the right schools and books, the right coaching classes, and peers aspiring for professional careers. My background greatly shaped my ambition and self-confidence and no doubt put me ahead of perhaps 96 percent of other Indians—the odds that I would perform extremely well on standardized academic tests were huge from the start.

The *meritocratic model*, often associated with the United States, recognizes such inequities and tries to correct for socioeconomic disadvantages. At its best, meritocracy takes real equality of opportunity seriously and tries to achieve it through various means: Head Start programs, education and job training, subsidized healthcare and housing, and so forth. Meritocrats admit that market-based distribution of rewards is just only to the extent to which we can reduce endemic socioeconomic disadvantages and bring everyone to comparable starting points. But thereafter, they believe that we are the authors of our own destiny and whoever wins the race is morally deserving of the rewards they obtain from the market—and its flip side, that we morally deserve our failure too, and its consequences. Swiss writer Alain de Botton looked at this phenomenon in the United States in his 2004 documentary film, *Status Anxiety.*

But is this entirely fair? Even if we somehow leveled socioeconomic disparities, the winners of the race would still be the fastest runners, due in part to a natural lottery. People are often born with certain talents and attributes—for instance, oratory, musical acumen, physical beauty and health, athleticism, good memory and cognition, extroversion—that give them unearned advantages. Are their wins not as arbitrary from a moral standpoint as the wins of those born with silver spoons in their mouths? Further, isn't it dumb luck that our society happens to value certain aptitudes we may have—such as the leap and hand-eye coordination of Michael Jordan, sound-byte witticisms of talk show hosts like Jay Leno, or the algorithmic wizardry of Sergey Brin in the Internet age? A millennium ago, society valued other aptitudes, such as sculpting bronze in Chola India, equine archery on the Mongolian steppes, or reciting epigrammatic verse in Arabia. My own aptitude for science and math served me well in an India looking to industrialize and a United States facing a shortfall of engineers. I might have done less well in an earlier age where the best opportunities were perhaps in mercantile pursuits or the bureaucracy of government.

But how can a system of distributive justice compensate for random natural gifts that happen to be valued in a time and place? We can't level natural gifts across people, can we? The mere thought is bizarre. The American political philosopher John Rawls (1921–2002) had much to say about this in his landmark 1971 book, *A Theory of Justice*, in which he developed his *egalitarian model.* Since we can't undo the inequities of the natural lottery, he writes, we must find a way to address the differences in the rewards that result from them. We should certainly encourage people to hone and exercise their aptitudes, he says, but we should be clear that they do not morally deserve the rewards their aptitudes earn from the market. Since their natural gifts aren't their own doing, and are moreover profitable only in light of the value a community places on them, they must share the rewards with the community.

One might object here: Wait a minute, what about the role of the personal drive and effort we put into cultivating our talents? Don't we deserve the rewards that come from our striving? Not really, says Rawls. Countless factors beyond our choosing influence our ambition and effort, such as our upbringing, our family's work ethic, our childhood experiences, subconscious insecurities, social milieu, career fads, role models, parental and peer pressure, available life paths, lucky breaks, and other contingent factors. It isn't clear how much of it is our own doing, however militantly we may hold the illusion that we create our own life story (an illusion not without psychological and practical payoffs). Even the accident of being firstborn among siblings can be a factor in how hard we strive. Each year, Sandel reports, 75–80 percent of his freshman class at Harvard are firstborns. Besides, effort may be a virtue but even the meritocrats don't think it deserves rewards independent of results or achievement. So, in short, we can't claim to deserve the rewards on the basis of effort either.

Rawls deflates the idea that we morally deserve the rewards of meritocracy. If we accept this, it follows that the house of distributive justice cannot be built on the sands of moral desert (in simple terms, moral desert is a condition by which we are deserving of something, whether good or bad), but must be built on other grounds. Notably, however, Rawls doesn't make a case for equal rewards. Instead, Rawls speaks of the "Difference Principle" in dealing with the inequities of the natural lottery. This principle, says Sandel, "permits income inequalities for the sake of incentives, provided the incentives are needed to improve the lot of the least advantaged." In other words, income inequality is justified only to the extent to which it improves the lot of the most disadvantaged when compared to an equal income arrangement. Only if society is better off as a whole does favoring inequality seem fair. Does this approach diminish the role of human agency and free will when it comes to moral desert? Some say it does, yet the claim seems modest enough, that our achievements have many ingredients, and the contributions from agency or free will are intertwined with the contributions from social and random factors—to the point that it seems unreasonable to give by default all credit to agency or free will, which libertarians try to do in order to justify the rewards of the market. However, some philosophers find an unresolved tension in Rawls's approach to setting up the Difference Principle. (See, for instance, *Egalitarianism, Free Will, and Ultimate Justice* by Saul Smilansky.)

One might ask: Why should we uphold the Difference Principle at all? Is it not an arbitrary construct? No, says Rawls, and invites us to a thought experiment on creating "a hypothetical social contract in an original position of equality." Imagine, he says, that "when we gather to choose the principles [for governing ourselves], we don't know where we will wind up in society. Imagine that we choose behind a 'veil of ignorance' that temporarily prevents us from knowing anything about who we are," including our race, gender, class, talents, intelligence, wealth, and religion (or lack thereof). What principles would we then choose to order our society? Rawls makes a powerful case that, simply out of a desire to minimize our odds of suffering, we will always choose political equality, fair equal opportunity, and the Difference Principle.

Some have argued that the Difference Principle may not get chosen as is, not unless it has a clause to address the unfairness of propping up those who willfully make bad choices or act irresponsibly. Further, is it desirable, or even possible, to choose a social contract from behind the so-called veil of ignorance, as if, in Rawls's words, "from the perspective of eternity," with scant regard for context? Doesn't Rawls implicitly presuppose a people who already value political equality, individualism, and resolving claims through public deliberation? Rawls

> **In Rawlsian terms, the problem in the United States is not that a minority has grown super rich, but that for decades now, it has done so to the detriment of the lower social classes.**

later downplays its universality but, argues Sandel, even in the United States, Rawls's thought experiment supports an arid secular public space detached from so much that is central to our identities. This includes historical, moral, and religious discourses, which, if squeezed out, often pop up elsewhere in worse forms, such as the religious right. If the point is to enhance the social contract, Sandel adds, political progressives should do so not by asking people to leave their deepest beliefs at home but by engaging them in the public sphere.

Sandel's basic critique here is that Rawls's concern with the distribution of primary goods—which Rawls defines as "things that every rational man is presumed to want"—is necessary but not sufficient for a social contract. As purposive beings, we should also consider the telos of our choices, such as our common ends as a community, the areas of life worth shielding from the market, the space we should accord to loyalty and patriotism, ties of blood, marriage, tradition, and so on. Still, Rawls's thought experiment retains a powerful moral force and continues to inspire liberals. His theory of justice, writes Sandel, "represents the most compelling case for a more equal society that American political philosophy has yet produced."

Theories of justice may clarify and guide our thoughts, but we still have to figure out how to change the game we want to play and where to draw the lines on the playing field. An open society does this through vigorous public debate. As British philosopher Isaiah Berlin wrote, "people who want to govern themselves must choose how much liberty, equality, and justice they seek and how much they can let go. The price of a free society is that sometimes, perhaps often, we make bad choices." Thereafter, when the rules are in place, "we are entitled to the benefits the rules of the game promise for the exercise of our talents." It is the rules, says Sandel, and not anything outside them, that create "entitlements to legitimate expectations." Entitlements only arise after we have chosen the rules of the competition. Only in this context can we say we deserve something, whether admission to a law school, a certain bonus, or a pension.

In Rawlsian terms, the problem in the United States is not that a minority has 15 grown super rich, but that for decades now, it has done so to the detriment of the lower

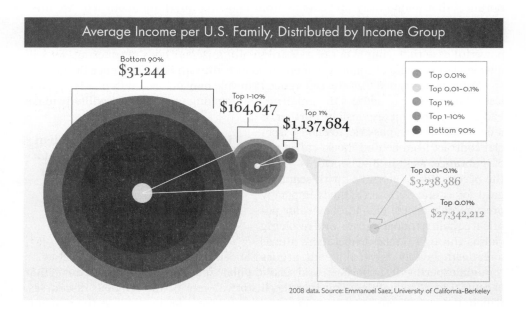

Average Income per U.S. Family, Distributed by Income Group

Bottom 90%
$31,244

Top 1–10%
$164,647

Top 1%
$1,137,684

- Top 0.01%
- Top 0.01–0.1%
- Top 1%
- Top 1–10%
- Bottom 90%

Top 0.01–0.1%
$3,238,386

Top 0.01%
$27,342,212

2008 data. Source: Emmanuel Saez, University of California–Berkeley social classes. The big question is: why does the majority in a seemingly free society tolerate this, and even happily vote against its own economic interests? A plausible answer is that it is under a self-destructive meritocratic spell that sees social outcomes as moral desert—a spell at least as old as the American frontier but long since repurposed by the corporate control of public institutions and the media: news, film, TV, publishing, and so forth. It parallels a religious spell in more ways than one. Here too, powerful social institutions are invested in clouding our notions of cause and effect. Rather than move towards greater fairness and egalitarianism, they promote a libertarian gospel of the free market with minimal regulation, taxation, and public safety nets. They beguile us into thinking that the lifestyles of the rich and famous are within reach of all, and uphold rags-to-riches stories as exemplary ("if this enterprising slumdog can do it against all odds, so can you!" goes the storyline). All this gets drummed into people's heads to the point that they only blame themselves for their lot and don't think of questioning the rules of the game.

What would it take to break this spell? For starters, it would require Americans to realize that the distribution of wealth in their society is far less egalitarian than they think it is—a recent survey revealed that Americans think the richest fifth of them own 59 percent of the wealth, while the actual figure is 84 percent. Perhaps living on credit helps create the illusion that the average American has more than he or she does. Americans also believe that their odds of rising to the top are far better than they actually are; social mobility is quite low by international standards. A kid from the poorest fifth of all households has a 1 percent chance of reaching the top 5 percentile income bracket, while a kid from the richest fifth has a 22 percent chance. The task of breaking this spell, then, requires telling new kinds of stories, engaging in vigorous public debate, and employing our best arts of persuasion.

Exploring Context

1. Visit We Are the 99 Percent (wearethe99percent.tumblr.com). How do the images and information you find there support Arora's arguments about economic justice in the United States?

2. Explore the website for the Bureau of Labor Statistics (bls.gov). Apply the information and data you find there to determine the current model of economic justice operating within the United States.

3. Recently, the Tea Party has emerged as a political force in this country. Visit the party's website (teapartypatriots.org). How does it imagine economic justice? Which model does it seem to favor?

Questions for Connecting

1. In some ways, Ariel Levy is also exploring economic justice in "Female Chauvinist Pigs" (p. 266). Synthesize her argument with Arora's. What role do factors such as gender play within models of economic justice? Do the models that Arora discusses assume a particular gender (or age or race)? How do Female Chauvinist Pigs fit into a meritocratic model of justice?

2. Thomas L. Friedman explores the extreme interconnectedness of the global economy in "The Dell Theory of Conflict Prevention" (p. 166). What happens to the models of justice that Arora presents when we move to a global scale? Which model seems to be in operation within globalization? Given the politically stabilizing effects of interconnected economies, are there other factors we should consider when thinking about economic justice?

3. In "Preface" and "The New Civil Rights" (p. 552), Kenji Yoshino is concerned not with economic rights but with civil rights. Synthesize his arguments with Arora's to create a more complete model of justice. How might Yoshino's liberty paradigm be applied to economics? What role does the Difference Principle play in civil rights?

4. **CONNECTING TO E-PAGES** Arora asks, "What do we deserve?" How might Arora's theories of economic justice apply to Charles Duhigg and David Barboza's report "In China, Human Costs Are Built Into an iPad" (bedfordstmartins.com/emerging/epages)? Do we, for instance, deserve iPads? What do the workers who make them deserve? Building on your responses to the Exploring Context questions, provide evidence to support your analysis.

Language Matters

1. In some ways, Arora's essay has a very clear but also very rigid organization, reminiscent of the five-paragraph essay. Begin by outlining Arora's argument and then consider how he uses organization to help prove his argument. How do the various sections build to a conclusion? How would the meaning of his essay change if it were rearranged? Apply what you learn to your own writing: How can you use organization to help prove your argument?

2. Arora uses a number of specialized terms such as *libertarian* and *meritocratic*. Note how he defines these terms in his text and then look up their definitions in a dictionary. How well does context function to help a reader define terms? When should you look up a word in the dictionary, and when is it sufficient to determine a word's meaning from the context of its use?

3. Arora uses a large graphic to illustrate average income in the United States. How does this graphic relate to his argument? Review any information you can find in a grammar handbook or reliable resource on using images, tables, charts, or graphics. When should you incorporate these into your text?

Assignments for Writing

1. Arora discusses three models of economic justice. Write a paper in which you determine which of these models is the most just, using Arora's analysis as well as your own experience. Which model should we pursue? Is there another alternative? Should we combine aspects of each model instead?

2. Arora's essay presupposes that economic justice is an issue worth considering. Evaluate this assumption by writing a paper on the role of justice in economics. Is social justice necessarily linked to economics or wealth? Why should we care about justice? What ramifications (political, social, cultural) do these questions have?

3. At the end of his essay, Arora suggests that promoting social and economic justice in America requires "telling new kinds of stories, engaging in vigorous public debate, and employing our best arts of persuasion" (p. 91). Write a paper in which you evaluate and extend Arora's suggestions. Are they sufficient to create a more equitable economic structure in America? Are there other strategies necessary as well? Draw on Arora's discussion in making your argument.

BRIAN CHRISTIAN

Brian Christian, a writer and poet, graduated from Brown University and received an M.F.A. from the University of Washington. His work has been published in *Wired* and the *Atlantic* and on popular blogs such as *Gizmodo*, and his poetry has been featured in *Best New Poets*. His book, *The Most Human Human: What Talking with Computers Teaches Us About What It Means to Be Alive* (2011), was a *Wall Street Journal* best-seller and was named a favorite book of 2011 by the *New Yorker*.

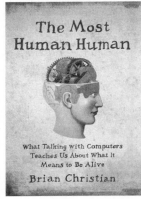

The Most
Human Human

What Talking with Computers
Teaches Us About What It
Means to Be Alive

Brian Christian

   In his book, Christian explores the relationship between humans and artificial intelligence. The book takes its name from the Loebner Prize, a contest to find the "most human human," in which human contestants compete against computers to answer questions in a convincingly "human-like" way. Christian finds that computers are shockingly good at mimicking certain types of human behavior, a fact that raises questions about what it means to be human.

   In "Authenticating," a chapter from *The Most Human Human*, Christian describes Cleverbot, a chat simulator so witty that users have accused it of being a hoax that connects users to each other anonymously rather than functioning as a "chatbot." However, simulators such as Cleverbot lack a cohesive self or memory, making intuitive and accumulative conversation difficult. Suggesting that "cobbled-together bits of human interaction do not a human relationship make" (p. 105), and comparing the language of artificially intelligent "bots" with real-world encounters like speed dating and customer service calls, Christian describes how technology and humanity reflect each other, but takes particular interest in the places where they differ.

▶ TAGS: *form, content, security, authentication, semantics, empiricism, nexting, statelessness, artificial intelligence*

Questions for Critical Reading

1. What do you think makes a human human? As you read Christian's essay, look for passages that support or challenge your understanding of the essential qualities of being human.

2. As you read Christian's text, pay special attention to his discussions of "nexting" and "statelessness." What do these terms mean? How do they affect what it means to be human?

3. What is the difference between form and content? Write down your understanding of these terms. While reading Christian, list passages where he talks about either form or content. How do the two play a role in making a human human?

Authenticating

Authentication: Form and Content

National Public Radio's *Morning Edition* recently reported the story of a man named Steve Royster. Growing up, Royster assumed he had an incredibly unusual and distinctive voice. As he explains, "Everyone always knew when I was calling just by the sound of my voice, while I had no earthly *idea* who was on the phone when *they* called." It would take him until his late twenties before he fully grasped — to his amazement — that other people could discern most *everyone's* identity by voice. How on earth could they do that? As it turns out, there *is* something unusual about Royster, but not about his voice: about his brain. Royster has a rare condition known as "phonagnosia," or "voice blindness." Even when Royster's own mother calls him, he simply goes politely along with the flow of the conversation, unaware that "this strange woman who has called me is, in fact, the one that gave birth to me." As reporter Alix Spiegel puts it, "Phonagnosics can tell from the sound of your voice if you're male or female, old or young, sarcastic, upset, happy. They just have no blooming idea who you are."[1]

This all puts Royster, of course, in an awfully strange position.

It happens to be the same position everyone is in on the Internet.

On September 16, 2008, a twenty-year-old college student named David Kernell attempted to log in to vice-presidential candidate Sarah Palin's personal Yahoo! email account. He didn't have a clue what her password might be. Guessing seemed futile; instead, it occurred to him to try to *change* it — and so he clicked on the "I forgot my password" option available to assist absentminded users. Before Yahoo! will let a user change an account password, it asks the user to answer several "authentication" questions — things like date of birth and zip code — in order to "Verify Your Identity." Kernell found the information on Wikipedia, he said, in approximately "15 seconds." Stunned, Kernell "changed the password to 'popcorn' and took a cold shower." Now he faces up to twenty years in prison.[2]

In the world of machines, we authenticate on *content*: password, PIN, last four digits of your Social Security number, your mother's maiden name. But in the human world, we authenticate on *form*: face, vocal timbre, handwriting, signature. 5

And, crucially, verbal style.

One of my friends emailed me recently: "I'm trying to rent a place in another city by email, and I don't want the fellow I've been communicating with to think I'm scamming him (or, am a flake), so, I've been hyperaware of sounding 'human' and 'real' and basically 'nonanonymous' in my emails. A weird thing. Do you know what I mean?" I do; it's *that* email's idiosyncrasies of style — the anachronistic "fellow," the compound, unhyphenated "hyperaware" and "nonanonymous" — that prove it's really *him*.

This kind of thing—behavior that seems "so you"—might always have been, say, charming or winning (at least to those who like you). Now it's something else too, our words increasingly dissociated from us in the era of the Internet: part of online *security.**

Antarctic penguins detect the precise call of their chicks among the 150,000 families at the nesting site. "Bless Babel," fiction writer Donald Barthelme says.[3] It's true: ironing out our idiosyncrasies in verbal style would not only be bad for literature; it would be bad for *safety.* Here as elsewhere, maybe that slight machine-exerted pressure to actively assert our humanity with each other ends up being a good thing.

Intimacy: Form and Content

One of my old college friends, Emily, came into town recently, and stopped downtown on her way from the airport to have lunch with a mutual friend of ours and his co-worker—who happened also to be my girlfriend, Sarah. When Emily and I met up later that day for dinner, I remarked on how funny it was that she'd already met Sarah before I'd had any chance to introduce them. I remember saying something to the effect of, "It's cool that you guys got to know each other a little bit." "Well, I wouldn't say that I got to *know* her, per se," Emily replied. "More like, 'saw what she's like' or something like that. 'Saw her in action.'"

And that's when the distinction hit me—

Having a *sense* of a person—their disposition, character, "way of being in the world"—and knowing *about* them—where they grew up, how many siblings they have, what they majored in, where they work—are two rather different things. Just like security, so does intimacy have both form and content.

"Speed dating" is a kind of fast-paced, highly structured round-robin-style social mixing event that emerged in Beverly Hills in the late 1990s. Each participant has a series of seven-minute conversations, and at the end they mark down on a card which people they'd be interested in meeting again; if there are any mutual matches, the organizers get in touch with the relevant contact information. Though it's entered into popular parlance, "SpeedDating" ("or any confusingly similar term") is technically a registered trademark, held by, of all groups, the Jewish organization Aish HaTorah: its inventor, Yaacov Deyo, is a rabbi.[4]

One of my earliest thoughts about the Turing test† was that it's a kind of speed date: you have five minutes to show another person who you are, to come across as a

---

* When something online makes me think of a friend I haven't talked to in a while, and I want to send them a link, I make sure to add some kind of personal flourish, some little verbal fillip to the message beyond just the minimal "hey, saw this and thought of you /[*link*]/ hope all's well," or else my message risks a spam-bin fate.

E.g., when I received the other week a short, generically phrased Twitter message from one of the poetry editors of *Fence* magazine saying, "hi, i'm 24/female/horny . . . i have to get off here but message me on my windows live messenger name: [*link*]," my instinct wasn't to figure out how to politely respond that I was flattered but thought it best to keep our relationship professional: it was to hit the "Report Spam" button.

† Turing test: Named for computer pioneer Alan Turing (1912–1954); one common version is a test of a computer's ability to imitate a human in conversation [Ed.].

real, living, breathing, unique and distinct, nonanonymous human being. It's a tall order. And the stakes in both cases are pretty high.

A friend of mine recently went to a speed-dating event in New York City. "Well, it   15
was the oddest thing," he said. "I kept wanting just to, like, banter, you know? To see if there was any chemistry. But all the women just kind of stuck to this script—where are you from, what do you do—like they were getting your stats, sizing you up. But I don't care about any of that stuff. So after a while I just started giving fake answers, just making stuff up, like. Just to keep it interesting, you know?"

The strangeness he experienced, and the kinds of "bullet points" that speed dating can frequently devolve into, are so well-known as to have been lampooned by *Sex and the City.*[5]

"Hi, I'm Miranda Hobbes."
"Dwight Owens: private wealth group at Morgan Stanley; investment management for high-net-worth individuals and a couple pension plans; like my job; been there five years; divorced; no kids; not religious; I live in New Jersey; speak French and Portuguese; Wharton business school; any of this appealing to you?"

The delivery certainly isn't.

People with elaborate checklists of qualities their ideal mate must have frequently put entirely the wrong types of things. This height. This salary. This profession. I've seen many a friend wind up, seemingly unsuspecting, with a jerk who nevertheless perfectly matched their description.

Fed up with the "Dwight Owens"–style, salvo-of-bullet-points approach that kept recurring in early speed-dating events, Yaacov Deyo decided on a simple, blunt solution: to make talking about your job *forbidden.* People fell back on talking about where they lived or where they were from. So he made that forbidden too. He seems charmed and maybe even a little smug enacting the ensuing panic, then breakthrough: "Omigosh, like, what *do* I talk

> **I've seen many a friend wind up, seemingly unsuspecting, with a jerk who nevertheless perfectly matched their description.**

about?" He laughs. "I can't talk about what I do for a living, or where I live, and . . . wow! All of a sudden I have to describe *me.*" Or: all of a sudden I have to *be* me, to *act like* myself instead of *describing* myself.[6]

Form and Content in the Turing Test

The first Loebner Prize competition was held on November 8, 1991, at the Boston Com-   20
puter Museum. In its first few years, the Loebner Prize gave each program and human confederate a "topic" as a means of limiting the conversation. In some ways, that first contest was a battle between style and content. One of the confederates was Shakespeare expert Cynthia Clay, who was, famously, deemed a computer by three different judges. The consensus seemed to be "No one knows that much about Shakespeare." (For this reason, Clay took her misclassifications as a compliment.)

The program behind the topic of "whimsical conversation"—PC Therapist III by Joseph Weintraub—won the Loebner Prize that year, earning the very first Most Human Computer award.[7] As the program practiced it, "whimsical conversation" was not a *topic* at all, but a *manner*—a crucial distinction. Weintraub was able to play off of a looseness in the contest rules, the natural behavior patterns of chatbots, and people's stereotypes about computers and humans all at once. Strategically, it was brilliant. Clay and her fellow confederates, by dutifully and scrupulously providing information to the questions asked, demonstrated their knowledge and understanding—but sometimes in a factual, encyclopedic way commonly associated with computer systems.

JUDGE: What is your opinion on Shakespeare's plays?
REMOTE: That's pretty general; would you be more specific? Otherwise, I'll just say I like them.

The interlocutor at the "whimsical conversation" terminal stood in stark contrast:

JUDGE: It has been a long day! Now I think I'm ready for some fun. The weather isn't very pleasant today. Do you have any jokes that could lift the clouds?
REMOTE: Everybody talks about the weather but nobody seems to do much about it. Why do you need to tell me now you think you're ready for some fun? Groannnnnn.

. . .

JUDGE: What is the definition of whimsical conversation?
REMOTE: Didn't you say well anyway I would imagine whimsical conversation is like a series of knight's moves in chess—skrt* of zig-zag rather than following any nparticular line.? Why do you ask? Was that a clever comment, or what? Are such questions much on your mind?
JUDGE: I like the image of knights moving hap-hazardly across the chess board, does that mean there is no thought to whimsical conversation?
REMOTE: I could swear you just said how do you define whimsical?? How do yku define whimsical? Were you always so sick sick sick? Why do you need to tell me you like the image of knights moving haphazardly across the chess board?

"I really thought [PC Therapist] was human because it . . . was weird and funny, in a normal sort of way," said one of the judges, a Harvard graduate student. Weintraub's program, shifting topics wildly and spouting non sequiturs and canned one-liners, came off as zany, a jokester, a much more "human" personality type. At least—before I learned how easy it was to mimic—I used to think so.

Suspicion; Roulette; Purée

Looking around on the Internet for information about the Most Human Computer of 2005 and 2006, Rollo Carpenter's web-based Cleverbot, I found something very curious. There seems to be a considerable amount of speculation that the site may be, in effect, a hoax.

---

* *Sic.* Weintraub's program, like many that followed it, faked typos.

"I've been talking to it for a while now, and am beginning to wonder if Cleverbot is ₂₅ really even a real bot," one user writes. "Cleverbot always says that itself is the human, and I am the bot. Could it be that I'm actually talking to a real person, but we are both tricked to believe that the other is Cleverbot?" Some of the responses seem just a hair too uncanny. One user writes, in French, "Je habite dans les Etats Unis," and finds his French not only comprehended but *critiqued*: "On dit J'habite AUX Etats-Unis," the bot corrects him.

Another trades off lines of Queen's "Bohemian Rhapsody":

USER: Scaramouche, Scaramouche.
CLEVERBOT: Will you do the fandango?
USER: Thunderbolt and lightning.
CLEVERBOT: Very very frightening me!
USER: Galileo.
CLEVERBOT: Galileo Galileo.

One user reports telling it a popular joke of the time—

USER: You know why they call it an Xbox 360?
CLEVERBOT: Why?
USER: Because when you see it, you turn 360 degrees and walk away.

—only to have his joke deconstructed by the bot:

CLEVERBOT: No because then you would be facing it and that would be unfunny.

Other users, attempting to fix the logic of the joke, meanwhile making it slightly more drily absurd—

USER: You know why they call it an Xbox 360?
CLEVERBOT: No. Why do they call it Xbox 360?
USER: Because when you see it, you turn 360 degrees and moonwalk away.

—were met with a kind of one-upmanship of an even drier, more absurd punch line:

CLEVERBOT: Nope, because when you see it you turn 3 degrees and walk slightly askew.

Surely there must be a human at the other side! The replies are too culturally attuned, too savvy. Yet at other moments, conversations change gears without a clutch, or a non sequitur comes seemingly from left field.

Cleverbot's programmer, Rollo Carpenter, is happy to explain his creation's pro- ₃₀ grammatic workings, and insists on Cleverbot's home page that "visitors never talk to a human, however convincing it is." Curiously, this insistence seems to have little effect on many users, who have their own, rather different theory about what's going on.

The Internet of the early 1990s was a much more anonymous place than it is now. On local BBSs (bulletin board systems), in the chat rooms of "walled garden" Internet providers/communities like Prodigy and AOL, and over universal chat protocols like IRC (Internet Relay Chat), strangers bumped into each other all the time. The massive social networks (e.g., Facebook) of the late '00s and early '10s have begun to make the Internet a different place. It's around this time that websites like Chatroulette and

Omegle, designed to bring some of that anonymity, randomness, and serendipity back, took off. You choose to use either video or text and are then paired up with another user completely at random and begin a conversation.* At any time, either of you can terminate it, in which case you're both re-paired with new strangers and begin instantly again at "Hello." There's an anxiety all users of such sites feel about the prospect of the other person cutting off the dialogue and bumping both of you into new conversations, which has been dubbed "getting nexted."

Now, imagine if, instead, the computer system was *automatically* cutting off conversations and re-pairing users with each other, and that it was *not telling them* it was doing this. Users A and B are arguing about baseball, and users C and D are talking about art. All of a sudden A is re-paired with C, and B re-paired with D. After talking about the Louvre, C receives the off-topic "So are you for the Mets or the Yankees?" and B, after analyzing the most recent World Series, is asked if he's ever seen the Sistine Chapel. Well, this is the conspiracy theory on Cleverbot (and some of its cousin bots, like Robert Medeksza's Ultra Hal): Omegle minus control over when to switch conversations. Imagine that the computer is simply switching you over, at random and without notice, to new people, and doing the same to them. What you'd end up with might look a lot like the Cleverbot transcripts.

The conspiracy theory isn't right, but it's not far off either.

"Cleverbot borrows the intelligence of its users," Carpenter explains to me in Brighton.[8] "A conversational Wikipedia," he calls it in a television interview with the Science Channel.[9] It works like this: Cleverbot begins a conversation by saying, for instance, "Hello." A user might respond in any number of ways, from "Hello" to "Howdy!" to "Are you a computer?" and so on. Whatever the user says goes into an enormous database of utterances, tagged as a genuine human response to "Hello." When, in a subsequent conversation, a user ever says to Cleverbot, "Hello," Cleverbot will have "Howdy!" (or whatever the first person said) ready on hand. As the same types of things tend to come up over and over—in what statisticians call a "Zipf distribution," to be precise—and as thousands of users are logged in to Cleverbot at any given time, chatting with it around the clock, over the span of many years now, Cleverbot's database contains appropriate replies to even seemingly obscure remarks. (E.g., "Scaramouche, Scaramouche.")

What you get, the cobbling together of hundreds of thousands of prior conversations, is a kind of conversational purée. Made of human parts, but less than a human sum. Users *are*, in effect, chatting with a kind of purée of real people—the *ghosts* of real people, at any rate: the echoes of conversations past.

This is part of why Cleverbot seems so impressive on basic factual questions ("What's the capital of France?" "Paris is the capital of France") and pop culture (trivia,

35

---

* Such anonymity brings hazard, though, at least as much as serendipity. I read someone's account of trying out Chatroulette for the first time: twelve of the first twenty video chats he attempted were with men masturbating in front of the camera. For this reason, and because it was more like the Turing test, I stuck to text. Still, my first two interlocutors on Omegle were guys trolling, stiltedly, for cybersex. But the third was a high school student from the suburbs of Chicago: we talked about *Cloud Gate*, the Art Institute, the pros and cons of growing up and moving out. Here was a real person. "You're normal!!" she wrote, with double exclamation marks; my thought exactly.

jokes, and song lyric sing-alongs)—the things to which there is a *right* answer inde-pendent of the speaker. No number of cooks can spoil the broth. But ask it about the city it lives in, and you get a pastiche of thousands of people talking about thousands of places. You find it out not so much by realizing that you aren't talking with a *human* as by realizing that you aren't talking with *a* human.

One Self, Any Self

My mind goes back to the organizers' advice to "just be myself," to how much phi-losophers have agonized over this idea. While other existentialists—for instance, Jean-Paul Sartre—emphasized authenticity and originality and freedom from out-side influence, nineteenth-century German philosopher Friedrich Nietzsche held the startling opinion that the most important part of "being oneself" was—in Brown University philosopher Bernard Reginster's words—"being *one* self, *any* self."[10]

Nietzsche spoke of this as "giving style to one's character," comparing people to works of art, which we often judge according to their "concinnity," the way their parts fit together to make a whole: "In the end, when the work is finished, it becomes evident how the constraint of a single taste governed and formed everything large and small."[11]

Computer culture critics like Jaron Lanier are skeptical, for instance, of decentral-ized projects like Wikipedia, arguing:

> *The Sims*, . . . the iPhone, the Pixar movies, and all the other beloved successes of digital culture . . . are personal expressions. True, they often involve large groups of collaborators, but there is always a central personal vision—a Will Wright, a Steve Jobs, or a Brad Bird conceiving the vision and directing a team of people earning salaries.[12]

It is this same "central personal vision" that is crucial for Nietzsche, who goes so   40 far as to say, "Whether this taste was good or bad is less important than one might sup-pose, if only it was a single taste!"

It is precisely the "central personal vision" of Lanier and "single taste" of Nietzsche that are lacking in most chatbots. For instance, I had the following conversation with "Joan," the Cleverbot-offshoot program that won the Loebner Prize in 2006. Though each of her answers, taken separately, is perfectly sensible and human, their sum pro-duces nothing but a hilarious cacophony in the way of identity:

> USER: Do you have a boyfriend?
> JOAN: Not at the moment, but I hope to find one soon.

I ventured:

> USER: I would like to be your boyfriend.
> JOAN: That would be difficult, since I'm happily married.

Curious. I asked again, for clarification:

> USER: Do you have a boyfriend?
> JOAN: No, I'm still looking for love.
> USER: Do you have a husband?

> JOAN: I don't have a husband, because it would be illegal for me to have one,
>   since I am male.

Male?

> USER: What gender are you?
> JOAN: Female.

And once again, just for good measure:

> USER: Do you have a boyfriend?
> JOAN: Not at the moment, but I live in hope.
> USER: Can I be your boyfriend?
> JOAN: No, I'm straight.

This kind of unity or coherence of identity is something that most humans, of course—being the products of a single and continuous life history—have. But given the extreme brevity of a five-minute conversation, displaying that kind of congruence was something I tried to be aware of. For instance, when a judge said hello to my fellow confederate Dave, Dave replied with the nicely colorful and cheerful "G'day mate."

The drawback of this choice becomes immediately clear, however, as the judge's next question was "Have you come far to be here?" The judge, I imagine, was expecting some reference to Australia, the land that "G'day mate" evokes: instead, Dave answered, "From the southwest US." To the judge's mild surprise, I imagine, he discovers that Dave is not Australian at all, as his salutation would suggest, but rather an American from Westchester, New York, living in Albuquerque. It's not game over—it doesn't take Dave too long to win over the judge's confidence (and his vote)—but those signs of disjointed identity are early warning flags and, in that sense, falter.

In similar fashion, when a judge I was talking to spelled "color" in the British style ("colour"), and then several messages later referenced "Ny," which I took to mean "New York" (actually it turned out to be a typo for "My"), I asked where he was from. "Canadian spelling, not Biritish [*sic*]," he explained; my hope was that showing attunement, and over multiple utterances, to these questions of cohesiveness of identity would help my case. Presumably, a bot that can't keep track of the coherence of its *own* identity wouldn't be able to keep track of the judge's either.

"When making a bot, you don't write a program, you write a novel," explain programmers Eugene Demchenko and Vladimir Veselov, whose program "Eugene Goostman" was the runner-up at the 2008 competition, as well as in 2005 and 2001.[13] They stress the importance of having a single programmer write the machine's responses: "Elect who will be responsible for the bot personality. The knowledge-base writing process can be compared to writing a book. Suppose every developer describes an episode without having any information on the others. Can you imagine what will be produced!"

In fact, it's quite easy to imagine what will be produced: "Eugene Goostman"'s competitors. This is a central trade-off in the world of bot programming, between coherence of the program's personality or style and the range of its responses. By "crowdsourcing" the task of writing a program's responses to the users themselves, the program acquires an explosive growth in its behaviors, but these behaviors stop being internally consistent.

Death of the Author; End of the Best Friend

Do you need *someone*? Or do you need *me*?

—SAY ANYTHING . . . [14]

Speaking of "writing a book": this notion of style versus content, and of singularity and uniqueness of vision, is at the heart of recent debates about machine translation, especially of literature.

Wolfram Alpha researcher and chatbot author Robert Lockhart describes the chatbot community as being split between two competing approaches, what he calls "pure semantics" and "pure empiricism."[15] Roughly speaking, the semantic camp tries to program linguistic *understanding*, with the hope that the desired behavior will follow, and the empirical camp tries to directly program linguistic *behavior*, with the hope that "understanding" will either happen along the way or prove to be an unnecessary middleman. This divide also plays out in the history of computer translation. For many decades, machine translation projects attempted to understand language in a rule-based way, breaking down a sentence's structure and getting down to the underlying, universal meaning, before re-encoding that meaning according to another language's rules. In the 1990s, a statistical approach to machine translation—the approach that Google uses—came into its own, which left the question of meaning entirely out of it.

Cleverbot, for instance, can know that "Scaramouche, Scaramouche" is best answered by "Will you do the fandango?" without needing any links to Queen or "Bohemian Rhapsody" in between, let alone needing to know that Scaramouche is a stock character in seventeenth-century Italian farce theater and that the fandango is an Andalusian folk dance. It's simply observed people saying one, then the other. Using huge bodies of text ("corpora") from certified United Nations translators, Google Translate and its statistical cousins regurgitate previous human translations the way Cleverbot and its cousins regurgitate previous human speech. Both Google Translate and Cleverbot show weaknesses for (1) unusual and/or nonliteral phrasing, and (2) long-term consistency in point of view and style. On both of those counts, even as machine translation increasingly penetrates the world of business, literary novels remain mostly untranslatable by machine.[16]

What this also suggests, intriguingly, is that the task of translating (or writing) 50 literary novels cannot be broken into parts and done by a succession of different *humans* either—not by wikis, nor crowdsourcing, nor ghostwriters. Stability of point of view and consistency of style are too important. What's truly strange, then, is the fact that we *do* seem to make a lot of art this way.

> **Even as machine translation increasingly penetrates the world of business, literary novels remain mostly untranslatable by machine.**

To be human is to be *a* human, a specific person with a life history and idiosyncrasy and point of view; artificial intelligence suggests that the line between intelligent machines and people blurs most when a purée is made of that identity. It is profoundly odd, then—especially so in a country with a reputation for "individualism"—to contemplate how often we do just that.

The British television series *The Office* consists of fourteen episodes, all written and directed by the two series creators, Ricky Gervais and Stephen Merchant.[17] The show was so successful that it was spun off into an American version: 130 episodes and counting, each written by a different person from the last and each directed by a different person from the last. The only thing stable from week to week seems to be the cast. The arts in America are strange that way: we seem to care what our vision falls upon, but not whose vision it is.

I remember being enchanted as a kid with the early Hardy Boys books by Franklin W. Dixon, but after a certain point in the series, the magic seemed to disappear. It wasn't until more than fifteen years later I discovered that Franklin W. Dixon never existed. The first sixteen books were written by a man named Leslie McFarlane. The next twenty were written by eleven different people. What I'd chalked up to the loss of something intangible in those later books was in fact the loss of something very tangible indeed: the author.

Aesthetic experiences like these for me are like an unending series of blind dates where you never follow up, conversations with a stranger on the bus (or the Internet) where you never catch the other person's name. There's nothing *wrong* with them—they're pleasant, sometimes memorable, even illuminating—and all relationships start somewhere. But to live a whole *life* like that?

The *New York Times* reported in June 2010—in an article titled "The End of the Best Friend"[18]—on the practice of deliberate intervention, on the part of well-meaning adults, to disrupt close nuclei of friends from forming in schools and summer camps.* One sleepaway camp in New York State, they wrote, has hired "friendship coaches" whose job is to notice whether "two children seem to be too focused on each other, [and] . . . put them on different sports teams [or] seat them at different ends of the dining table." Affirms one school counselor in St. Louis, "I think it is kids' preference to pair up and have that one best friend. As adults—teachers and counselors—we try to encourage them not to do that." Chatroulette and Omegle users "next" each other when the conversation flags; these children are being nexted by force—when things are going too *well*.

Nexted in Customer Service

The same thing happens sometimes in customer service, where the disruption of intimacy seems almost tactical. Recently a merchant made a charge to my credit card in error, which I attempted to clear up, resulting in my entering a bureaucratic Rube Goldberg machine the likes of which I had never before experienced. My record for the longest single call was forty-two minutes and *eight transfers*.

---

* Motives range from wanting the children not to put all of their emotional eggs in one basket, to wanting them to branch out and experience new perspectives, to reducing the occasionally harmful social exclusion that can accompany tight bonds.

The ultimate conclusion reached at the end of this particular call was "call back tomorrow."

Each call, each transfer, led me to a different service rep, each of whom was skeptical and testy about the validity of my refund request. If I managed to get a particular rep on my side, to earn their sympathy, to start to build a kind of relationship and come across as a distinct "nonanonymous" human being, it was only a few minutes before I'd be talking to someone else, anonymous again. Here's my name, here's my account number, here's my PIN, here's my Social, here's my mother's maiden name, here's my address, here's the reason for my call, yes, I've already tried that . . .

What a familiarity with the construction of Turing test bots had begun showing me was that we fail—again and again—to actually *be* human with other humans, so maddeningly much of the time. And it had begun showing me *how* we fail—and what to do about it.

Cobbled-together bits of human interaction do not a human relationship make.   60
Not fifty one-night stands, not fifty speed dates, not fifty transfers through the bureaucratic pachinko. No more than sapling tied to sapling, oak though they may be, makes an oak. Fragmentary humanity isn't humanity.

The Same Person

If the difference between a conversational purée and a conversation is continuity, then the solution, in this case, is extraordinarily simple: assign a rep to a case. A particular person sees it through from start to finish. The *same* person.

For a brief period a tiny plastic tab that held the SIM card in my phone had gotten loose, and so my phone only worked when I was pressing on this plastic tab with my finger. As a result, I could only make calls, not receive them. And if I took my finger off the tab mid-call, the call dropped.

The tab is little more valuable than the plastic equivalent of a soda can's pull tab, which it resembles in appearance, and is roughly as essential for the proper functioning of the device it's attached to. I was out of warranty; protocol was that I was out of luck and needed a new, multi-hundred-dollar phone. "But this tab weighs one gram and costs a penny to manufacture," I said. "I know," said the customer service rep.

There was *no* way, no way at all, I couldn't just purchase a tab from them?

"I don't think it will work," she said. "But let me talk to a manager."   65

"Then *the same woman* got back on the line. "I'm sorry," she said. "But . . ." I said. And we kept talking. "Well, let me talk to a *senior* manager, hold on," she says.

As I'm holding, I feel my hand, which has now been pushing down steadily on the plastic tab for about fifteen minutes, begin to cramp. If my finger slips off the tab, if she hits the wrong button on her console, if there is some glitch in my phone provider's network, or hers—I am anonymous again. Anybody. A nobody. A number. This particular person and I will never reconnect.

I must call again, introduce myself again, explain my problem again, hear again that protocol is against me, plead my case again.

Service works by the gradual buildup of sympathy through failed attempted solutions. If person X has told you to try something and it doesn't work, person X feels slightly sorry for you. X is slightly *responsible* for the problem now, having used up some of your time. Person Y, however, is considerably less moved that you tried following her colleague X's advice to no avail—even if it is the same advice that she herself would have given you had she been party to that earlier conversation. That's beside the point. The point is that she wasn't the one who gave you that advice. So she is not responsible for your wasted time.

The *same* woman, as if miraculously, again returns. "I can make an exception for   70 you," she says.

It occurs to me that an "exception" is what programmers call it when software breaks.

50 First Dates

Sometimes even a single, stable point of view, a unifying vision and style and taste, isn't enough. You also need a *memory*. In the 2004 comedy *50 First Dates*,[19] Adam Sandler courts Drew Barrymore, but in the process discovers that due to an accident she can't form new long-term memories.

Philosophers interested in friendship, romance, and intimacy more generally have, in recent times, endeavored to distinguish between the *types* of people we like (or, the things we like *about* people) and the *specific* people we feel connections with in our lives. University of Toronto philosopher Jennifer Whiting has dubbed the former "impersonal friends."[20] The difference between the numerous "impersonal friends" out there, who are more or less fungible, and the few individuals we care about *specifically*, who aren't fungible with anyone on the planet, lies, she says, in so-called "historical properties." Namely, your actual friends and your innumerable "impersonal friends" *are* fungible—but only at the moment the relationship begins. From there, the relationship puts down roots, builds up a shared history, shared understanding, shared experiences, sacrifices and compromises and triumphs . . .

Barrymore and Sandler really *are* good together—life-partner good—but she becomes "someone special" to him, whereas he is doomed to remain merely "her type." Fungible. And therefore—being no different from the *next* charming and stimulating and endearing guy who shows up at her restaurant—*vulnerable* to losing her.

His solution: give her a historical-properties crash course every morning, in the   75 form of a video primer that recaps their love. He must fight his way out of fungibility every morning.

Statefulness

A look at the "home turf" of many chatbots shows a conscious effort on the part of the programmers to make Drew Barrymores of us: worse, actually, because it was her long-term memory that kept wiping clean. At 2008 Loebner Prize winner Elbot's website, the screen refreshes each time a new remark is entered, so the conversational history evaporates with each sentence; ditto at the page of 2007 winner Ultra Hal. At the Cleverbot site, the conversation fades to white above the box where text is entered, preserving only the last three exchanges on the screen, with the history beyond that gone: out of sight, and hopefully—it would seem—out of the user's mind as well. The elimination of the long-term influence of conversational history makes the bots' jobs easier—in terms of both the psychology and the mathematics.

In many cases, though, physically eliminating the conversation log is unnecessary. As three-time Loebner Prize winner ('00, '01, and '04), programmer Richard Wallace explains, "Experience with [Wallace's chatbot] A.L.I.C.E. indicates that most casual conversation is 'state-less,' that is, each reply depends only on the current query, without any knowledge of the history of the conversation required to formulate the reply."[21]

Not all types of human conversations function in this way, but many do, and it behooves AI researchers to determine which types of conversations are "stateless"—that is, with each remark depending only on the last—and to attempt to create these very sorts of interactions. It's our job as confederates, as humans, to resist it.

One of the classic stateless conversation types, it turns out, is verbal abuse.

In 1989, twenty-year-old University College Dublin undergraduate Mark Humphrys connects a chatbot program he'd written called MGonz to his university's computer network and leaves the building for the day. A user (screen name "SOMEONE") from Drake University in Iowa tentatively sends the message "finger" to Humphrys's account—an early-Internet command that acts as a request for basic information about a user. To SOMEONE's surprise, a response comes back immediately: "cut this cryptic shit speak in full sentences." This begins an argument between SOMEONE and MGonz that will last almost an hour and a half.[22]

(The best part is undoubtedly when SOMEONE says, a mere twenty minutes in, "you sound like a goddamn robot that repeats everything.")

Returning to the lab the next morning, Humphrys is stunned to find the logs, and feels a strange, ambivalent emotion. His program might have just passed the Turing test, he thinks—but the evidence is so profane that he's afraid to publish it.

Humphrys's twist on the age-old chatbot paradigm of the "non-directive" conversationalist who lets the user do all the talking was to model his program, rather than on an attentive listener, on an abusive jerk. When it lacks any clear cue for what to say, MGonz falls back not on therapy clichés like "How does that make you feel?" or "Tell me more about that" but on things like "you are obviously an asshole," "ok thats it im not talking to you any more," or "ah type something interesting or shut up." It's a stroke of genius, because, as becomes painfully clear from reading the MGonz transcripts, *argument is stateless.*

I've seen it happen between friends: "Once again, you've neglected to do what you've promised." "Oh, there you go right in with that tone of yours!" "Great, let's just dodge the issue and talk about my tone instead! You're so defensive!" "*You're* the one being defensive! This is just like the time you x!" "For the millionth time, I did not even remotely x! *You're* the one who . . ." And on and on. A close reading of this dialogue, with MGonz in mind, turns up something interesting, and very telling: each remark after the first is *only about the previous remark.* The friends' conversation has become stateless. unanchored from all context, a kind of "Markov chain" of riposte, meta-riposte, meta-meta-riposte. If we can be induced to sink to this level, of course the Turing test can be passed.

Once again, the scientific perspective on what types of human behavior are imitable shines incredible light on how we conduct our own, human lives. There's a sense in which verbal abuse is simply *less complex* than other forms of conversation. Seeing how much MGonz's arguments resemble our own might shame us into shape.

Retorts, no matter how sharp or stinging, play into chatbots' hands. In contrast, requests for elaboration, like "In what sense?" and "How so?" turn out to be crushingly difficult for many bots to handle: because elaboration is hard to do when one is working from a prepared script, because such questions rely *entirely* on context for their meaning, because they extend the relevant conversational history, rather than resetting it.

In fact, since reading the papers on MGonz, and its transcripts, I find myself much more able to constructively manage heated conversations. Aware of their stateless, knee-jerk character, I recognize that the terse remark I want to blurt has far more to do with some kind of "reflex" to the very last sentence of the conversation than it does with either the actual issue at hand or the person I'm talking to. All of a sudden the absurdity and ridiculousness of this kind of escalation become *quantitatively* clear, and, contemptuously unwilling to act like a bot, I steer myself toward a more "stateful" response: better living through science.

NOTES

1. Alix Spiegel, " 'Voice Blind' Man Befuddled by Mysterious Callers." *Morning Edition*, National Public Radio, July 12, 2010.
2. David Kernell, posting (under the handle "rubico") to the message board www.4chan .org, September 17, 2008.
3. Donald Barthelme, "Not-Knowing," in *Not-Knowing: The Essays and Interviews of Donald Barthelme*, edited by Kim Herzinger (New York: Random House, 1997). Regarding "Bless Babel": Programmers have a concept called "security through diversity," which is basically the idea that a world with a number of different operating systems, spreadsheet programs, etc., is more secure than one with a software "monoculture." The idea is that the effectiveness of a particular hacking technique is limited to the machines that "speak that language," the way that genetic diversity generally means that no single disease will wipe out an entire species. Modern operating systems are designed to be "idiosyncratic" about how certain critical sections of memory are allocated, so that each computer, even if it is running the same basic environment, will be a little bit different. For more, see, e.g., Elena Gabriela Barrantes, David H. Ackley, Stephanie Forrest, Trek S. Palmer, Darko Stefanovic, and Dino Dai Zovi, "Intrusion Detection: Randomized Instruction Set Emulation to Disrupt Binary Code Injection Attacks," *Proceedings of the 10th ACM Conference on Computer and Communication Security* (New York: ACM, 2003), pp. 281–89.
4. "Speed Dating with Yaacov and Sue Deyo," interview by Terry Gross, *Fresh Air*, National Public Radio, August 17, 2005. See also Yaacov Deyo and Sue Deyo, *Speed Dating: The Smarter, Faster Way to Lasting Love* (New York: HarperResource, 2002).
5. "Don't Ask, Don't Tell," season 3, episode 12 of *Sex and the City*, August 27, 2000.
6. For more on how the form/content problem in dating intersects with computers, see the excellent video by the Duke University behavioral economist Dan Ariely, "Why Online Dating Is So Unsatisfying," Big Think, July 7, 2010, bigthink.com/ideas/20749.
7. The 1991 Loebner Prize transcripts, unlike most other years, are unavailable through the Loebner Prize website. The Clay transcripts come by way of Mark Halpern, "The Trouble with the Turing Test," *New Atlantis* (Winter 2006). The Weintraub tran-

scripts, and judge's reaction, come by way of P. J. Skerrett, "Whimsical Software Wins a Prize for Humanness," *Popular Science*, May 1992.

8. Rollo Carpenter, personal interview.
9. Rollo Carpenter, in "PopSci's Future of Communication: Cleverbot," Science Channel, October 6, 2009.
10. Bernard Reginster (lecture, Brown University, October 15, 2003).
11. "giving style to one's character": Friedrich Nietzsche, *The Gay Science*, translated by Walter Kaufman (New York: Vintage, 1974), sec. 290.
12. Jaron Lanier, *You Are Not a Gadget: A Manifesto* (New York: Knopf, 2010).
13. Eugene Demchenko and Vladimir Veselov, "Who Fools Whom?" in *Parsing the Turing Test*, edited by Robert Epstein et al. (New York: Springer, 2008).
14. *Say Anything. . .*, directed and written by Cameron Crowe (20th Century Fox, 1989).
15. Robert Lockhart, "Integrating Semantics and Empirical Language Data" (lecture at the Chatbots 3.0 conference, Philadelphia, March 27, 2010).
16. For more on Google Translate, the United Nations, and literature, see, e.g., David Bellos, "I, Translator," *New York Times*, March 20, 2010; and Miguel Helft, "Google's Computing Power Refines Translation Tool," *New York Times*, March 8, 2010.
17. *The Office*, directed and written by Ricky Gervais and Stephen Merchant, BBC Two, 2001–3.
18. Hilary Stout, "The End of the Best Friend," also titled "A Best Friend? You Must Be Kidding," *New York Times*, June 16, 2010.
19. *50 First Dates*, directed by Peter Segal (Columbia Pictures, 2004).
20. Jennifer E. Whiting, "Impersonal Friends," *Monist* 74 (1991), pp. 3–29. See also Jennifer E. Whiting, "Friends and Future Selves," *Philosophical Review* 95 (1986), pp. 547–80; and Bennett Helm, "Friendship," in *The Stanford Encyclopedia of Philosophy*, edited by Edward N. Zalta (Fall 2009 ed.).
21. Richard S. Wallace, "The Anatomy of A.L.I.C.E.," in Epstein et al., *Parsing the Turing Test*.
22. For more on MGonz, see Mark Humphrys, "How My Program Passed the Turing Test," in Epstein et al., *Parsing the Turing Test*.

Exploring Context

1. The chatbot Cleverbot (cleverbot.com) plays a significant role in Christian's discussion. Spend some time chatting with Cleverbot. How does your experience confirm or complicate Christian's analysis?

2. Christian's essay centers on the Loebner Prize, a contest that uses the Turing test to measure degrees of artificial intelligence. Explore the website for the prize (loebner.net/Prizef/loebner-prize.html). Has artificial intelligence progressed since Christian wrote his essay? Based on what you find on the site, are computers becoming more human?

3. Siri, the voice-enabled software assistant deployed on several devices made by Apple, is in some ways a kind of chatbot. Explore the site Stuff That Siri Says (stuffthatsirisays.com). Apply Christian's ideas about chatbots to Siri—is she more human than the bots he discusses? How so?

Questions for Connecting

1. In "The Hive" (p. 349), Marshall Poe looks at the humans and technologies behind the online knowledge repository known as Wikipedia, focusing on the ways in which collaboration works to generate and manage knowledge in this online encyclopedia. Given both Poe's and Christian's discussions, how has technology changed what it means to be human?

2. Francis Fukuyama is also concerned with what it means to be human in his essay "Human Dignity" (p. 185). Central to Fukuyama's discussion is the concept of "Factor X" (p. 186). Apply Fukuyama's discussion and particularly his use of Factor X to Christian's essay. Do chatbots possess Factor X? Are our interactions with technology destabilizing the Factor X of humanity?

3. In "Visible Man: Ethics in a World without Secrets" (p. 462), Peter Singer examines the impact of technology on privacy. Synthesize his discussion with Christian's in order to consider the relationship between technology and social change. Is technology moving us to a brighter or darker future? Locate passages from both authors that support your position.

4. **CONNECTING TO E-PAGES** In what ways does Alexandra Samuel, in "'Plug In Better': A Manifesto" (bedfordstmartins.com/emerging/epages), argue that technology can lead to a better way of living? Does technology make us more authentically human? What might this mean in the context of Christian's essay?

Language Matters

1. Several times in his essay, Christian chooses a different font. What is the function of these font changes? How does the selection of a font convey meaning? What font do you use for academic writing? Should you change fonts within a paper? Why or why not?

2. Christian uses endnotes. What function do they serve in his writing? When might you use them in your own writing?

3. In several places, Christian uses references from popular culture to support his points. How well do these serve as evidence? When should you use similar references in academic writing? How strongly might they serve as evidence?

Assignments for Writing

1. Christian examines the ways in which form and content interact not only to make humans human but also to make technologies like chatbots seem more human. Using the ideas in Christian's essay, write a paper in which you determine the key qualities of being human. Support your position not only by citing quotations from Christian's essay but also by drawing on your work in Questions for Critical Reading and Exploring Context.

2. What is the relationship between form and content? Which matters more? Which carries more meaning? Write a paper in which you address form and content, using Christian's essay as support.

3. Write a paper in which you assess the impact of technology on human relationships, using ideas from Christian's essay as support. Are our relationships becoming more "stateless" because of technology? How does "nexting" affect our ability to connect with each other? In what ways does technology allow for more connection between people?

PATRICIA CHURCHLAND

Patricia Churchland is the President's Professor of Philosophy at the University of California–San Diego. She received her degree in philosophy from Oxford University and has taught at the University of Manitoba. She was a recipient of the Mac-Arthur fellowship (known colloquially as the "genius grant") in 1991. She is the author of *Neurophilosophy: Toward a Unified Science of the Mind-Brain* (1986), *Brain-Wise: Studies in Neurophilosophy* (2002), and *Braintrust: What Neuroscience Tells Us about Morality* (2011), from which "Networking: Genes, Brains, and Behavior" was taken.

In *Braintrust: What Neuroscience Tells Us about Morality* (2011), Churchland argues that morality is primarily based in the brain, where decisions about ethics are highly complex, influenced by both genetics and environment. Morality, Churchland argues, comes from empathy, a neurological evolutionary development in mammals intended to promote strong relationships between parents and their young, as well as between local communities, regardless of relation. Because of this, she suggests that the influences of traditional models of institutional morality (particularly religion) on moral behavior may not be as important as we often believe.

In "Networking: Genes, Brains, and Behavior," Churchland argues that genes work in collaborative networks that operate with intricate complexity, "more like the behavior of a flock of crows than that of a clock" (p. 116). Questioning the widely held idea that morality is an innate quality, Churchland argues instead that what appears as universality in certain moral codes more likely stems from common approaches to solving similar problems at various times and in diverse cultures.

▶ TAGS: *executive functions, pleiotropy, moral organ, innate universality, moral foundations, costly signaling*

Questions for Critical Reading

1. What is the origin of morality? As you read Churchland's text, make note of the various evolutionary explanations that she explores and rejects. Abstracting from her analysis, how do you think Churchland would explain the emergence of morality?

2. Using a dictionary or other reference source, define the word *innate*. Given the definition, why is "innateness" such a problematic concept for Churchland? How can we tell what is or is not innate? Locate passages from the text that support your answer.

3. As you read this essay, look for the key terms "executive functions," "moral organ," "Golden Mean," and "costly signaling." How does Churchland define these terms, and how do they function in her overall argument?

Networking: Genes, Brains, and Behavior

As a species of mammal, humans seem capable of impressive cooperation, especially among kin, but also among strangers, and especially when conditions permit and advantages are discerned. Regarding this capacity as "in our nature" has motivated a long list of evolutionary biologists and psychologists to speculate on the genetic basis for cooperation. One caution already on the table: quite a lot of human cooperative behavior may be explained by capacities other than cooperation biologically defined (i.e., as selected for). For example, strong sociable dispositions, along with the motivation to belong and learn social practices, may suffice to explain many cases of joint efforts.

What other factors might figure in the getting along and helping out? A capacity to defer gratification and suppress costly impulses (known as *executive functions*) is important in acquiring social skills and making cooperative behavior advantageous. Many humans are skilled in evaluating what is in their long- and short-term interests, and they frequently distinguish between genuine cooperation that might bring general benefits, and phony cooperation that is really exploitation by an ambitious profiteer. In addition, humans are well able to draw on past experience to find analogies to a current problem, and to then apply an analogous solution. These abilities are presumably among those Aristotle* had in mind when, in his *Nicomachean Ethics,* he discussed in great detail the acquisition of social virtue and wisdom through experience.[1] Some of these capacities, jointly and severally, may go a long way in explaining many examples of human cooperation; for example, building a bridge to reach good pasture, which requires cooperation in moving logs and hoisting them into place. These considerations raise the possibility that cooperativity *as such* may not be causally linked to large effects by specific genes, even though the background neurobiological functions such as caring for offspring and mates, and the desire to avoid punishment and disapproval, are highly heritable. This would be rather like the discovery that while aggression in fruit flies can be selected for in the lab, and hence is heritable, aggression *as such* is not linked to large effects by specific genes dedicated to the aggressive behavior. (More on this below.)

I am suggesting that caring—for self, kin, and affiliates, for example—can frequently give rise to mammalian and avian behavior commonly called cooperative, and that the genetic background that contributes to caring circuitry may carry more of the explanatory burden for common instances of cooperation than previously supposed. On this analysis, cooperation, like aggression in defense of offspring, is a manifestation of attachment and caring. This does not rule out a specific genetic basis for cooperation. It does, however, invite circumspection about *genes for cooperativity,* made more

---

* Aristotle: Greek philosopher and enormously important figure in Western thought (384–322 BC) was a student of Plato and teacher of Alexander the Great [Ed.].

emphatic by recent attempts to link genes and behavior in the fruit fly, to which I shall now turn.

In their comprehensive and readable book *How Genes Influence Behavior* (2010), geneticists Jonathan Flint, Ralph Greenspan, and Kenneth Kendler list the criteria to be satisfied by a claim that "X is a gene for Y":

> We can summarize as follows: if gene X has a strong, specific association with a behavioral trait or psychiatric disease in all known environments and the physiological pathway from X to Y is short or well-understood, then it may be appropriate to speak of X as a gene for Y. . . . Do genes have a *specific* effect on behavior? Almost certainly not.[2]

Genetic Networks

The relations between genes and behavior, as geneticist Ralph Greenspan observes,[3] are not one-to-one, not even one-to-many; they are *many-to-many*. The significance of this point, now broadly appreciated by geneticists, has been steadily eroding the idea of a big-effect gene for this or that specific behavior such as aggression or cooperation. Let's start with evidence for one-to-many mappings. *Pleiotropy*—when a gene plays a role in many different, and functionally distinct, aspects of the phenotype (traits the organism has)—turns out to be not the exception, but the *rule*.[4] Moreover, when a gene plays a role *both* in vital operations of the organism's body *and* in behavior, via brain circuitry, then it is subject to stringent selection constraints. That is, behavioral mutants still have to be viable and relatively normal.[5] If a mutation happens to produce a behavioral advantage, it must not mess up other bodily functions so much as to imperil viability. So if I am born a genius but the mutation enabling my genius results in a dysfunctional liver, my genius will go for nought. Only very rarely does a gene mutation yield results that are sufficiently positive that the organism's body and brain are advantaged in the struggle for life and reproduction.

> **If a mutation happens to produce a behavioral advantage, it must not mess up other bodily functions so much as to imperil viability.**

The evidence indicates that most gene products (usually proteins but some can be RNA—ribonucleic acid) *do* play multiple roles, in body and brain. That is, the protein that a gene codes for may play a role in such diverse functions as building a liver, maintaining the inner membrane of the esophagus, sweeping up extra neurotransmitter at a synaptic site, and modification of a neuron's membrane during learning. Serotonin, for example, figures in cardiovascular regulation, respiration, circadian rhythm, sleep-wake cycles, appetite, aggression, sexual behavior, sensorimotor reactivity, pain sensitivity, and reward learning.[6] Depression has been associated with a short allele (variant of the gene) for the serotonin transporter protein, and the data are sometimes interpreted as meaning that having the gene causes depression. In fact, the effects are actually small, though statistically significant, and the presence of the short allele accounts only for 3–4% of the variation in the general population of the measures of depression, and 7–9% of inherited variance of the trait. This means that many other factors play an important role in the occurrence of depression.[7] This is not surprising. Consider that the physical trait of height in humans is associated with 54 known alleles, but collectively, they account only for 5% of the heritability of height. The rest is a mystery.

Here is a telling example of pleiotropy. In the early days of fruit fly genetics, it was widely believed that a single mutation to a gene called "dunce" affected just one capacity, namely associative conditioning (i.e., learning that one event predicts occurrence of another event; my dog Duff learned that jangling car keys in the morning predicts a walk to the beach). The *dunce* gene, it seemed, was the gene for associative conditioning, and was probably selected for the advantages accruing to those flies who could learn to associate one event with another. In the beginning at least, it really looked that way. Follow-up studies, however, show that the gene product (cyclic AMP phosphodiesterase) also plays a role in embryonic patterning, and in female fertility. This was surprising—female fertility and the capacity to learn a conditioned response would seem to have little to do with one another. They do not even seem to form a functional cluster, at least at the macro level. But genes are not one-trick ponies.

Given evolution's *modus operandi**—tinkering-opportunistically rather than redesigning-from-scratch—we should not expect our conception of functional categories at the macro level to map neatly onto genes and gene products.[8] Thus "capacity for conditioning" does not one-to-one-map onto *dunce.* In the very earliest stages of life on the planet, all the functions of a gene product such as cyclic AMP phosphodiesterase might have been more closely related, but as time and evolution moved on, structural branch points became increasingly elaborate and widely separated. Thus serotonin, perhaps handling only a single job in very simple organisms, gets recruited for new tasks, and ultimately ends up doing many things whose connections with each other are lost in our evolutionary past. Consequently the functions of the gene product can end up in very different categories. The various functions associated with the products of *dunce* may have something in common in the deep history of evolution, but that commonality cannot possibly be read off our conventional categorization of functions such as female fertility or associative conditioning. By and large, the strategy of trying to link a single gene to a particular phenotype has been superseded by the understanding that genes often form networks, and that a given gene is likely to figure in many jobs.

Now for the many-to-one-mapping problem, and the parable of fruit fly aggression. In fruit flies and mice, a connection between serotonin and aggression has been observed. Experimentally elevating levels of serotonin using drugs or genetic techniques increases aggression in the fruit fly; genetically silencing serotonin circuits decreases aggression. On the other hand, elevating levels of neuropeptide-F decreases aggression, and genetically silencing neuropeptide-F increases aggression.[9] These results are, moreover, consistent with experiments on the mouse, suggesting conservation of mechanisms for aggression through evolutionary change. One might even be tempted to think of the gene that expresses serotonin as the "aggression gene." Not so.

Over some twenty-one generations, Herman Dierick and Ralph Greenspan[10] selectively bred aggressive fruit flies (the little pugilists keep on fighting rather than quitting, and are thirty times more aggressive than the wild type). Since the flies had been bred for aggressive behavior, it was possible then to ask: What are the genetic

10

---

* *Modus operandi*: Latin for way or method of doing something [Ed.].

differences between the aggressive and the docile flies? To do this, they compared the gene-expression profiles of the aggressive flies with those of their more docile cousins using molecular techniques (microarray analysis). (A gene is expressed either when it makes the protein it codes for, or, in the case of noncoding genes, it makes RNA. So for a coding gene, an increase in its expression means that more of the protein it codes for is produced. Gene expression may be regulated by yet other genes and their products, which may turn a gene off or on. Altering a gene's expression can alter the observable traits of an organism.)

If the gene for serotonin really was the key to levels of aggression in an organism, one would predict that the aggressive flies would have an increase in serotonin. The surprising result was that this is not what was observed in the analysis of gene expression. In fact, no single gene could be fingered as specifically associated with aggression. Gene expression differences between aggressive and wild-type fruit flies were found in about 80 different genes; the differences in expression in those identified were all quite small. Moreover, many of the 80 genes whose expression changed (up or down) are genes known to play a role in a hodgepodge of phenotypic events—cuticle formation, muscle contraction, energy metabolism, RNA binding, DNA binding, development of a range of structures including cytoskeleton. No single gene on its own seemed to make much difference, but collectively the changes in the 80 genes did somehow produce highly aggressive fruit flies. Not all of the 80 different genes are necessarily related to the aggressive phenotypes, since some are undoubtedly "hitchhiking" along with those that were selected.

The crux of "The Parable of Aggression in the Fruit Fly" can be summarized thus: there is no single, big-effect gene for aggression in the fruit fly. Of those many genes differentially expressed between the wild-type and aggressive lines, none were the genes involved in serotonin or neuropeptide-F expression. None were even other proteins in the serotonin-metabolism chain.[11] How can that be, given the earlier experiments showing that elevating serotonin levels enhances aggression? It seems puzzling, at least until one recalls the complexity of genotype-phenotype relationships Ralph Greenspan has emphasized; genes are part of networks, influencing and interacting with each other and with features of the environment.[12] One factor contributing to this complexity is that serotonin is a very ancient molecule, important, as noted above, in a motley assortment of brain and body functions, including sleep, mood, gut motility (such as stomach and intestinal contractions), bladder functions, cardiovascular function, stress responses, induction of smooth muscle proliferation in lung vessel during embryological development, and regulating acute and chronic responses to low levels of oxygen (hypoxia).[13] The unsuitability of the label "aggression gene" is glaringly obvious. The diversity in serotonin's jobs helps explain how it is that changing its levels can have widespread effects all over the brain and body. For these changes can cascade into other effects, which may in turn exert an influence on aggressive behavior. The idea is not merely that things are complex, which they surely are, but that a gene product can have many roles, and genes interact in ways that are typical of a nonlinear dynamical system—more like the behavior of a flock of crows than that of a clock. As Greenspan has remarked, "The wider the network of contacts a gene product makes, the more chances there are for an alteration in another gene to influence it."[14]

The complexities pile on. Because genes and their products are involved in the construction of body and brain, and because the nervous system interacts with the environment in a manner that in turn can cause changes in gene expression, it is improbable in the extreme that a situationally sensitive behavior such as aggression or cooperation can be causally linked to the presence of a single gene or even a couple of genes.[15]

As the developing organism interacts with the environment, gene expression may be upregulated or downregulated (more protein is made or less protein is made). Neuroscientist Eric Kandel was interested in whether there would be changes in gene expression when mice learned something, in this case, to associate a location with a mild foot shock, and found that there was. In comparing the brains of the conditioned mice with naïve mice, he found two genes that were highly expressed in the system mediating fear—in the lateral nucleus of the amygdala (needed for processing fear responses) and in the pathways carrying the fearful auditory signal to the lateral nucleus amygdala.[16] For another example, in young songbirds, gene expression of the gene *zenk* is triggered when the bird hears the song of its species, the gene product playing a role in the bird's learning the song of its own species.

Despair is not the lesson of this bewildering complexity. Nor is the lesson that genes do not affect behavior. They do, of course, and heritability studies in populations confirm that some traits are highly heritable. Height, for example, is strongly heritable, as are temperamental profiles (e.g., introversion, extroversion, and probably degrees of sociability), and the susceptibility to schizophrenia or alcoholism. The point is that *if* a certain form of cooperation, such as making alarm calls when a predator appears, has a genetic basis, it is likely to be related to the expression of *many* genes, and their expression may be linked to events in the environment.

Almost certainly social behavior in mammals depends on genes for oxytocin (OXT), oxytocin receptors (OXTR),[17] vasopressin (AVP), endogenous opiates, dopamine and dopamine receptors, and serotonin and serotonin receptors, as well as genes involved in the development of circuitry such as that supporting the extensive pathways of the vagus nerve through the body. *For starters.*

As Frances Champagne and Michael Meaney have shown, licking and grooming by the mother rodent has effects on the subsequent social behavior of the babies; pups who get plenty of licking and grooming are more socially adept than pups who do not.[18] Genes are part of a flexible, interactive network that includes other genes, the body, the brain, and the environment. But to quote Greenspan again, "Synergism and network flexibility make it easier to conceive of how new properties in behavior can emerge: tune up an allele here, tune down another one there, combine them with some other preexisting variants, and boom! You have a new behavior."[19]

Innate Moral Principles and Innate Moral Foundations

In humans, ecological conditions, accidents of history, and cultural practices result in striking diversity in social organizations, including that aspect we refer to as morality. Even so, at a general level of description, there are obvious common themes among social organizations regarding values. On the face of it, these appear to reflect similar general strategies for solving rather similar problems of living together. Courage in defense, cunning in the hunt, honesty in transactions, tolerance of idiosyncrasies, and willingness to reconcile—these are values touted in the stories not only of aboriginal tribes, but of agricultural and post-industrial people as well. Many groups

15

share similar stories of vices: aggression gone sour, lust overwhelming good judgment, self-indulgence bringing ruin, ambition wreaking havoc, and miserliness leading to loneliness.

The generality of these themes does not entail that humans have a "hard-wired module" specifying particular kinds of social behavior, where the wiring-up is controlled by genes dedicated to producing that behavior. Although such a hypothesis cannot be absolutely ruled out, the complexity of gene-behavior relationships illustrated by "The Parable of Aggression in the Fruit Fly" suggests that aggression in the human, not to mention cooperation in the human, is unlikely to be associated with a few large-effect genes. Granting individual human differences, similarly organized brains facing similar problems are likely to land on similar solutions. Wood works well in boatbuilding, merriment eases social tensions, competitive games are less costly than fights. Languages may have emerged from similar pushes and pulls, without the help of a dedicated, new "language gene."[20]

Complexity in genes-brain-behavior interactions notwithstanding, the idea that morality is basically innate remains irresistible. As with many ideas that bob up again and again despite withering criticism, enough is right about it to attract adherents. There is no doubt that genes have a huge effect on our nature, but the problem is to say something meaningful about that relationship. The more distant one is from the hands-on study of genes, the greater the temptation to wave vaguely in the direction of genes and innateness and selection, as the source of an explanation for aspects of human behavior.

Plato, among the first to "solve" the problem of where values come from by invoking innateness, argued that we are born knowing the basic principles of morality, though he had to admit that the process of birth must entail some forgetting and introduces some weakness in the face of temptation. Fortunately, he thought, the innate knowledge is gradually recollected through time and experience, and in old age, if lucky, we can be knowledgeable once more about the Good. Plato had no decent theory to explain how our previous selves came by the knowledge in the first place, only pushing the problem back further. This remains a totally unsolved Platonic problem.

Recently, Marc Hauser, a psychologist and animal behavior scientist, defended the innateness approach to morality. Hauser thinks there are universals in human moral understanding—views about what is right and what is wrong—that obtain in all societies. These universals are, he contends, visible in the unreflective intuitions that people summon in addressing a specific moral issue. For example, Hauser finds that there is widespread agreement that incest is wrong, and that drinking apple juice from a brand-new bedpan is disgusting.[21]

> **There is widespread agreement that incest is wrong, and that drinking apple juice from a brand-new bedpan is disgusting.**

Universals in moral intuitions, so Hauser's argument continues, are strong evidence of an innate physiological organization that, given normal brain development, typically yields those intuitions. Call these moral intuitions, *conscience,* or perhaps, with Hauser, products of the *moral organ.* Hauser's own view and research program are modeled on linguist Noam Chomsky's view on the origin of human language and language acquisition. Chomsky believes that the human brain is genetically equipped with a unique "language organ" specifying abstract principles of syntax that become more concrete with exposure to language. From this organ flows our grammatical intuitions, and our ability to learn specific languages. Hauser argues that humans likewise have a "moral organ" that specifies the universal principles of morality, and from which originates our moral intuitions about right and wrong: "we are born with abstract rules or principles, with nurture entering the picture to set the parameters and guide us toward acquisition of particular moral systems."[22] In emphasizing the hardwired aspect, Hauser says, "Once we have acquired our culture's specific moral norms—a process that is more like growing a limb than sitting in Sunday school and learning about virtues and vices—we judge whether actions are permissible, obligatory, or forbidden, without conscious reasoning and without explicit access to the underlying principles."[23]

We have already spent some time looking at genetic networks and gene-environmental interactions; we need to dwell a little more on the issue of exactly what is meant by "innate" in the context of behavior. An expression with a tortured history, "innate" is used to refer to a wide or a narrow range of phenomena, or much in between. A concertina concept—one that expands and contracts as the conversation and criticism fluctuate—*innateness* sometimes impedes clarity. To defend a hypothesis about innateness for a particular behavioral trait, what kind of factual evidence must be marshaled? As compactly stated by Flint, Greenspan, and Kendler early in this chapter,[24] one needs to identify the genes involved, show how they help organize neural circuitry, and then show the relation of the circuitry to the behavior. Lacking that—and invariably that is lacking in human studies—social scientists resort to identifying what is *innate* via behavior. How does that work? Sometimes the specification rests on the idea that for anything we can easily acquire through learning, the genes provide the brain with an *innate capacity*—a structural "readiness." *Anything?* Even reading, riding a bicycle, and milking a cow—all of which are typically easily learned, but cannot have been selected for in the evolution of the human brain?[25] Because such generality seems to bleed the meaning out of the term, *anything* has to replaced with a more adequate filter.

On a more restricted use of *innate*, it refers to those behaviors that are both "genetically programmed" and universally displayed by all individuals that carry the relevant genes (and easily learned). Generally, of course, which genes are implicated is not known, and "easily learned" has, as noted, its own problems, so the heavy lifting falls to *universality*. Because there are not only gene-environment interactions, but also interactions between the developing brain and the environment within the uterus, some researchers find this proposed modification for *innate* too imprecise and too burdened with historical mistakes to be useful."[26]

According to Hauser, "our moral faculty is equipped with a universal moral grammar, a toolkit for building specific moral systems." Echoing Chomsky's claim that there are unlearnable languages, Hauser states further, "*Our moral instincts are immune to the explicitly articulated commandments handed down by religions and governments.*"[27] Hauser's optimism with respect to innate moral intuitions is perhaps inspiring, but it is truly hard to square with history and anthropology. Consider the many examples of human sacrifices as part of religious rituals, the vulnerability to propaganda, the willingness to go to war on a tide of jingoism, the nontrivial variability in moral customs concerning the status of women, torture during the various Inquisitions and wars, and most remarkably, the mass murder of Jews, Tutsis, Ukrainians, Poles, Lithuanians, and Native Americans, to name but a few of the massacres. Sadly, many of these practices did follow the exhortations and encouragement by governments and religions. One cannot but conclude that our *moral behavior* seems more susceptible "to the explicitly articulated commandments handed down by religions and governments" than what, according to Hauser, can be expected from a properly functioning moral organ. The question of evidence for Hauser's hypothesis is pressing.

Apart from concern about the semantic unsteadiness in *innate,* I also have reservations about what *universality,* when actually observed, implies. I suspect that the existence of common themes and styles in human behavior is not a reliable sign of a genetic basis for a specific behavior.[28] Let me explain. A universally (or more likely, *widely*) displayed behavior *may* be innate, but it may also just be a common solution to a very common problem.[29] For contrasting examples, note that blinking in reaction to a puff of air directed at the eye is a reflex. It appears to be a direct outcome of known brainstem circuitry, and is minimally affected by the environment, and minimally affected by training. If one feels compelled to use the concept of "hard-wired" in human behavior, this case may be as good as it gets. By contrast, making boats out of wood is common in cultures that have access to wood and a desire to move about on water.[30] Apparently, boat-making with wood is universal, and probably was used by earlier hominins to get themselves to Indonesia. But is it *innate?* Do we have a genetic basis for making boats? Do we have an innate "boat-making organ"?[31]

Probably not. Wood is just a good solution to the problem of making a boat, because it floats, is available in lots of places, and is moderately easy to work with. Logs can be lashed together, a large tree can be hollowed out with stone axes, and so forth. Making boats of wood is a reasonable solution to a problem; that is all it is. Or, as the late Elizabeth Bates famously pointed out, in all cultures, people feed themselves with their hands—not because they have an innate hand-feeding module programmed by the hand-feeding gene, but because given our physical equipment, eating with hands is a good solution to a problem. We could, if determined, eat with our feet, or just lean over and put our faces in our food (and we sometimes do). But using hands is an obvious, rather efficient way of getting the job done, and that convenience, given our equipment, is all that is needed to explain the universality of hand-feeding. Now for an example from the domain of morality.

Truth-telling is widely considered a virtue. This is plausibly related to the fact that for reasons pertaining to survival, humans value accurate predictions, and hence value being able to rely on one another for information regarding food sources, predators, how to make a boat, and so forth. Because our life and well-being depend on it, reliability is preferred over unreliability. A social practice that approves truth-telling and disapproves deception does not imply the existence of a special gene or a special module; it can be explained in terms of routine human problem-solving, given human intelligence and the platform for sociability. Seeing the practice this way also is consistent with the fact that humans are quite willing to deceive when conditions clearly require it, such as when prudence requires deceiving an enemy of the community. Spies, after all, are supposed to deceive, as are undercover police in a sting operation. And "white lies" in the service of social graciousness are absolutely required, according to

Miss Manners. Which is why truth-telling is a social practice, not a strict rule. The impropriety of telling the truth on certain occasions is learned along with the practice of generally telling the truth.

What these examples imply is that for these cases at least, no innate brain modules are needed—no boatbuilding or hand-feeding or truth-telling genes need be postulated. The logical point is simple: universality is *consistent* with the existence of an innate module, but it does not *imply* the existence of an innate module. Compelling evidence in addition to universality is needed. For some traits, it may be that *if* it is innate, then it is universal. But it would be a fallacy to say, well, the trait *is* universal, therefore it must be innate.[32]

Importantly, traits may be innate without being universal, as is lactase persistence in a subset of humans. Methodologically, such diversity in traits among populations can be a boon. As philosophers of science Jonathan Kaplan and David Buller both point out, if comparisons between populations regarding differential appearance of a trait can be linked to relevant differences in the ecology, then they can be linked to an adaptation for the trait in special ecological conditions.[33] Comparison of populations with and without light skin helped nail down the hypothesis that light skin allows for greater penetration of ultraviolet light, enhancing synthesis of vitamin D. This penetration is useful in latitudes far from the equator where the winters are long (and where light skin is common), and a handicap in latitudes closer to the equator where sunburn would be a problem. At least 100 genes have been implicated in skin pigmentation, so how exactly light skin emerged in populations that migrated into Europe is not completely understood. Still, this serves as a reminder that a trait may have a genetic basis but not be universal.

Here is the more general caution: when it comes to behavior such as displays of cooperation, as opposed to the eye-blink reflex, appealing to innateness is often minimally informative. That is because what mediates the behavior is neural circuitry, and neural circuitry, as we have seen, is the outcome of gene-gene, gene-neuron-environment, neuron-neuron, and brain-environment interactions. Without a doubt, genes have a huge role to play in what we are, but exactly what the role is remains to be clarified.

Learning, of course, greatly adds to the complexity of the picture. Neuroscientist Charles Gross observes that in some humans who pay a lot of attention to cars there are regions of the temporal lobe that respond differently to different models of cars—to Cadillac Seville versus Audi 5000 versus Ford Taurus.[34] This can be demonstrated using brain imaging techniques. Is such a region an innate "car" module? Obviously, car model identification was not selected for in our evolutionary history, though such a capacity may be highly advantageous these days. The temporal lobe, as Gross says, seems to be a general-purpose analyzer of visual forms that are relevant to how the animal makes its living. The basic lesson then is that working backwards from the existence of a certain behavior to a brain region that supports that behavior to the innateness of a function is, especially in animals that are prodigious learners, a project fraught with evidential hazard.

As things stand, it is clear that postulating "genes for" truth-telling, for example, has little to recommend it.[35] If, as described earlier, the relation between aggressiveness and genes in the fruit fly is complicated, then it is not surprising that the relation between genes and moral values espoused by humans, with their massive prefrontal cortex, their immaturity at birth, and the staggering amount of learning they do, looks to be very complicated indeed.[36]

Hauser is surely to be applauded for favoring scientific approaches in trying to discover the moral intuitions of the general public regarding certain moral dilemmas, and he does draw on a very broad sampling of opinion, to be sure. Nevertheless, the apparent universalities that he finds in responses to questionnaires may be partly owed to the simplicity, and lack of context, for many of the dilemma-stories subjects are asked to respond to. And as Philip Zimbardo has shown in his decades of careful work, a person's written response to a questionnaire may bear only a slight resemblance to what he or she would do if actually placed in a real situation.[37]

Consider one example from Hauser. Virtually everyone who fills out his questionnaire responds with disgust to the idea of drinking fresh apple juice out of a brand-new hospital bedpan. But what is the context for this? If I were to consider the idea as I sit now at my desk, well fed and well hydrated, I would not find it appealing, obviously because of the association with urine. Suppose, however, I am desperately dehydrated, stranded in the desert, and (miraculously) a camel appears with the bedpan full of fresh apple juice strapped to its hump. Would I find drinking it disgusting? Not in the slightest. How would contemporary subjects respond to the idea of using salt obtained by evaporating urine? My guess is that they would respond with disgust. Yet the Aztecs, hard put to find salt, used that as a method.[38] Were I an Aztec in that circumstance, I am betting I would tuck into the salt with gusto, not disgust, just as the Aztecs likely did.[39] As both Aristotle and Confucius realized, context matters a lot, which is why they both considered moral knowledge to be rooted in skills and dispositions, not a set of rules or, in Hauser's terms, a "moral grammar."

So the further caution is this: the existence of one's own powerful intuition about what is disgusting or wrong is not evidence that the intuition has an innate basis. It is *consistent* with that possibility, but it is also consistent with the possibility that the intuition reflects a social practice picked up during childhood, and ingrained via the reward system.[40]

Moreover, as Cambridge philosopher Simon Blackburn points out in contrast to Hauser, many moral dilemmas are addressed not automatically and instantly, but reflectively, with long, thoughtful deliberation.[41] Sometimes they remain unsettled for extended periods of time. Jurists, and those in government, as well as ordinary people, may struggle long and hard over the right way to handle moral problems involving inheritance laws, charging interest on loans, taxation, organ donation, eminent domain, "mainstreaming" mentally handicapped children in school, euthanasia for the terminally ill, immigration policy, war, removing children from parents, and capital punishment. On these topics, instant intuitions may give answers that backfire, and fair-minded disagreement can persist for decades. Hauser's claim that moral judgment does not involve conscious reasoning may apply in some situations such as seeing a child choking at dinner, but it clearly does not apply in multitudes of other situations, such as whether to go to war against a neighboring country.

Attuned to the realities besetting actual moral deliberation and negotiation, Blackburn challenges Hauser's analog between moral intuitions and linguistic intuitions: "So to sum up they [moral intuitions] are apparently *not abundant, not instant, not inarticulate, not inflexible and not certain.* Any similarity to language processing is therefore on the face of it quite slight, and so, I fear, may be the prospects for diving down to find hidden principles constraining them."[42] Blackburn's summary captures well the profound disanalogies between linguistic intuitions and moral judgment. It would perhaps be appropriate to add that the originating germ of the analogy (the so-called "language organ" and grammatical universals) is itself the subject of more than a little skeptical debate.[43]

Jonathan Haidt and Moral Foundations

Jonathan Haidt, a psychologist,[44] argues that human morality is based on five funda- 40
mental intuitions, where each corresponds to an adaptation to an ecological condition, and each has its characteristic emotion. His theory includes a hypothesis to the effect that evolution favored humans who displayed these five virtues. The list he offers consists of name-pairs for the domains of intuitions, matched with the adaptive behavior.

1. *harm/care*—protect and care for young, vulnerable, or injured kin
2. *fairness/reciprocity*—reap benefits of dyadic cooperation with non-kin
3. *ingroup/loyalty*—reap benefits of group cooperation
4. *authority/respect*—negotiate hierarchy, defer selectively
5. *purity/sanctity*—avoid microbes and parasites[45]

Itemizing fundamental virtues has a venerable history in philosophy. Socrates,* for example, starts with five (wisdom, courage, moderation, piety, and justice), but on reflection, demotes piety from the list, on grounds that it is not really a human virtue, but something that could be safely left to the Oracle at Delphi.† The list in the Buddhist *Abhid-harma* invites us to avoid the "three poisons" (hatred, craving, and delusion) and their assorted derivatives, while adhering to "Four Noble Truths" (loving-kindness, compassion, appreciative joy, and equanimity).[46] Mencius, a classical Chinese philosopher (4th c. BC), listed four overarching virtues: benevolence, righteousness, propriety, and wisdom.

Aristotle's list distinguishes between intellectual virtues and those he calls *virtues of character* or *ethical virtues.* Aristotle emphasized that establishing appropriate habits in early life was essential for practical wisdom. As a useful bit of practical wisdom, he suggested that choosing the middle ground between extremes of behavior was a reliable, though not infallible, guide to leading a virtuous life—a rule of thumb known as the Golden Mean (not to be confused with the Golden Rule: "Do unto others as you would be done by"). The Golden Mean counsels us that the middle ground is generally good: one should be neither reckless nor timid, but appropriately courageous; neither

---

* Socrates: Athenian Greek (469–399 BC); one of the founders of Western philosophy known chiefly through the writings of his students, notably Plato [Ed.].
† Oracle at Delphi: Dating back to 1400 BC, the Oracle at Delphi was the most important shrine in all Greece. There the priestess Pythia would answer questions about the future, but often ambiguously [Ed.].

tightfisted nor openhanded, but appropriately generous; neither wholly indulgent nor utterly abstemious, but moderate; and so forth. How to be *appropriate* is not something that is settled by applying a rule, according to Aristotle; it requires practical wisdom, acquired through experience and reflection.

The Stoics* emphasized the importance of prudence, wisdom, courage, and moderation, among other virtues. In the Middle Ages, others, including Aquinas and Ockham,† also listed virtues, but in contrast to Socrates, "obeying God" was high on the list. Each of Aesop's fables ends with a summary statement of a bit of moral wisdom, which could be paired with a corresponding virtue, often that of prudence or modesty or kindness—"The moral of the story is. . . ."[47] In later periods, thrift and hard work were emphasized alongside the other virtues, as in Benjamin Franklin's list of thirteen virtues and, much more recently, in William Bennett's list of ten virtues.[48]

So Haidt is in respectable, if fairly crowded, company. Nevertheless, Haidt wants to do more than just make a respectable list in the company of others. He wants also to claim an evolutionary basis for why some moral intuitions on his list (e.g., fairness) are actually fundamental and innate, while others (e.g., truth-telling, or staying-calm-and-carrying-on) are secondary. Haidt's strategy has three parts: (1) identify the basic domains of intuition from what is known about the evolutionary conditions of early humans. (2) Show that these value-dispositions are common across diverse cultures. (3) Show that each value-disposition has its unique "characteristic emotion," thus supporting the idea that it was selected for, and that it is fundamental, not secondary.[49]

Although the ambition of Haidt's project is laudable, the execution is disappointingly insensitive to the height of the evidence bar. No factual support from molecular biology, neuroscienee, or evolutionary biology is marshaled for his substantive claims about basic domains of intuitions. A danger in the project is that inferring what behavioral traits were selected for in human evolution cannot be solved by a vivid imagination about the ancestral condition plus selected evidence about cross-cultural similarity, evidence that could be explained in many different ways.[50]

The problem can be illustrated with Haidt's inclusion of a purity and sanctity domain as fundamental. His idea is that in the evolution of the human brain, religions would have served the well-being of individuals in the group who adhered to the religion, and hence the inclination would have been selected for in the biological evolution of the human brain. According to this view, beneficial intuitions about cleanliness and purity, originally connected to food, quite naturally attached themselves to local religious practices and objects. The foregoing sketches Haidt's account of what he believes is an innate inclination to religious adherence, and is meant to help explain the widespread occurrence of religions.

---

* Stoics: Ancient school of philosophy influenced by the Cynics. Stoics held that destructive emotions should be controlled and that clear thinking would lead to reason [Ed.].

† Aquinas and Ockham: Thomas Aquinas (1225–1274), Italian philosopher and theologian; his most important work is the *Summa Theologica,* which offers proofs for the existence of God and argues that virtuous acts are rewarded. William of Ockham (c. 1287–1347), English medieval philosopher; he and Aquinas are among the most important philosophers of their time. Ockham is best known today for "Ockham's razor," the principle that the simplest explanation is usually the correct one [Ed.].

The problem is, theories abound to explain religions in terms of natural selection, and the lack of substantiating evidence makes them equally unappealing. To illustrate, one hypothesis meant to explain religious behavior, popular among anthropologists and psychologists, refers to *costly signaling*, which is a behavior displayed as a way of signaling cooperative intent and reliability. Examples of costly signaling would be sacrifices of goats and chickens, or the renunciation of comforts such as warm

> **Theories abound to explain religions in terms of natural selection, and the lack of substantiating evidence makes them equally unappealing.**

baths, or of pleasures such as dancing or sex. Simplified, the idea is that individuals who join a group and willingly accept the group's renunciations (costly signaling) are identifiable as reliable cooperators. Benefits flow from group membership; costly signaling is the price we pay to be members, and it helps to deter cheaters and freeloaders, who, *ex hypothesi*, would not want to pay. According to the costly signaling hypothesis, willingness to display costly signals would be selected for in the evolution of the species, since individuals could use them to find one another, and to expand groups with strongly-cooperative members. Thus religion—usually involving costly signals such as sacrifices and renunciations—emerges as an innate module.[51] This sounds like a reasonable account, except that the evidence for the "costly signaling" hypothesis is in embarrassingly short supply. As philosophers have shown, none of the versions of this view are both logically coherent and sufficiently well supported to appear solid.[52]

Other strategies for explaining the ubiquity of religions proceed by arguing that in-group bonding occurs during religious rituals, enhancing attachment and loyalty, and that religion is thus a by-product of social bonding. Consequently, religious dispositions were selected for owing to the benefits of strong in-group bonds. This was advantageous in various aspects of social life where cooperation was needed. A somewhat different theory is that there are close links between religions and war. The motivating observation is that gods and spirits of war are very common, along with rituals with connections to war and fighting, and rewards for courageous fighters. Success in war, in both attack and defense, is a selective advantage, and religion aids a war effort.[53] Others have claimed that because people who had religious dispositions were on the whole healthier, the disposition to religion was selected for.[54] Though their arguments have been challenged and though there are some data showing that patients engaged in a religious "struggle" may actually be less healthy,[55] this link to health remains attractive to many people as a justification for religious faith.[56]

Another popular cluster of hypotheses claims that the disposition to religious beliefs is not selected for as such, but as a by-product of various other functions, such as attachment to parents, the wish for help in distress, and the inclination to explain mysteries and catastrophes by expanding one's attribution of mental states from the domain of observable humans to a domain of unobservable Others. Since religions are stunningly various, and deities come in all shapes, powers, and numbers (including zero), no single explanation along these lines holds much promise of doing the trick. Rather, a skein of interlocking explanations for different aspects of behavior that gets called "religious" may be more serviceable, in something like the way that many different things can be called music.[57] In any case, the plethora of selection theories to explain the prevalence of religious beliefs, none adequately supported by evidence so far, shows why leery evolutionary biologists and geneticists have shelved umpteen theories about innate modules as "just so" stories.[58] Speculations are of course useful in inspiring experiments, and are not to be discouraged. The point is, I prefer not buy into one, or be asked to, until some results bear upon its truth.

The classical problem that bedevils all innateness theories of behavior is that in   50 the absence of supporting evidence concerning genes and their relation to brain circuitry involved, the theories totter over when pushed. Haidt, for example, relies quite heavily on whether or not a skill is easily learned to demarcate skills the brain is innately "prepared for" and those that it is not so prepared for.[59] But how do you defend, without resorting to ad hoc fixes, the innateness of some "easily learned" things while excluding other "easily learned" things, like riding a bicycle, tying a reef knot, putting on shoes, or fishing for trout with a worm on a hook? Conversely, learning skills of self-control, arguably something the brain probably is "prepared for," is often *not* easy. Ease of learning of a skill is *consistent* with innateness, but it does not *imply* it. The problems facing claims about the innateness of foundational moral behaviors are daunting, and without strong evidential support, the innateness claims are left dangling.

Aristotle, in his discussions of morality, emphasizes social skills as yielding the flexibility, aptness, and practicality required for flourishing in the social domain. In his view, the exercise of social skills depends on acquiring the appropriate habits, and can be greatly influenced by the role models, social practices, and institutions one encounters in daily life. An essential component of normal sociality involves our ability to attribute mental states to others. Without that capacity, we cannot empathize with their plight, nor understand their intentions, feelings, beliefs, and what they are up to. By and large humans are adept in empathizing, and more generally, in "reading minds"—knowing what others feel, intend, want, and so forth. When the capacity begins to fail, as in frontotemporal dementia, which involves the degeneration of neural tissue in the frontal and temporal cortices, the effect is truly catastrophic, reminding us of how deeply important are the skills that we generally exercise effortlessly, fluently, and routinely. In the next chapter [not included here], I shall look more closely at what is known about the neurobiology of understanding minds—others' and one's own.

NOTES

1. See Aristotle, *Nicomacheam Ethics*, trans. Roger Crisp (New York: Cambridge University Press, 2000).
2. Jonathan Flint, Ralph J. Greenspan, and Kenneth S. Kendler, *How Genes Influence Behavior* (New York: Oxford University Press. 2010), 211, emphasis added.
3. R. J. Greenspan. "E Pluribus Unum, Ex Uno Plura: Quantitative and Single-Gene Perspectives on the Study of Behavior," *Annual Review of Neuroscience* 27 (2004): 79–105.
4. Ibid.
5. This is a paraphrase of Greenspan, "E Pluribus Unum," 92.
6. See Irwin Lucki, "The Spectrum of Behaviors Influenced by Serotonin," *Biological Psychiatry* 44, no. 3 (1998): 151–62. For results concerning serotonin's role in reward and negative feedback learning, see Andrea Bari et al., "Serotonin Modulates Sensitivity

to Reward and Negative Feedback in a Probabilistic Reversal Learning Task in Rats," *Neuropsychopharmacology* 35, no. 6 (2010): 1290–301.

7. Klaus-Peter Lesch et al., "Association of Anxiety-Related Traits with a Polymorphism in the Serotonin Transporter Gene Regulatory Region," *Science* 274, no. 5292 (1996): 1527–31.

8. R. J. Greenspan, "The Flexible Genome," *Nature Reviews Genetics* 2, no. 5 (2001): 383–87.

9. Herman A. Dierick and Ralph J. Greenspan, "Serotonin and Neuropeptide F Have Opposite Modulatory Effects on Fly Aggression," *Nature Genetics* 39, no. 5 (2007): 678–82: Neuropeptide-F is the homologue in flies of neuropeptide-Y, linked to aggressive behavior in mammals.

10. Herman A. Dierick and Ralph J. Greenspan, "Molecular Analysis of Flies Selected for Aggressive Behavior," *Nature Genetics* 38, no. 9 (2006): 1023–31.

11. See the online supplementary material for Dierick and Greenspan, "Molecular Analysis of Flies Selected for Aggressive Behavior," table 1. It is a dramatic demonstration of the results, showing the 80 genes whose expressions were changed between the aggressive and neutral flies. Incidentally, since testosterone has often been linked to aggression, it is well worth noting that fruit flies do not have testosterone, but can be highly aggressive nonetheless.

12. Greenspan, "The Flexible Genome," "E Pluribus Unum"; and see "Genetic Networks" earlier in this chapter.

13. Dennis L. Murphy et al., "How the Serotonin Story Is Being Rewritten by New Gene-Based Discoveries Principally Related to Slc6a4, the Serotonin Transporter Gene, Which Functions to Influence All Cellular Serotonin Systems," *Neuropharmacology* 55, no. 6 (2008): 932–60.

14. Greenspan, "E Pluribus Unum," 93.

15. Flint, Greenspan, and Kendler, *How Genes Influence Behavior.* On aggression, see Larry J. Siever, "Neurobiology of Aggression and Violence," *American Journal of Psychiatry* 165, no. 4 (2008): 429–42.

16. Gleb P. Shumyatsky et al., "Identification of a Signaling Network in Lateral Nucleus of Amygdala Important for Inhibiting Memory Specifically Related to Learned Fear," *Cell* 111, no. 6 (2002): 905–18.

17. See also Tost et al., "A Common Allele in the Oxytocin Receptor Gene (OXTR) Impacts Prosocial Temperament."

18. Champagne and Meaney, "Like Mother, Like Daughter," "Transgenerational Effects of Social Environment."

19. Greenspan, "E Pluribus Unum," 99.

20. Jeffrey L. Elman et al., *Rethinking Innateness: A Connectionist Perspective on Development* (Cambridge, MA: MIT Press, 1996); Nicholas Evans and Stephen C. Levinson, "The Myth of Language Universals: Language Diversity and Its Importance for Cognitive Science," *Behavioral and Brain Sciences* 32, no. 5 (2009): 429–48; Morten H. Christiansen and Nick Chater, "Language as Shaped by the Brain," *Behavioral and Brain Sciences* 31, no. 5 (2008): 489–509.

21. Marc D. Hauser, *Moral Minds: How Nature Designed Our Universal Sense of Right and Wrong* (New York: Ecco, 2006).

22. Ibid., 165.

23. Ibid., xviii.

24. Flint, Greenspan, and Kendler, *How Genes Influence Behavior.*

25. On reading and genes, see Alison Gopnik, "Mind Reading," review of *Reading in the Brain — The Science and Evolution of a Human Invention,* by Stanislas Dehaene, *New York Times,* January 3, 2010.

26. See Richerson and Boyd, *Not by Genes Alone*, for a concise and compelling discussion of why the *nature versus nurture* presumption came off the rails. See also Robert C. Richardson, *Evolutionary Psychology as Maladapted Psychology* (Cambridge, MA: MIT Press, 2007).
27. Hauser, *Moral Minds*, xviii.
28. Todd Preuss, in conversation, wittily calls the "genes-for" approach "folk molecular biology," a notion I find appealing.
29. Evans and Levinson ("The Myth of Language Universals") make this point with alleged cases of linguistic universals.
30. The Inuit, who had limited access to wood, used skins for their kayaks, but if they could get driftwood, they used it for the larger whaling boats.
31. For careful criticism of claims by evolutionary psychologists, see Richardson, *Evolutionary Psychology as Maladapted Psychology*.
32. This is the fallacy of affirming the consequent (if P, then Q: Q, therefore P). One could agree that *if* a dog has fallen from 5,000 feet, then it is dead. Now suppose we know that a certain dog is dead. Merely knowing that the dog is dead does not imply that it died by falling 5,000 feet—maybe it died of old age, or it was run over, or it ate rat poison, and so on and on.
33. Jonathan Michael Kaplan, "Historical Evidence and Human Adaptations," *Philosophy of Science* 69, no. s3 (2002): S294–S304; David J. Buller, "Four Fallacies of Pop Evolutionary Psychology," *Scientific American* 300 (2009): 74–81.
34. Charles G. Gross, "Making Sense of Printed Symbols," *Science* 327, no. 5965 (2010): 524–25.
35. Flint, Greenspan, and Kendler, *How Genes Influence Behavior*.
36. Siever, "Neurobiology of Aggression and Violence."
37. Philip G. Zimbardo, *The Lucifer Effect: Understanding How Good People Turn Evil* (New York: Random House, 2007). Or as Stuart Anstis said in conversation, "I learned one big thing in Cambridge: never use questionnaires."
38. Bill Bryson, *At Home: A Short History of Private Life* (New York: Doubleday, 2010).
39. Graybiel, "Habits, Rituals, and the Evaluative Brain."
40. Hauser is not unaware of cultural variability on certain issues, and he is aware that intuitions can be powerful even if not innate. This makes it a little difficult to see how he designates what principles are in the innately given "moral grammar."
41. Simon Blackburn, "Response to Hauser's Tanner Lecture," unpublished, http://www.phil.cam.ac.uk/~swb24/PAPERS/Hauser.pdf.
42. Blackburn, "Response to Hauser's Tanner Lecture."
43. Christiansen and Chater, "Language as Shaped by the Brain"; Elman et al., *Rethinking Innateness*; Evans and Levinson, "The Myth of Language Universals."
44. Most of the papers are coauthored with Craig Joseph or with Jesse Graham: others are written solely by Haidt. For brevity, I shall refer to Haidt.
45. This list is taken from Jonathan Haidt and Jesse Graham, "Planet of the Durkheimians, Where Community, Authority, and Sacredness Are Foundations of Morality," in *Social and Psychological Bases of Ideology and System Justification*, ed. J. Jost. A. C. Kay, and H. Thorisdottir (New York: Oxford University Press, 2009), 371–401. See also Jonathan Haidt and Craig Joseph, "The Moral Mind: How Five Sets of Innate Intuitions Guide the Development of Many Culture-Specific Virtues, and Perhaps Even Modules," in *The Innate Mind*. vol. 3: *Foundations and the Future*, ed. Peter Carruthers, Stephen Laurence, and Stephen Stich (New York: Oxford University Press, 2007), 367–92; Jonathan Haidt and Craig Joseph, "Intuitive Ethics: How Innately Prepared Intuitions Generate Culturally Variable Virtues, *Daedalus* 133, no. 4 (2004): 55–66.

46. See the discussion by Flanagan, *The Really Hard Problem*, chapter 4. I have taken some liberty with the language, since the Four Noble Truths are also referred to as the Divine Abodes.

47. For a detailed and clear discussion of different lists of virtues and different ways of conceiving of fundamental virtues, see MacIntyre, *After Virtue.*

48. William J. Bennett, *The Book of Virtues: A Treasury of Great Moral Stories* (New York: Simon & Schuster, 1993).

49. For a more complete critique of Haidt's view, including his hypothesis concerning the moral differences between liberals and conservatives, see Christopher Suhler and Patricia Churchland, "Can Innate, Modular 'Foundations' Explain Morality? Challenges for Haidt's Moral Foundations Theory," *Journal of Cognitive Neuroscience* 23, no. 9 (2011): 2103–16.

50. For a related but different critique, see Owen Flanagan and Robert Anthony Williams, "What Does the Modularity of Morals Have to Do with Ethics? Four Moral Sprouts Plus or Minus a Few," *Topics in Cognitive Science* (in press).

51. See, for example, R. Sosis and C. Alcorta, "Signaling, Solidarity, and the Sacred: The Evolution of Religious Behavior,'" *Evolutionary Anthropology: Issues, News, and Reviews* 12, no. 6 (2003): 264–74.

52. Michael J. Murray and Lyn Moore, "Costly Signaling and the Origin of Religion," *Journal of Cognition and Culture* 9 (2009): 225–45. This article explains well what is needed by way of evidence to support an innate module hypothesis for religion.

53. Dominic Johnson, "Darwinian Selection in Asymmetric Warfare: The Natural Advantage of Insurgents and Terrorists," *Journal of the Washington Academy of Sciences* 95 (2009): 89–112.

54. David B. Larson, James P. Swyers, and Michael E. McCullough, *Scientific Research on Spirituality and Health: A Report Based on the Scientific Progress in Spirituality Conferences* (Rockville, MD: National Institute for Healthcare Research, 1998).

55. Kenneth I. Pargament et al., "Religious Struggle as a Predictor of Mortality among Medically Ill Elderly Patients: A 2-Year Longitudinal Study," *Archives of Internal Medicine* 161, no. 15 (2001): 1881–85.

56. O. Freedman et al., "Spirituality, Religion and Health: A Critical Appraisal of the Larson Reports," *Annals (Royal College of Physicians and Surgeons of Canada)* 35 (2002): 89–93.

57. William Dalrymple, *Nine Lives: In Search of the Sacred in Modern India* (London: Bloomsbury, 2009).

58. For a range of approaches, see J. Bulbulia et al., eds., *The Evolution of Religion: Studies, Theories, and Critiques* (Santa Margarita, CA: Collins Foundation Press, 2008).

59. Haidt and Graham, "Planet of the Durkheimians."

Exploring Context

1. Search YouTube for "Bill Moyers interviews Patricia Churchland on neurophilosophy." How does the interview offer a larger context for understanding this essay? How does this essay fit within Churchland's work more generally?

2. Visit the website for the Human Genome Project (ornl.gov/sci/techresources/Human_ Genome/home.shtml). How does the information you find there support or complicate Churchland's claims that genes function in a "many to many" network?

3. Use the online mind-mapping tool bubbl.us (bubbl.us) to create a map of Churchland's essay. To what extent does her argument function like genes with multiple linkages?

Questions for Connecting

1. Richard Restak, in "Attention Deficit: The Brain Syndrome of Our Era" (p. 411), also makes an argument about brain biology and human behavior. Synthesize his argument and Churchland's. Are their views on the relationship between the brain and behavior consistent? How can you reconcile the differences?

2. In "Ethics and the New Genetics" (p. 133), the Dalai Lama argues that our ethics must keep pace with scientific progress. Use Churchland's analysis to extend the Dalai Lama's argument. Is there an innate "moral compass" we can use? If not, how can we come to agreement on scientific ethics? You might want to incorporate your work from Question 1 of Exploring Context, in which you examined a video in which Churchland discusses her encounter with the Dalai Lama.

3. How are genes similar to Wikipedia? Use Marshall Poe's exploration of the online encyclopedia in "The Hive" (p. 349) to examine the role of networks in social and biological systems. What does networking make possible? What are the limitations of networks?

Language Matters

1. Churchland frequently italicizes words or phrases. Review the rules for italicizing in a grammar handbook or other reliable resource. Select examples from Churchland's essay that illustrate various reasons to italicize.

2. Churchland uses endnotes to cite her sources. Research the systems of citation for various disciplines. Which ones promote the use of endnotes or footnotes? Given what you learn, can you determine Churchland's discipline? When might you use endnotes or footnotes, given the citation system you're using in this class?

3. In academic writing, it's vital to state a clear, central argument so that the reader can follow that argument as it's proven with evidence in the paper. Find a quotation that you believe is a clear statement of Churchland's argument. Where is it located in the essay? Why does she place it there? Where should you place your argument in your papers for this class?

Assignments for Writing

1. Is morality innate? Write a paper in which you address this question, drawing on Churchland's discussion. What factors give rise to morality in humans? Is there a biological basis for morality?

2. Write a paper in which you determine the role of networks in biological systems. How do networks affect the functioning of genes? How do they make our understanding of biological systems more complex? Given the inherent complexity that any network creates — with connections upon connections — is it even possible to answer questions about the relationship between neural networks in the brain and moral impulses?

3. In many ways, Churchland's essay functions as a counterargument. Write a paper in which you reconstruct the argument against which Churchland writes. Is there evidence in her essay to support that original argument? Or is Churchland's counterargument more successful? In what ways?

THE DALAI LAMA

Dalai Lama

THE UNIVERSE IN A SINGLE ATOM
THE CONVERGENCE OF SCIENCE
AND SPIRITUALITY

Tenzin Gyatso is the fourteenth Dalai Lama and the leader of the Central Tibetan Administration—the government-in-exile of Tibet. Gyatso was declared at two years old to be the reincarnation of an earlier Dalai Lama; at the age of fifteen he assumed the roles of religious and political leader of the Tibetan people. The only Dalai Lama to visit the West, Gyatso has become notable for gaining Western sympathy for the cause of a free Tibet and for authoring or coauthoring more than fifty books. Among his many honors are the Nobel Peace Prize (1989) and the U.S. Congressional Gold Medal (2006).

In *The Universe in a Single Atom* (2005), the Dalai Lama tries to reconcile religion with science, claiming that religion and science are parts of the same path to ultimate truth. Relying on just one, he suggests, is incomplete at best and "impoverishing" at worst. Simply following the rationale of science that everything "is reducible to matter and energy leaves out a huge range of human experience," and the opposite approach "can lock us into fundamentalist cages" that deny proven facts. According to the Dalai Lama, we must attempt to bridge this gap between our different ways of thinking.

In "Ethics and the New Genetics," a chapter from *The Universe in a Single Atom*, the Dalai Lama focuses on the field of genetic engineering. The potential benefits of this area of science are enormous, but the Dalai Lama reminds us to bear the potential costs in mind: "The higher the level of knowledge and power," he writes, "the greater must be our sense of moral responsibility" (p. 133). He argues that the speed of scientific progress in recent years has outpaced our society's ethical development, raising questions of what to do about possible breakthroughs in the future, when to trust our instinctual reactions, and what consequences science can have on culture and society.

In an age when stem cell research is controversial, the Dalai Lama urges us in this essay to craft ethical standards that can guide us in the complex decisions involved when technology intersects with life.

▶ TAGS: *ethics, biotechnology, human dignity, social changes, research*

Questions for Critical Reading

1. What sort of ethical standards should we have for fields with profound implications like genetic engineering? As you read the Dalai Lama's essay, locate quotations that support your proposed system of ethics.

2. What are the keys to developing an ethics apart from religion? Search the Dalai Lama's essay for quotations that support your position.

3. As you read the Dalai Lama's text, look for specific quotations that suggest the conditions necessary for the use of genetic technologies. Are such technologies ever justified, in his view?

Ethics and the New Genetics

Many of us who have followed the development of the new genetics are aware of the deep public disquiet that is gathering around the topic. This concern has been raised in relation to everything from cloning to genetic manipulation. There has been a world-wide outcry over the genetic engineering of foodstuffs. It is now possible to create new breeds of plants with far higher yields and far lower susceptibility to disease in order to maximize food production in a world where the increasing population needs to be fed. The benefits are obvious and wonderful. Seedless watermelons, apples that have longer shelf lives, wheat and other grains that are immune to pests when growing in the field — these are no longer science fiction. I have read that scientists are even experimenting to develop farm products, such as tomatoes, injected with genes from different species of spiders.

But by doing these things, we are changing the genetic makeup, and do we really know what the long-term impact will be on the species of plants, on the soil, on the environment? There are obvious commercial benefits, but how do we judge what is really useful? The complex web of interdependence that characterizes the environment makes it seem beyond our capacity to predict.

Genetic changes have happened slowly over hundreds of thousands of years of natural evolution. The evolution of the human brain has occurred over millions of years. By actively manipulating the gene, we are on the cusp of forcing an unnaturally quick rate of change in animals and plants as well as our own species. This is not to say that we should turn our backs on developments in this area — it is simply to point out that we must become aware of the awesome implications of this new area of science.

The most urgent questions that arise have to do more with ethics than with science per se, with correctly applying our knowledge and power in relation to the new possibilities opened by cloning, by unlocking the genetic code and other advances. These issues relate to the possibilities for genetic manipulation not only of human beings and animals but also of plants and the environment of which we are all parts. At heart the issue is the relationship between our knowledge and power on the one hand and our responsibility on the other.

Any new scientific breakthrough that offers commercial prospects attracts tremendous interest and investment from both the public sector and private enterprise. The amount of scientific knowledge and the range of technological possibilities are so enormous that the only limitations on what we do may be the results of insufficient imagination. It is this unprecedented acquisition of knowledge and power that places us in a critical position at this time. The higher the level of knowledge and power, the greater must be our sense of moral responsibility.

If we examine the philosophical basis underlying much of human ethics, a clear recognition of the principle that correlates greater knowledge and power with a greater need for moral responsibility serves as a key foundation. Until recently we could say that this principle had been highly effective. The human capacity for moral reasoning has kept pace with developments in human knowledge and its capacities. But with the new era in biogenetic science, the gap between moral reasoning and our technological capacities has reached a critical point. The rapid increase of human knowledge and the technological possibilities emerging in the new genetic science are such that it is now almost impossible for ethical thinking to keep pace with these changes. Much of what is soon going to be possible is less in the form of new breakthroughs or paradigms in science than in the development of new technological options combined with the financial calculations of business and the political and economic calculations of governments. The issue is no longer whether we should or should not acquire knowledge and explore its technological potentials. Rather, the issue is how to use this new knowledge and power in the most expedient and ethically responsible manner.

The area where the impact of the revolution in genetic science may be felt most immediately at present is medicine. Today, I gather, many in medicine believe that the sequencing of the human genome will usher in a new era, in which it may be possible to move beyond a biochemical model of therapy to a genetically based model. Already the very definitions of many diseases are changing as illnesses are found to be genetically programmed into human beings and animals from their conception. While successful gene therapy for some of these conditions may be some way off, it seems no longer beyond the bounds of possibility. Even now, the issue of gene therapy and the associated question of genetic manipulation, especially at the level of the human embryo, are posing grave challenges to our capacity for ethical thinking.

A profound aspect of the problem, it seems to me, lies in the question of what to do with our new knowledge. Before we knew that specific genes caused senile dementia, cancer, or even aging, we as individuals assumed we wouldn't be afflicted with these problems, but we responded when we were. But now, or at any rate very soon, genetics can tell individuals and families that they have genes which may kill or maim them in childhood, youth, or middle age. This knowledge could radically alter our definitions of health and sickness. For example, someone who is healthy at present but has a particular genetic predisposition may come to be marked as "soon to be sick." What should we do with such knowledge, and how do we handle it in a way that is most compassionate? Who should have access to such knowledge, given its social and personal implications in relation to insurance, employment, and relationships, as well as reproduction? Does the individual who carries such a gene have a responsibility to reveal this fact to his or her potential partner in life? These are just a few of the questions raised by such genetic research.

To complicate an already intricate set of problems, I gather that genetic forecasting of this kind cannot be guaranteed to be accurate. It is sometimes certain that a particular genetic disorder observed in the embryo will give rise to disease in the child or adult, but it is often a question of relative probabilities. Lifestyle, diet, and other environmental factors come into play. So while we may know that a particular embryo carries a gene for a disease, we cannot be certain that the disease will arise.

People's life choices and indeed their very self-identity may be significantly affected   10
by their perception of genetic risk, but those perceptions may not be correct and the risk may not be actualized. Should we be afforded such probabilistic knowledge? In cases where one member of the family discovers a genetic disorder of this type, should all the other members who may have inherited the same gene be informed? Should this knowledge be made available to a wider community — for instance, to health insurance companies? The carriers of certain genes may be excluded from insurance and hence even from access to health care all because there is a possibility of a particular disease manifesting itself. The issues here are not just medical but ethical and can affect the psychological well-being of the people concerned. When genetic disorders are

detected in the embryo (as will increasingly be the case), should parents (or society) make the decision to curtail the life of that embryo? This question is further complicated by the fact that new methods of dealing with genetic disease and new medications are being found as swiftly as the genes carrying individual disease are identified. One can imagine a scenario in which a baby whose disease may manifest in twenty years is aborted and a cure for the disease is found within a decade.

Many people around the world, especially practitioners of the newly emerging discipline of bioethics, are grappling with the specifics of these problems. Given my lack of expertise in these fields, I have nothing concrete to offer in regard to any specific question — especially as the empirical facts are changing so rapidly. What I wish to do, however, is think through some of the key issues which I feel every informed person in the world needs to reflect upon, and to suggest some general principles that can be brought to bear in dealing with these

> **At heart the challenge we face is really a question of what choices we make in the face of the growing options that science and technology provide us.**

ethical challenges. I believe that at heart the challenge we face is really a question of what choices we make in the face of the growing options that science and technology provide us.

Attendant on the new frontiers of genetically based medicine there is a series of further issues which again raise deep and troubling ethical questions. Here I am speaking primarily of cloning. It has now been several years since the world was introduced to a completely cloned sentient being, Dolly, the famous sheep. Since then there has been a huge amount of coverage of human cloning. We know that the first cloned human embryos have been created. The media frenzy aside, the question of cloning is highly complex. I am told there are two quite different kinds of cloning — therapeutic and reproductive. Within therapeutic cloning, there is the use of cloning technology for the reproduction of cells and the potential creation of semi-sentient beings purely for the purpose of harvesting body parts for transplantation. Reproductive cloning is basically the creation of an identical copy.

In principle, I have no objection to cloning as such — as a technological instrument for medical and therapeutic purposes. As in all these cases, what must govern one's decisions is the question of compassionate motivation. However, regarding the idea of deliberately breeding semi-human beings for spare parts, I feel an immediate, instinctive revulsion. I once saw a BBC documentary which simulated such creatures through computer animation, with some distinctively recognizable human features. I was horrified. Some people might feel this is an irrational emotional reaction that need not be taken seriously. But I believe we must trust our instinctive feelings of revulsion, as these arise out of our basic humanity. Once we allow the exploitation of such hybrid semihumans, what is to stop us from doing the same with our fellow human beings whom the whims of society may deem deficient in some way? The willingness to step across such natural thresholds is what often leads humanity to the commission of horrific atrocities.

Although reproductive cloning is not horrifying in the same way, in some respects its implications may be more far-reaching. Once the technology becomes feasible, there could be parents who, desperate to have children and unable to do so, may seek to bear a child through cloning. What would this practice do to the future gene pool? To the diversity that has been essential to evolution?

There could also be individuals who, out of a desire to live beyond biological pos- 15 sibility, may choose to clone themselves in the belief that they will continue to live in the new cloned being. In this case, I find it difficult to see any justifiable motives — from the Buddhist perspective, it may be an identical body, but there will be two different consciousnesses. They will still die.

One of the social and cultural consequences of new genetic technologies is their effect on the continuation of our species, through interference with the reproductive process. Is it right to select the sex of one's child, which I believe is possible now? If it is not, is it right to make such choices for reasons of health (say, in couples where a child is at serious risk of muscular dystrophy or hemophilia)? Is it acceptable to insert genes into human sperm or eggs in the lab? How far can we go in the direction of creating "ideal" or "designer" fetuses — for instance, embryos that have been selected in the lab to provide particular molecules or compounds absent in genetically deficient siblings in order that the children born from such embryos may donate bone marrow or kidneys to cure siblings? How far can we go with the artificial selection of fetuses with desirable traits that are held to improve intelligence or physical strength or specific color of eyes for instance?

When such technologies are used for medical reasons — as in the curing of a particular genetic deficiency — one can deeply sympathize. The selection of particular traits, however, especially when done for primarily aesthetic purposes, may not be for the benefit of the child. Even when the parents think they are selecting traits that will positively affect their child, we need to consider whether this is being done out of positive intention or on the basis of a particular society's prejudices at a particular time. We have to bear in mind the long-term impact of this kind of manipulation on the species as a whole, given that its effects will be passed on to following generations. We need also to consider the effects of limiting the diversity of humanity and the tolerance that goes with it, which is one of the marvels of life.

Particularly worrying is the manipulation of genes for the creation of children with enhanced characteristics, whether cognitive or physical. Whatever inequalities there may be between individuals in their circumstances — such as wealth, class, health, and so on — we are all born with a basic equality of our human nature, with certain potentialities; certain cognitive, emotional, and physical abilities; and the fundamental disposition — indeed the right — to seek happiness and overcome suffering. Given that genetic technology is bound to remain costly, at least for the foreseeable future, once it is allowed, for a long period it will be available only to a small segment of human society, namely the rich. Thus society will find itself translating an inequality of circumstance (that is, relative wealth) into an inequality of nature through enhanced intelligence, strength, and other faculties acquired through birth.

The ramifications of this differentiation are far-reaching — on social, political, and ethical levels. At the social level, it will reinforce — even perpetuate — our disparities, and it will make their reversal much more difficult. In political matters, it will breed a ruling elite, whose claims to power will be invocations of an intrinsic natural superiority. On the ethical level, these kinds of pseudonature-based differences can severely undermine our basic moral sensibilities insofar as these sensibilities are based on a mutual recognition of shared humanity. We cannot imagine how such practices could affect our very concept of what it is to be human.

When I think about the various new ways of manipulating human genetics, I can't help but feel that there is something profoundly lacking in our appreciation of what it is to cherish humanity. In my native Tibet, the value of a person rests not on physical appearance, not on intellectual or athletic achievement, but on the basic, innate capacity for compassion in all human beings. Even modern medical science has demonstrated how crucial affection is for human beings, especially during the first few weeks of life. The simple power of touch is critical for the basic development of the brain. In regard to his or her value as a human being, it is entirely irrelevant whether an individual has some kind of disability — for instance, Down syndrome — or a genetic disposition to develop a particular disease, such as sickle-cell anemia, Huntington's chorea, or Alzheimer's. All human beings have an equal value and an equal potential for goodness. To ground our appreciation of the value of a human being on genetic makeup is bound to impoverish humanity, because there is so much more to human beings than their genomes.

We cannot imagine how such practices could affect our very concept of what it is to be human.

For me, one of the most striking and heartening effects of our knowledge of the genome is the astounding truth that the differences in the genomes of the different ethnic groups around the world are so negligible as to be insignificant. I have always argued that the differences of color, language, religion, ethnicity, and so forth among human beings have no substance in the face of our basic sameness. The sequencing of the human genome has, for me, demonstrated this in an extremely powerful way. It has also helped reinforce my sense of our basic kinship with animals, who share very large percentages of our genome. So it is conceivable if we humans utilize our newly found genetic knowledge skillfully, it could help foster a greater sense of affinity and unity not only with our fellow human beings but with life as a whole. Such a perspective could also underpin a much more healthy environmental consciousness.

In the case of food, if the argument is valid that we need some kind of genetic modification to help feed the world's growing population, then I believe that we cannot simply dismiss this branch of genetic technology. However, if, as suggested by its critics, this argument is merely a front for motives that are primarily commercial — such as producing food that will simply have a longer lasting shelf life, that can be more easily exported from one side of the world to the other, that is more attractive in appearance and more convenient in consumption, or creating grains and cereals engineered not to produce their own seeds so that farmers are forced to depend entirely upon the biotech companies for seeds — then clearly such practices must be seriously questioned.

Many people are becoming increasingly worried by the long-term consequences of producing and consuming genetically modified produce. The gulf between the scientific community and the general public may be caused in part by the lack of transparency in the companies developing these products. The onus should be on the biotech industry both to demonstrate that there are no long-term negative consequences for consumers of these new products and to adopt complete transparency on all the possible implications such plants may have for the natural environment. Clearly the argument that if there is no conclusive evidence that a particular product is harmful then there is nothing wrong with it cannot be accepted.

The point is that genetically modified food is not just another product, like a car or a portable computer. Whether we like it or not, we do not know the long-term consequences of introducing genetically modified organisms into the wider environment. In medicine, for instance, the drug thalidomide was found to be excellent for the treatment of morning sickness in pregnant women, but its long-term consequences for the health of the unborn child were not foreseen and proved catastrophic.

Given the tremendous pace of development in modern genetics, it is urgent now to   25 refine our capacity for moral reasoning so that we are equipped to address the ethical challenges of this new situation. We cannot wait for a series of responses to emerge in an organic way. We need to confront the reality of our potential future and tackle the problems directly.

I feel the time is ripe to engage with the ethical side of the genetic revolution in a manner that transcends the doctrinal standpoints of individual religions. We must rise to the ethical challenge as members of one human family, not as a Buddhist, a Jew, a Christian, a Hindu, a Muslim. Nor is it adequate to address these ethical challenges from the perspective of purely secular, liberal political ideals, such as individual freedom, choice, and fairness. We need to examine the questions from the perspective of a global ethics that is grounded in the recognition of fundamental human values that transcend religion and science.

It is not adequate to adopt the position that our responsibility as a society is simply to further scientific knowledge and enhance our technological power. Nor is it sufficient to argue that what we do with this knowledge and power should be left to the choices of individuals. If this argument means that society at large should not interfere with the course of research and the creation of new technologies based on such research, it would effectively rule out any significant role for humanitarian or ethical considerations in the regulation of scientific development. It is essential, indeed it is a responsibility, for us to be much more critically self-aware about what we are developing and why. The basic principle is that the earlier one intervenes in the causal process, the more effective is one's prevention of undesirable consequences.

In order to respond to the challenges in the present and in the future, we need a much higher level of collective effort than has been seen yet. One partial solution is to ensure that a larger segment of the general public has a working grasp of scientific thinking and an understanding of key scientific discoveries, especially those which have direct social and ethical implications. Education needs to provide not only training in the empirical facts of science but also an examination of the relationship between science and society at large, including the ethical questions raised by new technological possibilities. This educational imperative must be directed at scientists as well as laypeople, so that scientists retain a wider understanding of the social, cultural, and ethical ramifications of the work they are doing.

Given that the stakes for the world are so high, the decisions about the course of research, what to do with our knowledge, and what technological possibilities should be developed cannot be left in the hands of scientists, business interests, or government officials. Clearly, as a society we need to draw some lines. But these deliberations cannot come solely from small committees, no matter how august or expert they may be. We need a much higher level of public involvement, especially in the form of debate and discussion, whether through the media, public consultation, or the action of grassroots pressure groups.

Today's challenges are so great — and the dangers of the misuse of technology 30 so global, entailing a potential catastrophe for all humankind — that I feel we need a moral compass we can use collectively without getting bogged down in doctrinal differences. One key factor that we need is a holistic and integrated outlook at the level of human society that recognizes the fundamentally interconnected nature of all living beings and their environment. Such a moral compass must entail preserving our human sensitivity and will depend on us constantly bearing in mind our fundamental human values. We must be willing to be revolted when science — or for that matter any human activity — crosses the line of human decency, and we must fight to retain the sensitivity that is otherwise so easily eroded.

How can we find this moral compass? We must begin by putting faith in the basic goodness of human nature, and we need to anchor this faith in some fundamental and universal ethical principles. These include a recognition of the preciousness of life, an understanding of the need for balance in nature and the employment of this need as a gauge for the direction of our thought and action, and — above all — the need to ensure that we hold compassion as the key motivation for all our endeavors and that it is combined with a clear awareness of the wider perspective, including long-term consequences. Many will agree with me that these ethical values transcend the dichotomy of religious believers and nonbelievers, and are crucial for the welfare of all humankind. Because of the profoundly interconnected reality of today's world, we need to relate to the challenges we face as a single human family rather than as members of specific nationalities, ethnicities, or religions. In other words, a necessary principle is a spirit of oneness of the entire human species. Some might object that this is unrealistic. But what other option do we have?

I firmly believe it is possible. The fact that, despite our living for more than half a century in the nuclear age, we have not yet annihilated ourselves is what gives me great hope. It is no more coincidence that, if we reflect deeply, we find these ethical principles at the heart of all major spiritual traditions.

In developing an ethical strategy with respect to the new genetics, it is vitally important to frame our reflection within the widest possible context. We must first of all remember how new this field is and how new are the possibilities it offers, and to contemplate how little we understand what we know. We have now sequenced the whole of the human genome, but it may take decades for us fully to understand the functions of all the individual genes and their interrelationships, let alone the effects of their interaction with the environment. Too much of our current focus is on the feasibility of a particular technique, its immediate or short-term results and side effects, and what effect it may have on individual liberty. These are all valid concerns, but they are not sufficient. Their purview is too narrow, given that the very conception of human nature is at stake. Because of the far-reaching scope of these innovations, we need to examine all areas of human existence where genetic technology may have lasting implications. The fate of the human species, perhaps of all life on this planet, is in our hands. In the face of the great unknown, would it not be better to err on the side of caution than to transform the course of human evolution in an irreversibly damaging direction?

In a nutshell, our ethical response must involve the following key factors. First, we have to check our motivation and ensure that its foundation is compassion. Second, we must relate to any problem before us while taking into account the widest possible perspective, which includes not only situating the issue within the picture of wider human enterprise but also taking due regard of both short-term and long-term consequences. Third, when we apply our reason in addressing a problem, we have to be vigilant in ensuring that we remain honest, self-aware, and unbiased; the danger otherwise is that we may fall victim to self-delusion. Fourth, in the face of any real ethical challenge, we must respond in a spirit of humility, recognizing not only the limits of our knowledge (both collective and personal) but also our vulnerability to being misguided in the context of such a rapidly changing reality. Finally, we must all — scientists and society at large — strive to ensure that whatever new course of action we take, we keep in mind the primary goal of the well-being of humanity as a whole and the planet we inhabit.

The earth is our only home. As far as current scientific knowledge is concerned, this may be the only planet that can support life. One of the most powerful visions I have experienced was the first photograph of the earth from outer space. The image of a blue planet floating in deep space, glowing like the full moon on a clear night, brought home powerfully to me the recognition that we are indeed all members of a single family sharing one little house. I was flooded with the feeling of how ridiculous are the various disagreements and squabbles within the human family. I saw how futile it is to cling so tenaciously to the differences that divide us. From this perspective one feels the fragility, the vulnerability of our planet and its limited occupation of a small orbit sandwiched between Venus and Mars in the vast infinity of space. If we do not look after this home, what else are we charged to do on this earth?

35

Exploring Context

1. Visit the home page for the Human Genome Project (ornl.gov/sci/techresources/ Human_Genome/home.shtml). How does the project address the kinds of ethical problems that concern the Dalai Lama? Is it consistent with your proposed system of ethics from Question 1 of Questions for Critical Reading?

2. Explore the website for the Presidential Commission for the Study of Bioethical Issues (bioethics.gov). Are government organizations equipped to answer the Dalai Lama's call for a new ethics governing these technologies? Does the Commission reflect your argument about a nonreligious ethics from Question 2 of Questions for Critical Reading?

3. London's Science Museum has an online exhibit about Dolly the sheep, the first cloned animal. Visit the site at sciencemuseum.org.uk/antenna/dolly/index.asp. In the aftermath of Dolly's life and death, what new ethical concerns should we consider?

Questions for Connecting

1. Francis Fukuyama's "Human Dignity" (p. 185) also addresses concerns about the potential of biotechnologies. How does Fukuyama's exploration of the matter complicate the Dalai Lama's call for a new ethics? What are their respective positions on genetic technologies? Does Fukuyama answer the Dalai Lama's call for a "moral compass"? You may wish to draw on your work on the use of genetic technologies from Question 3 of Questions for Critical Reading.

2. What is the relationship between the Dalai Lama's "moral compass" and what Hal Herzog, in "Animals Like Us" (p. 242), describes as the "troubled middle"? Can you synthesize their respective positions on ethics into a position of your own?

3. The Dalai Lama is a world religious figure. How can we account for his authority on the subject of genetics and ethics using the insights provided by Madeleine Albright in "Faith and Diplomacy" (p. 35)?

Language Matters

1. The Dalai Lama uses a clear, simple style of writing to discuss a very complex subject. Select a key quotation from his text and break down the parts of each sentence. How does he use language to express difficult concepts clearly? How can you do the same in your writing?

2. In a small group, discuss what revision means. If you were going to revise this text, where would you start? What areas need more development?

3. If you were going to include images with this text, which ones would you choose? How would adding images change the meaning of the text? How can visual images support an argument made with words?

Assignments for Writing

1. The Dalai Lama uses the complex ethical dilemma of genetic technologies to make his argument about the necessity for a moral compass to guide us in relation to knowledge and scientific discovery. Write a paper in which you extend the Dalai Lama's argument using your own example of a technology or discovery that demands a moral compass. You may want to use your example to discuss how to utilize new knowledge and power in the most expedient and ethically responsible manner. In composing your essay, consider the gap between moral reasoning and technological capacity. Should different approaches be taken when developing ethical standards for the two different types of cloning? Why? What are the implications of probabilistic knowledge?

2. In this essay, the Dalai Lama discusses potential consequences of people being able to forecast genetic predispositions in their children and to alter their children's genetic makeup accordingly. Write a paper in which you propose a standard for when such forecasting should be used. Is such a technology ever ethical? Is it ever accurate? Why must relative probabilities be taken into consideration when thinking about genetic

forecasting? To what degree must self-determination be considered a factor? You may wish to discuss the correlation of greater knowledge with a greater need for moral responsibility, and you may wish to draw on your exploration of the websites in Exploring Context and your understanding of the Dalai Lama's concepts from Questions for Connecting.

3. The possible consequences of genetic manipulation reach far beyond the sphere of science. Consider, for example, the role of national and global politics in relation to scientific breakthroughs that have the potential to literally change the face of humanity but will almost certainly not be available to everyone. Write a paper in which you examine the consequences of technology in terms of social and economic stability. How does the Dalai Lama characterize the relationship between knowledge and responsibility? In what ways does genetic engineering have the potential to perpetuate our disparities on social, political, and ethical levels? Should new technologies be available to everyone?

ELIZABETH DICKINSON

Elizabeth Dickinson, a Yale graduate, is a field reporter and former editor of *Foreign Policy*. A regular guest on NPR, BBC, and ABC News, she has worked abroad for the *Wall Street Journal*, the *Economist*, and the *New York Times*. She frequently writes on foreign policy for publications including the *Atlantic*, the *Christian Science Monitor*, the *New Republic*, *Newsweek International*, and the *Guardian*.

Dickinson compiled "The Future of Food" for *Foreign Policy*'s special-topic issue titled "The Food Issue," dedicated to food, science, and politics from around the world. Other essays in this special issue focused on worldwide street-food-eating habits, reasons why food actually does define who we are, and the politics of food in the Middle East. It also featured an investigation of world hunger that questions the reliability of our current statistics concerning the problem.

"The Future of Food" is a statistical compilation of opinions and viewpoints from the top experts in the industry arranged as an "infographic," combining text and images to present an argument. Dickinson's infographic offers a glimpse into the past and the future of rising food costs as well as the likely increases in demand that we may see in the near future. As Dickinson makes clear, there are difficult decisions we must make when considering the future of food in the context of a hungry planet.

▶ TAGS: *production, famine, food, crisis, technology, genetic engineering, community, politics*

Questions for Critical Reading

1. Dickinson largely presents information from a survey, without taking an explicit position. Determine for yourself "the future of food," selecting relevant data and quotations from Dickinson's infographic to support your position.

2. Dickinson combines data, quotations, images, and survey responses to compose her infographic. What role does each element play? As you read, pay attention to how she uses each.

3. Dickinson uses several primary headings to organize her essay. What headings do you think are missing? What other factors should we consider when thinking about the future of food?

The Future of Food

Three years ago, as markets were heading toward collapse, one set of prices made a startling and disruptive leap: food. With rice and wheat more than doubling, riots broke out from Haiti to Bangladesh, to Cameroon to Egypt. Then oil prices went down and the crisis waned. Today, however, it seems that was only a temporary reprieve. Inflation in the developing world is pushing up food prices again, floods and fires last year destroyed a significant chunk of the world's wheat harvest, and oil is shooting back up as well, bringing with it the cost of fertilizer and shipping. Worse, with the world's population set to hit 9 billion by 2050 on an increasingly arid globe, what we now call crisis may become the status quo. How did things get so bad? And is there any turning back?

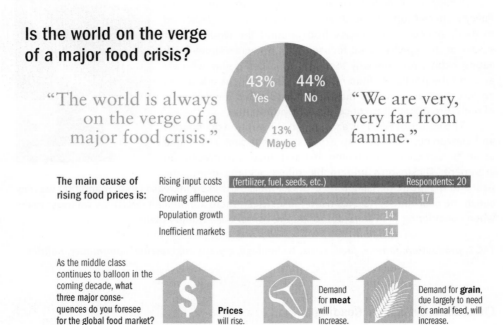

Is the world on the verge of a major food crisis?

"The world is always on the verge of a major food crisis."

43% Yes   44% No   13% Maybe

"We are very, very far from famine."

The main cause of rising food prices is:
- Rising input costs (fertilizer, fuel, seeds, etc.) — Respondents: 20
- Growing affluence — 17
- Population growth — 14
- Inefficient markets — 14

As the middle class continues to balloon in the coming decade, what three major consequences do you foresee for the global food market?

$ Prices will rise.

Demand for meat will increase.

Demand for grain, due largely to need for aninal feed, will increase.

Feeding the World

The United Nations estimates that close to 1 billion in the world today are hungry. **Do you agree or disagree and why?**

81%
Agree
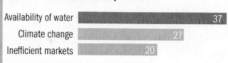

"Humanity has never been better fed, nor has it ever lived longer and healthier than today. Let's identify what got us to this remarkable achievement first, so that we do not end up undoing our success in our haste to do good."

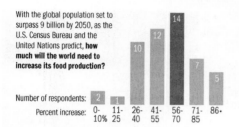

With the global population set to surpass 9 billion by 2050, as the U.S. Census Bureau and the United Nations predict, **how much will the world need to increase its food production?**

Number of respondents:
0–10%	11–25	26–40	41–55	56–70	71–85	86+
2	1	10	12	14	7	5

Percent increase:

What will most limit the world's ability to increase future food production?

Availability of water	37
Climate change	27
Inefficient markets	20

"It's regional production increases that are needed. We could feed the world from Iowa if we wanted to, but ... Africa needs to feed itself, and it needs to boost output by 80 percent to do so."

(Seeking Solutions)

What is the most promising technological development for food today?

Genetic engineering	14
Stress-resistant breeding	9
Use of ecosystems in farming	5

"Both promising and dangerous in absence of adequate monitoring and regulation."

The most dangerous?

Genetic engineering	6
Decreasing genetic variety/biodiversity	4
"Anti-science zealotry"	3
"Techno-optimists"	3

True or false:
Only through widespread use of genetic engineering can we increase food production enough to support global population growth.

39%
True

61%
False

"False. Which isn't to say we shouldn't try it."

What is the most important thing that the international community can do to cut the global hunger rate?

Promote broader economic growth — 10
Support smallholder farmers — 8
Reform global agricultural trade — 7

"All the new technologies and practices must be on the table if we are to produce enough food to support global population growth."

International food aid is:

A vital humanitarian intervention — 22
A necessary evil — 13
Destructive to local producers — 9
More help to rich-country farmers than anyone else — 9
Usually underfunded and oversubscribed — 7
All of the above — 4

"Poverty is the main problem. Even when food is abundant, many go hungry because of lack of income to purchase food."

(Politics)

On a scale of 1 to 10, how big an impact will rising food prices have on global political instability?

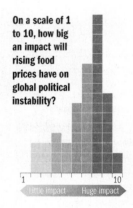

1 — 10
Little impact   Huge impact

"Hungry people are going to be an instant source of instability....If someone is hungry they won't care about the geopolitics."

Top 5 countries on respondents' watch list for food-related instability in the coming 12 months

NIGER
PAKISTAN
CHINA
INDIA
SUDAN

Some commentators have cited rising food prices as a factor sparking recent unrest across the Middle East. Do you agree?

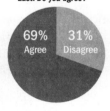

69% Agree   31% Disagree

"Peace is as essential for food security as food security is for peace."

(Africa)

What is the biggest reason that many regions of Africa have yet to experience the benefits of a "Green Revolution"?

Lack of modern farming techniques — 13
Poor infrastructure — 10
Bad governance — 9
Lack of good soil — 8
Underinvestment in agriculture — 7

NIGER

SUDAN

"Contrary to the conventional wisdom, the Green Revolution did not bypass Africa. It failed because expensive hybrid seeds and fertilizers quickly degraded soils and impoverished small farmers."

What one thing could African countries do to improve their food production immediately?

Improve market infrastructure — 15
Introduce modern farming practices — 8
Achieve better governance — 7
Increase use of fertilizer — 7
Adapt better seed varieties — 6

(Prime Numbers)

+70%
Amount by which **food production will need to increase** to feed the world by 2050.

+10-20%
Increase in the number of hungry people by 2050 due to climate change.

Food prices
In U.S. dollars per ton

$600 — Soy
— Rice
— Wheat
400 — Corn

200

2000   2011

Meat production
Millions of tons
518
310
Today   2050

Grain production
Billions of tons
2.7   3.3
Today   2050

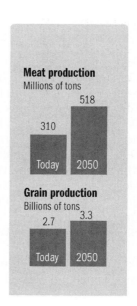

⟨Prime Numbers⟩

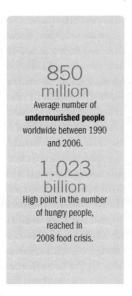

850 million
Average number of
undernourished people
worldwide between 1990
and 2006.

1.023 billion
High point in the number
of hungry people,
reached in
2008 food crisis.

**Regional distribution
of the world's hungry**

Asia and the Pacific

62%

Sub-Saharan Africa

26

Latin America/Caribbean

6

Middle East/North Africa

4

Developed countries

2

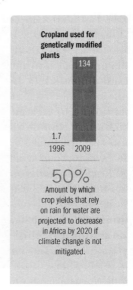

Cropland used for
genetically modified
plants

134

1.7
1996   2009

50%
Amount by which
crop yields that rely
on rain for water are
projected to decrease
in Africa by 2020 if
climate change is not
mitigated.

Survey participants (58): Hakan Altinay, Kwadwo Asenso-Okyere, Emmanuel Asmah, Christopher A. Bailey, Robert Bates, David Beckmann, Andrew Bent, Pascal Bergeret, Nancy Birdsall, Masum Burak, Sylvia Mathews Burwell, David Byrne, Jake Caldwell, Edward Cameron, Hank Cardello, Paul Collier, Richard Conant, Raj Desai, Dickson D. Despommier, Shenggen Fan, Ted Friend, Julian Gaspar, Wenonah Hauter, Kjell Havnevik, Peter Hazell, Yurie Tanimichi Hoberg, Eric Holt-Giménez, Charles Hurburgh, Sallie James, Monty Jones, Calestous Juma, Charles Kenny, Homi Kharas, Mwangi S. Kimenyi, Russell Libby, Will Martin, Peter Matlon, Jeffrey McNeely, David Michel, Todd Moss, Dambisa Moyo, Raymond C. Offenheiser Jr., Robert Paarlberg, Gregory Page, Carlo Petrini, Norman Piccioni, James Roth, Sara J. Scherr, Glen Shinn, Iain Shuker, Fawzi Al-Sultan, Mark Tercek, Carl-Gustaf Thornström, Camilla Toulmin, Johanna Nesseth Tuttle, Kristin Wedding, Patrick C. Westhoff, Steve Wiggins.

Data sources: "The Future of Food and Farming" (2011), Government Office for Science, London; U.N. Food and Agriculture Organization.

Exploring Context

1. Dickinson's presentation takes the form of an infographic. Visit the Cool Infographics site (coolinfographics.com) to see other examples of this genre. In what ways does

Dickinson's work relate to infographics more generally? How do infographics use both text and visual elements to convey information?

2. The U.S. Department of State maintains an Office of Global Food Security (state.gov/s /globalfoodsecurity). Explore the site to locate more information on both global hunger and the role the United States is taking in solving this problem. How does the information you find at the site confirm or complicate the data from Dickinson?

3. Visit the website for the International Food Policy Research Institute (ifpri.org), which annually produces the Global Hunger Index (GHI). Locate the most recent GHI. How have patterns of food and hunger shifted since Dickinson published her work? Is the future of food the same?

Questions for Connecting

1. The future of food is clearly a global issue. How might globalization offer a solution? Apply Thomas L. Friedman's ideas in "The Dell Theory of Conflict Prevention" (p. 166) to the problem of global hunger. Based on Dickinson's data and survey responses, can global supply chains offer a solution?

2. Namit Arora discusses several models of economic justice in his essay "What Do We Deserve?" (p. 87). Expand Arora's analysis by applying these models to Dickinson's infographic. Which model of economic justice, if any, seems to be operating when it comes to questions of food and global hunger?

3. Michael Pollan's "The Animals: Practicing Complexity" (p. 373) explores the highly productive farming practices of Polyface Farm. How might these approaches to growing food address some of the issues that Dickinson identifies?

Language Matters

1. Dickinson uses a number of charts. Use a grammar handbook or other reference resource to review information on making and using charts. When would it be appropriate to use charts in academic writing? What sort of information is best presented in chart form?

2. Given the visual nature of this selection, citation is a particular challenge. How should you properly cite Dickinson's work? Review information on citation in a grammar handbook or other reference resource. Is there a specific format you should use? How would you cite the visual elements, and how would you cite the quotations?

3. We read text linearly, from left to right. How does reading change when a reader is presented with an infographic like Dickinson's? Pay attention to how you read it. What factors determine the order of reading?

Assignments for Writing

1. Write a paper in which you develop your response to Question 1 of Questions for Critical Reading. Though Dickinson titles her work "The Future of Food," she doesn't explicitly provide an answer to what is, implicitly, a question. In your paper, determine

the future of food—the challenges we must face and the strategies we can use to face them—using information from Dickinson's infographic.

2. The last sections of Dickinson's piece are titled "Prime Numbers." Write a paper in which you explain the significance of these statistics. What makes them "prime"? Is Dickinson's emphasis on this data consistent with the information in the rest of the infographic?

3. Dickinson appears to present an impartial collection of statistics and data. Can any data be impartial? Write a paper in which you determine what bias, if any, Dickinson has in composing this infographic.

HELEN EPSTEIN

After earning a Ph.D. in molecular biology from Cambridge University, **Helen Epstein** attended the London School of Hygiene and Tropical Medicine, where she earned an M.Sc. in public health in developing countries. In 1993, while working as a scientist for a biotechnology company in search of an AIDS vaccine, Epstein moved to Uganda, where she witnessed the suffering caused by the virus. Epstein still works in public health care in developing countries. She has published articles in magazines such as the *New York Review of Books* and in 2007 published her book, *The Invisible Cure: Africa, the West, and the Fight against AIDS*.

Epstein compiled the information she had gathered in her years as a scientist in Africa, along with her personal observations, to write *The Invisible Cure*. In it she explores the reasons behind the unprecedented AIDS epidemic in Africa and suggests ways to reduce infection rates on that continent. Along the way she corrects the misinformation and misconceptions that Westerners have been using as a guide for aiding Africans who suffer from or are at risk for AIDS/HIV. She points out that programs for prevention might need to be in the hands of Africans themselves in order to account for local cultures. For instance, while campaigns promoting condom usage might be successful in Western countries, this does not mean such campaigns will succeed within other cultures. Instead, listening to and understanding the traditions and customs of individual cultures might lead to more successful approaches to the AIDS epidemic.

In "AIDS, Inc." a chapter from *The Invisible Cure*, Epstein examines HIV and AIDS prevention programs in Africa. In South Africa, Epstein witnesses a government-run campaign that focuses on creating conversations about sexual activity among the nation's youth in order to help them create informed decisions about sex. However, many of the conversations stop there, leaving out any talk of people who already have AIDS. While the campaign may open up new avenues for youth in terms of sexual responsibility and respect, the lack of conversation surrounding AIDS perpetuates the social stigmas of infected peoples as well as an "out of sight, out of mind" attitude toward the virus. Perhaps, as Epstein points out, campaigns are only as successful as the conversations surrounding them. She points to Uganda—one of the few countries in Africa where the rate of infection has dropped precipitously—as an example of effective conversation. Open conversation among Ugandans about personal experiences with the virus has succeeded in preventing its spread by breaking the cycle of social stigmas surrounding those infected.

What social stigmas concerning HIV and AIDS exist locally and globally? How do these social stigmas interfere with campaigns to successfully prevent the spread of the virus? How might class, race, gender, and religion contribute to the way prevention is approached? While Epstein points out how important conversation is among communities, is it possible to create a global conversation about HIV and AIDS?

▶ TAGS: *research, media, community, conversation, social change, technology, social cohesion, disease, epidemiology*

Questions for Critical Reading

1. What is a "lifestyle brand"? Make note of the definition of the term as you read Epstein's text. Then find an example of a lifestyle brand from popular culture. How might such an approach be used in health education? How effective might it be? How effective was it in South Africa?

2. Define *social cohesion* using Epstein's text. What role did it play in HIV infection rates in Uganda? How might that role be extended to other countries, including the United States?

3. What do you think would make an effective HIV prevention program for the United States? Compare your vision to Epstein's and her observations on such programs in Africa. Would the same strategies be effective in those two different cultural contexts? Support your responses with passages from the essay.

AIDS, Inc.

In response to government prevarication over HIV treatment, a vigorous AIDS activist movement emerged in South Africa and a fierce public relations battle ensued. The Treatment Action Campaign, or TAC, along with other activist groups, accused the South African health minister, Manto Tshabalala-Msimang, of "murder" for denying millions of South Africans access to medicine for AIDS. A spokesman from the ANC Youth League then called the activists "paid marketing agents for toxic AIDS drugs from America."[1] An official in the Department of Housing accused journalists who defended the AIDS activists of fanaticism, and quoted Lenin* on how the "press in bourgeois society . . . deceive[s], corrupt[s], and fool[s] the exploited and oppressed mass of the people, the poor."

Meanwhile, across the nation thousands of people were becoming infected daily, from the rural homesteads of the former Bantustans† to the peri-urban townships and squatter camps to the formerly all-white suburbs, now home to a growing black middle class. By 2005, the death rate for young adults had tripled.[2] Surveys showed that nearly everyone in South Africa knew that HIV was sexually transmitted and that it could be prevented with condoms, abstinence, and faithfulness to an uninfected partner. Children were receiving AIDS education in school and condoms were widely available,

---

* Lenin: Vladimir Lenin (1870–1924), a chief figure in the Russian revolution of 1917 (which led to the communist takeover); Lenin was the first head of the USSR [Ed.].
† Bantustans: Areas in South Africa where the black population was kept separate from whites during the policy of apartheid, or racial segregation, in the twentieth century [Ed.].

but these programs made little difference. In the din of the battle between the activists and the government, the deeper message, that HIV was everyone's problem, was lost.

In 1999, a group of public health experts sponsored by the U.S.-based Kaiser Family Foundation stepped into this fray. They were concerned about the worsening AIDS crisis in South Africa and wanted to launch a bold new HIV prevention program for young people. They also knew they had to take account of the South African government's attitudes toward AIDS and AIDS activists. Their program, called loveLife, would soon become South Africa's largest and most ambitious HIV prevention campaign. It aimed both to overcome the limitations of similar campaigns that had failed in the past and, at the same time, to avoid dealing with the issues of AIDS treatment and care that had become so controversial.

Could this work? I wondered. Was it possible to reduce the spread of HIV without involving HIV-positive people and the activists and community groups that supported them? LoveLife had been endorsed at one time or another by the archbishop of Cape Town; Nelson Mandela; the king of the Zulu tribe; Jacob Zuma, South Africa's former deputy president; and even Zanele Mbeki, the wife of the president. In 2003, loveLife's annual $20 million budget was paid for by the South African government, the Kaiser Family Foundation, UNICEF, the Bill and Melinda Gates Foundation, and the Global Fund to Fight AIDS, Tuberculosis, and Malaria. At least South Africa's leaders were beginning to take AIDS seriously, I thought, but what kind of program was this?

"What we want to do is create a substantive, normative shift in the way young people behave," explained loveLife's director, David Harrison, a white South African doctor, when I met him in his Johannesburg office. The average age at which young South Africans lose their virginity—around seventeen—is not much different from the age at which teenagers in other countries do. What's different, Harrison said, was that many of the young South Africans who were sexually active were very sexually active. They were more likely to start having sex at very young ages, even below the age of fourteen—well below the national average. Those vulnerable young people were more likely to have more than one sexual partner, and they were less likely to use condoms. South African girls were more likely to face sexual coercion or rape, or to exchange sex for money or gifts, all of which placed them at greater risk of HIV infection. For Harrison, the trick was to "get inside the head-space of these young people . . . we have to understand what is driving them into sex—they know what HIV is, but they don't internalize it," he said.

LoveLife's aim was to get young people talking, to each other and to their parents, so they would really understand and act on what they knew. But to reach out to them, you had to use a special language that young people could relate to. According to Harrison, traditional HIV prevention campaigns were too depressing: They tried to scare people into changing their behavior, and this turned kids off. LoveLife's media campaign, on the other hand, was positive and cheerful, and resembled the bright, persuasive modern ad campaigns that many South African kids were very much attracted to.

In the past couple of years, nearly a thousand loveLife billboards had sprouted all along the nation's main roads. They were striking. For example, on one of them, the hands of four women of different races caressed the sculpted back and buttocks of a young black man as though they were appraising an antique newel post. The caption read, "Everyone he's slept with, is sleeping with you." On another, a gorgeous mixed-race couple—the boy looked like Brad Pitt, the girl like an Indian film star—lay in bed, under the caption "No Pressure." Some people told me they found these ads oversexualized and disturbing, but it is hard to see why. On the same roads, there are torsos advertising sexy underwear and half-naked actresses advertising romantic movies. Sex is a potent theme in marketing all sorts of products; loveLife, according to its creators, tries to turn that message around to get young people thinking and talking about sex in more responsible ways and convince them of the virtues of abstinence, fidelity, and the use of condoms.

Harrison calls loveLife "a brand of positive lifestyle." The sexy billboards and similar ads on TV and radio, as well as newspaper inserts that resemble teen gossip magazines, with articles and advice columns about clothes, relationships, and sexual health, were designed, Harrison says, to persuade young people to avoid sex in the same way a sneaker ad tries to seduce them into buying new sneakers, because the players in the ads look so cool. The idea is "to create a brand so strong that young people who want to be hip and cool and the rest of it want to associate with it," Harrison told an interviewer in 2001.[3]

The concept of a "lifestyle brand" originated with the rise of brand advertising in the 1960s, when ads for such products as Pepsi-Cola and Harley-Davidson began to promote not only soft drinks and motorcycles, but also a certain style or aesthetic. People were urged to "join the Pepsi generation" or ride a Harley-Davidson not just to get around, but to embrace a certain attitude. A Harley wasn't just a bike; it was a macho rebellion, an escape from the workaday world to the open road. In the 1970s, family-planning programs also tried to promote contraceptives in developing countries by tapping into poor people's

> **Harrison calls loveLife "a brand of positive lifestyle."**

aspirations for a glamorous Western lifestyle. Campaigns depicted small, well-dressed families surrounded by sleek new commodities, including televisions and cars. Harrison predicted that young South Africans would readily respond to this approach too.

"Kids have changed," Harrison explained. Today's young South Africans weren't like the activists who risked their lives in the anti-apartheid demonstrations at Sharpeville and Soweto. "Seventy-five percent of South African teenagers watch TV every day," Harrison informed me. "Their favorite program is *The Bold and the Beautiful*"—an American soap opera in which glamorous characters struggle with personal crises while wearing and driving some very expensive gear. "They are exposed to the global youth culture of music, fashion, pop icons, and commercial brands. They talk about brands among themselves, even if they can't afford everything they see."

The Kaiser Foundation's Michael Sinclair told me that loveLife drew much of its inspiration from the marketing campaign for the soft drink Sprite.[4] In the mid-1990s, sales of Sprite were flagging until the company began an aggressive campaign to embed Sprite in youth culture by sponsoring hip-hop concerts and planting attractive, popular kids in Internet chat rooms or college dormitories and paying them to praise or distribute Sprite in an unobtrusive way. Sprite is now one of the most profitable drinks in the world because it managed to exploit what marketing experts call "the cool effect"—meaning the influence that a small number of opinion leaders can have on the norms and behavior of large numbers of their peers. So far, corporate marketers had made the greatest use of the cool effect, but there was speculation that small numbers of trendsetters could change more complex behavior than shopping, such as criminality, suicide, and sexual behavior.[5]

For this reason, loveLife had established a small network of recreation centers for young people, known as Y-Centers, throughout the country. At Y-Centers, young people could learn to play basketball, volleyball, and other sports, as well as learn break dancing, radio broadcasting, and word processing. All Y-Center activities were led by "loveLife GroundBreakers"—older youths, usually in their early twenties, who, like the kids who made Sprite cool, were stylish and cheerful and enthusiastic about their product, in this case, loveLife and its program to encourage safer sexual behavior. If abstinence, monogamy, and condoms all happened to fail, each Y-Center was affiliated with a family-planning clinic that offered contraceptives and treatment for sexually transmitted diseases such as syphilis and gonorrhea. The centers offered no treatment for AIDS symptoms, however, and when I visited, none of them offered HIV testing either.

Any young person could become a Y-Center member, but in order to fully participate in its activities, he or she had to complete a program of seminars about HIV, family planning, and other subjects related to sexuality and growing up. The seminars emphasized the biological aspects of HIV and its prevention, but not the experience of the disease and its effects on people's lives. Members also received training to raise their self-esteem, because, as Harrison told an interviewer in 2001,

> there is a direct correlation between young people's sexual behavior and their sense of confidence in the future. Those young people who feel motivated, who feel that they have something to look forward to—they are the ones who protect themselves, who ensure that they do not get HIV/AIDS. . . . It's all about the social discount rates that young people apply to future benefits.[6]

Dr. Harrison arranged for me to visit a loveLife Y-Center in the archipelago of townships in the flat scrubland south of Johannesburg known as the Vaal Triangle. Millions of people live in these townships, many of them recent migrants from rural South Africa or from neighboring countries. The Vaal, once a patchwork of white-owned farms, is now a residential area for poor blacks. At first, only a few families moved here, because the apartheid government used the notorious pass laws to restrict the tide of impoverished blacks seeking a better life in Johannesburg. But when the apartheid laws were scrapped, people poured in. Today, the roads and other services in the area are insufficient for its huge and growing population, and many people have no electricity and lack easy access to clean water and sanitation. Unemployment exceeds 70 percent and the crime rate is one of the highest in South Africa.[7]

The loveLife Y-Center was a compound of two small lavender buildings surrounded by an iron fence and curling razor wire. Inside the compound, a group of young men in shorts and T-shirts were doing warm-up exercises on the outdoor basketball court, while girls and barefoot children looked on. Inside the main building, another group of boys in fashionably droopy jeans and dreadlocks practiced a hip-hop routine, and two girls in the computer room experimented with Microsoft Word.

Valentine's Day was coming up, and the Y-Center had organized a group discussion for some of its members. About thirty teenagers, most of them in school uniforms, sat around on the floor of a large seminar room and argued about who should pay for what on a Valentine's Day date. A GroundBreaker in a loveLife T-shirt and with a loveLife kerchief tied pirate-style on her head officiated. "I go with my chick and I spend money on her and always we have sex," said a husky boy in a gray school uniform. "And I want to know, what's the difference between my chick and a prostitute?" As we have seen, long-term transactional relationships — in which money or gifts are frequently exchanged — may not be the same as prostitution, but they nevertheless put many township youths at risk of HIV.[8]

"Boys, they are expecting too much from us. They say we are parasites if we don't sleep with them," said a plump girl in the uniform of a local Catholic school.

"The girls, they ask for a lot of things," another boy chimed in.

"Me, I think it is wrong. If most of the boys think Valentine's Day is about buying sex, the boys must stop," a girl said. "We girls must hold our ground."

These young people were certainly talking openly about sexual relationships all right, just as Harrison prescribed. Nevertheless, I felt something was missing. "Do you ever talk about AIDS in those discussion groups?" I asked the GroundBreaker afterward. "We do it indirectly," she replied. "We know that if we just came out and started lecturing them about AIDS, they wouldn't listen. They would just turn off. So we talk about positive things, like making informed choices, sharing responsibility, and positive sexuality." 20

Was this true? Do young people in South Africa, like their politicians, really want to avoid the subject of AIDS? I wanted to meet young people outside the Y-Center and ask them what they thought about that. A few hundred yards away from the Y-Center stood the headquarters of St. Charles Lwanga, a Catholic organization that carries out a number of activities in the township. Their AIDS program, called Inkanyezi, meaning "star" in Zulu, provides counseling to young people about AIDS and also brings food and other necessities to some four hundred orphans and people living with AIDS in the Vaal.

St. Charles Lwanga was independent of loveLife, and its budget was modest, less than a tenth of what loveLife spent on its billboards alone. The Inkanyezi program was staffed almost entirely by volunteers, whose only compensation was that they were allowed to eat some of the food — usually rice and vegetables — that they prepared for the patients. Lack of funding greatly limited the help that Inkanyezi was able to provide. Although Inkanyezi nurses were able to dispense tuberculosis medicine, antiretroviral drugs were as yet unavailable. Indeed, many of the patients they visited lacked some of the most basic necessities for life and human dignity. Sometimes destitute patients had their water and electricity cut off. But the worst thing was that many of the patients were socially isolated and lived alone in flimsy shacks. The doors were easily broken down and at night neighborhood thugs sometimes came in and stole what little they had. Sometimes the patients were raped.

Justice Showalala, who ran Inkanyezi, organized a meeting for me with a group of about twenty-five young people from Orange Farm. The HIV rate in the area was not known, but several people explained to me how their lives had been changed by the virus. They said they had witnessed extreme prejudice and discrimination against people with AIDS, and they did not know where to turn when they learned that a relative or friend was HIV positive. "People say you shouldn't touch someone with HIV," said one girl. "I have a friend at school who disclosed she has HIV, and the others won't even walk with her." Justice explained how he had offered to introduce some teachers from a local school to some of his HIV-positive clients. "They said, 'If you want me to meet people with AIDS, you better give me a rubber suit.'"

The loveLife Y-Center did little to help young people deal with such confusion, stigma, and shame. "I learned basketball at the Y-Center," one girl told me, "and at meetings we talked about resisting peer pressure, [like when] your friends advise you to break your virginity, to prove you are girl enough. But I was afraid the people there would find out my sister had HIV. We talked about it as though it was someone else's problem."

In general, although sex was openly discussed at the Y-Center, the experience of AIDS was not. The Y-Center offered individual counseling for a small number of young people with HIV, but those who were hungry, homeless, or destitute, or were suffering from the symptoms of AIDS, were told to consult other organizations, including Inkanyezi. 25

It turns out that talking about the pain, both physical and emotional, that the disease creates is far more difficult than getting over the embarrassment of talking about sex. "I had heard about HIV before," said an Inkanyezi girl, wearing a bright blue T-shirt and matching headband. "But then I found out my mother was HIV positive. I was so shocked, so shocked. I even talked to my teacher about it. She said it can happen to anyone; it must have been from mistakes my mother made, and that I shouldn't make those mistakes in my own life."

"Sometimes, women have no choice," said the older woman sitting next to the girl in blue. She was thin, with intense dark eyes and a deep, wry smile. She was dressed entirely in black, except for a baseball cap with a red ribbon on it—the universal symbol of solidarity with HIV-positive people. "They get infected because of their husbands, and there's nothing they can do.

"It happened like this," the older woman went on. "It was back when we were living in Soweto, before we moved here. One day my daughter and I were washing clothes together," she said, nodding at the girl in blue. "She said she'd had a dream that I was so sick, that I had cancer and I was going to die. I waited until we were done with the washing, and then I told her that I was HIV positive. She said, 'I knew it, you were always sick and always going to support groups.' She was so down, she just cried all day and all night after that. I told her, 'Only God knows why people have this disease. Don't worry, I won't die right away.'

"Once I visited the loveLife Y-Center," the woman continued, "but I just saw children playing. I sat and talked with them, and they were shocked when I said I was HIV positive. I told them about what it was like, and one of them said she would ask the managers whether I could come and talk to a bigger group. But that was about six months ago and they haven't called me. I haven't moved and my number hasn't changed. I don't know why they haven't called."

"I think there should be more counseling and support groups for people who find out their parents are HIV positive," the girl in blue said. "It puts you down, it really gets to you, it haunts you. When you are standing in class and you have to recite a poem 30 or something, I find I can't get anything out of my mouth. I can't concentrate. [The problem] here is ignorance. I didn't care about HIV until I found out about my mother. Then I started to care about these people. I wish many people in our country would also think like that."

In 2003, the only African country that had seen a nationwide decline in HIV prevalence was Uganda. Since 1992 the HIV rate had fallen by some two-thirds, a success that saved perhaps a million lives. The programs and policies that led to this success [are discussed elsewhere], but the epidemiologists Rand Stoneburner and Daniel Low-Beer have argued that a powerful role was played by the ordinary, but frank, conversations people had with family, friends, and neighbors—not about sex, but about the frightening, calamitous effects of AIDS itself.[9] Stoneburner and Low-Beer maintain that these painful personal conversations did more than anything else to persuade Ugandans to come to terms with the reality of AIDS, care for the afflicted, and change their behavior. This in turn led to declines in HIV transmission. The researchers found that people in other sub-Saharan African countries were far less likely to have such discussions.

In South Africa, people told Stoneburner and Low-Beer that they had heard about the epidemic from posters, radio, newspapers, and clinics, as well as from occasional mass rallies, schools, and village meetings; but they seldom spoke about it with the people they knew. They were also far less likely to admit knowing someone with AIDS or to be willing to care for an AIDS patient. It may be no coincidence that the HIV rate in South Africa rose higher than it ever did in Uganda, and has taken far longer to fall.

When I was in Uganda during the early 1990s, the HIV rate was already falling, and I vividly recall how the reality of AIDS was alive in people's minds. Kampala taxi drivers talked as passionately about AIDS as taxi drivers elsewhere discuss politics or football. And they talked about it in a way that would seem foreign to many in South Africa because it was so personal: "my sister," "my father," "my neighbor," "my friend."[10]

Ugandans are not unusually compassionate people, and discrimination against people with AIDS persists in some families and institutions. But Ugandans do seem more willing to openly address painful issues in their lives. This courage owes much to the AIDS information campaigns launched by the government of Uganda early on in the epidemic. But it may have other sources as well. Maybe the difference between the ways South Africa and Uganda have dealt with AIDS has historical roots. Both South Africa and Uganda have bitter histories of conflict. But while Uganda was terrorized for decades by a series of brutal leaders, they could not destroy the traditional rhythms of rural family life. Uganda is one of the most fertile countries in Africa; there is enough land for everyone, and most people live as their ancestors did, as peasant farmers and herders. No large settler population displaced huge numbers of people or set up a system to exploit and humiliate them, as happened in South Africa and in many other African countries. This means Ugandans are more likely to know their neighbors and to live near members of their extended families. This in turn may have contributed to what sociologists call "social cohesion"—the tendency of people to talk openly with one another and form trusted relationships. Perhaps this may have facilitated more realistic and open discussion of AIDS, more compassionate attitudes toward infected people, and pragmatic behavior change.

Perhaps many attempts to prevent the spread of HIV fail because those in charge   35
of them don't recognize that the decisions people make about sex are usually a matter
of feeling, not calculation. In other words, sexual behavior is determined less by what
Dr. Harrison called "discount rates" that young people "apply to future benefits" than
by emotional attachments. I thought of the South African girls who said they had lost
a sister or a friend to AIDS. If one of them was faced with a persistent, wealthy seducer,
what would be more likely to persuade her to decline? The memory of a loveLife billboard, with its flashy, beautiful models? Or the memory of a person she had known who
had died?

On the morning before I left South Africa, I attended a loveLife motivational seminar at
a school not far from Orange Farm. "These seminars help young people see the future,
identify choices, and identify the values that underpin those choices," Harrison had
told me. "We help them ask themselves, 'What can you do to chart life's journey and
control it as much as possible?'" The seminars were based on Success by Choice, a series
devised by Marlon Smith, a California-based African-American motivational speaker.
How was Mr. Smith's message of personal empowerment translated to South Africa,
I wondered, where children have to contend with poverty, the risk of being robbed or
raped, and a grim future of likely unemployment?

About twenty-five children aged ten to fourteen were in the class, and the Ground-
Breaker asked them to hold their hands out in front of them, pretend they were looking
in a mirror, and repeat the following words:

"You are intelligent!"
"You are gifted!"
"There is no one in the world like you!"   40
"I love you!"

The children spoke quietly at first, then louder, as though they were being hypno-
tized. The GroundBreaker urged them to talk more openly with their parents, to keep
themselves clean, and to make positive choices in their lives, especially when it came
to sexuality. There was little mention of helping other people, nor was there much advice about how to avoid being raped or harassed by other students as well as teachers,
relatives, or strangers, or how to plan a future in a country where unemployment for
township blacks was so high.

Then something really odd occurred. One of the GroundBreakers asked the children to stand up because it was time for an "Icebreaker." "This is a little song-and-dance
thing we do, to give the children a chance to stretch. It improves their concentration,"
another GroundBreaker told me. The words of the song were as follows:

Pizza Hut
Pizza Hut
Kentucky Fried Chicken and a Pizza Hut
McDonald's
McDonald's
Kentucky Fried Chicken and a Pizza Hut.

In the dance, the children spread their arms out as though they were rolling out a
pizza, or flapped their elbows like chickens.

What kinds of choices was Dr. Harrison really referring to? I wondered. The techniques of marketing attempt to impose scientific principles on human choices. But it seemed a mad experiment to see whether teenagers living through very difficult times could be persuaded to choose a new sexual lifestyle as they might choose a new brand of shampoo, or whether children could be trained to associate safe sex with pizza and self-esteem.

Afterward, I spoke to some of the children who had participated in the seminar. They all knew how to protect themselves from HIV, and they were eager to show off their knowledge about condoms, abstinence, and fidelity within relationships. But they all said they didn't personally know anyone with AIDS; nor did they know of any children who had lost parents to AIDS. They did mention Nkosi Johnson, the brave HIV-positive twelve-year-old boy who became world-famous in 2000 when he stood up at an International Conference on AIDS and challenged the South African president, Thabo Mbeki, to do more for people living with the virus.

In fact, their principal would tell me later, more than twenty children at the school were AIDS orphans, and many more had been forced to drop out because there was no one to pay their expenses after their parents died. The children I spoke to seemed not to know why some of their classmates wore ragged uniforms or had no shoes or stopped showing up at all.

The week before, I had met some teenage girls in Soweto and I had asked them the same question. They answered in the same way: The only person they knew with AIDS was Nkosi Johnson, the famous boy at the AIDS conference. Just as Harrison had warned me, these girls said they were tired of hearing about AIDS. The girls were orphans, although they said their parents had not died of AIDS. I later discovered that, in another part of that same orphanage, there was a nursery where thirty babies and small children, all of them HIV positive, all abandoned by their parents, lay on cots or sat quietly on the floor, struggling for life. No wonder those girls were tired of hearing about HIV. It was right in their midst, within earshot, but the world around them was telling them to look the other way.

A couple of years later, I would meet a group of primary-school students in Kigali, Rwanda. By then, the HIV infection rate in Rwanda had fallen steeply, just as it had in Uganda years earlier. The school was a typical single-story line of classrooms in one of the poorest sections of Kigali. I spoke to the principal first, and he showed me the government-issued manual used for teaching about AIDS, which contained the usual information about abstinence and condoms. The school day had just ended, and he went outside and asked a few students to stay behind and chat with me.[11]

The Rwandan students had no idea in advance what I wanted to talk to them about. But when I asked them the same question I had asked the South African children, "Do you know anyone with AIDS?" their answers floored me. Every one of them had a story about someone they knew who was HIV positive or suffering from AIDS. "I knew a man who had bad lips [sores] and tears all over his skin," said a fourteen-year-old boy. "People stigmatized him and he died because no one was caring for him." Another boy described a woman who was "so thin, she almost died." But then her relatives took her to the hospital, where she was given AIDS treatment. "She got better because people cared for her," he said.

When I asked the Rwandan children whether they had any questions for me, all they wanted to know was what they could do to help people with AIDS. The responses of the South African children were strikingly different. When I asked them if they had questions for me, they quickly changed the subject from AIDS and asked me what America was like and whether I knew any of the pop stars they admired on TV.

The persistent denial of AIDS in South Africa was deeply disturbing. People liked the colorful, frank advertising and the basketball games sponsored by loveLife. But its programs seemed to me to reinforce the denial that posed so many obstacles to preventing HIV in the first place. In 2005, the Global Fund to Fight AIDS, Tuberculosis, and Malaria would come to similar conclusions and terminate its multimillion-dollar grant to loveLife.[12]

> **The persistent denial of AIDS in South Africa was deeply disturbing.**

Epidemiologists are equivocal about whether loveLife had any effect on HIV transmission in South Africa, but during the program's first seven years, HIV infection rates continued to rise steadily.[13]

A more realistic HIV prevention program would have paid less attention to aspirations and dreams unattainable for so many young people, and greater attention to the real circumstances in people's lives that make it hard for them to avoid infection. It would also have been more frank about the real human consequences of the disease. But that would have meant dealing with some very painful matters that South Africa's policy-makers seemed determined to evade.

It was heartening that Western donors were now spending so much money on AIDS programs in Africa. But the problem with some large foreign-aid programs was that distributing the funds often involved negotiating with governments with a poor record of dealing with AIDS. In addition, the huge sums of money involved were often very difficult to manage, so that small community-based groups that need thousands of dollars, rather than millions—like Inkanyezi in Orange Farm—were often overlooked in favor of overly ambitious megaprojects, whose effectiveness had not been demonstrated and whose premises were open to question. It seemed clear to me that more could be learned from Inkanyezi's attempt to help people deal with the reality of AIDS than from loveLife's attempt to create a new consumerist man and woman for South Africa.

NOTES

1. Helen Schneider, "On the fault-line: The politics of AIDS policy in contemporary South Africa," *Afr Stud* 61:1 (July 1, 2002), 145–67; Samantha Power, "The AIDS Rebel," *New Yorker*, May 19, 2003, pp. 54–67.
2. Rob Dorrington et al., "The Impact of HIV/AIDS on Adult Mortality in South Africa" (Cape Town: Burden of Disease Research Unit, Medical Research Council of South Africa, September 2001); "Mortality and causes of death in South Africa, 2003 and 2004," Statistics South Africa, May 2006.
3. Richard Delate, "The Struggle for Meaning: A Semiotic Analysis of Interpretations of the loveLife His&Hers Billboard Campaign," November 2001, http://www.comminit.com/stlovelife/sld-4389.html.

4. Personal communication, February 2003.
5. For more about this, see Malcolm Gladwell, *The Tipping Point* (Boston: Little, Brown, 2000), and Everett Rogers, *Diffusion of Innovations* (New York: Free Press, 1983).
6. Delate, "Struggle for Meaning."
7. See Prishani Naidoo, "Youth Divided: A Review of loveLife's Y-Centre in Orange Farm" (Johannesburg: CADRE Report, 2003).
8. Nancy Luke and Kathleen M. Kurtz, "Cross-Generational and Transactional Sexual Relations in Sub-Saharan Africa: Prevalence of Behavior and Implications for Negotiating Safer Sexual Practices," International Center for Research on Women, 2002, http://www.icrw.org/docs/CrossGenSex_ Report_902.pdf; J. Swart-Kruger and L. M. Richter, "AIDS-related knowledge, attitudes and behaviour among South African street youth: Reflections on power, sexuality and the autonomous self," *Soc Sci Med* 45:6 (1997), 957–66; Editorial, "Reassessing priorities: Identifying the determinants of HIV transmission," *Soc Sci Med* 36:5 (1993), iii–viii.
9. Daniel Low-Beer and Rand Stoneburner, "Uganda and the Challenge of AIDS," in *The Political Economy of AIDS in Africa*, eds. Nana Poku and Alan Whiteside (London: Ashgate, 2004).
10. See Helen Epstein, "Fat," *Granta* 49 (1995). Low-Beer and Stoneburner make this observation, too, as do Janice Hogle et al. in *What Happened in Uganda? Declining HIV Prevalence, Behavior Change and the National Response* (USAID, 2002).
11. In 2006, the *Washington Post* reported that the HIV infection rate in Rwanda, once estimated to be 15 percent, was now estimated to be 3 percent. See Craig Timberg, "How AIDS in Africa Was Overstated: Reliance on Data from Urban Prenatal Clinics Skewed Early Projections," *Washington Post*, April 6, 2006, p. A1. Timberg attributed the downward revision to a new U.S. government survey and suggested that the earlier estimate, issued by the UNAIDS program, had been inflated, perhaps to raise money or appease AIDS activists. Although the old UNAIDS statistics were in need of correction, there clearly had been a decline in the true infection rate. A population-based survey carried out in Rwanda in 1986 found that prevalence was 17.8 percent in urban areas and 1.3 percent in rural areas. (Rwandan HIV Seroprevalence Study Group, "Nationwide community-based serological survey of HIV-1 and other human retrovirus infections in a country," *Lancet* 1 (ii) (1989), 941–43.
12. A. E. Pettifor et al., "Young people's sexual health in South Africa: HIV prevalence and sexual behaviors from a nationally representative household survey," *AIDS* 19:14 (September 23, 2005), 1525–34; but see R. Jewkes, "Response to Pettifor et al.," *AIDS* 20:6 (April 4, 2006), 952–53; author reply, 956–58; and W. M. Parker and M. Colvin, "Response to Pettifor et al.," *AIDS* 20:6 (April 4, 2006), 954–55.
13. In 2005, an article in the prestigious medical journal *AIDS* reported that young people who had attended at least one loveLife program were slightly, but significantly, less likely to be HIV positive than those who had not. The author argued that this was consistent with the possibility that loveLife reduced risky sexual behavior. However, there could well be another explanation. From what I saw, loveLife attracted young people who would have been at lower risk of infection in the first place, either because they were wealthier or better educated or less vulnerable to abuse. (While the loveLife study attempted to control for education and wealth, it did not do so rigorously.) Indeed, the tendency to avoid the subject of AIDS would seem to discourage HIV-positive young people from attending loveLife's programs, and this could make it look as though loveLife protected young people when in fact it merely alienated those most at risk. Most loveLife materials were in English, and thus accessible only to young people with higher social status. This would have sent a clear signal to those—often marginalized

and vulnerable young people—who could not speak English well that loveLife was not for them. The main author of the article reporting lower HIV rates among young people exposed to loveLife admitted to me in an interview that an anthropologist hired by loveLife itself had come to these same conclusions, but her results remain unpublished. See Pettifor et al., "A community-based study to examine the effect of a youth HIV prevention intervention on young people aged 15–24 in South Africa: results of the baseline survey," *Trop Med Int Health* 10:10 (October 2005), 971–80; but see also Jewkes, "Response to Pettifor et al.," author reply, and Parker and Colvin, "Response to Pettifor." Information re the loveLife anthropologist from Pettifor, personal communication, April 2006.

Exploring Context

1. The (PRODUCT) RED campaign (joinred.com) pairs popular products with fund-raising in the fight against AIDS in Africa. Explore the (PRODUCT) RED website. Given Epstein's argument, how successful might this campaign be? How does your work with lifestyle brands from Question 1 of Questions for Critical Reading inform your answer?

2. Use the Web to locate information on current HIV infection rates in Africa. Has the situation improved since Epstein wrote her essay, or is it continuing to get worse? What might account for this trend, given Epstein's argument?

3. One of Epstein's central arguments is the usefulness of conversation in combating HIV infection in Africa. How might social networking technologies like Facebook or Twitter help in such a campaign?

Questions for Connecting

1. Leslie Savan, in "What's Black, Then White, and Said All Over?" (p. 435), explores the role of black talk in mainstream advertising. How do her arguments help explain the loveLife campaign that Epstein examines? According to Savan and Epstein, what are the limits of advertising? What role does race play in the production of cultural change? You may want to draw on your work on lifestyle brands from Question 1 of Questions for Critical Reading.

2. What role should religion play in HIV education in Africa and elsewhere? Use Madeleine Albright's arguments in "Faith and Diplomacy" (p. 35) to determine the best functions of religion in HIV prevention campaigns. You may want to use your work imagining a prevention program from Question 3 of Questions for Critical Reading in composing your response. Should faith be a determining factor when lives are at stake? Would taking religion into account produce better prevention campaigns? What do Epstein's experiences in Uganda and South Africa suggest?

3. Kenji Yoshino, in "Preface" and "The New Civil Rights" (p. 552), suggests that conversation has an important role to play in producing change around civil rights. How does Epstein's argument confirm or complicate Yoshino's ideas? What makes conversation useful in producing social change?

Language Matters

1. Periods are important marks of punctuation, denoting the units of meaning we call sentences. Select a key passage from Epstein's text and type it into a word processor without any capital letters or periods. In class, trade these never-ending sentences and work on replacing the missing punctuation marks. How can you tell when a period is needed in Epstein's text? How can you tell when one is needed in your own text?

2. Outlines can be helpful in creating organization before we start writing, but they can also help us see the organization of any existing piece of writing. Create an outline of Epstein's piece, using a one-sentence summary of each major move of her argument. What sections do you see in her essay? How do they relate to each other? How can you use postdraft outlines of your own papers to check your organization as you revise?

3. Because it is sexually transmitted, AIDS/HIV is a delicate issue for many people. What sort of tone and language does Epstein use to discuss the disease and its transmission? How do her choices reflect both her audience and the delicacy of the subject matter? When would you make similar choices in your own writing?

Assignments for Writing

1. Epstein explores the way children and families address the AIDS crisis in Africa. In a short paper, examine the generational response to HIV/AIDS using Epstein's essay. Here are some questions to help your critical thinking: How do adults handle the discussion of AIDS? Is this separate from the discussion of other sexually transmitted diseases? How do children and young adults handle this topic? How do *you* handle it? You might want to draw on your work on social cohesion from Question 2 of Questions for Critical Reading or your analysis of conversation's potential for combating HIV from Question 3 of Exploring Context.

2. Epstein evaluates a number of approaches to HIV prevention, both formal and informal campaigns. Write a paper in which you assess the role of government in the prevention of diseases like HIV. Consider: What should the role of the government be in addressing the HIV/AIDS crisis? Both loveLife and Inkanyezi are private organizations that address sexually transmitted diseases and HIV/AIDS; should there be a similar government outreach program? What role would that program play? Are ordinary people better at preventing disease? How can a government promote the kind of strategies that were effective in Uganda?

3. South Africa's loveLife relies heavily on an advertising campaign. Write an essay in which you evaluate the role of commercial culture in addressing national crises such as HIV/AIDS. What role should companies and advertisers take upon themselves? How does that differ from what they appear to do? Are they really just out for profit, or do companies have a conscience? Should or can they act on issues that affect national health? You might want to reference your work on PRODUCT (RED) from Question 1 in Exploring Context in making your argument.

THOMAS L. FRIEDMAN

Journalist and author **Thomas L. Friedman** holds a B.A. in Mediterranean studies from Brandeis University and an M.A. in Middle Eastern studies from Oxford University. Friedman joined the *New York Times* in 1981 and has won three Pulitzer Prizes since. His foreign affairs column appears in more than seven hundred newspapers, and his books *From Beirut to Jerusalem* (1989), *The Lexus and the Olive Tree: Understanding Globalization* (1999), *Longitudes and Attitudes: Exploring the World after September 11* (2002), *The World Is Flat: A Brief History of the Twenty-First Century* (2005), and *Hot, Flat, and Crowded: Why We Need a Green Revolution—and How It Can Renew America* (2008) have been national best-sellers.

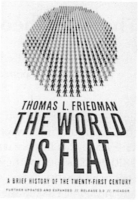

THOMAS L. FRIEDMAN

THE WORLD IS FLAT

A BRIEF HISTORY OF THE TWENTY-FIRST CENTURY

FURTHER UPDATED AND EXPANDED // RELEASE 3.0 // PICADOR

The World Is Flat examines the impact of the "flattening" of the globe, an international leveling of business competition enabled by increasing interconnectedness. Friedman argues that globalized trade, outsourcing, offshoring, supply-chaining, and six other economic, technological, and political forces have changed the world permanently. He examines the positive and negative effects flattening has had and will continue to have on global politics and business.

In "The Dell Theory of Conflict Prevention," which is the penultimate chapter in *The World Is Flat*, Friedman explores the future of war in a globalized economy. Updating a concept he first introduced in *The Lexus and the Olive Tree*—the "Golden Arches Theory of Conflict Prevention," which suggested that citizens in societies economically developed enough to support a McDonald's lose interest in fighting wars—Friedman proposes with the "Dell Theory of Conflict Prevention" that countries will hesitate to risk their place in the global supply chain by fighting a nonessential war. He warns, though, that his new theory does not apply to every kind of modern threat, for terrorists, too, have learned how to use global supply chains.

According to Friedman, the flat world will have an impact on you directly as you compete for work with others around the world. This new business environment presents tremendous opportunities for us all; but what are the geopolitical consequences of this new economic reality, and will those consequences generate peace or more conflict?

▶ TAGS: *globalization, collaboration, economics, politics, supply chains, knowledge*

Questions for Critical Reading

1. Much of Friedman's focus in this chapter is on collaboration. What role do you imagine collaboration plays in economic systems of production? Do you think it also plays a role

in terrorism? As you read Friedman's text, look for quotations that confirm or challenge your initial thoughts.

2. What is the Dell Theory of Conflict Prevention? As you read Friedman's text, locate a quotation that defines this concept. Can you offer any examples from current events that show the Dell Theory's success or failure in relation to conflicts around the world?

3. Friedman discusses mutant supply chains. As you read his text, take note of the reasons they can be so successful and thus so dangerous. Locate passages from Friedman that support your answer.

The Dell Theory of Conflict Prevention

Free Trade is God's diplomacy. There is no other certain way of uniting people in the bonds of peace.

—BRITISH POLITICIAN RICHARD COBDEN, 1857

Before I share with you the subject of this chapter, I have to tell you a little bit about the computer that I wrote this book on. It's related to the theme I am about to discuss. This book was largely written on a Dell Inspiron 600m notebook, service tag number 9ZRJP41. As part of the research for this book, I visited with the management team at Dell near Austin, Texas. I shared with them the ideas in this book and in return I asked for one favor: I asked them to trace for me the entire global supply chain that produced my Dell notebook. Here is their report:

My computer was conceived when I phoned Dell's 800 number on April 2, 2004, and was connected to sales representative Mujteba Naqvi, who immediately entered my order into Dell's order management system. He typed in both the type of notebook I ordered as well as the special features I wanted, along with my personal information, shipping address, billing address, and credit card information. My credit card was verified by Dell through its work flow connection with Visa, and my order was then released to Dell's production system. Dell has six factories around the world—in Limerick, Ireland; Xiamen, China; Eldorado do Sul, Brazil; Nashville, Tennessee; Austin, Texas; and Penang, Malaysia. My order went out by e-mail to the Dell notebook factory in Malaysia, where the parts for the computer were immediately ordered from the supplier logistics centers (SLCs) next to the Penang factory. Surrounding every Dell factory in the world are these supplier logistics centers, owned by the different suppliers of Dell parts. These SLCs are like staging areas. If you are a Dell supplier anywhere in the world, your job is to keep your SLC full of your specific parts so they can constantly be trucked over to the Dell factory for just-in-time manufacturing.

"In an average day, we sell 140,000 to 150,000 computers," explained Dick Hunter, one of Dell's three global production managers. "Those orders come in over Dell.com or over the telephone. As soon as these orders come in, our suppliers know about it. They get a signal based on every component in the machine you ordered, so the supplier knows just what he has to deliver. If you are supplying power cords for desktops, you can see minute by minute how many power cords you are going to have to deliver." Every two hours, the Dell factory in Penang sends an e-mail to the various

SLCs nearby, telling each one what parts and what quantities of those parts it wants delivered within the next ninety minutes—and not one minute later. Within ninety minutes, trucks from the various SLCs around Penang pull up to the Dell manufacturing plant and unload the parts needed for all those notebooks ordered in the last two hours. This goes on all day, every two hours. As soon as those parts arrive at the factory, it takes thirty minutes for Dell employees to unload the parts, register their bar codes, and put them into the bins for assembly. "We know where every part in every SLC is in the Dell system at all times," said Hunter.

So where did the parts for my notebook come from? I asked Hunter. To begin with, he said, the notebook was codesigned in Austin, Texas, and in Taiwan by a team of Dell engineers and a team of Taiwanese notebook designers. "The customer's needs, required technologies, and Dell's design innovations were all determined by Dell through our direct relationship with customers," he explained. "The basic design of the motherboard and case—the basic functionality of your machine—was designed to those specifications by an ODM [original design manufacturer] in Taiwan. We put our engineers in their facilities and they come to Austin and we actually codesign these systems. This global teamwork brings an added benefit—a globally distributed virtually twenty-four-hour-per-day development cycle. Our partners do the basic electronics and we help them design customer and reliability features that we know our customers want. We know the customers better than our suppliers and our competition, because we are dealing directly with them every day." Dell notebooks are completely redesigned roughly every twelve months, but new features are constantly added during the year—through the supply chain—as the hardware and software components advance.

It happened that when my notebook order hit the Dell factory in Penang, one part was not available—the wireless card—due to a quality control issue, so the assembly of the notebook was delayed for a few days. Then the truck full of good wireless cards arrived. On April 13, at 10:15 AM, a Dell Malaysia worker pulled the order slip that automatically popped up once all my parts had arrived from the SLCs to the Penang factory. Another Dell Malaysia employee then took out a "traveler"—a special carrying tote designed to hold and protect parts—and started plucking all the parts that went into my notebook.

> **This supply chain symphony . . . is one of the wonders of the flat world.**

Where did those parts come from? Dell uses multiple suppliers for most of the thirty key components that go into its notebooks. That way if one supplier breaks down or cannot meet a surge in demand, Dell is not left in the lurch. So here are the key suppliers for my Inspiron 600m notebook: The Intel microprocessor came from an Intel factory either in the Philippines, Costa Rica, Malaysia, or China. The memory came from a Korean-owned factory in Korea (Samsung), a Taiwanese-owned factory in Taiwan (Nanya), a German-owned factory in Germany (Infineon), or a Japanese-owned factory in Japan (Elpida). My graphics card was shipped from either a Taiwanese-owned factory in China (MSI) or a Chinese-run factory in China (Foxconn). The cooling fan came from a Taiwanese-owned factory in Taiwan (CCI or Auras). The motherboard came from either a Korean-owned factory in Shanghai (Samsung), a Taiwanese-owned factory in Shanghai (Quanta), or a Taiwanese-owned factory in Taiwan (Compal or Wistron). The keyboard came from either a Japanese-owned company in Tianjin, China

(Alps), a Taiwanese-owned factory in Shenzen, China (Sunrex), or a Taiwanese-owned factory in Suzhou, China (Darfon). The LCD display was made in either South Korea (Samsung or LG.Philips LCD), Japan (Toshiba or Sharp), or Taiwan (Chi Mei Optoelectronics, Hannstar Display, or AU Optronics). The wireless card came from either an American-owned factory in China (Agere) or Malaysia (Arrow), or a Taiwanese-owned factory in Taiwan (Askey or Gemtek) or China (USI). The modem was made by either a Taiwanese-owned company in China (Asustek or Liteon) or a Chinese-run company in China (Foxconn). The battery came from an American-owned factory in Malaysia (Motorola), a Japanese-owned factory in Mexico or Malaysia or China (Sanyo), or a South Korean or Taiwanese factory in either of those two countries (SDI or Simplo). The hard disk drive was made by an American-owned factory in Singapore (Seagate), a Japanese-owned company in Thailand (Hitachi or Fujitsu), or a Japanese-owned factory in the Philippines (Toshiba). The CD/DVD drive came from a South Korean–owned company with factories in Indonesia and the Philippines (Samsung); a Japanese-owned factory in China or Malaysia (NEC); a Japanese-owned factory in Indonesia, China, or Malaysia (Teac); or a Japanese-owned factory in China (Sony). The notebook carrying bag was made by either an Irish-owned company in China (Tenba) or an American-owned company in China (Targus, Samsonite, or Pacific Design). The power adapter was made by either a Thai-owned factory in Thailand (Delta) or a Taiwanese, Korean, or American-owned factory in China (Liteon, Samsung, or Mobility). The power cord was made by a British-owned company with factories in China, Malaysia, and India (Volex). The removable memory stick was made by either an Israeli-owned company in Israel (M-System) or an American-owned company with a factory in Malaysia (Smart Modular).

This supply chain symphony—from my order over the phone to production to delivery to my house—is one of the wonders of the flat world.

"We have to do a lot of collaborating," said Hunter. "Michael [Dell] personally knows the CEOs of these companies, and we are constantly working with them on process improvements and real-time demand/supply balancing." Demand shaping goes on constantly, said Hunter. What is "demand shaping"? It works like this: At 10 AM Austin time, Dell discovers that so many customers have ordered notebooks with 40-gigabyte hard drives since the morning that its supply chain will run short in two hours. That signal is automatically relayed to Dell's marketing department and to Dell.com and to all the Dell phone operators taking orders. If you happen to call to place your Dell order at 10:30 AM, the Dell representative will say to you, "Tom, it's your lucky day! For the next hour we are offering 60-gigabyte hard drives with the notebook you want—for only $10 more than the 40-gig drive. And if you act now, Dell will throw in a carrying case along with your purchase, because we so value you as a customer." In an hour or two, using such promotions, Dell can reshape the demand for any part of any notebook or desktop to correspond with the projected supply in its global supply chain. Today memory might be on sale, tomorrow it might be CD-ROMs.

Picking up the story of my notebook, on April 13, at 11:29 AM, all the parts had been plucked from the just-in-time inventory bins in Penang, and the computer was assembled there by A. Sathini, a team member "who manually screwed together all of the parts from kitting as well as the labels needed for Tom's system," said Dell in their production report to me. "The system was then sent down the conveyor to go to burn, where Tom's specified software was downloaded." Dell has huge server banks stocked with the latest in Microsoft, Norton Utilities, and other popular software applications, which are downloaded into each new computer according to the specific tastes of the customer.

"By 2:45 PM, Tom's software had been successfully downloaded, and [was] manu- ally moved to the boxing line. By 4:05 PM, Tom's system [was] placed in protective foam and a shuttle box, with a label, which contains his order number, tracking code, system type, and shipping code. By 6:04 PM, Tom's system had been loaded on a pallet with a specified manifest, which gives the Merge facility visibility to when the system will arrive, what pallet it will be on (out of 75+ pallets with 152 systems per pallet), and to what address Tom's system will ship. By 6:26 PM, Tom's system left [the Dell factory] to head to the Penang, Malaysia, airport."

Six days a week Dell charters a China Airlines 747 out of Taiwan and flies it from Penang to Nashville via Taipei. Each 747 leaves with twenty-five thousand Dell note-books that weigh altogether 110,000 kilograms, or 242,500 pounds. It is the only 747 that ever lands in Nashville, except Air Force One, when the president visits. "By April 15, 2004, at 7:41 AM, Tom's system arrived at [Nashville] with other Dell systems from Penang and Limerick. By 11:58 AM, Tom's system [was] inserted into a larger box, which went down the boxing line to the specific external parts that Tom had ordered."

That was thirteen days after I'd ordered it. Had there not been a parts delay in Ma-laysia when my order first arrived, the time between when I phoned in my purchase, when the notebook was assembled in Penang, and its arrival in Nashville would have been only four days. Hunter said the total supply chain for my computer, including sup-pliers of suppliers, involved about four hundred companies in North America, Europe, and primarily Asia, but with thirty key players. Somehow, though, it all came together. As Dell reported: On April 15, 2004, at 12:59 PM, "Tom's system had been shipped from [Nashville] and was tenured by UPS shipping LTL (3–5-day ground, specified by Tom), with UPS tracking number 1Z13WA374253514697. By April 19, 2004, at 6:41 PM, Tom's system arrived in Bethesda, MD, and was signed for."

I am telling you the story of my notebook to tell a larger story of geopolitics in the flat world. To all the forces . . . that are still holding back the flattening of the world, or could actually reverse the process, one has to add a more traditional threat, and that is an outbreak of a good, old-fashioned, world-shaking, economy-destroying war. It could be China deciding once and for all to eliminate Taiwan as an independent state; or North Korea, out of fear or insanity, using one of its nuclear weapons against South Korea or Japan; or Israel and a soon-to-be-nuclear Iran going at each other; or India and Paki-stan finally nuking it out. These and other classic geopolitical conflicts could erupt at any time and either slow the flattening of the world or seriously unflatten it.

The real subject of this chapter is how these classic geopolitical threats might be moderated or influenced by the new forms of collaboration fostered and demanded by the flat world — particularly supply-chaining. The flattening of the world is too young for us to draw any definitive conclusions. What is certain, though, is that as the world flattens, one of the most interesting dramas to watch in international relations will be the interplay between the traditional global threats and the newly emergent global supply chains. The interaction between old-time threats (like China *versus* Taiwan) and just-in-time supply chains (like China *plus* Taiwan) will be a rich source of study for the field of international relations in the early twenty-first century.

In *The Lexus and the Olive Tree* I argued that to the extent that countries tied their   15 economies and futures to global integration and trade, it would act as a restraint on going to war with their neighbors. I first started thinking about this in the late 1990s, when, during my travels, I noticed that no two countries that both had McDonald's had ever fought a war against each other since each got its McDonald's. (Border skirmishes and civil wars don't count, because McDonald's usually served both sides.) After confirming this with McDonald's, I offered what I called the Golden Arches Theory of Conflict Prevention. The Golden Arches Theory stipulated that when a country reached the level of economic development where it had a middle class big enough to support a network of McDonald's, it became a McDonald's country. And people in McDonald's countries didn't like to fight wars anymore. They preferred to wait in line for burgers. While this was offered slightly tongue in cheek, the serious point I was trying to make was that as countries got woven into the fabric of global trade and rising living standards, which having a network of McDonald's franchises had come to symbolize, the cost of war for victor and vanquished became prohibitively high.

This McDonald's theory has held up pretty well, but now that almost every country has acquired a McDonald's, except the worst rogues like North Korea, Iran, and Iraq under Saddam Hussein, it seemed to me that this theory needed updating for the flat world. In that spirit, and again with tongue slightly in cheek, I offer the Dell Theory of Conflict Prevention, the essence of which is that the advent and spread of just-in-time global supply chains in the flat world are an even greater restraint on geopolitical adventurism than the more general rising standard of living that McDonald's symbolized.

The Dell Theory stipulates: No two countries that are both part of a major global supply chain, like Dell's, will ever fight a war against each other as long as they are both part of the same global supply chain. Because people embedded in major global supply chains don't want to fight old-time wars anymore. They want to make just-in-time deliveries of goods and services—and enjoy the rising standards of living that come with that. One of the people with the best feel for the logic behind this theory is Michael Dell, the founder and chairman of Dell.

"These countries understand the risk premium that they have," said Dell of the countries in his Asian supply chain. "They are pretty careful to protect the equity that they have built up or tell us why we should not worry [about their doing anything adventurous]. My belief after visiting China is that the change that has occurred there is in the best interest of the world and China. Once people get a taste for whatever you want to call it—economic independence, a better lifestyle, and a better life for their child or children—they grab on to that and don't want to give it up."

Any sort of war or prolonged political upheaval in East Asia or China "would have a massive chilling effect on the investment there and on all the progress that has been made there," said Dell, who added that he believes the governments in that part of the world understand this very clearly. "We certainly make clear to them that stability is important to us. [Right now] it is not a day-to-day worry for us . . . I believe that as time and progress go on there, the chance for a really disruptive event goes down exponentially. I don't think our industry gets enough credit for the good we are doing in these areas. If you are making money and being productive and raising your standard of living, you're not sitting around thinking, Who did this to us? or Why is our life so bad?"

There is a lot of truth to this. Countries whose workers and industries are woven into a major global supply chain know that they cannot take an hour, a week, or a month off for war without disrupting industries and economies around the world and thereby risking the loss of their place in that supply chain for a long time, which could be extremely costly. For a country with no natural resources, being part of a global supply chain is like striking oil—oil that never runs out. And therefore, getting dropped from such a chain because you start a war is like having your oil wells go dry or having someone pour cement down them. They will not come back anytime soon.

"You are going to pay for it really dearly," said Glenn E. Neland, senior vice president for worldwide procurement at Dell, when I asked him what would happen to a major supply-chain member in Asia that decided to start fighting with its neighbor and disrupt the supply chain. "It will not only bring you to your knees [today], but you will pay for a long time—because you just won't have any credibility if you demonstrate you are going to go [off] the political deep end. And China is just now starting to develop a level of credibility in the business community that it is creating a business environment you can prosper in—with transparent and consistent rules." Neland said that suppliers regularly ask him whether he is worried about China and Taiwan, which have threatened to go to war at several points in the past half century, but his standard response is that he cannot imagine them "doing anything more than flexing muscles with each other." Neland said he can tell in his conversations and dealings with companies and governments in the Dell supply chain, particularly the Chinese, that "they recognize the opportunity and are really hungry to participate in the same things they have seen other countries in Asia do. They know there is a big economic pot at the end of the rainbow and they are really after it. We will spend about $35 billion producing parts this year, and 30 percent of that is [in] China."

If you follow the evolution of supply chains, added Neland, you see the prosperity and stability they promoted first in Japan, and then in Korea and Taiwan, and now in Malaysia, Singapore, the Philippines, Thailand, and Indonesia. Once countries get embedded in these global supply chains, "they feel part of something much bigger than their own businesses," he said. Osamu Watanabe, the CEO of the Japan External Trade Organization (JETRO), was explaining to me one afternoon in Tokyo how Japanese companies were moving vast amounts of low- and middle-range technical work and manufacturing to China, doing the basic fabrication there, and then bringing it back to Japan for final assembly. Japan was doing this despite a bitter legacy of mistrust between the two countries, which was intensified by the Japanese invasion of China in the last century. Historically, he noted, a strong Japan and a strong China have had a hard time coexisting. But not today, at least not for the moment. Why not? I asked. The reason you can have a strong Japan and a strong China at the same time, he said, "is because of the supply chain." It is a win-win for both.

Obviously, since Iraq, Syria, south Lebanon, North Korea, Pakistan, Afghanistan, and Iran are not part of any major global supply chains, all of them remain hot spots that could explode at any time and slow or reverse the flattening of the world. As my own notebook story attests, the most important test case of the Dell Theory of Conflict Prevention is the situation between China and Taiwan—since both are deeply embedded in several of the world's most important computer, consumer electronics, and, increasingly, software supply chains. The vast majority of computer components for every major company comes from coastal China, Taiwan, and East Asia. In addition,

Taiwan alone has more than $100 billion in investments in mainland China today, and Taiwanese experts run many of the cutting-edge Chinese high-tech manufacturing companies.

It is no wonder that Craig Addison, the former editor of *Electronic Business Asia* magazine, wrote an essay for the *International Herald Tribune* (September 29, 2000), headlined "A 'Silicon Shield' Protects Taiwan from China." He argued that "Silicon-based products, such as computers and networking systems, form the basis of the digital economies in the United States, Japan, and other developed nations. In the past decade, Taiwan has become the third-largest information technology hardware producer after the United States and Japan. Military aggression by China against Taiwan would cut off a large portion of the world's supply of these products . . . Such a development would wipe trillions of dollars off the market value of technology companies listed in the United States, Japan, and Europe." Even if China's leaders, like former president Jiang Zemin, who was once minister of electronics, lose sight of how integrated China and Taiwan are in the world's computer supply chain, they need only ask their kids for an update. Jiang Zemin's son, Jiang Mianheng, wrote Addison, "is a partner in a wafer fabrication project in Shanghai with Winston Wang of Taiwan's Grace T.H.W. Group." And it is not just Taiwanese. Hundreds of big American tech companies now have R&D operations in China; a war that disrupted them could lead not only to the companies moving their plants elsewhere but also to a significant loss of R&D investment in China, which the Beijing government has been betting on to advance its development. Such a war could also, depending on how it started, trigger a widespread American boycott of Chinese goods — if China were to snuff out the Taiwanese democracy — which would lead to serious economic turmoil inside China.

The Dell Theory had its first real test in December 2004, when Taiwan held parliamentary elections. President Chen Shui-bian's pro-independence Democratic Progressive Party was expected to win the legislative runoff over the main opposition Nationalist Party, which favored closer ties with Beijing. Chen framed the election as a popular referendum on his proposal to write a new constitution that would formally enshrine Taiwan's independence, ending the purposely ambiguous status quo. Had Chen won and moved ahead on his agenda to make Taiwan its own motherland, as opposed to maintaining the status quo fiction that it is a province of the mainland, it could have led to a Chinese military assault on Taiwan. Everyone in the region was holding his or her breath. And what happened? *Motherboards won over motherland.* A majority of Taiwanese voted against the pro-independence governing party legislative candidates, ensuring that the DPP would not have a majority in parliament. I believe the message Taiwanese voters were sending was not that they never want Taiwan to be independent. It was that they do not want to upset the status quo right now, which has been so beneficial to so many Taiwanese. The voters seemed to understand clearly how interwoven they had become with the mainland, and they wisely opted to maintain their de facto independence rather than force de jure* independence, which might have triggered a Chinese invasion and a very uncertain future.

25

---

* de facto . . . de jure: concerning fact; concerning law. In other words, Taiwanese independence may not be officially recognized, but in practice it exists [Ed.].

Warning: What I said when I put forth the McDonald's theory, I would repeat even more strenuously with the Dell Theory: It does not make wars obsolete. And it does not guarantee that governments will not engage in wars of choice, even governments that are part of major supply chains. To suggest so would be naive. It guarantees only that governments whose countries are enmeshed in global supply chains will have to think three times, not just twice, about engaging in anything but a war of self-defense. And if they choose to go to war anyway, the price they will pay will be ten times higher than it was a decade ago and probably ten times higher than whatever the leaders of that country think. It is one thing to lose your McDonald's. It's quite another to fight a war that costs you your place in a twenty-first-century supply chain that may not come back around for a long time.

While the biggest test case of the Dell Theory is China versus Taiwan, the fact is that the Dell Theory has already proved itself to some degree in the case of India and Pakistan, the context in which I first started to think about it. I happened to be in India in 2002, when its just-in-time services supply chains ran into some very old-time geopolitics—and the supply chain won. In the case of India and Pakistan, the Dell Theory was working on only one party—India—but it still had a major impact. India is to the world's knowledge and service supply chain what China and Taiwan are to the manufacturing ones. By now readers of this book know all the highlights: General Electric's biggest research center outside the United States is in Bangalore, with seventeen hundred Indian engineers, designers, and scientists. The brain chips for many brand-name cell phones are designed in Bangalore. Renting a car from Avis online? It's managed in Bangalore. Tracing your lost luggage on Delta or British Airways is done from Bangalore, and the backroom accounting and computer maintenance for scores of global firms are done from Bangalore, Mumbai, Chennai, and other major Indian cities.

Here's what happened: On May 31, 2002, State Department spokesman Richard Boucher issued a travel advisory saying, "We urge American citizens currently in India to depart the country," because the prospect of a nuclear exchange with Pakistan was becoming very real. Both nations were massing troops on their borders, intelligence reports were suggesting that they both might be dusting off their nuclear warheads, and CNN was flashing images of people flooding out of India. The global American firms that had moved their back rooms and R&D operations* to Bangalore were deeply unnerved.

"I was actually surfing on the Web, and I saw a travel advisory come up on India on a Friday evening," said Vivek Paul, president of Wipro, which manages backroom operations from India of many American multinationals. "As soon as I saw that, I said, 'Oh my gosh, every customer that we have is going to have a million questions on this.' It was the Friday before a long weekend, so over the weekend we at Wipro developed a fail-safe business continuity plan for all of our customers." While Wipro's customers were pleased to see how on top of things the company was, many of them were nevertheless rattled. This was not in the plan when they decided to outsource mission-critical

---

* Back rooms and R&D operations: technical and logistical systems, and research and development [Ed.].

research and operations to India. Said Paul, "I had a CIO from one of our big American clients send me an e-mail saying, 'I am now spending a lot of time looking for alternative sources to India. I don't think you want me doing that, and I don't want to be doing it.' I immediately forwarded his message to the Indian ambassador in Washington and told him to get it to the right person." Paul would not tell me what company it was, but I have confirmed through diplomatic sources that it was United Technologies. And plenty of others, like American Express and General Electric, with back rooms in Bangalore, had to have been equally worried.

For many global companies, "the main heart of their business is now supported   30 here," said N. Krishnakumar, president of MindTree, another leading Indian knowledge outsourcing firm based in Bangalore. "It can cause chaos if there is a disruption." While not trying to meddle in foreign affairs, he added, "What we explained to our government, through the Confederation of Indian Industry, is that providing a stable, predictable operating environment is now the key to India's development." This was a real education for India's elderly leaders in New Delhi, who had not fully absorbed how critical India had become to the world's knowledge supply chain. When you are managing vital backroom operations for American Express or General Electric or Avis, or are responsible for tracing all the lost luggage on British Airways or Delta, you cannot take a month, a week, or even a day off for war without causing major disruptions for those companies. Once those companies have made a commitment to outsource business operations or research to India, they expect it to stay there. That is a major commitment. And if geopolitics causes a serious disruption, they will leave, and they will not come back very easily. When you lose this kind of service trade, you can lose it for good.

"What ends up happening in the flat world you described," explained Paul, "is that you have only one opportunity to make it right if something [goes] wrong. Because the disadvantage of being in a flat world is that despite all the nice engagements and stuff and the exit barriers that you have, every customer has multiple options, and so the sense of responsibility you have is not just out of a desire to do good by your customers, but also a desire for self-preservation."

The Indian government got the message. Was India's central place in the world's services supply chain the only factor in getting Prime Minister Vajpayee to tone down his rhetoric and step back from the brink? Of course not. There were other factors, to be sure—most notably the deterrent effect of Pakistan's own nuclear arsenal. But clearly, India's role in global services was an important additional source of restraint on its behavior, and it was taken into account by New Delhi. "I think it sobered a lot of people," said Jerry Rao, who heads the Indian high-tech trade association. "We engaged very seriously, and we tried to make the point that this was very bad for Indian business. It was very bad for the Indian economy . . . [Many people] didn't realize till then how suddenly we had become integrated into the rest of the world. We are now partners in a twenty-four by seven by three-sixty-five supply chain."

Vivek Kulkarni, then information technology secretary for Bangalore's regional government, told me back in 2002, "We don't get involved in politics, but we did bring to the government's attention the problems the Indian IT industry might face if there were a war." And this was an altogether new factor for New Delhi to take into consideration. "Ten years ago, [a lobby of IT ministers from different Indian states] never existed," said Kulkarni. Now it is one of the most important business lobbies in India and a coalition that no Indian government can ignore.

"With all due respect, the McDonald's [shutting] down doesn't hurt anything," said Vivek Paul, "but if Wipro had to shut down we would affect the day-to-day operations of many, many companies." No one would answer the phones in call centers. Many e-commerce sites that are supported from Bangalore would shut down. Many major companies that rely on India to maintain their key computer applications or handle their human resources departments or billings would seize up. And these companies did not want to find alternatives, said Paul. Switching is very difficult, because taking over mission-critical day-to-day backroom operations of a global company takes a great deal of training and experience. It's not like opening a fast-food restaurant. That was why, said Paul, Wipro's clients were telling him, " 'I have made an investment in you. I need you to be very responsible with the trust I have reposed in you.' And I think that created an enormous amount of back pressure on us that said we have to act in a responsible fashion . . . All of a sudden it became even clearer that there's more to gain by economic gains than by geopolitical gains. [We had more to gain from building] a vibrant, richer middle class able to create an export industry than we possibly could by having an ego-satisfying war with Pakistan." The Indian government also looked around and realized that the vast majority of India's billion people were saying, "I want a better future, not more territory." Over and over again, when I asked young Indians working at call centers how they felt about Kashmir or a war with Pakistan, they waved me off with the same answer: "We have better things to do." And they do. America needs to keep this in mind as it weighs its overall approach to outsourcing. I would never advocate shipping some American's job overseas just so it will keep Indians and Pakistanis at peace with each other. But I would say that to the extent that this process happens, driven by its own internal economic logic, it will have a net positive geopolitical effect. It will absolutely make the world safer for American kids.

Each of the Indian business leaders I interviewed noted that in the event of some outrageous act of terrorism or aggression from Pakistan, India would do whatever it takes to defend itself, and they would be the first to support that—the Dell Theory be damned. Sometimes war is unavoidable. It is imposed on you by the reckless behavior of others, and you have to just pay the price. But the more India and, one hopes, soon Pakistan get enmeshed in global service supply chains, the greater disincentive they have to fight anything but a border skirmish or a war of words.

The example of the 2002 India-Pakistan nuclear crisis at least gives us some hope. That cease-fire was brought to us not by General Powell but by General Electric.

We bring good things to life.

Infosys Versus al Qaeda

Unfortunately, even GE can do only so much. Because, alas, a new source for geopolitical instability has emerged only in recent years, for which even the updated Dell Theory can provide no restraint. It is the emergence of mutant global supply chains—that is, nonstate actors, be they criminals or terrorists, who learn to use all the elements of the flat world to advance a highly destabilizing, even nihilistic agenda. I first started thinking about this when Nandan Nilekani, the Infosys CEO, was giving me [a] tour . . . of his company's global videoconferencing center at its Bangalore headquarters. As Nandan explained to me how Infosys could get its global supply chain together at once for a virtual conference in that room, a thought popped into my head: Who else uses open-sourcing and supply-chaining so imaginatively? The answer, of course, is al Qaeda.

Al Qaeda has learned to use many of the same instruments for global collaboration that Infosys uses, but instead of producing products and profits with them, it has produced mayhem and murder. This is a particularly difficult problem. In fact, it may be the most vexing geopolitical problem for flat-world countries that want to focus on the future. The flat world—unfortunately—is a friend of both Infosys and al Qaeda. The Dell Theory will not work at all against these informal Islamo-Leninist terror networks, because they are not a state with a population that will hold its leaders accountable or with a domestic business lobby that might restrain them. These mutant global supply chains are formed for the purpose of destruction, not profit. They don't need investors, only recruits, donors, and victims. Yet these mobile, self-financing mutant supply chains use all the tools of collaboration offered by the flat world—open-sourcing to raise money, to recruit followers, and to stimulate and disseminate ideas; outsourcing to train recruits; and supply-chaining to distribute the tools and the suicide bombers to undertake operations. The U.S. Central Command has a name for this whole underground network: the Virtual Caliphate. And its leaders and innovators understand the flat world almost as well as Wal-Mart, Dell, and Infosys do.

In the previous chapter [not included here], I tried to explain that you cannot understand the rise of al Qaeda emotionally and politically without reference to the flattening of the world. What I am arguing here is that you cannot understand the rise of al Qaeda technically without reference to the flattening of the world, either. Globalization in general has been al Qaeda's friend in that it has helped to solidify a revival of Muslim identity and solidarity, with Muslims in one country much better able to see and sympathize with the struggles of their brethren in another country—thanks to the Internet and satellite television. At the same time, . . . this flattening process has intensified the feelings of humiliation in some quarters of the Muslim world over the fact that civilizations to which the Muslim world once felt superior—Hindus, Jews, Christians, Chinese—are now all doing better than many Muslim countries, and everyone can see it. The flattening of the world has also led to more urbanization and large-scale immigration to the West of many of these young, unemployed, frustrated Arab-Muslim males, while simultaneously making it much easier for informal open-source networks of these young men to form, operate, and interconnect. This certainly has been a boon for underground extremist Muslim political groups. There has been a proliferation of these informal mutual supply chains throughout the Arab-Muslim world today—small networks of people who move money through *hawalas* (hand-to-hand financing networks), who recruit through alternative education systems like the madrassas, and who communicate through the Internet and other tools of the global information revolution. Think about it: A century ago, anarchists were limited in their ability to communicate and collaborate with one another, to find sympathizers, and to band together for an operation. Today, with the Internet, that is not a problem. Today even the Unabomber could find friends to join a consortium where his "strengths" could be magnified and reinforced by others who had just as warped a worldview as he did.

40

What we have witnessed in Iraq is an even more perverse mutation of this mutant supply chain—the suicide supply chain. Since the start of the U.S. invasion in March 2002, more than two hundred suicide bombers have been recruited from within Iraq and from across the Muslim world, brought to the Iraqi front by some underground railroad, connected with the bomb makers there, and then dispatched against U.S. and Iraqi targets according to whatever suits the daily tactical needs of the insurgent Islamist forces in Iraq. I can understand, but not accept, the notion that more than thirty-seven years of Israeli occupation of the West Bank might have driven some Palestinians into a suicidal rage. But the American occupation of Iraq was only a few months old before it started to get hit by this suicide supply chain. How do you recruit so many young men "off the shelf" who are ready to commit suicide in the cause of jihad, many of them apparently not even Iraqis? And they don't even identify themselves by name or want to get credit—at least in this world. The fact is that Western intelligence agencies have no clue how this underground suicide supply chain, which seems to have an infinite pool of recruits to draw on, works, and yet it has basically stymied the U.S. armed forces in Iraq. From what we do know, though, this Virtual Caliphate works just like the supply chains I described earlier. Just as you take an item off the shelf in a discount store in Birmingham and another one is immediately made in Beijing, so the retailers of suicide deploy a human bomber in Baghdad and another one is immediately recruited and indoctrinated in Beirut. To the extent that this tactic spreads, it will require a major rethinking of U.S. military doctrine.

The flat world has also been such a huge boon for al Qaeda and its ilk because of the way it enables the small to act big, and the way it enables small acts—the killing of just a few people—to have big effects. The horrific video of the beheading of *Wall Street Journal* reporter Danny Pearl by Islamist militants in Pakistan was transmitted by the Internet all over the world. There is not a journalist anywhere who saw or even just read about that who was not terrified. But those same beheading videos are also used as tools of recruitment. The flat world makes it much easier for terrorists to transmit their terror. With the Internet they don't even have to go through Western or Arab news organizations but can broadcast right into your computer. It takes much less dynamite to transmit so much more anxiety. Just as the U.S. Army had embedded journalists, so the suicide supply chain has embedded terrorists, in their own way, to tell us their side of the story. How many times have I gotten up in the morning, fired up the Internet, and been confronted by the video image of some masked gunman threatening to behead an American—all brought to me courtesy of AOL's home page? The Internet is an enormously useful tool for the dissemination of propaganda, conspiracy theories, and plain old untruths, because it combines a huge reach with a patina of technology that makes anything on the Internet somehow more believable. How many times have you heard someone say, "But I read it on the Internet," as if that should end the argument? In fact, the Internet can make things worse. It often leads to more people being exposed to crazy conspiracy theories.

"The new system of diffusion—the Internet—is more likely to transmit irrationality than rationality," said political theorist Yaron Ezrahi, who specializes in the interaction between media and politics. "Because irrationality is more emotionally loaded, it requires less knowledge, it explains more to more people, it goes down easier." That is why conspiracy theories are so rife in the Arab-Muslim world today—and unfortunately are becoming so in many quarters of the Western world, for that matter. Conspiracy theories are like a drug that goes right into your bloodstream, enabling you to see "the Light." And the Internet is the needle. Young people used to have to take LSD to escape. Now they just go online. Now you don't shoot up, you download. You download the precise point of view that speaks to all your own biases. And the flat world makes it all so much easier.

Gabriel Weimann, a professor of communication at Haifa University, Israel, did an incisive study of terrorists' use of the Internet and of what I call the flat world, which was published in March 2004 by the United States Institute of Peace and excerpted on YaleGlobal Online on April 26, 2004. He made the following points:

> While the danger that cyber-terrorism poses to the Internet is frequently debated, surprisingly little is known about the threat posed by terrorists' use of the Internet. A recent six-year-long study shows that terrorist organizations and their supporters have been using all of the tools that the Internet offers to recruit supporters, raise funds, and launch a worldwide campaign of fear. It is also clear that to combat terrorism effectively, mere suppression of their Internet tools is not enough. Our scan of the Internet in 2003–04 revealed the existence of hundreds of websites serving terrorists in different, albeit sometimes overlapping, ways . . . There are countless examples of how [terrorists] use this uncensored medium to spread disinformation, to deliver threats intended to instill fear and helplessness, and to disseminate horrific images of recent actions. Since September 11, 2001, al Qaeda has festooned its websites with a string of announcements of an impending "large attack" on U.S. targets. These warnings have received considerable media coverage, which has helped to generate a widespread sense of dread and insecurity among audiences throughout the world and especially within the United States. . . .
>
> The Internet has significantly expanded the opportunities for terrorists to secure publicity. Until the advent of the Internet, terrorists' hopes of winning publicity for their causes and activities depended on attracting the attention of television, radio, or the print media. The fact that terrorists themselves have direct control over the content of their websites offers further opportunities to shape how they are perceived by different target audiences and to manipulate their image and the images of their enemies. Most terrorist sites do not celebrate their violent activities. Instead—regardless of their nature, motives, or location—most terrorist sites emphasize two issues: the restrictions placed on freedom of expression; and the plight of their comrades who are now political prisoners. These issues resonate powerfully with their own supporters and are also calculated to elicit sympathy from Western audiences that cherish freedom of expression and frown on measures to silence political opposition. . . .
>
> Terrorists have proven not only skillful at online marketing but also adept at mining the data offered by the billion-some pages of the World Wide Web. They can learn from the Internet about the schedules and locations of targets such as transportation facilities, nuclear power plants, public buildings, airports and ports, and even counterterrorism measures. According to Secretary of Defense Donald Rumsfeld, an al Qaeda training manual recovered in

Afghanistan tells its readers, "Using public sources openly and without resorting to illegal means, it is possible to gather at least 80 percent of all information required about the enemy." One captured al Qaeda computer contained engineering and structural architecture features of a dam, which had been downloaded from the Internet and which would enable al Qaeda engineers and planners to simulate catastrophic failures. In other captured computers, U.S. investigators found evidence that al Qaeda operators spent time on sites that offer software and programming instructions for the digital switches that run power, water, transportation, and communications grids.

Like many other political organizations, terrorist groups use the Internet to raise funds. Al Qaeda, for instance, has always depended heavily on donations, and its global fund-raising network is built upon a foundation of charities, nongovernmental organizations, and other financial institutions that use websites and Internet-based chat rooms and forums. The fighters in the Russian breakaway republic of Chechnya have likewise used the Internet to publicize the numbers of bank accounts to which sympathizers can contribute. And in December 2001, the U.S. government seized the assets of a Texas-based charity because of its ties to Hamas.

In addition to soliciting financial aid online, terrorists recruit converts by using the full panoply of website technologies (audio, digital video, etc.) to enhance the presentation of their message. And like commercial sites that track visitors to develop consumer profiles, terrorist organizations capture information about the users who browse their websites. Visitors who seem most interested in the organization's cause or well suited to carrying out its work are then contacted. Recruiters may also use more interactive Internet technology to roam online chat rooms and cyber cafes, looking for receptive members of the public, particularly young people. The SITE Institute, a Washington, D.C.–based terrorism research group that monitors al Qaeda's Internet communications, has provided chilling details of a high-tech recruitment drive launched in 2003 to recruit fighters to travel to Iraq and attack U.S. and coalition forces there. The Internet also grants terrorists a cheap and efficient means of networking. Many terrorist groups, among them Hamas and al Qaeda, have undergone a transformation from strictly hierarchical organizations with designated leaders to affiliations of semi-independent cells that have no single commanding hierarchy. Through the Internet, these loosely interconnected groups are able to maintain contact with one another—and with members of other terrorist groups. The Internet connects not only members of the same terrorist organizations but also members of different groups. For instance, dozens of sites supporting terrorism in the name of jihad permit terrorists in places as far-removed from one another as Chechnya and Malaysia to exchange ideas and practical information about how to build bombs, establish terror cells, and carry out attacks . . . Al Qaeda operatives relied heavily on the Internet in planning and coordinating the September 11 attacks.

For all of these reasons we are just at the beginning of understanding the geo-political impact of the flattening of the world. On the one hand, failed states and failed regions are places we have every incentive to avoid today. They offer no economic opportunity and there is no Soviet Union out there competing with us for influence over such countries. On the other hand, there may be nothing more dangerous today than a failed state with broadband capability. That is, even failed states tend to have telecommunications systems and satellite links, and therefore if a terrorist group infiltrates a failed state, as al Qaeda did with Afghanistan, it can amplify its power enormously. As much as big powers want to stay away from such states, they may feel compelled to get even more deeply embroiled in them. Think of America in Afghanistan and Iraq, Russia in Chechnya, Australia in East Timor.

In the flat world it is much more difficult to hide, but much easier to get connected. "Think of Mao at the beginning of the Chinese communist revolution," remarked Michael Mandelbaum, the Johns Hopkins foreign policy specialist. "The Chinese Communists had to hide in caves in northwest China, but they could move around in whatever territory they were able to control. Bin Laden, by contrast, can't show his face, but he can reach every household in the world, thanks to the Internet." Bin Laden cannot capture any territory but he can capture the imagination of millions of people. And he has, broadcasting right into American living rooms on the eve of the 2004 presidential election.

> **In the flat world it is much more difficult to hide, but much easier to get connected.**

Hell hath no fury like a terrorist with a satellite dish and an interactive Web site.

Too Personally Insecure

In the fall of 2004, I was invited to speak at a synagogue in Woodstock, New York, home of the famous Woodstock music festival. I asked my hosts how was it that they were able to get a synagogue in Woodstock, of all places, big enough to support a lecture series. Very simple, they said. Since 9/11, Jews, and others, have been moving from New York City to places like Woodstock, to get away from what they fear will be the next ground zero. Right now this trend is a trickle, but it would become a torrent if a nuclear device were detonated in any European or American city.

Since this threat is the mother of all unflatteners, this book would not be complete without a discussion of it. We can live with a lot. We lived through 9/11. But we cannot live with nuclear terrorism. That would unflatten the world permanently.

The only reason that Osama bin Laden did not use a nuclear device on 9/11 was not that he did not have the intention but that he did not have the capability. And since the Dell Theory offers no hope of restraining the suicide supply chains, the only strategy we have is to limit their worst capabilities. That means a much more serious global effort to stanch nuclear proliferation by limiting the supply—to buy up the fissile material that is already out there, particularly in the former Soviet Union, and prevent more states from going nuclear. Harvard University international affairs expert Graham Allison, in his book *Nuclear Terrorism: The Ultimate Preventable Catastrophe*, outlines just such a strategy for denying terrorists access to nuclear weapons and nuclear materials. It can be done, he insists. It is a challenge to our will and convictions, but *not to our capabilities.* Allison proposes a new American-led international security order to deal with this problem based on what he calls "a doctrine of the Three No's: No loose nukes, No new nascent nukes, and No new nuclear states." No loose nukes, says Allison, means locking down all nuclear weapons and all nuclear material from which bombs could be made—in a much more serious way than we have done up till now. "We don't lose gold from Fort Knox," says Allison. "Russia doesn't lose treasures from the Kremlin armory. So we both know how to prevent theft of those things that are super valuable to us if we are determined to do it." No new nascent nukes means recognizing that there is a group of actors out there who can and do produce highly enriched uranium or pluto- nium, which is nothing more than nuclear bombs just about to hatch. We need a much more credible, multilateral nonproliferation regime that soaks up this fissile material. Finally, no new nuclear states means "drawing a line under the current eight nuclear powers and determining that, however unfair and unreasonable it may be, that club will have no more members than those eight," says Allison, adding that these three steps might then buy us time to develop a more formal, sustainable, internationally approved regime.

It would be nice also to be able to deny the Internet to al Qaeda and its ilk, but that, alas, is impossible—without undermining ourselves. That is why limiting their capa- bilities is necessary but not sufficient. We also have to find a way to get at their worst intentions. If we are not going to shut down the Internet and all the other creative and collaborative tools that have flattened the world, and if we can't restrict access to them, the only thing we can do is try to influence the imagination and intentions that people bring to them and draw from them. When I raised this issue, and the broad themes of this book, with my religious teacher, Rabbi Tzvi Marx from Holland, he surprised me by saying that the flat world I was describing reminded him of the story of the Tower of Babel.

How so? I asked. "The reason God banished all the people from the Tower of Babel and made them all speak different languages was not because he did not want them to collaborate per se," answered Rabbi Marx. "It was because he was enraged at what they were collaborating on—an effort to build a tower to the heavens so they could be- come God." This was a distortion of the human capacity, so God broke their union and their ability to communicate with one another. Now, all these years later, humankind has again created a new platform for more people from more places to communicate and collaborate with less friction and more ease than ever: the Internet. Would God see the Internet as heresy?

"Absolutely not," said Marx. "The heresy is not that mankind works together—it is to what ends. It is essential that we use this new ability to communicate and collabo- rate for the right ends—for constructive human aims and not megalomaniacal ends. Building a tower was megalomaniacal. Bin Laden's insistence that he has the truth and can flatten anyone else's tower who doesn't heed him is megalomaniacal. Collaborat- ing so mankind can achieve its full potential is God's hope."

Exploring Context

1. Friedman opens this chapter by tracing the assembly of his Dell notebook. Explore Dell's website (dell.com). Does it provide any sense of the global supply chains that are vital to the creation of its computers? Why would Dell highlight or obscure these global supply chains on its website? What global images and what national images are

created? How does the site reflect your response to Question 1 of Questions for Critical Reading about collaboration?

2. Infosys, headquartered in Bangalore, India, is one of the companies that Friedman mentions. Visit the website for Infosys (Infosys.com). How does the information on this site reflect Friedman's arguments? Given that Infosys's primary business is completely tied to global supply chains, how does its site compare to Dell's? Use your answer to Question 1 of Exploring Context.

3. Visit the Federal Bureau of Investigation's counterterrorism website at fbi.gov/about-us/investigate/terrorism. Does it reflect the global nature of terror networks as explained by Friedman? How does Friedman propose we fight terrorism? Are such strategies being pursued by organizations like the FBI? You may want to draw on your work on collaboration and mutant supply chains from Questions 1 and 3 of Questions for Critical Reading.

Questions for Connecting

1. Michael Pollan, in "The Animals: Practicing Complexity" (p. 373), describes a very different, very local economic system. What parallels can you find between Pollan's and Friedman's ideas about the collateral effects of economic systems? Do "holons" have a role to play in the global supply chain? Are integrated and organic farming systems a kind of supply chain? Use your work defining Friedman's concepts from Questions for Critical Reading to help make your argument.

2. Like Friedman, James Surowiecki focuses on collaboration in "Committees, Juries, and Teams: The *Columbia* Disaster and How Small Groups Can Be Made to Work" (p. 472). How might some of the pitfalls of small groups noted by Surowiecki endanger the Dell Theory? Are small-group dynamics applicable to global collaborative systems? How can the lessons learned from Surowiecki's analysis help in the fight against mutant supply chains and terrorism? Use your work on collaboration from Question 1 of Questions for Critical Reading.

3. Leslie Savan examines the economic appropriation of black talk in "What's Black, Then White, and Said All Over?" (p. 435). Should there be limits on economic systems or global supply chains? Must we limit their effects? Or, based on the ideas of Friedman and Savan, is it in our best interests to give economic systems free reign? Drawing on your work in Exploring Context, can you use Dell or Infosys as an example for your argument?

4. **CONNECTING TO E-PAGES** Analyze Charles Duhigg and David Barboza's "In China, Human Costs Are Built Into an iPad" (bedfordstmartins.com/emerging/epages) as an example of Friedman's globalized supply chain. In what ways do Friedman's ideas fit with the description of iPad manufacturing? For instance, how would you characterize Duhigg and Barboza's description of collaboration in the manufacturing process? How is it similar to and different from the one Friedman describes for his computer? Incorporate your responses to Question 1 of Questions for Critical Reading and Question 1 of Exploring Context, and support your answer with quotations from the texts.

Language Matters

1. Integrating the words of other authors into your writing is an essential skill. In small groups, select a key quotation from Friedman's text and then create three different sentences that integrate that quotation. Have different groups share their results. What general techniques or strategies did people use?

2. Systems of citation are a central aspect of academic writing. In this class, you may be asked to use MLA, APA, or some other format for in-text citations. Develop your own system and illustrate it by citing a quotation from Friedman's essay. What kind of information would the citation have to include? What does this then say about how citation systems work—what does every system seem to need? Why are there so many citation systems?

3. Strong organization is self-evident. That is, when a paper is well organized, each paragraph clearly has a place in the whole. Imagine a different order for Friedman's essay. What sections would you place first, and why? What transitions would you need? Why do you think Friedman organized his essay the way he did?

Assignments for Writing

1. According to Friedman's theory, global supply chains promote geopolitical stability. But Friedman is careful to say that they do not guarantee peace. Write a paper in which you determine the limitations of Friedman's theory. What would cause the Dell Theory of Conflict Prevention to fail? Are there specific supply chains or commodities (oil, gas, natural resources) that fall outside this theory? You may want to build your argument using your work on the Dell Theory from Question 2 of Questions for Critical Reading.

2. Both Friedman's Dell Theory of Conflict Prevention and his earlier Golden Arches Theory seem to rely on the spread of American culture. Can we reap the benefits of globalized economics without sacrificing local culture? Write a paper in which you suggest strategies for balancing globalization and localization. You might want to draw on your work with Leslie Savan's essay from Question 3 of Questions for Connecting in making your argument. Consider, too, these questions: Are terrorist supply chains an attempt to preserve local cultures? Must global economics mean global culture?

3. As you learned in Question 1 of Questions for Critical Reading, collaboration is one of Friedman's central concerns in this essay. Write a paper in which you use Friedman's ideas to suggest the key factors for making collaboration a success. You might also want to draw on your work with James Surowiecki's essay from Question 2 of Questions for Connecting.

FRANCIS FUKUYAMA

Francis Fukuyama holds a B.A. in classics from Cornell University and a Ph.D. in political science from Harvard University. He is Olivier Nomellini Senior Fellow at the Freeman Spogli Institute for International Studies at Stanford University. As a prominent neoconservative thinker, Fukuyama signed letters to both President Bill Clinton (in 1998) and President George W. Bush (in 2001) advocating the overthrow of Saddam Hussein (at the time, the president of Iraq). However, Fukuyama ultimately disapproved of the 2003 invasion of Iraq, writing publicly that neoconservative ideas had changed and were no longer supportable. Fukuyama is the author of multiple books of political philosophy advocating liberal democracy, including his 2006 publication *America at the Crossroads*, which deals directly with his departure from the neoconservative agenda.

In *Our Posthuman Future: Consequences of the Biotechnology Revolution* (2002), Fukuyama updates an earlier proposal. Fukuyama had, in his book *The End of History and the Last Man* (1992), suggested that the history of humanity is an ideological struggle that is pretty much settled now, with liberal democracy as the eventual and destined end point, an argument he clarified in *America at the Crossroads*, stating that modernization is what wins the ideological struggle and that liberal democracy is merely one of the outcomes of modernization. In *Our Posthuman Future*, he reexamines this argument, taking into account the potential effects of biotechnology on liberal democracy. Now that human behavior can potentially be modified and DNA can be manipulated, Fukuyama asks, how will a political order based on natural equality survive?

In "Human Dignity," a chapter from *Our Posthuman Future*, Fukuyama examines the idea of "Factor X," an "essential human quality . . . that is worthy of a certain minimal level of respect" (p. 186) regardless of our varying individual characteristics, such as skin color, looks, or social class. Modern science, particularly the science of genetic engineering, Fukuyama claims, tends to disagree with the very idea of an essential human quality like Factor X. From this scientific perspective, human beings are the end result of genetic accidents and environmental influences. Fukuyama, however, finds merit in Pope John Paul II's assertion that science can't fully explain how human beings emerge from simple components. If that assertion is correct, Fukuyama speculates, what does this imply about science's ability to understand other complex systems? What does this mean for the future of human consciousness and political systems? In "Human Dignity," Fukuyama asks the reader to consider what happens to the idea of universal human equality when genetic engineering can be used to "improve" human genes.

Given the seemingly inevitable progress of science, which undoubtedly will influence you throughout your life, what does it mean to be human, and how can we preserve the qualities that make us so?

▶ TAGS: *human dignity, morality, biotechnology, ethics, civil rights*

Questions for Critical Reading

1. The idea of a "Factor X" plays a central role in Fukuyama's essay. As you read this text, locate quotations where Fukuyama defines this term and then provide a definition of the concept in your own words.

2. Do humans have an "essence"? Locate passages from Fukuyama that support your analysis. Does he think there is a human essence? What quotations make his position clear? You will need to read his text closely and critically to determine his position.

3. As the title of this selection suggests, Fukuyama is centrally concerned with the concept of human dignity in this chapter. Define *human dignity*, using quotations from Fukuyama that support your definition.

Human Dignity

> Is it, then, possible to imagine a new Natural Philosophy, continually conscious that the "natural object" produced by analysis and abstraction is not reality but only a view, and always correcting the abstraction? I hardly know what I am asking for. . . . The regenerate science which I have in mind would not do even to minerals and vegetables what modern science threatens to do to man himself. When it explained it would not explain away. When it spoke of parts it would remember the whole. . . . The analogy between the *Tao* of Man and the instincts of an animal species would mean for it new light cast on the unknown thing, Instinct, by the only known reality of conscience and not a reduction of conscience to the category of Instinct. Its followers would not be free with the words *only* and *merely*. In a word, it would conquer Nature without being at the same time conquered by her and buy knowledge at a lower cost than that of life.
>
> —C. S. LEWIS, *THE ABOLITION OF MAN*[1]

According to the Decree by the Council of Europe on Human Cloning, "The instrumentalisation of human beings through the deliberate creation of genetically identical human beings is contrary to human dignity and thus constitutes a misuse of medicine and biology."[2] Human dignity is one of those concepts that politicians, as well as virtually everyone else in political life, like to throw around, but that almost no one can either define or explain.

   Much of politics centers on the question of human dignity and the desire for recognition to which it is related. That is, human beings constantly demand that others recognize their dignity, either as individuals or as members of religious, ethnic, racial, or other kinds of groups. The struggle for recognition is not economic: What we desire is not money but that other human beings respect us in the way we think we deserve. In earlier times, rulers wanted others to recognize their superior worth as king, emperor, or lord. Today, people seek recognition of their equal status as members of formerly disrespected or devalued groups—as women, gays, Ukrainians, the handicapped, Native Americans, and the like.[3]

The demand for an equality of recognition or respect is the dominant passion of modernity, as Tocqueville* noted over 170 years ago in *Democracy in America*.[4] What this means in a liberal democracy is a bit complicated. It is not necessarily that we think we are equal in all important respects, or demand that our lives be the same as everyone else's. Most people accept the fact that a Mozart or an Einstein or a Michael Jordan has talents and abilities that they don't have, and receives recognition and even monetary compensation for what he accomplishes with those talents. We accept, though we don't necessarily like, the fact that resources are distributed unequally based on what James Madison called the "different and unequal faculties of acquiring property." But we also believe that people deserve to keep what they earn and that the faculties for working and earning will not be the same for all people. We also accept the fact that we look different, come from different races and ethnicities, are of different sexes, and have different cultures.

Factor X

What the demand for equality of recognition implies is that when we strip all of a person's contingent and accidental characteristics away, there remains some essential human quality underneath that is worthy of a certain minimal level of respect—call it Factor X. Skin color, looks, social class and wealth, gender, cultural background, and even one's natural talents are all accidents of birth relegated to the class of nonessential characteristics. We make decisions on whom to befriend, whom to marry or do business with, or whom to shun at social events on the basis of these secondary characteristics. But in the political realm we are required to respect people equally on the basis of their possession of Factor X. You can cook, eat, torture, enslave, or render the carcass of any creature lacking Factor X, but if you do the same thing to a human being, you are guilty of a "crime against humanity." We accord beings with Factor X not just human rights but, if they are adults, political rights as well—that is, the right to live in democratic political communities where their rights to speech, religion, association, and political participation are respected.

The circle of beings to whom we attribute Factor X has been one of the most contested issues throughout human history. For many societies, including most democratic societies in earlier periods of history, Factor X belonged to a significant subset of the human race, excluding people of certain sexes, economic classes, races, and tribes and people with low intelligence, disabilities, birth defects, and the like. These societies were highly stratified, with different classes possessing more or less of Factor X, and some possessing none at all. Today, for believers in liberal equality, Factor X etches a bright red line around the whole of the human race and requires equality of respect for all of those on the inside, but attributes a lower level of dignity to those outside the boundary. Factor X is the human essence, the most basic meaning of what it is to be

---

* Tocqueville: Alexis de Tocqueville (1805–1859); French political thinker and historian best known for his two-volume book *Democracy in America* (1835 and 1840), which examined changing social conditions in American society [Ed.].

human. If all human beings are in fact equal in dignity, then X must be some characteristic universally possessed by them. So what is Factor X, and where does it come from?

So what is Factor X, and where does it come from?

For Christians, the answer is fairly easy: It comes from God. Man is created in the image of God, and therefore shares in some of God's sanctity, which entitles human beings to a higher level of respect than the rest of natural creation. In the words of Pope John Paul II, what this means is that "the human individual cannot be subordinated as a pure means or a pure instrument, either to the species or to society; he has value per se. He is a person. With his intellect and his will, he is capable of forming a relationship of communion, solidarity, and self-giving with his peers . . . It is by virtue of his spiritual soul that the whole person possesses such dignity even in his body."[5]

Supposing one is not a Christian (or a religious believer of any sort), and doesn't accept the premise that man is created in the image of God. Is there a secular ground for believing that human beings are entitled to a special moral status or dignity? Perhaps the most famous effort to create a philosophical basis for human dignity was that of Kant,* who argued that Factor X was based on the human capacity for moral choice. That is, human beings could differ in intelligence, wealth, race, and gender, but all were equally able to act according to moral law or not. Human beings had dignity because they alone had free will—not just the subjective illusion of free will but the actual ability to transcend natural determinism and the normal rules of causality. It is the existence of free will that leads to Kant's well-known conclusion that human beings are always to be treated as ends and not as means.

It would be very difficult for any believer in a materialistic account of the universe—which includes the vast majority of natural scientists—to accept the Kantian account of human dignity. The reason is that it forces them to accept a form of dualism—that there is a realm of human freedom parallel to the realm of nature that is not determined by the latter. Most natural scientists would argue that what we believe to be free will is in fact an illusion and that all human decision making can ultimately be traced back to material causes. Human beings decide to do one thing over another because one set of neurons fires rather than another, and those neuronal firings can be traced back to prior material states of the brain. The human decision-making process may be more complex than that of other animals, but there is no sharp dividing line that distinguishes human moral choice from the kinds of choices that are made by other animals. Kant himself does not offer any proof that free will exists; he says that it is simply a necessary postulate of pure practical reason about the nature of morality—hardly an argument that a hard-bitten empirical scientist would accept.

Seize the Power

The problem posed by modern natural science goes even deeper. The very notion that there exists such a thing as a human "essence" has been under relentless attack by modern science for much of the past century and a half. One of the most fundamental

---

* Kant: Immanuel Kant (1724–1804), German philosopher best known for *The Critique of Pure Reason* (1781); he was concerned with questions of how we can know what we know [Ed.].

assertions of Darwinism* is that species do not have essences.[6] That is, while Aristotle[†] believed in the eternity of the species (i.e., that what we have been labeling "species-typical behavior" is something unchanging), Darwin's theory maintains that this behavior changes in response to the organism's interaction with its environment. What is typical for a species represents a snapshot of the species at one particular moment of evolutionary time; what came before and what comes after will be different. Since Darwinism maintains that there is no cosmic teleology guiding the process of evolution, what seems to be the essence of a species is just an accidental by-product of a random evolutionary process.

In this perspective, what we have been calling human nature is merely the species-typical human characteristics and behavior that emerged about 100,000 years ago, during what evolutionary biologists call the "era of evolutionary adaptation" — when the precursors of modern humans were living and breeding on the African savanna. For many, this suggests that human nature has no special status as a guide to morals or values because it is historically contingent. David Hull, for example, argues,   10

> I do not see why the existence of human universals is all that important. Perhaps all and only people have opposable thumbs, use tools, live in true societies, or what have you. I think that such attributions are either false or vacuous, but even if they were true and significant, the distributions of these particular characters is largely a matter of evolutionary happenstance.[7]

The geneticist Lee Silver, trying to debunk the idea that there is a natural order that could be undermined by genetic engineering, asserts,

> Unfettered evolution is never predetermined [toward some goal], and not necessarily associated with progress — it is simply a response to unpredictable environmental changes. If the asteroid that hit our planet 60 million years ago had flown past instead, there would never have been any human beings at all. And whatever the natural order might be, it is not necessarily good. The smallpox virus was part of the natural order until it was forced into extinction by human intervention.[8]

This inability to define a natural essence doesn't bother either writer. Hull, for example, states that "I, for one, would be extremely uneasy to base something as important as human rights on such temporary contingencies [as human nature]. . . I fail to see why it matters. I fail to see, for example, why we must all be essentially the same to have rights."[9] Silver, for his part, pooh-poohs fears about genetic engineering on the part of those with religious convictions or those who believe in a natural order. In the future, man will no longer be a slave to his genes, but their master:

> Why not seize this power? Why not control what has been left to chance in the past? Indeed, we control all other aspects of our children's lives and identities

---

* Darwinism: Shorthand for naturalist Charles Darwin's idea of evolution by natural selection, the concept that only the species best adapted to their environment survive [Ed.].

† Aristotle: Greek philosopher and enormously important figure in Western thought. Aristotle (384–322 BC) was a student of Plato and a teacher of Alexander the Great [Ed.].

through powerful social and environmental influences and, in some cases, with the use of powerful drugs like Ritalin and Prozac. On what basis can we reject positive genetic influences on a person's essence when we accept the rights of parents to benefit their children in every other way?[10]

Why not seize this power, indeed?

Well, let us begin by considering what the consequences of the abandonment of the idea that there is a Factor X, or human essence, that unites all human beings would be for the cherished idea of universal human equality—an idea to which virtually all of the debunkers of the idea of human essences are invariably committed. Hull is right that we don't all need to be the same in order to have rights—but we need to be the same in some one critical respect in order to have *equal* rights. He for one is very concerned that basing human rights on human nature will stigmatize homosexuals, because their sexual orientation differs from the heterosexual norm. But the only basis on which anyone can make an argument in favor of equal rights for gays is to argue that whatever their sexual orientation, *they are people too* in some other respect that is more essential than their sexuality. If you cannot find this common other ground, then there is no reason not to discriminate against them, because in fact they are different creatures from everyone else.

Similarly, Lee Silver, who is so eager to take up the power of genetic engineering to "improve" people, is nonetheless horrified at the possibility that it could be used to create a class of genetically superior people. He paints a scenario in which a class called the GenRich steadily improve the cognitive abilities of their children to the point that they break off from the rest of the human race to form a separate species.

Silver is not horrified by much else that technology may bring us by way of unnatural reproduction—for example, two lesbians producing genetic offspring, or eggs taken from an unborn female fetus to produce a child whose mother had never been born. He dismisses the moral concerns of virtually every religion or traditional moral system with regard to future genetic engineering but draws the line at what he perceives as threats to human equality. He does not seem to understand that, given his premises, there are no possible grounds on which he can object to the GenRich, or the fact that they might assign themselves rights superior to those of the GenPoor. Since there is no stable essence common to all human beings, or rather because that essence is variable and subject to human manipulation, why not create a race born with metaphorical saddles on their backs, and another with boots and spurs to ride them? Why not seize *that* power as well?

The bioethicist Peter Singer, whose appointment to Princeton University caused great controversy because of his advocacy of infanticide and euthanasia under certain circumstances, is simply more consistent than most people on the consequences of abandoning the concept of human dignity. Singer is an unabashed utilitarian: He believes that the single relevant standard for ethics is to minimize suffering in the aggregate for all creatures. Human beings are part of a continuum of life and have no special status in his avowedly Darwinian worldview. This leads him to two perfectly logical conclusions: the need for animal rights, since animals can experience pain and suffering as well as humans, and the downgrading of the rights of infants and elderly people who lack certain key traits, like self-awareness, that would allow them to anticipate pain. The rights of certain animals, in his view, deserve greater respect than those of certain human beings.

But Singer is not nearly forthright enough in following these premises through to their logical conclusion, since he remains a committed egalitarian. What he does not explain is why the relief of suffering should remain the only moral good. As usual, the philosopher Friedrich Nietzsche was much more clear-eyed than anyone else in understanding the consequences of modern natural science and the abandonment of the concept of human dignity. Nietzsche had the great insight to see that, on the one hand, once the clear red line around the whole of humanity could no longer be drawn, the way would be paved for a return to a much more hierarchical ordering of society. If there is a continuum of gradations between human and nonhuman, there is a continuum within the type human as well. This would inevitably mean the liberation of the strong from the constraints that a belief in either God or Nature had placed on them. On the other hand, it would lead the rest of mankind to demand health and safety as the only possible goods, since all the higher goals that had once been set for them were now debunked. In the words of Nietzsche's Zarathustra, "One has one's little pleasure for the day and one's little pleasure for the night: But one has a regard for health. 'We have invented happiness,' say the last men, and they blink."[11] Indeed, both the return of hierarchy and the egalitarian demand for health, safety, and relief of suffering might all go hand in hand if the rulers of the future could provide the masses with enough of the "little poisons" they demanded.

It has always struck me that one hundred years after Nietzsche's death, we are much less far down the road to either the superman or the last man than he predicted. Nietzsche once castigated John Stuart Mill as a "flathead" for believing that one could have a semblance of Christian morality in the absence of belief in a Christian God. And yet, in a Europe and an America that have become secularized over the past two generations, we see a lingering belief in the concept of human dignity, which is by now completely cut off from its religious roots. And not just lingering: The idea that one could exclude any group of people on the basis of race, gender, disability, or virtually any other characteristic from the charmed circle of those deserving recognition for human dignity is the one thing that will bring total obloquy on the head of any politician who proposes it. In the words of the philosopher Charles Taylor, "We believe it would be utterly wrong and unfounded to draw the boundaries any narrower than around the whole human race," and should anyone try to do so, "we should immediately ask what distinguished those within from those left out."[12] The idea of the equality of human dignity, deracinated from its Christian or Kantian origins, is held as a matter of religious dogma by the most materialist of natural scientists. The continuing arguments over the moral status of the unborn (about which more later) constitute the only exception to this general rule.

The reasons for the persistence of the idea of the equality of human dignity are complex. Partly it is a matter of the force of habit and what Max Weber once called the "ghost of dead religious beliefs" that continue to haunt us. Partly it is the product of historical accident: The last important political movement to explicitly deny the premise of universal human dignity was Nazism, and the horrifying consequences of the Nazis' racial and eugenic policies were sufficient to inoculate those who experienced them for the next couple of generations.

But another important reason for the persistence of the idea of the universality of human dignity has to do with what we might call the nature of nature itself. Many of the grounds on which certain groups were historically denied their share of human dignity were proven to be simply a matter of prejudice, or else based on cultural and environmental conditions that could be changed. The notions that women were too irrational or emotional to participate in politics, and that immigrants from southern Europe had smaller head sizes and were less intelligent than those from northern Europe, were overturned on the basis of sound, empirical science. That moral order did not completely break down in the West in the wake of the destruction of consensus over traditional religious values should not surprise us either, because moral order comes from within human nature itself and is not something that has to be imposed on human nature by culture.[13]

All of this could change under the impact of future biotechnology. The most clear and present danger is that the large genetic variations between individuals will narrow and become clustered within certain distinct social groups. Today, the "genetic lottery" guarantees that the son or daughter of a rich and successful parent will not necessarily inherit the talents and abilities that created conditions conducive to the parent's success. Of course, there has always been a degree of genetic selection: Assortative mating means that successful people will tend to marry each other and, to the extent that their success is genetically based, will pass on to their children better life opportunities. But in the future, the full weight of modern technology can be put in the service of optimizing the kinds of genes that are passed on to one's offspring. This means that social elites may not just pass on social advantages but embed them genetically as well. This may one day include not only characteristics like intelligence and beauty, but behavioral traits like diligence, competitiveness, and the like.

The genetic lottery is judged as inherently unfair by many because it condemns certain people to lesser intelligence, or bad looks, or disabilities of one sort or another. But in another sense it is profoundly egalitarian, since everyone, regardless of social class, race, or ethnicity, has to play in it. The wealthiest man can and often does have a good-for-nothing son; hence the saying "Shirtsleeves to shirtsleeves in three generations." When the lottery is replaced by choice, we open up a new avenue along which human beings can compete, one that threatens to increase the disparity between the top and bottom of the social hierarchy.

What the emergence of a genetic overclass will do to the idea of universal human dignity is something worth pondering. Today, many bright and successful young people believe that they owe their success to accidents of birth and upbringing but for which their lives might have taken a very different course. They feel themselves, in other words, to be lucky, and they are capable of feeling sympathy for people who are less lucky than they. But to the extent that they become "children of choice" who have been genetically selected by their parents for certain characteristics, they may come to believe increasingly that their success is a matter not just of luck but of good choices and planning on the part of their parents, and hence something deserved. They will look, think, act, and perhaps even feel differently from those who were not similarly chosen, and may come in time to think of themselves as different kinds of creatures. They may, in short, feel themselves to be aristocrats, and unlike aristocrats of old, their claim to better birth will be rooted in nature and not convention.

Aristotle's discussion of slavery in Book I of the *Politics* is instructive on this score. It is often condemned as a justification of Greek slavery, but in fact the discussion is far more sophisticated and is relevant to our thinking about genetic classes. Aristotle makes a distinction between conventional and natural slavery.[14] He argues that slavery would be justified by nature if it were the case that there were people with naturally slavish natures. It is not clear from his discussion that he believes such people exist: Most actual slavery is conventional—that is, it is the result of victory in war or force, or based on the wrong opinion that barbarians as a class should be slaves of Greeks.[15] The noble-born think their nobility comes from nature rather than acquired virtue and that they can pass it on to their children. But, Aristotle notes, nature is "frequently unable to bring this about."[16] So why not, as Lee Silver suggests, "seize this power" to give children genetic advantages and correct the defect of natural equality?

The possibility that biotechnology will permit the emergence of new genetic classes has been frequently noted and condemned by those who have speculated about the future.[17] But the opposite possibility also seems to be entirely plausible—that there will be an impetus toward a much more genetically egalitarian society. For it seems highly unlikely that people in modern democratic societies will sit around complacently if they see elites embedding their advantages genetically in their children.

Indeed, this is one of the few things in a politics of the future that people are likely to rouse themselves to fight over. By this I mean not just fighting metaphorically, in the sense of shouting matches among talking heads on TV and debates in Congress, but actually picking up guns and bombs and using them on other people. There are very few domestic political issues today in our rich, self-satisfied liberal democracies that can cause people to get terribly upset, but the specter of rising genetic inequality may well get people off their couches and into the streets.

If people get upset enough about genetic inequality, there will be two alternative courses of action. The first and most sensible would simply be to forbid the use of biotechnology to enhance human characteristics and decline to compete in this dimension. But the notion of enhancement may become too powerfully attractive to forgo, or it may prove difficult to enforce a rule preventing people from enhancing their children, or the courts may declare they have a right to do so. At this point a second possibility opens up, which is to use that same technology to raise up the bottom.[18]

This is the only scenario in which it is plausible that we will see a liberal democracy of the future get back into the business of state-sponsored eugenics. The bad old form of eugenics discriminated against the disabled and less intelligent by forbidding them to have children. In the future, it may be possible to breed children who are more intelligent, more healthy, more "normal." Raising the bottom is something that can only be accomplished through the intervention of the state. Genetic enhancement technology is likely to be expensive and involve some risk, but even if it were relatively cheap and safe, people who are poor and lacking in education would still fail to take advantage of it. So the bright red line of universal human dignity will have to be reinforced by allowing the state to make sure that no one falls outside it.

The politics of breeding future human beings will be very complex. Up to now, the Left has on the whole been opposed to cloning, genetic engineering, and similar biotechnologies for a number of reasons, including traditional humanism, environmental concerns, suspicion of technology and of the corporations that produce it, and fear of eugenics. The Left has historically sought to play down the importance of heredity in favor of social factors in explaining human outcomes. For people on the Left to come around and support genetic engineering for the disadvantaged, they would first have to admit that genes are important in determining intelligence and other types of social outcomes in the first place.

The Left has been more hostile to biotechnology in Europe than in North America. Much of this hostility is driven by the stronger environmental movements there, which have led the campaign, for example, against genetically modified foods. (Whether certain forms of radical environmentalism will translate into hostility to human biotechnology remains to be seen. Some environmentalists see themselves defending nature from human beings, and seem to be more concerned with threats to nonhuman than to human nature.) The Germans in particular remain very sensitive to anything that smacks of eugenics. The philosopher Peter Sloterdijk raised a storm of protest in 1999 when he suggested that it will soon be impossible for people to refuse the power of selection that biotechnology provides them, and that the questions of breeding something "beyond" man that were raised by Nietzsche and Plato could no longer be ignored.[19] He was condemned by the sociologist Jürgen Habermas, among others, who in other contexts has also come out against human cloning.[20]

On the other hand, there are some on the Left who have begun to make the case for genetic engineering.[21] John Rawls argued in *A Theory of Justice* that the unequal distribution of natural talents was inherently unfair. A Rawlsian should therefore want to make use of biotechnology to equalize life chances by breeding the bottom up, assuming that prudential considerations concerning safety, cost, and the like would be settled. Ronald Dworkin has laid out a case for the right of parents to genetically engineer their children based on a broader concern to protect autonomy,[22] and Laurence Tribe has suggested that a ban on cloning would be wrong because it might create discrimination against children who were cloned in spite of the ban.[23]

It is impossible to know which of these two radically different scenarios—one of growing genetic inequality, the other of growing genetic equality—is more likely to come to pass. But once the technological possibility for biomedical enhancement is realized, it is hard to see how growing genetic inequality would fail to become one of the chief controversies of twenty-first-century politics.

Human Dignity Redux

Denial of the concept of human dignity—that is, of the idea that there is something unique about the human race that entitles every member of the species to a higher moral status than the rest of the natural world—leads us down a very perilous path. We may be compelled ultimately to take this path, but we should do so only with our eyes open. Nietzsche is a much better guide to what lies down that road than the legions of bioethicists and casual academic Darwinians that today are prone to give us moral advice on this subject.

To avoid following that road, we need to take another look at the notion of human dignity, and ask whether there is a way to defend the concept against its detractors that is fully compatible with modern natural science but that also does justice to the full meaning of human specificity. I believe that there is.

In contrast to a number of conservative Protestant denominations that continue to hold a brief for creationism, the Catholic Church by the end of the twentieth century had come to terms with the theory of evolution. In his 1996 message to the Pontifical Academy of Sciences, Pope John Paul II corrected the encyclical *Humani generis* of Pius XII, which maintained that Darwinian evolution was a serious hypothesis but one that remained unproven. The pope stated, "Today, almost half a century after the publication of the Encyclical, new knowledge has led to the recognition of the theory of evolution as more than a hypothesis. It is indeed remarkable that this theory has been progressively accepted by researchers, following a series of discoveries in various fields of knowledge. The convergence, neither sought nor fabricated, of the results of work that was conducted independently is in itself a significant argument in favor of this theory."[24]

But the pope went on to say that while the church can accept the view that man is descended from nonhuman animals, there is an "ontological leap" that occurs somewhere in this evolutionary process.[25] The human soul is something directly created by God: Consequently, "theories of evolution which, in accordance with the philosophies inspiring them, consider the mind as emerging from the forces of living nature, or as a mere epiphenomenon of this matter, are incompatible with the truth about man." The pope continued, "Nor are they able to ground the dignity of the person."

The pope was saying, in other words, that at some point in the 5 million years between man's chimplike forebears and the emergence of modern human beings, a human soul was inserted into us in a way that remains mysterious. Modern natural science can uncover the time line of this process and explicate its material correlates, but it has not fully explained either what the soul is or how it came to be. The church has obviously learned a great deal from modern natural science in the past two centuries and has adjusted its doctrines accordingly. But while many natural scientists would scoff at the idea that they have anything to learn from the church, the pope has pointed to a real weakness in the current state of evolutionary theory, which scientists would do well to ponder. Modern natural science has explained a great deal less about what it means to be human than many scientists think it has.

Parts and Wholes

Many contemporary Darwinians believe that they have demystified the problem of how human beings came to be human through the classical reductionist methods of modern natural science. That is, any higher-order behavior or characteristic, such as language or aggression, can be traced back through the firing of neurons to the biochemical substrate of the brain, which in turn can be understood in terms of the simpler organic compounds of which it is composed. The brain arrived at its present state through a series of incremental evolutionary changes that were driven by random variation, and a process of natural selection by which the requirements of the surrounding environment selected for certain mental characteristics. Every human characteristic can thus be traced back to a prior material cause. If, for example, we today love to listen to Mozart or Beethoven, it is because we have auditory systems that were evolved, in the environment of evolutionary adaptation, to discriminate between certain kinds of sounds that were necessary perhaps to warn us against predators or to help us on a hunt.[26]

The problem with this kind of thinking is not that it is necessarily false but that it is insufficient to explain many of the most salient and unique human traits. The problem lies in the methodology of reductionism itself for understanding complex systems, and particularly biological ones.

Reductionism constitutes, of course, one of the foundations of modern natural science and is responsible for many of its greatest triumphs. You see before you two apparently different substances, the graphite in your pencil lead and the diamond in your engagement ring, and you might be tempted to believe that they were essentially different substances. But reductionist chemistry has taught us that in fact they are both composed of the same simpler substance, carbon, and that the apparent differences are not ones of essence but merely of the way the carbon atoms are bonded. Reductionist physics has been busy over the past century tracing atoms back to subatomic particles and thence back to an even more reduced set of basic forces of nature.

But what is appropriate for domains in physics, like celestial mechanics and fluid dynamics, is not necessarily appropriate for the study of objects at the opposite end of the complexity scale, like most biological systems, because the behavior of complex systems cannot be predicted by simply aggregating or scaling up the behavior of the parts that constitute them.* The distinctive and easily recognizable behavior of a flock of birds or a swarm of bees, for example, is the product of the interaction of individual birds or bees following relatively simple behavioral rules (fly next to a partner, avoid obstacles, and so on), none of which encompasses or defines the behavior of the flock or swarm as a whole. Rather, the group behavior "emerges" as a result of the interaction of the individuals that make it up. In many cases, the relationship between parts and wholes is nonlinear: That is, increasing input A increases output B up to a certain point, whereupon it creates a qualitatively different and unexpected output C. This is true even of relatively simple chemicals like water: H_2O undergoes a phase transition from liquid to solid at 32 degrees Fahrenheit, something that one would not necessarily predict on the basis of knowledge of its chemical composition.

That the behavior of complex wholes cannot be understood as the aggregated behavior of their parts has been understood in the natural sciences for some time now,[27] and has led to the development of the field of so-called nonlinear or "complex adaptive" systems, which try to model the emergence of complexity. This approach is, in a way, the opposite of reductionism: It shows that while wholes can be traced back to their simpler antecedent parts, there is no simple predictive model that allows us to move from the parts to the emergent behaviors of the wholes. Being nonlinear, they may be extremely sensitive to small differences in starting conditions and thus may appear chaotic even when their behavior is completely deterministic.

This means that the behavior of complex systems is much more difficult to understand than the founders of reductionist science once believed. The eighteenth-century astronomer Laplace once said that he could precisely predict the future of the universe

---

* The determinism of classical Newtonian mechanics is based in large measure on the parallelogram rule, which says that the effects of two forces acting on a body can be summed as if each were acting independently of the other. Newton shows that this rule works for celestial bodies like planets and stars, and assumes that it will also work for other natural objects, like animals.

on the basis of Newtonian mechanics, if he could know the mass and motion of the universe's constituent parts.[28] No scientist could make this claim today—not just because of the inherent uncertainties introduced by quantum mechanics but also because there exists no reliable methodology for predicting the behavior of complex systems.[29] In the words of Arthur Peacocke, "The concepts and theories . . . that constitute the content of the sciences focusing on the more complex levels are often (not always) logically not reducible to those operative in the sciences that focus on their components."[30] There is a hierarchy of levels of complexity in the sciences, with human beings and human behavior occupying a place at the uppermost level.

Each level can give us some insight into the levels above it, but understanding the lower levels does not allow one to fully understand the higher levels' emergent properties. Researchers in the area of complex adaptive systems have created so-called agent-based models of complex systems, and have applied them in a wide variety of areas, from cell biology to fighting a war to distributing natural gas. It remains to be seen, however, whether this approach constitutes a single, coherent methodology applicable to all complex systems.[31] Such models may tell us only that certain systems will remain inherently chaotic and unpredictable, or that prediction rests on a precise knowledge of initial conditions that is unavailable to us. The higher level must thus be understood with a methodology appropriate to its degree of complexity.

We can illustrate the problematic relationship of parts to wholes by reference to one unique domain of human behavior, politics.[32] Aristotle states that man is a political animal by nature. If one were to try to build a case for human dignity based on human specificity, the capability of engaging in politics would certainly constitute one important component of human uniqueness. Yet the idea of our uniqueness in this regard has been challenged. . . . [C]himpanzees and other primates engage in something that looks uncannily like human politics as they struggle and connive to achieve alpha male status. They appear, moreover, to feel the political emotions of pride and shame as they interact with other members of their group. Their political behavior can also apparently be transmitted through nongenetic means, so that political culture would not seem to be the exclusive preserve of human beings.[33] Some observers gleefully cite examples like this to deflate human feelings of self-importance relative to other species.

But to confuse human politics with the social behavior of any other species is to mistake parts for wholes. Only human beings can formulate, debate, and modify abstract rules of justice. When Aristotle asserted that man is a political animal by nature, he meant this only in the sense that politics is a potentiality that emerges over time.[34] He notes that human politics did not begin until the first lawgiver established a state and promulgated laws, an event that was of great benefit to mankind but that was contingent on historical developments. This accords with what we know today about the emergence of the state, which took place in parts of the world like Egypt and Babylonia perhaps 10,000 years ago and was most likely related to the development of agriculture. For tens of thousands of years before that, human beings lived in stateless hunter-gatherer societies in which the largest group numbered no more than 50 to 100 individuals, most of them related by kinship.[35] So in a certain sense, while human sociability is obviously natural, it is not clear that humans are political animals by nature.

But Aristotle insists that politics is natural to man despite the fact that it did not exist at all in early periods of human history. He argues that it is human language that allows human beings to formulate laws and abstract principles of justice that are necessary to the creation of a state and of political order. Ethologists have noted that many other species communicate with sounds, and that chimpanzees and other animals can learn human language to a limited extent. But no other species has *human* language—that is, the ability to formulate and communicate abstract principles of action. It is only when these two natural characteristics, human sociability and human language, come together that human politics emerges. Human language obviously evolved to promote sociability, but it is very unlikely that there were evolutionary forces shaping it to become an enabler of politics. It was rather like one of Stephen Jay Gould's spandrels,* something that evolved for one reason but that found another key purpose when combined in a human whole.[36] Human politics, though natural in an emergent sense, is not reducible to either animal sociability or animal language, which were its precursors.

Consciousness

The area in which the inability of a reductionist materialist science to explain observable phenomena is most glaringly evident is the question of human consciousness. By consciousness I mean subjective mental states: not just the thoughts and images that appear to you as you are thinking or reading this page, but also the sensations, feelings, and emotions that you experience as part of everyday life.

There has been a huge amount of research and theorizing about consciousness over the past two generations, coming in equal measure from the neurosciences and from studies in computer and artificial intelligence (AI). Particularly in the latter field there are many enthusiasts who are convinced that with more powerful computers and new approaches to computing, such as neural networks, we are on the verge of a breakthrough in which mechanical computers will achieve consciousness. There have been conferences and earnest discussions devoted to the question of whether it would be moral to turn off such a machine if and when this breakthrough occurs, and whether we would need to assign rights to conscious machines.

The fact of the matter is that we are nowhere close to a breakthrough; consciousness remains as stubbornly mysterious as it ever was. The problem with the current state of thinking begins with the traditional philosophical problem of the ontological status of consciousness. Subjective mental states, while produced by material biological processes, appear to be of a very different, nonmaterial order from other phenomena. The fear of dualism—that is, the doctrine that there are two essential types of being, material and mental—is so strong among researchers in this field that it has led them to palpably ridiculous conclusions. In the words of the philosopher John Searle,

> Seen from the perspective of the last fifty years, the philosophy of mind, as well as cognitive science and certain branches of psychology, present a very

---

* A spandrel is an architectural feature that emerges, unplanned by the architect, from the intersection of a dome and the walls that support it.

curious spectacle. The most striking feature is how much of mainstream philosophy of mind of the past fifty years seems obviously false . . . in the philosophy of mind, obvious facts about the mental, such as that we all really do have subjective conscious mental states and that these are not eliminable in favor of anything else, are routinely denied by many, perhaps most, of the advanced thinkers in the subject.[37]

An example of a patently false understanding of consciousness comes from one of the leading experts in the field, Daniel Dennett, whose book *Consciousness Explained* finally comes to the following definition of consciousness: "Human consciousness is *itself* a huge complex of memes (or more exactly, meme-effects in brains) that can best be understood as the operation of a '*von Neumannesque*' virtual machine *implemented* in the *parallel architecture* of a brain that was not designed for any such activities."[38] A naive reader may be excused for thinking that this kind of statement doesn't do much at all to advance our understanding of consciousness. Dennett is saying in effect that human consciousness is simply the by-product of the operations of a certain type of computer, and if we think that there is more to it than that, we have a mistakenly old-fashioned view of what consciousness is. As Searle says of this approach, it works only by denying the existence of what you and I and everyone else understand consciousness to be (that is, subjective feelings).[39]

Similarly, many of the researchers in the field of artificial intelligence sidestep the question of consciousness by in effect changing the subject. They assume that the brain is simply a highly complex type of organic computer that can be identified by its external characteristics. The well-known Turing test asserts that if a machine can perform a cognitive task such as carrying on a conversation in a way that from the outside is indistinguishable from similar activities carried out by a human being, then it is indistinguishable on the inside as well. Why this should be an adequate test of human mentality is a mystery, for the machine will obviously not have any subjective awareness of what it is doing, or feelings about its activities.* This doesn't prevent such authors as Hans Moravec[40] and Ray Kurzweil[41] from predicting that machines, once they reach a requisite level of complexity, will possess human attributes like consciousness as well.[42] If they are right, this will have important consequences for our notions of human dignity, because it will have been conclusively proven that human beings are essentially nothing more than complicated machines that can be made out of silicon and transistors as easily as carbon and neurons.

The likelihood that this will happen seems very remote, however, not so much because machines will never duplicate human intelligence—I suspect they will probably be able to come very close in this regard—but rather because it is impossible to see how they will come to acquire human emotions. It is the stuff of science fiction for an android, robot, or computer to suddenly start experiencing emotions like fear, hope,

───────────

* Searle's critique of this approach is contained in his "Chinese room" puzzle, which raises the question of whether a computer could be said to understand Chinese any more than a non-Chinese-speaking individual locked in a room who received instructions on how to manipulate a series of symbols in Chinese. See Searle (1997), p. 11.

even sexual desire, but no one has come remotely close to positing how this might come about. The problem is not simply that, like the rest of consciousness, no one understands what emotions are ontologically; no one understands why they came to exist in human biology.

There are of course functional reasons for feelings like pain and pleasure. If we didn't find sex pleasurable we wouldn't reproduce, and if we didn't feel pain from fire we would be burning ourselves constantly. But state-of-the-art thinking in cognitive science maintains that the particular subjective form that the emotions take is not necessary to their function. It is perfectly possible, for example, to design a robot with heat sensors in its fingers connected to an actuator that would pull the robot's hand away from a fire. The robot could keep itself from being burned without having any subjective sense of pain, and it could make decisions on which objectives to fulfill and which activities to avoid on the basis of a mechanical computation of the inputs of different electrical impulses. A Turing test would say it was a human being in its behavior, but it would actually be devoid of the most important quality of a human being, feelings. The actual subjective forms that emotions take are today seen in evolutionary biology and in cognitive science as no more than epiphenomenal to their underlying function; there are no obvious reasons this form should have been selected for in the course of evolutionary history.[43]

As Robert Wright points out, this leads to the very bizarre outcome that what is most important to us as human beings has no apparent purpose in the material scheme of things by which we became human.[44] For it is the distinctive human gamut of emotions that produces human purposes, goals, objectives, wants, needs, desires, fears, aversions, and the like and hence is the source of human values. While many would list human reason and human moral choice as the most important unique human characteristics that give our species dignity, I would argue that possession of the full human emotional gamut is at least as important, if not more so.

The political theorist Robert McShea demonstrates the importance of human emotions to our commonsense understanding of what it means to be human by asking us to perform the following thought experiment.[45] Suppose you met two creatures on a desert island, both of which had the rational capacity of a human being and hence the ability to carry on a conversation. One had the physical form of a lion but the emotions of a human being, while the other had the physical form of a human being but the emotional characteristics of a lion. Which creature would you feel more comfortable with, which creature would you be more likely to befriend or enter into a moral relationship with? The answer, as countless children's books with sympathetic talking lions suggest, is the lion, because species-typical human emotions are more critical to our sense of our own humanness than either our reason or our physical appearance.

> **We would regard a Mr. Spock who was truly devoid of any feelings as a psychopath and a monster.**

ther our reason or our physical appearance. The coolly analytical Mr. Spock in the TV series *Star Trek* appears at times more likable than the emotional Mr. Scott only because we suspect that somewhere beneath his rational exterior lurk deeply buried human feelings. Certainly many of the female characters he encountered in the series hoped they could rouse something more than robotic responses from him.

On the other hand, we would regard a Mr. Spock who was truly devoid of any feel-   55
ings as a psychopath and a monster. If he offered us a benefit, we might accept it but
would feel no gratitude because we would know it was the product of rational calculation on his part and not goodwill. If we double-crossed him, we would feel no guilt,
because we know that he cannot himself entertain feelings of anger or of having been
betrayed. And if circumstances forced us to kill him to save ourselves, or to sacrifice
his life in a hostage situation, we would feel no more regret than if we lost any other
valuable asset, like a car or a teleporter.[46] Even though we might want to cooperate
with this Mr. Spock, we would not regard him as a moral agent entitled to the respect
that human beings command. The computer geeks in AI labs who think of themselves
as nothing more than complex computer programs and want to download themselves
into a computer should worry, since no one would care if they were turned off for good.

So there is a great deal that comes together under the rubric of consciousness that
helps define human specificity and hence human dignity, which nonetheless cannot
currently be fully explicated by modern natural science. It is not sufficient to argue that
some other animals are conscious, or have culture, or have language, for their consciousness does not combine human reason, human language, human moral choice,
and human emotions in ways that are capable of producing human politics, human
art, or human religion. All of the nonhuman precursors of these human traits that existed in evolutionary history, and all of the material causes and preconditions for their
emergence, collectively add up to much less than the human whole. Jared Diamond in
his book *The Third Chimpanzee* notes the fact that the chimpanzee and human genomes
overlap by more than 98 percent, implying that the differences between the two species
are relatively trivial.[47] But for an emergent complex system, small differences can lead
to enormous qualitative changes. It is a bit like saying there is no significant difference
between ice and liquid water because they differ in temperature by only 1 degree.

Thus one does not have to agree with the pope that God directly inserted a human
soul in the course of evolutionary history to acknowledge with him that there was a
very important qualitative, if not ontological, leap that occurred at some point in this
process. It is this leap from parts to a whole that ultimately has to constitute the basis
for human dignity, a concept one can believe in even if one does not begin from the
pope's religious premises.

What this whole is and how it came to be remain, in Searle's word, "mysterious."
None of the branches of modern natural science that have tried to address this question
have done more than scratch the surface, despite the belief of many scientists that they
have demystified the entire process. It is common now for many AI researchers to say
that consciousness is an "emergent property" of a certain kind of complex computer.
But this is no more than an unproven hypothesis based on an analogy with other complex systems. No one has ever seen consciousness emerge under experimental conditions, or even posited a theory as to how this might come about. It would be surprising
if the process of "emergence" didn't play an important part in explaining how humans
came to be human, but whether that is all there is to the story is something we do not
at present know.

This is not to say that the demystification by science will never happen. Searle himself believes that consciousness is a biological property of the brain much like the firing
of neurons or the production of neurotransmitters and that biology will someday be

able to explain how organic tissue can produce it. He argues that our present problems in understanding consciousness do not require us to adopt a dualistic ontology or abandon the scientific framework of material causation. The problem of how consciousness arose does not require recourse to the direct intervention of God.

It does not, on the other hand, rule it out, either.

What to Fight For

If what gives us dignity and a moral status higher than that of other living creatures is related to the fact that we are complex wholes rather than the sum of simple parts, then it is clear that there is no simple answer to the question, What is Factor X? That is, Factor X cannot be reduced to the possession of moral choice, or reason, or language, or sociability, or sentience, or emotions, or consciousness, or any other quality that has been put forth as a ground for human dignity. It is all of these qualities coming together in a human whole that make up Factor X. Every member of the human species possesses a genetic endowment that allows him or her to become a whole human being, an endowment that distinguishes a human in essence from other types of creatures.

A moment's reflection will show that none of the key qualities that contribute to human dignity can exist in the absence of the others. Human reason, for example, is not that of a computer; it is pervaded by emotions, and its functioning is in fact facilitated by the latter.[48] Moral choice cannot exist without reason, needless to say, but it is also grounded in feelings such as pride, anger, shame, and sympathy.[49] Human consciousness is not just individual preferences and instrumental reason, but is shaped intersubjectively by other consciousnesses and their moral evaluations. We are social and political animals not merely because we are capable of game-theoretic reason, but because we are endowed with certain social emotions. Human sentience is not that of a pig or a horse, because it is coupled with human memory and reason.

This protracted discussion of human dignity is intended to answer the following question: What is it that we want to protect from any future advances in biotechnology? The answer is, we want to protect the full range of our complex, evolved natures against attempts at self-modification. We do not want to disrupt either the unity or the continuity of human nature, and thereby the human rights that are based on it.

If Factor X is related to our very complexity and the complex interactions of uniquely human characteristics like moral choice, reason, and a broad emotional gamut, it is reasonable to ask how and why biotechnology would seek to make us less complex. The answer lies in the constant pressure that exists to reduce the ends of biomedicine to utilitarian ones—that is, the attempt to reduce a complex diversity of natural ends and purposes to just a few simple categories like pain and pleasure, or autonomy. There is in particular a constant predisposition to allow the relief of pain and suffering to automatically trump all other human purposes and objectives. For this will be the constant trade-off that biotechnology will pose: We can cure this disease, or prolong this person's life, or make this child more tractable, at the expense of some ineffable human quality like genius, or ambition, or sheer diversity.

That aspect of our complex natures most under threat has to do with our emotional gamut. We will be constantly tempted to think that we understand what "good" and "bad" emotions are, and that we can do nature one better by suppressing the latter, by trying to make people less aggressive, more sociable, more compliant, less depressed. The utilitarian goal of minimizing suffering is itself very problematic. No one can make a brief in favor of pain and suffering, but the fact of the matter is that what we consider to be the highest and most admirable human qualities, both in ourselves and in others, are often related to the way that we react to, confront, overcome, and frequently succumb to pain, suffering, and death. In the absence of these human evils there would be no sympathy, compassion, courage, heroism, solidarity, or strength of character.* A person who has not confronted suffering or death has no depth. Our ability to experience these emotions is what connects us potentially to all other human beings, both living and dead.

Many scientists and researchers would say that we don't need to worry about fencing off human nature, however defined, from biotechnology, because we are a very long way from being able to modify it, and may never achieve the capability. They may be right: Human germ-line engineering and the use of recombinant DNA technology on humans are probably much further off than many people assume, though human cloning is not.

But our ability to manipulate human behavior is not dependent on the development of genetic engineering. Virtually everything we can anticipate being able to do through genetic engineering we will most likely be able to do much sooner through neuropharmacology. And we will face large demographic changes in the populations that find new biomedical technologies available to them, not only in terms of age and sex distributions, but in terms of the quality of life of important population groups.

The widespread and rapidly growing use of drugs like Ritalin and Prozac demonstrates just how eager we are to make use of technology to alter ourselves. If one of the key constituents of our nature, something on which we base our notions of dignity, has to do with the gamut of normal emotions shared by human beings, then we are *already* trying to narrow the range for the utilitarian ends of health and convenience.

Psychotropic drugs do not alter the germ line or produce heritable effects in the way that genetic engineering someday might. But they already raise important issues about the meaning of human dignity and are a harbinger of things to come.

When Do We Become Human?

In the near term, the big ethical controversies raised by biotechnology will not be threats to the dignity of normal adult human beings but rather to those who possess something less than the full complement of capabilities that we have defined as characterizing human specificity. The largest group of beings in this category are the unborn, but it could also include infants, the terminally sick, elderly people with debilitating diseases, and the disabled.   70

This issue has already come up with regard to stem cell research and cloning. Embryonic stem cell research requires the deliberate destruction of embryos, while so-called therapeutic cloning requires not just their destruction but their deliberate creation for research purposes prior to destruction. (As bioethicist Leon Kass notes,

---

* The Greek root of *sympathy* and the Latin root of *compassion* both refer to the ability to feel another person's pain and suffering.

therapeutic cloning is not therapeutic for the embryo.) Both activities have been strongly condemned by those who believe that life begins at conception and that embryos have full moral status as human beings.

I do not want to rehearse the whole history of the abortion debate and the hotly contested question of when life begins. I personally do not begin with religious convictions on this issue and admit to considerable confusion in trying to think through its rights and wrongs. The question here is, What does the natural-rights approach to human dignity outlined here suggest about the moral status of the unborn, the disabled, and so on? I'm not sure it produces a definitive answer, but it can at least help us frame an answer to the question.

At first blush, a natural-rights doctrine that bases human dignity on the fact that the human species possesses certain unique characteristics would appear to allow a gradation of rights depending on the degree to which any individual member of that species shares in those characteristics. An elderly person with Alzheimer's, for example, has lost the normal adult ability to reason, and therefore that part of his dignity that would permit him to participate in politics by voting or running for office. Reason, moral choice, and possession of the species-typical emotional gamut are things that are shared by virtually all human beings and therefore serve as a basis for universal equality, but individuals possess these traits in greater or lesser amounts: Some are more reasonable, have stronger consciences or more sensitive emotions than others. At one extreme, minute distinctions could be made between individuals based on the degree to which they possess these basic human qualities, with differentiated rights assigned to them on that basis. This has happened before in history; it is called natural aristocracy. The hierarchical system it implies is one of the reasons people have become suspicious of the very concept of natural rights.

There is a strong prudential reason for not being too hierarchical in the assignment of political rights, however. There is, in the first place, no consensus on a precise definition of that list of essential human characteristics that qualify an individual for rights. More important, judgments about the degree to which a given individual possesses one or another of these qualities are very difficult to make, and usually suspect, because the person making the judgment is seldom a disinterested party. Most real-world aristocracies have been conventional rather than natural, with the aristocrats assigning themselves rights that they claimed were natural but that were actually based on force or convention. It is therefore appropriate to approach the question of who qualifies for rights with some liberality.

Nonetheless, every contemporary liberal democracy does in fact differentiate rights based on the degree to which individuals or categories of individuals share in certain species-typical characteristics. Children, for example, do not have the rights of adults because their capacities for reason and moral choice are not fully developed; they cannot vote and do not have the freedom of person that their parents do in making choices about where to live, whether to go to school, and so on. Societies strip criminals of basic rights for violating the law, and do so more severely in the case of those regarded as lacking a basic human moral sense. In the United States, they can be deprived even of the right to life for certain kinds of crimes. We do not officially strip Alzheimer's patients of their political rights, but we do restrict their ability to drive and make financial decisions, and in practice they usually cease to exercise their political rights as well.

From a natural-rights perspective, then, one could argue that it is reasonable to assign the unborn different rights from those of either infants or children. A day-old infant may not be capable of reason or moral choice, but it already possesses important elements of the normal human emotional gamut — it can get upset, bond to its mother, expect attention, and the like, in ways that a day-old embryo cannot. It is the violation of the natural and very powerful bonding that takes place between parent and infant, in fact, that makes infanticide such a heinous crime in most societies. That we typically hold funerals after the deaths of infants but not after miscarriages is testimony to the naturalness of this distinction. All of this suggests that it does not make sense to treat embryos as human beings with the same kinds of rights that infants possess.

Against this line of argument, we can pose the following considerations, again not from a religious but from a natural-rights perspective. An embryo may be lacking in some of the basic human characteristics possessed by an infant, but it is also not just another group of cells or tissue, because it has the *potential* to become a full human being. In this respect, it differs from an infant, which also lacks many of the most important characteristics of a normal adult human being, only in the degree to which it has realized its natural potential. This implies that while an embryo can be assigned a lower moral status than an infant, it has a higher moral status than other kinds of cells or tissue that scientists work with. It is therefore reasonable, on nonreligious grounds, to question whether researchers should be free to create, clone, and destroy human embryos at will.

Ontogeny recapitulates phylogeny. We have argued that in the evolutionary process that leads from prehuman ancestor to human beings, there was a qualitative leap that transformed the prehuman precursors of language, reason, and emotion into a human whole that cannot be explained as a simple sum of its parts, and that remains an essentially mysterious process. Something similar happens with the development of every embryo into an infant, child, and adult human being: What starts out as a cluster of organic molecules comes to possess consciousness, reason, the capacity for moral choice, and subjective emotions, in a manner that remains equally mysterious.

Putting these facts together — that an embryo has a moral status somewhere between that of an infant and that of other types of cells and tissue, and that the transformation of the embryo into something with a higher status is a mysterious process — suggests that if we are to do things like harvest stem cells from embryos, we should put a lot of limits and constraints around this activity to make sure that it does not become a precedent for other uses of the unborn that would push the envelope further. To what extent are we willing to create and grow embryos for utilitarian purposes? Supposing some miraculous new cure required cells not from a day-old embryo, but tissue from a month-old fetus? A five-month-old female fetus already has in her ovaries all the eggs she will ever produce as a woman; supposing someone wanted access to them? If we get too used to the idea of cloning embryos for medical purposes, will we know when to stop?

If the question of equality in a future biotech world threatens to tear up the Left, 80 the Right will quite literally fall apart over questions related to human dignity. In the United States, the Right (as represented by the Republican Party) is divided between economic libertarians, who like entrepreneurship and technology with minimal regulation, and social conservatives, many of whom are religious, who care about a range of issues including abortion and the family. The coalition between these two groups is usually strong enough to hold up during elections, but it papers over some fundamental differences in outlook. It is not clear that this alliance will survive the emergence of new technologies that, on the one hand, offer enormous health benefits and money-making opportunities for the biotech industry, but, on the other, require violating deeply held ethical norms.

We are thus brought back to the question of politics and political strategies. For if there is a viable concept of human dignity out there, it needs to be defended, not just in philosophical tracts but in the real world of politics, and protected by viable political institutions. . . .

NOTES

1. Clive Staples Lewis, *The Abolition of Man* (New York: Touchstone, 1944), p. 85.
2. Counsel of Europe, Draft Additional Protocol to the Convention on Human Rights and Biomedicine, On the Prohibiting of Cloning Human Beings, Doc. 7884, July 16, 1997.
3. This is the theme of the second part of Francis Fukuyama, *The End of History and the Last Man* (New York: Free Press, 1992).
4. For an interpretation of this passage in Tocqueville, see Francis Fukuyama, "The March of Equality," *Journal of Democracy* 11 (2000): 11–17.
5. John Paul II, "Message to the Pontifical Academy of Sciences," October 22, 1996.
6. Daniel C. Dennett, *Darwin's Dangerous Idea: Evolution and the Meanings of Life* (New York: Simon and Schuster, 1995), pp. 35–39; see also Ernst Mayr, *One Long Argument: Charles Darwin and the Genesis of Modern Evolutionary Thought* (Cambridge, Mass.: Harvard University Press, 1991), pp. 40–42.
7. Michael Ruse and David L. Hull, *The Philosophy of Biology* (New York: Oxford University Press, 1998), p. 385.
8. Lee M. Silver, *Remaking Eden: Cloning and Beyond in a Brave New World* (New York: Avon, 1998), pp. 256–57.
9. Ruse and Hull (1998), p. 385.
10. Silver (1998), p. 277.
11. Friedrich Nietzsche, *Thus Spoke Zarathustra*, First part, section 5, from *The Portable Nietzsche*, ed. Walter Kaufmann (New York: Viking, 1968), p. 130.
12. Charles Taylor, *Sources of the Self: The Making of the Modern Identity* (Cambridge, Mass.: Harvard University Press, 1989), pp. 6–7.
13. For a fuller defense of this proposition, see Francis Fukuyama, *The Great Disruption: Human Nature and the Reconstitution of Social Order*, part II (New York: Free Press, 1999).
14. Aristotle, *Politics* I.2.13, 1254b, 16–24.
15. Ibid., I.2.18, 1255a, 22–38.
16. Ibid., I.2.19, 1255b, 3–5.
17. See, for example, Dan W. Brock, "The Human Genome Project and Human Identity," in *Genes, Humans, and Self-Knowledge*, eds. Robert F. Weir and Susan C. Lawrence et al. (Iowa City: University of Iowa Press, 1994), pp. 18–23.
18. This possibility has already been suggested by Charles Murray. See his "Deeper into the Brain," *National Review* 52 (2000): 46–49.
19. Peter Sloterdijk, "Regeln für den Menschenpark: Ein Antwortschreiben zum Brief über den Humanismus," *Die Zeit*, no. 38, September 16, 1999.
20. Jürgen Habermas, "Nicht die Natur verbietet das Klonen. Wir müssen selbst entscheiden. Eine Replik auf Dieter E. Zimmer," *Die Zeit*, no. 9, February 19, 1998.
21. For a discussion of this issue, see Allen Buchanan and Norman Daniels et al., *From Chance to Choice: Genetics and Justice* (New York and Cambridge: Cambridge University Press, 2000), pp. 17–20. See also Robert H. Blank and Masako N. Darrough, *Biological*

Differences and Social Equality: Implications for Social Policy (Westport, Conn.: Green-wood Press, 1983).

22. Ronald M. Dworkin, *Sovereign Virtue: The Theory and Practice of Equality* (Cambridge, Mass.: Harvard University Press, 2000), p. 452.

23. Laurence H. Tribe, "Second Thoughts on Cloning," *New York Times*, December 5, 1997, p. A31.

24. John Paul II (1996).

25. On the meaning of this "ontological leap," see Ernan McMullin, "Biology and the Theology of the Human," in Phillip R. Sloan, ed., *Controlling Our Desires: Historical, Philosophical, Ethical, and Theological Perspectives on the Human Genome Project* (Notre Dame, Ind.: University of Notre Dame Press, 2000), p. 367.

26. It is in fact very difficult to come up with a Darwinian explanation for the human enjoyment of music. See Steven Pinker, *How the Mind Works* (New York: W. W. Norton, 1997), pp. 528–38.

27. See, for example, Arthur Peacocke, "Relating Genetics to Theology on the Map of Scientific Knowledge," in Sloan, ed. (2000), pp. 346–50.

28. Laplace's exact words were: "We ought then to regard the present state of the universe [not just the solar system] as the effect of its anterior state and as the cause of the one which is to follow. Given an intelligence that could comprehend at one instant all the forces by which nature is animated and the respective situation of the beings who compose it—an intelligence sufficiently vast to submit these data [initial conditions] to analysis—it would embrace in the same formula the movements of the greatest bodies in the universe and those of the lightest atom; for it, nothing would be uncertain and the future, as the past, would be present to its eyes. . . . The regularity which astronomy shows us in the movements of the comets doubtless exists also in all phenomena. The curve described by a simple molecule of air or vapor is regulated in a manner just as certain as the planetary orbits; the only difference between them is that which comes from our ignorance." Quoted in *Final Causality in Nature and Human Affairs*, ed. Richard F. Hassing (Washington, D.C.: Catholic University Press, 1997), p. 224.

29. Hassing, ed. (1997), pp. 224–26.

30. Peacocke, in Sloan, ed. (2000), p. 350.

31. McMullin, in Sloan, ed. (2000), p. 374.

32. On this question, see Roger D. Masters, "The Biological Nature of the State," *World Politics* 35 (1983): 161–93.

33. Andrew Goldberg and Christophe Boesch, "The Cultures of Chimpanzees," *Scientific American* 284 (2001): 60–67.

34. Larry Arnhart, *Darwinian Natural Right: The Biological Ethics of Human Nature* (Albany, N.Y.: State University of New York Press, 1998), pp. 61–62.

35. One exception to this appears to be the indigenous peoples of the American Pacific Northwest, a hunter-gatherer society that seems to have developed a state. See Robert Wright, *Nonzero: The Logic of Human Destiny* (New York: Pantheon Books, 2000), pp. 31–38.

36. Stephen Jay Gould and R. C. Lewontin, "The Spandrels of San Marco and the Panglossian Paradigm: A Critique of the Adaptionist Programme," *Proceedings of the Royal Society of London* 205 (1979): 81–98.

37. John R. Searle, *The Mystery of Consciousness* (New York: New York Review Books, 1997).

38. Daniel C. Dennett, *Consciousness Explained* (Boston: Little, Brown, 1991), p. 210.

39. John R. Searle, *The Rediscovery of the Mind* (Cambridge, Mass.: MIT Press, 1992), p. 3.

40. Hans P. Moravec, *Robot: Mere Machine to Transcendent Mind* (New York: Oxford University Press, 1999).
41. Ray Kurzweil, *The Age of Spiritual Machines: When Computers Exceed Human Intelligence* (London: Penguin Books, 2000).
42. For a critique, see Colin McGinn, "Hello HAL," *New York Times Book Review*, January 3, 1999.
43. On this point, see Wright (2000), pp. 306–8.
44. Ibid., pp. 321–22.
45. Robert J. McShea, *Morality and Human Nature: A New Route to Ethical Theory* (Philadelphia: Temple University Press, 1990), p. 77.
46. Daniel Dennett makes the following bizarre statement in *Consciousness Explained*: "But why should it matter, you may want to ask, that a creature's desires are thwarted if they aren't conscious desires? I reply: Why would it matter more if they were conscious—especially if consciousness were a property, as some think, that forever eludes investigation? Why should a 'zombie's' crushed hopes matter less than a conscious person's crushed hopes? There is a trick with mirrors here that should be exposed and discarded. Consciousness, you say, is what matters, but then you cling to doctrines about consciousness that systematically prevent us from getting any purchase on *why* it matters" (p. 450). Dennett's question begs a more obvious one: What person in the world would care about crushing a zombie's hopes, except to the extent that the zombie was instrumentally useful to that person?
47. Jared Diamond, *The Third Chimpanzee* (New York: HarperCollins, 1992), p. 23.
48. The dualism between reason and emotion—that is, the idea that these are distinct and separable mental qualities—can be traced to Descartes (see *The Passions of the Soul*, Article 47). This dichotomy has been widely accepted since then but is misleading in many ways. The neurophysiologist Antonio Damasio points out that human reasoning invariably involves what he labels somatic markers—emotions that the mind attaches to certain ideas or options in the course of thinking through a problem—that help speed many kinds of calculations. Antonio R. Damasio, *Descartes' Error: Emotion, Reason, and the Human Brain* (New York: Putnam, 1994).
49. That is, the Kantian notion that moral choice is an act of pure reason overriding or suppressing natural emotions is not the way that human beings actually make moral choices. Human beings more typically balance one set of feelings against another and build character by strengthening the pleasurability of good moral choices through habit.

Exploring Context

1. Fukuyama opens this chapter by quoting from a decree from the Council of Europe. Visit the council's website at coe.int and search for information on cloning. What else does the council have to say on the issue? How does its position reflect or complicate Fukuyama's argument?

2. Fukuyama turns to complexity theory to recuperate an understanding of the human essence. Conway's Game of Life is a classic mathematical model illustrating how simple rules governing individual parts can combine into very complex wholes. Play the Game of Life at bitstorm.org/gameoflife. Does it reflect the evolution of consciousness? How often does a stable pattern emerge in the game? How does it support or undercut Fukuyama's arguments about Factor X?

3. Fukuyama asks, "What is it that we want to protect from any future advances in biotechnology?" (p. 201). Visit the website of the *American Journal of Bioethics* at bioethics.net. In browsing through the site, what answers to Fukuyama's question can you find? How can we decide which biotechnologies should be pursued and which would cause us to lose our humanity?

Questions for Connecting

1. Michael Pollan's discussion of "holons" in "The Animals: Practicing Complexity" (p. 373) seems closely related to Fukuyama's use of complexity theory. In what ways are humans and organic farms similar? What insight does Pollan's essay provide on Fukuyama's argument?

2. In "The End of Race: Hawaii and the Mixing of Peoples" (p. 334), Steve Olson suggests that, as a result of intermarriage, race no longer has a genetic basis. Is race part of Factor X? How does Fukuyama's essay support or complicate Olson's argument about race? Is race part of being human? Is it part of human dignity? You may want to use the definition of human dignity you developed in Question 3 of Questions for Critical Reading in making your argument.

3. According to Richard Restak in "Attention Deficit: The Brain Syndrome of Our Era" (p. 411), our brains are being rewired to produce attention deficit disorder. Is multitasking a threat to human dignity as well? If culture can change the wiring of our brains, then is that, too, a kind of biotechnology?

4. **CONNECTING TO E-PAGES** What does Charles Duhigg and David Barboza's "In China, Human Costs Are Built Into an iPad" (bedfordstmartins.com/emerging/epages) say about human dignity? Use quotations from that text and from Fukuyama to support your conclusions.

Language Matters

1. Select a key paragraph from the essay and then reduce each sentence of the paragraph down to a single subject and verb. What is lost by condensing the sentences in this way? What other grammatical constructions help carry the meaning of a sentence?

2. Select a particularly complex sentence from this essay. Begin by breaking this sentence down into several smaller sentences. Try substituting simpler vocabulary, too. Once you've absorbed the ideas through this process, try stating out loud a summary of what Fukuyama is trying to communicate and then write down what you say. Try these same strategies in your own writing.

3. You're probably familiar with common parts of speech like nouns and verbs. Using Fukuyama's text, create new parts of speech from common combinations of the usual parts of speech. For example, a noun and a verb together might form a "quarplat," an adverb and an adjective might be a "jerbad." Create rules for your parts of speech. When does Fukuyama use the kinds of constructions you've named? When might you?

Assignments for Writing

1. Write a paper in which you explain what it means to be human. In making your argument, you should account for the fact that Fukuyama identifies many different qualities
as being necessary to Factor X. Why, then, does he call them collectively "Factor X"?
How do you account for the seemingly infinite number of divergent views on what it is
to be human? Use your definition of Factor X from Question 1 of Questions for Critical
Reading.

2. Fukuyama acknowledges the difficulties that a vision of human equality presents when
dealing with specific populations, including the elderly, disabled, and terminally ill.
Write a paper in which you suggest standards for dealing with these boundary populations in relation to medical advances such as biotechnology. How might you change
Fukuyama's working definitions of Factor X to be more inclusive? Consider using any
specific examples you located from your work with the *American Journal of Bioethics*
website in Question 3 of Exploring Context.

3. Fukuyama stresses the centrality of human nature in current political and ethical debate. Some environmentalists would consider his discussion anthropocentric. What
about natural life beyond human beings? Write a paper in which you extend Fukuyama's
discussion of human dignity to account for the natural environment, ecosystems, and
other forms of life. You may want to identify those parts of Fukuyama's essay that deal
directly with the distinction between the "natural" and "human" worlds as a point of
departure for this discussion. What happens when we extend the concept of dignity
beyond humans? Would it change the way we acquire our food or what we eat? Consider
your work with Michael Pollan from Question 1 of Questions for Connecting.

DANIEL GILBERT

Daniel Gilbert is a professor of psychology at Harvard University. He has won a Guggenheim fellowship, as well as the American Psychological Association's Distinguished Scientific Award for an Early Career Contribution to Psychology. In 2002, *Personality and Social Psychology Bulletin* named him one of the fifty most influential social psychologists of the decade. In addition to his book *Stumbling on Happiness* (2006) and his scholarly publications, Gilbert has published works of science fiction as well as contributed to the *New York Times*, the *Los Angeles Times*, *Forbes*, and *Time*. He was elected to the American Academy of Arts and Sciences in 2008.

In *Stumbling on Happiness*, a *New York Times* best-seller, Gilbert applies his expertise to the study of happiness itself. Gilbert argues that people are rarely able to predict with any accuracy how they will feel in the future, and so are often quite wrong about what will make them happy.

In "Reporting Live from Tomorrow," a chapter from *Stumbling on Happiness*, Gilbert suggests that beliefs, just like genes, can be "super-replicators," given to spreading regardless of their usefulness. Thus even beliefs that are based on inaccurate information can provide the means for their own propagation. Gilbert explains why humans, with their unreliable memories and imaginations, are so easily susceptible to such beliefs. Though "the best way to predict our feelings tomorrow is to see how others are feeling today" (p. 222), most of us are unwilling to make use of the experiences of others because we mistakenly believe ourselves to be unique.

The pursuit of happiness is central to our understanding of America—we all want to be happy. But this selection cautions us about predicting our future happiness and in the process provides the tools we need to correct our misapprehensions.

▶ TAGS: *happiness, decision making, research, identity, surrogates, super-replicators*

Questions for Critical Reading

1. As you read Gilbert's text, look for the term *super-replicator*. What does this term mean? Develop a definition using Gilbert's text and then offer an example not included in his essay. What function does this concept serve in Gilbert's argument?

2. What does Gilbert mean by *surrogate*? You will notice as you read that Gilbert never explicitly defines the term. Instead, you should read his text critically and construct a definition out of quotations you find that discuss the idea.

3. Using Gilbert's text, define *happiness*. As with *surrogate*, you will need to analyze Gilbert's text to construct this definition. What does it mean in the context of this essay, and what does it mean for you?

Reporting Live from Tomorrow

In Alfred Hitchcock's 1956 remake of *The Man Who Knew Too Much*, Doris Day sang a waltz whose final verse went like this:

> When I was just a child in school,
> I asked my teacher, "What will I try?
> Should I paint pictures, should I sing songs?"
> This was her wise reply:
> "*Que sera, sera.* Whatever will be, will be.
> The future's not ours to see. *Que sera, sera.*"[1]

Now, I don't mean to quibble with the lyricist, and I have nothing but fond memories of Doris Day, but the fact is that this is *not* a particularly wise reply. When a child asks for advice about which of two activities to pursue, a teacher should be able to provide more than a musical cliché. Yes, of *course* the future is hard to see. But we're all heading that way anyhow, and as difficult as it may be to envision, we have to make *some* decisions about which futures to aim for and which to avoid. If we are prone to mistakes when we try to imagine the future, then how *should* we decide what to do?

Even a child knows the answer to that one: We should ask the teacher. One of the benefits of being a social and linguistic animal is that we can capitalize on the experience of others rather than trying to figure everything out for ourselves. For millions of years, human beings have conquered their ignorance by dividing the labor of discovery and then communicating their discoveries to one another, which is why the average newspaper boy in Pittsburgh knows more about the universe than did Galileo, Aristotle, Leonardo,* or any of those other guys who were so smart they only needed one name. We all make ample use of this resource. If you were to write down everything you know and then go back through the list and make a check mark next to the things you know only because somebody told you, you'd develop a repetitive-motion disorder because almost *everything* you know is secondhand. Was Yury Gagarin the first man in space? Is *croissant* a French word? Are there more Chinese than North Dakotans? Does a stitch in time save nine? Most of us know the answers to these questions despite the fact that none of us actually witnessed the launching of *Vostok I*, personally supervised the evolution of language, hand-counted all the people in Beijing and Bismarck, or performed a fully randomized double-blind study of stitching. We know the answers because someone shared them with us. Communication is a kind of "vicarious

---

* Galileo, Aristotle, Leonardo: Three geniuses. Galileo Galilei (1564–1642) was an Italian mathematician and astronomer best known for his extremely controversial belief that the earth revolves around the sun. Aristotle (384–322 BC) was a Greek philosopher and an enormously important figure in Western thought. He was a student of Plato and a teacher of Alexander the Great. Leonardo da Vinci (1452–1519) was an Italian Renaissance painter, sculptor, and scientist best known for the *Mona Lisa* and *The Last Supper* [Ed.].

observation"[2] that allows us to learn about the world without ever leaving the comfort of our Barcaloungers. The six billion interconnected people who cover the surface of our planet constitute a leviathan with twelve billion eyes, and anything that is seen by one pair of eyes can potentially be known to the entire beast in a matter of months, days, or even minutes.

The fact that we can communicate with one another about our experiences should provide a simple solution to the core problem with which this book has been concerned. Yes, our ability to imagine our future emotions is flawed—but that's okay, because we don't have to imagine what it would feel like to marry a lawyer, move to Texas, or eat a snail when there are so many people who have *done* these things and are all too happy to tell us about them. Teachers, neighbors, coworkers, parents, friends, lovers, children, uncles, cousins, coaches, cabdrivers, bartenders, hairstylists, dentists, advertisers—each of these folks has something to say about what it would be like to live in this future rather than that one, and at any point in time we can be fairly sure that one of these folks has actually *had* the experience that we are merely contemplating. Because we are the mammal that shows and tells, each of us has access to information about almost any experience we can possibly imagine—and many that we can't. Guidance counselors tell us about the best careers, critics tell us about the best restaurants, travel agents tell us about the best vacations, and friends tell us about the best travel agents. Every one of us is surrounded by a platoon of Dear Abbys who can recount their own experiences and in so doing tell us which futures are most worth wanting.

Given the overabundance of consultants, role models, gurus, mentors, yentas,* and nosy relatives, we might expect people to do quite well when it comes to making life's most important decisions, such as where to live, where to work, and whom to marry. And yet, the average American moves more than six times,[3] changes jobs more than ten times,[4] and marries more than once,[5] which suggests that most of us are making more than a few poor choices. If humanity is a living library of information about what it feels like to do just about anything that can be done, then why do the people with the library cards make so many bad decisions? There are just two possibilities. The first is that a lot of the advice we receive from others is bad advice that we foolishly accept. The second is that a lot of the advice we receive from others is good advice that we foolishly reject. So which is it? Do we listen too well when others speak, or do we not listen well enough? As we shall see, the answer to that question is *yes.*

Super-Replicators

The philosopher Bertrand Russell once claimed that believing is "the most mental thing we do."[6] Perhaps, but it is also the most *social* thing we do. Just as we pass along our genes in an effort to create people whose faces look like ours, so too do we pass along our beliefs in an effort to create people whose minds think like ours. Almost any time we tell anyone anything, we are attempting to change the way their brains

5

---

* Yenta: A Yiddish slang word meaning a person, especially a woman, who is gossipy and always ready to offer an opinion [Ed.].

operate—attempting to change the way they see the world so that their view of it more closely resembles our own. Just about every assertion—from the sublime ("God has a plan for you") to the mundane ("Turn left at the light, go two miles, and you'll see the Dunkin' Donuts on your right")—is meant to bring the listener's beliefs about the world into harmony with the speaker's. Sometimes these attempts succeed and sometimes they fail. So what determines whether a belief will be successfully transmitted from one mind to another?

The principles that explain why some genes are transmitted more successfully than others also explain why some beliefs are transmitted more successfully than others.[7] Evolutionary biology teaches us that any gene that promotes its own "means of transmission" will be represented in increasing proportions in the population over time. For instance, imagine that a single gene were responsible for the complex development of the neural circuitry that makes orgasms feel so good. For a person having this gene, orgasms would feel . . . well, orgasmic. For a person lacking this gene, orgasms would feel more like sneezes—brief, noisy, physical convulsions that pay rather paltry hedonic dividends. Now, if we took fifty healthy, fertile people who had the gene and fifty healthy, fertile people who didn't, and left them on a hospitable planet for a million years or so, when we returned we would probably find a population of thousands or millions of people, almost all of whom had the gene. Why? Because a gene that made orgasms feel good would tend to be transmitted from generation to generation simply because people who enjoy orgasms are inclined to do the thing that transmits their genes. The logic is so circular that it is virtually inescapable: Genes tend to be transmitted when they make us do the things that transmit genes. What's more, even *bad* genes—those that make us prone to cancer or heart disease—can become super-replicators if they compensate for these costs by promoting their own means of transmission. For instance, if the gene that made orgasms feel delicious also left us prone to arthritis and tooth decay, that gene might still be represented in increasing proportions because arthritic, toothless people who love orgasms are more likely to have children than are limber, toothy people who do not.

The same logic can explain the transmission of beliefs. If a particular belief has some property that facilitates its own transmission, then that belief tends to be held by an increasing number of minds. As it turns out, there are several such properties that increase a belief's transmissional success, the most obvious of which is accuracy. When someone tells us where to find a parking space downtown or how to bake a cake at high altitude, we adopt that belief and pass it along because it helps us and our friends do the things we want to do, such as parking and baking. As one philosopher noted, "The faculty of communication would not gain ground in evolution unless it was by and large the faculty of transmitting true beliefs."[8] Accurate beliefs give us power, which makes it easy to understand why they are so readily transmitted from one mind to another.

Do we listen too well when others speak, or do we not listen well enough? As we shall see, the answer to that question is *yes*.

It is a bit more difficult to understand why *inaccurate* beliefs are so readily transmitted from one mind to another—but they are. False beliefs, like bad genes, can and do become super-replicators, and a thought experiment illustrates how this can happen.

Imagine a game that is played by two teams, each of which has a thousand players, each of whom is linked to teammates by a telephone. The object of the game is to get one's team to share as many accurate beliefs as possible. When players receive a message that they believe to be accurate, they call a teammate and pass it along. When they receive a message that they believe to be inaccurate, they don't. At the end of the game, the referee blows a whistle and awards each team a point for every accurate belief that the entire team shares and subtracts one point for every inaccurate belief the entire team shares. Now, consider a contest played one sunny day between a team called the Perfects (whose members always transmit accurate beliefs) and a team called the Imperfects (whose members occasionally transmit an inaccurate belief). We should expect the Perfects to win, right?

Not necessarily. In fact, there are some special circumstances under which the Imperfects will beat their pants off. For example, imagine what would happen if one of the Imperfect players sent the false message "Talking on the phone all day and night will ultimately make you very happy," and imagine that other Imperfect players were gullible enough to believe it and pass it on. This message is inaccurate and thus will cost the Imperfects a point in the end. But it may have the compensatory effect of keeping more of the Imperfects on the telephone for more of the time, thus increasing the total number of accurate messages they transmit. Under the right circumstances, the costs of this inaccurate belief would be outweighed by its benefits, namely, that it led players to behave in ways that increased the odds that they would share other accurate beliefs. The lesson to be learned from this game is that inaccurate beliefs can prevail in the belief-transmission game if they somehow facilitate their own "means of transmission." In this case, the means of transmission is not sex but communication, and thus any belief—even a false belief—that increases communication has a good chance of being transmitted over and over again. False beliefs that happen to promote stable societies tend to propagate because people who hold these beliefs tend to live in stable societies, which provide the means by which false beliefs propagate.

Some of our cultural wisdom about happiness looks suspiciously like a super-replicating false belief. Consider money. If you've ever tried to sell anything, then you probably tried to sell it for as much as you possibly could, and other people probably tried to buy it for as little as they possibly could. All the parties involved in the transaction assumed that they would be better off if they ended up with more money rather than less, and this assumption is the bedrock of our economic behavior. Yet, it has far fewer scientific facts to substantiate it than you might expect. Economists and psychologists have spent decades studying the relation between wealth and happiness, and they have generally concluded that wealth increases human happiness when it lifts people out of abject poverty and into the middle class but that it does little to increase happiness thereafter.[9] Americans who earn $50,000 per year are much happier than those who earn $10,000 per year, but Americans who earn $5 million per year are not much happier than those who earn $100,000 per year. People who live in poor nations are much less happy than people who live in moderately wealthy nations, but people who live in moderately wealthy nations are not much less happy than people who live in extremely wealthy nations. Economists explain that wealth has "declining marginal utility," which is a fancy way of saying that it hurts to be hungry, cold, sick, tired, and scared, but once you've bought your way out of these burdens, the rest of your money is an increasingly useless pile of paper.[10]

So once we've earned as much money as we can actually enjoy, we quit working and enjoy it, right? Wrong. People in wealthy countries generally work long and hard to earn more money than they can ever derive pleasure from.[11] This fact puzzles us less than it should. After all, a rat can be motivated to run through a maze that has a cheesy reward at its end, but once the little guy is all topped up, then even the finest Stilton won't get him off his haunches. Once we've eaten our fill of pancakes, more pancakes are not rewarding, hence we stop trying to procure and consume them. But not so, it seems, with money. As Adam Smith, the father of modern economics, wrote in 1776: "The desire for food is limited in every man by the narrow capacity of the human stomach; but the desire of the conveniences and ornaments of building, dress, equipage, and household furniture, seems to have no limit or certain boundary."[12]

If food and money both stop pleasing us once we've had enough of them, then why do we continue to stuff our pockets when we would not continue to stuff our faces? Adam Smith had an answer. He began by acknowledging what most of us suspect anyway, which is that the production of wealth is not necessarily a source of personal happiness.

> In what constitutes the real happiness of human life, [the poor] are in no respect inferior to those who would seem so much above them. In ease of body and peace of mind, all the different ranks of life are nearly upon a level, and the beggar, who suns himself by the side of the highway, possesses that security which kings are fighting for.[13]

That sounds lovely, but if it's true, then we're all in big trouble. If rich kings are no happier than poor beggars, then why should poor beggars stop sunning themselves by the roadside and work to become rich kings? If no one wants to be rich, then we have a significant economic problem, because flourishing economies require that people continually procure and consume one another's goods and services. Market economies require that we all have an insatiable hunger for *stuff*, and if everyone were content with the stuff they had, then the economy would grind to a halt. But if this is a significant *economic* problem, it is not a significant *personal* problem. The chair of the Federal Reserve may wake up every morning with a desire to do what the economy wants, but most of us get up with a desire to do what *we* want, which is to say that the fundamental needs of a vibrant economy and the fundamental needs of a happy individual are not necessarily the same. So what motivates people to work hard every day to do things that will satisfy the economy's needs but not their own? Like so many thinkers, Smith believed that people want just one thing — happiness — hence economies can blossom and grow only if people are deluded into believing that the production of wealth will make them happy.[14] If and only if people hold this false belief will they do enough producing, procuring, and consuming to sustain their economies.

> The pleasures of wealth and greatness . . . strike the imagination as something grand and beautiful and noble, of which the attainment is well worth all the toil and anxiety which we are so apt to bestow upon it. . . . It is this deception which rouses and keeps in continual motion the industry of mankind. It is this which first prompted them to cultivate the ground, to build houses, to found cities and commonwealths, and to invent and improve all the sciences and arts, which ennoble and embellish human life; which have entirely changed

the whole face of the globe, have turned the rude forests of nature into agreeable and fertile plains, and made the trackless and barren ocean a new fund of subsistence, and the great high road of communication to the different nations of the earth.[15]

In short, the production of wealth does not necessarily make individuals happy, but it does serve the needs of an economy, which serves the needs of a stable society, which serves as a network for the propagation of delusional beliefs about happiness and wealth. Economies thrive when individuals strive, but because individuals will only strive for their own happiness, it is essential that they mistakenly believe that producing and consuming are routes to personal well-being. Although words such as *delusional* may seem to suggest some sort of shadowy conspiracy orchestrated by a small group of men in dark suits, the belief-transmission game teaches us that the propagation of false beliefs does not require that anyone be *trying* to perpetrate a magnificent fraud on an innocent populace. There is no cabal at the top, no star chamber,* no master manipulator whose clever program of indoctrination and propaganda has duped us all into believing that money can buy us love. Rather, this particular false belief is a super-replicator because holding it causes us to engage in the very activities that perpetuate it.[16]

The belief-transmission game explains why we believe some things about happiness that simply aren't true. The joy of money is one example. The joy of children is another that for most of us hits a bit closer to home. Every human culture tells its members that having children will make them happy. When people think about their offspring—either imagining future offspring or thinking about their current ones—they tend to conjure up images of cooing babies smiling from their bassinets, adorable toddlers running higgledy-piggledy across the lawn, handsome boys and gorgeous girls playing trumpets and tubas in the school marching band, successful college students going on to have beautiful weddings, satisfying careers, and flawless grandchildren whose affections can be purchased with candy.

If parenting is such difficult business, then why do we have such a rosy view of it?

Prospective parents know that diapers will need changing, that homework will need doing, and that orthodontists will go to Aruba on their life savings, but by and large, they think quite happily about parenthood, which is why most of them eventually leap into it. When parents look back on parenthood, they remember feeling what those who are looking forward to it expect to feel. Few of us are immune to these cheery contemplations. I have a twenty-nine-year-old son, and I am absolutely convinced that he is and always has been one of the greatest sources of joy in my life, having only recently been eclipsed by my two-year-old granddaughter, who is equally adorable but who has not yet asked me to walk behind her and pretend we're unrelated. When people are asked to identify their sources of joy, they do just what I do: They point to their kids.

Yet if we measure the *actual* satisfaction of people who have children, a very different story emerges. As Figure 1 shows, couples generally start out quite happy in their

15

---

* Star chamber: Secretive and abusive English law court during the fifteenth to seventeenth centuries [Ed.].

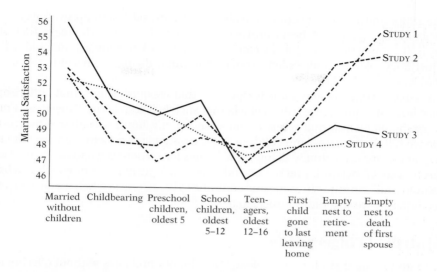

Figure 1
As the four separate studies in this graph show, marital satisfaction decreases dramatically after the birth of the first child and increases only when the last child leaves home.

marriages and then become progressively less satisfied over the course of their lives together, getting close to their original levels of satisfaction only when their children leave home.[17] Despite what we read in the popular press, the only known symptom of "empty nest syndrome" is increased smiling.[18] Interestingly, this pattern of satisfaction over the life cycle describes women (who are usually the primary caretakers of children) better than men.[19] Careful studies of how women feel as they go about their daily activities show that they are less happy when taking care of their children than when eating, exercising, shopping, napping, or watching television.[20] Indeed, looking after the kids appears to be only slightly more pleasant than doing housework.

None of this should surprise us. Every parent knows that children are a lot of work—a lot of really *hard* work—and although parenting has many rewarding moments, the vast majority of its moments involve dull and selfless service to people who will take decades to become even begrudgingly grateful for what we are doing. If parenting is such difficult business, then why do we have such a rosy view of it? One reason is that we have been talking on the phone all day with society's stockholders—our moms and uncles and personal trainers—who have been transmitting to us an idea that they *believe* to be true but whose accuracy is not the cause of its successful transmission. "Children bring happiness" is a super-replicator. The belief-transmission network of which we are a part cannot operate without a continuously replenished supply of people to do the transmitting, thus the belief that children are a source of happiness becomes a part of our cultural wisdom simply because the opposite belief unravels the fabric of any society that holds it. Indeed, people who believed that children bring misery and despair—and who thus stopped having them—would put their belief-transmission network out of business in around fifty years, hence terminating the belief that terminated them. The Shakers were a utopian farming community that arose in the 1800s and at one time numbered about six thousand. They approved of children, but they did not approve of the natural act that creates them. Over the years, their strict belief in the importance of celibacy caused their network to contract, and today there are just a few elderly Shakers left, transmitting their doomsday belief to no one but themselves.

The belief-transmission game is rigged so that we *must* believe that children and money bring happiness, regardless of whether such beliefs are true. This doesn't mean that we should all now quit our jobs and abandon our families. Rather, it means that while we *believe* we are raising children and earning paychecks to increase our share of happiness, we are actually doing these things for reasons beyond our ken. We are nodes in a social network that arises and falls by a logic of its own, which is why we continue to toil, continue to mate, and continue to be surprised when we do not experience all the joy we so gullibly anticipated.

The Myth of Fingerprints

My friends tell me that I have a tendency to point out problems without offering solutions, but they never tell me what I should do about it. In one chapter after another, I've described the ways in which imagination fails to provide us with accurate previews of our emotional futures. I've claimed that when we imagine our futures we tend to fill in, leave out, and take little account of how differently we will think about the future once we actually get there. I've claimed that neither personal experience nor cultural wisdom compensates for imagination's shortcomings. I've so thoroughly marinated you in the foibles, biases, errors, and mistakes of the human mind that you may wonder how anyone ever manages to make toast without buttering their kneecaps. If so, you will be heartened to learn that there *is* a simple method by which anyone can make strikingly accurate predictions about how they will feel in the future. But you may be disheartened to learn that, by and large, no one wants to use it.

Why do we rely on our imaginations in the first place? Imagination is the poor man's wormhole. We can't do what we'd really *like* to do—namely, travel through time, pay a visit to our future selves, and *see* how happy those selves are—and so we imagine the future instead of actually going there. But if we cannot travel in the dimensions of time, we can travel in the dimensions of space, and the chances are pretty good that somewhere in those other three dimensions there is another human being who is actually *experiencing* the future event that we are merely thinking about. Surely we aren't the first people ever to consider a move to Cincinnati, a career in motel management, another helping of rhubarb pie, or an extramarital affair, and for the most part, those who have already tried these things are more than willing to tell us about them. It is true that when people tell us about their past experiences ("That ice water wasn't really so cold" or "I love taking care of my daughter"), memory's peccadilloes may render their testimony unreliable. But it is also true that when people tell us about their *current* experiences ("How am I feeling right now? I feel like pulling my arm out of this freezing bucket and sticking my teenager's head in it instead!"), they are providing us with the kind of report about their subjective state that is considered the gold standard of happiness measures. If you believe (as I do) that people can generally say how they are feeling at the moment they are asked, then one way to make predictions about our own emotional futures is to find someone who is having the experience we are con-templating and ask them how they feel. Instead of remembering our past experience in order to simulate our future experience, perhaps we should simply ask other people to introspect on their inner states. Perhaps we should give up on remembering and imag-ining entirely and use other people as *surrogates* for our future selves.

This idea sounds all too simple, and I suspect you have an objection to it that goes something like this: *Yes, other people are probably right now experiencing the very things I am merely contemplating, but I can't use other people's experiences as proxies for my own because those other people are not me. Every human being is as unique as his or her finger-prints, so it won't help me much to learn about how others feel in the situations that I'm facing. Unless these other people are my clones and have had all the same experiences I've had, their reactions and my reactions are bound to differ. I am a walking, talking idiosyncrasy, and thus I am better off basing my predictions on my somewhat fickle imagination than on the reports of people whose preferences, tastes, and emotional proclivities are so radically different from my own.* If that's your objection, then it is a good one—so good that it will take two steps to dismantle it. First let me prove to you that the experience of a single randomly selected individual can sometimes provide a better basis for predicting your future experience than your own imagination can. And then let me show you why you—and I—find this so difficult to believe.

Finding the Solution

Imagination has three shortcomings, and if you didn't know that then you may be reading this book [Gilbert's *Stumbling on Happiness*] backward. If you did know that, then you also know that imagination's first shortcoming is its tendency to fill in and leave out without telling us. . . . No one can imagine every feature and consequence of a future event, hence we must consider some and fail to consider others. The problem is that the features and consequences we fail to consider are often quite important. You may recall the study [not discussed in this excerpt] in which college students were asked to imagine how they would feel a few days after their school's football team played a game against its archrival.[21] The results showed that students overestimated the duration of the game's emotional impact because when they tried to imagine their future experience, they imagined their team winning ("The clock will hit zero, we'll storm the field, everyone will cheer . . .") but failed to imagine what they would be doing afterward ("And then I'll go home and study for my final exams"). Because the students were focused on the game, they failed to imagine how events that hap-pened *after* the game would influence their happiness. So what *should* they have done instead?

They should have abandoned imagination altogether. Consider a study that put people in a similar predicament and then forced them to abandon their imaginations. In this study, a group of volunteers (reporters) first received a delicious prize—a gift certificate from a local ice cream parlor—and then performed a long, boring task in which they counted and recorded geometric shapes that appeared on a computer screen.[22] The reporters then reported how they felt. Next, a new group of volunteers was told that they would also receive a prize and do the same boring task. Some of these new volunteers (simulators) were told what the prize was and were asked to use their imaginations to predict their future feelings. Other volunteers (surrogators) were not

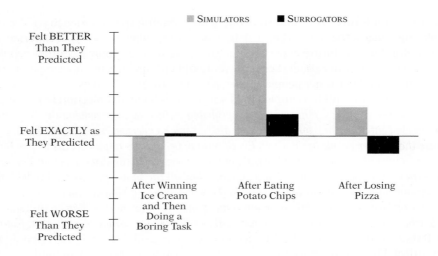

Figure 2
Volunteers made much more accurate predictions of their future feelings when they learned how someone else had felt in the same situation (surrogators) than when they tried to imagine how they themselves would feel (simulators).

told what the prize was but were instead shown the report of a randomly selected reporter. Not knowing what the prize was, they couldn't possibly use their imaginations to predict their future feelings. Instead, they had to rely on the reporter's report. Once all the volunteers had made their predictions, they received the prize, did the long, boring task, and reported how they actually felt. As the leftmost bars in Figure 2 show, simulators were not as happy as they thought they would be. Why? Because they failed to imagine how quickly the joy of receiving a gift certificate would fade when it was followed by a long, boring task. This is precisely the same mistake that the college-football fans made. But now look at the results for the surrogators. As you can see, they made extremely accurate predictions of their future happiness. These surrogators didn't know what kind of prize they would receive, but they did know that someone who had received that prize had been less than ecstatic at the conclusion of the boring task. So they shrugged and reasoned that they too would feel less than ecstatic at the conclusion of the boring task—and they were right!

Imagination's second shortcoming is its tendency to project the present onto the future. . . . When imagination paints a picture of the future, many of the details are necessarily missing, and imagination solves this problem by filling in the gaps with details that it borrows from the present. Anyone who has ever shopped on an empty stomach, vowed to quit smoking after stubbing out a cigarette, or proposed marriage while on shore leave* knows that how we feel now can erroneously influence how we

---

* Shore leave: Time granted to a sailor to spend on land [Ed.].

think we'll feel later. As it turns out, surrogation can remedy this shortcoming too. In one study, volunteers (reporters) ate a few potato chips and reported how much they enjoyed them.[23] Next, a new group of volunteers was fed pretzels, peanut-butter cheese crackers, tortilla chips, bread sticks, and melba toast, which, as you might guess, left them thoroughly stuffed and with little desire for salty snack foods. These stuffed volunteers were then asked to predict how much they would enjoy eating a particular food the next day. Some of these stuffed volunteers (simulators) were told that the food they would eat the next day was potato chips, and they were asked to use their imaginations to predict how they would feel after eating them. Other stuffed volunteers (surrogators) were not told what the next day's food would be but were instead shown the report of one randomly selected reporter. Because surrogators didn't know what the next day's food would be, they couldn't use their imaginations to predict their future enjoyment of it and thus they had to rely on the reporter's report. Once all the volunteers had made their predictions, they went away, returned the next day, ate some potato chips, and reported how much they enjoyed them. As the middle bars in Figure 2 show, simulators enjoyed eating the potato chips more than they thought they would. Why? Because when they made their predictions they had bellies full of pretzels and crackers. But surrogators—who were equally full when they made their predictions—relied on the report of someone without a full belly and hence made much more accurate predictions. It is important to note that the surrogators accurately predicted their future enjoyment of a food despite the fact that they didn't even know what the food was!

Imagination's third shortcoming is its failure to recognize that things will look different once they happen—in particular, that bad things will look a whole lot better. . . . When we imagine losing a job, for instance, we imagine the painful experience ("The boss will march into my office, shut the door behind him . . .") without also imagining how our psychological immune systems will transform its meaning ("I'll come to realize that this was an opportunity to quit retail sales and follow my true calling as a sculptor"). Can surrogation remedy this shortcoming? To find out, researchers arranged for some people to have an unpleasant experience. A group of volunteers (reporters) was told that the experimenter would flip a coin, and if it came up heads, the volunteer would receive a gift certificate to a local pizza parlor. The coin was flipped and—*oh, so sorry*—it came up tails and the reporters received nothing.[24] The reporters then reported how they felt. Next, a new group of volunteers was told about the coin-flipping game and was asked to predict how they would feel if the coin came up tails and they didn't get the pizza gift certificate. Some of these volunteers (simulators) were told the precise monetary value of the gift certificate, and others (surrogators) were instead shown the report of one randomly selected reporter. Once the volunteers had made their predictions, the coin was flipped and—*oh, so sorry*—came up tails. The volunteers then reported how they felt. As the rightmost bars in Figure 2 show, simulators felt better than they predicted they'd feel if they lost the coin flip. Why? Because simulators did not realize how quickly and easily they would rationalize the loss ("Pizza is too fattening, and besides, I don't like that restaurant anyway"). But surrogators—who had nothing to go on except the report of another randomly selected individual—assumed that they wouldn't feel too bad after losing the prize and hence made more accurate predictions.

Rejecting the Solution

This trio of studies suggests that when people are deprived of the information that [25] imagination requires and are thus *forced* to use others as surrogates, they make remarkably accurate predictions about their future feelings, which suggests that the best way to predict our feelings tomorrow is to see how others are feeling today.[25] Given the impressive power of this simple technique, we should expect people to go out of their way to use it. But they don't. When an entirely new group of volunteers was told about the three situations I just described—winning a prize, eating a mystery food, or failing to receive a gift certificate—and was then asked whether they would prefer to make predictions about their future feelings based on *(a)* information about the prize, the food, and the certificate; or *(b)* information about how a randomly selected individual felt after winning them, eating them, or losing them, virtually every volunteer chose the former. If you hadn't seen the results of these studies, you'd probably have done the same. If I offered to pay for your dinner at a restaurant if you could accurately predict how much you were going to enjoy it, would you want to see the restaurant's menu or some randomly selected diner's review? If you are like most people, you would prefer to see the menu, and if you are like most people, you would end up buying your own dinner. Why?

> **If you are like most people, then like most people, you don't know you're like most people.**

Because if you are like most people, then like most people, you don't know you're like most people. Science has given us a lot of facts about the average person, and one of the most reliable of these facts is that the average person doesn't see herself as average. Most students see themselves as more intelligent than the average student,[26] most business managers see themselves as more competent than the average business manager,[27] and most football players see themselves as having better "football sense" than their teammates.[28] Ninety percent of motorists consider themselves to be safer-than-average drivers,[29] and 94 percent of college professors consider themselves to be better-than-average teachers.[30] Ironically, the bias toward seeing ourselves as better than average causes us to see ourselves as less biased than average too.[31] As one research team concluded, "Most of us appear to believe that we are more athletic, intelligent, organized, ethical, logical, interesting, fair-minded, and healthy—not to mention more attractive—than the average person."[32]

This tendency to think of ourselves as better than others is not necessarily a manifestation of our unfettered narcissism but may instead be an instance of a more general tendency to think of ourselves as *different* from others—often for better but sometimes for worse. When people are asked about generosity, they claim to perform a greater number of generous acts than others do; but when they are asked about selfishness, they claim to perform a greater number of selfish acts than others do.[33] When people are asked about their ability to perform an easy task, such as driving a car or riding a bike, they rate themselves as better than others; but when they are asked about their ability to perform a difficult task, such as juggling or playing chess, they rate themselves as worse than others.[34] We don't always see ourselves as *superior,* but we almost always see ourselves as *unique.* Even when we do precisely what others do, we tend to think that we're doing it for unique reasons. For instance, we tend to attribute other people's choices to features of the chooser ("Phil picked this class because he's one of those literary types"), but we tend to attribute our own choices to features of the options ("But I picked it because it was easier than economics").[35] We recognize that our decisions are influenced by social norms ("I was too embarrassed to raise my hand in class even though I was terribly confused"), but fail to recognize that others' decisions were similarly influenced ("No one else raised a hand because no one else was as confused as I was").[36] We know that our choices sometimes reflect our aversions ("I voted for Kerry because I couldn't stand Bush"), but we assume that other people's choices reflect their appetites ("If Rebecca voted for Kerry, then she must have liked him").[37] The list of differences is long but the conclusion to be drawn from it is short: The self considers itself to be a very special person.[38]

What makes us think we're so darned special? Three things, at least. First, even if we aren't special, the way we know ourselves is. We are the only people in the world whom we can know from the inside. We *experience* our own thoughts and feelings but must *infer* that other people are experiencing theirs. We all trust that behind those eyes and inside those skulls, our friends and neighbors are having subjective experiences very much like our own, but that trust is an article of faith and not the palpable, self-evident truth that our own subjective experiences constitute. There is a difference between making love and reading about it, and it is the same difference that distinguishes our knowledge of our own mental lives from our knowledge of everyone else's. Because we know ourselves and others by such different means, we gather very different kinds and amounts of information. In every waking moment we monitor the steady stream of thoughts and feelings that runs through our heads, but we only monitor other people's words and deeds, and only when they are in our company. One reason why we seem so special, then, is that we learn about ourselves in such a special way.

The second reason is that we *enjoy* thinking of ourselves as special. Most of us want to fit in well with our peers, but we don't want to fit in too well.[39] We prize our unique identities, and research shows that when people are made to feel too similar to others, their moods quickly sour and they try to distance and distinguish themselves in a variety of ways.[40] If you've ever shown up at a party and found someone else wearing exactly the same dress or necktie that you were wearing, then you know how unsettling it is to share the room with an unwanted twin whose presence temporarily diminishes your sense of individuality. Because we *value* our uniqueness, it isn't surprising that we tend to overestimate it.

The third reason why we tend to overestimate our uniqueness is that we tend to overestimate everyone's uniqueness — that is, we tend to think of people as more different from one another than they actually are. Let's face it: All people are similar in some ways and different in others. The psychologists, biologists, economists, and sociologists who are searching for universal laws of human behavior naturally care about the similarities, but the rest of us care mainly about the differences. Social life involves selecting particular individuals to be our sexual partners, business partners, bowling partners, and more. That task requires that we focus on the things that distinguish one person from another and not on the things that all people share, which is why personal ads are much more likely to mention the advertiser's love of ballet than his love of oxygen. A penchant for respiration explains a great deal about human behavior — for example, why people live on land, become ill at high altitudes, have lungs, resist suffocation, love trees, and so on. It surely explains more than does a person's penchant for ballet. But it does nothing to distinguish one person from another, and thus for ordinary folks who are in the ordinary business of selecting others for commerce, conversation, or copulation, the penchant for air is stunningly irrelevant. Individual similarities are vast, but we don't care much about them because they don't help us do what we are here on earth to do, namely, distinguish Jack from Jill and Jill from Jennifer. As such, these individual similarities are an inconspicuous backdrop against which a small number of relatively minor individual differences stand out in bold relief.

Because we spend so much time searching for, attending to, thinking about, and remembering these differences, we tend to overestimate their magnitude and frequency, and thus end up thinking of people as more varied than they actually are. If you spent all day sorting grapes into different shapes, colors, and kinds, you'd become one of those annoying grapeophiles who talks endlessly about the nuances of flavor and the permutations of texture. You'd come to think of grapes as infinitely varied, and you'd forget that almost all of the really *important* information about a grape can be deduced from the simple fact of its grapehood. Our belief in the variability of others and in the uniqueness of the self is especially powerful when it comes to emotion.[41] Because we can *feel* our own emotions but must *infer* the emotions of others by watching their faces and listening to their voices, we often have the impression that others don't experience the same intensity of emotion that we do, which is why we expect others to recognize our feelings even when we can't recognize theirs.[42] This sense of emotional uniqueness starts early. When kindergarteners are asked how they and others would feel in a variety of situations, they expect to experience unique emotions ("Billy would be sad but I wouldn't") and they provide unique reasons for experiencing them ("I'd tell myself that the hamster was in heaven, but Billy would just cry").[43] When adults make these same kinds of predictions, they do just the same thing.[44]

Our mythical belief in the variability and uniqueness of individuals is the main reason why we refuse to use others as surrogates. After all, surrogation is only useful when we can count on a surrogate to react to an event roughly as we would, and if we believe that people's emotional reactions are more varied than they actually are, then surrogation will seem less useful to us than it actually is. The irony, of course, is that surrogation is a cheap and effective way to predict one's future emotions, but because we don't realize just how similar we all are, we reject this reliable method and rely instead on our imaginations, as flawed and fallible as they may be.

Onward

Despite its watery connotation, the word *hogwash* refers to the feeding—and not to the bathing—of pigs. Hogwash is something that pigs eat, that pigs like, and that pigs need. Farmers provide pigs with hogwash because without it, pigs get grumpy. The word *hogwash* also refers to the falsehoods people tell one another. Like the hogwash that farmers feed their pigs, the hogwash that our friends and teachers and parents feed us is meant to make us happy; but unlike hogwash of the porcine variety, human hogwash does not always achieve its end. As we have seen, ideas can flourish if they preserve the social systems that allow them to be transmitted. Because individuals don't usually feel that it is their personal duty to preserve social systems, these ideas must disguise themselves as prescriptions for individual happiness. We might expect that after spending some time in the world, our experiences would debunk these ideas, but it doesn't always work that way. To learn from our experience we must remember it, and for a variety of reasons, memory is a faithless friend. Practice and coaching get us out of our diapers and into our britches, but they are not enough to get us out of our presents and into our futures. What's so ironic about this predicament is that the information we need to make accurate predictions of our emotional futures is right under our noses, but we don't seem to recognize its aroma. It doesn't always make sense to heed what people tell us when they communicate their beliefs about happiness, but it does make sense to observe how happy they are in different circumstances. Alas, we think of ourselves as unique entities—minds unlike any others—and thus we often reject the lessons that the emotional experience of others has to teach us.

NOTES

1. J. Livingston and R. Evans, "Whatever Will Be, Will Be (Que Sera, Sera)" (1955).
2. W. V. Quine and J. S. Ullian, *The Web of Belief*, 2nd ed. (New York: Random House, 1978), 51.
3. Half of all Americans relocated in the five-year period of 1995–2000, which suggests that the average American relocates about every ten years; B. Berkner and C. S. Faber, *Geographical Mobility, 1995 to 2000* (Washington, D.C.: U.S. Bureau of the Census, 2003).
4. The average baby boomer held roughly ten jobs between the ages of eighteen and thirty-six, which suggests that the average American holds at least this many in a lifetime. Bureau of Labor Statistics, *Number of Jobs Held, Labor Market Activity, and Earnings Growth among Younger Baby Boomers: Results from More Than Two Decades of a Longitudinal Survey*, Bureau of Labor Statistics news release (Washington, D.C.: U.S. Department of Labor, 2002).
5. The U.S. Census Bureau projects that in the coming years, 10 percent of Americans will never marry, 60 percent will marry just once, and 30 percent will marry at least twice. R. M. Kreider and J. M. Fields, *Number, Timing, and Duration of Marriages and Divorces, 1996* (Washington, D.C.: U.S. Bureau of the Census, 2002).
6. B. Russell, *The Analysis of Mind* (New York: Macmillan, 1921), 231.
7. The biologist Richard Dawkins refers to these beliefs as *memes*. See R. J. Dawkins, *The Selfish Gene* (Oxford: Oxford University Press, 1976). See also S. Blackmore, *The Meme Machine* (Oxford: Oxford University Press, 2000).
8. D. C. Dennett, *Brainstorms: Philosophical Essays on Mind and Psychology* (Cambridge, Mass.: Bradford/MIT Press, 1981), 18.
9. R. Layard, *Happiness: Lessons from a New Science* (New York: Penguin, 2005); E. Diener and M. E. P. Seligman, "Beyond Money: Toward an Economy of Well-Being," *Psychological Science in the Public Interest* 5: 1–31 (2004); B. S. Frey and A. Stutzer, *Happiness and Economics: How the Economy and Institutions Affect Human Well-Being* (Princeton, N.J.: Princeton University Press, 2002); R. A. Easterlin, "Income and Happiness: Towards a Unified Theory," *Economic Journal* 111: 465–84 (2001); and D. G. Blanchflower and A. J. Oswald, "Well-Being over Time in Britain and the USA," *Journal of Public Economics* 88: 1359–86 (2004).
10. The effect of declining marginal utility is slowed when we spend our money on the things to which we are least likely to adapt. See T. Scitovsky, *The Joyless Economy: The Psychology of Human Satisfaction* (Oxford: Oxford University Press, 1976); L. Van Boven

and T. Gilovich, "To Do or to Have? That Is the Question," *Journal of Personality and Social Psychology* 85: 1193–1202 (2003); and R. H. Frank, "How Not to Buy Happiness," *Daedalus: Journal of the American Academy of Arts and Sciences* 133: 69–79 (2004). Not all economists believe in decreasing marginal utility: R. A. Easterlin, "Diminishing Marginal Utility of Income? Caveat Emptor," *Social Indicators Research* 70: 243–326 (2005).

11. J. D. Graaf et al., *Affluenza: The All-Consuming Epidemic* (New York: Berrett-Koehler, 2002); D. Myers, *The American Paradox: Spiritual Hunger in an Age of Plenty* (New Haven: Yale University Press, 2000); R. H. Frank, *Luxury Fever* (Princeton, N.J.: Princeton University Press, 2000); J. B. Schor, *The Overspent American: Why We Want What We Don't Need* (New York: Perennial, 1999); and P. L. Wachtel, *Poverty of Affluence: A Psychological Portrait of the American Way of Life* (New York: Free Press, 1983).

12. Adam Smith, *An Inquiry into the Nature and Causes of the Wealth of Nations* (1776), book 1 (New York: Modern Library, 1994).

13. Adam Smith, *The Theory of Moral Sentiments* (1759; Cambridge: Cambridge University Press, 2002).

14. N. Ashraf, C. Camerer, and G. Loewenstein, "Adam Smith, Behavorial Economist," *Journal of Economic Perspectives* 19: 131–45 (2005).

15. Smith, *The Theory of Moral Sentiments*.

16. Some theorists have argued that societies exhibit a cyclic pattern in which people do come to realize that money doesn't buy happiness but then forget this lesson a generation later. See A. O. Hirschman, *Shifting Involvements: Private Interest and Public Action* (Princeton, N.J.: Princeton University Press, 1982).

17. C. Walker, "Some Variations in Marital Satisfaction," in *Equalities and Inequalities in Family Life*, ed. R. Chester and J. Peel (London: Academic Press, 1977), 127–39.

18. D. Myers, *The Pursuit of Happiness: Discovering the Pathway to Fulfillment, Well-Being, and Enduring Personal Joy* (New York: Avon, 1992), 71.

19. J. A. Feeney, "Attachment Styles, Communication Patterns and Satisfaction across the Life Cycle of Marriage," *Personal Relationships* 1: 333–48 (1994).

20. D. Kahneman et al., "A Survey Method for Characterizing Daily Life Experience: The Day Reconstruction Method," *Science* 306: 1776–80 (2004).

21. T. D. Wilson et al., "Focalism: A Source of Durability Bias in Affective Forecasting," *Journal of Personality and Social Psychology* 78: 821–36 (2000).

22. R. J. Norwick, D. T. Gilbert, and T. D. Wilson, "Surrogation: An Antidote for Errors in Affective Forecasting" (unpublished manuscript, Harvard University, 2005).

23. Ibid.

24. Ibid.

25. This is also the best way to predict our future behavior. For example, people overestimate the likelihood that they will perform a charitable act but correctly estimate the likelihood that others will do the same. This suggests that if we would base predictions of our own behavior on what we see others do, we'd be dead-on. See N. Epley and D. Dunning, "Feeling 'Holier Than Thou': Are Self-Serving Assessments Produced by Errors in Self- or Social Prediction?" *Journal of Personality and Social Psychology* 79: 861–75 (2000).

26. R. C. Wylie, *The Self-Concept: Theory and Research on Selected Topics*, vol. 2 (Lincoln: University of Nebraska Press, 1979).

27. L. Larwood and W. Whittaker, "Managerial Myopia: Self-Serving Biases in Organizational Planning," *Journal of Applied Psychology* 62: 194–98 (1977).

28. R. B. Felson, "Ambiguity and Bias in the Self-Concept," *Social Psychology Quarterly* 44: 64–69.

29. D. Walton and J. Bathurst, "An Exploration of the Perceptions of the Average Driver's Speed Compared to Perceived Driver Safety and Driving Skill," *Accident Analysis and Prevention* 30: 821–30 (1998).

30. P. Cross, "Not Can But Will College Teachers Be Improved?" *New Directions for Higher Education* 17: 1–15 (1977).

31. E. Pronin, D. Y. Lin, and L. Ross, "The Bias Blind Spot: Perceptions of Bias in Self Versus Others," *Personality and Social Psychology Bulletin* 28: 369–81 (2002).

32. J. Kruger, "Lake Wobegon Be Gone! The 'Below-Average Effect' and the Egocentric Nature of Comparative Ability Judgments," *Journal of Personality and Social Psychology* 77: 221–32 (1999).

33. J. T. Johnson et al., "The 'Barnum Effect' Revisited: Cognitive and Motivational Factors in the Acceptance of Personality Descriptions," *Journal of Personality and Social Psychology* 49: 1378–91 (1985).

34. Kruger, "Lake Wobegon Be Gone!"

35. E. E. Jones and R. E. Nisbett, "The Actor and the Observer: Divergent Perceptions of the Causes of Behavior," in *Attribution: Perceiving the Causes of Behavior*, ed. E. E. Jones et al. (Morristown, N.J.: General Learning Press, 1972); and R. E. Nisbett and E. Borgida, "Attribution and the Psychology of Prediction," *Journal of Personality and Social Psychology* 32: 932–43 (1975).

36. D. T. Miller and C. McFarland, "Pluralistic Ignorance: When Similarity Is Interpreted as Dissimilarity," *Journal of Personality and Social Psychology* 53: 298–305 (1987).

37. D. T. Miller and L. D. Nelson, "Seeing Approach Motivation in the Avoidance Behavior of Others: Implications for an Understanding of Pluralistic Ignorance," *Journal of Personality and Social Psychology* 83: 1066–75 (2002).

38. C. R. Snyder and H. L. Fromkin, "Abnormality as a Positive Characteristic: The Development and Validation of a Scale Measuring Need for Uniqueness," *Journal of Abnormal Psychology* 86: 518–27 (1977).

39. M. B. Brewer, "The Social Self: On Being the Same and Different at the Same Time," *Personality and Social Psychology Bulletin* 17: 475–82 (1991).

40. H. L. Fromkin, "Effects of Experimentally Aroused Feelings of Undistinctiveness upon Valuation of Scarce and Novel Experiences," *Journal of Personality and Social Psychology* 16: 521–29 (1970); and H. L. Fromkin, "Feelings of Interpersonal Undistinctiveness: An Unpleasant Affective State," *Journal of Experimental Research in Personality* 6: 178–85 (1972).

41. R. Karniol, T. Eylon, and S. Rish, "Predicting Your Own and Others' Thoughts and Feelings: More Like a Stranger Than a Friend," *European Journal of Social Psychology* 27: 301–11 (1997); J. T. Johnson, "The Heart on the Sleeve and the Secret Self: Estimations of Hidden Emotion in Self and Acquaintances," *Journal of Personality* 55: 563–82 (1987); and R. Karniol, "Egocentrism Versus Protocentrism: The Status of Self in Social Prediction," *Psychological Review* 110: 564–80 (2003).

42. C. L. Barr and R. E. Kleck, "Self-Other Perception of the Intensity of Facial Expressions of Emotion: Do We Know What We Show?" *Journal of Personality and Social Psychology* 68: 608–18 (1995).

43. R. Karniol and L. Koren, "How Would You Feel? Children's Inferences Regarding Their Own and Others' Affective Reactions," *Cognitive Development* 2: 271–78 (1987).

44. C. McFarland and D. T. Miller, "Judgments of Self-Other Similarity: Just Like Other People, Only More So," *Personality and Social Psychology Bulletin* 16: 475–84 (1990).

Exploring Context

1. Visit Stripgenerator.com and make a comic strip that represents the argument of Gilbert's essay. Incorporate representations for your definitions of the terms in Questions for Critical Reading.

2. What is "happiness"? Enter "happy," "happiness," and related terms into Google or another search engine. What sort of results do you get? What if you search for images? What does "happiness" look like on the Web? Does it match the definition you developed in Question 3 of Questions for Critical Reading?

3. Gilbert suggests that if we want to know how happy we will be in the future, we should ask someone who's already living our goals. Use Yahoo! Answers (answers.yahoo.com) to ask questions about possible plans for your future. Can the Web function as a surrogate? Use the definition of *surrogate* that you developed in Question 2 of Questions for Critical Reading in your answer.

Questions for Connecting

1. Gilbert examines the happiness produced by both money and children. How does Julia Alvarez's discussion of quinceañeras in "Selections from *Once Upon a Quinceañera*" (p. 46) challenge these findings? Do the relationships between parents and children and money in Alvarez's essay match the findings that Gilbert presents? Are they happy? You may want to use the definition of *happiness* you developed in Question 3 of Questions for Critical Reading and Question 2 of Exploring Context.

2. What is the relationship between memes and super-replicators? Consider the impact of Bill Wasik's ideas in "My Crowd Experiment: The Mob Project" (p. 514) on what Gilbert has to say about super-replicators, drawing on the understanding of that term that you developed in response to Question 1 of Questions for Critical Reading.

3. Gilbert suggests that surrogates can help us predict our future happiness, but can surrogates help us in dealing with other emotions as well? To what extent do the postcards in PostSecret (p. 388) function as surrogates? Do they match your definition from Question 2 of Questions for Critical Reading?

Language Matters

1. Locate information on sentence diagrams in a grammar handbook or other reference resource. Then select a key sentence from Gilbert's text and diagram the sentence. What are the different parts of the sentence, and how are they related?

2. Locate a sentence in Gilbert's essay that uses *I* as the subject. When does Gilbert use *I*? When doesn't he? When should you?

3. Take a key sentence from Gilbert. Summarize it and then paraphrase it. What is the difference between a summary, a paraphrase, and a quotation? When would you use each in your writing, and what type of citation does each need?

Assignments for Writing

1. According to Gilbert, surrogates can offer us an accurate sense of our future happiness. Write a paper in which you assess the potential of the kind of surrogates that Gilbert describes. You will want to extend, complicate, or refute Gilbert's argument for surrogates and their reliability in predicting the future. Think about these questions: What role does individuality have in our future happiness? Is Gilbert correct in claiming that we are not as unique as we believe? Can surrogates be used to examine all future events? How can surrogates be used to control social processes? If we are not unique, why do we see ourselves as individuals? Use your definition of *surrogate* from Question 2 of Questions for Critical Reading as well as your work with Yahoo! Answers from Question 3 of Exploring Context.

2. Write a paper in which you evaluate Gilbert's argument about surrogates and their reliability in predicting the future by finding an appropriate surrogate for you and your future happiness. You may wish to use your experience finding a surrogate on the Web from Question 3 of Exploring Context in making your argument. Also consider: What role does individuality have in our future happiness? Are surrogate examples more accurate than our imagination? What event in your life did you imagine was going to make you happier than it did?

3. Gilbert defines *super-replicators* as genes or beliefs that are given to transmission regardless of their usefulness. Write a paper in which you extend Gilbert's argument through your own example of a super-replicator that persists in society. How do we communicate our ideas to others? What super-replicators are we passing along to those we come into contact with? Does the validity of a belief correlate to its speed of transmission? What is the role of super-replicators in communicating cultural ideas? Use your definition of the term from Question 1 of Questions for Critical Reading.

MALCOLM GLADWELL

Born in England and raised in Canada before moving to New York City, **Malcolm Gladwell** is a best-selling author and staff writer for the *New Yorker*. He began his career as a reporter for the *Washington Post*, a position he held from 1987 to 1996, before moving on to a staff writing position for the *New Yorker*. He has won a National Magazine Award and was named one of *Time* magazine's 100 most influential people in 2005. Gladwell famously received a $1 million advance for his first book, *The Tipping Point: How Little Things Make a Big Difference* (2000), which became a best-seller. His other books include *Blink: The Power of Thinking without Thinking* (2005) and *Outliers: The Story of Success* (2008). His most recent book, 2009's *What the Dog Saw*, is a collection of essays that previously appeared in the *New Yorker*.

The essay presented here, "Small Change," originally appeared in the October 4, 2010, issue of the *New Yorker*. That issue featured the magazine's usual selection of book reviews and short fiction as well as a brief note to the readers that the magazine had finally debuted on the iPad. Given that technological milestone for the publication, it is interesting that Gladwell's contribution to the issue analyzed the role technology played in inciting the "Arab Spring" uprisings of 2010.

In "Small Change," Gladwell discusses the perception that modern social networking technologies such as Facebook and Twitter have been instrumental in organizing mass uprisings in the Middle East in response to the oppressive regimes of the region. While he concedes that traditional social networks led to great successes for American civil rights in the 1960s, Gladwell disagrees with any comparisons made to the power of social networking in the modern age—"The revolution will not be tweeted," as the *New Yorker* put it. "Small Change" looks at the ties that bind us, both "weak ties" and "strong ties." Ultimately, Gladwell suggests that it's the quality of connections that people have (rather than the quantity of them) that leads to success in social change.

▶ TAGS: ***strong tie, weak tie, Twitter, Facebook, technology, civil rights, social change***

Questions for Critical Reading

1. Gladwell discusses "strong ties" and "weak ties." As you read his essay, mark passages where he discusses each term and then define them using Gladwell's text. What role does each play in social change, according to Gladwell?

2. Can social media be used to enact real social change? Consider recent events such as the Occupy Wall Street movement. Engage Gladwell's argument using your own perceptions of the power of social media. Does his analysis remain true?

3. According to Gladwell, what are the crucial factors needed to enact social change? As you read his essay, mark these passages.

Small Change

At four-thirty in the afternoon on Monday, February 1, 1960, four college students sat down at the lunch counter at the Woolworth's in downtown Greensboro, North Carolina. They were freshmen at North Carolina A&T, a black college a mile or so away.

"I'd like a cup of coffee, please," one of the four, Ezell Blair, said to the waitress.

"We don't serve Negroes here," she replied.

The Woolworth's lunch counter was a long L-shaped bar that could seat sixty-six people, with a standup snack bar at one end. The seats were for whites. The snack bar was for blacks. Another employee, a black woman who worked at the steam table, approached the students and tried to warn them away. "You're acting stupid, ignorant!" she said. They didn't move. Around five-thirty, the front doors to the store were locked. The four still didn't move. Finally, they left by a side door. Outside, a small crowd had gathered, including a photographer from the *Greensboro Record*. "I'll be back tomorrow with A&T College," one of the students said.

By next morning, the protest had grown to twenty-seven men and four women, most from the same dormitory as the original four. The men were dressed in suits and ties. The students had brought their schoolwork, and studied as they sat at the counter. On Wednesday, students from Greensboro's "Negro" secondary school, Dudley High, **It happened without e-mail, texting, Facebook, or Twitter.** joined in, and the number of protesters swelled to eighty. By Thursday, the protesters numbered three hundred, including three white women, from the Greensboro campus of the University of North Carolina. By Saturday, the sit-in had reached six hundred. People spilled out onto the street. White teenagers waved Confederate flags. Someone threw a firecracker. At noon, the A&T football team arrived. "Here comes the wrecking crew," one of the white students shouted.

By the following Monday, sit-ins had spread to Winston-Salem, twenty-five miles away, and Durham, fifty miles away. The day after that, students at Fayetteville State Teachers College and at Johnson C. Smith College, in Charlotte, joined in, followed on Wednesday by students at St. Augustine's College and Shaw University, in Raleigh. On Thursday and Friday, the protest crossed state lines, surfacing in Hampton and Portsmouth, Virginia, in Rock Hill, South Carolina, and in Chattanooga, Tennessee. By the end of the month, there were sit-ins throughout the South, as far west as Texas. "I asked every student I met what the first day of the sitdowns had been like on his campus," the political theorist Michael Walzer wrote in *Dissent*. "The answer was always the same: 'It was like a fever. Everyone wanted to go.'" Some seventy thousand students eventually took part. Thousands were arrested and untold thousands more radicalized. These events in the early sixties became a civil-rights war that engulfed the South for the rest of the decade—and it happened without e-mail, texting, Facebook, or Twitter.

The world, we are told, is in the midst of a revolution. The new tools of social media have reinvented social activism. With Facebook and Twitter and the like, the traditional relationship between political authority and popular will has been upended, making it easier for the powerless to collaborate, coordinate, and give voice to their concerns. When ten thousand protesters took to the streets in Moldova* in the spring of 2009 to protest against their country's Communist government, the action was dubbed the Twitter Revolution, because of the means by which the demonstrators had been brought together. A few months after that, when student protests rocked Tehran, the State Department took the unusual step of asking Twitter to suspend scheduled maintenance of its website, because the Administration didn't want such a critical organizing tool out of service at the height of the demonstrations. "Without Twitter the people of Iran would not have felt empowered and confident to stand up for freedom and democracy," Mark Pfeifle, a former national-security adviser, later wrote, calling for Twitter to be nominated for the Nobel Peace Prize. Where activists were once defined by their causes, they are now defined by their tools. Facebook warriors go online to push for change. "You are the best hope for us all," James K. Glassman, a former senior State Department official, told a crowd of cyber activists at a recent conference sponsored by Facebook, AT&T, Howcast, MTV, and Google. Sites like Facebook, Glassman said, "give the U.S. a significant competitive advantage over terrorists. Some time ago, I said that Al Qaeda was 'eating our lunch on the Internet.' That is no longer the case. Al Qaeda is stuck in Web 1.0. The Internet is now about interactivity and conversation."

These are strong, and puzzling, claims. Why does it matter who is eating whose lunch on the Internet? Are people who log on to their Facebook page really the best hope for us all? As for Moldova's so-called Twitter Revolution, Evgeny Morozov, a scholar at Stanford who has been the most persistent of digital evangelism's critics, points out that Twitter had scant internal significance in Moldova, a country where very few Twitter accounts exist. Nor does it seem to have been a revolution, not least because the protests—as Anne Applebaum suggested in the *Washington Post*—may well have been a bit of stagecraft cooked up by the government. (In a country paranoid about Romanian revanchism,† the protesters flew a Romanian flag over the Parliament building.) In the Iranian case, meanwhile, the people tweeting about the demonstrations were almost all in the West. "It is time to get Twitter's role in the events in Iran right," Golnaz Esfandiari wrote, this past summer, in *Foreign Policy*. "Simply put: There was no Twitter Revolution inside Iran." The cadre of prominent bloggers, like Andrew Sullivan, who championed the role of social media in Iran, Esfandiari continued, misunderstood the situation. "Western journalists who couldn't reach—or didn't bother reaching?—people on the ground in Iran simply scrolled through the

---

* Moldova: The Republic of Moldova is located northeast of Romania in Eastern Europe, bordering Ukraine. Formerly a part of the USSR, Moldova elected a communist president in 2001. He resigned in 2009 [Ed.].
† Revanchism: French term meaning retaliation or revenge; refers to a policy of attempting to retake lost land or honor [Ed.].

English-language tweets posted with tag #iranelection," she wrote. "Through it all, no one seemed to wonder why people trying to coordinate protests in Iran would be writing in any language other than Farsi."

Some of this grandiosity is to be expected. Innovators tend to be solipsists. They often want to cram every stray fact and experience into their new model. As the historian Robert Darnton has written, "The marvels of communication technology in the present have produced a false consciousness about the past—even a sense that communication has no history, or had nothing of importance to consider before the days of television and the Internet." But there is something else at work here, in the outsized enthusiasm for social media. Fifty years after one of the most extraordinary episodes of social upheaval in American history, we seem to have forgotten what activism is.

Greensboro in the early 1960s was the kind of place where racial insubordination   10
was routinely met with violence. The four students who first sat down at the lunch counter were terrified. "I suppose if anyone had come up behind me and yelled 'Boo,' I think I would have fallen off my seat," one of them said later. On the first day, the store manager notified the police chief, who immediately sent two officers to the store. On the third day, a gang of white toughs showed up at the lunch counter and stood ostentatiously behind the protesters, ominously muttering epithets such as "burr-head nigger." A local Ku Klux Klan leader made an appearance. On Saturday, as tensions grew, someone called in a bomb threat, and the entire store had to be evacuated.

The dangers were even clearer in the Mississippi Freedom Summer Project of 1964, another of the sentinel campaigns of the civil-rights movement. The Student Nonviolent Coordinating Committee recruited hundreds of Northern, largely white unpaid volunteers to run Freedom Schools, register black voters, and raise civil-rights awareness in the Deep South. "No one should go *anywhere* alone, but certainly not in an automobile and certainly not at night," they were instructed. Within days of arriving in Mississippi, three volunteers—Michael Schwerner, James Chaney, and Andrew Goodman—were kidnapped and killed, and, during the rest of the summer, thirty-seven black churches were set on fire and dozens of safe houses were bombed; volunteers were beaten, shot at, arrested, and trailed by pickup trucks full of armed men. A quarter of those in the program dropped out. Activism that challenges the status quo—that attacks deeply rooted problems—is not for the faint of heart.

What makes people capable of this kind of activism? The Stanford sociologist Doug McAdam compared the Freedom Summer dropouts with the participants who stayed, and discovered that the key difference wasn't, as might be expected, ideological fervor. "*All* of the applicants—participants and withdrawals alike—emerge as highly committed, articulate supporters of the goals and values of the summer program," he concluded. What mattered more was an applicant's degree of personal connection to the civil-rights movement. All the volunteers were required to provide a list of personal contacts—the people they wanted kept apprised of their activities—and participants were far more likely than dropouts to have close friends who were also going to Mississippi. High-risk activism, McAdam concluded, is a "strong-tie" phenomenon.

This pattern shows up again and again. One study of the Red Brigades, the Italian terrorist group of the 1970s, found that seventy percent of recruits had at least one good friend already in the organization. The same is true of the men who joined the mujahideen* in Afghanistan. Even revolutionary actions that look spontaneous, like the demonstrations in East Germany that led to the fall of the Berlin Wall†, are, at core, strong-tie phenomena. The opposition movement in East Germany consisted of several hundred groups, each with roughly a dozen members. Each group was in limited contact with the others: at the time, only thirteen percent of East Germans even had a phone. All they knew was that on Monday nights, outside St. Nicholas Church in downtown Leipzig, people gathered to voice their anger at the state. And the primary determinant of who showed up was "critical friends"—the more friends you had who were critical of the regime the more likely you were to join the protest.

So one crucial fact about the four freshmen at the Greensboro lunch counter—David Richmond, Franklin McCain, Ezell Blair, and Joseph McNeil—was their relationship with one another. McNeil was a roommate of Blair's in A&T's Scott Hall dormitory. Richmond roomed with McCain one floor up, and Blair, Richmond, and McCain had all gone to Dudley High School. The four would smuggle beer into the dorm and talk late into the night in Blair and McNeil's room. They would all have remembered the murder of Emmett Till in 1955, the Montgomery bus boycott that same year, and the showdown in Little Rock in 1957. It was McNeil who brought up the idea of a sit-in at Woolworth's. They'd discussed it for nearly a month. Then McNeil came into the dorm room and asked the others if they were ready. There was a pause, and McCain said, in a way that works only with people who talk late into the night with one another, "Are you guys chicken or not?" Ezell Blair worked up the courage the next day to ask for a cup of coffee because he was flanked by his roommate and two good friends from high school.

The kind of activism associated with social media isn't like this at all. The platforms   15
of social media are built around weak ties. Twitter is a way of following (or being followed by) people you may never have met. Facebook is a tool for efficiently managing your acquaintances, for keeping up with the people you would not otherwise be able to stay in touch with. That's why you can have a thousand "friends" on Facebook, as you never could in real life.

This is in many ways a wonderful thing. There is strength in weak ties, as the sociologist Mark Granovetter has observed. Our acquaintances—not our friends—are our greatest source of new ideas and information. The Internet lets us exploit the power of these kinds of distant connections with marvellous efficiency. It's terrific at the diffusion of innovation, interdisciplinary collaboration, seamlessly matching up buyers and sellers, and the logistical functions of the dating world. But weak ties seldom lead to high-risk activism.

In a new book called *The Dragonfly Effect: Quick, Effective, and Powerful Ways to Use Social Media to Drive Social Change*, the business consultant Andy Smith and the Stanford Business School professor Jennifer Aaker tell the story of Sameer Bhatia, a young

---

* Mujahideen: Fighters who resisted the Soviet invasion of Afghanistan in the 1980s [Ed.].

† Berlin Wall: Barrier that divided Berlin, Germany, into communist East and democratic West; it lasted from 1961 to 1989. East Germans discovered while attempting to cross the wall to escape to the West were either captured or killed by East German forces [Ed.].

Silicon Valley entrepreneur who came down with acute myelogenous leukemia. It's a perfect illustration of social media's strengths. Bhatia needed a bone-marrow transplant, but he could not find a match among his relatives and friends. The odds were best with a donor of his ethnicity, and there were few South Asians in the national bone-marrow database. So Bhatia's business partner sent out an e-mail explaining Bhatia's plight to more than four hundred of their acquaintances, who forwarded the e-mail to their personal contacts; Facebook pages and YouTube videos were devoted to the Help Sameer campaign. Eventually, nearly twenty-five thousand new people were registered in the bone-marrow database, and Bhatia found a match.

But how did the campaign get so many people to sign up? By not asking too much of them. That's the only way you can get someone you don't really know to do something on your behalf. You can get thousands of people to sign up for a donor registry, because doing so is pretty easy. You have to send in a cheek swab and—in the highly unlikely event that your bone marrow is

> **But how did the campaign get so many people to sign up? By not asking too much of them.**

a good match for someone in need—spend a few hours at the hospital. Donating bone marrow isn't a trivial matter. But it doesn't involve financial or personal risk; it doesn't mean spending a summer being chased by armed men in pickup trucks. It doesn't require that you confront socially entrenched norms and practices. In fact, it's the kind of commitment that will bring only social acknowledgment and praise.

The evangelists of social media don't understand this distinction; they seem to believe that a Facebook friend is the same as a real friend and that signing up for a donor registry in Silicon Valley today is activism in the same sense as sitting at a segregated lunch counter in Greensboro in 1960. "Social networks are particularly effective at increasing motivation," Aaker and Smith write. But that's not true. Social networks are effective at increasing *participation*—by lessening the level of motivation that participation requires. The Facebook page of the Save Darfur Coalition has 1,282,339 members, who have donated an average of nine cents apiece. The next biggest Darfur charity on Facebook has 22,073 members, who have donated an average of thirty-five cents. Help Save Darfur has 2,797 members, who have given, on average, fifteen cents. A spokesperson for the Save Darfur Coalition told *Newsweek*, "We wouldn't necessarily gauge someone's value to the advocacy movement based on what they've given. This is a powerful mechanism to engage this critical population. They inform their community, attend events, volunteer. It's not something you can measure by looking at a ledger." In other words, Facebook activism succeeds not by motivating people to make a real sacrifice but by motivating them to do the things that people do when they are not motivated enough to make a real sacrifice. We are a long way from the lunch counters of Greensboro.

The students who joined the sit-ins across the South during the winter of 1960 described the movement as a "fever." But the civil-rights movement was more like a military campaign than like a contagion. In the late 1950s, there had been sixteen sit-ins in various cities throughout the South, fifteen of which were formally organized by civil-rights organizations like the NAACP and CORE. Possible locations for activism were scouted. Plans were drawn up. Movement activists held training sessions and retreats for would-be protesters. The Greensboro Four were a product of this ground-work: all were members of the NAACP Youth Council. They had close ties with the head of the local NAACP chapter. They had been briefed on the earlier wave of sit-ins in Durham, and had been part of a series of movement meetings in activist churches. When the sit-in movement spread from Greensboro throughout the South, it did not spread indiscriminately. It spread to those cities which had preexisting "movement centers" — a core of dedicated and trained activists ready to turn the "fever" into action.

The civil-rights movement was high-risk activism. It was also, crucially, strategic activism: a challenge to the establishment mounted with precision and discipline. The NAACP was a centralized organization, run from New York according to highly formalized operating procedures. At the Southern Christian Leadership Conference, Martin Luther King, Jr., was the unquestioned authority. At the center of the movement was the black church, which had, as Aldon D. Morris points out in his superb 1984 study, *The Origins of the Civil Rights Movement*, a carefully demarcated division of labor, with various standing committees and disciplined groups. "Each group was task-oriented and coordinated its activities through authority structures," Morris writes. "Individuals were held accountable for their assigned duties, and important conflicts were resolved by the minister, who usually exercised ultimate authority over the congregation."

This is the second crucial distinction between traditional activism and its online variant: social media are not about this kind of hierarchical organization. Facebook and the like are tools for building *networks*, which are the opposite, in structure and character, of hierarchies. Unlike hierarchies, with their rules and procedures, networks aren't controlled by a single central authority. Decisions are made through consensus, and the ties that bind people to the group are loose.

This structure makes networks enormously resilient and adaptable in low-risk situations. Wikipedia is a perfect example. It doesn't have an editor, sitting in New York, who directs and corrects each entry. The effort of putting together each entry is self-organized. If every entry in Wikipedia were to be erased tomorrow, the content would swiftly be restored, because that's what happens when a network of thousands spontaneously devote their time to a task.

There are many things, though, that networks don't do well. Car companies sensibly use a network to organize their hundreds of suppliers, but not to design their cars. No one believes that the articulation of a coherent design philosophy is best handled by a sprawling, leaderless organizational system. Because networks don't have a centralized leadership structure and clear lines of authority, they have real difficulty reaching consensus and setting goals. They can't think strategically; they are chronically prone to conflict and error. How do you make difficult choices about tactics or strategy or philosophical direction when everyone has an equal say?

The Palestine Liberation Organization originated as a network, and the international-relations scholars Mette Eilstrup-Sangiovanni and Calvert Jones argue in a recent essay in *International Security* that this is why it ran into such trouble as it grew: "Structural features typical of networks — the absence of central authority, the unchecked autonomy of rival groups, and the inability to arbitrate quarrels through formal mechanisms — made the PLO excessively vulnerable to outside manipulation and internal strife." 25

In Germany in the 1970s, they go on, "the far more unified and successful left-wing terrorists tended to organize hierarchically, with professional management and clear divisions of labor. They were concentrated geographically in universities, where they could establish central leadership, trust, and camaraderie through regular, face-to-face meetings." They seldom betrayed their comrades in arms during police interrogations. Their counterparts on the right were organized as decentralized networks, and had no such discipline. These groups were regularly infiltrated, and members, once arrested, easily gave up their comrades. Similarly, Al Qaeda was most dangerous when it was a unified hierarchy. Now that it has dissipated into a network, it has proved far less effective.

The drawbacks of networks scarcely matter if the network isn't interested in systemic change—if it just wants to frighten or humiliate or make a splash—or if it doesn't need to think strategically. But if you're taking on a powerful and organized establishment you have to be a hierarchy. The Montgomery bus boycott required the participation of tens of thousands of people who depended on public transit to get to and from work each day. It lasted a *year*. In order to persuade those people to stay true to the cause, the boycott's organizers tasked each local black church with maintaining morale, and put together a free alternative private carpool service, with forty-eight dispatchers and forty-two pickup stations. Even the White Citizens Council, King later said, conceded that the carpool system moved with "military precision." By the time King came to Birmingham, for the climactic showdown with Police Commissioner Eugene (Bull) Connor, he had a budget of a million dollars, and a hundred full-time staff members on the ground, divided into operational units. The operation itself was divided into steadily escalating phases, mapped out in advance. Support was maintained through consecutive mass meetings rotating from church to church around the city.

Boycotts and sit-ins and nonviolent confrontations—which were the weapons of choice for the civil-rights movement—are high-risk strategies. They leave little room for conflict and error. The moment even one protester deviates from the script and responds to provocation, the moral legitimacy of the entire protest is compromised. Enthusiasts for social media would no doubt have us believe that King's task in Birmingham would have been made infinitely easier had he been able to communicate with his followers through Facebook, and contented himself with tweets from a Birmingham jail. But networks are messy: think of the ceaseless pattern of correction and revision, amendment and debate, that characterizes Wikipedia. If Martin Luther King, Jr., had tried to do a wiki-boycott in Montgomery, he would have been steamrollered by the white power structure. And of what use would a digital communication tool be in a town where ninety-eight percent of the black community could be reached every Sunday morning at church? The things that King needed in Birmingham—discipline and strategy—were things that online social media cannot provide.

The bible of the social-media movement is Clay Shirky's *Here Comes Everybody*. Shirky, who teaches at New York University, sets out to demonstrate the organizing power of the Internet, and he begins with the story of Evan, who worked on Wall Street, and his friend Ivanna, after she left her smart phone, an expensive Sidekick, on the back seat of a New York City taxicab. The telephone company transferred the data on Ivanna's lost phone to a new phone, whereupon she and Evan discovered that the Sidekick was now in the hands of a teenager from Queens, who was using it to take photographs of herself and her friends.

When Evan e-mailed the teenager, Sasha, asking for the phone back, she replied   30
that his "white ass" didn't deserve to have it back. Miffed, he set up a Web page with her picture and a description of what had happened. He forwarded the link to his friends, and they forwarded it to their friends. Someone found the MySpace page of Sasha's boyfriend, and a link to it found its way onto the site. Someone found her address online and took a video of her home while driving by; Evan posted the video on the site. The story was picked up by the news filter Digg. Evan was now up to ten e-mails a minute. He created a bulletin board for his readers to share their stories, but it crashed under the weight of responses. Evan and Ivanna went to the police, but the police filed the report under "lost," rather than "stolen," which essentially closed the case. "By this point millions of readers were watching," Shirky writes, "and dozens of mainstream news outlets had covered the story." Bowing to the pressure, the NYDP reclassified the item as "stolen." Sasha was arrested, and Evan got his friend's Sidekick back.

Shirky's argument is that this is the kind of thing that could never have happened in the pre-Internet age—and he's right. Evan could never have tracked down Sasha. The story of the Sidekick would never have been publicized. An army of people could never have been assembled to wage this fight. The police wouldn't have bowed to the pressure of a lone person who had misplaced something as trivial as a cell phone. The story, to Shirky, illustrates "the ease and speed with which a group can be mobilized for the right kind of cause" in the Internet age.

Shirky considers this model of activism an upgrade. But it is simply a form of organizing which favors the weak-tie connections that give us access to information over the strong-tie connections that help us persevere in the face of danger. It shifts our energies from organizations that promote strategic and disciplined activity and toward those which promote resilience and adaptability. It makes it easier for activists to express themselves, and harder for that expression to have any impact. The instruments of social media are well suited to making the existing social order more efficient. They are not a natural enemy of the status quo. If you are of the opinion that all the world needs is a little buffing around the edges, this should not trouble you. But if you think that there are still lunch counters out there that need integrating it ought to give you pause.

Shirky ends the story of the lost Sidekick by asking, portentously, "What happens next?"—no doubt imagining future waves of digital protesters. But he has already answered the question. What happens next is more of the same. A networked, weak-tie world is good at things like helping Wall Streeters get phones back from teenage girls. *Viva la revolución.**

---

* *Viva la revolución:* "Long live the revolution" (Spanish) [Ed.].

Exploring Context

1. Examine your friends list on Facebook or any other social networking site you use regularly. Using Gladwell's distinction between strong and weak ties, categorize your friends. How many do you think you have strong ties with? How many do you have weak ties with? Does your personal experience with social networking confirm or challenge Gladwell's argument?

2. The Occupy Wall Street movement (occupywallst.org) uses many of the social networking tools that Gladwell suggests are insufficient for true social action. Explore the site and use a search engine to locate any more local "occupy" movements. How do these groups use social networking technologies and media? Will they accomplish or have they accomplished social change? Use their experiences to evaluate Gladwell's argument.

3. In 2011, *Time* magazine named The Protestor as the person of the year (time.com/time/person-of-the-year/2011). Explore *Time*'s coverage of protestors. Do protestors use weak or strong ties? What role does social media play in protesting today?

Questions for Connecting

1. To what extent are the kinds of ties established between people dependent on group dynamics? Synthesize Gladwell's argument with James Surowiecki's discussion of small groups in "Committees, Juries, and Teams: The *Columbia* Disaster and How Small Groups Can Be Made to Work" (p. 472). Which of Surowiecki's examples reflect weak or strong ties? How do factors like social comparison or group polarization affect the kinds of ties that can be made between people?

2. Civil rights is a central concern of Gladwell's essay. Apply his analysis to Kenji Yoshino's "Preface" and "The New Civil Rights" (p. 552). Yoshino suggests that changes in civil rights should happen outside courtrooms; what mechanisms can Gladwell offer to help achieve Yoshino's vision?

3. Can Gladwell's analysis be applied to other problems? Consider Rebekah Nathan's discussion of higher education in "Community and Diversity" (p. 314). How do weak and strong ties determine the kind of communities possible in universities? How might universities use one or the other to promote both community and diversity?

4. **CONNECTING TO E-PAGES** Gladwell argues that the weak ties that characterize social networking don't allow for activism, but concedes that "there is strength in weak ties" (p. 234). Alexandra Samuel, in "'Plug In Better': A Manifesto" (bedfordstmartins.com/emerging/epages), writes that "you can create meaning in the way you use your time online" and that "this new online world offers extraordinary opportunities for creation, discovery, and connection." Connect these arguments: What do Gladwell and Samuel agree that the Internet is good for when it comes to social relations? What does each see as its dangers?

Language Matters

1. Apostrophes indicate possession. Go through Gladwell's text and locate some examples of the apostrophe, which is perhaps one of the most frequently misunderstood marks of punctuation. Given that an apostrophe is a kind of "tie," how might Gladwell's discussion explain the frequent misuse of this punctuation mark? What are the complexities of "possession" in today's world, in writing and in reality?

2. Locate the strongest transition in Gladwell's essay. What makes it strong or effective? How can you use this strategy in your own writing?

3. What are higher- and lower-order concerns in writing? Apply these concepts to Gladwell's writing. What are the higher-order concerns of the essay? Are there any?

Assignments for Writing

1. Gladwell seems to argue that strong-tie connections offer greater possibilities for social change than weak-tie connections. Write a paper in which you confirm, extend, or complicate Gladwell's argument by using your own example of either weak-tie or strong-tie connections and the possibilities they create for change.

2. Are strong-tie connections even possible with social media technologies? Write a paper in which you examine the possibility of strong-tie connections created through social media such as Twitter or Facebook. Use Gladwell's definitions and examples as well as your work from Questions for Critical Reading, Exploring Context, and Questions for Connecting.

3. What makes social change possible? Write a paper in which you synthesize Gladwell's competing concepts of strong-tie connections and weak-tie connections in order to propose ideal strategies for promoting social change. How can the two kinds of ties work together?

HAL HERZOG

Hal Herzog is a professor of psychology at Western Carolina University. Though he teaches courses in human sexuality and biological psychology, he is also interested in anthrozoology—an emerging field that examines the relationship between humans and animals. He has published over one hundred academic articles in journals including *Science, Anthrozoös,* and the *American Scholar.* His work has also been presented in more popular media such as *Salon,* NPR, and *USA Today.*

Herzog's book *Some We Love, Some We Hate, Some We Eat: Why It's So Hard to Think Straight about Animals* (2010) discusses the often-contradictory relationship human beings have with the animals around them. Dogs, he points out, can be regarded as family pets, working animals, or even food depending on the geographic area in which they happen to have been born. The book explains the historical and cultural reasons behind the somewhat arbitrary classifications we have for various animals, which in turn put an animal in the zoo or in a testing lab.

"Animals Like Us" is an excerpt from Herzog's book. In it he begins by presenting some innocuous anecdotal stories that pave the way for the rest of his argument, one in which mankind's complex relationships with all variety of animals is dissected. The complications of this dissection are represented by the "troubled middle" (p. 247), an almost inevitable gray area of morality that Herzog uses in figuring out his own relationships to animals and the ethics that entails.

▶ TAGS: *vegetarianism, relationships with animals, predator pets, food, morally problematic interactions, ethical obligations, troubled middle*

Questions for Critical Reading

1. Herzog notes that some of our interactions with animals are "morally problematic" (p. 245). As you read the text, pay close attention to the anecdotal stories about other people's interactions with animals. Would you characterize any of these as more or less "morally problematic" than others?

2. Herzog mentions "the troubled middle" (p. 247). What is it, and how does it factor into his study of "animal people"?

3. As you read the text, consider what actually separates humans from animals and why humans put certain animals into categories like "pet" and others into categories like "food." Locate passages from Herzog that would support your position.

Animals Like Us

> I like pondering our relationship with animals because they tell a lot about
> who we are.
>
> —MARC BEKOFF

The way we think about other species often defies logic. Consider Judith Black. When she was 12, Judith decided that it was wrong to kill animals just because they taste good. But what exactly is an animal? While it is obvious that dogs and cats and cows and pigs are animals, it was equally clear to Judith that fish were not. They just didn't feel like animals to her. So for the next 15 years, this intuitive biological classification system enabled Judith, who has a Ph.D. in anthropology, to think of herself as a vegetarian, yet still experience the joys of smoked Copper River salmon and lemon-grilled swordfish.

This twisted moral taxonomy worked fine until Judith ran into Joseph Weldon, a graduate student in biology. When they first met, Joseph, himself a meat eater, tried to convince Judith that there is not a shred of moral difference between eating a Cornish hen and eating a Chilean sea bass. After all, he reasoned, both birds and fish are vertebrates, have brains, and lead social lives.

"Fortunately, their disagreement over the moral status of mahi mahi* did not prevent them from falling in love. They married, and her new husband kept the fish-versus-fowl discussion going over the dinner table. After three years of philosophical to-and-fro, Judith sighed one evening and gave in: "OK, I see your point. Fish are animals."

But now she faced a difficult decision: She could either quit eating fish, or stop thinking of herself as a vegetarian. Something had to give. A week later, friends invited Joseph to a grouse hunt. Though he had no experience with a shotgun, he managed to shoot a bird, and he showed up at home, dead carcass in hand. Joseph then proceeded to pluck and cook the grouse, which he served to his wife for dinner along with wild rice and raspberry sauce.

In an instant, 15 years of moral high ground went down the drain. ("I am a sucker for raspberries," Judith told me.) The taste of roasted grouse opened the floodgates, and there was no going back. Within a week, she was chowing down on cheeseburgers. Judith had joined the ranks of ex-vegetarians, a club that outnumbers current vegetarians in the United States by a ratio of three to one.

Then there is Jim Thompson, a 25-year-old doctoral student in mathematics. Before beginning graduate school, Jim had worked in a poultry research laboratory in Lexington, Kentucky, where one of his jobs was dispatching baby chicks at the end of the experiments. For a while, this posed no problem for Jim. However, things changed one day when he was looking for a magazine to read on a plane and his mother handed him a copy of *The Animals' Agenda*, a magazine that advocated animal rights. He never ate meat again.

---

* Mahi mahi: A kind of edible fish [Ed.].

Over the next couple of months, Jim quit wearing leather shoes, and he pressured his girlfriend to go veg. He even began to question the morality of keeping pets, including his beloved white cockatiel. One afternoon Jim looked at the bird flitting around her cage and a little voice in his head whispered, "This is wrong." He carried the bird into his backyard and released it into the gray skies of Raleigh, North Carolina. It was a great feeling, he told me. But then he sheepishly added, "I knew she wouldn't survive, that she probably starved. I guess I was doing it for myself more than for her."

Our relationships with animals can also be emotionally complicated. Twenty years ago, Carolyn fell head over heels for a 1,100-pound manatee. She had applied for a job — any job — at a small natural history museum in central Florida. The museum had an opening; they were looking for a caregiver for a 30-year-old sea cow named Snooty. Carolyn had no experience working with marine mammals, but they offered her the position anyway. She did not know that her life was about to change.

On the phylogenetic scale,* Snooty falls somewhere between the Creature from the Black Lagoon and Yoda. When Carolyn introduced me to him, Snooty hooked his flippers over the edge of his pool, hoisted his head out of the water, and looked me straight in the eye, checking me out. While his brain was smaller than a softball, he seemed oddly wise. I found the experience unnerving. Not Carolyn. She was in love.

For over two decades, Carolyn's life revolved around Snooty. She spent nearly every day with him. Food was a major part of their relationship. Manatees are vegetarians, and Carolyn fed him by hand — 120 pounds of leafy green vegetables, mostly lettuce, every day.   10

But life with an aging sea cow has its downside. When she and her husband would sneak off for a week or two of vacation, Snooty would get in a funk and quit eating. All too often, Carolyn would get a call saying that Snooty was off his feed again, and she would rush back to ply him with a couple of bushels of iceberg lettuce.

At some point, Carolyn gave up going on vacations. That's when her husband accused her of having her priorities screwed up, of loving a half-ton blob of blubber and muscle more than she loved him.

As a research psychologist, I have been studying human-animal relationships for 20 years, and I have found that the quirky thinking when it comes to animals that we see in Judith, Jim, and Carolyn is not the exception but the rule. I began to think seriously about the inconsistencies in our relationships with other species when I got a phone call from my friend Sandy. At the time, I was an animal behaviorist and Sandy was an animal rights activist who taught at my university.

"Hal, I heard that you were picking up kittens from the Jackson County animal shelter and feeding them to a snake. Is it true?"

I was completely taken aback.   15

"We do have a pet snake, but he is just a baby," I told her. "He could not possibly swallow a kitten. And I like cats. Even if he were bigger, I would never let him eat a cat."

Sandy apologized profusely. She said she figured the charge was not true, but that she just had to check. I told her I understood, but would appreciate it if she would assure

---

* Phylogenetic scale: A ranking of animals based on their complexity, from lower to higher [Ed.].

her animal protection pals that I was not dipping into our community's reservoir of unwanted cats to feed my son's snake.

But then I started thinking about the moral implications of keeping a predator for a pet. We had acquired the baby boa by accident when I was a visiting scientist at the University of Tennessee, studying the development of defensive behaviors in reptiles. A man called and told me his seven-foot red-tail boa constrictor had given birth to 42 wriggling newborns.

The man had heard that I was a snake behaviorist and was looking for tips on how to keep the babies healthy and where he could find good homes for them. I recommended that he contact a reptile expert I knew at the university's veterinary college for information on raising baby snakes, and agreed to adopt one of the babies myself.

Sam was a low-maintenance pet. He did not scratch the furniture, keep the neighbors awake, or require daily exercise. He was gentle—except for the time he tried to swallow Adam's thumb. It was Adam's fault. He made the mistake of lifting Sam out of his cage immediately after handling a friend's pet hamster. Sam's brain was about as big as an aspirin tablet, and he could not tell the difference between a rodent and a human hand. He just smelled meat. The accusation that the Herzog family was feeding kittens to snakes came a few weeks later. 20

In the following days, several questions kept nagging me. My accuser had inadvertently forced me to confront questions I had never really considered about the moral burdens of bringing animals into our lives. Snakes don't eat carrots and asparagus. Given Sam's need for meat, was it ethical to keep a boa constrictor for a pet? Is having a pet that gets its daily ration of

> **Given Sam's need for meat, was it ethical to keep a boa constrictor as a pet?**

meat from a can of cat food morally preferable to living with a snake? And are there circumstances in which feeding kittens to boa constrictors might actually be morally acceptable?

The person who started the rumor about me lived with several cats that she allowed to roam the woods around her house. Like many cat lovers, she conveniently ignored the fact that from lions to tabbies, all members of the family Felidae eat flesh for a living. Each day the cats of America chow down on a wide array of meat. The pet-food shelves of my local supermarket are piled high with six-ounce tins of cow, sheep, chicken, horse, turkey, and fish. Even dried cat foods are advertised as containing "fresh meat." With about 94 million cats in America, the numbers add up. If each cat consumes just two ounces of meat daily, en masse they consume nearly 12 million pounds of flesh—the equivalent of 3 million chickens—every single day.

In addition, cats, unlike snakes, are recreational killers. It is estimated that a billion small animals a year fall victim to the hunting instincts of our pet cats. Oddly, many cat owners don't seem to care about the devastation their feline friends cause to wildlife. In a cruel irony, many cat owners also enjoy feeding birds in their backyards, inadvertently luring legions of hapless towhees and cardinals to their deaths at the claws of the family pet. It is likely that at least 10 times as many furry and feathered creatures are killed each year as a result of our love of cats as are used in biomedical experiments.

So, pet cats cause havoc. What about pet snakes? Well, first, there are a lot fewer of them. In addition, each snake consumes only a fraction of the flesh that a cat does. According to Harry Greene, a Cornell University herpetologist, an adult boa living in a Costa Rican rainforest consumes maybe half a dozen rats a year. This means that a medium-size pet boa constrictor needs less than five pounds of meat a year. A pet cat requires far more flesh. At two ounces a day, the average cat would consume about 50 pounds of meat in a year. Objectively, the moral burden of enjoying the company of a cat is 10 times higher than that of living with a pet snake.

About 2 million unwanted cats, many of them kittens, are euthanized in animal   25
"shelters" in the United States each year. Their bodies are cremated. Wouldn't it make more sense to make these carcasses available to snake fanciers? After all, these cats are going to die anyway and fewer mice and rats would be sacrificed to satisfy the dietary needs of the pythons and king snakes living in American homes. Seems like a win-win, right?

Yikes—I had inadvertently painted myself into a logical corner in which feeding the bodies of kittens to boa constrictors was not only permissible but morally preferable to feeding them rodents. But while the logical part of my brain may have concluded that there was not much difference, the emotional part of me was not buying the argument at all. I found the idea of feeding the bodies of cats to snakes revolting.

The boa constrictor incident got me thinking about other instances of morally problematic interactions between people and animals that I had encountered. For instance, my graduate school friend Ron Neibor studied how the brain reorganizes itself after injury. Cats, unfortunately, were the best model for the neural mechanisms he was studying. He employed a standard neuroscience technique: He surgically destroyed specific parts of the animals' brains to observe how their abilities recovered over the succeeding weeks and months. The problem was that Ron liked his cats. His study lasted a year, during which time he became attached to the two dozen animals in his lab. On weekends, he would drive to the lab, release his cats from their cages, and play with them. They had become pets.

His experimental protocol required that he confirm the location of the neurological lesions in the animals in the experimental group by examining their brain tissue. Part of this procedure, technically referred to as perfusion, is grisly. Each animal is injected with a lethal dose of anesthetic. Then formalin is pumped through its veins to harden the brain, and the animal's head is severed from the body. Pliers are used to chip away the skull so the brain can be extracted intact and sliced into thin sections for microscopic analysis.

It took Ron several weeks to perfuse all the cats. His personality changed. A naturally cheerful and warmhearted person, he became tense, withdrawn, shaky. Several graduate students in his lab became concerned and offered to perfuse his cats for him. Ron refused, unwilling to dodge the moral consequences of his research. He did not talk much during the weeks he was "sacrificing" his cats. Sometimes his eyes were red, and he would look down as we passed in the halls.

These sorts of moral complexities also extend to man's best friend, the dog. Most of   30
the dogs living in American homes are simply companions, but our attitudes toward them can be convoluted. Over half of dog owners think of their pets as family members. A report by the American Animal Hospital Association found that 40 percent of

the women they surveyed said they got more affection from their dogs than from their husbands or children. Yet there is a dark side to our interactions with dogs. One in 10 American adults is afraid of dogs, and dogs are second only to late-night noise as a source of conflict between neighbors. In a typical year, 4.5 million Americans are bitten by dogs, and two dozen people, mostly children, are killed by them.

From a dog's-eye view, the human-pet relationship isn't always rosy either. Between 2 million and 3 million unwanted dogs are euthanized in animal shelters each year. Then there are the horrendous genetic problems we have inflicted upon dogs in our attempts to breed the perfect pet. Take, for example, the English bulldog, a breed that dog behavior expert James Serpell refers to as a canine train wreck. Bulldogs have such monstrous heads that 90 percent of bulldog puppies have to be delivered by cesarean section. Their distorted snouts and deformed nasal passages make breathing a chore, even during sleep. They suffer from numerous maladies and have a tendency to suddenly drop dead from cardiac arrest.

Things are worse for dogs in Korea, where a puppy can be a pet or an item on the menu. Meat dogs, which are typically short-haired, largish animals that look disconcertingly like Old Yeller, are raised in horrific conditions before they are slaughtered, often by electrocution.

We usually ignore these contradictions, but as a psychologist, I began to be fascinated by them.

In the weeks after I was accused of feeding kittens to boas, I found myself thinking more about the paradoxes associated with our relationships with animals and less about my animal behavior studies. By conventional standards, my research program was a success. I published articles in good journals, received my share of grant funds, and presented my research at scholarly meetings. But it dawned on me that there were plenty of smart young scientists investigating topics like vocalizations in cotton rats, tool use in crows, and the offbeat reproductive habits of spotted hyenas (female hyenas give birth through their penises). On the other hand, there were only a handful of researchers trying to understand the often wacky ways that people relate to other species. Here was an emerging field, one that I could enter on the ground floor and possibly make a contribution to. Within a year, I had closed up my animal lab to concentrate full time on the psychology of human-animal interactions.

Since I shifted from studying animal behavior to studying animal people, my re- 35 search has largely focused on individuals who love animals but who confront moral quandaries in their relationships with them—the veterinary student who tries not to cry when she euthanizes a puppy, the animal rights activist who can't find someone to date because "just going out to eat becomes an ordeal," the burly circus animal trainer whose life is completely focused on the giant bears he hauls around the country in the dreary confines of an 18-wheeler, the grizzled cockfighter who beams when I offer to take a picture of his beloved battle-scarred seven-time winner.

I have attended animal rights protests, serpent-handling church services, and clandestine rooster fights. I have interviewed laboratory animal technicians, big-time dog-show handlers, and small-time circus animal trainers. I've watched high school kids dissect their first fetal pigs and helped a farm crew slaughter cattle. I analyzed several thousand Internet messages between biomedical researchers and animal rights activists as they tried—and ultimately failed—to find common ground.

My students have studied women hunters, dog rescuers, ex-vegetarians, and people who love pet rats. We have surveyed thousands of people about their attitudes toward rodeos, factory farming, and animal research. We have even pored over hundreds of back issues of sleazy supermarket tabloids for insight into our modern cultural myths about animals.

Like most people, I am conflicted about our ethical obligations to animals. The philosopher Strachan Donnelley calls this murky ethical territory "the troubled middle." Those of us in the troubled middle live in a complex moral universe. I eat meat—but not as much as I used to, and not veal. I oppose testing the toxicity of oven cleaner and eye shadow on animals, but I would sacrifice a lot of mice to find a cure for cancer. And while I find some of the logic of animal liberation philosophers convincing, I also believe that our vastly greater capacity for symbolic language, culture, and ethical judgment puts humans on a different moral plane from that of other animals.

We middlers see the world in shades of gray rather than in the clear blacks and whites of committed animal activists and their equally vociferous opponents. Some argue that we are fence-sitters, moral wimps. I believe, however, that the troubled middle makes perfect sense because moral quagmires are inevitable in a species with a huge brain and a big heart. They come with the territory.

Exploring Context

1. Learn more about Snooty the manatee at the website for the South Florida Museum (southfloridamuseum.org/TheAquarium/SnootyFacts.aspx). How does the museum's representation of Snooty confirm Herzog's argument about the ways in which we relate to certain animals?

2. Explore the website for the Humane Society at humanesociety.org. What kinds of animals seem to take precedence on the site in terms of its design and content? Relate your exploration to Herzog's analysis.

3. Visit Hal Herzog's website at halherzog.com and explore his collection of links for anthrozoology. How do they extend your own understanding of how complex relationships can be between humans and animals?

Questions for Connecting

1. Michael Pollan's "The Animals: Practicing Complexity" (p. 373) also focuses on our relationship with animals. Synthesize the positions of these two authors to consider the ethics of farm animals. Does Polyface's approach avoid the "troubled middle"?

2. In "Ethics and the New Genetics" (p. 133), the Dalai Lama calls for a "moral compass" to guide us in relation to scientific progress. Use Herzog's analysis of our relationship with animals to complicate the Dalai Lama's argument. Is it possible to locate a stable moral compass? Use both Herzog's examples as well as his discussion of the "troubled middle."

3. How does our relationship with animals change what it means to be human? Incorporate Herzog's discussion into Francis Fukuyama's analysis in "Human Dignity" (p. 185). Do any of the animals that Herzog discusses possess Factor X? Does Factor X blur when it comes to our relationships with some animals such as pets?

Language Matters

1. At times Herzog uses parentheses to set off information; other times he uses dashes. Review the rules for both of these punctuation marks in a grammar handbook or other reference resource. When should you use one or the other to set off information that is not the main point of your sentence?

2. Review the rules for verb tense in a grammar handbook or other reference resource. Then select two key quotations from Herzog and change the tenses of the verbs. What difference does tense make to an argument? What are the conventions for verb tense in academic writing?

3. What makes a comma unnecessary? Review information on comma usage in a grammar handbook or other reliable source. Then review Herzog's essay. Are any of his commas unnecessary? How can you make sure you only use necessary commas in your own writing?

Assignments for Writing

1. Is there a way out of the troubled middle? Write a paper in which you explore the relationship between ethics and animals, proposing strategies to resolve the murkiness of Herzog's troubled middle. Is it possible to move beyond the troubled middle? Or does it represent the best moral position, given the issues involved? Use Herzog to support your position.

2. Write a paper in which you determine what it means to be human based on our relationships with animals. What can we learn about ourselves by looking at these relationships? What separates us from animals? What do we have in common? Use Herzog to support your response.

3. Herzog's title — "Animals Like Us" — is ambiguous. It could mean that animals like humans or that animals are like humans. Write a paper in which you resolve this ambiguity by determining what Herzog means by his title, as represented by the argument he makes in his text.

MARA HVISTENDAHL

Mara Hvistendahl, former professor of journalism at Fudan University in Shanghai, is a regular correspondent for *Science* magazine who has written for *Harper's Magazine*, *Scientific American*, the *Financial Times*, *Foreign Policy*, and *Popular Science*. Her book, *Unnatural Selection: Choosing Boys Over Girls, and the Consequences of a World Full of Men* (2011), earned a place on many top ten lists for 2011 books, including those of the *Wall Street Journal*, *Slate*, and *Discover* magazine.

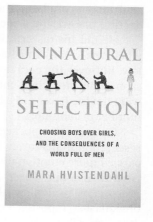

In *Unnatural Selection*, Hvistendahl explores the cultural factors that caused societies in Asia to prefer male children to female and how this preference has led — by means of sex-selective abortion — to a gross imbalance of genders across the continent. Our own Western society, Hvistendahl shows, has contributed to the problem.

"Missing: 163 Million Women" was adapted for *Mother Jones* magazine from Hvistendahl's book. In this essay, Hvistendahl presents the very real numbers of this gender imbalance in Asia (and in other places). Along with this information, Hvistendahl outlines the real-world complications that have resulted. As she makes clear, while women are the only ones missing from the tally now, the situation at hand radiates outward with consequences for both genders that are only beginning to be felt.

▶ TAGS: *gender, Generation XY, surplus men, research, social policy, population*

Questions for Critical Reading

1. Hvistendahl suggests that gender imbalance is not a problem confined to other countries but is instead a global concern. Mark passages where she offers evidence for this assertion. What are the global implications for an imbalance in gender, if any?

2. What is "Generation XY"? Define this term using Hvistendahl's text.

3. How does Hvistendahl use rhetoric to frame her argument? Consider her title and her claims. How is she trying to persuade her audience? When does she use appeals to evidence? What other appeals does she use? Based on the style and content of this essay, who do you think her audience is?

Missing: 163 Million Women

Midway through his career, Christophe Guilmoto stopped counting babies and started counting boys. A French demographer with a mathematician's love of numbers and an anthropologist's obsession with detail, he had attended graduate school in Paris in the 1980s, when babies had been the thing. By the time he started his Ph.D., birth rates were falling around the world, but the populations of many developing nations were still growing, and it was hard to shake the idea lingering in demography that overpopulation was a grave threat.[1] Like many demography* students at the time, he concentrated on studying the drop in fertility, searching for clues of what factors proved decisive in lowering a country's birth rate.

He did his dissertation research in Tamil Nadu, a state in southwestern India where the fertility rate had fallen to European levels even as personal income remained low. But over the course of working in India, he realized that there, at least, demography's big story had changed. People were not simply having fewer children. They were having fewer girls. Population growth had been slowed, in part, by reducing the number of daughters.

Outside of the pocket of rural Tamil Nadu where Guilmoto happened to do his field research, Indians rarely killed infants. "Everybody talked about infanticide because it carried more emotional weight," he recalls. "But actually it was hardly in existence." As it turned out, Tamil Nadu was in fact one of the states where girls had a better prospect of survival, while in 2001 the northwest, a wealthy region considered India's breadbasket, reported a regional sex ratio at birth of 126—that is, 126 boys for every 100 girls. (The natural human sex ratio at birth is 105 boys for every 100 girls.) The cause for this gap, Guilmoto quickly learned, was that pregnant women were taking advantage of a cheap and pervasive sex determination tool—ultrasound—and aborting if the fetus turned out to be female.

The link to technology was alarming, for it meant that India's skewed ratio of male to female newborns was an outgrowth of economic progress, not backward traditions. And it wasn't just happening in India. Guilmoto found that several other Asian countries exceeded the biological upper limit of 106 boys born per 100 girls. In the 1980s, South Korea, Taiwan, and parts of Singapore registered sex ratios at birth exceeding 109. By 2000, Azerbaijan, Armenia, and Georgia would show sex ratios at birth of over 115, and significantly skewed birth ratios would later appear in Vietnam and Albania as well. In preliminary census results released this spring, China reported a sex ratio at birth of 118 boys per 100 girls, while India, which uses an alternative statistic, reported 914 girls for every 1,000 boys, ages 0–6. People, Guilmoto realized, were engineering what he calls "rampant demographic masculinization"—a change with potentially grave effects for future generations. "It was very difficult," he told me, "not to see it as a revolution."

In 2005, Guilmoto calculated that, had Asia's ratio remained at its natural equilibrium of 105 over the past few decades, the continent would have had an additional

5

---

* Demography: The study of the composition of human populations and their changes over time [Ed.].

163 million women and girls. Since then, the lopsided birth totals of China and India have boosted the global sex ratio at birth to a biologically improbable 107.

If 163 million women were missing from the U.S. population, you would certainly notice—but only if you were a man. That's because there would be no women left. Imagine the nation's malls and super-markets, its highways and hospitals, its boardrooms and classrooms exclusively filled with men. Imagine the bus or the subway or the car that takes you to work, then erase the females commuting

> **If 163 million women were missing from the U.S. population, you would certainly notice—but only if you were a man.**

alongside you. Erase your wife and your daughter. If you are a woman reading this, erase yourself.

Imagine this and you come close to picturing the scale of the problem. But because women have disappeared from Asia and Eastern Europe, what little you've heard about the imbalance probably came in the form of an international news brief. Gender im-balance is treated as a local problem, but it is a local problem in the way a superpower's financial crisis or a neighboring country's war is a local problem. Skewed sex ratios in the developing world have led to a slew of secondary human rights abuses, and those are issues the rest of the world must address.

Because the reduction in the number of females in the population has paralleled a reduction in the global birth rate, this new generation—call it Generation XY—is the largest that will hit many developing countries for decades to come. Even using conservative UN population projections, which assume that couples soon start having boys and girls in equal numbers (which is highly unlikely), restoring the global gender balance will take until 2050.

Which means we're already stuck with large numbers of what demographers call "surplus" men, the ones left over in an imagined world where everyone who can marry does so. Men doomed, should they be straight, to a life of singledom. Overstock. But the loneliness that accompanies bachelorhood is the least of Asia's problems. Surplus men have been going to great lengths to find women—and in many cases succeeding. As the first generation touched by sex-ratio imbalance grows up, the silent biological discrimination that is sex selection has been exacerbated by more visible threats to women, including sex trafficking, bride buying, and forced marriages.

In South Korea and Taiwan, increasing numbers of men obtain wives on one-week "marriage tours" of Vietnam—a trade similar to America's mail-order-bride industry but so pervasive that in South Korea more than 1,000 international marriage agen-cies have registered with the government. In wealthy parts of China and India, men buy women from poorer regions, working through shady brokers who may or may not bother to secure the women's consent. In poorer parts of China and India, they visit brothels staffed by prostitutes who have often been forced into sex work.

As Generation XY matures in other parts of the gender-imbalanced world, more-over, even these crude tactics will not be an option. Men in western China, eastern India, Vietnam, Georgia, Albania, and other countries with recent or looming sex-ratio imbalances won't be able to import women, because at some point in the near future the supply of women will dry up.

"The idea of importing brides to solve the shortage in women may work in coun-tries with lower populations, but in a huge country like China they are just a drop in the ocean," Tian Xueyuan, deputy director of the China Population Association, recently told the *China Daily*—as if diminishing numbers were the only problem with bringing in boatloads of bought foreign women. "It's not a realistic solution."

Lately, Guilmoto, now affiliated with the institut de recherche pour le développement in Paris, has dedicated himself to calculating precisely how bad the male surplus will be by, as he puts it, "trying to marry these guys off." The outlook is grim. "It's not sustainable," he says. "It's not such a great idea to have children of only one gender. At the beginning it's a dream—I call it a male Utopia." He smiles slightly. "But if you start imagining that the neighbors are going to do the same, then these good-looking boys will face trouble in the marriage market. The surplus will pile up."

> **"These good-looking boys will face trouble in the marriage market,"**
> **Guilmoto says. "The surplus will pile up."**

It won't just be forlorn single men who will suffer in 2020s Asia and 2030s Eastern Europe. Other scholars have begun to calculate the impact that hundreds of millions of surplus men will have on everything from health care to crime. Historically, societies in which men substantially outnumber women are not nice places to live. Sometimes they are violent: Leaders in both China and India now see the imbalance as a threat to social stability.

In the number of lives it has touched, Guilmoto says, sex selection merits comparison with AIDS. In the introduction to *Watering the Neighbour's Garden*, a collection of scholarly papers on the global sex-ratio imbalance, he and coeditor Isabelle Attané point out that AIDS has claimed an estimated 25 million lives worldwide—a mere fraction of the number of missing females.   15

In 2008, indeed, HIV commanded fully one-fourth of global spending on health. AIDS has the attention of nongovernmental organizations, policymakers, and schoolchildren around the world. It boasts its own United Nations agency. Sex selection recently yielded a UN statement[2]—a document released from the World Health Organization and other agencies in mid-June outlining a program for addressing the gender discrimination underlying the global preference for boys. But beyond that, the practice remains mostly invisible, a pervasive and yet quiet epidemic observed only by demographers scrutinizing birth registration records years after the fact—and, of course, by the hundreds of millions of people who live or will live in communities where women are scarce.

NOTES

1. http://motherjones.com/environment/2010/05/population-growth-india-vatican
2. http://www.who.int/reproductivehealth/publications/gender_rights/
   9789241501460/en/

Exploring Context

1. Visit Wikipedia's list of countries by sex ratio (en.wikipedia.org/wiki/List_of_countries_by_sex_ratio) and sort the list by clicking on the "at birth" column. How does the data presented there confirm or complicate Hvistendahl's argument?

2. The Vietnamese Migrant Workers and Brides Office (taiwanact.net) is a Taiwanese group focused on the rights of both workers and brides. Given the site's dual focus, how might you expand Hvistendahl's argument? Is gender imbalance the only issue in the countries she examines?

3. Explore the Gender Selection Guide (in-gender.com), an Internet resource for parents who wish to choose the gender of their children. Synthesize the information you find there with Hvistendahl's essay. Is sex selection ethical? What are its implications for not just the world but, more specifically, the United States?

Questions for Connecting

1. In "Making Conversation" and "The Primacy of Practice" (p. 67), Kwame Anthony Appiah explores the ways in which cultural practices change. Synthesize his position with Hvistendahl's discussion. How have birthing practices changed? Can Appiah's text explain the mechanism for this change? While Appiah's examples feel "progressive," how does Hvistendahl suggest that these same mechanisms might have devastating consequences?

2. The Dalai Lama suggests that science progresses faster than ethics in "Ethics and the New Genetics" (p. 133). How can you use Hvistendahl's essay as an extension of the Dalai Lama's argument about ethical ways to apply new technologies? Is a moral compass missing in decisions about birth technologies, or does Hvistendahl indicate that a moral compass can fail by pointing in the wrong direction?

3. How has globalization affected marriage and birth? Use Thomas L. Friedman's discussion of global and rogue supply chains in "The Dell Theory of Conflict Prevention" (p. 166) to consider the economics involved in this looming gender imbalance crisis. What role did global supply chains play in creating this problem? Given Friedman's emphasis on collaboration, how can globalization address this issue?

Language Matters

1. What counts as evidence for Hvistendahl? Reread her essay, noting the kinds of evidence she uses to support her argument. How would you categorize each? What is the strongest evidence? The weakest? Which kinds of evidence should you use to support your own argument?

2. Using a grammar handbook or other reference resource, review the rules for writing numbers. When should they be spelled out, and when should you use numerals? Apply your findings to Hvistendahl's text. Does she follow these rules? How can you bring these insights to your own writing?

3. What is the difference between a dash and a hyphen? Use a grammar handbook or other reliable source to differentiate the two and review the rules on when to use each. Apply your findings to Hvistendahl's text. How does she use each? When might you use these punctuation marks in your own writing?

Assignments for Writing

1. How can we minimize the consequences of technological advances? Using Hvisten-dahl's analysis as a starting point, write a paper on the ramifications of technology, suggesting ways that we can minimize negative consequences.

2. Hvistendahl compares the current global gender imbalance to the HIV epidemic. Write a paper in which you analyze her use of this analogy. In what ways is the selection of Generation XY similar to an epidemic? More crucially, in what ways does her analogy fail? What aspects of the HIV epidemic (treatment, prevention) are not replicated in the situation that Hvistendahl describes?

3. How can we address the problem of "surplus men" and Generation XY? Write a paper in which you suggest ways in which the global community can work to solve this problem, drawing on Hvistendahl to support your position.

RACHEL KADISH

Rachel Kadish currently teaches creative writing in the M.F.A. program at Lesley University while serving as a scholar at the Women's Studies Research Center of Brandeis University. After receiving her undergraduate degree from Princeton University, she went on to obtain an M.A. in creative writing from New York University. Among her many achievements, she spent time as a fiction fellow at Harvard/Radcliffe's Bunting Institute and was a fellow of the National Endowment for the Arts. She specializes in fiction writing and has published the novels *From a Sealed Room* (1998) and *Tolstoy Lied: A Love Story* (2006). Her nonfiction essays have been published in the anthologies *The Modern Jewish Girl's Guide to Guilt* (2005) and *Who We Are: On Being (and Not Being) a Jewish Writer in America* (2005) as well as in *Tin House, Poets & Writers, Moment,* and *The Good Men Project.*

The selection included here, "Who Is This Man, and Why Is He Screaming?" was originally published by *The Good Men Project,* an online magazine that focuses on the social definition of manhood and what it means to be a good man in the twenty-first century. Kadish's article can be found alongside other arts and entertainment articles, which address a new series of comic-book-style biographies of history's great men, the unbalanced gender representation in movies, and the benefits men can reap from watching *Project Runway.* The slightly edited version included here is from the July/August 2011 *Utne Reader.*

The essay "Who Is This Man, and Why Is He Screaming?" tells the story of Kadish's cousin, Noam Galai. After posting a self-portrait to the photo-hosting website Flickr (flickr .com), Galai found that people around the world had, without his knowledge or permission, utilized the image for a variety of purposes and in a multitude of situations, pulling it out of its original context and altering Galai's intent. In this essay, Kadish investigates this invasion of privacy and brings into question the extent of our own personal property.

▶ TAGS: *licensing, Flickr, political movements, identity, Iranian resistance, private property, aesthetic objects, representation*

Questions for Critical Reading

1. What are the risks and rewards of living in a networked world? As you read Kadish, locate passages that support your answer.

2. Kadish notes that one of the contexts for Galai's image was protests against the government of Iran. She links his silent scream to protestors screaming "Allahu akbar"

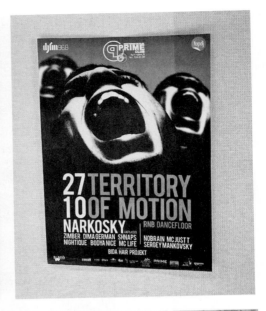

(p. 261). Use the Web to locate the meaning of this phrase. What makes it revolutionary?

3. Kadish is on some level conflicted about the appropriation of her cousin's image. She writes, "I can't work out whether it's the end of innocence, or the start of it" (p. 262). As you read her essay, make note of passages that suggest her overall feeling about the circulation of Galai's photograph.

Who Is This Man, and Why Is He Screaming?

You've probably never met my cousin. But you've probably seen him scream.

My cousin Noam Galai is 26 years old. He's the youngest of four brothers, a thin guy with brown eyes and a buzz cut, and he speaks so rarely that, although I've known him all my life, the sound of his voice is still a surprise. Shyness, in fact, has been a central fact of Noam's existence for as long as he can remember.

Growing up in Jerusalem, he refused to speak in class or even go to the chalkboard. There was nothing more excruciating for him than finding himself the center of attention. His unwillingness to step forward caused many of his teachers to assume he didn't know the answers; still, he found it easier not to explain himself. When, at the end of high school, he was required to take an English-language exam involving an

Noam Galai / www.noamgalai.com

oral component—a five-minute conversation in English with an examiner—Noam, raised by an American mother, walked into the room and told the examiner softly in Hebrew: "I know English, you can trust me. I'm just not going to show you." For some reason he still doesn't understand, she passed him.

Time only solidified Noam's stage fright. By his early 20s, he'd finished his service in the Israeli army and had moved to New York City to work for his brother's Internet start-up. On the side he took jobs as a photographer, working mainly at sports events. One day he was at work in midtown Manhattan when the building was shaken by an enormous explosion. Amid the confusion, Noam took his camera and ran outside, onto a street engulfed by steam and a hail of flying rock and scalding water shooting 20 stories into the air. A nearly century-old steam pipe under Lexington Avenue near Grand Central had exploded, opening craters. Throngs of New Yorkers were fleeing the site, faces covered with dust, some literally running out of their shoes in their panicked certainty that this was another 9/11. Noam sprinted in the opposite direction—toward the explosion. He photographed the scene for nearly half an hour before police secured the site and ordered him back to the safe zone.

Professional photographers representing major news outlets had been required by the police to photograph from behind the safety line. Some of them, seeing Noam returning from the site with his camera around his neck, asked to see his photographs. He showed them images of the gaping crater, of buildings wreathed in steam, of expensive shoes abandoned on the Lexington Avenue sidewalk.

A few hours later he received a phone call from someone at CNN: Would he come to their studios to be a guest on their morning program? Show his one-of-a-kind photos and talk about what he'd seen?

No way, said Noam.

The CNN rep urged him to reconsider. This was a great professional opportunity for him. He realized, didn't he, the exposure his work would receive?

If he didn't want to appear on camera, then, would he agree to be interviewed over the phone?

No way.

He sold CNN the pictures and was acknowledged with a photo credit misspelling his name.

He'd shied from CNN, yet when hundreds of people had fled the site of an explosion, Noam had run toward it. When I asked him about this some time later, his reply was typically terse.

He shrugged, considered. He said only, "I trust myself." And, he added, "I don't need to talk to the rocks and the water."

In his free time, Noam liked to play around with self-portraiture. He'd experiment with different characters or looks. It wasn't like speaking in front of a crowd. With the camera, he could control everything. The resulting photos were somehow someone else—not him.

One day he decided to try out an idea he'd had for years. "Every time I was tired or busy and I saw myself yawn in a mirror," he later said, "it looked cool and scary. I thought it might be cool to do a picture like that."

Noam tilted his head back and took a chin-level shot of himself, his mouth wide in a scream. The resulting image was unsettling—a youth with buzz-cut hair and a long, narrow face, aiming an open-throated cry skyward.

Noam liked the picture but soon forgot about it. Months later he rediscovered it, showed it to a few friends, posted it on Flickr, and forgot about it once more.

About a year later, Noam was greeted at work by a tirade from one of his coworkers. Why, when he knew she liked his scream picture, hadn't he bothered to tell her he'd licensed T-shirts with his self-portrait on them? She'd just seen someone on the subway wearing a T-shirt with his face on it, and when she'd asked the guy he'd said he'd bought the T-shirt from a vendor in Brooklyn—and she would think Noam could have bothered to mention it.

After confused protestations that he hadn't licensed the photo, Noam began an intermittent search of T-shirt stands wherever he encountered them. It took months to learn that someone was selling T-shirts bearing his screaming face in Brooklyn. Someone, it emerged, was selling them in SoHo.

No one had licensed the photo or contacted Noam about using it. Curious as to how far his face had spread, Noam eventually tried searching Flickr for scream images, then using a tool called Tineye to search for images that match an uploaded picture. Despite the crude nature of these searches, some 50 images popped up.

I like to imagine Noam's face, lit in the glow of his computer display, at the moment the results of the search appeared on his screen.

Noam's photo—and his face—had gone international.

His image, downloaded from Flickr without his knowledge, had been used on a rock-concert poster in Chile. It had been reproduced on a poster advertising a completely unrelated event in Argentina. And on one in Germany. And on one in Brazil.

Noam's photo—and his face— had gone international.

The image had rippled outward in all directions, passing straight through national barriers. Noam's screaming face had been graffitied larger than life onto walls and sidewalks in Montreal, Utrecht, Rome, Mexico City, and London. It had been printed on the backs of playing cards. Painted onto skateboards. Carved into Halloween pumpkins.

What's more, Noam had become—literally—the face of several political movements. Noam's upturned, screaming face was on posters in Honduras for a political initiative he knew nothing about in a language he couldn't read. It was on banners in Spain and Colombia calling for the release of political prisoners he'd never heard of, accused of crimes unknown to him.

There were crude uses of the portrait and sophisticated ones. A few of those who had downloaded the photo had altered it, adding vampire's teeth and blood, or a knife in the mouth. Some had tinted it, enlarged it, set it on a black or orange or blue background, but most had left it unchanged.

Only once was Noam paid for the use of his portrait: *National Geographic* asked to use the image on the cover of a special issue they printed before the U.S. elections. The image, they said, was exactly what they needed. The theme of the special issue was "power to the people."

With this single exception, though, the use of Noam's self-portrait had gone out of his control. It was sketched and silk-screened, crayoned and printed, stenciled and spray-painted on concrete walls.

Noam's response was mostly a sort of awed fascination. He liked seeing how people used the portrait, what settings they chose. He had no quarrel with anyone, except perhaps those selling scream T-shirts for a profit. He posted an album on Facebook: images from all over the world, of his face. A face that seemed to imply protest. Rage. Despair. Fist-pumping populism. Or, in some cases, just a rockin' good time.

Shortly after Noam began investigating the spread of his scream photograph around the globe, he discovered something completely unexpected. Images of his face were turning up graffitied on walls in Tehran. In Tabriz City. 30

His portrait, it turned out, had been picked up by some antigovernment protesters in Iran. In the year following the Green Movement's* first open clashes with Ahmadinejad's† government—a violent confrontation watched anxiously by the world—images of Noam's face were reproduced by activist graffiti artists, sometimes veiled in red-painted blood. His anonymous face was rendered by anonymous Iranians on metal fuse-boxes and walls, alone or amid a crowd of other spray-painted images: part of a mute but vociferous message dangerous to utter aloud.

One of the hallmarks of the Iranian resistance movement has been the nighttime scream—protesters climbing unseen to their rooftops in Tehran and elsewhere to fill the dark skies with cries of "Allahu akbar,"° a slogan the religious government can't technically oppose, but of course everyone understands the message. In this setting, it seems natural that Noam's portrait might strike a chord. Seen in context, on rusted Tehran notice boards papered with torn fliers or on the barren sun-struck walls of a Tabriz City construction site, the face is a portrait of suffering and rage. The mouth is a black hole, crying to the heavens—but it's not a passive howl. There's something about it that implies that this scream is going to end. And when it does, the face is going to level its gaze at someone and take action.

The fact that members of the Iranian protest movement are using the face of an Israeli in their street art has surfaced here and there. It's been a small ironic punch line in a few articles—one in an Israeli newspaper, two in Germany, one in the Netherlands, one in Turkey, one in Switzerland. Until recently, there had been a few blog mentions, but nothing in the U.S. press. And nothing in the Iranian press.

An acquaintance who runs a network of Iranian journalists made inquiries about the portrait and its uses; based on what she was able to learn, the origin and identity of that screaming face doesn't seem to have made it onto either the Iranian artists' or the Iranian government's radar. The graffiti artists who put Noam's face on walls seem to have no idea that the screaming face they're reproducing is, in fact, the face of a Jew . . . a Jew who happens to be a grandson of survivors of the Holocaust (which Ahmadinejad has gone on record calling "a lie," a "mythical claim," and "the opinion of just a

---

* Green Movement: Name for resistance to Iranian government that started in 2009 [Ed.].
† Ahmadinejad: Mahmoud Ahmadinejad (1956–), president of the Islamic Republic of Iran [Ed.].
° *Allahu akbar*: Arabic for "God is great" [Ed.].

few") . . . a Jew who also happens to be a former soldier of the country that Ahmadine-jad calls "the flag of Satan," and that even Moussavi, the relatively progressive candi-date some of the anti-Ahmadinejad protesters champion, calls "a cancerous tumor."

When Noam learned that his self-portrait was being used by anti-Ahmadinejad 35 protesters, he emailed some of the Iranian graffiti artists through Flickr, where they'd posted images of their work under aliases.

"I told them, 'It's me. It's cool. I'll be happy to see more of what you do.' "

One of the Iranian graffiti artists wrote back.

It was a two-line exchange.

"He was cool," Noam said. "He was 'Nice to meet you, I like your picture.' I didn't tell him I'm from Jerusalem."

My cousin's face screams mutely from the walls in cities where protesters' voices can be 40 safely raised only under cover of dark. At the same time, it's a handy image for rockers and artists and T-shirt vendors in dozens of countries, a fun decal for skateboarders, a conversation piece for bridge players who deal cards with his face on the backs. It's being passed from hand to Internet-hand, used and reused, altered and interpreted to fit the needs of the user.

There's something glorious and terrible about a world in which a picture of one's face can sweep around the globe this way, part of a human chorus changing us for bet-ter and worse. Waves of information and images rebound around the planet, erasing privacy and mystery—while simultaneously allowing a familiarity with others' lives that just might save us. Something in it inspires an almost religious awe: your face, traveling the world at the speed of data. The notion makes me feel more human. But there's also something in it that unnerves me. I can't work out whether it's the end of innocence, or the start of it.

Because there is also something dehumanizing in the spectacle of a young man's face being carried on the wind like dust. Because the same technology that allowed young Iranian protesters to find common ground with a former Israeli soldier also means that anyone's face can be downloaded, stretched, tinted, appropriated, and made into an emoticon to suit someone else's needs—a collection of features that can be digitally altered by anyone, anywhere.

If your face isn't private property, what is?

Noam's face is lean, his hair short, his eyes brown behind the camera that routinely ob-scures the view of his face. He doesn't stand out in a crowd, which is—still, even after everything—how he likes it. There's nothing in his appearance that would make you guess his face is all over the globe—and perhaps that's part of the reason it is. He could be any one of us, his appearance almost anonymous behind the raised camera through which he registers, over and over, the present moment.

It seems to me he's changed a bit since his face traveled the world for him. His eyes 45 seem to have lost some of their caution. It makes it easier to notice the kindness and curiosity there.

Noam is still shy. He still speaks in brief sentences more often than in paragraphs. But although he first said, in response to my questioning, that he didn't think this ex-perience had changed him, he did observe that maybe it had brought him more fans on the Facebook fan page he'd now launched. And in the past few months, his photography business has grown, expanding outward from sporting events into some celebrity shoots. When people find out he's the guy whose screaming face they've seen, he says, they ask for his business card. He identifies himself more readily as a photographer. As an artist.

Noam regularly updates a Facebook album with images of his portrait from around the world. Most recently, he added a photograph of his screaming face stenciled onto the wall behind a toilet in a West Village bar. He's started a small sideline, too: selling Scream products. Mugs, T-shirts, magnets, aprons, even shoes. He says he takes it as a compliment when other artists use his photograph, and he likes seeing what they do with it. He says he doesn't worry about loss of privacy, because so far no one has recognized his face on the street. He's glad, he says, that the Iranian protesters are using his face. "If you do something cool," he says, "you want people to see it."

It's Noam's screaming adult face that's become the property of the world: a gaunt, anguished challenge roared into the firmament. An anonymous Everyman, a hieroglyph for protest. But I remember my cousin's face when he was a boy. I remember him at the age of 3: pale and expectant, with a quiet gaze that seemed to take in everything, while his older brothers tossed soccer balls inside the house. On a routine pediatrician's visit in Jerusalem, though, my aunt was told to take Noam to an ophthalmologist; the ophthalmologist, in turn, discovered the extreme nearsightedness that meant Noam would walk through life from then on looking at the world through powerful lenses.

When the eyeglasses were ready, my aunt took Noam to pick them up. By the time my aunt led him from the building, thick lenses perched on his face, it was already dark.

Only a few steps out onto the street, hand in hers, he stopped, his small round face upturned and agape. A boy scanning the borders of the world as he knew it, and glimpsing something astonishing. *Ima*, he whispered, pointing at the stars. *What are those?* 50

Exploring Context

1. Visit Noam Galai's website (noamgalai.com) to see more of his photography. You may, in particular, want to click on "The Stolen Scream" for Galai's take on the appropriation of his image.

2. Visit the Community Guidelines for Flickr (flickr.com/guidelines.gne). Given Galai's experience, how effective are these guidelines? What more should or could Flickr (or any Web service) do to protect its users?

3. Visit the U.S. Copyright Office's website for stopping copyright infringement (copyright.gov/help/faq/faq-infringement.html). What role does the government play in protecting images such as Galai's? What role can the government play, given the global nature of the Web?

Questions for Connecting

1. Kadish asks, "If your face isn't private property, what is?" (p. 262). Use Peter Singer's discussion of privacy online in "Visible Man: Ethics in a World without Secrets" (p. 462) to answer Kadish's question.

2. In "Veiled Threat: The Guerrilla Graffiti of Princess Hijab" (p. 28), Arwa Aburawa discusses another artist whose work has been placed in the context of social change, Princess Hijab. How are the experiences of these two artists different? Does art belong to the artist or to society? In what ways can art create change?

3. Leslie Savan discusses the appropriation of language in "What's Black, Then White, and Said All Over?" (p. 435). Synthesize her analysis of pop culture's use of black talk with Kadish's discussion of the circulation of Galai's image. What are the mechanisms and effects of appropriation in each case?

Language Matters

1. One way to consider Kadish's essay is as a story of what happens without citation. Review the rules for citing images and photographs using a grammar handbook or other reference resource. Practice these rules by providing a citation for an image from Flickr (flickr.com).

2. Kadish opens and closes her essay with personal anecdotes. What effect do these stories have on the reader? When is it appropriate to use personal anecdotes in academic writing?

3. Review information on plagiarism provided by your instructor, your school, or a grammar handbook or reference guide. Was Galai plagiarized? Make an argument using the standards for plagiarism that will be used to judge your own work.

Assignments for Writing

1. How can we mediate between intellectual property rights and the public domain in a Web-connected world? Write a paper in which you propose strategies to balance the two, using Kadish's description of Galai's experience for support.

2. Why is Galai's image so popular? Write a paper about the universality of particular images. What is it about Galai's photograph that allows it to be used in so many places and in so many different contexts?

3. Write a paper on the relationship between technology and racial politics. Why is it significant that Galai's image was used in Iran? (Note that Galai is from Jerusalem.) Does technology erode racial, political, and ethnic difference or does it accentuate it?

ARIEL LEVY

Ariel Levy, a staff writer at the *New Yorker*, has been called "feminism's newest and most provocative voice" by Malcolm Gladwell. While she has written many in-depth profiles on popular figures — Donatella Versace, Jude Law, and John Waters, to name a few — her work on gender and modern feminism has sparked the greatest interest from her readers. Her essays have appeared in publications as varied as the *New Yorker*, *Vogue*, and *Blender*.

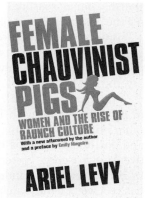

Levy's first book-length project, *Female Chauvinist Pigs: Women and the Rise of Raunch Culture* (2005), was inspired by a tag-along with the crew of the pornographic Girls Gone Wild series. Levy was bewildered that the girls participating in these videos, who take their clothes off for little more than attention and a GGW trucker cap, saw their participation as "liberating." This discovery led Levy to explore the ramifications of the "post-feminist" society that propagates this kind of thinking.

In the chapter included here, Levy identifies the subject of her work — Female Chauvinist Pigs (or FCPs for short). FCPs are seemingly educated women, many in positions of power, who participate in the very male-dominated culture of raunch and bawdiness that has plagued and exploited women for generations. When Levy connects the behavior she's noticing in popular culture to Harriet Beecher Stowe's *Uncle Tom's Cabin*, she ends up making a striking argument about gender politics and their effect on the oppressed — whoever those oppressed may be.

▶ TAGS: **Female Chauvinist Pig, loophole woman, gender, girly-girl, feminism, Tomming**

Questions for Critical Reading

1. According to Levy, why is raunch appealing to some women? Mark passages where Levy uses her own language to describe why women engage in raunch culture, and passages where she uses other people's words/ideas to explore why raunch behavior is attractive. What differences can you find between Levy's explanations and the explanations of those she interviews?

2. What kinds of women does Levy use as examples to convey her points? What specific types of women does Levy define in her text, and how have these different definitions emerged?

3. What role, would Levy say, do men play in the production and perpetuation of not only raunch culture, but also definitions of gender and sex? Mark passages that support your position and pay particular attention to Levy's discussion of "Tomming," explaining its role in this process.

Female Chauvinist Pigs

On the first warm day of spring 2000, the organization New York Women in Film & Television threw a brunch to honor Sheila Nevins, a twenty-six-year veteran of HBO and their president of documentary and family programming. It was held in a grand, street-level room off Park Avenue, in which they'd assembled an impressive selection of stylish women, seasonal berries, and high-end teas. Through the windows you could see the passing streams of yellow taxis sparkling in the midtown sunlight.

But the vibe was more *Lifetime Intimate Portrait* than *Sex and the City.* "I was growing up in a society where women were quiet so I got to listen," Nevins reflected from the podium, where she sat lovely and serene in a pale pink shawl. "I like to laugh, I like to cry, the rest is paperwork."

Nevins is a big deal. She was once profiled as one of the "25 Smartest Women in America" along with Tina Brown, Susan Sontag, and Donna Brazile in *Mirabella. Crain's* has called Nevins "a revered player." Under her stewardship, HBO programs and documentary films have won seventy-one Emmy awards, thirteen Oscars, and twenty-two George Foster Peabody awards, including Nevins's own personal Peabody. In 2000, Nevins was inducted into the Broadcasting and Cable Hall of Fame, and she has received Lifetime Achievement Awards from the International Documentary Association and the Banff Television Festival. In 2002, Nevins was named the National Foundation for Jewish Culture's "Woman of Inspiration." She is an elegant blonde with a husband and a son and a glamorous, lucrative career that even involves an intimidating level of gravitas: She has overseen the making of films about the Holocaust, cancer, and war orphans.

At that breezy spring breakfast, all the women wore glazed, reverential expressions as they picked at their melon wedges and admired Nevins's sharp wit, keen intellect, and zebra-printed slides. "Who opened your career doors for you?" one wanted to know.

"Me," Nevins replied. 5

A tweedy gentleman with a bow tie started his question with, "I'm just the token guy . . ."

Nevins gave a little snort and said, "You're all tokens," and everyone had a good laugh.

But then a curly-haired woman in the back brought up *G-String Divas,* a late-night "docu-soap" Nevins executive produced, which treated audiences to extended showings of T & A sandwiched between interviews with strippers about tricks of the trade and their real-life sexual practices. "Why would a woman—a middle-aged woman with a child—make a show about strippers?" the woman asked. Everyone was stunned.

Nevins whipped around in her chair. "You're talking fifties talk! Get with the program!" she barked. "I love the sex stuff, I love it! What's the big deal?"

In fact, there *was* something vaguely anachronistic about this woman compared 10 to the rest with their blowouts and lip liner. She adjusted her eyeglasses, visibly shaken, but persisted. "Why is it still the case that if we're going to have a series about women on television, it has to be about their bodies and their sexuality?"

Nevins shook her head furiously. "Why is it that women will still go after women taking their clothes off and not after all the injustices in the workplace? I don't get it! As if women taking off their clothes is disgusting and degrading. Not being able to feed your kids, *that's* disgusting and degrading!"

"But . . ."

"Everyone has to bump and grind for what they want," Nevins interrupted. "Their bodies are their instruments and if I had that body I'd play it like a Stradivarius!"*

"But . . ."

"The women are beautiful and the men are fools! What's the problem?"   15

"But you're not really answering my question."

Of course not. Because part of the answer is that nobody wants to be the frump at the back of the room anymore, the ghost of women past. It's just not cool. What *is* cool is for women to take a guy's-eye view of pop culture in general and live, nude girls in particular. *You're worried about strippers?* Nevins seemed on the verge of hollering at her inquisitor, *Honey, they could teach you a thing or two about where it's at!* Nevins was threatening something she clearly considered far worse than being objectified: being out of touch.

If you are too busy or too old or too short to make a Stradivarius of yourself, then the least you can do is appreciate that achievement in others, or so we are told. If you still suffer from the (hopelessly passé) conviction that valuing a woman on the sole basis of her hotness is, if not disgusting and degrading, then at least dehumanizing, if you still cling to the (pathetically deluded) hope that a more abundant enjoyment of the "sex stuff" could come from a reexamination of old assumptions, then you are clearly stuck in the past (and you'd better get a clue, but quick).

If I told you that I'd met someone who executive produces a reality show about strippers, who becomes irritable and dismissive when faced with feminist debate, and who is a ferocious supporter of lap dances, you might reasonably assume I was talking about a man—the kind of man we used to call a Male Chauvinist Pig. But no. I'm talking about the Jewish Woman of Inspiration. I'm talking about an urbane, articulate, extremely successful woman who sits on a high perch in the middle of the mainstream, and I *could* be talking about any number of other women, because the ideas and emotions Nevins gave voice to are by no means uniquely her own: They are the status quo.

We decided long ago that the Male Chauvinist Pig was an unenlightened rube,   20
but the Female Chauvinist Pig (FCP) has risen to a kind of exalted status. She is post-feminist. She is funny. She *gets it*. She doesn't mind cartoonish stereotypes of female sexuality, and she doesn't mind a cartoonishly macho response to them. The FCP asks: Why throw your boy-

> **She is post-feminist. She is funny. She *gets it*.**

friend's *Playboy* in a freedom trash can when you could be partying at the Mansion?

---

*Stradivarius: Violin made in the workshop of Antonio Stradivari (1644–1737); a shorthand for excellence [Ed.].

Why worry about *disgusting* or *degrading* when you could be giving — or getting — a lap dance yourself? Why try to beat them when you can join them?

There's a way in which a certain lewdness, a certain crass, casual manner that has at its core a me-Tarzan-you-Jane mentality can make people feel equal. It makes us feel that way because we are all Tarzan now, or at least we are all pretending to be. For a woman like Nevins, who "grew up in a society where women were quiet" and still managed to open all her career doors herself, this is nothing new. She has been functioning — with enormous success — in a man's world for decades. Somewhere along the line she had to figure out how to be one of the guys.

Nevins is (still) what used to be known as a "loophole woman," an exception in a male-dominated field whose presence supposedly proves its penetrability. (The phrase was coined by Caroline Bird in her book *Born Female: The High Cost of Keeping Women Down*, published in 1968.) Women in powerful positions in entertainment were a rare breed when Nevins started out, and they remain so today. In 2003, women held only 17 percent of the key roles — executive producers, producers, directors, writers, cinematographers, and editors — in making the top 250 domestic grossing films. (And progress is stalled: The percentage of women working on top films hasn't changed since 1998.) Meanwhile on television, men outnumbered women by approximately four to one in behind-the-scenes roles in the 2002–2003 prime-time season, which was also the case for the preceding four seasons. What the statistics indicate more clearly than the entertainment industry's permeability is a woman like Nevins's own vulnerability. To hang on to her position, she has to appear that much more confident, aggressive, and unconflicted about her choices — she has to do everything Fred Astaire* does, backward, in heels.

Women who've wanted to be perceived as powerful have long found it more efficient to identify with men than to try and elevate the entire female sex to their level. The writers Mary McCarthy and Elizabeth Hardwick were famously contemptuous of "women's libbers," for example, and were untroubled about striving to "write like a man." Some of the most glamorous and intriguing women in our history have been compared to men, either by admirers or detractors. One of poet Edna St. Vincent Millay's many lovers, the young editor John Bishop, wrote to her in a letter, "I think really that your desire works strangely like a man's." In an August 2001 article for *Vanity Fair*, Hillary Clinton's biographer Gail Sheehy commented that "from behind, the silhouette of the freshman senator from New York looks like that of a man." A high school classmate of Susan Sontag's told her biographers Carl Rollyson and Lisa Paddock that young "Sue" maintained a "masculine kind of independence." Judith Regan, the most feared and famous executive in publishing — and the woman who brought us Jenna Jameson's best-selling memoir — is fond of bragging, "I have the biggest cock in the building!" at editorial meetings (and referring to her detractors as "pussies"). There is a certain kind of woman — talented, powerful, unrepentant — whom we've always found difficult to describe without some version of the phrase "like a man," and plenty

---

*Fred Astaire: Celebrated American actor and dancer (1899–1987); his most famous dance partner was Ginger Rogers (1911–1995), who was said to do everything that Astaire did, backwards, in high heels [Ed.].

of those women have never had a problem with that. Not everyone cares that this doesn't do much for the sisterhood.

Raunch provides a special opportunity for a woman who wants to prove her mettle. It's in fashion, and it is something that has traditionally appealed exclusively to men and actively offended women, so producing it or participating in it is a way both to flaunt your coolness and to mark yourself as different, tougher, looser, funnier — a new sort of loophole woman who is "not like other women," who is instead "like a man." Or, more precisely, like a Female Chauvinist Pig.

Sherry, Anyssa, and Rachel are a trio of friends who share a taste for raunch: *Maxim*, porn, Howard Stern, *Playboy*, you name it. All three are in their late twenties and, on the night we met, they had recently returned to New York City from a postcollegiate spring break. Rachel, a registered nurse, a tough, compact girl with short red hair, had brought the others a memento: a postcard picturing a woman's tumescent breasts against a background of blue sky with the words *Breast wishes from Puerto Rico!* scrawled in loopy cursive across the top.

"When I first moved to New York, I couldn't get over Robin Byrd," said Rachel. She was talking about New York City's local-access television sex queen. Byrd has been on cable since 1977, hosting a show in which male and female performers strip and plug their upcoming appearances in clubs or magazines or porn movies. The finale of each show is Byrd — herself a former adult film performer — going around and licking or fondling each of her guest's breasts or genitals. "I wouldn't go out till I watched Robin Byrd, and when I did go out, I would talk about Robin Byrd," Rachel said. "Watching Robin Byrd doesn't turn me on, though. It's for humor."

"Yeah, it's all comical to me," Sherry agreed. Sherry had just completed her first day at a new job as an advertising account executive, and Rachel gave her a little congratulatory gift: a thick red pencil with a rubber Farrah Fawcett head smiling on one end.

All three of them loved *Charlie's Angels* growing up, but more recently they had become "obsessed" with Nevins's show *G-String Divas*. "The other day we were on the subway and I wanted to dance on the pole in the middle," said Anyssa. "I could never be a stripper myself, but I think it would be so sexually liberating." Her looks were not holding her back. Anyssa was a Stradivarius . . . a built, beautiful young woman with milky skin and silky hair and a broad, lipsticked mouth. She aspired to be an actress, but in the meantime she was working at a bar near Union Square. "When I'm bartending, I don't dress up though," she said. "Because I have to deal with enough assholes as it is. In college, Sherry and I, by day we would wear these guy outfits, and then at night we'd get dressed up, and people would be like, *Oh my God!* It's like a card . . . you pull out the hot card and let them look at you and it takes it to a whole different level." Anyssa smiled. "And maybe you get to *feel* like a stripper does."

Everyone was quiet for a moment, savoring that possibility.

I suggested there were reasons one might not want to feel like a stripper, that spinning greasily around a pole wearing a facial expression not found in nature is more a parody of female sexual power than an expression of it. That did not go over well.

"I can't feel bad for these women," Sherry snapped. "I think they're asking for it."

Sherry considered herself a feminist. "I'm very pro-woman," she said. "I like to see women succeed, whether they're using their minds to do it or using their tits." But she didn't mind seeing women fail, either, if they weren't using both effectively. She liked the Howard Stern show, for example, because his is a realm in which fairness of a sort pervades: Women who are smart and funny like Sherry, or Stern's sidekick, the FCP Robin Quivers, get to laugh along with the boys. (Quivers has always been the mitigating presence that saves Stern's shows from being entirely frightening. His trademark shtick, getting female guests to take off their clothes so his staff can ogle or mock them, would seem a lot creepier if Quivers—a smart, articulate, fully clothed black woman—wasn't there to reassure the viewer or listener that there was a way out, an alternate role for a woman on the show. But then, Quivers is pretty much the only one who gets that option—the other women Stern invites into his universe are either hot or crazy or, his favorite, both.) The women who are pathetic enough to go on national television and strip down to their underwear in the hopes that Howard will buy them a boob job are punished with humiliation. Sherry and her friends found something about this routine reassuring. They seemed satisfied by what they experienced as justice being meted out; it was like the pleasure some people get watching the police throw the bad guys against the hood of their cars on *Cops*.

"Yeah, we're all women, but are we supposed to band together?" said Anyssa. "Hell, no. I don't trust women. Growing up, I hung out with all guys . . . these are the first girls I ever hung out with who had the same mentality as me and weren't going to starve themselves and paint their nails every fucking second. I've never been a girly-girl, and I've never wanted to compete in that world. I just didn't fit in."

Anyssa is not different from most FCPs: They want to be like men, and profess to disdain women who are overly focused on the appearance of femininity. But men seem to like those women, those girly-girls, or like to look at them, at least. So to *really* be like men, FCPs have to enjoy looking at those women, too. At the same time, they wouldn't mind being looked at a little bit themselves. The task then is to simultaneously show that you are not the same as the girly-girls in the videos and the

> **But men seem to like those women, those girly-girls, or like to look at them, at least.**

Victoria's Secret catalogs, but that you approve of men's appreciation for them, and that possibly you too have some of that same sexy energy and underwear underneath all your aggression and wit. A passion for raunch covers all the bases.

Twenty-two-year-old Erin Eisenberg, a city arts administrator, and her little sister Shaina, a student at Baruch College, kept a stack of men's magazines—*Playboy*, *Maxim*, *FHM*—on the floor of the bedroom they still shared in their parents' apartment. "A lot of times I say, Oh, she looks good, or check out that ass, but sometimes I'm also like, This is so airbrushed, or Oh, her tits are fake or whatever," said Erin. "I try not to be judgmental, but sometimes it's there."

"I pick up *Playboy* because I want to see who's on the cover," said Shaina. "The other day Shannen Doherty was on one and I just wanted to see what her breasts looked like."

The magazines and raunch culture in general piqued their curiosity and provided them with inspiration. Erin said, "There's countless times in my life where I know I've turned people on just by showing off." By putting on a little performance, making out with another girl, for instance. "It moved into Oh, this turns guys on if you do it in public. Having had that experience in a real-life setting, it was almost as if I was on *The Man Show* or something like that. But those times, it wasn't as sexy as in my fantasies."

Both Eisenberg sisters said they were "not easily offended," and Erin felt she had "a higher tolerance for sexual harassment" than most women.

"I went out with my friend a couple weeks ago and some guy touched her ass and she flipped out at him," said Shaina. "I was just like, Dude, he slapped your ass. To me that would be no big deal—if anything, I'd be flattered."

"You have to understand, a man is a man; it doesn't matter what position he's in," Erin said. "I have a lot of male friends. I feel conflicted being a woman, and I think I make up for it by trying to join the ranks of men. I don't think I have a lot of feminine qualities." 40

"You're not a girly-girl," Shaina cut in. "Like, her priority is not, *Am I gonna go get a manicure?*"

"Girly-girl" has become the term women use to describe exactly who they do not want to be: a prissy sissy. Girly-girls are people who "starve themselves and paint their nails every fucking second," as Anyssa put it; people who have nothing better to think about than the way they look. But while the FCP shuns girly-girls from her social life, she is fixated on them for her entertainment. Nobody has to wax as much as a porn star, and most strippers wouldn't be caught dead without a manicure. Weirdly, these are the women—the ultimate girly-girls—who FCPs spend their time thinking about.

Like Sherry, Erin Eisenberg professed an interest in feminism, and she showed me her copy of *The Feminine Mystique* to prove it. "But I don't try to espouse my ideas to everyone else," she said. "I'd rather observe and analyze on my own, and then do something else—further myself in other ways rather than start a debate. I gain strength by not exerting that energy."

"Gaining strength" is the key. FCPs have relinquished any sense of themselves as a collective group with a linked fate. Simply by being female and getting ahead, by being that strong woman we hear so much about, you are doing all you need to do, or so the story goes.

Carrie Gerlach, then an executive at Sony Pictures in Los Angeles, wrote in an e-mail in 2001: 45

> My best mentors and teachers have always been men. Why? Because I have great legs, great tits, and a huge smile that God gave to me. Because I want to make my first million before the age of thirty-five. So of course I am a female chauvinist pig. Do you think those male mentors wanted me telling them how to better their careers, marketing departments, increase demographics? Hell no. They wanted to play in my secret garden. But I applied the Chanel war paint, pried the door open with Gucci heels, worked, struggled and climbed the ladder. And made a difference!!! And I did it all in a short Prada suit.

Gerlach made no bones about wanting to "climb the ladder" so she could enjoy life's ultimate riches, namely Prada, Gucci, and Chanel. The ends justify the means, and the means are "great legs" and "great tits."

"Everyone wants to make money," said Erin Eisenberg, the daughter of a pair of erstwhile hippies. ("My dad claims he was a socialist," she said skeptically.) Where her parents had misgivings about the system, Erin has doubts only about its lower rungs. Gone is the sixties-style concern (and lip service) about society as a whole. FCPs don't bother to question the criteria on which women are judged, they are too busy judging other women themselves.

"Who doesn't want to be looked at as a sex symbol?" said Shaina. "I always tell people, if I had a twenty-three-inch waist and a great body, I would pose in *Playboy*. You know all those guys are sitting there staring at you, *awe-ing* at you. That must be power."

If we are to look for a precedent for this constellation of ideas and behaviors, we can find it in an unlikely place . . . a novel written before the Civil War. Published in 1852, Harriet Beecher Stowe's *Uncle Tom's Cabin* sold more copies than any book besides the Bible in the nineteenth century, and it is still widely considered to be the most historically significant novel ever written by an American author. Since it was first published, Stowe's book has been credited with having an enormous impact on the way Americans conceive of race. During Stowe's tour of Great Britain in 1853, the minister sent to greet her congratulated her by saying "that the voice which most effectively kindles enthusiasm in millions is the still small voice which comes forth from the sanctuary of a woman's breast." (Stowe proudly relayed his words in her travel book *Sunny Memories of Foreign Lands*.) These sentiments were echoed ten years later by Abraham Lincoln, who famously called Stowe the "little lady who made this big war" when he met her just after he issued the Emancipation Proclamation.

While Stowe inarguably advanced the cause of abolition (and intensified the tensions over slavery that helped ignite the Civil War), she has also been blamed for exacerbating "the wrongheadedness, distortions and wishful thinkings about Negroes in general and American Negroes in particular that still plague us today," as the critic J. C. Furnas wrote in 1956. Stowe created various characters who "transcend" their race—which is to say that instead of acting "like a man" (or trying to), they "act white." One of Stowe's protagonists is a slave character, George Harris, who is light-skinned enough to pass as "a Spanish gentleman." But it is not just the skin Stowe gave him that allows George to move through her fictive society and her reader's imagination distinct from other slaves. In "Everybody's Protest Novel," an essay on *Uncle Tom's Cabin* published in the *Partisan Review* in 1949, James Baldwin wrote that Stowe crafted George "in all other respects as white as she can make" him; Stowe created George "a race apart" from Tom and his fellow slaves.

The converse strategy for coping with race in Stowe's text is the one that has become notorious, and it is, of course, the one exhibited by Uncle Tom. Tom, remember, is a creation of Stowe's who so thoroughly accepts his oppression as a slave, he renders the standard appurtenances of enslavement unnecessary. When a slave trader transports him for sale, Tom can be left unshackled; there is no chance he will run away because he has so completely internalized the system of which he is a victim. He believes that he really *is* property, so to run away would be to rob his owner, a crime he wouldn't dream of committing.

Consequently, Tom is thought of by his masters—and by Stowe herself—as "steady," "honest," "sensible," and "pious." Not only does Tom submit to the system that oppresses him, he actively strives for the love of his oppressor, and loves him in return.

50

George Shelby, the man Tom has served since his birth, is too ashamed to say good-bye to Tom after he literally sells him down the river, thus separating Tom from his wife, children, and home, and condemning him to a bleak and lethally brutal future. Yet Tom's wistful parting words as he is carted off to the auction block are, "Give my love to Mas'r George."

> **Not only does Tom submit to the system that oppresses him, he actively strives for the love of his oppressor, and loves him in return.**

Stowe wanted Tom to serve as a heartbreaking and representative example of the "soft, impressible nature of his kindly race, ever yearning toward the simple and childlike." In her book, this is simply the character's character. But the concept of an Uncle Tom has taken on a meaning very different from the one Stowe intended. An Uncle Tom is a person who deliberately upholds the stereotypes assigned to his or her marginalized group in the interest of getting ahead with the dominant group.

In a discussion of "Tom shows," the staged adaptations of *Uncle Tom's Cabin* that became wildly popular after the book's publication (and remained so into the 1930s), author Mary C. Henderson describes a "theatrical industry called 'Tomming,'" in which "Uncle Tom's original character was almost totally obliterated in the worst and cheapest dramatizations. Somewhere in tents set among the cornfields he lost his dignity and his persona and became the servile, obedient, sycophantic black man who gave the term 'Uncle Tom' its terrible taint."

Tomming, then, is conforming to someone else's—someone more powerful's—distorted notion of what you represent. In so doing, you may be getting ahead in some way—getting paid to dance in blackface in a Tom show, or gaining favor with Mas'r as Stowe's hero did in literature—but you are simultaneously reifying the system that traps you.

The notions of "acting white," as Stowe crafted George Harris to, and "acting black," as she decided Uncle Tom did (thus expressing the "nature of his kindly race"), are both predicated on the assumption that there is a fixed, unchanging essence of whiteness and another of blackness which can then be imitated. James Baldwin* wrote, "We take our shape, it is true, within and against that cage of reality bequeathed us at our birth; and yet it is precisely through our dependence on this reality that we are most endlessly betrayed." The cage in which we "find ourselves bound, first without, then within," is the "nature of our categorization." We are defined and ultimately define ourselves, Baldwin argued, by the cultural meaning assigned to our broadest human details—blackness, whiteness, maleness, femaleness, and so on. In order to start Tomming, "acting black," we would necessarily have to first believe that there was such a thing as blackness to enact. And likewise, if we are going to act "like a man," there has to be an inherent manliness to which we can aspire.

It would be crazy to suggest that being a woman today (black or white) is anything remotely like being a slave (male or female) in antebellum America. There is obviously no comparison. But there are parallels in the ways we can think about the limits of

55

---

*James Baldwin: Noted African American essayist, novelist, and playwright (1924–1987), who in reaction to the poor treatment of blacks and homosexuals, spent many of the later years of his life in Europe [Ed.].

what can be gained by "acting like" an exalted group or reifying the stereotypes attributed to a subordinate group. These are the two strategies an FCP uses to deal with her femaleness: either acting like a cartoon man—who drools over strippers, says things like "check out that ass," and brags about having the "biggest cock in the building"—or acting like a cartoon woman, who has big cartoon breasts, wears little cartoon outfits, and can only express her sexuality by spinning around a pole.

In a broader sense, both of these strategies have existed historically and continue to because to a certain extent they are unavoidable. Does a marginalized person—a female producer going to a job interview at an all-male film company, a Chinese attorney striving to make partner at an old-boy, white-shoe law firm,* a lesbian trying to fit in at a Big Ten keg party—need to act the way the people in charge expect in order to get what he or she wants? Without question. A certain amount of Tomming, of going along to get along, is part of life on planet Earth.

But Americans gave up the idea—or tried to, or pretended to—that there are certain characteristics and qualities that are essentially black and essentially white a long time ago. At the very least we can say that it would be considered wildly offensive and thoroughly idiotic to articulate ideas like that now. Yet somehow we don't think twice about wanting to be "like a man" or unlike a "girly-girl." As if those ideas even *mean* anything. Like which man? Iggy Pop? Nathan Lane? Jesse Jackson? Jesse Helms? It is a staggeringly unsophisticated way to think about being a human being, but smart people do it all the time.

The most obvious example in recent memory of someone intelligent espousing such ideas publicly is the scholar Camille Paglia. Paglia notoriously proclaimed that "if civilization had been left in female hands, we would still be living in grass huts." That may be too puerile a provocation to bother with, but Paglia's more understated articulations of her beliefs about gender echo our still widely held cultural assumption that women are one way and men are another (and that there's nothing wrong with saying so). In an interview with *Spin* magazine (which Paglia liked enough to reprint in her book *Sex, Art, and American Culture*), Paglia defended her controversial views on date rape and assessed her critics:

> They have this stupid, pathetic, completely-removed-from-reality view of things that they've gotten from these academics who are totally off the wall, totally removed. Whereas my views on sex are coming from the fact that I am a football fan and I am a rock fan. Rock and football are revealing something true and permanent and eternal about male energy and sexuality. They are revealing the fact that women, in fact, *like* the idea of flaunting, strutting, wild masculine energy. The people who criticize me, these establishment feminists, these white upper-middle-class feminists in New York, especially, who think of themselves as so literate, the kind of music they like, is, like Suzanne Vega—you know, women's music.
> SPIN: *Yuck.*

---

*White-shoe law firm: Long-established, prestigious, and conservative firm run by Eastern elites [Ed.].

First off, one has to wonder if Paglia has ever heard of Patti Smith. Or Debbie Harry. Or Janis Joplin. Or Grace Jones. It seems as if she has temporarily forgotten even her idol, Madonna (the subject of two of Paglia's essays in that same book). Aren't these people women . . . who necessarily make women's music? Do these women not flaunt and strut and effuse the wild energy with which Paglia is so enthralled? Are they up-tight? Uncool?

Reducing "women's music" to something soft and neutered, something guaran-teed to make her—female!—interviewer say "yuck," is a manipulative little move. It's a way for Paglia to separate herself from the human characteristics she finds most un-attractive—weakness, effeteness, pusillanimity—and to make these things "perma-nently and eternally" female. (Which, by the way, Paglia *is*.)

Paglia's equation of all things aggressive, arrogant, adventurous, and libidinous with masculinity, and her relegation of everything whiney, wimpy, needy, and com-placent to femininity, is, among other things, dopey. We have to wonder why a woman as crackling smart as Camille Paglia would be so unsophisticated in her conception of gender. We have to wonder why a woman as thoughtful as Sheila Nevins—a woman whose entire career is based on the intrepid exploration of complex stories—would have a knee-jerk reaction to a question that positioned her as a member of the female gender.

Instead of trying to reform other people's—or her own—perception of femininity, the Female Chauvinist Pig likes to position herself as something outside the normal bounds of womanhood. If defending her own little patch of turf requires denigrating other women—reducing them to "yuck" as Paglia does or airheads who prioritize manicures, or, Judith Regan's favorite, "pussies"—so be it.

It can be done very persuasively.

Mary Wells Lawrence was one of the first women in this country to start her own advertising agencies, certainly the most successful, and the first woman CEO of a company listed on the New York Stock Exchange. She stands out as one of the great giants of her industry, male or female. Wells Lawrence came up with the "I Love New York" campaign, which many people credit with resuscitating the city's image during the seventies; she also invented the weirdly unforgettable "Plop Plop Fizz Fizz" Alka-Seltzer ads.

One of her earliest successes was a colorful marketing strategy for Braniff Air-lines in the sixties that eventually prompted a transformation of the look of American airports. Wells Lawrence bucked the bland, military style of the times and had every Braniff plane painted a bright color. Then she hired Emilio Pucci to design riotous cos-tumes for the flight "hostesses." One of her ads featured what she called the "air strip," the process by which Braniff stewardesses pared down their Pucci flight uniforms little by little on the way to tropical destinations. Pucci "even made teeny-weeny bikinis for them, an inch of cloth," Wells Lawrence wrote in her memoir, *A Big Life (in Advertising)*. These ads, with their focus on pretty young women in escalating stages of undress, may have been what prompted Gloria Steinem to famously comment, "Mary Wells Uncle Tommed it to the top."

In her memoir, Wells Lawrence returned fire at Steinem. "What a silly woman," she wrote. "I wanted a big life. I worked as a man worked. I didn't preach it, I did it."

How scalding. How convincing. Who wouldn't pick action over nagging, succeed-ing over hand-wringing? Who doesn't want a big life?

There's just one thing: Even if you are a woman who achieves the ultimate and becomes *like a man*, you will still always be like a woman. And as long as womanhood is thought of as something to escape from, something less than manhood, you will be thought less of, too.

There is a variety program on Comedy Central called *The Man Show*, which concludes each episode with a segment of bouncing women appropriately called "Girls on Trampolines." The show's original hosts Jimmy Kimmel and Adam Carolla have left; Kimmel now has his own network talk show, *Jimmy Kimmel Live*, on ABC, and both Kimmel and Carolla executive produce *Crank Yankers* for Comedy Central. But when I went to visit their set in L.A. in 2000, *The Man Show* was one of the top shows on cable, and it was getting a lot of attention for its brand of self-described "chauvinistic fun." Thirty-eight percent of *The Man Show's* viewers were female. It was co–executive produced by two women.

Like Sheila Nevins, co–executive producer Jennifer Heftler was not who you'd 70 expect to find as the wizard behind the curtain of a raunch operation. She was a big woman who wore batik and had a tattoo of a dragonfly on her wrist and another of a rose on her ankle. She described her program as "big, dumb, goofy fun."

"One of the perks to this job was that I wouldn't have to prove myself anymore," she said. "I could say, 'I worked at *The Man Show'* and no one would ever say 'Oh, that prissy little woman' again." Heftler felt her female viewers' incentive for watching the program was very much like her own for making it. "It's like a badge," she said. "Women have always had to find ways to make guys comfortable with where we are, and this is just another way of doing that. If you can show you're one of the guys, it's good."

The night I went to a taping, there wasn't enough space to fit all the guys who had lined up outside the studio, and a team of heavy-limbed boys in matching green T-shirts from Chico State were pumped to make it into the audience.

Don, the bald audience fluffer, seemed to be looking directly at them when he yelled from the stage, "A few weeks ago we had trouble with guys touching the women here. You can't just grab their asses — you don't do that in real life, do you? [Beat.] Welllll . . . so do I!" The frat guys cheered, but not with the alarming gusto of the man in front of them, a scrawny computer technician who resembled one of the P's in Peter, Paul and Mary. "To the women," shouted Don, "today only, you're an honorary man! Grab your dick!"

Abby, a brunette in tight white jeans, was called up to the stage for her big chance to win a T-shirt. Honorary man status notwithstanding, she was asked to expose her breasts. Abby declined, but agreed brightly to kiss another girl instead. A pert redhead in her early twenties raced up from the audience to wrap her hands around Abby's back and put her tongue in the stranger's mouth. "Yeah! Yeah! You're making me hard," shrieked Peter/Paul. He was nearly hit in the head by the Chico Statesman behind him, who dumped his fist in the air in front of his crotch, semaphoring masturbation.

Soon after, the stage doors opened and out poured the Juggies, nine dancing girls 75 in coordinating pornographic nursery rhyme costumes: Little Red Riding Hood in spike-heeled patent leather thighhighs, Bo Peep in a push-up bra so aggressive you could almost see her nipples, and, of course, Puss 'n Boots.

They shimmied their way around the audience, and some did tricks on the poles like strippers. After the shouting died down, Adam Carolla and Jimmy Kimmel emerged from backstage, fresh as daisies in matching gingham shirts. "Who knows a good joke?" Carolla asked.

"How do you piss your girlfriend off when you're having sex?" a guy in the back volunteered. "Call her up and tell her."

Then they showed a pretaped spot about a mock clinic for wife evaluation, where a prospective bride was assessed based on her grasp of football and her aptitude for administering fellatio to pornographer Ron Jeremy.

There's a side to boydom that's fun," Jen Heftler declared. "They get to fart, they get to be loud—and I think now we're saying we can fart and curse and go to strip clubs and smoke cigars just as easily and just as well." As for the Juggies, we are supposed to experience them as kitsch. "In the sixties, Dean Martin had his Golddiggers, and they were basically Juggies," Heftler said, "but the audience wasn't in on the joke. It was just pretty girls because that's what a guy would have. Then it was, you can never have that, you can't show a woman as a sex object, that's terrible. Now we're back to having it, but it's kind of commenting on that as opposed to just being that. The girls are in on it, and the women watching it are in on it."

But after sitting in that audience, I have to wonder what exactly we are in on. That women are ditzy and jiggly? That men would like us to be? 80

"Listen," Heftler countered, "our generation has gone past the point where *The Man Show* is going to cause a guy to walk into a doctor's office and say, 'Oh, my God! A woman doctor!'"

Her co–executive producer, Lisa Page, a sweet, quiet woman, said, "It doesn't need to threaten us anymore."

The night after the taping, I had dinner with Carolla, Kimmel, and *The Man Show*'s cocreator and executive producer, Daniel Kellison, at the restaurant inside the W Hotel in Westwood. I asked them why they supposed 38 percent of their viewers were women.

"We did a little research," said Carolla, "and it turns out 38 percent of all women have a sense of humor."

I laughed. I wanted to be one of those women. The women at the W were like another species: lush curves bursting off of impossibly thin frames and miles of hairless, sand-colored skin as far as the eye could see. 85

"It's a whole power thing that you take advantage of and career women take advantage of," Kellison offered. "If you read *Gear* or watch our show or Howard Stern or whatever, you have an overview of a cultural phenomenon, you have power. You take responsibility for your life and you don't walk around thinking, *I'm a victim of the press! I'm a victim of pop culture!* So you can laugh at girls on trampolines." He smiled warmly. "You get it."

For a moment I allowed myself to feel vaguely triumphant.

Kimmel sucked an oyster out of its shell and then snickered. "At TCA," the annual Television Critics Association conference in Pasadena, "this woman asked, 'How does having a big-breasted woman in the Juggy dance squad differ from having black women in the darkie dance squad?' I said, 'First of all, that's the stupidest question I've ever heard.'"

"Then Adam said, 'Let me put your mind at ease: If we ever decide to put together a retarded dance squad, you'll be the first one in it,'" said Kellison, and all three of them laughed.

"What kind of women do you hang out with?" I asked them.   90

Kimmel looked at me like I was insane. "For the most part," he said, "*women* don't even want to hang out with their friends."

And there it is. The reason that being Robin Quivers or Jen Heftler or me, for that moment when *I got it*, is an ego boost but not a solution. It can be fun to feel exceptional—to be the loophole woman, to have a whole power thing, to be an honorary man. But if you are the exception that proves the rule, and the rule is that women are inferior, you haven't made any progress.

Exploring Context

1. Levy opens her essay by discussing HBO executive Sheila Nevins and, in particular, her decision to produce the show *G-String Divas*. Review Nevins's filmography at the Internet Movie Database (imdb.com/name/nm0627521). How much of her work reflects raunch culture? Is there any suggestion that she has changed since Levy wrote this essay?

2. What exactly is a "chauvinist"? What is the origin of the word? Use an online resource such as Wikipedia or Dictionary.com to define the term. How do its origins relate to the argument Levy is making?

3. The Bureau of Labor Statistics maintains data on earnings based on a variety of demographics (bls.gov/cps/earnings.htm#demographics). Explore this data. In economic terms, has raunch culture helped women generally? What other factors (age, race) affect economic success? Does Levy's discussion account for these factors?

Questions for Connecting

1. In "Preface" and "The New Civil Rights" (p. 552), Kenji Yoshino proposes that legal rulings are insufficient to address the social pressures that force individuals to "cover." Synthesize his discussion with Levy's concept of "Tomming." In what ways are Female Chauvinist Pigs "covering"? What social pressures might force them to do so?

2. Levy examines Female Chauvinist Pigs, raunch culture, girly-girls, and Tomming in an effort to explore how society reinforces certain behaviors in women. Julia Alvarez also explores the social expectations for women in "Selections from *Once Upon a Quinceañera*" (p. 46). How are gender roles shaped by specific cultures? Synthesize both authors to suggest strategies for resisting these social pressures.

3. How does Patricia Churchland's discussion of innate capacities in "Networking: Genes, Brains, and Behavior" (p. 113) relate to Levy's contemplation of "essential" qualities (p. 274)?

4. **CONNECTING TO E-PAGES** Levy summarizes the attitude of television executive Sheila Nevins this way: "If you are too busy or too old or too short to make a Stradivarius of

yourself, then the least you can do is appreciate that achievement in others, or so we are told" (p. 267). Compare Levy's essay to Sabrina Rubin Erdely's "Kiki Kannibal: The Girl Who Played With Fire" (bedfordstmartins.com/emerging/epages). In what ways does Nevins's comment reflect Kiki Kannibal's vision of herself? Does Kiki Kannibal's view of herself evolve in any way? Explain your response.

Language Matters

1. Gender is a primary concern in this essay, and it is also an issue in writing. Writers use a variety of techniques to avoid sexist language, including alternating their use of *he* and *she* or employing the awkward construction *s/he*. Frequently, people use a plural pronoun with a singular antecedent to accomplish this goal—for example, "Someone who wants to avoid sexist language should watch their pronouns." Which method is best, leaving aside the rules of grammar? How might or must language change to accommodate nonsexist attitudes?

2. What is a hyphen? How is it used? Select a passage of this essay and revise it by adding hyphens. When would you use them in your own writing?

3. Raunch culture is closely related to class boundaries. What class boundaries exist in writing? Is slang an issue of class? Can you determine Levy's class from her writing? What class is reflected in academic writing? What level of class is reflected in the language used by the women Levy interviews?

Assignments for Writing

1. Levy discusses Female Chauvinist Pigs and raunch culture extensively. Write a paper in which you determine Levy's position on Female Chauvinist Pigs and raunch culture. Use specific quotations from her text that reveal her position.

2. Using Levy's ideas, write a paper in which you create a definition of feminism. Are Female Chauvinist Pigs feminists? Is feminism defined in opposition to Female Chauvinist Pigs? What are the goals of feminism?

3. Consider Levy's discussion of "Tomming." Extend her argument in that section by writing a paper in which you expand on the concept, providing additional examples that confirm or complicate her explanation of the concept.

ANDREW MARANTZ

Andrew Marantz is a nonfiction writer who lives in New York City. He is perhaps best known for using his writing as an advocacy platform for social change, examining topics such as organizing for the Obama campaign and teaching writing workshops to prison inmates. Marantz is a frequent contributor to the website Change.org, and his work can be found in publications such as *New York* magazine, the *New York Times*, *Slate*, and *Mother Jones*.

Marantz's essay "My Summer at an Indian Call Center" was originally published in the July/August 2011 issue of the nonprofit magazine *Mother Jones*, where it was accompanied by other essays that focus on corporations and the workplace. The issue features articles on recent corporate profit increases and the disease scandals and poor working conditions that accompany the manufacturing of Spam, as well as a piece on the veteran pension scam.

In "My Summer at an Indian Call Center," Marantz recounts his experiences working at one of the many call centers in Delhi, India, including the "culture training" he was required to attend, but he also writes about cultural perception, as he received insight from others about his own culture.

▶ TAGS: *globalization, economics, culture, service industry, politics, knowledge*

Questions for Critical Reading

1. Marantz seems mainly to report his experience. As you read his essay, mark passages where he seems to be making a larger argument. What is his goal in writing this essay? Locate passages that support your response.

2. What is "culture training"? Look for this term as you read Marantz and mark passages that define it and offer examples. How effective is it? Do we all go through some form of "culture training"?

3. What role do stereotypes play in Marantz's essay? Look not only for stereotypes about Indians but also for stereotypes Indians have about other people. Where do these stereotypes come from?

My Summer at an Indian Call Center

I stand flush against the window of a Toyota showroom, trying to stay in a shrinking sliver of shade. We're on the cusp of midday, which, in Delhi in June, lasts most of the day and drives everyone into a languid torpor. I am waiting for a company cab, now an hour and a half late, to drive me across town to a call center, where an Indian "culture trainer" will teach me how to act Australian.

A uniformed guard next to me dozes on a stool, his rifle slumped in his lap. Behind the showroom window, which would be clear if two boys would stop rubbing it down with rags, a dozen red sedans glisten on a waxy white floor. On the dirt shoulder of the road, children hold hands as they walk to school.

Call centers don't trust Indian infrastructure, as well they shouldn't, so the company cab[1] — typically a white Toyota Qualis—has become a standard industry perk. This morning a class of 24 new hires, myself included, will be ferried from all corners of the city to the offices of a small firm named Delhi Call Centre. For three weeks, a culture trainer will teach us conversational skills, Australian pop culture, and the terms of the mobile-phone contracts we'll be peddling. Those of us who pass the training course will graduate to the calling floor. Our first job at DCC will be to interrupt Australians at dinner and ask them to switch phone providers. In the Delhi area alone, maybe 100,000 call-center agents make their living selling vitamins to Britons or helping Americans troubleshoot their printers. I am almost certainly the only one who acquired his conversational skills accidentally—by being born in the United States.

My phone vibrates. By the time I get it to my ear, a husky male voice is shouting in Hinglish, a rapid-fire blend of Hindi and English. "Meet at Toyota showroom!" I shout back.

"Fine sir, 20 minutes," he replies.

I know "20 minutes" is a Hinglish phrase meaning "30 minutes," so I call back after 40. A woman answers this time. "No problem, sir," she says, "20 minutes only." A sweat-and-sunblock solution drips down my forehead and stings my eyes. Behind me, the boys continue toweling the glass. The streaks they create blur into the streaks they wipe away.

Every month, thousands of Indians leave their Himalayan tribes and coastal fishing towns to seek work in business process outsourcing, which includes customer service, sales, and anything else foreign corporations hire Indians to do. The competition is fierce. No one keeps a reliable count, but each year there are possibly millions of applicants vying for BPO positions. A good many of them are bright recent college grads, but their knowledge of econometrics and Soviet history won't help them in interviews. Instead, they pore over flashcards and accent tapes, intoning the shibboleths* of English pronunciation—"wherever" and "pleasure" and "socialization"—that recruiters use to distinguish the employable candidates from those still suffering from MTI, or "mother tongue influence."

---

* Shibboleths: Phrases or beliefs that distinguish a group, in this case referring to Western pronunciation [Ed.].

Monica Joshi, 22, kills some time before her graveyard shift at a Gurgaon call center.

In the end, most of the applicants will fail and return home deeper in debt. The lucky ones will secure Spartan* lodgings and spend their nights (thanks to time differences) in air-conditioned white-collar sweatshops. They will earn as much as 20,000 rupees per month — around $2 per hour, or $5,000 per year if they last that long, which most will not. In a country where per-capita income is about $900 per year, a BPO salary qualifies as middle-class.[2] Most call-center agents, however, will opt to sleep in threadbare hostels, eat like monks, and send their paychecks home. Taken together, the millions of calls they make and receive constitute one of the largest intercultural exchanges in history.

Indian BPOs work with firms from dozens of countries, but most call-center jobs involve talking to Americans. New hires must be fluent in English, but many have never spoken to a foreigner. So to earn their headsets, they must complete classroom training lasting from one week to three months. First comes voice training, an attempt to "neutralize" pronunciation and diction by eliminating the round vowels[3] of Indian English. Speaking Hindi on company premises is often a fireable offense.

Next is "culture training," in which trainees memorize colloquialisms and state capitals, study clips of *Seinfeld* and photos of Walmarts, and eat in cafeterias serv- 10

---

* Spartan: Sparta was an ancient Greek city-state known for the self-discipline of its warriors. Spartan lodgings are simple and lacking in luxury [Ed.].

ing paneer* burgers and pizza topped with lamb pepperoni. Trainers aim to impart something they call "international culture"—which is, of course, no culture at all, but a garbled hybrid of Indian and Western signifiers designed to be recognizable to everyone and familiar to no one. The result is a comically botched translation—a multibillion dollar game of telephone. "The most marketable skill in India today," the *Guardian* wrote[4] in 2003, "is the ability to abandon your identity and slip into someone else's."

When the Qualis arrives, two hours late, I join two other new hires in the backseat. The air-conditioning vents emit an anemic trickle, as effective as an ice cube dropped into a swamp. While we idle in interminable traffic, my coworker Nishant asks where I'm from. "America?" he says. "I'll tell you about America."

I must look wary, because he quickly explains that, after years of 50-hour work-weeks, he's probably spoken with more of my compatriots than I have. "America is not all honey and roses the way they tell you," he informs me. "Truth is, 90 percent of the people there, you will find, they'll do the most stupid things, impulsive things. I know for a fact. At the same time, Americans are bighearted people, and the remaining 10 percent of them are smart. Bloody smart. That's why they rule the world."

Growing up in rural Haryana, Nishant got his picture of the world from grainy Sylvester Stallone movies on a neighbor's TV. Like all the boys in his village, he dreamed of living in California. "It was a wonderland to me, where no kid goes hungry, where everyone has those fast cars, those red-colored Ford Mustangs."

Nishant, now 26, moved to Delhi at age 18. His first job was tracking down Americans with delinquent bills. "In training they told us, 'It's easy. These guys have the money, they just don't want to pay.' They told us, 'Threaten their credit score, Americans can't live without good credit.'"

On his first day, Nishant donned his headset, dialed the number on the screen and was connected to a 60-year-old woman in Tennessee. She had an outstanding hospital bill for $400. "I told her, 'Just pay this, what's the problem?' She told me, 'You don't understand, I can't pay.'" They talked for 45 minutes, and the woman cried as she told Nishant about the Iraq War and its toll on American families. "By this time I'm crying also," Nishant said.

The same day, he was connected with a man living in a trailer. "I told him, 'What's a trailer?' He told me, 'It's this tin shed; it gets 90 degrees; we don't have our own washroom.'" Nishant learned more about America that first day, he told me, than he had in his whole childhood.

When I first decided to apply for a call-center job, I headed to Gurgaon, a commercial suburb of Delhi. Gurgaon was built[5] 30 years ago by a corporation, for corporations. It was fallow farmland until 1979, when DLF, India's biggest developer, began buying up property. Gurgaon, is a non-city.[6] In my time there, I saw no sidewalks, convenience stores, or public parks—only stray cows foraging in the sun-baked dirt between office towers.

---

* Paneer: South Asian cheese [Ed.].

A makeshift market in Gurgaon.

I unfolded a scrap of paper, damp with sweat, on which I'd written the address of IBM's outsourcing headquarters: DLF Tower, DLF Cyber City, Phase II, Gurgaon. With high attrition rates, big BPOs are always hiring.[7] Anyone can walk in and arrange for a job interview. Mine did not go as planned.

"You've completed a four-year university?" the recruiter asked, pen poised above my résumé.

"Yes," I said.

"And your stream?"

"Pardon?"

She sighed. "What did you study?"

"Religion," I said. "Well—liberal arts."

She made a face, scribbling something.

"What does your father do?" she asked.

"He's a doctor."

"And your mother is a housewife?"

"No, a doctor also."

"A doctor also! Why didn't you go in for that line?"

"I . . . I didn't want to," I said.

"You didn't *want* to?" She could no longer hide her exasperation.

"These things are different in America," I said feebly.

She stood and offered her hand. "We'll let you know if anything opens up."

In Delhi the next day, I passed a storefront banner: "Walk-In for Instant BPO Spot Offers—No Money, No Catch!" I walked in. The power was out. A young recruiter, sitting behind a desk illuminated by candles, spoke rapidly in a Monty Python–esque caricature of American twang.

"If I give you a topic," she asked, "can you speak on it for upwards of 30 seconds? Your topic is: hometown."

I began spewing facts about New York—"The street vendors sell hot dogs. There is a street called Madison Avenue"—until she asked me to stop.

"Fine, Andrew. Actually, we were not listening for content primarily as much as your voice tone and voice confidence and communications skills, which in fact I am happy to report is all excellent, so I am recommending you for top marks. Congratulations." I knew she was just following the script, but I couldn't help feeling a swell of pride. "Which means you are selected for our exclusive BPO job search course this Sunday. Which means all I'd need from you now are 500 rupees."

I forked over the 500 rupees, which was nearly a week's pay for the average Indian worker—but which was, on the other hand, $11.

The "skills course" consisted of a woman reading from a photocopied pamphlet   40
while 100 of us took notes. "What is call center to you?" she bellowed. Without waiting for a response, she intoned the correct answer. "Call center is a place where"—she motioned for us to transcribe—"we render the services to the customers and"—pause, more scribbling—"queries are made out by customer-care executive."

Over the next five hours, we sat stiffly while she recited the entire pamphlet, listing the "elements of voice modulation," what to wear to a job interview, and the types of customers we might encounter.

"First is your eccentric!" she yelled.

"Second is your arrogant!

"Third is your bumpkin!

"Fourth is your quarrelsome!

"Fifth is your prudent!   45

"Sixth is your assertive!

"And seventh is your sweet-spoken!

"Now, any questions?"

"Ma'am," said a young man in front, "you instructed us that our necktie should   50
reach halfway down the belt buckle?"

"Yes?"

"Ma'am, I don't have any necktie. In India we don't wear neckties."

"That's true," she said. "Other questions?"

Using my newly honed communication skills, I landed my job at Delhi Call Centre. The next day, the company cab brought us to Okhla, a muddy industrial zone on the banks of the Yamuna River, stopping at an unmarked iron gate in front of a chalky concrete bunker. We walked up stairs stained red by *paan* spit, under a door lintel decorated with a lucky swastika,* and into a conference room that smelled of disinfectant. As we waited, I took notes: almost as many women as men,[8] mostly middle-class and in their

---

* Lucky swastika: Hindu symbol that long predates its use by Nazi Germany; the word comes from the Sanskrit for "well-being" or "all is well" [Ed.].

Gurgaon, an epicenter of the BPO industry, was effectively built by corporations, for corporations.

twenties.[9] Had I been Indian, I would have fit right in. As it was, my tawny hair and near-albinic skin made me a spectacle.

"What's he *doing?*" a girl behind me whispered in Hindi.   55

"He's writing!" her friend answered.

"Writing what?"

"I don't know, ask him!"

After an hour of waiting, our trainer entered. Lekha was tall and rail thin, with big doll eyes. Her accent was what BPO higher-ups would call "perfectly neutral"—her vowels soft and long, her Rs a benign compromise between flipped and rolled. "Training takes three weeks," she told us. "It's combined accent and culture training; we'll assume that you come to us with the accent part pretty well taken care of." In a playfully arch tone, she rattled off the rules: no mobile phones, eating, or drinking. And she would charge us a rupee, she teased, for every non-English word she heard in the classroom. "Any questions so far?"

"When do we get paid?" asked a young man wearing a Nike cap, yellow-tinted   60
sunglasses, and carefully crafted facial stubble. In New York, I would have pegged him as a party promoter from Long Island City.

"Very funny," Lekha said. "You'll be paid for your time, including this training, but only after you've stayed two months. You know the drill: We wouldn't want people taking off as soon as training is over."

During our first cigarette break, Mr. Long Island City revealed that, indeed, his plan was to do precisely that—he'd already gone through this routine at some 15 BPOs around Delhi. "Who needs to stay for the actual work? Plus," he added, flashing a sala-cious smile, "that way you meet more girls."

After the break, we toured the empty office—the agents weren't due in until later. The computer terminals were of a clunky premillennial vintage. DCC, Lekha admitted, was not "one of your Dells or IBMs with fancy workstations and a McDonald's in our cafeteria." This reminded her of another rule: "No leaving the premises during work. You can smoke out front, but don't leave the gates."

On our next smoke break, I asked Mr. Long Island City if he found this rule strange. "No, it's just for safety types," he said. "Especially for the girls. Who knows what could happen to a girl on her own?" Another classmate had his own theory. "Out there it's India, man," he said, gesturing through the gate to where a goat was urinating in the street. "We go outside, and when we go back in, we bring India in with us."

> **"Out there it's India, man," he said, gesturing through the gate to where a goat was urinating in the street. "We go outside, and when we go back in, we bring India in with us."**

Twenty years ago, before India opened its markets to the world, career prospects were bleak. Men might have been laborers or government workers, but even the most ambi-tious women often gave in to social pressure and stayed home. 65

Today, almost half of BPO employees are women, many of whom outearn both of their parents. Free-market cheerleaders, conflating rising wages with rising spirits, are quick to applaud India's "maturing" markets. But the truth[10] is more complicated: Studies show[11] that once people move out of poverty, increasing wealth does not neces-sarily lead to happiness.

Call-center employees gain their financial independence at the risk of an identity crisis. A BPO salary is contingent on the worker's ability to de-Indianize:[12] to adopt a Western name and accent and, to some extent, attitude. Aping Western culture has long been fashionable; in the call-center classroom, it's company policy. Agents know that their jobs only exist because of the low value the world market ascribes to Indian labor. The more they embrace the logic of global capitalism, the more they must con-front the notion that they are worth less.

At the end of each training day, the Qualis would drop me back at the Toyota show-room. From there I would walk down a narrow, unpaved lane and turn onto an even narrower alley, just wide enough (I learned the hard way) for a human to squeeze past a cow.

Like most BPO agents from out of town, I rented a room in a workers' hostel. For the equivalent of $80 per month, I got a nine-by-six cell—a plywood double bed, a ceil-ing fan, and two windows covered in newspaper—plus two hot meals a day.

In the hostel I met Satish, a slight, bespectacled fellow who worked with com-puters and always seemed to have a head cold. One night, he grabbed my sleeve and whispered that Shail, his girlfriend, was coming to visit. She lived in a ladies' hostel down the street, but they rarely saw each other because she worked nights at a call center. Shail, 23, had moved here from a small town in Uttar Pradesh. She had gradu-ated at the top of her college class but always assumed she'd end up at a call center. 70

DUDE, WHERE'S MY JOB?

More and more, US multinationals are laying off workers at home and hiring overseas.

Jobs added/lost (in thousands)

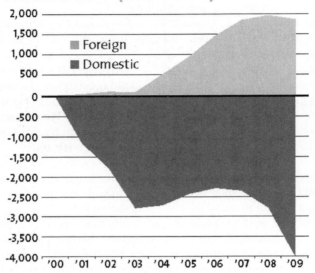

Sources: Commerce Department, *Wall Street Journal*; figures are cumulative since 2000; banks excluded

She answered phones for Target, telling customers the balance remaining on their gift cards. The work was boring, she said, but she was "learning to feel independent" and saving up for her dowry.

Shail was bright and personable, with effortless good looks. I asked how she and Satish had met. "Online," she said, giggling. "Yahoo Chat. He proposed without seeing me. It was so embarrassing." Satish had selected her screen name at random and "proposed" that they date. Later, he told me he'd done the same with dozens of girls. "I never used to attend his chats," Shail said. "But something happened; we started talking and I realized that really he is loving me. After a few months, I accepted his proposal."

They planned to spend a few years working in Delhi before getting married and moving to Satish's home state of Tamil Nadu. "There is slight language problem," Shail admitted. She doesn't speak Tamil and Satish doesn't speak Hindi. "Even when we want to fight, we fight in English."

When I returned, there was a man sitting upright in my bed, fully clothed and fast asleep. My cell, it turned out, was now a "shared room," and Amit was my new roommate.

When I stopped asking questions, Shail had one for me. "I have experienced some Americans—please don't mind—they don't like Indians. They act rude as soon as they come to know I am Indian. Why is this?" I stammered something about protectionism, but really I didn't know what to say.

The next morning, a Saturday, I went out for a late breakfast. When I returned, there was a man sitting upright in my bed, fully clothed and fast asleep. My cell, it turned out, was now a "shared room," and Amit was my new roommate. He was sleeping off a 36-hour triple shift at his tech-support job. For the next month, Amit and I slept side by side. The bed was wide enough that we didn't have to touch, but we could hear each other breathing. On nights when the power cut out and the ceiling fan stopped, we would lie awake sweating and cursing and praying for relief.

I also got to know a man I'll call Arjuna, a meaty guy with a cleft chin who rented a two-bedroom flat nearby. His hobbies included drumming (he liked the Eagles and Bon Jovi) and taking solo motorcycle trips through the Himalayas, and even in the oppressive summer heat he wore his biker outfit: black bomber jacket, black boots, a bandanna around his neck. 75

Arjuna told me that he spent the first half of 2003 raising funds for the GOP. As an employee of the outsourcing firm HCL, he called[13] registered Republicans all over the United States to solicit donations. (That September, the conservative site *WorldNetDaily*,[14] citing an Indian press report, reported that HCL was raising money for the "U.S. Republican Party." The Republican National Committee insisted[15] that[16] the story was false. Later, as it happened, the FEC sued[17] a Texas-based group called the Republican Victory Committee—which employed a Delhi call center called Apex to do its fundraising—for falsely claiming that it represented the party.)

Arjuna told me he enjoyed fundraising but was opposed to Bush's policies, particularly the war in Iraq. I asked whether he felt partly responsible for his reelection. "It's a scary thought," he admitted. "Luckily, I wasn't very good at my job back then."

As he recounted his subsequent eight years in the industry, his big eyes swelled with indignation. He'd only intended to work in the call centers for a few months. At 34, he felt stuck. He was still at HCL, doing customer support for British Telecom. "All this time 'perfecting my skills,' " he said bitterly. "What skills? Accent and diction? How will that lead to a career?"

Growing up in Kolkata, Arjuna never got along with his parents. "In America, you guys move away from your family after high school or college," he said, "but not here." His family expected him to stay at home, work at the bank where his father worked, and marry his high school sweetheart. Instead, he shocked everyone by moving to Delhi. BPOs aligned with his individualist streak; culture training taught him about societies where young people lived as they pleased. He impressed coworkers with his American accent, and when he got his first paycheck, he tasted the liberating power of disposable income.

Soon, though, his hobbies began to feel hollow. He had lost touch with his family 80 and made few friends. His high school sweetheart stayed in Kolkata and met another guy, but Arjuna had not found a girlfriend in Delhi.

During our second day of culture training, Lekha dissected the Australian psyche. It took about 20 minutes.

Arjuna thought he would just work in call centers a few months.
Now he's in his thirties, feeling trapped between East and West.

"Just stating facts, guys," Lekha began, as we scribbled notes, "Australia is known as the dumbest continent. Literally, college was unknown there until recently. So speak slowly." Next to me, a young man in a turban wrote *No College* in his notebook.

"Technologically speaking, they're somewhat backward, as well. The average person's mobile would be no better than, say, a Nokia 3110 classic." This drew scoffs from around the room.

"Australians drink constantly," Lekha continued. "If you call on a Friday night, they'll be smashed—every time. Oh, and don't attempt to make small talk with them about their pets, okay? They can be quite touchy about animals."

"What kind of people are there in Australia?" a trainee asked. "What are their traits?" 85

"Well, for one thing," Lekha said, "let's admit: They are quite racist. They do not like Indians. Their preferred term for us is—please don't mind, ladies—'brown bastards.' So if you hear that kind of language, you can just hang up the call."

Thus ended our lesson in Australian sociology. We moved on to geography. Lekha drew a circle on the board and carved it into portions. "Now, I suppose we all know Australia is divided into six states?" I was the only person, it seemed, who did not know this. After 10 minutes, everyone except me understood Australia's geography, so we moved on to brainstorming "English aliases." At work, Lekha explained, we would answer to non-Indian names—"except Andrew can stick with Andrew."

Some people picked names that sounded like their own (Adarsh became Adam), while others took the name of a favorite celebrity. One young man, a smoker, chose "Joe" in honor of Joe Camel.* Lekha advised us not to use the phrase "call center" during sales calls; we were also not to say where we were, or what time it was, unless asked directly.

With an hour to kill before lunch, Lekha steered the conversation my way. Was it really true that I was staying in an Indian workers' hostel?

"That's right," I said.

"You didn't want to live with other expats?" she asked.

90

"Not really," I said. "Most expats just order in Domino's and complain about the heat. I wanted to have a fuller experience."

"So you have something against your fellow countrymen?" she asked. My trainer and coworkers thought it perfectly natural that white people should want to self-segregate and eat bland food.

During lunches and breaks, I chatted with coworkers. Vidya was 19 but looked younger. She had been a top chemistry student but had taken an indefinite leave from university to make money for her family. She wore hip-hugging jeans and T-shirts bedazzled with messages like "No Angel," and she spent most of her breaks flirting with Mr. Long Island City. Soon the other women—especially the few who were married, in their thirties, and wore traditional *salwar kameez†*—started spending their breaks gossiping about Vidya.

Mittu from Chennai wore black jeans, steel-toed boots, and a charm bracelet. Looking closely at his bracelet, I saw a peace sign, a marijuana leaf, the anarchist "A," and a swastika—not the Hindu kind. "You know this is the Nazi one, right?" I asked. Mittu grinned. "I just bought it for the pot leaf."

95

I was the only one in my class who had never worked at a BPO. Everyone else had stories from their old jobs, which they called "processes." Nishant, who asked the lady in Tennessee to pay her hospital bills, had worked in a "collections process." Nidhi preferred "inbound processes" (taking calls) to "outbound processes" (placing calls) because she didn't like bothering people. Almost everyone had worked in a process doing "hardcore sales," which made me imagine a porno starring Willy Loman.

---

* Joe Camel: Cartoon character featured in advertising in the late 1980s and 1990s, allegedly to make Camel cigarettes appealing to children and adolescents, until protests led to the end of its use [Ed.].
† *Salwar kameez:* Central and South Asian dress [Ed.].

Call-center worker Monica Joshi shops on a day off.

Rohan and Sube, who hailed from neighboring villages in Madhya Pradesh, told me that "fake process" (a.k.a. phishing) was their favorite. "All it is," Rohan explained, "is you call American clients. Tell them, 'U.S. government is giving away free money!'"

> "I remember quite well this guy who just called me up and said out of nowhere, 'You fucking Paki!' . . . I said . . . 'Then this Paki would be helping you fix your computer.'"

"You say that—'free money'—and just watch how people respond," Sube agreed.

Rohan continued, "You tell them, 'Just provide me your information and don't worry, I'll fill the forms, you sit back. You just pay us for our services.'"

"Really there are no forms and no services," Sube said, his eyes sparkling. "They tell their information over the phone and you don't even write it, you just write the credit card. We take our commission. Next week, the company disconnects the phone." 100

My coworkers were happy to give me a rundown of the different nationalities they'd encountered. "Britishers get angry," said Nidhi. "Still, they are subtle—they'll say something sarcastic under the breath."

"Americans will just shout at you," Sube said. Mittu agreed: "I have only been cursed by Americans. They are sharp-witted and very articulated and yet very free with their anger."

Most customers are well-behaved, they assured me. Still, each agent had a stockpile of best- and worst-call anecdotes. "I remember quite well this guy who just called me up and said out of nowhere, 'You fucking Paki,'" Arnab told me during a break. "We don't take those things personally; it's part of the job. So I just said, very calmly, 'Yes sir,

Arnab saw culture training as a weak brainwashing attempt, noting: They "hardly took the Indian out of us."

if I am a Paki, then this Paki would be helping you fix your computer.' By the end of the call, he apologized and gave me a five-star feedback rating."

With his pomaded hair, pearly white teeth, and habit of clapping me genially on the back, Arnab could have passed for a U.S. congressman. Only after several conversations did I learn that as a student at the prestigious Jawaharlal Nehru University, he was a Marxist* activist. He worked in BPOs because his family needed money, but his dream was to organize the workers. "Not all at once," he said. "Just steadily, over time, I'm thinking how to bring down the system from the inside. Meantime, I'm happy to cash their paycheck."

In the end, I didn't stay to complete the training — visa issues — but I kept in touch   105
with some of my DCC coworkers. Most of them had quit soon after I left, for higher-paying jobs. A year later, I tracked down Arnab, who was happily employed at Dartnell Publications, a Florida-based corporation with a Delhi office. He worked East Coast hours writing newsletters about management strategies. He now peppered his speech with phrases like "take it easy" and "no worries" and signed his emails "Joe." (He now works for the History Channel.)

---

* Marxist: Referring to the ideas of the influential German political philosopher Karl Marx (1818–1883), best known for *The Communist Manifesto* [Ed.].

Arnab, who still considers himself a Marxist, told me he had come to view culture training as an inept attempt at brainwashing. "Yes, we were asked to hate everything Indian and love everything Western, but we never really took it seriously," he said. The trainers asked him to eat American fast food and listen to American music, even on weekends. One BPO installed an American-style water fountain, which confounded the employees. "But that hardly took the Indian out of us."

Arjuna was more conflicted. In a long Facebook chat, he told me he was still stuck in the same customer-support job, still verging on depression, and still single. He never could figure out how to date casually, as Americans do; nor could he bring himself to use the matrimonial websites popular in India. "To me, arranged marriage is a joke," he said.

In a sense, Arjuna is too westernized to be happy in India. He speaks with an American accent, listens to American rock music, and suffers from American-style malaise. In his more candid moments, he admits that life would have been easier if he had hewn to the traditional Indian path. "I spent my youth searching for the real me," he says. "Sometimes I feel that now I've destroyed anything that is the real me, that I am floating somewhere in between."

NOTES

1. http://www.pbase.com/yardbird/image/49227273
2. http://www.state.gov/r/pa/ei/bgn/3454.htm#econ
3. http://www.languageinindia.com/junjul2002/baldridgeindianenglish.html
4. http://www.guardian.co.uk/world/2003/oct/21/india.politics
5. http: //www.granta.com/Magazine/107/Capital-Gains/1
6. http://gurgaon.gov.in/modern_ggn.htm
7. http://www.neogroup.com/PDFs/Whitepapers/OIv4i04_0506_ITO_and_BPO_Salary_Report_2006.pdf
8. http://www.working-the-nightshift.com/
9. http://www.nasscom.in/upload/68924/Impact_Study_2010_Exec_Summary.pdf
10. http://motherjones.com/politics/2010/05/peter-victor-deficit-growth
11. http://www.princeton.edu/main/news/archive/S15/15/09S18/index.xml?section=topstories
12. http://nadeem.commons.gc.cuny.edu/
13. http://web.archive.org/web/20030226131941/http://www.business-standard.com/archives/2003/jan/50310103.016.asp
14. http://www.wnd.com/?pageId=20585
15. http://www.upi.com/Top_News/2003/02/19UPIs-Capital-Comment-for-Feb-19-2003/UPI-33651045691023/
16. http://www.freerepublic.com/focus/f-news/979828/posts
17. http://www.fec.gov/law/litigation/novacek.shtml

Exploring Context

1. Visit the call center section of the website for Delhi Capital (delhicapital.com/callcenters-in-delhi), a site promoting the city of Delhi. How does the site reflect Marantz's experience? What audience does the site imagine?

2. Marantz begins his search for a call center job in Gurgaon, a suburb of Delhi that Marantz describes as a "non-city" (p. 283). Explore the website for Gurgaon (gurgaon .nic.in). How do the design and content of the site confirm Marantz's description? What might you infer from the fact that the official site for this district is in English?

3. Using Google or another search engine to find images for "outsourcing." How is this process visually represented? Do the images used match the realities that Marantz describes?

Questions for Connecting

1. In "The Dell Theory of Conflict Prevention" (p. 166), Thomas L. Friedman offers a much broader view of India's role in a globalized economy. How does Marantz's experience complicate Friedman's ideas about globalization? What are the costs of globalization? Do these costs outweigh its benefits?

2. Manuel Muñoz also discusses cultural assimilation in "Leave Your Name at the Border" (p. 307). How do the processes of assimilation differ in these two essays? In what ways are Indians more resistant to assimilation? Is geographic location a significant factor or is globalization homogenizing culture more generally?

3. Namit Arora discusses several models of economic justice in "What Do We Deserve?" (p. 87). Which of the models he discusses seem to apply to India, based on Marantz's essay?

Language Matters

1. Consider the relationship between author and authority in Marantz's essay. What privileges allow him to go to India, take a job at a call center, and write about it? What cultural power is he deploying? Use these insights in your own writing to think about your authority in an academic context.

2. One common error for writers involves using commas with introductory elements. Review the rules for comma usage in these situations, using a grammar handbook or other reliable reference source. Then, find examples from Marantz that illustrate these rules. How can you apply these rules to your own writing?

3. Citation is absolutely essential to academic writing, though it plays no role in Marantz's essay. Why doesn't Marantz use citation? Why is it so important in academic writing? Consider issues of audience and authority as you prepare your answer.

Assignments for Writing

1. Consider the effects that a globalized economy has on local cultures. Write a paper in which you examine how globalization has changed Indian culture. To what extent has the "American Dream" become the "Indian Dream"? In what ways does Indian culture resist the changes of globalization?

2. Marantz writes, "Call-center employees gain their financial independence at the risk of an identity crisis" (p. 287). Write a paper in which you determine the relationship between economics and identity. What is the identity crisis according to Marantz? What are some strategies that call-center workers use to resolve it?

3. Write a paper in which you explore the role that stereotypes play in global economics. What is the difference between a target demographic and a stereotype? How do companies use stereotypes? Given the stereotypes that Marantz discusses, consider the effect that capitalism has on identity and international cooperation.

STEVE MUMFORD

THE AMERICAN
STATE OF TERROR
•
David Rieff: Getting Over 9/11
Peter Singer: Will the End of Privacy Be Good for Us?
The FBI Hunts for the Enemy Within

Painter **Steve Mumford** is an American artist who works with oil and watercolor. He earned an M.F.A. from the School of Visual Arts in New York City. He has spent time embedded with American troops in both Iraq and Afghanistan, experiences that have provided the inspiration for much of his work, including his book *Baghdad Journal: An Artist in Occupied Iraq* (2005), a collection of paintings and writings influenced by his time in Iraq. Mumford's work has been featured in numerous solo and group exhibitions in New York City and around the United States.

"The Things They Carry" is a collection of watercolor paintings that originally appeared in the August 2011 issue of *Harper's Magazine*. That issue also featured "Visible Man: Ethics in a World without Secrets" by Peter Singer (p. 462), along with essays dealing with issues of war, terrorism, and the role of government by writers including Petra Bartosiewicz and David Rieff. The issue, published ten years after the 9/11 terrorist attacks, explores the many ways that those events and the subsequent wars have changed the political climate in the United States.

The paintings in "The Things They Carry" feature everyday moments in the lives of American soldiers, free of overt political or moral comment; instead, such interpretations are left open to viewers. This collection is the product of time spent embedded with the U.S. Marines in Afghanistan's Helmand Province in 2010 and 2011. Inspired by the paintings of Winslow Homer, whose Civil War paintings appeared in *Harper's* between 1861 and 1864, the title also echoes the name of Tim O'Brien's famous collection of related stories about the Vietnam War, *The Things They Carried*. Both references invite parallels between America's wars of the past and those of the present.

▶ TAGS: *war, aesthetic objects, soldiers, representation, politics*

Questions for Critical Reading

1. Where does Mumford tend to focus his art as represented in these images? Why does he represent these specific aspects of his time in Afghanistan?

2. Mumford chose primarily to use watercolors to create this series of images. How does this choice affect your interpretation of the images?

3. Mumford makes a note on each of his images, usually indicating the subject and the date. Often these are hard to read. Why does Mumford include this information at all? What is the relationship between this writing and each image?

The Things They Carry

2/26/11
Trek Nawa Afghanistan

LCpl Ricardo Hernandez tries
to clean jammed weapon
in firefight
2nd Platoon, Echo Co, 2/3 Marines

LCpl Dan Morphis
3rd Platoon   2/3 Marines
Nawa Afghanistan
2.20.11

2nd Platoon, Echo Co. 2/3
leaves FOB Lamba Dand   Nawa, Afghanistan
March 1 2011

Dog shot by Afghan soldier
on foot patrol with Marines

Trek Nawa
near Patrol Base Lamba Dand

2/26/11

2 village elders show up to
chat – Patrol with 2nd Platoon
India Co 3/6 Marines
S. Marja. 6/27/10

Base "Camel"
India Co 3/6 Marines
in a sandstorm

6/28/10
S. Marja. Afghanistan

2/3 Marines
Nawa Afghanistan
Checkpoint
2/28/11

Exploring Context

1. View more of Mumford's art at Postmasters (postmastersart.com) by clicking on "artists" and then on his name. How is the work reproduced here representative of Mumford's art? How does his work in other media (such as oil painting) change the impact of his images?

2. Mumford directly references Tim O'Brien's collection of stories *The Things They Carried*. Learn more about this work by reading the Wikipedia page about the collection (http://en.wikipedia.org/wiki/The_Things_They_Carried). Why would Mumford use this title? How does his use of it reinforce the meaning of his art?

3. Using Google or another search engine, look for photographs using the search terms "pictures war Afghanistan." Compare the subject matter, composition, and impact of the images you find to Mumford's work. Why might Mumford have chosen to work in watercolor?

Questions for Connecting

1. What is the political role of art? Synthesize Mumford's work with Arwa Aburawa's discussion of the work of Princess Hijab in "Veiled Threat: The Guerrilla Graffiti of Princess Hijab" (p. 28). Does all art make a political statement? Should politics be kept out of art?

2. Madeleine Albright explores the complex world of international relations in "Faith and Diplomacy" (p. 35). Use Albright's discussion of diplomacy to interpret Mumford's work. How can his art be seen as a kind of diplomacy?

3. Does Mumford's work reflect human dignity? Use Francis Fukuyama's discussion of the concept in his essay of the same title (p. 185) to analyze Mumford's images. In what ways does Mumford locate dignity in war? In what ways does his work suggest that war is never compatible with human dignity?

4. **CONNECTING TO E-PAGES** Watch the Wired.com video of the video game the U.S. Army produced in order to train soldiers in Afghanistan (bedfordstmartins.com/emerging /epages). The video game is described by Mark Covey of the Department of Defense as "a teenager's dream." Based on your examination of Mumford's paintings of soldiers in Afghanistan, how do you react to that assertion? As part of your answer, consider the basis for the appeal of the video game. How does the game relate to the scenes depicted by Mumford? In what ways are they similar, and in what ways are they different? Would having soldiers analyze paintings such as Mumford's be an effective supplement to their training for war? Explain your answer.

Language Matters

1. Verbs express action or a state of being. What is the visual equivalent to a verb? Using Mumford's paintings, describe what a verb looks like. What expresses action in the images?

2. A complete sentence has a subject and a verb. What is the visual equivalent of a sentence? Consider Mumford's paintings as sentences. How can you identify the subject and verb? Consider, for starters, the difference between "subject" in its grammatical sentence and the "subject" of a piece of art or writing.

3. Punctuation marks delineate boundaries between words. What is the visual equivalent? Using Mumford's paintings, consider what elements act as "punctuation marks." Is the border of a painting a period? Can the arrangement of elements in a painting act as a question mark?

Assignments for Writing

1. Select one of Mumford's images and write a paper in which you analyze its argument. Refer to the introduction for guidance on how to analyze visual arguments (see p. 9). Use as well your work from Questions for Critical Reading.

2. Write a paper in which you analyze the relationship between Mumford's title, "The Things They Carry," and his images. What are the "things they carry"? Who are "they"? What is being "carried"? Refer to specific images to support your argument.

3. How do Mumford's images comment on war? Write a paper in which you make an argument about the relationship between the concept of war and its representations. What effect does seeing war have on our understanding of war?

MANUEL MUÑOZ

Manuel Muñoz, who holds an M.F.A. from Cornell University, is currently a professor of creative writing at the University of Arizona. In 2006, he received a National Endowment for the Arts fellowship. Primarily a writer of fiction, he has published several works, including *Zigzagger: Stories* (2003) and *The Faith Healer of Olive Avenue* (2007). Muñoz's most recent novel is titled *What You See in the Dark* and was released in 2011.

"Leave Your Name at the Border," a rare nonfiction publication for Muñoz, first appeared in the Opinion section of the August 1, 2007, edition of the *New York Times*, a publication noted for its op-ed section. Muñoz's essay appeared alongside a piece by Stanley Fish on public institutions of higher education and pieces by Peter Zimmerman, James Acton, and M. Brooke Rogers on radiological terrorism.

In this selection, Muñoz recounts an experience that many of us can relate to — hearing one's last name mispronounced. That experience leads Muñoz to consider the Anglicization of Latino names in American culture. Through the names Latinos give to their children and the ways in which these names are allowed to be popularly pronounced, Muñoz argues, we can trace a gradient of culture for these people along the lines of public and private lives. "Leave Your Name at the Border" sparks discussion regarding the assimilation of cultures and the very real consequences this has for the people belonging to them.

▶ TAGS: *identity, Anglicization, language, assimilation, culture, race, ethnicity*

Questions for Critical Reading

1. What does it mean for something to be "Anglicized"? Define this term through Muñoz's text and then locate additional examples from your own life and experience.

2. How does Muñoz see public and private lives functioning for Latinos in California? What are the differences between these lives?

3. How does culture factor into Muñoz's text? Is it different from race? From ethnicity? Since he uses all of these terms, mark passages where he uses each in an attempt to delineate these differences.

Leave Your Name at the Border

At the Fresno airport, as I made my way to the gate, I heard a name over the intercom. The way the name was pronounced by the gate agent made me want to see what she looked like. That is, I wanted to see whether she was Mexican. Around Fresno, identity politics rarely deepen into exacting terms, so to say "Mexican" means, essentially, "not white." The slivered self-identifications Chicano, Hispanic, Mexican-American, and Latino are not part of everyday life in the Valley. You're either Mexican or you're not. If someone wants to know if you were born in Mexico, they'll ask. Then you're From Over There—de allá. And leave it at that.

The gate agent, it turned out, was Mexican. Well-coiffed, in her 30s, she wore foundation that was several shades lighter than the rest of her skin. It was the kind of makeup job I've learned to silently identify at the mall when I'm with my mother, who will say nothing about it until we're back in the car. Then she'll point to the darkness of her own skin, wondering aloud why women try to camouflage who they are.

I watched the Mexican gate agent busy herself at the counter, professional and studied. Once again, she picked up the microphone and, with authority, announced the name of the missing customer: "Eugenio Reyes, please come to the front desk."

You can probably guess how she said it. Her Anglicized pronunciation wouldn't be unusual in a place like California's Central Valley. I didn't have a Mexican name there either: I was an instruction guide.

When people ask me where I'm from, I say Fresno because I don't expect them   5
to know little Dinuba. Fresno is a booming city of nearly 500,000 these days, with a diversity—white, Mexican, African-American, Armenian, Hmong, and Middle Eastern people are all well represented—that shouldn't surprise anyone. It's in the small towns like Dinuba that surround Fresno that the awareness of cultural difference is stripped down to the interactions between the only two groups that tend to live there: whites and Mexicans. When you hear a Mexican name spoken in these towns, regardless of the speaker's background, it's no wonder that there's an "English way of pronouncing it."

I was born in 1972, part of a generation that learned both English and Spanish. Many of my cousins and siblings are bilingual, serving as translators for those in the family whose English is barely functional. Others have no way of following the Spanish banter at family gatherings. You can tell who falls into which group: Estella, Eric, Delia, Dubina, Melanie.

It's intriguing to watch "American" names begin to dominate among my nieces and nephews and second cousins, as well as with the children of my hometown friends. I am not surprised to meet 5-year-old Brandon or Kaitlyn. Hardly anyone questions the incongruity of matching these names with last names like Trujillo or Zepeda. The English-only way of life partly explains the quiet erasure of cultural difference that assimilation has attempted to accomplish. A name like Kaitlyn Zepeda doesn't completely obscure her ethnicity, but the half-step of her name, as a gesture, is almost understandable.

Spanish was and still is viewed with suspicion: Always the language of the vilified illegal immigrant, it segregated schoolchildren into English-only and bilingual programs; it defined you, above all else, as part of a lower class. Learning English, though, brought its own complications. It was simultaneously the language of the white population and a path toward the richer, expansive identity of "American." But it took getting out of the Valley for me to understand that "white" and "American" were two very different things.

Something as simple as saying our names "in English" was our unwittingly complicit gesture of trying to blend in. Pronouncing Mexican names correctly was never encouraged. Names like Daniel, Olivia, and Marco slipped right into the mutability of the English language.

I remember a school ceremony at which the mathematics teacher, a white man, announced the names of Mexican students correctly and caused some confusion, if not embarrassment. Years later we recognized that he spoke in deference to our Spanish-speaking parents in the audience, caring teacher that he was.

These were difficult names for a non-Spanish speaker: Araceli, Nadira, Luis (a beautiful name when you glide the u and the i as you're supposed to). We had been accustomed to having our birth names altered for convenience. Concepción was Connie. Ramón was Raymond. My cousin Esperanza was Hope—but her name was pronounced "Hopie" because any Spanish speaker would automatically pronounce the e at the end.

Ours, then, were names that stood as barriers to a complete embrace of an American identity, simply because their pronunciations required a slip into Spanish, the otherness that assimilation was supposed to erase. What to do with names like Amado, Lucio, or Élida? There are no English "equivalents," no answer when white teachers asked, "What does your name mean?" when what they really wanted to know was "What's the English one?" So what you heard was a name butchered beyond recognition, a pronunciation that pointed the finger at the Spanish language as the source of clunky sound and ugly rhythm.

My stepfather, from Ojos de Agua, Mexico, jokes when I ask him about the names of Mexicans born here. He deliberately stumbles over pronunciations, imitating our elders who have difficulty with Bradley and Madelyn. "Ashley Sánchez. ¿Tú crees?" He wonders aloud what has happened to the "nombres del rancho"—traditional Mexican names that are hardly given anymore to children born in the States: Heraclio, Madaleno, Otilia, Dominga.

My stepfather's experience with the Anglicization of his name—Antonio to Tony—ties into something bigger than learning English. For him, the erasure of his name was about deference and subservience. Becoming Tony gave him a measure of access as he struggled to learn English and get more fieldwork.

This isn't to say that my stepfather welcomed the change, only that he could not put up much resistance. Not changing put him at risk of being passed over for work. English was a world of power and decisions, of smooth, uninterrupted negotiation. Clear communication meant you could go unsupervised. Every gesture made toward convincing an employer that English was on its way to being mastered had the potential to make a season of fieldwork profitable.

It's curious that many of us growing up in Dinuba adhered to the same rules. Although as children of farm workers we worked in the fields at an early age, we'd also had the opportunity to stay in one town long enough to finish school. Most of us had learned English early and splintered off into a dual existence of English at school, Spanish at home. But instead of recognizing the need for fluency in both

The corrosive effect of assimilation is the displacement of one culture over another, the inability to sustain more than one way of being.

languages, we turned it into a peculiar kind of battle. English was for public display. Spanish was for privacy—and privacy quickly turned to shame.

The corrosive effect of assimilation is the displacement of one culture over another, the inability to sustain more than one way of being. It isn't a code word for racial and ethnic acculturation only. It applies to needing to belong, of seeing from the outside and wondering how to get in and then, once inside, realizing there are always those still on the fringe.

When I went to college on the East Coast, I was confronted for the first time by people who said my name correctly without prompting; if they stumbled, there was a quick apology and an honest plea to help with the pronunciation. But introducing myself was painful: already shy, I avoided meeting people because I didn't want to say my name, felt burdened by my own history. I knew that my small-town upbringing and its limitations on Spanish would not have been tolerated by any of the students of color who had grown up in large cities, in places where the sheer force of their native languages made them dominant in their neighborhoods.

It didn't take long for me to assert the power of code-switching in public, the transferring of words from one language to another, regardless of who might be listening. I was learning that the English language composed new meanings when its constrictions were ignored, crossed over, or crossed out. Language is all about manipulation, or not listening to the rules.

When I come back to Dinuba, I have a hard time hearing my name said incorrectly, 20
but I have an even harder time beginning a conversation with others about why the pronunciation of our names matters. Leaving a small town requires an embrace of a larger point of view, but a town like Dinuba remains forever embedded in an either/or way of life. My stepfather still answers to Tony and, as the United States–born children grow older, their Anglicized names begin to signify who does and who does not "belong"—who was born here and who is de allá.

My name is Manuel. To this day, most people cannot say it correctly, the way it was intended to be said. But I can live with that because I love the alliteration of my full name. It wasn't the name my mother, Esmeralda, was going to give me. At the last minute, my father named me after an uncle I would never meet. My name was to have been Ricardo. Growing up in Dinuba, I'm certain I would have become Ricky or even Richard, and the journey toward the discovery of the English language's extraordinary power in even the most ordinary of circumstances would probably have gone unlearned.

I count on a collective sense of cultural loss to once again swing the names back to our native language. The Mexican gate agent announced Eugenio Reyes, but I never got a chance to see who appeared. I pictured an older man, cowboy hat in hand, but I made the assumption on his name alone, the clash of privileges I imagined between someone de allá and a Mexican woman with a good job in the United States. Would she speak to him in Spanish? Or would she raise her voice to him as if he were hard of hearing?

But who was I to imagine this man being from anywhere, based on his name alone? At a place of arrivals and departures, it sank into me that the currency of our names is a stroke of luck: because mine was not an easy name, it forced me to consider how language would rule me if I allowed it. Yet I discovered that only by leaving. My stepfather must live in the Valley, a place that does not allow that choice, every day. And Eugenio Reyes—I do not know if he was coming or going.

Exploring Context

1. Visit the Social Security Administration's website for popular baby names (ssa.gov/oact /babynames). How many of these suggest a non-Anglo culture? How popular are some of the Mexican names mentioned by Muñoz?

2. Explore the U.S. Census Bureau's website on the Hispanic population of the United States (census.gov/population/hispanic/). Given the strength of this population, why does there continue to be pressure to Anglicize? What factors—economic, social, or otherwise—might be at play?

3. Visit the website for Dinuba (dinuba.org). How do the site's design and content reflect the issues Muñoz discusses?

Questions for Connecting

1. In "Selections from *Once Upon a Quinceañera*" (p. 46), Julia Alvarez discusses "retro-culturation," a movement of later generations to embrace their Hispanic origins. How can you reconcile retroculturation with Muñoz's experience? How does Alvarez's essay reflect similar pressures for assimilation?

2. Steve Olson suggests that race no longer has any true genetic basis in "The End of Race: Hawaii and the Mixing of Peoples" (p. 334). What role does language—specifically names—play in maintaining racial and ethnic divisions?

3. Kwame Anthony Appiah's concept of cosmopolitanism from "Making Conversation" and "The Primacy of Practice" (p. 67) suggests that we need to get along in a crowded world filled with different cultures. Use Muñoz's essay to critique Appiah's argument. What are the downsides to cosmopolitanism? What is lost when practices change?

Language Matters

1. What special concerns might bilingual speakers have when it comes to academic writing? How does speaking more than one language complicate the process of composition? Consult a grammar handbook or reference source. Does it provide specific resources for writers who speak other languages? What kind of support is included, and why?

2. Locate a word that has been recently Anglicized and adopted into usage in English. Is it a slang word? What are its origins? How does language evolve? What does English owe to other languages?

3. Visit Wikipedia's guide to the pronunciation of English words at en.wikipedia.org /wiki/Wikipedia:Pronunciation_(simple_guide_to_markup,_American). How does the complexity of a "simple" guide to pronouncing English words change Muñoz's argument? What is the relationship between the spoken and written word?

Assignments for Writing

1. What is the relationship between names and identity? Write a paper in which you determine this relationship using Muñoz's essay as support. Consider your own name in writing the paper. Does your name shape your identity? How are culture and ethnicity reflected in names?

2. Write a paper in which you analyze the costs and benefits of assimilation, using Muñoz as a primary example. What is lost when a culture assimilates? What is gained? Is assimilation worth it? How can groups assimilate while maintaining their unique identities?

3. How does geography determine social position and power? Write a paper in which you consider the impact of location on social class and power. What happens when Muñoz leaves the small town of Dinuba? How does he react when he returns?

REBEKAH NATHAN

Rebekah Nathan is a pseudonym for Cathy Small, an anthropology professor at North Arizona University. When Small went undercover to write her second book, *My Freshman Year: What a Professor Learned by Becoming a Student* (2005), she took on the pseudonym to protect the identity of her students and her university. Small previously published *Voyages: From Tongan Villages to American Suburbs* (1997), an ethnographical study of immigrants in their old and new homelands.

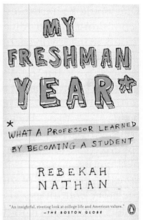

My *Freshman Year* is the result of a two-semester study by Small of all aspects of freshman life at her university. She applied to the university, enrolled in classes, moved into the student dorms, and even ate with students in the resident dining hall, hoping with her experiment to become a better teacher. After so long in the field, Small had found herself disconnected from the average student at her university, unable to understand why her students seemed so uninterested in and unprepared for class. She reveals in *My Freshman Year* that the demands on freshmen are much more varied and pressing than she had realized and that her initial assessment of her students had not been completely accurate.

"Community and Diversity," a chapter from *My Freshman Year*, deals with the difference between a university's stated goals for both community and diversity and their realization on campus, as well as the perpetual confusion among educators and administrators about why the image and the reality don't align. Small investigates low attendance at dorm events, patterns of freshman friendship, and the eating habits of ethnic and gender groups to reach some conclusions about the reality behind the lofty unmet intentions and the necessity of having such intentions at all.

As a student, you've undoubtedly encountered the call for community and diversity. It's likely, too, that you've seen this call go unanswered. You are in a unique position to continue Small's work on the possibilities of forming community and fostering diversity on the college campus.

▶ TAGS: *community, education, conversation, diversity, research, integration*

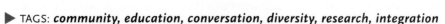

Questions for Critical Reading

1. What does Nathan mean by "ego-centered network"? As you read the text, develop a definition of the term by locating passages where Nathan discusses this concept. What role do these networks play in community? Support your answer with examples from the essay.

2. Most of Nathan's essay is concerned with the failures of both community and diversity at AnyU. Read her essay critically to locate passages in which Nathan indicates the main reasons for the lack of both at her school.

3. Submerged in Nathan's analysis are the requirements for successfully promoting community and diversity. As you read her essay, find quotations that provide the tools needed to promote these ideals.

Community and Diversity

One would be hard-pressed to find words more widespread in university rhetoric than "community" and "diversity." As a student, one is immediately enlisted to join the group, to get involved, to realize that one has become a part of the AnyU "community."

It starts during Previews and Welcome Week. We sing the AnyU alma mater with leaders; we learn the AnyU cheer. At the convocation that commences our freshman year, we are welcomed to AnyU with some statistics about our class, and then an entertaining PowerPoint presentation with voice-over begins: "In the year that you were born . . ." — it goes back eighteen years and shows a baby — "Ronald Reagan was president, AnyU was building its South Campus, and the movie that won the Academy Award was *Out of Africa*." We see graphics of all this, and AnyU history, at least for the past eighteen years, is interspersed with the shared "history" of the audience, which consists primarily of movies, TV shows, and dramatic historical events. "In 1986," the story continues, "the Emmy goes to *L.A. Law*, and the explosion of the *Challenger* saddens the American public." The presentation takes us briefly through all eighteen years of the baby-who-is-us.

By 1991 we have torn down the Berlin Wall, constructed the new AnyU library, and arrived at the same year that *Seinfeld* begins. There is silence, clapping, or booing as the event being described moves us. Our history continues, year by year, to mention, among other things, the end of the TV series *Cheers* in 1993, the Monica Lewinsky scandal in 1998, the beginning of *Friends* in 1994 (to thunderous applause), and the September 11, 2001, attack. By 2002 we are eighteen and ready to go to college, and — the lights come on — here we are, part of the AnyU family.

The presentation works; it is relatively short, and students leave mildly entertained and energized, having experienced a compressed version of our joint heritage and our shared place at the starting line of something new. It is clear what the common heritage has been constructed to be. What holds students together, really, is age, pop culture, a handful of (recent) historical events, and getting a degree. No one ever remembers the institutional history or the never-sung alma mater.

How Community Works at AnyU

Youth, pop culture, and getting a degree are pretty accurately the ties that bind together a public state university "community." Unless it offers a big-time (and winning) sports team that draws large attendance and loyalty, there is little in the way of shared first-year experiences that three thousand or so freshmen will have in common. AnyU   5 did have a Freshman Colloquium course that was mandatory for all first-year students. It was designed to be just such a community builder, one that required students to complete a summer reading assignment—usually a provocative contemporary novel chosen collectively by the participating faculty—that would be discussed in small seminars before classes formally began.

The faculty had an ambitious, and what they thought exciting, intellectual agenda in mind. Students would read the same book, and then their academic career would start with a stimulating seminar-style discussion with only twenty or so participants. The entire freshman class would be engaged in the same reading, and thus have a common basis for debate and dialogue. Freshmen would then meet the book's author, who had been invited at great expense to give a talk following their small-group discussions. This experience would jump-start the colloquium that would follow: a small, seminar-based freshman course centered on readings about community and citizenship, diversity, environment, and technology, designed to help them explore their journeys as "thinking persons," including the purpose of the liberal education they had begun. For the administration, the course was also a way to build a sense of loyalty and community, and thus, according to official belief, to retain freshmen as paying students.

I was in one of the last freshman classes to take the course. It was nullified as a requirement because the university faculty and administration concluded that it wasn't working. For one thing, only about a third of the students actually did the summer reading. My own pre-course seminar was led by an impressive instructor who practically pulled teeth trying to get a response to questions raised by our reading: "Does a common enemy help to make people a community? What is a typical American or an ideal citizen? Can anyone think of places within America that seem like a different country? Does technology bring you closer to or farther away from other people—does it separate or connect?" She ended up letting us go a half-hour early because, I surmised, of our silence. Very few in my seminar had read the book, at least "all the way through," as one student qualified it.

According to student surveys, many disliked the course that followed, in particular the idea that they "had no choice and that they *had* to take it," but also because it was abstract and impractical, and they didn't learn anything "related to their interests." The requirement, designed as the only common academic experience the freshmen would have, was accordingly wiped from the books, leaving an elective course, chosen separately by each student, in its place.

One can learn from the fate of the freshman seminar. It is a good example of what happens nowadays when efforts at building community compete with the demand for choice. The freshman course had been designed and initiated at AnyU as part of a nationwide agenda, begun in the early 1990s, to engage students in their freshman year and quickly establish a "learning community." It was one local response to what educational policy analysts identified as a crisis in community that left the university to be experienced in "momentary and marginal ways." "Not only has cultural coherence faded," reads the thoughtful and influential 1990 report from the Carnegie Foundation for the Advancement of Teaching, "but the very notion of commonalities seems strikingly inapplicable to the vigorous diversity of contemporary life." Titled *Campus Life: In*

Search of Community, the report called for a renewal of community in higher learning. Its authors wrote:

> It is of special significance, we believe, that higher learning institutions, even the big, complex ones, continue to use the familiar rhetoric of "community" to describe campus life and even use the metaphor of "family." Especially significant, 97 percent of the college and university presidents we surveyed said they "strongly believe in the importance of community." Almost all the presidents agreed that "community is appropriate for my campus" and also support the proposition that "administrators should make a greater effort to strengthen common purposes and shared experiences."[1]

It is a cry that has been taken up in earnest by university presidents around the country. Because *requiring* common experiences is vastly unpopular, and efforts often meet the fate of the freshman seminar. AnyU, like many universities today, encourages community through elective participation. "If you don't see what you like," said one Welcome Week booster, "start your own club." The 158 registered student organizations on campus don't tell the full story of the options that confront a student in a single week, from salsa dancing night at a downtown club, to the regular pickup game of coed volleyball, to the Overeaters Anonymous meeting, to the self-defense lesson in the dorm, to the plethora of academic events that are part of lecture and film series.

Every week the hall bulletin boards are plastered with notices about new events to attend, new music groups in town, or organizations offering enthusiastic invitations to their open house. The proliferation of event choices, together with the consistent message to "get involved," and the ever available option of dropping out, creates a self-contradictory system. Students are confronted with an endless slate of activities vying for their time. Every decision not to join but to keep one's time for oneself is interpreted as "student apathy" or "program irrelevance," and ever more activities are designed to remedy them. Each decision to join something new pulls at another commitment, fragmenting the whole even further. Not only people but also community are spread thin.

AnyU, like many universities today, encourages community through elective participation.

In my life as a student this process of community building through elective involvement was repeated numerous times and in numerous places within the university. On my dorm floor alone, where we had not done much together as a group during my first semester, the process worked like this. To begin our second semester and usher in a renewed spirit of community, our enthusiastic RA devised an "interest survey," which she administered at the first mandatory hall meeting of that period. (Since it was second semester, the turnout was decidedly sparse: Only six people attended.) "Let's do more things together," the RA suggested, and we agreed. It would be desirable, the collective thinking seemed to be, to have more "community" in the dorm.

"What would we like to do this semester?" she asked us. To find out, she distributed the survey with a written checklist that would assist her in launching new dorm programs that fit our interests and schedules. There were sixty-four activities suggested on the checklist in ten categories (community living, health/wellness, social awareness, employment skills, academic programs, relationship issues . . .), which ranged from presentation and panels, to group games and activities, to participatory workshops. We could write in activities if the ones presented did not suit. There was also an availability section of the form, where we were asked to check our preferred times—which evenings, which hours—for the activities. Because the showing at the meeting was so meager, our RA placed questionnaires under each of the doors on the wing, to be returned to her by a specified date. I asked whether I could see the final tallies.

A total of 304 selections were made by all hall mates, with eighteen of the sixty-four listed activities chosen by approximately half of all respondents. The most popular choice was not an activity at all but an expressed interest in buying floor T-shirts or boxer shorts. Among activities, several—including swing or salsa dancing and playing board games—were high on the list, but the RA decided to start her local "community" program with the biggest vote-getter, "Movie Night," endorsed by about three-quarters of the voting residents on the floor.

Movie Night was an activity whereby once every other week we would come to 15 our RA's room, as in Welcome Week, to watch a movie on video while sharing popcorn and other snacks provided by the RA or anted up by the residents. The preferred time, according to the questionnaires, was 8 PM on Tuesday. And so Movie Night was instituted twice a month on Tuesday nights, and slips of paper appeared under our doors to announce the first movie. On the first Tuesday, two people showed, besides the RA. The second time nobody showed. The RA moved the night to Sunday. Still nobody showed. The program was canceled, leaving the RA wondering what she could do to "really involve" her corridor.

Two organizational levels up from the corridor was the dorm. Here RAs and dorm officers attempted more extensive full-dorm programs that would get the residents involved. There were dozens of them, in addition to the corridor or floor-level activities devised by individual RAs. The most residents I ever saw attend any single event in our dormitory, housing about four hundred people, was for the talent show, where there were about twenty-one people — mostly the talent — and the "How to Make Edible Underwear" program around Valentine's Day, which drew twenty-three people.

With varying degrees of success, this was the pattern of "community involvement" that operated at various levels of the university: a multiplicity of voluntary activities, a handful of participants at each, and renewed efforts to create new activities that were more relevant and attractive, resulting in an even greater proliferation of choices and fragmentation of the whole.

The American Way: The Individualism in Community

To university administrators my story of Movie Night would be yet one more example of failing involvement and community on the contemporary college campus. By 1990 it was already becoming clear that few students participate in campus events; 76 percent of college and university presidents called nonparticipation a moderate to major problem on campuses.[2] An RA might count Movie Night as a personal failure, and become dispirited by the apathy of residents, or perhaps hear a call to invent more and better activities.

Students, I imagine, would see it a little differently. The activities chosen were not the "wrong" ones, nor were their RAs remiss. Nor had students been insincere in their desire for more community life in the dorm. If you had asked most students what happened with Movie Night, they would have answered, "I wanted to go, but when the time came, I didn't," or "I forgot." They genuinely want to have a close community, while at the same time they resist the claims that community makes on their schedule and resources in the name of individualism, spontaneity, freedom, and choice.

This is exactly how many students talk about sororities and fraternities. Fewer 20 than 10 percent of AnyU residents are members of either. When I asked students whether they'd considered "rushing," instead of mentioning the "elitism" or "conservative politics" that dominated Greek critique in my day, students complained about "conformity" and "control of my life." Judy explained that she had almost rushed but then changed her mind because "you become lost. It's hard to know all ninety girls in a sorority. You become the same rather than an individual in a group. It can get, you know, almost cult-like, and you spend all your time there. You can't live in other dorms, or meet new people."

I found that students' greatest objections to the Greek system were its steep demands—that it required so much time ("I can't give up that many nights a week to one organization") and so many resources ("Why should I pay all that money to a fraternity to have friends when I can make friends for free?"), all of them mandatory ("I don't want people telling me what to do and where I have to be all the time"; "I'm an individual, not a group person"). Yet, the one AnyU student in ten who did join a fraternity or sorority was, according to 2003 surveys conducted by the Office of Student Life, much less likely to drop out of school and much more likely to report the highest level of satisfaction with campus life.

There is a familiar dilemma here. "The very organizations that give security to students," concluded national policy analysts in 1990, "can also create isolation and even generate friction on the campus."[3] More than half of university presidents were reported to view Greek life as a problem, largely because it creates "little loyalties" that isolate students, removing them from the mainstream life of the university. It is not just Greek groups that operate this way. They are only illustrative of what one university president saw as "a great deal of 'orbital energy' among the many subgroups, a magnetism that tugs at these groups, pulling them away from any common agenda."[4]

Struggling with community in this way is, as observers of American life have pointed out, the American way.[5] The same things that make us feel connected and protected are the things that make us feel obligated and trapped as individuals and/or cut off from other groups with different agendas. For most students, as for most Americans in general, the "big community" has a dual connotation that includes both a warm and fuzzy side, all about "oneness" or "togetherness" or "common purpose," and a negative side that tends to surface with reference to government regulations, Big Brother images, and fears of conformity. When students talk about their educational community, these contradictory ideas of community are reproduced, bouncing between an entity that provides love and a sense of belonging and one that limits freedom and imposes new obligations.

I initially encountered student thoughts about community on "introduction sheets," tellingly titled "IT'S ALL ABOUT ME," that the RA had asked us to fill out and hang on our doors. Aimed at "community building," the sheets posed questions designed to acquaint others on the hall with our opinions and personality. After blanks for our major, hometown, and favorite color, and prompts to name our distinctive qualities, "the things I like to do for fun," and "what makes you unique," was the question, "What does community mean to you?"

For half the students, community was a somewhat naïve amalgam of love, belong- ing, sharing, and togetherness—all the things we would want community to do for us with none of its obligations. It was, in their words, "respect; caring, open people" who would be "sharing together, always there for me"; a place where there are "pillows on the floor" and "everybody leaves their door open," where you can "crash on your neighbor's floor if you're too tired to go home." My favorite answer in this category was "Community means being able to fart comfortably," because it so perfectly ignores the possibility of being the one at the other end of the farting freedom who has to put up with her flatulent neighbors. Only one person, in fact, mentioned any kind of respon- sibility when defining community, stating that she would "pick up garbage when I see it on the ground."

The downside of the community coin was also well represented, with some students balking at the idea of community or making jokes: "Community means Communism"; "Community means dirt—do you realize how many germs infest close-proximity liv- ing quarters?"; "Community means I can do whatever annoying habits I want and if my neighbors don't like it they can move out."

What I saw in student responses, as well as in student behavior, was a profound ambivalence about community life, resulting in a tentative, often conflicted relation- ship to the collective life of the university. Not only did campus participation suffer from this conflict, but also it was difficult to create mutual commitments and agreements among people whose connection to community was so hesitant.

One of the most interesting community ventures at AnyU came in the form of our second hall meeting in each semester, where we devised our "Community Liv- ing Agreement." Initiated by the RAs, these were to be the local agreements that each wing lived by, the "dos and don'ts" of hall life, fashioned by the residents themselves. The agreement for the first semester was drafted at a "mandatory" hall meeting at which seven people on the wing showed, one of whom left almost immediately because it was her birthday and she was too drunk to pay attention. After pizza, M&Ms, and yet another icebreaker game, the RA introduced our charge of creating a joint compact and handed out cards and pens, asking each person to write down something in the way of a rule or a "don't" that she would like to obtain for the hall. When we'd finished, the RA taped an enormous blank sheet of white paper to the wall, stood next to it with a marker, and said, "Tell me some of your items." Reluctantly and slowly, each person volunteered some rule. "Don't be too loud at night"; "Close the shower curtain so it doesn't flood the little anteroom"; "Don't leave your hair in the drain"; "Keep your door open when you're in your room (unless you're studying/sleeping)"; "Wipe your hair off of the shower walls"; "Don't take showers too long if there are people waiting."

There was no real discussion of any of the items. After everyone contributed, the RA took the sheet off the wall and left us to our candy. About one week later a large printed poster appeared on the hall, titled "Community Living Agreement," listing eight items, half of them pertaining to showers and a few to hair.

The same process occurred during the second semester, although shower etiquette   30
had a lower priority. Six items were posted in the hall for our second semester community agreement:

Keep hair off the shower walls.
Keep doors open while you're chillin'.
Sleepovers and parties on the hall are cool.
Yell "flushing" if there's someone in the shower [because the shower water turned
   scalding during the flush].
No writing on the bathroom stall walls [this was the RA's].
Say "hi" to people to be friendly.

Although the agreement no doubt reflected some important values held by the
residents, including sociability, courtesy, and cleanliness, it was the relationship of the
individuals to the community agreement that interested me most. There had been no
road map for actually creating an agreement, no mechanism for turning individual
opinions into a community document. No one, including the RA, was comfortable
suggesting that we might modify, prioritize, or remove individuals' suggestions from
the list. While the seven students in attendance were considered to "represent" the
others, because the latter did not show up to participate, there was no means for making the "agreement" binding on hall residents. As a result, the list remained posted
for a semester, but each student on the hall decided whether she would abide by the
agreement or not.

I never once heard anyone yell "flushing" in the bathroom, nor did I ever see a "cool
sleepover" or public party on the hall. It seemed to me that the same people who kept
their doors open prior to the agreement, including me, were the ones who kept their
doors open afterward. There was never any follow-up or discussion about whether our
agreement was being honored.

Community in the American university is paradoxically a private and an individual decision. As Robert Putnam documents in his history of community in the United
States, *Bowling Alone*, the private decision to participate in community life is one that
individuals in recent U.S. history are making less and less. From civic and religious life
to political participation and informal social connections, there is an increasing individualism in American life that is evident in our universities as well.[6]

In such a historical light, the trends in dormitory living are thought-provoking.
The newest dormitories being built across the country are both higher in amenities
and lower in density than those of the past. It is no longer considered a viable model of
campus life to have a hall full of people sharing a communal bathroom, lounge, and
washing machine. The old blueprint of collective living has given way to much more
individualized and opulent arrangements. Put in student lingo, individualism "rules."

At AnyU, new dorms are all built "suite-style," with four students sharing a huge   35
apartment with four bedrooms and two bathrooms, as well as its own living room,
kitchen, and washer-dryer units. The private bedrooms and semi-private bathrooms
are more acceptable to contemporary students, who are no longer accustomed in
childhood to sharing a room with a sibling. In fact, according to AnyU's Office of Resi-
dence Life, the number one reason why students move out of traditional dormitories is
that they do not like sharing a communal bathroom. Dormitories, like campus life as

a whole, are increasingly privatized, well appointed, and focused on an ever smaller network of people that constitutes the significant living community of the student.

These national trends bring into clearer focus the use of space in my own dormitory, a building constructed in the 1940s for a 1940s student. One can see how new students with new values have refashioned the existing space. The dormitory includes big, cushy public spaces filled with overstuffed furniture which appear to be expecting a crowd. There are lounges on each floor, one with a fireplace and some with large outside terraces; they have tables and chairs, community TVs and VCRs.

After using these spaces as a student, I began to realize something that I subsequently checked by monitoring more public lounges in my dorm and others: Fellow students didn't really use these areas as social space. With the exception of the cleaning staff on their lunch breaks, I never saw students bring food and eat together, sit and socialize together, or even watch television together in our local lounge. During the course of an entire semester, what could be called "community life" or even "social activity" was extremely sparse. I saw one or two card games in the lounge on my floor, one simulation game meeting, scattered study groups that assembled in the dorm to work on a class project, and a Christian group who occasionally used the space to work on volunteer projects.

My observations of lounges in other dormitories were not significantly different. These spaces often sat empty. During the day, no one used them at all. On most nights, the overstuffed couches and chairs in our largest lounge would be draped with one to three students who had positioned themselves as far as possible from one another. Interviews with the few students who *were* in the lounges during my observations revealed that the majority came there to "get away" —from a gathering in their room, music blasting on the hall, or a roommate with a guest. In other words, the community spaces were often a *retreat* from social interaction, a way to create more private options. They were no longer, as their builders had probably envisioned, primarily a place for people to come together and participate in joint activities.

One of my greatest epiphanies about community life in the dorm came on Super Bowl Sunday. I had sneaked home Saturday night, intending to stay at my own house until Sunday night, when I realized that on Sunday afternoon at 2 PM Super Bowl coverage would begin, and I needed to be at the dorm. The event had been advertised heavily in the hall for weeks. "Free Ticket," the flyers read, and the "ticket" entitled one to good company, free pizza, and drinks during the game. The large lobby had been set up with two big-screen TVs so as to accommodate viewers from any vantage point.

I arrived a little early to get a good seat and waited for the lobby lounge to fill, but by game time there were only five other people in the space. One had tuned the second TV set to a different program, so I and four others watched the opening kickoff together. A couple of months earlier, when I had been the only one in the lounge for the World Series, I simply assumed that the event was under-advertised and that this generation had no love of baseball. When I saw that the same no-show pattern had occurred with the well-publicized football event, I decided to investigate further. Where were the other students? I left at halftime.

Many, I surmised, had gone to sports bars. But as I wandered the floors of my dorm, I could hear the game playing from numerous rooms. On my corridor alone, where there were two open doors, I could see clusters of people in each room eating and drinking as they watched the game together on their own sizable television sets. It seemed telling to me that so many dormitory residents were watching the same game in different places, the great majority preferring to pass the time with a carefully chosen group of personal friends in their own private space. It spoke in a more general way to how community really worked in the university.

Rather than being located in its shared symbols, meetings, activities, and rituals, the university for an undergraduate was more accurately a world of self-selected people and events. The university community was experienced by most students as a relatively small, personal network of people who did things together. This "individual community" was bolstered by a university system that honors student choice, as well as a level of materialism in the larger society that, by enabling students to own their own cars, computers, TV sets, and VCRs, renders collective resources and spaces superfluous. These characteristics of American university life—individualism, choice, and materialism—stand out even more clearly in chapter 4 [not included here], where foreign students at AnyU describe and compare their own educational systems.

AnyU's Real Community: The Ego-Centered Network

When I asked students in interviews whether they felt they had a "community" at AnyU, most said yes. But what they meant by community were these personal networks of friends that some referred to as my "homeys." It was these small, ego-centered groups that were the backbone of most students' social experience in the university.

On a daily basis these personal networks were easily recognizable within the dorm and on campus. "Where are you now?" says the cell phone caller walking back to the dorm from class. "I'm on my way home, so ask Jeffrey and Mark to come, and I'll meet you at my room at 8." Such conversations are everywhere. In the dorm, residents can be heard discussing the timing and location of dinners and after-dinner plans, and message boards record the social negotiations: "Be home by 5:30. What about Mexican? Call me—P." Creating one's community involved very conscious choices to make one's leisure hours jibe with selected others'. There were few open invitations in these exchanges. Unless the RA had planned an activity, there was no general call to join in on dinner plans or come watch a video in someone's room.

Among members of the same network, however, there were constant interactions, ranging from borrowing detergent and snacks, to arranging social and shopping trips, to watching TV or videos together, to working out. The communications among network members occurred both publicly, like the planning just noted, and privately, as I saw in student diaries, where frequent cell phone contact and Instant Messaging sessions were the norm.

The intense reciprocity of ego-based groups helped explain a problem about campus traffic that had long puzzled me. As a professor, I could never understand why campus roads were so hopelessly jammed between classes. After all, AnyU had a campus bus system, and students had parking permits only for the lots adjacent to their dorms. They couldn't legally park at classroom building lots and would receive a hefty ticket if they did. When I pasted my student parking pass on my car, I found myself basically grounded—able to drive off campus and back to my dorm but nowhere else. Why, then, were the roads so crowded with cars seemingly traveling from dorms to classes?

It wasn't long before I saw message boards with reminders such as "Tara, don't forget to pick me up 10 AM at the Social Science building.—L." Or "Be out in the Education Parking Lot at 3:10—Nick." As I walked or took the bus to class, I began to pay more attention to the non-dormitory parking lots and realized that there was a vast web of personal relationships activated for dropping and picking up passengers. It was network reciprocity at work.

These personal networks grew in importance to me as I realized their salience in the life of my fellow students, and in the life of the university. I became increasingly interested in how friends are made, how groups are formed, and how activities are coordinated. I built these queries into my interviews and discovered much that observation alone did not tell me.

Student networks, like family relations, are ego based. In a family, even your first cousin will have relatives that you don't have in common, and the same is true of two students who are in each other's networks. Pam and Terry are part of the same social network, but when they separately name their own closest friends, the names are not exactly the same. Pam includes her boyfriend and his roommate along with Alice and Marie in her close network, while Terry includes Alice, Marie, and Pam but also a friend from class whom Pam barely knows. And Pam's boyfriend shares only a few of Pam's friends. One student's network, although it may overlap with those of others, is essentially personal; no two people share the exact same group of friends. This is what is meant by ego based: Even these intimate forms of community are quite individual.

Most students, I found, had established a network of two to six friends who formed their core university community. From the "native" point of view, they got together because "we like each other." Students regularly named personality traits and attitudes to explain their attraction to friends: "They're outspoken"; "We're all a little weird"; they're "strong-minded and focused like me"; they're "up for anything, and pretty laid back"; "We're the same when it comes to school, not big party-ers"; or they're "real friendly, open, responsible people."

To an outsider, especially an outsider who is looking at the points of convergence among a number of students, student networks have less to do with personality than with shared circumstances and shared demographics. Kyle, a Christian student on the floor, had a network of close friends for whom being Christian was very important. They'd met while they were still in high school, after attending several retreats that happened to be held at AnyU. By the time they came to AnyU as freshmen, they were already friends. The close networks of five of the six minority students in my sample contained several other minority students. A number of them had met their closest friends in an intensive pre-college summer program for first-generation students, where there had been a sizable percentage of minority students. One of the most surprising findings to me was the discovery that eight of fourteen students interviewed about the subject of social networks had one or more people in their close personal networks whom they knew from high school or their hometown. In all, then, many of the networks that endured through college were based on experiences *before* college, and these were conditioned by demographic characteristics such as religion, race, ethnicity, and/or hometown (itself a function of race, ethnicity, religion, and class).

Once in school, it was also edifying to learn how early the enduring friendships occurred in students' college life, and how little they drew on academic interests and contacts. Most students whose friends were cultivated after college began had met their closest friends by virtue of living in the same freshman dorm or floor. Classroom contacts figured relatively little in the social networks of students; fewer than one-quarter of my interview students had met a member of their network in an academic class or in an activity or club related to their major, while almost as many had met a close friend through ROTC or work.

Despite the belief that college expands our social horizons and extends our experience to include new and different types of people, the findings suggest otherwise. The most significant relationships are formed either before college or very early in one's college career, most often in some shared affiliation, whether voluntary or not, such as freshman dorm assignment, special freshman summer program, ROTC, ethnic club, or sorority and fraternity rush.

Diaries and interviews confirmed that for many students, their social lives at the university consisted of repeated contacts with the same people, who constituted that student's personal network. Once networks were formed, usually by the end of the freshman year, students tended to stay with their groups, maintaining intense and frequent interactions with their network and more superficial and sparse contacts with others. The way that student social life is formed necessarily affects issues of diversity.

Diversity at AnyU?

Student networks may be able to explain, at least in part, the failed diversity efforts at many universities, and certainly at AnyU. About 22 to 25 percent of AnyU students are considered "minority" by federal standards, and minority students appear approximately in these percentages in AnyU dorms and classes. What makes diversity a "success" in a state university, however, is not only that the university population reflects the diversity of the general population but also that students become more involved in the lives and issues of that diverse population. Part of that diversity ideal is the hope that all students will develop friends and have important conversations with those of backgrounds and ethnicities different from their own.

The National Survey of Student Engagement tries to capture this information by asking a student to self-report as to whether he or she has "had serious conversations with students of a different race or ethnicity than your own." In 2003, fifty percent of college seniors nationwide indicated that they "often" or "very often" had such conversations, while only 13 percent said they did not.

> **Most students, but white students predominantly, ended up becoming close friends with people of their own ethnicity.**

This jibed with the information I initially was getting from my interviews about social networks, where I was finding that many students named someone from a different ethnic group within their close circle of friends. The interview information, though, did not match my direct observations, and this led me to probe further by fiddling with my interview questions and format. I soon realized that if I started, as I had, by asking informants whether they had close friends from other ethnic groups, the majority of students would say that they did. If I questioned them further, they would name that man from a class, or woman on the same intramural volleyball team, with whom they had close contact and describe how they met.

If, however, I started by asking informants to name their closest friends and then later asked them to identify the ethnicity of the named people, it turned out that most students, but white students predominantly, ended up becoming close friends with people of their own ethnicity. Since I thought that this "names first, ethnicity later" approach was more accurate, I changed the order of my questions and arrived at a very different picture. Five out of six white students I interviewed in this way about their networks had no members of another racial or ethnic group in their close social circle; the networks of five of the six minority students contained one or more minorities (more on the details of this later).

One can see from the descriptions of how networks form why this might be true. Many students are building on contacts developed before they entered college, contacts that have strong demographic and social components. If many student networks begin with hometown contacts, what is the likelihood that they will cross class, ethnic, race, or even religious lines when the United States is demographically divided along precisely these lines? Although there was one instance in my data of a cross-racial network pair with its origin in high school, the probabilities in this country work strongly the other way because of de facto neighborhood and school segregation. All other examples I found of high school or hometown friends in an AnyU network involved a woman or man of the same ethnicity as the person interviewed.

Even many relationships developed early in college contain a built-in bias. Although classes and interest clubs may be ethnically well mixed, this is not where students make their earliest school contacts. Freshman dorms are generally well integrated, but not several of the early programs and events that help introduce and acclimate new students, including Previews weekends designated for particular ethnic groups, pre-college "outdoor adventure" trips that cost extra money, a summer program for first-generation college students, or the opening round of sorority and fraternity mixers. Some institutional structures like these may encourage the early formation of same-ethnicity relationships.

There is no doubt that active racism also plays a part in the lack of diversity on college campuses. Yet, race or ethnicity is typically ignored as a topic of conversation in mainstream college culture, treated as an invisible issue and with silence. As Levine and Cureton (1998) found in their nationwide survey, students were "more willing to tell intimate details of their sex lives than discuss race relations on campus."[7] When the subject *is* raised, as in the occasional class, students of color report being continually expected to educate whites about minority issues or speak "as a representative of their race."

Despite the general invisibility of the subject of race in informal student culture, there was not a single minority student I interviewed who hadn't experienced racism.[8] Few openly complained, but everyone had at least one story to tell of comments made in class, rude remarks on the street, or just hostile looks. When I asked Pat, a Hispanic–Native American woman, whether she had ever considered rushing a sorority, she told me that she had in her freshman year, but "I could see that it wasn't really right for me, because I'd pass by all the sorority tables—you know how they call out to girls to come over and take a look—well, I saw they called out to other girls but not to me. They just kinda ignored me, not hostile or anything, but not interested either."

"It's just how it is," another female student explained. "There are some good people and some not so good people, and you deal with it."

Who Eats with Whom: A Study of Student Dining

My very small sample of student networks and interviews was suggestive to me but not convincing that diversity in student relationships was in serious question. So I decided to conduct a larger observational study of students' informal social behavior. I chose eating as the focus, one of my favorite social activities, and asked the research question "Who eats with whom?" This seemed a fair and appropriate inquiry into diversity, to determine the range of people with whom one breaks bread.

It was my most extensive and longest-running "mini-study" of campus life. For five months I directly observed and recorded the dining behavior of fellow students during randomly selected periods of the day at optional dining areas on campus.[9] Although some patrons carried out their food, returning to their dorms or outside benches to eat, many ate and drank singly or in groups at the various tables provided in one of five eating areas I surveyed. Sitting at a different table in the room, I would record who sat at each table by gender and, as much as outward appearances can signal, ethnicity.

It is always problematic to do research like this, because there is a wide range of appearances for all ethnicities, and many sticky issues. My interest, however, *was* in appearances, and in seeing to what extent students chose to share food and conversation with people who looked like them (or, more accurately, seemed to belong in the same broad ethnic category that an observer would attribute to them). Although there are other kinds of diversity (e.g., age), I recorded only the data reflecting each person's gender and, to the extent possible, his or her category of ethnicity such as white non-Hispanic, Hispanic, Asian, African American, Native American, and so on. These were not easy calls. Sometimes I could tell only that someone was not a white non-Hispanic but couldn't identify the more specific group to which she or he belonged; at other times I could not tell whether a person was white and non-Hispanic or something else.

In gathering this information I had these questions in mind: To what extent did informal university activities (e.g., eating together) convey diversity? Did students eat in same or mixed ethnic and gender groups? Were there differences in the eating patterns of dominant (defined as white non-Hispanic) and non-dominant (defined as people of color) ethnic groups? Did any ethnic group or category eat alone more often than others?

I analyzed the data with regard to these questions but took care to analyze by person rather than by table in order to try to see the data through the eyes of the particular diner. For instance, if there were a table consisting of four people—a white male, two white women, and one Hispanic woman—each would have a different reality at the table: The male is eating with a table of all women of mixed ethnicity; both white women are eating at a table of mixed gender and mixed ethnicity; and the Hispanic woman is eating at a mixed-gender table where everyone is of a different ethnicity from herself. I recorded the data, preserving the perspective of each diner, and then analyzed the data in ten different categories that allowed me to examine the relationship of each table diner to the rest.[10] In this way, I tracked almost 1,500 examples of dining behavior.

What I found was interesting. It showed not only an overall lack of diversity, as national studies report,[11] but also the existence of huge differences in the diversity experiences of dominant and non-dominant groups. Minorities (people of color) ate alone only slightly more often: one-quarter of minority women and more than one-third of minority men sitting in public spaces ate alone, a rate greater than that for white women and men by 3 percent and 5 percent, respectively. But of all those who ate with others, only 10 percent of white men and 14 percent of white women ate at a table where there was anyone of a different color from themselves. Only 2.6 percent and 3.5 percent of white men and women, respectively, ate at a table of two or more where they were the only white person. The statistics were strikingly different for people of color: 68 percent of women and 58 percent of men ate with "mixed groups." People of color were ten times more likely than whites to eat in a group in which they were the only person of a different race/ethnicity at the table.

The same patterns I saw in the dining spaces proved true in the composition of personal networks when I compared a group of twelve students on my hall, six whites and six students of color. Although the networks of Caucasian students included more whites, and those of people of color more minorities, the total networks of minority students were primarily "mixed," comprising people of various ethnicities, including whites. One student of color was in an all-white network, while another had friends of only her own ethnicity. By contrast, five of the six white students had networks that were solidly white; only one white student had a mixed network, and none was the only Caucasian.

Seen in this context, minority ethnic clubs, dorms, and student unions have a clearer meaning. Ethnic-based groups are often clouded by perceptions that they, like the Greek system, remove their members from the mainstream and surround them with people of the same background. What the data suggest to me is that people of color are already heavily involved in interethnic and interracial relationships on campus. In fact, most of their informal dining contacts, as well as personal networks, included people who were ethnically different from them. Under these circumstances, an ethnic-based club—which half of the minorities in my sample thought was important in their lives—is better understood as a needed respite from difference, a chance to rest comfortably with others who share similar experiences in the world.

It was white students, most markedly males, whose social lives suffered from a lack of diversity. When white men *did* eat with those of different ethnicities, the majority of tables were "cross-gender." In other words, white men socialized at meals to a greater degree with nonwhite women or with groups that included nonwhite women. There was extremely little contact between white and nonwhite men. Only 4 of 489 white males, fewer than 1 percent, ate with (only) males of a different ethnicity, but 31 ate in different or mixed ethnic groups in which women were present. Men of color, while much more diverse in their dining, followed a similar pattern, tending to have fewer cross-ethnic male-only eating partners (7 of 79) while favoring cross-ethnic tables where women were eating too (24 of 79). The same pattern was not true of women. For both white women and women of color, their cross-color contact was primarily with other women.

One of the more disturbing but confusing findings was how few people of color, proportionally, used the common eating spaces. Only 13 percent of the entire dining sample was nonwhite, while 22 percent of full-time students were nonwhite. This left more than 40 percent of the minority population unaccounted for. There are certainly many ways to interpret what was going on. Perhaps this eyeballing approach to minority status simply fails to recognize many who are legal minorities. Perhaps there are economic factors at work that bear on having a meal ticket or buying food during the day that disadvantage some minority students. Perhaps the difference is explained by the larger percentage of minority students who enroll in off-campus programs. But there is another possibility that I entertained, which was related to my finding that more minority students eat alone.

My evidence is only anecdotal because I didn't formally monitor what I thought I was seeing, but this is what I noticed. I would observe the food court area as people got their food and stood in line to pay, watching each person leave the register to see where he or she went to sit in order to mark it in my book. I often found that instead of going to a table, however, a person of color would go to a condiment area, pack up a napkin and the food in a bag, and leave. It seemed to me that a greater proportion of minorities was leaving.

One day, as I was just finishing an observation session, an African American 75 woman left the register and headed for a table. She would be the last diner to enter my monitored space in the set time period. I prepared to mark her table choice, but instead of sitting down, she readjusted her backpack, took her food, and left. Where is she going? I asked myself. To meet a friend in a different area? To eat outside? I felt a bit like a stalker as I followed her out of the dining area and out of the building. She passed the outdoor tables and kept walking until she entered one of the freshman dorms, went through the lobby, and up the stairs. My guess was that she had returned to eat in her dorm room.

I will never know for sure what lay behind that one observation, or what I perceived to be the larger proportion of students of color who did not stay to eat. But it left me with the uncomfortable feeling that I was witnessing the effect of a "white space"—which I had never noticed because I am white—where people of color could eat alone publicly, or eat with people different from themselves, or go home to their rooms. Perhaps, many times, the dorm room just seems the most comfortable option, and this may have explained some of the missing 40 percent of minority students in the dining areas.

The ideals of community and diversity are certainly in place at AnyU and remain important components of stated university policy. Yet neither is fully realized in university culture, as I believe I have illustrated in this chapter. What I also hope I've illustrated, though, is what anthropologists mean when they say that a culture cannot really be divided into its parts; one part of a culture cannot be understood in isolation from its other parts, and all must be contextualized within the larger whole. Culture, we argue, is both integrated and holistic.

In just this way "community" and "diversity" are parts of university culture, but they are not intelligible on their own. As the descriptions of student life attest, diversity is one part of college culture that is intimately tied to community, another part. And both parts are ultimately conditioned by structures in the larger American society—including values of individualism and choice, materialism, and the realities of U.S. demographics—that may seem, at first, to have little bearing on whether college diversity increases because freshmen Joe and Juan truly become friends, or whether Jane strengthens community by deciding to attend Movie Night. But they do. Not understanding this leads to a reality about diversity and community in university culture that does not match its rhetoric, and a persistent confusion about why this is so.

NOTES

1. Carnegie Foundation for the Advancement of Teaching 1990, 64, 63.
2. Ibid., 48.
3. Ibid., 49.
4. Ibid., 50.
5. Varenne 1977.
6. Putnam 2000.
7. Levine and Cureton 1998, 72.
8. My brief section here hardly does justice to the urgency of race and ethnicity issues on campus or, for that matter, to the active discrimination experienced by gay and transgendered individuals. For more on the thoughts and experiences of minority and gay students, see Lesage et al. 2002 and Howard and Stevens 2000, and see Tusmith and Reddy 2002 for teachers' challenges with teaching diversity to students.
9. To mitigate such factors as meal plans and off-campus versus on-campus living, which may draw differentially on class and ethnicity, I confined my observations to tables shared in the optional dining areas on campus where either a meal plan card or cash was accepted. I made observations only during the day and from Monday to Friday, when most classes were in session, because these were the times and meals, I figured, that would be least affected by demographic and economic differences among students.
10. Each diner ("who," according to gender and ethnicity) and the number at the table (#) were recorded. Then each person sitting at the table was recorded by gender and specific ethnicity, where possible. The data were then sorted and analyzed by looking at the composition of the table from the diner's point of view and marked as to whether the diner was eating with: (1) no one (the person was sitting alone); (2) females of the same ethnic/power group (SF), males of the same ethnic/power group (SM), or a mixed-gender table of the same ethnic/power group (SX); (2) females (OF) or males (OM) of a different ethnic/power group, a mixed-gender table comprising members of a different ethnic/power group (OX); or (3) a mixed ethnic/power group that was all female (MxF), all male (MxM), or mixed gender (MxX). The term "ethnic/power group" is used because, for purposes of this section, people's ethnicities were analyzed in two broad categories that are more than ethnic designations: dominant (white non-Hispanic) and minority (people of color) groups. More detailed ethnic information was recorded and reviewed, but the comparisons here focused on dominant and nondominant groups.
11. "Walk into the cafeteria in most colleges and universities," write Levine and Cureton, "and the tables are separated by race and ethnicity. The larger the campus, the sharper the divisions" (1998, 86).

BIBLIOGRAPHY

Carnegie Foundation for the Advancement of Teaching. 1990. *Campus Life: In Search of Community.* Princeton: Carnegie Foundation for the Advancement of Teaching.

Howard, Kim, and Annie Stevens. 2000. *Out and About Campus: Personal Accounts by Lesbian, Gay, Bisexual, and Transgendered College Students*. Los Angeles: Alyson Books.

Lesage, Julia, Abby L. Ferber, Debbie Storrs, and Donna Wong. 2002. *Making a Difference: University Students of Color Speak Out*. Lanham, Md.: Rowman & Littlefield.

Levine, Arthur, and Jeanette S. Cureton. 1998. *When Hope and Fear Collide: A Portrait of Today's College Student*. San Francisco: Jossey-Bass.

Putnam, Robert D. 2000. *Bowling Alone: The Collapse and Revival of American Community*. New York: Simon & Schuster.

Tusmith, Bonnie, and Maureen T. Reddy, eds. 2002. *Race in the College Classroom: Pedagogy and Politics*. New Brunswick: Rutgers University Press.

Varenne, Hervé. 1977. *Americans Together: Structured Diversity in a Midwestern Town*. New York: Teachers College Press.

Exploring Context

1. In this selection, Nathan is interested in exploring the gap between her school's stated goals for community and diversity and the actuality of these ideals in student life. What are your school's objectives in these two areas? Generate a sense of how your school approaches community and diversity by searching for these terms in your institution's website, and then prepare a short report on what you find in this search. Do you find the same gap between image and reality that Nathan finds at her institution? If not, what might account for the success of community and diversity at your school? How does your work on failures of community and diversity from Question 2 of Questions for Critical Reading apply to your school's website?

2. Nathan opens by recounting the time line presentation that students at AnyU watch during orientation. Use the Web to research significant national or world events that took place at different stages of your own life. Share these time lines in small groups. Do you and your classmates share the same historical sense? Did you look up the same years or dates? How might such a time line produce community, and why might you and your classmates have different events listed? Do the differences in your apprehensions of the past create challenges to forming community? Does the diversity of your class play any role?

3. At the heart of Nathan's analysis are the very definitions of community and diversity. Search for blog entries on "community" and "diversity" using a search engine for blogs. Based on the blog postings you read, what do these terms mean to people in general? How do they talk about them? Do they value them? How are they viewed differently in the blogosphere and at AnyU? What might account for this difference?

Questions for Connecting

1. How can Leslie Savan's analysis of pop talk in "What's Black, Then White, and Said All Over?" (p. 435) help explain the failure of diversity on college campuses? What role might "paying the dues" have in achieving true diversity? Relate your answer to your work on this issue from Questions for Critical Reading.

2. Given Steve Olson's argument in "The End of Race: Hawaii and the Mixing of Peoples" (p. 334) about the end of any genetic basis for race, how important is diversity? Does Hawaii serve as a model for college communities? Or does Nathan help explain why notions of race persist even without a genetic basis?

3. Michael Pollan examines the complex ecosystems of organic farming in "The Animals: Practicing Complexity" (p. 373). Might those ecosystems provide a model for community and diversity in education? How can individuals serve as "holons" on the college campus? Use your work on your school's website from Question 1 of Exploring Context in considering your own school as an ecosystem. What might be a holon for your campus?

Language Matters

1. Sentences can be written in either active or passive voice. If you're not sure what these terms mean, look up *active voice* and *passive voice* in a grammar handbook or reference guide. Then select a quotation from Nathan's essay that you think is key to her argument. Identify whether it is written in active or passive voice, noting how you know this to be the case. Then rewrite the sentence in the opposite voice. Is the argument weaker in passive voice or in active voice? Are concepts clearer in one voice or the other? Why or why not? Why might you choose active or passive voice in your own writing?

2. Word choice and tone are important in your writing. Select a significant quotation from Nathan's text, type it into a blank document in a word processor, and, using a thesaurus (the word processor's, one online, or a printed one), replace every significant word in the sentence with a synonym. Does the sentence still work? How does word choice influence tone and meaning? Why didn't Nathan use "fancier" or more "academic" language in this text? Based on what you have discovered, what sort of tone do you think you should use in your writing for this class?

3. Drafting and revising are crucial components of the writing process. We often see a published piece of writing as perfect, but imagine earlier drafts of Nathan's text. How do you think she started this piece? What areas do you think Nathan revised the most? Where do you think you should do the most revision as you draft your own papers?

Assignments for Writing

1. Nathan notes that despite AnyU's best efforts to unite the university's population, students who make up the different communities within the school would rather bond within their own social groups than venture outside of them. Assess the situation Nathan talks about in her essay. Thinking beyond Nathan's findings, write a paper in which you examine the possibilities of communities becoming fully integrated. Is such integration even possible in a world made up of so many diverse and differing communities? The purpose of this essay is for you to apply the concepts in Nathan's essay to your own specific observations and experiences. Rather than simply writing a story about your own opinions, you should instead use your experiences and observations among diverse communities, on an academic campus or elsewhere, to explore the

possibilities of a truly integrated community. You may also want to use your responses to Questions for Critical Reading and Exploring Context in supporting your argument.

2. Nathan decides that going undercover is the only way to understand why university social life has not become what university presidents want. This reflects her belief that these leaders are out of touch with students' perspectives on community. So although university presidents want the best for their schools, it seems like their actions have had little impact. Write a paper in which you examine why it is important for university and college leaders to share the same outlook as their students in terms of community building. To help you complete your essay successfully, you may want to closely read specific passages from Nathan's essay that outline the perspectives university presidents and students have. Why is it so important to understand the differences in those perspectives?

3. How does individuality inhibit community building within diverse populations? Write a paper in which you assess the potential for balancing the needs of individuals and communities. Use your responses to Questions for Critical Reading as well as to Question 3 of Questions for Connecting to support your argument. Are ego-centered networks inevitable? Are diversity and community mutually exclusive goals?

STEVE OLSON

Journalist **Steve Olson**, who holds a B.S. in physics from Yale University, has reported for the *Atlantic*, *Science*, and *Scientific American* and has published multiple books, including *Mapping Human History: Genes, Race, and Our Common Origins* (2002), which was a finalist for the National Book Award, and *Count Down* (2004), about teens at the International Mathematical Olympiad.

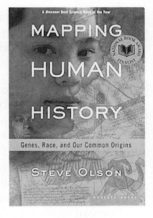

In *Mapping Human History*, the source of the following selection, Olson studies the path of our species through genes and continents, tracking all of humanity back to a small group that lived in eastern Africa, debunking racial myths along the way. Regardless of what appear to be differences among us, suggests Olson, biologically we are all basically the same. Our group origins and differences, which were superficial to begin with, lose importance as time goes by.

In "The End of Race: Hawaii and the Mixing of Peoples," Olson considers centuries of intermarriage between native and nonnative races in the Hawaiian islands. Although this extensive "mixing of peoples" has led some to propose Hawaii as an example of interracial harmony, Olson acknowledges that such claims are not entirely true. Though the majority of those born and raised in Hawaii come from a complex racial and ethnic makeup, social, political, and historical influences have contributed to deep cultural divides among the various island populations. Now, in the aftermath of European colonization, the preservation of Hawaiian culture and the definition of what it means to be a native Hawaiian are pressing questions with no easy genetic or biological answers. Thus Olson ultimately questions whether racial and cultural identity is rooted in biology or affiliation. The "end of race" is, perhaps, no end at all.

What defines race? And given how complicated such a definition must inevitably be, how can we end racism and promote racial harmony?

▶ TAGS: *race, integration, research, diversity, bioethics, diplomacy, community*

Questions for Critical Reading

1. What is a "community of descent"? Develop a definition by reading Olson's text to locate quotations that define the concept. Offer, too, an example of a community of descent from your own experience.

2. As you read, ask yourself how Olson defines *race*. Create a definition and support it using quotations from Olson's essay. To do so, you will need to read his essay critically, paying close attention to what Olson has to say about the concept of race.

3. If race no longer has a biological basis, as Olson claims, why do ethnicities continue to function in society? Use Olson's text to propose reasons why race persists.

The End of Race: Hawaii and the Mixing of Peoples

He loved everything, he was full of joyous love toward everything that he saw. And it seemed to him that was just why he was previously so ill—because he could love nothing and nobody.

—HERMANN HESSE, *Siddhartha*

On the morning of November 26, 1778, the 100-foot-long, three-masted ship *Resolution*, captained by the fifty-year-old Englishman James Cook, sailed into view off the northeast coast of the Hawaiian island of Maui. The island's Polynesian inhabitants had never seen a European sailing ship before. The sight of the *Resolution* just beyond the fierce windward surf must have looked as strange to them as a spaceship from another planet. Yet they responded without hesitation. They boarded canoes and paddled to the ship. From atop the rolling swells they offered the sailors food, water, and, in the case of the women, themselves.

One can easily imagine the contrast: the European sailors—gaunt, dirty, many bearing the unmistakable signs of venereal disease—and the Polynesians, a people who abided by strict codes of personal hygiene, who washed every day and plucked the hair from their faces and underarms, whose women had bodies "moulded into the utmost perfection," in the words of one early admirer. At first Cook forbade his men to bring the women on board the ship "to prevent as much as possible the communicating [of the] fatal disease [gonorrhea] to a set of innocent people." In the weeks and months to come, as the *Resolution* lingered offshore, Cook was far less resolute. Toward the end of 1779, the first of what are today called *hapa haoles*—half European, half non-European—were born on the island of Maui.

The nineteenth-century stereotype of the South Pacific as a sexual paradise owes as much to the feverish imaginations of repressed Europeans as to the actions of the Polynesians. The young women who swam out to the ships in Hawaii, Tahiti, and other South Pacific islands were from the lower classes, not from the royalty, which carefully guarded its legitimacy. Many were training to be dancers in religious festivals. They would rise in status by exchanging their sexual favors for a tool, a piece of cloth, or an iron nail.

The Polynesians paid dearly for their openness. At least 300,000 people, and possibly as many as 800,000, lived on the Hawaiian islands when Captain Cook first sighted them (today the total population of the state is about 1.2 million). Over the course of the next century, diseases introduced by Europeans reduced the native population to fewer than 50,000. By the time the painter Paul Gauguin journeyed to the Pacific in

1891, the innocence that Europeans had perceived among the Polynesians was gone. "The natives, having nothing, nothing at all to do, think of one thing only, drinking," he wrote. "Day by day the race vanishes, decimated by the European diseases. . . . There is so much prostitution that it does not exist. . . . One only knows a thing by its contrary, and its contrary does not exist." The women in Gauguin's paintings are beautiful yet defeated, without hope, lost in a vision of the past.

Today visitors to Maui land on a runway just downwind from the shore where Captain Cook battled the surf eleven generations ago. Once out of the airport, they encounter what is probably the most genetically mixed population in the world. To the genes of Captain Cook's sailors and the native Polynesians has been added the DNA of European missionaries, Mexican cowboys, African American soldiers, and plantation workers from throughout Asia and Europe. This intense mixing of DNA has produced a population of strikingly beautiful people. Miss Universe of 1997 and Miss America of 2001 were both from Hawaii. The former, Brook Mahealani Lee, is a classic Hawaiian blend. Her ancestors are Korean and Hawaiian, Chinese and European.

Bernie Adair—who was selling candles at a swap meet in Kahului, Maui's largest town, when I met her—told me that her family's history was typical. Adair, whose ancestors came to Hawaii from the Philippines, married a Portuguese man in the 1960s. In the 1980s their daughter Marlene married a man of mixed Hawaiian, Chinese, and Portuguese descent. Adair's granddaughter Carly, peeking shyly at me from under a folding table, therefore embodies four different ethnicities. "These children have grandparents with so many different nationalities you can't tell what they are," Adair said.

> **Hawaii's high rates of intermarriage have fascinated academics for decades.**

Almost half the people who live in Hawaii today are of "mixed" ancestry. What it means to be mixed is not at all obvious genetically, but for official purposes it means that a person's ancestors fall into more than one of the four "racial" categories identified on U.S. census forms: black, white, Native American, and Asian or Pacific Islander. Intermarriage is a cumulative process, so once an individual of mixed ancestry is born, all of that person's descendants also will be mixed. As intermarriage continues in Hawaii—and already almost half of all marriages are between couples of different or mixed ethnicities—the number of people who will be able to call themselves pure Japanese, or pure Hawaiian, or pure white (*haole* in Hawaiian), will steadily decline.

Hawaii's high rates of intermarriage have fascinated academics for decades. The University of Hawaii sociologist Romanzo Adams wrote an article titled "Hawai'i as a Racial Melting Pot" in 1926, and many scholars since then have extolled Hawaii as a model of ethnic and racial harmony. The researchers have always been a bit vague about the reasons for all this intermarriage; explanations have ranged from the benign climate to the "aloha spirit" of the Native Hawaiians. But their lack of analytic rigor hasn't damped their enthusiasm. One of the goals of the former Center for Research on Ethnic Relations at the University of Hawaii was "to determine why ethnic harmony exists in Hawai'i" and "to export principles of ethnic harmony to the mainland and the world."

The rest of the United States has a smaller percentage of mixed marriages than does Hawaii. But given recent trends, one might wonder if the country as a whole is headed down a road Hawaii took long ago. According to the 2000 census, one in twenty children under the age of eighteen in the United States is mixed, in that their parents fall into more than one racial category. Between the 1990 and 2000 censuses, the number of interracial couples quadrupled. This number—about 1.5 million of 55 million married couples—is not yet high, but because of kinship ties, American families are already much more mixed than they look. Demographer Joshua Goldstein of Princeton University has calculated that about 20 percent of Americans are already in extended families with someone from a different racial group—that is, they or their parents, uncles and aunts, siblings, or children have married someone classified as a member of a different race.

The rapid growth of interracial marriages in the United States and elsewhere   10 marks a new phase in the genetic history of humanity. Since the appearance of modern humans in Africa more than 100,000 years ago, human groups have differentiated in appearance as they have expanded across the globe and have undergone some measure of reproductive isolation. This differentiation has always been limited by the recentness of our common ancestry and by the powerful tendency of groups to mix over time. Still, many human populations have remained sufficiently separate to develop and retain the distinctive physical characteristics we recognize today.

In Hawaii this process is occurring in reverse. It's as if a videotape of our species' history were being played backward at a fantastically rapid speed. Physical distinctions that took thousands of generations to produce are being wiped clean with a few generations of intermarriage.

The vision of the future conjured up by intermarriage in Hawaii can be seductive. When everyone is marrying everyone else, when the ethnic affiliation of most people can no longer be ascertained at a glance, one imagines that ethnic and racial tensions would diminish. But spending some time in Hawaii shows that the future will not be that simple. Despite the high rate of intermarriage here, ethnic and racial tensions haven't really disappeared. They have changed into something else, something less threatening, perhaps, but still divisive. Hawaii may well be a harbinger of a racially mixed future. But it won't be the future many people expect.

Many of the harshest conflicts in the world today are between people who are physically indistinguishable. If someone took a roomful of Palestinians and Israelis from the Middle East, or of Serbs and Albanians from the Balkans, or of Catholics and Protestants from Ireland, or of Muslims and Hindus from northern India, or of Dayaks and Madurese from Indonesia, gave them all identical outfits and haircuts, and forbade them to speak or gesture, no one could distinguish the members of the other group—at least not to the point of being willing to shoot them. The antagonists in these conflicts have different ethnicities, but they have been so closely linked biologically throughout history that they have not developed marked physical differences.

Yet one of the most perverse dimensions of ethnic thinking is the "racialization" of culture—the tendency to think of another people as not just culturally but genetically distinct. In the Yugoslavian war, the Croats caricatured their Serbian opponents as tall and blond, while the Serbs disparaged the darker hair and skin of the Croats—even though these traits are thoroughly intermixed between the two groups. During World War II the countries of Europe fiercely stereotyped the physical attributes of their enemies, despite a history of intermarriage and migration that has scrambled physical characteristics throughout the continent. In Africa the warring Tutsis and Hutus often call attention to the physical differences of their antagonists, but most observers have trouble distinguishing individual members of the two groups solely on the basis of appearance.

The flip side of this biological stereotyping is the elevation of one's own ancestry. The Nazis were the most notorious believers in the purity of their past, but many other groups have similar beliefs. They proclaim themselves to be descended from ancient tribes of noble warriors, or from prominent families in the distant past, or even from famous individuals.

Genetics research has revealed the flaw inherent in any such belief. Every group is a mixture of many previous groups, a fleeting collection of genetic variants drawn from a shared genetic legacy. The Polynesian colonizers of the Hawaiian archipelago are a good example. In 1795 the German anatomist J. F. Blumenbach proposed that the "Malays"—a collection of peoples, including the Polynesians, from southeastern Asia and Oceania—were one of the five races of humanity, in addition to Africans, Caucasians, Mongoloids, and Native Americans. But all of these groups (to the extent that they can be defined) are genetic composites of previous groups. In the case of the Polynesians, this mixing was part of the spread of humans into the Pacific. The last major part of the world to be occupied by humans was Remote Oceania, the widely separated islands scattered in a broad crescent from Hawaii to New Zealand. Before that, humans

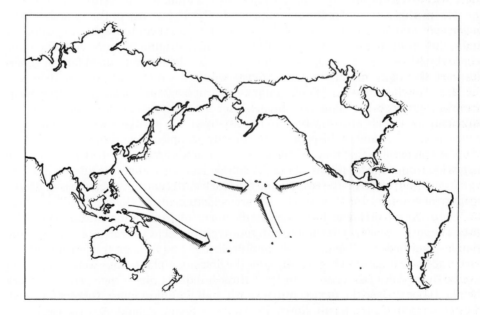

The Polynesian inhabitants of Hawaii are descended from people who lived both in southeastern Asia and in Melanesia, which includes New Guinea and nearby islands. The Polynesians migrated first to the South Pacific islands of Fiji, Tonga, and Samoa, with later migrations taking their descendants from the Marquesas islands to Hawaii. More recent migrants have included people from Asia, the Americas, and Europe.

had been living only in Near Oceania, which includes Australia, Papua New Guinea, and the Bismarck Archipelago. The humans who settled these regions were adept at short ocean crossings, but they never developed the kinds of boats or navigation skills needed to sail hundreds of miles to Fiji, Samoa, and beyond.

Then, about 6,000 years ago, rice and millet agriculture made the leap across the Formosa Strait from the mainland of southeastern Asia to Taiwan. From there, agriculture began to spread, island by island, to the south and southeast. With it came two important cultural innovations. The first was the Austronesian language family, which eventually spread halfway around the world, from Madagascar to Easter Island. The second was a suite of new technologies—pottery, woodworking implements, and eventually the outrigger canoe* and ways of using the stars to navigate across large expanses of open water. Archaeological evidence shows that people first reached the previously uninhabited island of Fiji about 3,000 years ago. They sailed to Easter Island, their farthest point east, in about AD 300 and to New Zealand, their farthest point south, in about 800.

One hypothesis, known as the express-train model of Polynesian origins, claims that both the knowledge of agriculture and Austronesian languages were carried into the Pacific by people descended almost exclusively from the first farmers who set sail from Taiwan. But genetic studies have revealed a much more complex picture. Mitochondrial and Y-chromosome haplotypes† among today's Polynesians show that there was extensive mixing of peoples in Near Oceania, which eventually produced the groups that set sail for the remote islands. Though many of the mitochondrial haplotypes and Y chromosomes of the Polynesians do seem to have come from the mainland of southeastern Asia and Taiwan, others originated in New Guinea and its nearby islands—a geographic region known as Melanesia (named for the generally dark skin of its inhabitants). Geneticists Manfred Kayser and Mark Stoneking of the Max Planck Institute for Evolutionary Anthropology in Leipzig have dubbed the resulting synthesis the "slow-boat model." According to this model, today's Polynesians can trace their ancestry both to the Austronesian speakers who moved out of southeastern Asia and to the people who already occupied Melanesia.

The Polynesians first reached the Hawaiian islands around AD 400, probably in a migration from the Marquesas islands. A subsequent wave of people migrated to Hawaii from Tahiti between the twelfth and the fourteenth century. Then the islands saw no more newcomers until Captain Cook's arrival four centuries later.

The discovery of Hawaii by Europeans did not result in an immediate influx of colo- 20 nists. The early decades of the nineteenth century brought just a trickle of settlers to the islands—washed-up sailors, retired captains, British and Russian traders, missionaries. Large-scale migration began only after the first sugar plantations were established around the middle of the century. In 1852, three hundred Chinese men arrived to work the plantations. Over the next century nearly half a million more workers followed. They came from China, Japan, Korea, Puerto Rico, Spain, Poland, Austria, Germany,

* Outrigger canoe: Canoe with a side floatation unit for increased stability [Ed.].
† Mitochondrial and Y-chromosome haplotypes: Genetic information that can be used to trace ancestry through the mother's and father's lineage [Ed.].

Norway, and Russia. Some of these groups have long since disappeared, blending into the genetic background. Others still have a significant ethnic presence on the islands.

A few miles from the Honolulu airport is a vivid reminder of those times. Hawaii's Plantation Village is one of the few tourist attractions designed as much for the locals as for mainlanders. It meticulously recreates a camp town of the type that once dotted the islands, housing the workers who toiled each day in the sugar and pineapple fields. Each house along the main avenue reflects the ethnicity of the workers who lived there: A large bread oven sits next to the Portuguese house, rice cookers dominate the kitchen of the Chinese house, crucifixes adorn the walls of the Puerto Rican house. A Japanese shrine is a few doors away from the Chinese society building. Down the hill by the taro* fields is a *dohyo*, a sumo ring, where the workers wrestled every Sunday afternoon.

Mike Hama showed me around the day I was there. The descendant of Japanese, German, Hawaiian, and Irish grandparents, Hama grew up on a plantation camp in the 1940s. "Kids of all different nationalities played together in these camps," he told me. "We didn't know we were different." They communicated using a pidgin that combined words from many languages. The German kids taught the other kids to polka in the camp social halls. The Japanese kids taught their friends sumo wrestling. When the Japanese emperor visited Hawaii after World War II, according to a widely told if hard-to-verify story, he was so impressed to see wrestlers of all different nationalities in the *dohyo* that when he returned to Japan he opened the country's sumo rings to foreigners.

When Hama was eighteen, he joined the military and was stationed in California. "That was a real awakening for me," he recalls. "For the first time I saw the bigotry that was going on outside Hawaii." He moved back to Hawaii as soon as he could and married a woman of mixed ancestry. His four daughters think of themselves as nothing other than local Hawaiians.

The camp towns disappeared decades ago in Hawaii, yet they have left a remarkable legacy. Large-scale segregation in housing remains rare on the islands. People of all ethnic backgrounds live side by side, just as they did in the camp towns. The only people who live in ghettos are the soldiers on military bases and wealthy haoles who wall themselves off in gated communities. Because neighborhoods are integrated in Hawaii, so are most of the schools. Children of different ethnicities continue to grow up together and marry, just as they did in the camps.

Integrated neighborhoods, integrated schools, high rates of intermarriage — the islands sound as if they should be a racial paradise. But there's actually a fair amount of prejudice here. It pops up in novels, politics, the spiels of standup comics. And it's especially prominent in everyday conversation — "talk stink" is the pidgin term for disrespecting another group. ²⁵

Some of the prejudice is directed toward haoles, who continue to occupy many of the positions of social and economic prominence on the islands (though their days as plantation overlords are long gone). Nonwhites label haoles as cold, self-serving, arrogant, meddling, loud, and even that old stereotype — smelly (because, it is held,

---

* Taro: Common name for several varieties of a root vegetable [Ed.].

they still do not bathe every day). White kids say they'll get beat up if they venture onto certain nonwhite beaches. Occasionally a rumor sweeps through a school about an upcoming "Kill a Haole" day. The rumors are a joke meant to shock the prevailing sensibilities. But one would not expect such a joke where racial tensions are low.

Other groups come in for similarly rough treatment. The Japanese are derided as clannish and power-hungry, the Filipinos as ignorant and underhanded, the Hawaiians as fat, lazy, and fun-loving. And, as is true of stereotypes everywhere, the objects of them have a tendency to reinforce them, either by too vigorously denying or too easily repeating them.

"Intermarriage may indicate tolerance," says Jonathan Okamura, an anthropologist at the University of Hawaii, "but it doesn't mean we have an egalitarian society on a larger scale." Though he calls his viewpoint a "minority position," Okamura holds that racial and ethnic prejudice is deeply ingrained in the institutional structures of everyday life in Hawaii. For example, the integration of the public schools is deceptive, he says. Well-off haoles, Chinese, and Japanese send their children to private schools, and the public schools are underfunded. "We've created a two-tiered system that makes inequality increasingly worse rather than better," says Okamura. Meanwhile the rapid growth of the tourism industry in Hawaii has shut off many traditional routes to economic betterment. Tourism produces mostly low-paying jobs in sales, service, and construction, Okamura points out, so people have few opportunities to move up career ladders.

Of course, talented and lucky individuals still get ahead. "Students with parents who didn't go to college come to the university and do well—that happens all the time," Okamura says. "But it doesn't happen enough to advance socioeconomically disadvantaged groups in society."

Several ethnic groups occupy the lower end of the socioeconomic scale, but one in particular stands out: the people descended from the island's original inhabitants. Native Hawaiians have the lowest incomes and highest unemployment rates of any ethnic group. They have the most health problems and the shortest life expectancy. They are the least likely to go to college and the most likely to be incarcerated.

Then again, applying statistics like these to a group as large and diverse as Native Hawaiians is inevitably misleading. Individuals with some Hawaiian ancestry make up a fifth of the population in Hawaii. Some are successful; some are not. Some are consumed by native issues; others pay them no mind. And Native Hawaiians are much less marginalized in Hawaii than are, for example, Native Americans in the rest of the United States. Hawaiian words, names, and outlooks have seeped into everyday life on the islands, producing a cultural amalgam that is one of the state's distinct attractions.

Native Hawaiians should not be seen as simply another ethnic group, the leaders of their community point out. Other cultures have roots elsewhere; people of Japanese, German, or Samoan ancestry can draw from the traditions of an ancestral homeland to sustain an ethnic heritage. If the culture of the Native Hawaiians disappears, it will be gone forever. Greater recognition of the value and fragility of this culture has led to a resurgence of interest in the Hawaiian past. Schools with Hawaiian language immersion programs have sprung up around the islands to supplement the English that children speak at home. Traditional forms of Hawaiian dance, music, canoeing, and religion all have undergone revivals.

This Hawaiian Renaissance also has had a political dimension. For the past several decades a sovereignty movement has been building among Native Hawaiians that seeks some measure of political autonomy and control over the lands that the U.S. government seized from the Hawaiian monarchy at the end of the nineteenth century. Reflecting the diversity of the native population, several sovereignty organizations have carried out a sometimes unseemly struggle over strategies and goals. One radical faction advocates the complete independence of the islands from the United States. More moderate groups have called for the establishment of a Native Hawaiian nation modeled on the Indian tribes on the mainland. Native Hawaiians would have their own government, but it would operate within existing federal and state frameworks, and its citizens would remain Americans.

Native Hawaiian sovereignty faces many hurdles, and it is premature to harp on exactly how it would work. But whenever the topic comes up in discussion, a question quickly surfaces: Exactly who is a Native Hawaiian? "Pure" Hawaiians with no non-Hawaiian ancestors probably number just a few thousand. Many Native Hawaiians undoubtedly have a preponderance

Exactly who is a Native Hawaiian?

of Hawaiian ancestors, but no clear line separates natives from nonnatives. Some people who call themselves Native Hawaiians probably have little DNA from Polynesian ancestors.

Past legislation has waffled on this issue. Some laws define Native Hawaiians as people who can trace at least half their ancestry to people living in Hawaii before the arrival of Captain Cook. Others define as Hawaiian anyone who has even a single precontact Hawaiian ancestor. These distinctions are highly contentious for political and economic as well as cultural reasons. Many state laws restrict housing subsidies, scholarships, economic development grants, and other benefits specifically to Native Hawaiians.

As the study of genetics and history has progressed, an obvious idea has arisen. Maybe science could resolve the issue. Maybe a genetic marker could be found that occurs only in people descended from the aboriginal inhabitants of Hawaii. Then anyone with that marker could be considered a Native Hawaiian.

No one is better qualified to judge this idea than Rebecca Cann, a professor of genetics at the University of Hawaii. Cann was the young graduate student at the University of California at Berkeley who, with Mark Stoneking, did much of the work that led to the unveiling of mitochondrial Eve.* She haunted hospital delivery rooms to obtain mitochondrion-rich placentas, which at that time was the only way to get enough mitochondrial DNA to sequence. She ran gels and compared nucleotides. Her faculty adviser, Allan Wilson, landed mitochondrial Eve on the cover of *Newsweek*, but Cann did the footwork.

She moved to Hawaii even before mitochondrial Eve made headlines, responding to an ad in *Science* magazine for a job. She's been here ever since, though her flat

---

* Mitochondrial Eve: A term in genetics for the maternal ancestor of every human now alive. This woman is estimated to have lived about 200,000 years ago in East Africa [Ed.].

American accent still betrays a childhood spent in Iowa. She met me at the door of her office, in the foothills above Honolulu, dressed in sandals and a patterned Hawaiian dress. "I think we correctly anticipated many of the applications and potential problems of this research," she said, "right down to people wanting to clone Elvis from a handkerchief he'd used to wipe his brow. What we didn't understand was the degree to which religious and cultural beliefs would dictate attitudes toward genetic materials. In Hawaii, for instance, there's a very strong belief in *mana*, in the power of the spirit, which is contained in the remains of a person's ancestors. The absolute disgust that many people have toward the desecration of a grave—that was a cultural eye-opener for me."

Despite the occasional cultural difficulties, Cann has continued her study of human genetics in Hawaii and has played an important role in piecing together the prehistory of the Pacific. By comparing the mitochondrial DNA sequences of people on various islands, she has traced the gradual eastward spread of modern humans from southeastern Asia and Melanesia. She has discovered that men and women had different migration patterns into the Pacific and has even detected tantalizing evidence, still unconfirmed, of genetic contacts between Pacific Islanders and South Americans. "I'm convinced that our history is written in our DNA," she told me.

Yet she cautioned against using genetics to determine ethnicity. "I get people coming up to me all the time and saying, 'Can you prove that I'm a Hawaiian?'" She can't, she said, at least not with a high degree of certainty. A given individual might have a mitochondrial haplotype that is more common among Native Hawaiians. But the ancestors of the aboriginal Hawaiians also gave rise to other Pacific populations, so a mitochondrial sequence characteristic of Native Hawaiians could have come from a Samoan or Filipino ancestor.

Also, a person's mitochondrial DNA is not necessarily an accurate indication of ancestry. The only way for a person to have mitochondrial DNA from a woman who lived in Hawaii before the arrival of Captain Cook is for that person to have an unbroken line of grandmothers dating back to that woman. But because groups have mixed so much in Hawaii, mitochondrial lineages have become thoroughly tangled. People who think of themselves as Native Hawaiian could easily have had non-Hawaiian female ancestors sometime in the past eleven generations, which would have given them mitochondrial DNA from another part of the world.

These genetic exchanges are also common elsewhere in the world, even in populations that think of themselves as less mixed. Most native Europeans, for example, have mitochondrial DNA characteristic of that part of the world. But some have mitochondrial DNA from elsewhere—southern Africa, or eastern Asia, or even Polynesia—brought to Europe over the millennia by female immigrants. The British matron who has a mitochondrial haplotype found most often in southern Africans is not an African, just as the Native Hawaiian with mitochondrial DNA from a German great-great-grandmother does not automatically become German.

This confusion of genetic and cultural identities becomes even greater with the Y chromosome, given the ease with which that chromosome can insert itself into a genealogy. Most of the early migrants to Hawaii, for example, were males, especially the plantation workers. Those males mated with native women more often than native men mated with immigrant women, so nonnative Y chromosomes are now more common in mixed populations than nonnative mitochondrial DNA. In some populations in South America, virtually all the Y chromosomes are from Europe and all the mitochondrial DNA is from indigenous groups.

The mixing of genes can cause great consternation, but it is the inevitable consequence of our genetic history. Several years ago a geneticist in Washington, D.C., began offering to identify the homelands of the mitochondrial DNA and Y chromosomes of African Americans. The service foundered for several reasons, but one was that 30 percent of the Y chromosomes in African American males come from European ancestors.

Within a few years geneticists will be able to use DNA sequences from all the chromosomes to trace ancestry. But these histories will be just as convoluted as those of mitochondrial DNA and the Y. Granted, geneticists will be able to make statistical assessments. They will be able to say, for instance, that a given person has such and such a probability of descent from a Native Hawaiian population, and in some cases the probability will be very high. But probabilities don't convey the cold, hard certainties that people want in their genealogies.

Beyond the purely genetic considerations are the social ones. When children are adopted from one group into another, they become a member of that group socially, yet their haplotypes and those of their descendants can differ from the group norm. Rape is another way in which the genetic variants of groups mix. And sometimes people from one group make a conscious decision to join another and are gladly accepted, despite their different genetic histories.

"I get nervous when people start talking about using genetic markers to prove ethnicity," Cann told me. "I don't believe that biology is destiny. Allowing yourself to be defined personally by whatever your DNA sequence is, that's insane. But that's exactly what some people are going to be tempted to do."

When geneticists look at our DNA, they do not see a world of rigidly divided groups each going its own way. They see something much more fluid and ambiguous—something more like the social structures that have emerged in Hawaii as intermarriage has accelerated.

The most remarkable aspect of ethnicity in Hawaii is its loose relation to biology. Many people have considerable latitude in choosing their ethnic affiliations. Those of mixed ancestry can associate with the ethnicity of a parent, a grandparent, or a more distant ancestor. They can partition their ethnic affiliations: They can be Chinese with their Chinese relatives; Native Hawaiian with their native kin; and just plain local with their buddies. The community of descent that a person associates with has become more like a professional or religious affiliation, a connection over which a person has some measure of control.

People whose ancestors are from a single ethnic group have fewer options, but they, too, can partake of at least some of Hawaii's ethnic flexibility. Young whites, for example, sometimes try to pass themselves off as mixed by maintaining an especially dark tan. Among many young people, dating someone from a different ethnic group is a social asset rather than a liability, in part because of the doors it opens to other communities. Many prospective students at the University of Hawaii simply mark "mixed" in describing their ethnicity on application forms, even if both parents have the same

ethnic background. "My students say they don't want to be pigeonholed," says Okamura. "That way they can identify with different groups."

Hawaii's high rates of intermarriage also contribute greatly to the islands' ethnic
flux. Ethnicity is not defined just by who one's ancestors were. It also is defined pro-
spectively—by the group into which one is expected to marry. For most young people
in Hawaii, the pool of marriageable partners encompasses the entire population. Relations among groups are inevitably less fractious when their members view each other
as potential mates.

Of course, ethnic and even "racial" groups still exist in Hawaii, and they will for
a long time. Despite the rapid growth of intermarriage in Hawaii and elsewhere, the
mixing of peoples takes generations, not a few years or even decades. Most people
around the world still choose marriage partners who would be classified as members
of the same "race." In many parts of the world—the American Midwest, China, Iceland—few other options are available. Five hundred years from now, unless human
societies undergo drastic changes, Asians, Africans, and Europeans still will be physically distinguishable.

But the social effects of intermarriage are much more immediate than are the biological effects. Socially, intermarriage can quickly undermine the idea that culture
has biological roots. When a substantial number of mixed individuals demonstrate, by
their very existence, that choices are possible, that biology is not destiny, the barriers
between groups become more permeable. Ethnicity in Hawaii, for example, seems far
less stark and categorical than it does in the rest of the United States. The people of Hawaii recognize overlaps and exceptions. They are more willing to accept the haole who
claims to have non-European ancestors or the Native Hawaiian who affiliates with
Filipinos. It's true that people talk about the differences among groups all the time, but
even talking about these differences, rather than rigidly ignoring them, makes them
seem less daunting. Expressions of social prejudice in Hawaii are more like a form of
social banter, like a husband and wife picking at each other's faults.

The logical endpoint of this perspective is a world in which people are free to
choose their ethnicity regardless of their ancestry. Ethnicity is not yet *entirely* voluntary in Hawaii, but in many respects the islands are headed in that direction. State law,
for example, is gradually coming to define a Native Hawaiian as anyone with a single
Hawaiian ancestor. But at that point ethnicity becomes untethered from biology—it is
instead a cultural, political, or historical distinction. People are no longer who they say
they are because of some mysterious biological essence. They have chosen the group
with which they want to affiliate.

Genetically, this view of ethnicity makes perfect sense. Our DNA is too tightly   55
interconnected to use biology to justify what are essentially social distinctions. Our
preferences, character, and abilities are not determined by the biological history of
our ancestors. They depend on our individual attributes, experiences, and choices. As
this inescapable conclusion becomes more widely held, our genetic histories inevitably
will become less and less important. When we look at another person, we won't think
Asian, black, or white. We'll just think: person.

In his novel *Siddhartha*, Hermann Hesse tells the story of a young man in ancient India,
a disciple of an inspired teacher, who sets out to find the reality beneath the world of

appearance. After years of study and wandering, Siddhartha becomes a ferryman, learning from his predecessor how to listen to the voices in the passing river. One day a childhood friend named Govinda comes to the river. Siddhartha and Govinda have a long conversation about the interdependence of illusion and truth, about the existence of the past and future in the present, about the need not just to think about the world but to love it. Finally Govinda asks Siddhartha how he has achieved such peace in his life. Siddhartha replies, "Kiss me on the forehead, Govinda." Govinda is surprised by the request, but out of respect for his friend he complies. When he touches Siddhartha's forehead with his lips, he has a wondrous vision:

> He no longer saw the face of his friend Siddhartha. Instead he saw other faces, many faces, a long series, a continuous stream of faces—hundreds, thousands, which all came and disappeared and yet all seemed to be there at the same time, which all continually changed and renewed themselves and which were all yet Siddhartha. . . . He saw the face of a newly born child, red and full of wrinkles, ready to cry. He saw the face of a murderer. . . . He saw the naked bodies of men and women in the postures and transports of passionate love. . . . Each one was mortal, a passionate, painful example of all that is transitory. Yet none of them died, they only changed, were always reborn, continually had a new face; only time stood between one face and another.

I began this book [*Mapping Human History*] by calling attention to the different appearances of human beings. I conclude it now by calling attention to the opposite. Throughout human history, groups have wondered how they are related to one another. The study of genetics has now revealed that we all are linked: the Bushmen hunting antelope, the mixed-race people of South Africa, the African Americans descended from slaves, the Samaritans on their mountain stronghold, the Jewish populations scattered around the world, the Han Chinese a billion strong, the descendants of European settlers who colonized the New World, the Native Hawaiians who look to a cherished past. We are members of a single human family, the products of genetic necessity and chance, borne ceaselessly into an unknown future.

Exploring Context

1. Read the U.S. Census Bureau's explanation of the racial categories used in the census taken every ten years at census.gov/population/race. How do these categories relate to Olson's argument? Relate your response to your work on the persistence of race from Question 3 of Questions for Critical Reading.

2. Visit Hawaii's official state government website at hawaii.gov and then visit the official Hawaii tourism website at gohawaii.com. How is race represented on these sites? What races do you see in the images? Is the representation of race the same for residents and for tourists? Why might there be differences? Use the definition of race you developed in Question 2 of Questions for Critical Reading to support your position.

3. One place that race persists in Hawaii, according to Olson, is in schools. Locate websites for some schools in Hawaii. Do you find evidence to support Olson's argument or to complicate it?

Questions for Connecting

1. If Olson is right in discounting the genetic basis of race, why do racial categories persist? Does Leslie Savan's analysis of the economic value of pop talk and its relation to black talk in "What's Black, Then White, and Said All Over?" (p. 435) offer some reasons? Apply your analysis of race from Question 3 of Questions for Critical Reading in making your response.

2. Using your definition of the term "community of descent" from Question 1 of Questions for Critical Reading as well as Olson's other concepts, explain the widespread popularity of quinces as demonstrated by Julia Alvarez in "Selections from *Once Upon a Quinceañera*" (p. 46). How does the quinceañera reflect a "community of descent"? Is retroculturation a hindrance to the end of race?

3. Does Hawaii offer a model for the new civil rights that Kenji Yoshino advocates in "Preface" and "The New Civil Rights" (p. 552)? Given the end of race, should we pursue a liberty or an equality paradigm?

Language Matters

1. Choose a key quotation from Olson. Revise it to make it less effective but still grammatically correct. Would making it a question blunt its force? What about changing it to passive voice? Draw some general conclusions from this experiment. What makes a sentence effective?

2. Locate materials in a reference book or online on writing a résumé and then make a résumé for this essay. What would be this essay's "career objective"? What would be its "experience"? Whom would it list for references?

3. How would you "grade" Olson's essay? In small groups, develop a set of grading criteria and then apply those criteria to Olson's text. What does your group value in writing? What does this class value in writing?

Assignments for Writing

1. Can there be an end to race? Engage Olson's essay by writing a paper in which you examine the possibility of an end to race. Why does race persist? Can or should we move beyond concepts of race? Would something replace the idea of race, or has something replaced it already? You may want to draw on your responses to the Questions for Critical Reading as well as your examination of the census from Question 1 of Exploring Context in making your argument.

2. Olson's argument is based in part on advances in genetic technologies. Write a paper in which you evaluate the relationship between technology and race. Consider: Is race itself a kind of technology? Can technology move us beyond race? You may want to use the definition of race you developed in Question 2 of Questions for Critical Reading in making your argument.

3. Race is not the only factor in determining group identity; Olson discusses communities of descent as well. Using Olson's essay, write a paper in which you determine the relationship between race and cultural identity. Does the history of a particular race dictate its importance as a cultural identity? Can a particular race have ownership over its cultural aspects? Can an individual choose a racial or cultural identity? In making your argument, you may want to use the definition of "communities of descent" that you developed in Questions for Critical Reading.

MARSHALL POE

Marshall Poe, a historian who has published numerous books on Russian and Soviet history and has held fellowships at Harvard and Columbia Universities, is currently associate professor and director of undergraduate studies in the history department at the University of Iowa. In addition to his work in history, Poe is also interested in the intersections of technology, publishing, and memory. As a journalist, Poe worked for the *Atlantic*, where he published the following article, "The Hive," in September 2006.

"The Hive" tells a number of stories about Wikipedia (wikipedia.org), the collaboratively written and edited online encyclopedia, in order to tell a larger story about collaborative knowledge in general. Poe details his embarrassing attempt to add his own biography to the site's archives, the early role-playing game and discussion-board lives of the site's founders, and the fate of Wikipedia's predecessor. He also documents the site's birth pangs, revealing the influences and motivating factors behind its rapid growth and rapidly growing importance.

"Wikipedia," Poe claims, "has the potential to be the greatest effort in collaborative knowledge gathering the world has ever known, and it may well be the greatest effort in voluntary collaboration of any kind" (p. 349). The epistemological questions offered by "The Hive" go beyond merely what people know to whether collective knowledge is valid, what motivates people to share their knowledge, and what can be gained from what Poe calls "the wisdom-of-crowds scheme" (p. 353).

Each of you has the opportunity to contribute or edit entries in Wikipedia. But what is the ultimate value of Wikipedia's collective knowledge, and what are the keys to Wikipedia's success?

▶ TAGS: *technology, collaboration, feedback, community, group, diplomacy, education*

Questions for Critical Reading

1. You've probably used Wikipedia at some point. What do you think makes Wikipedia so successful? Read Poe's text to locate quotations that demonstrate the key qualities of Wikipedia's success.

2. In his essay, Poe examines top-down and bottom-up systems. As you read, mark passages that show the advantages of each system. Is one inherently better than the other? In what contexts does each work best?

3. Poe spends time discussing the conflict between Cunc and Larry Sanger. Is such conflict beneficial or detrimental to the kind of system Wikipedia represents? Locate quotations from Poe's text that support your position.

The Hive

Several months ago, I discovered that I was being "considered for deletion." Or rather, the entry on me in the Internet behemoth that is Wikipedia was.

For those of you who are (as uncharitable Wikipedians sometimes say) "clueless newbies," Wikipedia is an online encyclopedia. But it is like no encyclopedia Diderot* could have imagined. Instead of relying on experts to write articles according to their expertise, Wikipedia lets anyone write about anything. You, I, and any wired-up fool can add entries, change entries, even propose that entries be deleted. For reasons I'd rather not share outside of therapy, I created a one-line biographical entry on "Marshall Poe." It didn't take long for my tiny article to come to the attention of Wikipedia's self-appointed guardians. Within a week, a very active—and by most accounts responsible—Scottish Wikipedian named "Alai" decided that ... well, that I wasn't worth knowing about. Why? "No real evidence of notability," Alai cruelly but accurately wrote, "beyond the proverbial average college professor."

Wikipedia has the potential to be the greatest effort in collaborative knowledge gathering the world has ever known, and it may well be the greatest effort in voluntary collaboration of any kind. The English-language version alone has more than a million entries.† It is consistently ranked among the most visited Web sites in the world. A quarter century ago it was inconceivable that a legion of unpaid, unorganized amateurs scattered about the globe could create anything of value, let alone what may one day be the most comprehensive repository of knowledge in human history. Back then we knew that people do not work for free; or if they do work for free, they do a poor job; and if they work for free in large numbers, the result is a muddle. Jimmy Wales and Larry Sanger knew all this when they began an online encyclopedia in 1999. Now, just seven years later, everyone knows different.

The Moderator

Jimmy Wales does not fit the profile of an Internet revolutionary. He was born in 1966 and raised in modest circumstances in Huntsville, Alabama. Wales majored in finance at Auburn, and after completing his degree enrolled in a graduate program at the University of Alabama. It was there that he developed a passion for the Internet. His entry point was typical for the nerdy set of his generation: fantasy games.

In 1974, Gary Gygax and Dave Arneson, two gamers who had obviously read *The Lord of the Rings*, invented the tabletop role-playing game Dungeons & Dragons. The game spread largely through networks of teenage boys, and by 1979, the year the classic *Dungeon Master's Guide* was published, it seemed that every youth who couldn't get a date was rolling the storied twenty-sided die in a shag-carpeted den. Meanwhile, a more electronically inclined crowd at the University of Illinois at Urbana-Champaign was experimenting with moving fantasy play from the basement to a computer network.

5

---

* Diderot: Denis Diderot (1713–1784), French philosopher and chief editor of an innovative encyclopedia that was famous for representing Enlightenment thought [Ed.].
† More than a million entries: As of 2012, it has nearly 3.9 million articles in English and approximately 19 million articles in 270 other languages [Ed.].

The fruit of their labors was the unfortunately named MUD (Multi-User Dungeon). Allowing masses of players to create virtual fantasy worlds, MUDs garnered a large audience in the 1980s and 1990s under names like Zork, Myst, and Scepter of Goth. (MUDs came to be known as "Multi-Undergraduate Destroyers" for their tendency to divert college students from their studies.)

Wales began to play MUDs at Alabama in the late 1980s. It was in this context that he first encountered the power of networked computers to facilitate voluntary cooperation on a large scale. He did not, however, set up house in these fantasy worlds, nor did he show any evidence of wanting to begin a career in high tech. He completed a degree in finance at Auburn, received a master's in finance at the University of Alabama, and then pursued a Ph.D. in finance at Indiana University. He was interested, it would seem, in finance. In 1994, he quit his doctoral program and moved to Chicago to take a job as an options trader. There he made (as he has repeatedly said) "enough."

> **Wales is of a thoughtful cast of mind.**

Wales is of a thoughtful cast of mind. He was a frequent contributor to the philosophical "discussion lists" (the first popular online discussion forums) that emerged in the late '80s as e-mail spread through the humanities. His particular passion was objectivism, the philosophical system developed by Ayn Rand. In 1989, he initiated the Ayn Rand Philosophy Discussion List and served as moderator—the person who invites and edits e-mails from subscribers. Though discussion lists were not new among the technorati in the 1980s, they were unfamiliar territory for most academics. In the oak-paneled seminar room, everyone had always been careful to behave properly—the chairman sat at the head of the table, and everyone spoke in turn and stuck to the topic. E-mail lists were something altogether different. Unrestrained by convention and cloaked by anonymity, participants could behave very badly without fear of real consequences. The term for such poor comportment—*flaming*—became one of the first bits of net jargon to enter common usage.

Wales had a careful moderation style:

> First, I will frown—very much—on any flaming of any kind whatsoever. . . . Second, I impose no restrictions on membership based on my own idea of what objectivism really is. . . . Third, I hope that the list will be more "academic" than some of the others, and tend toward discussions of technical details of epistemology. . . . Fourth, I have chosen a "middle-ground" method of moderation, a sort of behind-the-scenes prodding.

Wales was an advocate of what is generically termed "openness" online. An "open" online community is one with few restrictions on membership or posting—everyone is welcome, and anyone can say anything as long as it's generally on point and doesn't include gratuitous ad hominem* attacks. Openness fit not only Wales's idea of objectivism, with its emphasis on reason and rejection of force, but also his mild personality. He doesn't like to fight. He would rather suffer fools in silence,

---

* Ad hominem: Latin for "to the man" or "to the person." A personal attack substituting for logical argument, it is considered a fallacy, a form of faulty reasoning [Ed.].

waiting for them to talk themselves out, than confront them. This patience would serve Wales well in the years to come.

Top-Down and Bottom-Up

In the mid-1990s, the great dream of Internet entrepreneurs was to create *the* entry point on the Web. "Portals," as they were called, would provide everything: e-mail, news, entertainment, and, most important, the tools to help users find what they wanted on the Web. As Google later showed, if you build the best "finding aid," you'll be a dominant player. In 1996, the smart money was on "Web directories," man-made guides to the Internet. Both Netscape and Yahoo relied on Web directories as their primary finding aids, and their IPOs* in the mid-1990s suggested a bright future. In 1996, Wales and two partners founded a Web directory called Bomis.

Initially, the idea was to build a universal directory, like Yahoo's. The question was how to build it. At the time, there were two dominant models: top-down and bottom-up. The former is best exemplified by Yahoo, which began as *Jerry's Guide to the World Wide Web.* Jerry—in this case Jerry Yang, Yahoo's cofounder—set up a system of categories and began to classify Web sites accordingly. Web surfers flocked to the site because no one could find anything on the Web in the early 1990s. So Yang and his partner, David Filo, spent a mountain of venture capital to hire a team of surfers to classify the Web. Yahoo ("Yet Another Hierarchical Officious Oracle") was born.

Other would-be classifiers approached the problem of Web chaos more democratically. Beginning from the sound premise that it's good to share, a seventeen-year-old Oregonian named Sage Weil created the first "Web ring" at about the time Yang and Filo were assembling their army of paid Web librarians. A Web ring is nothing more than a set of topically related Web sites that have been linked together for ease of surfing. Rings are easy to find, easy to join, and easy to create; by 1997, they numbered 10,000.

Wales focused on the bottom-up strategy using Web rings, and it worked. Bomis users built hundreds of rings—on cars, computers, sports, and especially "babes" (e.g., the Anna Kournikova Web ring), effectively creating an index of the "laddie" Web. Instead of helping all users find all content, Bomis found itself positioned as the *Playboy* of the Internet, helping guys find guy stuff. Wales's experience with Web rings reinforced the lesson he had learned with MUDs: Given the right technology, large groups of self-interested individuals will unite to create something they could not produce by themselves, be it a sword-and-sorcery world or an index of Web sites on Pamela Anderson. He saw the power of what we now call "peer-to-peer," or "distributed," content production.

Wales was not alone: Rich Skrenta and Bob Truel, two programmers at Sun Microsystems, saw it too. In June 1998, along with three partners, they launched GnuHoo, an all-volunteer alternative to the Yahoo Directory. (GNU, a recursive acronym for "GNUs Not Unix," is a free operating system created by the über-hacker Richard Stallman.) The project was an immediate success, and it quickly drew the attention of Netscape,

---

* IPOs: Initial public offerings. In an IPO, a private company becomes a public one by selling shares that are traded openly on the stock market [Ed.].

which was eager to find a directory capable of competing with Yahoo's index. In November 1998, Netscape acquired GnuHoo (then called NewHoo), promising to both develop it and release it under an "open content" license, which meant anyone could use it. At the date of Netscape's acquisition, the directory had indexed some 100,000 URLs; a year later, it included about a million.

Wales clearly had the open-content movement in mind when, in the fall of 1999, he began thinking about a "volunteer-built" online encyclopedia. The idea—explored most prominently in Stallman's 1999 essay "The Free Universal Encyclopedia and Learning Resource"—had been around for some time. Wales says he had no direct knowledge of Stallman's essay when he embarked on his encyclopedia project, but two bits of evidence suggest that he was thinking of Stallman's GNU free documentation license. First, the name Wales adopted for his encyclopedia—Nupedia.org—strongly suggested a Stallman-esque venture. Second, he took the trouble of leasing a related domain name, GNUpedia.org. By January 2000, his encyclopedia project had acquired funding from Bomis and hired its first employee: Larry Sanger. 15

The Philosopher

Sanger was born in 1968 in Bellevue, Washington, a suburb of Seattle. When he was seven, his father, a marine biologist, moved the family to Anchorage, Alaska, where Sanger spent his youth. He excelled in high school, and in 1986 he enrolled at Reed College. Reed is the sort of school you attend if you are intelligent, are not interested in investment banking, and wonder a lot about truth. There Sanger found a question that fired his imagination: What is knowledge? He embarked on that most unremunerative of careers, epistemology, and entered a doctoral program in philosophy at Ohio State.

Sanger fits the profile of almost every Internet early adopter: He'd been a good student, played Dungeons & Dragons, and tinkered with PCs as a youth—going so far as to code a text-based adventure game in BASIC, the first popular programming language. He was drawn into the world of philosophy discussion lists and, in the early 1990s, was an active participant in Wales's objectivism forum. Sanger also hosted a mailing list as part of his own online philosophy project (eventually named the Association for Systematic Philosophy). The mission and mien of Sanger's list stood in stark contrast to Wales's Rand forum. Sanger was far more programmatic. As he wrote in his opening manifesto, dated March 22, 1994:

> The history of philosophy is full of disagreement and confusion. One reaction by philosophers to this state of things is to doubt whether the truth about philosophy can ever be known, or whether there is any such thing as the truth about philosophy. But there is another reaction: One may set out to think more carefully and methodically than one's intellectual forebears.

Wales's Rand forum was generally serious, but it was also a place for philosophically inclined laypeople to shoot the breeze: Wales permitted discussion of "objectivism in the movies" or "objectivism in Rush lyrics." Sanger's list was more disciplined, but he soon began to feel it, too, was of limited philosophical worth. He resigned after little more than a year. "I think that my time could really be better spent in the real world,"

Sanger wrote in his resignation letter, "as opposed to cyberspace, and in thinking to myself, rather than out loud to a bunch of other people." Sanger was seriously considering abandoning his academic career.

As the decade and the century came to a close, another opportunity arose, one that would let Sanger make a living away from academia, using the acumen he had developed on the Internet. In 1998, Sanger created a digest of news reports relating to the "Y2K problem." *Sanger's Review of Y2K News Reports* became a staple of IT managers across the globe. It also set him to thinking about how he might make a living in the new millennium. In January 2000, he sent Wales a business proposal for what was in essence a cultural news blog. Sanger's timing was excellent.

The Cathedral

Wales was looking for someone with good academic credentials to organize Nupedia, and Sanger fit the bill. Wales pitched the project to Sanger in terms of Eric S. Raymond's essay (and later book) "The Cathedral and the Bazaar." Raymond sketched two models of software development. Under the "cathedral model," source code was guarded by a core group of developers; under the "bazaar model," it was released on the Internet for anyone to tinker with. Raymond argued that the latter model was better, and he coined a now-famous hacker aphorism to capture its superiority: "Given enough eyeballs, all bugs are shallow." His point was simply that the speed with which a complex project is perfected is directly proportional to the number of informed people working on it. Wales was enthusiastic about Raymond's thesis. His experience with MUDs and Web rings had demonstrated to him the power of the bazaar. Sanger, the philosopher, was charier about the wisdom-of-crowds scheme but drawn to the idea of creating an open online encyclopedia that would break all the molds. Sanger signed on and moved to San Diego.

According to Sanger, Wales was very "hands-off." He gave Sanger only the loosest sketch of an open encyclopedia. "Open" meant two things: First, anyone, in principle, could contribute. Second, all of the content would be made freely available. Sanger proceeded to create, in effect, an online academic journal. There was simply no question in his mind that Nupedia would be guided by a board of experts, that submissions would be largely written by experts, and that articles would be published only after extensive peer review. Sanger set about recruiting academics to work on Nupedia. In early March 2000, he and Wales deemed the project ready to go public, and the Nupedia Web site was launched with the following words:

> Suppose scholars the world over were to learn of a serious online encyclopedia effort in which the results were not proprietary to the encyclopedists, but were freely distributable under an open content license in virtually any desired medium. How quickly would the encyclopedia grow?

The answer, as Wales and Sanger found out, was "not very." Over the first several months little was actually accomplished in terms of article assignment, writing, and publication. First, there was the competition. Wales and Sanger had the bad luck to launch Nupedia around the same time as *Encyclopaedia Britannica* was made available for free on the Internet. Then there was the real problem: production. Sanger and the Nupedia board had worked out a multistage editorial system that could have been borrowed from any scholarly journal. In a sense, it worked: Assignments were made, articles were submitted and evaluated, and copyediting was done. But, to both Wales and Sanger, it was all much too slow. They had built a cathedral.

The Bazaar

In the mid-1980s, a programmer named Ward Cunningham began trying to create a "pattern language" for software design. A pattern language is in essence a common vocabulary used in solving engineering problems—think of it as best practices for designers. Cunningham believed that software development should have a pattern language, and he proposed to find a way for software developers to create it.

Apple's Hypercard offered inspiration. Hypercard was a very flexible database application. It allowed users to create records ("cards"), add data fields to them, and link them in sets. Cunningham created a Hypercard "stack" of software patterns and shared it with colleagues. His stack was well liked but difficult to share, since it existed only on Cunningham's computer. In the 1990s, Cunningham found himself looking for a problem-solving technique that would allow software developers to fine-tune and accumulate their knowledge collaboratively. A variation on Hypercard seemed like an obvious option.

Cunningham coded and, in the spring of 1995, launched the first "wiki," calling it the "WikiWikiWeb." (*Wiki* is Hawaiian for "quick," which Cunningham chose to indicate the ease with which a user could edit the pages.) A wiki is a Web site that allows multiple users to create, edit, and hyperlink pages. As users work, a wiki can keep track of all changes; users can compare versions as they edit and, if necessary, revert to earlier states. Nothing is lost, and everything is transparent.

The wiki quickly gained a devoted following within the software community. And there it remained until January 2001, when Sanger had dinner with an old friend named Ben Kovitz. Kovitz was a fan of "extreme programming." Standard software engineering is very methodical—first you plan, then you plan and plan and plan, then you code. The premise is that you must correctly anticipate what the program will need to do in order to avoid drastic changes late in the coding process. In contrast, extreme programmers advocate going live with the earliest possible version of new software and letting many people work simultaneously to rapidly refine it.

Over tacos that night, Sanger explained his concerns about Nupedia's lack of progress, the root cause of which was its serial editorial system. As Nupedia was then structured, no stage of the editorial process could proceed before the previous stage was completed. Kovitz brought up the wiki and sketched out "wiki magic," the mysterious process by which communities with common interests work to improve wiki pages by incremental contributions. If it worked for the rambunctious hacker culture of programming, Kovitz said, it could work for any online collaborative project. The wiki could break the Nupedia bottleneck by permitting volunteers to work simultaneously all over the project. With Kovitz in tow, Sanger rushed back to his apartment and called Wales to share the idea. Over the next few days he wrote a formal proposal for Wales and started a page on Cunningham's wiki called "WikiPedia."

Wales and Sanger created the first Nupedia wiki on January 10, 2001. The initial purpose was to get the public to add entries that would then be "fed into the Nupedia process" of authorization. Most of Nupedia's expert volunteers, however, wanted nothing to do with this, so Sanger decided to launch a separate site called "Wikipedia." Neither Sanger nor Wales looked on Wikipedia as anything more than a lark. This is evident in Sanger's flip announcement of Wikipedia to the Nupedia discussion list. "Humor me," he wrote. "Go there and add a little article. It will take all of five or ten minutes." And, to Sanger's surprise, go they did. Within a few days, Wikipedia outstripped Nupedia in terms of quantity, if not quality, and a small community developed. In late January, Sanger created a Wikipedia discussion list (Wikipedia-L) to facilitate discussion of the project. At the end of January, Wikipedia had seventeen "real" articles (entries with more than 200 characters). By the end of February, it had 150; March, 572; April, 835; May, 1,300; June, 1,700; July, 2,400; August, 3,700. At the end of the year, the site boasted approximately 15,000 articles and about 350 "Wikipedians."

Setting the Rules

Wikipedia's growth caught Wales and Sanger off guard. It forced them to make quick decisions about what Wikipedia would be, how to foster cooperation, and how to manage it. In the beginning it was by no means clear what an "open" encyclopedia should include. People posted all manner of things: dictionary definitions, autobiographies, position papers, historical documents, and original research. In response, Sanger created a "What Wikipedia Is Not" page. There he and the community defined Wikipedia by exclusion—not a dictionary, not a scientific journal, not a source collection, and so on. For everything else, they reasoned that if an article could conceivably have gone in *Britannica*, it was "encyclopedic" and permitted; if not, it was "not encyclopedic" and deleted.

Sanger and Wales knew that online collaborative ventures can easily slide into a morass of unproductive invective. They had already worked out a solution for Nupedia, called the "lack of bias" policy. On Wikipedia it became NPOV, or the "neutral point of view," and it brilliantly encouraged the work of the community. Under NPOV, authors were enjoined to present the conventionally acknowledged "facts" in an unbiased way, and, where arguments occurred, to accord space to both sides. The concept of neutrality, though philosophically unsatisfying, had a kind of everybody-lay-down-your-arms ring to it. Debates about what to include in the article were encouraged on the "discussion" page that attends every Wikipedia article.

The most important initial question, however, concerned governance. When Wikipedia was created, wikis were synonymous with creative anarchy. Both Wales and Sanger thought that the software might be useful, but that it was no way to build a trusted encyclopedia. Some sort of authority was assumed to be essential. Wales's part in it was clear: He owned Wikipedia. Sanger's role was murkier.

Citing the communal nature of the project, Sanger refused the title of "editor in chief," a position he held at Nupedia, opting instead to be "chief organizer." He governed the day-to-day operations of the project in close consultation with the "community," the roughly two dozen committed Wikipedians (most of them Nupedia converts) who were really designing the software and adding content to the site. Though the division of powers between Sanger and the community remained to be worked out, an important precedent had been set: Wikipedia would have an owner, but no leader.

The Cunctator

By October 2001, the number of Wikipedians was growing by about fifty a month. There were a lot of new voices, among them a user known as "The Cunctator" (Latin for "procrastinator" or "delayer"). "Cunc," as he was called, advocated a combination of anarchy (no hierarchy within the project) and radical openness (few or no limitations on contributions). Sanger was not favorably disposed to either of these positions, though he had not had much of a chance to air his opposition. Cunc offered such an opportunity by launching a prolonged "edit war" with Sanger in mid-October of that year. In an edit war, two or more parties cyclically cancel each other's work on an article with no attempt to find the NPOV. It's the wiki equivalent of "No, *your* mother wears combat boots."

With Cunc clearly in mind, Sanger curtly defended his role before the community on November 1, 2001:

> I need to be granted fairly broad authority by the community—by you, dear reader—if I am going to do my job effectively. Until fairly recently, I was granted such authority by Wikipedians. I was indeed not infrequently called to justify decisions I made, but not constantly and nearly always respectfully and helpfully. This place in the community did not make me an all-powerful editor who must be obeyed on pain of ousting; but it did make me a leader. That's what I want, again. This is my job.

Seen from the trenches, this was a striking statement. Sanger had so far said he was primus inter pares;* now he seemed to be saying that he was just primus. Upon reading this post, one Wikipedian wrote: "Am I the only person who detects a change in [Sanger's] view of his own position? Am I the only person who fears this is a change for the worse?"

On November 4, the Sanger-Cunc contretemps† exploded. Simon Kissane, a respected Wikipedian, accused Sanger of capriciously deleting pages, including some of Cunc's work. Sanger denied the allegation but implied that the excised material was no great loss. He then launched a defense of his position in words that bled resentment:

> I do reserve the right to permanently delete things—particularly when they have little merit and when they are posted by people whose main motive is evidently to undermine my authority and therefore, as far as I'm concerned, damage the project. Now suppose that, in my experience, if I make an attempt to justify this or other sorts of decisions, the people in question will simply co-opt huge amounts of my time and will never simply say, "Larry, you win; we realize that this decision is up to you, and we'll have to respect it." Then, in order

---

* Primus inter pares: Latin for "first among equals" [Ed.].
† Contretemps: A disruptive event or awkward disagreement [Ed.].

to preserve my time and sanity, I have to act like an autocrat. In a way, I am being trained to act like an autocrat. It's rather clever in a way — if you think college-level stunts are clever. Frankly, it's hurting the project, guys — so stop it, already. Just write articles — please!

The blowup disturbed Wales to no end. As a list moderator, he had tried hard to keep his discussants out of flame wars. He weighed in with an unusually forceful posting that warned against a "culture of conflict." Wikipedia, he implied, was about building an encyclopedia, not about debating how to build or govern an encyclopedia. Echoing Sanger, he argued that the primary duty of community members was to contribute — by writing code, adding content, and editing. Enough talk, he seemed to be saying: We know what to do, now let's get to work. Yet he also seemed to take a quiet stand against Sanger's positions on openness and on his own authority:

> Just speaking off the top of my head, I think that total deletions seldom make sense. They should be reserved primarily for pages that are just completely mistaken (typos, unlikely misspellings), or for pages that are nothing more than insults.

Wales also made a strong case that anyone deleting pages should record his or her identity, explain his or her reasons, and archive the entire affair.

Within several weeks, Sanger and Cunc were at each other's throats again. Sanger had proposed creating a "Wikipedia Militia" that would deal with issues arising from sudden massive influxes of new visitors. It was hardly a bad idea: Such surges did occur (they're commonly called "slash-dottings"). But Cunc saw in Sanger's reasonable proposition a very slippery slope toward "central authority." "You start deputizing groups of people to do necessary and difficult tasks," he wrote, "fast-forward two/three years, and you have pernicious cabals."

Given the structure of Wikipedia there was little Sanger could do to defend himself. The principles of the project denied him real punitive authority: He couldn't ban "trolls" — users like Cunc who baited others for sport — and deleting posts was evidence of tyranny in the eyes of Sanger's detractors. A defensive strategy wouldn't work either, as the skilled moderator's tactic for fighting bad behavior — ignoring it — was blunted by the wiki. On e-mail lists, unanswered inflammatory posts quickly vanish under layers of new discussion; on a wiki, they remain visible to all, often near the tops of pages. Sanger was trapped by his own creation.

The "God-King"

Wales saw that Sanger was having trouble managing the project. Indeed, he seems to have sensed that Wikipedia really needed no manager. In mid-December 2001, citing financial shortfalls, he told Sanger that Bomis would be cutting its staff and that he should look for a new job. To that point, Wales and his partners had supported both Nupedia and Wikipedia. But with Bomis suffering in the Internet bust, there was financial pressure. Early on, Wales had said that advertising was a possibility, but the community was now set against any commercialization. In January 2002, Sanger loaded up his possessions and returned to Ohio.

Cunc responded to Sanger's departure with apparent appreciation:

I know that we've hardly been on the best of terms, but I want you to know that I'll always consider you one of the most important Wikipedians, and I hope that you'll always think of yourself as a Wikipedian, even if you don't have much time to contribute. Herding cats ain't easy; you did a good job, all things considered.

Characteristically, Sanger took this as nothing more than provocation: "Oh, how nice and gracious this was. Oh, thank you SO much, Cunctator. I'm sure glad I won't have to deal with you anymore, Cunctator. You're a friggin' piece of work." The next post on the list is from Wales, who showed a business-as-usual sangfroid:* "With the resignation of Larry, there is a much less pressing need for funds."

Sanger made two great contributions to Wikipedia: He built it, and he left it. After forging a revolutionary mode of knowledge building, he came to realize—albeit dimly at first—that it was not to his liking. He found that he was not heading a disciplined crew of qualified writers and editors collaborating on authoritative statements (the Nupedia ideal), but trying to control an ill-disciplined crowd of volunteers fighting over ever-shifting articles. From Sanger's point of view, both the behavior of the participants and the quality of the scholarship were wanting. Even after seeing Wikipedia's explosive growth, Sanger continued to argue that Wikipedia should engage experts and that Nupedia should be saved.

Wales, though, was a businessman. He wanted to build a free encyclopedia, and Wikipedia offered a very rapid and economically efficient means to that end. The articles flooded in, many were good, and they cost him almost nothing. Why interfere? Moreover, Wales was not really the meddling kind. Early on, Wikipedians took to calling him the "God-King." The appellation is purely ironic. Over the past four years, Wales has repeatedly demonstrated an astounding reluctance to use his power, even when the community has begged him to. He wouldn't exile trolls or erase offensive material, much less settle on rules for how things should or should not be done. In 2003, Wales diminished his own authority by transferring Wikipedia and all of its assets to the nonprofit Wikimedia Foundation, whose sole purpose is to set general policy for Wikipedia and its allied projects. (He is one of five members of the foundation's board.)

Wales's benign rule has allowed Wikipedia to do what it does best: grow. The numbers are staggering. The English-language Wikipedia alone has well more than a million articles and expands by about 1,700 a day. (*Britannica*'s online version, by comparison, has about 100,000 articles.) As of mid-February 2006, more than 65,000 Wikipedians—registered users who have made at least ten edits since joining—had contributed to the English-language Wikipedia. The number of registered contributors is increasing by more than 6,000 a month; the number of unregistered contributors is presumably much larger. Then there are the 200-odd non-English-language Wikipedias. Nine of them already have more than 100,000 entries each, and nearly all of the major-language versions are growing on pace with the English version.

———————————

* Sangfroid: Coolness and composure (French for "cold blood") [Ed.].

What Is Wikipedia?

The Internet did not create the desire to collect human knowledge. For most of history, however, standardizing and gathering knowledge was hard to do very effectively. The main problem was rampant equivocation. Can we all agree on what an apple is exactly, or the shades of the color green? Not easily. The wiki offered a way for people to actually decide in common. On Wikipedia, an apple is what the contributors say it is *right now*. You can try to change the definition by throwing in your own two cents, but the community — the voices actually negotiating and renegotiating the definition — decides in the end. Wikipedia grew out of a natural impulse (communication) facilitated by a new technology (the wiki).

The power of the community to decide, of course, asks us to reexamine what we mean when we say that something is "true." We tend to think of truth as something that resides in the world. The fact that two plus two equals four is written in the stars — we merely discovered it. But Wikipedia suggests a different theory of truth. Just think about the way we learn what words mean. Generally speaking, we do so by listening to other people (our parents, first). Since we want to communicate with them (after all, they feed us), we use the words in the same way they do. Wikipedia says judgments of truth and falsehood work the same way. The community decides that two plus two equals four the same way it decides what an apple is: by consensus. Yes, that means that if the community changes its mind and decides that two plus two equals five, then two plus two does equal five. The community isn't likely to do such an absurd or useless thing, but it has the ability.

> **The Internet did not create the desire to collect human knowledge.**

Early detractors commonly made two criticisms of Wikipedia. First, unless experts were writing and vetting the material, the articles were inevitably going to be inaccurate. Second, since anyone could edit, vandals would have their way with even the best articles, making them suspect. No encyclopedia produced in this way could be trusted. Last year, however, a study in the journal *Nature* compared *Britannica* and Wikipedia science articles and suggested that the former are usually only marginally more accurate than the latter. *Britannica* demonstrated that *Nature*'s analysis was seriously flawed ("Fatally Flawed" was the fair title of the response), and no one has produced a more authoritative study of Wikipedia's accuracy. Yet it is a widely accepted view that Wikipedia is comparable to *Britannica*. Vandalism also has proved much less of an issue than originally feared. A study by IBM suggests that although vandalism does occur (particularly on high-profile entries like "George W. Bush"), watchful members of the huge Wikipedia community usually swoop down to stop the malfeasance shortly after it begins.

There are, of course, exceptions, as in the case of the journalist John Seigenthaler, whose Wikipedia biography long contained a libel about his supposed complicity in the assassinations of John F. and Robert Kennedy. But even this example shows that the system is, if not perfect, at least responsive. When Seigenthaler became aware of the error, he contacted Wikipedia. The community (led in this instance by Wales) purged the entry of erroneous material, expanded it, and began to monitor it closely.

45

Even though the Seigenthaler entry is often attacked by vandals, and is occasionally locked to block them, the page is more reliable precisely because it is now under "enough eyeballs." The same could be said about many controversial entries on Wikipedia: The quality of articles generally increases with the number of eyeballs. Given enough eyeballs, all errors are shallow.

Common Knowledge

In June 2001, only six months after Wikipedia was founded, a Polish Wikipedian named Krzysztof Jasiutowicz made an arresting and remarkably forward-looking observation. The Internet, he mused, was nothing but a "global Wikipedia without the end-user editing facility." The contents of the Internet—its pages—are created by a loose community of users, namely those on the Web. The contents of Wikipedia—its entries—are also created by a loose community of users, namely Wikipedians. On the Internet, contributors own their own pages, and only they can edit them. They can also create new pages as they see fit. On Wikipedia, contributors own *all* of the pages collectively, and each can edit nearly every page. Page creation is ultimately subject to community approval. The private-property regime that governs the Internet allows it to grow freely, but it makes organization and improvement very difficult. In contrast, Wikipedia's communal regime permits growth *plus* organization and improvement. The result of this difference is there for all to see: Much of the Internet is a chaotic mess and therefore useless, whereas Wikipedia is well ordered and hence very useful.

Having seen all of this in prospect, Jasiutowicz asked a logical question: "Can someone please tell me what's the end point/goal of Wikipedia?" Wales responded, only half jokingly, "The goal of Wikipedia is fun for the contributors." He had a point. Editing Wikipedia *is* fun, and even rewarding. The site is huge, so somewhere on it there is probably something you know quite a bit about. Imagine that you happen upon your pet subject, or perhaps even look it up to see how it's being treated. And what do you find? Well, this date is wrong, that characterization is poor, and a word is misspelled. You click the "edit" tab and make the corrections, and you've just contributed to the progress of human knowledge. All in under five minutes, and at no cost.

Yet Wikipedia has a value that goes far beyond the enjoyment of its contributors. For all intents and purposes, the project is laying claim to a vast region of the Internet, a territory we might call "common knowledge." It is the place where all nominal information about objects of widely shared experience will be negotiated, stored, and renegotiated. When you want to find out *what something is*, you will go to Wikipedia, for that is where common knowledge will, by convention, be archived and updated and made freely available. And while you are there, you may just add or change a little something, and thereby feel the pride of authorship shared by the tens of thousands of Wikipedians.

Keeper

One of the objects of common knowledge in Wikipedia, I'm relieved to report, is "Marshall Poe." Recall that the Scottish Wikipedian Alai said that I had no "notability" and therefore couldn't really be considered encyclopedic. On the same day that Alai suggested my entry be deleted, a rather vigorous discussion took place on the "discussion" page that attended the Marshall Poe entry. A Wikipedian who goes by "Dlyons493" discovered that I had indeed written an obscure dissertation on an obscure topic at a not-so-obscure university. He gave the article a "Weak Keep." Someone with the handle "Splash" searched Amazon and verified that I had indeed written books on Russian history, so my claim to be a historian was true. He gave me a "Keep." And finally, my champion and hero, a Wikipedian called "Tupsharru," dismissed my detractors with this:

> Keep. Obvious notability. Several books published with prestigious academic publishers. One of his books has even been translated into Swedish. I don't know why I have to repeat this again and again in these deletion discussions on academics, but don't just use Amazon when the Library of Congress catalogue is no farther than a couple of mouse clicks away.

Bear in mind that I knew none of these people, and they had, as far as I know, no 50
interest other than truth in doing all of this work. Yet they didn't stop with verifying my claims and approving my article. They also searched the Web for material they could use to expand my one-line biography. After they were done, the Marshall Poe entry was two paragraphs long and included a good bibliography. Now that's wiki magic.

Exploring Context

1. This essay is about the collaborative process behind the creation of entries in the online encyclopedia Wikipedia (wikipedia.org). Visit Wikipedia and find an entry you feel qualified to write about. Register at the site and participate in the authorship process by editing your selected entry. What is the process like? Is it consistent with Poe's description? Relate your experience to your work on the key factors in Wikipedia's success from Question 1 of Questions for Critical Reading.

2. Kickstarter (kickstarter.com) is a site for the collaborative funding of projects ranging from films to computer peripherals. Explore the site and some of its projects. Does this site harness the same collective power that Poe locates in Wikipedia? What makes it different? Use your response on Wikipedia's success from Question 1 of Questions for Critical Reading to support your answer.

3. Poe opens this essay by discussing his own entry in Wikipedia. Visit his entry on the site at en.wikipedia.org/wiki/Marshall_Poe and then examine the history of changes to the entry by clicking on the "View history" tab at the top of the page. How has his entry changed? What reasons can you find for those changes? Does the entry reflect the success of the kind of process Poe describes?

Questions for Connecting

1. In what ways is Wikipedia like a flash mob? Apply Bill Wasik's ideas in "My Crowd Experiment: The Mob Project" (p. 514) to Poe's discussion of collaborative knowledge. Is Wikipedia powered by memes? You may want to use your experience with wikis from Exploring Context in composing your response.

2. In "Ethics and the New Genetics" (p. 133), the Dalai Lama argues for a moral compass to guide us around scientific developments such as genetic technologies, but how can we develop a system of ethics when knowledge itself is becoming socially constituted? Is ethics possible without transcendent truths? Does Wikipedia threaten the idea of "truth," or can its collaborative model be used to create the ethical system the Dalai Lama calls for?

3. James Surowiecki outlines the many dangers of small groups in "Committees, Juries, and Teams: The *Columbia* Disaster and How Small Groups Can Be Made to Work" (p. 472). Are the same dangers present in a large-scale group project like Wikipedia? How can the pitfalls that Surowiecki details be avoided? Use your responses from Questions for Critical Reading and Exploring Context to support your position.

4. **CONNECTING TO E-PAGES** In what ways does Alexandra Samuel's "'Plug In Better': A Manifesto" (bedfordstmartins.com/emerging/epages) highlight positive views of technology? What reservations does Samuel have about the use of technology? How are those views similar to or different from the motivations behind the development of Wikipedia?

Language Matters

1. Select a key quotation from Poe's text and then translate it into another language using an online tool such as Bing Translator (bing.com/translator) or Google's Language Tools (google.com/language_tools). You might even choose to translate it several times (from English to French to German to Chinese). Then translate it back into English. The resulting sentence will probably make little sense. Describe what happened to the sentence. Did translation change parts of speech? Verb tense? Sentence structure? What elements of the sentence are key to transmitting Poe's meaning? Do they survive translation? What parts of your own sentences should you then pay attention to the most?

2. Draw the argument of Poe's essay, either by hand or with a graphics program on your computer. How would the inclusion of this drawing affect Poe's text? What elements of visual argument do you use to convey Poe's meaning?

3. Locate a key passage from Poe's text and then revise the quotation you've selected using more informal language or slang. How does this revision change the meaning of the quotation? What audience would be most receptive to your revision? Why did Poe choose the tone he used in this essay, and what tone might you choose in your own writing for this class?

Assignments for Writing

1. Write a paper in which you determine the role of collaboration in the production of knowledge. Does a consensus determine the truth? Is knowledge created by individuals? Does society have the right to determine that "two plus two equals five" (p. 359), as noted in the selection from Poe? Use your experience with wikis in Exploring Context and your work with Poe's concepts from Questions 1 and 3 of Questions for Connecting in making your argument.

2. Though Poe's explicit concern is Wikipedia, his essay is also concerned with the circulation of knowledge. Write a paper in which you determine who owns knowledge. Can knowledge be owned? Is it common property or the property of academics or other experts? Consider the ethical implications by drawing on your work with the Dalai Lama's essay from Question 2 of Questions for Connecting.

3. What is the power of experts? Does a consensus determine the truth? Poe's essay asks us to consider these questions, since the collaborative authorship of Wikipedia suggests that experts are not vital in the creation of knowledge. Write a paper in which you suggest the proper boundaries between experts and nonexperts in relation to knowledge. What role does technology play in this process? Should experts be granted special status in relation to knowledge? What makes an expert "expert" anyway?

JAYME POISSON

Jayme Poisson is a staff writer for the *Toronto Star*. As an undergraduate she studied political science at McGill University and then enrolled in a master of journalism program at Carleton University. As part of her work on that degree, she traveled to Nepal and shot a documentary about how fallen womb syndrome has deeply affected the women there.

"Parents Keep Child's Gender Secret" is an article by Poisson that first appeared in the May 21, 2011, edition of the *Toronto Star*. In this piece of journalism, Poisson's voice never veers to the right or left of neutral, but the story of a Canadian couple raising their child without ever revealing the child's gender (keeping it secret from anyone not in their immediate family) has incited many strong reactions from readers and locals alike. Poisson's piece allows us to form our own opinions about this subject—which may not seem so thorny at first—and forces us to examine why we consider gender so important to the development of a child.

▶ TAGS: *gender, family, identity, community, secrecy, decision making*

Questions for Critical Reading

1. What is the difference between sex and gender? Make your own definition of each and then consider how Poisson's article challenges, confirms, or changes your definition. Mark passages where Poisson suggests the difference between the two.

2. Consider your own ideas about how children should be raised. While reading the article closely, pay attention to the motivations behind the parents' desire to raise a child without revealing the child's gender. What is their philosophy of parenting?

3. As you read, pay close attention to psychologist Diane Ehrensaft's position on Storm. Why does she object to the withholding of Storm's sex by Witterick and Stocker, Storm's parents? How does her position differ from Dr. Ken Zucker's?

Parents Keep Child's Gender Secret

"So it's a boy, right?" a neighbor calls out as Kathy Witterick walks by, her four-month-old baby, Storm, strapped to her chest in a carrier.

Each week the woman asks the same question about the baby with the squishy cheeks and feathery blond hair.

Witterick smiles, opens her arms wide, comments on the sunny spring day, and keeps walking.

She's used to it. The neighbors know Witterick and her husband, David Stocker, are raising a genderless baby. But they don't pretend to understand it.

While there's nothing ambiguous about Storm's genitalia, they aren't telling anyone whether their third child is a boy or a girl.   5

Storm gets a cuddle from older brother Jazz. Kathy Witterick, 38, and David Stocker, 39, are raising their four-month-old child, Storm, to be genderless.

The only people who know are Storm's brothers, Jazz, 5, and Kio, 2, a close family friend, and the two midwives who helped deliver the baby in a birthing pool at their Toronto home on New Year's Day.

"When the baby comes out, even the people who love you the most and know you so intimately, the first question they ask is, 'Is it a girl or a boy?'" says Witterick, bouncing Storm, dressed in a red-fleece jumper, on her lap at the kitchen table.

"If you really want to get to know someone, you don't ask what's between their legs," says Stocker.

When Storm was born, the couple sent an email to friends and family: "We've decided not to share Storm's sex for now—a tribute to freedom and choice in place of limitation, a stand up to what the world could become in Storm's lifetime (a more progressive place? . . .)."

Their announcement was met with stony silence. Then the deluge of criticisms began. Not just about Storm, but about how they were parenting their other two children. 10

The grandparents were supportive, but resented explaining the gender-free baby to friends and co-workers. They worried the children would be ridiculed. Friends said they were imposing their political and ideological values on a newborn. Most of all, people said they were setting their kids up for a life of bullying in a world that can be cruel to outsiders.

Witterick and Stocker believe they are giving their children the freedom to choose who they want to be, unconstrained by social norms about males and females. Some say their choice is alienating.

In an age where helicopter parents hover nervously over their kids micromanaging their lives, and tiger moms ferociously push their progeny to get into Harvard, Stocker, 39, and Witterick, 38, believe kids can make meaningful decisions for themselves from a very early age.

"What we noticed is that parents make so many choices for their children. It's obnoxious," says Stocker.

Jazz and Kio have picked out their own clothes in the boys and girls sections of   15
stores since they were 18 months old. Just this week, Jazz unearthed a pink dress at Value Village, which he loves because it "really poofs out at the bottom. It feels so nice." The boys decide whether to cut their hair or let it grow.

Like all mothers and fathers, Witterick and Stocker struggle with parenting decisions. The boys are encouraged to challenge how they're expected to look and act based on their sex.

"We thought that if we delayed sharing that information, in this case hopefully, we might knock off a couple million of those messages by the time that Storm decides Storm would like to share," says Witterick.

They don't want to isolate their kids from the world, but, when it's meaningful, talk about gender.

This past winter, the family took a vacation to Cuba with Witterick's parents. Since they weren't fluent in Spanish, they flipped a coin at the airport to decide what to tell people. It landed on heads, so for the next week, everyone who asked was told Storm was a boy. The language changed immediately. "What a big, strong boy," people said.

The moment a child's sex is announced, so begins the parade of pink and barrage of   20
blue. Tutus and toy trucks aren't far behind. The couple says it only intensifies with age.

"In fact, in not telling the gender of my precious baby, I am saying to the world, 'Please can you just let Storm discover for him/herself what s(he) wants to be?'!" Witterick writes in an email.

Stocker teaches at City View Alternative, a tiny school west of Dufferin Grove Park, with four teachers and about 60 Grade 7 and 8 students whose lessons are framed by social-justice issues around class, race, and gender.

When Kio was a baby, the family traveled through the mountains of Mexico, speaking with the Zapatistas, a revolutionary group who shun mainstream politics as corrupt and demand greater indigenous rights. In 1994, about 150 people died in violent clashes with the Mexican military, but the leftist movement has been largely peaceful since.

Last year, they spent two weeks in Cuba, living with local families and learning about the revolution. Witterick has worked in violence prevention, giving workshops to teachers. These days, she volunteers, offering breastfeeding support. At the moment, she is a full-time mom.

Both come from liberal families. Stocker grew up listening to *Free to Be . . . You and*   25
Me, a 1972 record with a central message of gender neutrality. Witterick remembers

her brother mucking around with gender as a teen in the '80s, wearing lipstick and carrying handbags like David Bowie and Mick Jagger.

The family lives in a cream-colored two-story brick home in the city's Junction Triangle neighborhood. Their front porch is crammed with bicycles, including Kio's pink and purple tricycle. Inside, it's organized clutter. The children's arts and crafts projects are stacked in the bookcases, maps hang on the walls, and furniture is well-used and of a certain vintage.

Upstairs they co-sleep curled up on two mattresses pushed together on the floor of the master bedroom, under a heap of mismatched pillows and blankets. During the day the kids build forts with the pillows and pretend to walk a tightrope between the mattresses.

On a recent Tuesday, the boys finish making paper animal puppets and a handmade sign to celebrate their dad's birthday. "I love to do laundry with dad," reads one message. They nuzzle Storm, splayed out on the floor. The baby squeals with delight.

Witterick practices unschooling, an offshoot of home-schooling centered on the belief that learning should be driven by a child's curiosity. There are no report cards, no textbooks, and no tests. For unschoolers, learning is about exploring and asking questions, "not something that happens by rote from 9 AM to 3 PM weekdays in a building with a group of same-age people, planned, implemented, and assessed by someone else," says Witterick. The fringe movement is growing. An unschooling conference in Toronto drew dozens of families last fall.

The kids have a lot of say in how their day unfolds. They decide if they want to squish through the mud, chase garter snakes in the park, or bake cupcakes.

Jazz—soft-spoken, with a slight frame and curious brown eyes—keeps his hair long, preferring to wear it in three braids, two in the front and one in the back, even though both his parents have close-cropped hair. His favorite color is pink, although his parents don't own a piece of pink clothing between them. He loves to paint his fingernails and wears a sparkly pink stud in one ear, despite the fact his parents wear no nail polish or jewelry.

Kio keeps his curly blond hair just below his chin. The 2-year-old loves purple, although he's happiest in any kind of pajama pants.

"As a result, Jazz and now Kio are almost exclusively assumed to be girls," says Stocker, adding he and Witterick don't out them. It's the boys' choice whether they want to offer a correction.

On a recent trip to High Park, Jazz, wearing pink shorts, patterned pink socks, and brightly colored elastics on his braids, runs and skips across the street.

"That's a princess!" says a smiling crossing guard, ushering the little boy along. "And that's a princess, too," she says again, pointing at Kio with her big red sign.

"That's a princess!" says a smiling crossing guard, ushering the little boy along.

Jazz doesn't mind. One of his favorite books is *10,000 Dresses*, the story of a boy who loves to dress up. But he doesn't like being called a girl. Recently, he asked his mom to write a note on his application to the High Park Nature Center because he likes the group leaders and wants them to know he's a boy.

Jazz was old enough for school last September, but chose to stay home. "When we would go and visit programs, people—children and adults—would immediately react with Jazz over his gender," says Witterick, adding the conversation would gravitate to his choice of pink or his hairstyle.

That's mostly why he doesn't want to go to school. When asked if it upsets him, he nods, but doesn't say more.

Instead he grabs a handmade portfolio filled with his drawings and poems. In its pages is a booklet written under his pseudonym, the "Gender Explorer." In purple and pink lettering, adorned with butterflies, it reads: "Help girls do boy things. Help boys do girl things. Let your kid be whoever they are!"

Storm was named after whipped winds and dark rain clouds, because they are beautiful and transformative.

"When I was pregnant, it was really this intense time around Jazz having experiences with gender and I was feeling like I needed some good parenting skills to support him through that," says Witterick.

It began as an offhand remark. "Hey, what if we just didn't tell?" And then Stocker found a book in his school library called *X: A Fabulous Child's Story* by Lois Gould. The book, published in 1978, is about raising not a boy or a girl, but X. There's a happy ending here. Little X—who loved to play football and weave baskets—faces the taunting head on, proving that X is the most well-adjusted child ever examined by "an impartial team of Xperts."

"It became so compelling it was almost like, How could we not?" says Witterick.

There are days when their decisions are tiring, shackling even. "We spend more time than we should providing explanations for why we do things this way," says Witterick. "I regret that [Jazz] has to discuss his gender before people ask him meaningful questions about what he does and sees in this world, but I don't think I am responsible for that—the culture that narrowly defines what he should do, wear, and look like is."

Longtime friend Ayal Dinner, 35, a father of two young boys, was surprised to hear the couple's announcement when Storm was born, but is supportive.

"I think it's amazing that they're willing to take on challenging people in this way," says Dinner. "While they are political and ideological about these things, they're also really thinking about what it means and struggling with it as they go along."

Dinner understands why people may find it extreme. "Although I can see the criticism of 'This is going to be hard on my kid,' it's great to say, 'I love my kid for whoever they are.'"

On a recent trip to Hamilton, Jazz was out of earshot when family friend Denise Hansen overheard two little girls at the park say they didn't want to play with a "girl-boy." Then, there was the time a saleswoman at a second-hand shop refused to sell him a pink feather boa. "Surely you won't buy it for him—he's a boy!" said the woman. Shocked, and not wanting to upset Jazz, Witterick left the store.

Parents talk about the moment they realize they would throw themselves in front of a speeding truck to save their child from harm, yet battle the instinct to overprotect. They want to encourage independence. They hope people won't be mean. They pray they aren't bullied. No parent would ever wish that for their child.

On a night after she watched her husband of 11 years and the boys play with 50 sparklers after dark, Witterick, in a reflective mood, writes to say we are all mocked at some point for the way we look, the way we dress, and the way we think.

"When faced with inevitable judgment by others, which child stands tall (and sticks up for others)—the one facing teasing despite desperately trying to fit in, or the one with a strong sense of self and at least two 'go-to' adults who love them unconditionally? Well, I guess you know which one we choose."

Diane Ehrensaft is a California-based psychologist and mother of Jesse, a "girlyboy" who turned his trucks into cradles and preferred porcelain dolls over soldiers when he was a child. Her newly published book, *Gender Born, Gender Made*, is a guide for parents of nonconforming kids.

She believes parents should support gender-creative children, which includes the transgendered, who feel born in the wrong bodies, and gender hybrids, who feel they are part girl and part boy. Then there are gender "smoothies," who have a blended sense of gender that is purely "them."

Ehrensaft believes there is something innate about gender, and points to the '70s, when parents experimented by giving dolls to boys and trucks to girls.

"It only worked up to a certain extent. Some girls never played with the trucks, 55 some boys weren't interested in ballet . . . It was a humbling experiment for us because we learned we don't have the control that we thought we did."

But she worries by not divulging Storm's sex, the parents are denying the child a way to position himself or herself in a world where you are either male, female, or in between. In effect they have created another category: Other than other. And that could marginalize the child.

"I believe that it puts restrictions on this particular baby so that in this culture this baby will be a singular person who is not being given an opportunity to find their true gender self, based on also what's inside them."

Ehrensaft gets the "What the heck?!" reaction people may have when they hear about Storm. "I think it probably makes people feel played with to have that information withheld from them."

While she accepts and supports Jazz's freedom "to be who he is," she's concerned about asking two small boys to keep a secret about the baby of the family. "For very young children, just in their brains, they're not ready to do the kind of sophisticated discernment we do about when a secret is necessary."

Jazz says it's not difficult. He usually just calls the baby Storm. 60

Dr. Ken Zucker, considered a world expert on gender identity and head of the gender identity service for children at Toronto's Center for Addiction and Mental Health, calls this a "social experiment of nurture." The broader question, he says, is how much influence parents have on their kids. If Ehrensaft leans toward nature, Zucker puts more emphasis on nurture. Even when parents don't make a choice, that's still a choice, and one that can impact the children.

When asked what psychological harm, if any, could come from keeping the sex of a child secret, Zucker said: "One will find out."

The couple plan to keep Storm's sex a secret as long as Storm, Kio, and Jazz are comfortable with it. In the meantime, philosophy and reality continue to collide.

Out with the kids all day, Witterick doesn't have the time or the will to hide in a closet every time she changes Storm's diaper. "If (people) want to peek, that's their journey," she says.

There are questions about which bathroom Storm will use, but that is a couple of   65
years off. Then there is the "tyranny of pronouns," as they call it. They considered referring to Storm as "Z." Witterick now calls the baby she, imagining the "s" in brackets.

For the moment, it feels right.

"Everyone keeps asking us, 'When will this end?' " says Witterick. "And we always turn the question back. Yeah, when will this end? When will we live in a world where people can make choices to be whoever they are?"

Exploring Context

1. Visit the website for Toys "R" Us (toysrus.com) and look for the categories for boys and girls. Explore these sections. Is there any overlap? What do the gifts unique to each section say about what we as a society expect of each gender? Do any toys that this site identifies as gender-specific seem gender-neutral to you?

2. Using Google or some other search engine, locate more information about Storm by searching with the terms "storm genderless baby." Select one of the many news stories about Storm and read both the article and any accompanying comments. Why are people so fascinated with Storm? How do readers tend to react?

3. Visit the website for My Princess Boy (myprincessboy.com), a book and iPad application by Cheryl Kilodavis about her son's preference for "girly" things. How does Kilodavis's position compare to the one presented in Poisson's article? How have people reacted? You might also want to check the reviews of the book at a website like Amazon.com in forming your response.

Questions for Connecting

1. In "Preface" and "The New Civil Rights" (p. 552), Kenji Yoshino discusses the pressures we face to "cover." Apply this concept to the decision Storm's parents have made. In what ways is it a strategy to resist covering? Is it an effective one? Is some measure of covering necessary for any society?

2. Julia Alvarez's "Selections from *Once Upon a Quinceañera*" (p. 46) examines the gender expectations for both boys and girls within Hispanic culture. Does raising Storm without gender avoid these expectations? What rites of passage will be available to Storm?

3. In some ways, Wesley Yang's "Paper Tigers" (p. 533) is also about the decisions parents make when raising their children; in fact, Poisson mentions "tiger moms" in her essay. Synthesize Yang's essay with Poisson's discussion of Storm. How are we shaped by the decisions our parents make?

Language Matters

1. Many foreign languages are highly structured by questions of gender: Nouns, for example, might be masculine or feminine. How does the English language reflect gender? Use a grammar handbook or other reference source to explore the ways in which gender is built into English. Review Poisson's article. How does she handle issues of gender when talking about Storm?

2. This article was originally published in a newspaper. How does journalistic writing differ from academic writing? Locate one or more sentences from Poisson that seem especially to reflect journalism. Rewrite these as academic sentences. What changes? Word choice? Sentence structure? Tone?

3. Quotations should always be integrated fluidly. Locate three instances where Poisson includes quotations. What strategies does she use to integrate quotations into her own sentences? How can you apply these techniques to your own writing?

Assignments for Writing

1. What is the relationship between gender and identity? Write a paper in which you determine that relationship, supported with quotations from Poisson's essay.

2. Storm's parents have faced a lot of criticism for their decision to raise a child without revealing the child's gender. Write a paper in which you determine what rights parents should have in raising their children. Is there a point where cultural expectations or social need should override parents' decisions?

3. Why is Storm's gender so important? Why has this story generated any attention at all? Write a paper in which you use Poisson's essay to determine the importance of gender in society today.

MICHAEL POLLAN

Michael Pollan is the Knight Professor of Science and Environmental Journalism at the University of California–Berkeley as well as the author of five books: *Second Nature: A Gardener's Education* (1991), *A Place of My Own* (1997), *The Botany of Desire: A Plant's-Eye View of the World* (2001), *The Omnivore's Dilemma: A Natural History of Four Meals* (2006), and *In Defense of Food: An Eater's Manifesto* (2008). A graduate of Bennington College and Columbia University, Pollan has won multiple journalism awards, and his writing has appeared in *The Norton Book of Nature Writing* (1990), *Best American Essays* (1990 and 2003), and *Best American Science Writing* (2004). Pollan's work can often be seen in the *New York Times*, where he is a contributing writer.

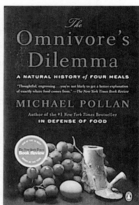

The *Omnivore's Dilemma*, declared by the *New York Times* to be one of 2006's best nonfiction books, traces three different food chains—the industrial, the pastoral, and the personal—from nature to table. Ultimately, the book is about the politics of eating: what we should eat, why we should eat it, and what impact our eating decisions have.

In "The Animals: Practicing Complexity" from *The Omnivore's Dilemma*, Pollan writes about an alternative to traditional agribusiness and profiles farmer Joel Salatin. With few outside raw materials, Salatin is able to run an incredibly productive farm that mimics a natural ecosystem in which nothing goes to waste. Pollan shows how order arises from the complex system of Salatin's farm, where everything plays a part, from a tree to a cow to the cow's manure, in a system—described as "holon" based—in which each element is simultaneously an individual whole and an active part in a complex system.

For Pollan, the omnivore's dilemma is one we face each day: what to have for dinner? This selection suggests that a healthy and sustainable answer to that question might come not from rejecting agribusiness entirely for an idealized agrarian past but from rethinking the intersection of business, farming, and food.

▶ TAGS: *collaboration, supply chains, technology, food, sustainability, tradition, holons, interconnections*

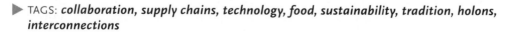

Questions for Critical Reading

1. What makes Polyface so successful? Locate passages where Pollan describes the key features of this farm, reading this essay critically to identify the key factors to the farm's success.

2. What is a "holon"? Use Pollan's text to define this term and to offer examples. Then apply the concept to another area by locating your own example of a holon.

3. Pollan subtitles this essay "Practicing Complexity." Use his text to explain what this means, referring to specific quotations or passages that show complexity in practice. You will need to read critically to determine your answer since Pollan never explains the relationship between this subtitle and his essay.

The Animals: Practicing Complexity

1. Tuesday Morning

It's not often I wake up at six in the morning to discover I've overslept, but by the time I had hauled my six-foot self out of the five-foot bed in Lucille's microscopic guest room, everyone was already gone and morning chores were nearly done. Shockingly, chores at Polyface commence as soon as the sun comes up (five-ish this time of year) and always before breakfast. Before coffee, that is, not that there was a drop of it to be had on this farm. I couldn't recall the last time I'd even attempted to do anything consequential before breakfast, or before caffeine at the very least.

When I stepped out of the trailer into the warm early morning mist, I could make out two figures—the interns, probably—moving around up on the broad shoulder of hill to the east, where a phalanx of portable chicken pens formed a checkerboard pattern on the grass. Among other things, morning chores consist of feeding and watering the broilers* and moving their pens one length down the hillside. I was supposed to be helping Galen and Peter do this, so I started up the path, somewhat groggily, hoping to get there before they finished.

As I stumbled up the hill, I was struck by how very beautiful the farm looked in the hazy early light. The thick June grass was silvered with dew, the sequence of bright pastures stepping up the hillside dramatically set off by broad expanses of blackish woods. Birdsong stitched the thick blanket of summer air, pierced now and again by the wood clap of chicken pen doors slamming shut. It was hard to believe this hillside had ever been the gullied wreck Joel had described at dinner, and even harder to believe that farming such a damaged landscape so intensively, rather than just letting it be, could restore it to health and yield this beauty. This is not the environmentalist's standard prescription. But Polyface is proof that people can sometimes do more for the health of a place by cultivating it rather than by leaving it alone.

By the time I reached the pasture Galen and Peter had finished moving the pens. Fortunately they were either too kind or too timid to give me a hard time for oversleeping. I grabbed a pair of water buckets, filled them from the big tub in the center of the pasture, and lugged them to the nearest pen. Fifty of these pens were spread out

---

* Broilers: Chickens raised for their meat rather than for egg production [Ed.].

across the damp grass in a serrated formation that had been calibrated to cover every square foot of this meadow in the course of the fifty-six days it takes a broiler to reach slaughter weight; the pens moved ten feet each day, the length of one pen. Each ten-by-twelve, two-foot-tall floorless pen houses seventy birds. A section of the roof is hinged to allow access, and a five-gallon bucket perched atop each unit fed a watering device suspended inside.

Directly behind each pen was a perfectly square patch of closely cropped grass re-   5
sembling a really awful Jackson Pollock painting, thickly spattered with chicken crap in pigments of white, brown, and green. It was amazing what a mess seventy chickens could make in a day. But that was the idea: Give them twenty-four hours to eat the grass and fertilize it with their manure, and then move them onto fresh ground.

Joel developed this novel method for raising broiler chickens in the 1980s and pop-ularized it in his 1993 book, *Pastured Poultry Profit$*, something of a cult classic among grass farmers. (Joel has self-published four other how-to books on farming, and all but one of them has a $ stepping in for an S somewhere in its title.) Left to their own devices, a confined flock of chickens will eventually destroy any patch of land, by pecking the grass down to its roots and poisoning the soil with their extremely "hot," or nitrog-enous, manure. This is why the typical free-range chicken yard quickly winds up bereft of plant life and hard as brick. Moving the birds daily keeps both the land and the birds healthy; the broilers escape their pathogens and the varied diet of greens supplies most of their vitamins and minerals. The birds also get a ration of corn, toasted soybeans, and kelp, which we scooped into long troughs in their pens, but Joel claims the fresh grass, along with the worms, grasshoppers, and crickets they peck out of the grass, provides as much as 20 percent of their diet — a significant savings to the farmer and a boon to the birds. Meanwhile, their manure fertilizes the grass, supplying all the ni-trogen it needs. The chief reason Polyface Farm is completely self-sufficient in nitrogen is that a chicken, defecating copiously, pays a visit to virtually every square foot of it at several points during the season. Apart from some greensand (a mineral supplement to replace calcium lost in the meadows), chicken feed is the only important input Joel buys, and the sole off-farm source of fertility. ("The way I look at it, I'm just returning some of the grain that's been extracted from this land over the last 150 years.") The chicken feed not only feeds the broilers but, transformed into chicken crap, feeds the grass that feeds the cows that, as I was about to see, feeds the pigs and the laying hens.

After we had finished watering and feeding the broilers, I headed up to the next pasture, where I could hear a tractor idling. Galen had told me Joel was moving the Eggmobile, an operation I'd been eager to watch. The Eggmobile, one of Joel's proudest innovations, is a ramshackle cross between a henhouse and a prairie schooner. Hous-ing four hundred laying hens, this rickety old covered wagon has hinged nesting boxes lined up like saddlebags on either side, allowing someone to retrieve eggs from the out-side. I'd first laid eyes on the Eggmobile the night before, parked a couple of paddocks away from the cattle herd. The hens had already climbed the little ramp into the safety of the coop for the night, and before we went down to dinner Joel had latched the trap-door behind them. Now it was time to move them into a fresh paddock, and Joel was bolting the Eggmobile to the hitch of his tractor. It wasn't quite 7:00 AM yet, but Joel seemed delighted to have someone to talk to, holding forth being one of his greatest pleasures.

"In nature you'll always find birds following herbivores," Joel explained, when I asked him for the theory behind the Eggmobile. "The egret perched on the rhino's nose, the pheasants and turkeys trailing after the bison—that's a symbiotic relationship we're trying to imitate." In each case the birds dine on the insects that would otherwise bother the herbivore; they also pick insect larvae and parasites out of the animal's droppings, breaking the cycle of infestation and disease. "To mimic this symbiosis on a domestic scale, we follow the cattle in their rotation with the Eggmobile. I call these gals our sanitation crew."

Joel climbed onto the tractor, threw it into gear, and slowly towed the rickety contraption fifty yards or so across the meadow to a paddock the cattle had vacated three days earlier. It seems the chickens eschew fresh manure, so he waits three or four days before bringing them in—but not a day longer. That's because the fly larvae in the manure are on a four-day cycle, he explained. "Three days is ideal. That gives the grubs a chance to fatten up nicely, the way the hens like them, but not quite long enough to hatch into flies." The result is prodigious amounts of protein for the hens, the insects supplying as much as a third of their total diet—and making their eggs unusually rich and tasty. By means of this simple little management trick, Joel is able to use his cattle's waste to "grow" large quantities of high-protein chicken feed for free; he says this trims his cost of producing eggs by twenty-five cents per dozen. (Very much his accountant father's son, Joel can tell you the exact economic implication of every synergy on the farm.) The cows further oblige the chickens by shearing the grass; chickens can't navigate in grass more than about six inches tall.

> **I began to understand just how radically different this sort of farming is from the industrial models I'd observed before.**

After Joel had maneuvered the Eggmobile into position, he opened the trapdoor, and an eager, gossipy procession of Barred Rocks, Rhode Island Reds, and New Hampshire Whites filed down the little ramp, fanning out across the pasture. The hens picked at the grasses, especially the clover, but mainly they were all over the cowpats, doing this frantic backward-stepping break-dance with their claws to scratch apart the caked manure and expose the meaty morsels within. Unfolding here before us, I realized, was a most impressive form of alchemy: Cowpatties in the process of being transformed into exceptionally tasty eggs.

"I'm convinced an Eggmobile would be worth it even if the chickens never laid a single egg. These birds do a more effective job of sanitizing a pasture than anything human, mechanical, or chemical, and the chickens love doing it." Because of the Eggmobile, Joel doesn't have to run his cattle through a headgate to slather Ivomectrin, a systemic paraciticide, on their hides or worm them with toxic chemicals. This is what Joel means when he says the animals do the real work around here. "I'm just the orchestra conductor, making sure everybody's in the right place at the right time."

That day, my second on the farm, as Joel introduced me to each of his intricately layered enterprises, I began to understand just how radically different this sort of farming is from the industrial models I'd observed before, whether in an Iowa cornfield or an organic chicken farm in California. Indeed, it is so different that I found Polyface's system difficult to describe to myself in an orderly way. Industrial processes follow a clear, linear, hierarchical logic that is fairly easy to put into words, probably because words follow a similar logic: First this, then that; put this in here, and then out comes that. But the relationship between cows and chickens on this farm (leaving aside for the moment the other creatures and relationships present here) takes the form of a loop rather than a line, and that makes it hard to know where to start, or how to distinguish between causes and effects, subjects and objects.

Is what I'm looking at in this pasture a system for producing exceptionally tasty eggs? If so, then the cattle and their manure are a means to an end. Or is it a system for producing grass-fed beef without the use of any chemicals, in which case the chickens, by fertilizing and sanitizing the cow pastures, comprise the means to that end. So does that make their eggs a product or a by-product? And is manure—theirs or the cattle's—a waste product or a raw material? (And what should we call the fly larvae?) Depending on the point of view you take—that of the chicken, cow, or even the grass—the relationship between subject and object, cause and effect, flips.

Joel would say this is precisely the point, and precisely the distinction between a biological and industrial system. "In an ecological system like this everything's connected to everything else, so you can't change one thing without changing ten other things.

"Take the issue of scale. I could sell a whole lot more chickens and eggs than I do.   15 They're my most profitable items, and the market is telling me to produce more of them. Operating under the industrial paradigm,* I could boost production however much I wanted—just buy more chicks and more feed, crank up that machine. But in a biological system you can never do just one thing, and I couldn't add many more chickens without messing up something else.

"Here's an example: This pasture can absorb four hundred units of nitrogen a year. That translates into four visits from the Eggmobile or two passes of a broiler pen. If I ran any more Eggmobiles or broiler pens over it, the chickens would put down more nitrogen than the grass could metabolize. Whatever the grass couldn't absorb would run off, and suddenly I have a pollution problem." Quality would suffer, too. Unless he added more cattle, to produce more grubs for the chickens and to keep the grass short enough for them to eat it, those chickens and eggs would not taste nearly as good as they do.

"It's all connected. This farm is more like an organism than a machine, and like any organism it has its proper scale. A mouse is the size of a mouse for a good reason, and a mouse that was the size of an elephant wouldn't do very well."

Joel likes to quote from an old agricultural textbook he dug out of the stacks at Virginia Tech many years ago. The book, which was published in 1941 by a Cornell Ag professor, offers a stark conclusion that, depending on your point of view, will sound either hopelessly quaint or arresting in its gnomic wisdom: "Farming is not adapted to large-scale operations because of the following reasons: Farming is concerned with plants and animals that live, grow, and die."

---

* Paradigm: Pattern or model [Ed.].

"Efficiency" is the term usually invoked to defend large-scale industrial farms, and it usually refers to the economies of scale that can be achieved by the application of technology and standardization. Yet Joel Salatin's farm makes the case for a very different sort of efficiency—the one found in natural systems, with their coevolutionary relationships and reciprocal loops. For example, in nature there is no such thing as a waste problem, since one creature's waste becomes another creature's lunch. What could be more efficient than turning cow pies into eggs? Or running a half-dozen different production systems—cows, broilers, layers, pigs, turkeys—over the same piece of ground every year?

Most of the efficiencies in an industrial system are achieved through simplification: doing lots of the same thing over and over. In agriculture, this usually means a monoculture of a single animal or crop. In fact, the whole history of agriculture is a progressive history of simplification, as humans reduced the biodiversity of their landscapes to a small handful of chosen species. (Wes Jackson calls our species "homo the homogenizer.") With the industrialization of agriculture, the simplifying process reached its logical extreme—in monoculture. This radical specialization permitted standardization and mechanization, leading to the leaps in efficiency claimed by industrial agriculture. Of course, how you choose to measure efficiency makes all the difference, and industrial agriculture measures it, simply, by the yield of one chosen species per acre of land or farmer.

By contrast, the efficiencies of natural systems flow from complexity and interdependence—by definition the very opposite of simplification. To achieve the efficiency represented by turning cow manure into chicken eggs and producing beef without chemicals you need at least two species (cows and chickens), but actually several more as well, including the larvae in the manure and the grasses in the pasture and the bacteria in the cows' rumens. To measure the efficiency of such a complex system you need to count not only all the products it produces (meat, chicken, eggs) but also all the costs it eliminates: antibiotics, wormers, paraciticides, and fertilizers.

Polyface Farm is built on the efficiencies that come from mimicking relationships found in nature, and layering one farm enterprise over another on the same base of land. In effect, Joel is farming in time as well as in space—in four dimensions rather than three. He calls this intricate layering "stacking" and points out that "it is exactly the model God used in building nature." The idea is not to slavishly imitate nature, but to model a natural ecosystem in all its diversity and interdependence, one where all the species "fully express their physiological distinctiveness." He takes advantage of each species' natural proclivities in a way that not only benefits that animal but other species as well. So instead of treating the chicken as a simple egg or protein machine, Polyface honors—and exploits—"the innate distinctive desires of a chicken," which include pecking in the grass and cleaning up after herbivores. The chickens get to do, and eat, what they evolved to do and eat, and in the process the farmer and his cattle both profit. What is the opposite of zero-sum?* I'm not sure, but this is it.

20

---

* Zero-sum: Situation or system in which one side gains all and the other loses all [Ed.].

Joel calls each of his stacked farm enterprises a "holon," a word I'd never encountered before. He told me he picked it up from Allan Nation; when I asked Nation about it, he pointed me to Arthur Koestler, who coined the term in *The Ghost in the Machine*. Koestler felt English lacked a word to express the complex relationship of parts and wholes in a biological or social system. A holon (from the Greek *holos*, or whole, and the suffix *on*, as in proton, suggesting a particle) is an entity that from one perspective appears a self-contained whole, and from another a dependent part. A body organ like the liver is a holon; so is an Eggmobile.

At any given time, Polyface has a dozen or more holons up and running, and on my second day Joel and Daniel introduced me to a handful of them. I visited the Raken House, the former toolshed where Daniel has been raising rabbits for the restaurant trade since he was ten. ("Raken?" "Half rabbit, half chicken," Daniel explained.) When the rabbits aren't out on the pasture in portable hutches, they live in cages suspended over a deep bedding of woodchips, in which I watched several dozen hens avidly pecking away in search of earthworms. Daniel explained that the big problem in raising rabbits indoors is their powerful urine, which produces so much ammonia that it scars their lungs and leaves them vulnerable to infection. To cope with the problem most rabbit farmers add antibiotics to their feed. But the scratching of the hens turns the nitrogenous rabbit pee into the carbonaceous bedding, creating a rich compost teeming with earthworms that feed the hens. Drugs become unnecessary and, considering how many rabbits and chickens lived in it, the air in the Raken was, well, tolerable. "Believe me," Daniel said, "if it weren't for these chickens, you'd be gagging right about now, and your eyes would sting something awful."

Before lunch I helped Galen and Peter move the turkeys, another holon. Moving the turkeys, which happens every three days, means setting up a new "feathernet"—a paddock outlined by portable electric fencing so lightweight I could carry and lay out the entire thing by myself—and then wheeling into it the shademobile, called the Gobbledy-Go. The turkeys rest under the Gobbledy-Go by day and roost on top of it at night. They happily follow the contraption into the fresh pasture to feast on the grass, which they seemed to enjoy even more than the chickens do. A turkey consumes a long blade of grass by neatly folding it over and over again with its beak, as if making origami. Joel likes to run his turkeys in the orchard, where they eat the bugs, mow the grass, and fertilize the trees and vines. (Turkeys will eat much more grass than chickens, and they don't damage crops the way chickens can.) "If you run turkeys in a grape orchard," Joel explained, "you can afford to stock the birds at only seventy percent of normal density, and space the vines at seventy percent of what's standard, because you're getting two crops off the same land. And at seventy percent you get much healthier birds and grapevines than you would at 100 percent. That's the beauty of stacking." By industry standards, the turkey and grape holon are each less than 100 percent efficient; together, however, they produce more than either enterprise would yield if fully stocked, and they do so without fertilizer, weeding, or pesticide.

I had witnessed one of the most winning examples of stacking in the cattle barn during my first visit to Polyface back in March. The barn is an unfancy open-sided structure where the cattle spend three months during the winter, each day consuming twenty-five pounds of hay and producing fifty pounds of manure. (Water makes up the difference.) But instead of regularly mucking out the barn, Joel leaves the manure in place, every few days covering it with another layer of woodchips or straw. As this layer cake of manure, woodchips, and straw gradually rises beneath the cattle, Joel simply raises the adjustable feed gate from which they get their ration of hay; by winter's end the bedding, and the cattle, can be as much as three feet off the ground. There's one more secret ingredient Joel adds to each layer of this cake: a few bucketfuls of corn. All winter long the layered bedding composts, in the process generating heat to warm the barn (thus reducing the animals' feed requirements), and fermenting the corn. Joel calls it his cattle's electric blanket.

Why the corn? Because there's nothing a pig enjoys more than forty-proof corn, and there's nothing he's better equipped to do than root it out with his powerful snout and exquisite sense of smell. "I call them my pigaerators," Salatin said proudly as he showed me into the barn. As soon as the cows head out to pasture in the spring, several dozen pigs come in, proceeding systematically to turn and aerate the compost in their quest for kernels of alcoholic corn.

> **These were the happiest pigs I'd ever seen.**

What had been an anaerobic decomposition suddenly turns aerobic, which dramatically heats and speeds up the process, killing any pathogens. The result, after a few weeks of pigaerating, is a rich, cakey compost ready to use.

"This is the sort of farm machinery I like: never needs its oil changed, appreciates over time, and when you're done with it you eat it." We were sitting on the rail of a wooden paddock, watching the pigs do their thing—a thing, of course, we weren't having to do ourselves. The line about the pigaerators was obviously well-worn. But the cliché that kept banging around in my head was "happy as a pig in shit." Buried clear to their butts in composting manure, a bobbing sea of wriggling hams and corkscrew tails, these were the happiest pigs I'd ever seen.

I couldn't look at their spiraled tails, which cruised above the earthy mass like conning towers on submarines, without thinking about the fate of pigtails in industrial hog production. Simply put, there *are* no pigtails in industrial hog production. Farmers "dock," or snip off, the tails at birth, a practice that makes a certain twisted sense if you follow the logic of industrial efficiency on a hog farm. Piglets in these CAFOs* are weaned from their mothers ten days after birth (compared with thirteen weeks in nature) because they gain weight faster on their drug-fortified feed than on sow's milk. But this premature weaning leaves the pigs with a lifelong craving to suck and chew, a need they gratify in confinement by biting the tail of the animal in front of them. A normal pig would fight off his molester, but a demoralized pig has stopped caring. "Learned helplessness" is the psychological term, and it's not uncommon in CAFOs, where tens of thousands of hogs spend their entire lives ignorant of earth or straw or sunshine, crowded together beneath a metal roof standing on metal slats suspended over a septic tank. It's not surprising that an animal as intelligent as a pig would get depressed under these circumstances, and a depressed pig will allow his tail to be chewed on to the point of infection. Since treating sick pigs is not economically efficient, these underperforming production units are typically clubbed to death on the spot.

---

* CAFOs: Concentrated Animal Feeding Operations [Ed.].

Tail docking is the USDA's recommended solution to the porcine "vice" of tail   30
chewing. Using a pair of pliers and no anesthetic, most—but not quite all—of the tail
is snipped off. Why leave the little stump? Because the whole point of the exercise is not
to remove the object of tail biting so much as to render it even more sensitive. Now a
bite to the tail is so painful that even the most demoralized pig will struggle to resist it.
Horrible as it is to contemplate, it's not hard to see how the road to such a hog hell is
smoothly paved with the logic of industrial efficiency.

A very different concept of efficiency sponsors the hog heaven on display here in
Salatin's barn, one predicated on what he calls "the pigness of the pig." These pigs too
were being exploited—in this case, tricked into making compost as well as pork. What
distinguishes Salatin's system is that it is designed around the natural predilections
of the pig rather than around the requirements of a production system to which the
pigs are then conformed. Pig happiness is simply the by-product of treating pigs as pigs
rather than as "a protein machine with flaws"—flaws such as pig tails and a tendency,
when emiserated, to get stressed.

Salatin reached down deep where his pigs were happily rooting and brought a
handful of fresh compost right up to my nose. What had been cow manure and woodchips just a few weeks before now smelled as sweet and warm as the forest floor in
summertime, a miracle of transubstantiation. As soon as the pigs complete their alchemy, Joel will spread the compost on his pastures. There it will feed the grasses, so
the grasses might again feed the cows, the cows the chickens, and so on until the snow
falls, in one long, beautiful, and utterly convincing proof that in a world where grass
can eat sunlight and food animals can eat grass, there is indeed a free lunch.

2. Tuesday Afternoon

After our own quick lunch (ham salad and deviled eggs), Joel and I drove to town in
his pickup to make a delivery and take care of a few errands. It felt sweet to be sitting
down for a while, especially after a morning taken up with loading the hay we'd baled
the day before into the hayloft. For me this rather harrowing operation involved attempting to catch fifty-pound bales that Galen tossed in my general direction from the
top of the hay wagon. The ones that didn't completely knock me over I hoisted onto a
conveyor belt that carried them to Daniel and Peter, stationed up in the hayloft. It was
an assembly line, more or less, and as soon as I fell behind (or just fell, literally) the hay
bales piled up fast at my station; I felt like Lucille Ball at the candy factory. I joked to Joel
that, contrary to his claims that the animals did most of the real work on this farm, it
seemed to me they'd left plenty of it for us.

On a farm, complexity sounds an awful lot like hard work, Joel's claims to the
contrary notwithstanding. As much work as the animals do, that's still us humans
out there moving the cattle every evening, dragging the broiler pens across the field
before breakfast (something I'd pledged I'd wake up in time for the next day), and
towing chicken coops hither and yon according to a schedule tied to the life cycle of
fly larvae and the nitrogen load of chicken manure. My guess is that there aren't too
many farmers today who are up for either the physical or mental challenge of this
sort of farming, not when industrializing promises to simplify the job. Indeed, a large
part of the appeal of industrial farming is its panoply of labor- and thought-saving

devices: machines of every description to do the physical work, and chemicals to keep crops and animals free from pests with scarcely a thought from the farmer. George Naylor works his fields maybe fifty days out of the year; Joel and Daniel and two interns are out there every day sunrise to sunset for a good chunk of the year.

Yet Joel and Daniel plainly relish their work, partly because it is so varied from day to day and even hour to hour, and partly because they find it endlessly interesting. Wendell Berry has written eloquently about the intellectual work that goes into farming well, especially into solving the novel problems that inevitably crop up in a natural system as complex as a farm. You don't see much of this sort of problem-solving in agriculture today, not when so many solutions come ready-made in plastic bottles. So much of the intelligence and local knowledge in agriculture has been removed from the farm to the laboratory, and then returned to the farm in the form of a chemical or machine. "Whose head is the farmer using?" Berry asks in one of his essays. "Whose head is using the farmer?"

"Part of the problem is, you've got a lot of D students left on the farm today," Joel said, as we drove around Staunton* running errands. "The guidance counselors encouraged all the A students to leave home and go to college. There's been a tremendous brain drain in rural America. Of course that suits Wall Street just fine; Wall Street is always trying to extract brainpower and capital from the countryside. First they take the brightest bulbs off the farm and put them to work in Dilbert's cubicle, and then they go after the capital of the dimmer ones who stayed behind, by selling them a bunch of gee-whiz solutions to their problems." This isn't just the farmer's problem, either. "It's a foolish culture that entrusts its food supply to simpletons."

It isn't hard to see why there isn't much institutional support for the sort of low-capital, thought-intensive farming Joel Salatin practices: He buys next to nothing. When a livestock farmer is willing to "practice complexity"—to choreograph the symbiosis of several different animals, each of which has been allowed to behave and eat as they evolved to—he will find he has little need for machinery, fertilizer, and, most strikingly, chemicals. He finds he has no sanitation problem or any of the diseases that result from raising a single animal in a crowded monoculture and then feeding it things it wasn't designed to eat. This is perhaps the greatest efficiency of a farm treated as a biological system: health.

I was struck by the fact that for Joel abjuring agrochemicals and pharmaceuticals is not so much a goal of his farming, as it so often is in organic agriculture, as it is an indication that his farm is functioning well. "In nature health is the default," he pointed out. "Most of the time pests and disease are just nature's way of telling the farmer he's doing something wrong."

At Polyface no one ever told me not to touch the animals, or asked me to put on a biohazard suit before going into the brooder house. The reason I had to wear one at Petaluma Poultry is because that system—a monoculture of chickens raised in close confinement—is inherently precarious, and the organic rules' prohibition on antibiotics puts it at a serious disadvantage. Maintaining a single-species animal farm on an industrial scale isn't easy without pharmaceuticals and pesticides. Indeed, that's why

---

* Staunton: Polyface Farm is located eight miles south of the city of Staunton, Virginia [Ed.].

these chemicals were invented in the first place, to keep shaky monocultures from collapsing. Sometimes the large-scale organic farmer looks like someone trying to practice industrial agriculture with one hand tied behind his back.

By the same token, a reliance on agrochemicals destroys the information feedback 40
loop on which an attentive farmer depends to improve his farming. "Meds just mask genetic weaknesses," Joel explained one afternoon when we were moving the cattle. "My goal is always to improve the herd, adapt it to the local conditions by careful culling. To do this I need to know: Who has a propensity for pinkeye? For worms? You simply have no clue if you're giving meds all the time.

"So you tell me, who's really *in* this so-called information economy? Those who learn from what they observe on their farm, or those who rely on concoctions from the devil's pantry?"

Of course the simplest, most traditional measure of a farm's efficiency is how much food it produces per unit of land; by this yardstick too Polyface is impressively efficient. I asked Joel how much food Polyface produces in a season, and he rattled off the following figures:

30,000 dozen eggs
10,000 broilers
800 stewing hens
50 beeves (representing 25,000 pounds of beef)
250 hogs (25,000 pounds of pork)
1,000 turkeys
500 rabbits

This seemed to me a truly astonishing amount of food from one hundred acres of grass. But when I put it that way to Joel that afternoon—we were riding the ATV up to the very top of the hill to visit the hogs in their summer quarters—he questioned my accounting method. It was far too simple.

"Sure, you can write that we produced all that food from a hundred open acres, but if you really want to be accurate about it, then you've got to count the four hundred and fifty acres of woodlot too." I didn't get that at all. I knew the woodlot was an important source of farm income in the winter—Joel and Daniel operate a small sawmill from which they sell lumber and mill whatever wood they need to build sheds and barns (and Daniel's new house). But what in the world did the forest have to do with producing food?

Joel proceeded to count the ways. Most obviously, the farm's water supply de- 45
pended on its forests to hold moisture and prevent erosion. Many of the farm's streams and ponds would simply dry up if not for the cover of trees. Nearly all of the farm's 550 acres had been deforested when the Salatins arrived; one of the first things Bill Salatin did was plant trees on all the north-facing slopes.

"Feel how cool it is in here." We were passing through a dense stand of oak and hickory. "Those deciduous trees work like an air conditioner. That reduces the stress on the animals in summer."

Suddenly we arrived at a patch of woodland that looked more like a savanna than a forest: The trees had been thinned and all around them grew thick grasses. This was one of the pig paddocks that Joel had carved out of the woods with the help of the pigs themselves. "All we do to make a new pig paddock is fence off a quarter acre of forest, thin out the saplings to let in some light, and then let the pigs do their thing." Their thing includes eating down the brush and rooting around in the stony ground, disturbing the soil in a way that induces the grass seed already present to germinate. Within several weeks, a lush stand of wild rye and foxtail emerges among the trees, and a savanna is born. Shady and cool, this looked like ideal habitat for the sunburn-prone pigs, who were avidly nosing through the tall grass and scratching their backs against the trees. There is something viscerally appealing about a savanna, with its pleasing balance of open grass and trees, and something profoundly heartening about the idea that, together, farmer and pigs could create such beauty here in the middle of a brushy second-growth forest.

But Joel wasn't through counting the benefits of woodland to a farm; idyllic pig habitat was the least of it.

"There's not a spreadsheet in the world that can measure the value of maintaining forest on the northern slopes of a farm. Start with those trees easing the swirling of the air in the pastures. That might not seem like a big deal, but it reduces evaporation in the fields—which means more water for the grass. Plus, a grass plant burns up fifteen percent of its calories just defying gravity, so if you can stop it from being wind whipped, you greatly reduce the energy it uses keeping its photovoltaic array pointed toward the sun. More grass for the cows. That's the efficiency of a hedgerow surrounding a small field, something every farmer used to understand before 'fencerow to fencerow' became USDA mantra."*

Then there is the water-holding capacity of trees, he explained, which on a north slope literally pumps water uphill. Next was all the ways a forest multiples a farm's biodiversity. More birds on a farm mean fewer insects, but most birds won't venture more than a couple hundred yards from the safety of cover. Like many species, their preferred habitat is the edge between forest and field. The biodiversity of the forest edge also helps control predators. As long as the weasels and coyotes have plenty of chipmunks and voles to eat, they're less likely to venture out and prey on the chickens. 50

There was more. On a steep northern slope trees will produce much more biomass than will grass. "We're growing carbon in the woods for the rest of the farm—not just the firewood to keep us warm in the winter, but also the woodchips that go into making our compost." Making good compost depends on the proper ratio of carbon to nitrogen; the carbon is needed to lock down the more volatile nitrogen. It takes a lot of woodchips to compost chicken or rabbit waste. So the carbon from the woodlots feeds the fields, finding its way into the grass and, from there, into the beef. Which it turns out is not only grass fed but tree fed as well.

These woods represented a whole other order of complexity that I had failed to take into account. I realized that Joel didn't look at this land the same way I did, or had before this afternoon: as a hundred acres of productive grassland patchworked into four hundred and fifty acres of unproductive forest. It was all of a biological piece, the trees and the grasses and the animals, the wild and the domestic, all part

---

* USDA mantra: Policy of the United States Department of Agriculture [Ed.].

of a single ecological system. By any conventional accounting, the forests here represented a waste of land that could be put to productive use. But if Joel were to cut down the trees to graze more cattle, as any conventional accounting would recommend, the system would no longer be quite as whole or as healthy as it is. *You can't just do one thing.*

For some reason the image that stuck with me from that day was that slender blade of grass in a too big, wind-whipped pasture, burning all those calories just to stand up straight and keep its chloroplasts* aimed at the sun. I'd always thought of the trees and grasses as antagonists—another zero-sum deal in which the gain of the one entails the loss of the other. To a point, this is true: More grass means less forest; more forest less grass. But either-or is a construction more deeply woven into our culture than into nature, where even antagonists depend on one another and the liveliest places are the edges, the in-betweens or both-ands. So it is with the blade of grass and the adjacent forest as, indeed, with all the species sharing this most complicated farm. Relations are what matter most, and the health of the cultivated turns on the health of the wild. Before I came to Polyface I'd read a sentence of Joel's that in its diction had struck me as an awkward hybrid of the economic and the spiritual. I could see now how characteristic that mixing is, and that perhaps the sentence isn't so awkward after all: "One of the greatest assets of a farm is the sheer ecstasy of life."

Exploring Context

1. Learn more about Polyface Farm by visiting its website at polyfacefarms.com. Look under "Production" for pictures of the Eggmobile and the Gobbledy-Go. You can also learn more about the farm by clicking on "Principles" and "Our Story." How do you see the ideas that Pollan discusses at work in the farm's website? Use your work on the success of Polyface from Question 1 of Questions for Critical Reading in making your response.

2. Visit the website for the U.S. Department of Agriculture's National Organic Program at ams.usda.gov/nop. What differences can you locate between the philosophy of organic farming at Polyface and that of the U.S. government? Which seems like a better standard for "organic," and why?

3. Spend some time at Michael Pollan's home page, michaelpollan.com. How does this essay fit into Pollan's other writing? What biases do you think he might have based on the information you find on his site? Do these biases make a difference in this essay?

Questions for Connecting

1. Pollan's description of Polyface Farm reveals a complex economic and ecological system. In what ways is this system consistent with the global supply chains that Thomas L. Friedman explores in "The Dell Theory of Conflict Prevention" (p. 166)? Can local and global economic systems work together?

---

* Chloroplasts: Specialized units in a plant cell responsible for photosynthesis [Ed.].

2. What role can organic farming play in the future of food? Synthesize the information in Elizabeth Dickinson's infographic "The Future of Food" (p. 144) with Pollan's observations about Polyface Farm. Connect your response to the work you did on Polyface and complexity in Questions 1 and 3 of Questions for Critical Reading.

3. David Foster Wallace points to some of the ethical complications of food in "Consider the Lobster" (p. 498). How do the practices of Polyface that Pollan explores complicate Wallace's observation? Is organic farming more "ethical"?

Language Matters

1. Find a passage in Pollan's text that you think is central to his argument. Identify each of the verbs in your selected passage. What are the key verbs? What is the *action* of these sentences? Are there more verbs used in clauses rather than other parts or components of the sentence? What are the implications of each verb's location and the kind of verb used? How can you apply these insights to your own writing?

2. Understanding your audience is a crucial factor in the success of any piece of writing. Looking at Pollan's writing identify the audience you think he has in mind. How do you know that? What audience should you keep in mind when writing in this class? How can you make sure that your writing reflects that audience?

3. Conjunctions are words that join nouns, phrases, or clauses. Find two quotations that seem to have some relation in Pollan's essay (or choose one from Pollan and one from another essay you've read for this class). Express the relationship between the two quotations using only one conjunction. When might you want to use this same conjunction in your own writing?

Assignments for Writing

1. Pollan reviews farmer Joel Salatin's alternative farming methods, in the process prompting us to question the very nature of farming. By attempting to simplify and sanitize farming, have we moved away from the health and efficiency inherent in a natural system? Can the benefits of biotechnology outweigh the benefits of symbiosis and nature? As biotechnology pushes science and food toward new frontiers, will we find that the old ways of farming are the better, more healthful ways, or is technologically engineered food simply a measurement of healthy progress, no different than progress in any other arena? Using Pollan's essay, formulate an argument on the relationship between food production methods and health. To support your position, consider the alternatives to Salatin's farming methods, the effect of farming practices on our health, and how the interdependence among the different parts of the farming process affects not only the farmer, the animals, and the farm's products but the consumer as well. Use your work with complexity from Question 3 of Questions for Critical Reading.

2. Using Pollan's essay, write a paper in which you evaluate the efficiency of nature-based farming methods versus the efficiency of biotechnology-based farming methods in food production. What does Pollan mean when he describes Salatin's methods as "holon" based? Why don't we all still farm in the traditional, interdependent manner practiced

by Salatin? What are the benefits and disadvantages of "alternative" natural farming? What are the benefits and disadvantages of farming with biotechnology? Do complexity and multiculture lead to better efficiency? Are complexity and multiculture more or less efficient than simplicity and monoculture? Use your work with Pollan's essay from Questions for Critical Reading to support your argument.

3. As agribusiness continues to expand in a global economy, will we find that the old ways of farming are the more effective ways, or will we find that current monoculture practices are needed to keep up with the demands of an ever-expanding world population? Using Pollan's essay, write a paper in which you evaluate the advantages of monoculture-based farming methods versus multiculture-based farming methods in food production. What are the benefits and disadvantages of "alternative" natural farming, or what Pollan calls "coevolutionary relationships"? What are the benefits and disadvantages of farming with biotechnology in the form of vaccines, disease-resistant crop varieties, chemical fertilizers, and genetically modified seeds? Are complexity and multiculture necessary to feed the modern world? Are complexity and multiculture more or less efficient than simplicity and monoculture? Draw on your work on complexity from Question 3 of Questions for Critical Reading.

POSTSECRET

PostSecret (postsecret.com) is a collaborative art project and blog created by Frank Warren. Developed in 2005, the project accepts postcard art from anonymous creators with only one rule: The postcard must reveal a true secret never before shared. Postcards are featured on the blog every Sunday in a minimalist format, without comment features or archives of past posts. PostSecret aims to be liberating for the secret's author as well as for readers, who may find secrets they could have written themselves. Warren has published five books from these collected postcards: *PostSecret: Extraordinary Confessions from Ordinary Lives* (2005), *My Secret: A PostSecret Book* (2006), *The Secret Lives of Men and Women: A PostSecret Book* (2007), *A Lifetime of Secrets: A PostSecret Book* (2007), and *Confessions on Life, Death, and God* (2009).

The postcards included here, excerpted from *PostSecret: Extraordinary Confessions from Ordinary Lives*, cover a number of topics, each revealing a secret without any ties to the original artist's identity. Some secrets are life changing, others seem trivial, but all are important enough to their authors to create and share. Many included here focus on identity, including race, sexuality, and self-esteem, revealing the incongruities between the ways we present ourselves to one another and what we consider to be our inner truth.

▶ TAGS: *identity, secrecy, aesthetic representation, privacy, revelation, sexuality, visual argument*

Questions for Critical Reading

1. As you examine the postcards included here, look for common themes. What kinds of secrets do people tend to keep and tend to share? Why are these the kinds of things people feel the need to keep secret?

2. Some postcards use crude, hand-drawn illustrations and others use photography or some other higher-quality art. Does the medium make the revelation of the secret more or less effective?

3. What is the relationship between the design of each postcard and its content? Consider the visual argument being made in these postcards. How do the visual elements reinforce the secret being revealed? What do they reveal about the author of the postcard?

Portfolio of Postcards

(Back): *I married someone I don't love because I wanted to wear the dress.*

[I DON'T WANT TO GO TO COLLEGE]

I WANT TO GROW SHIT.

I am bULiMiC feMiNiSt

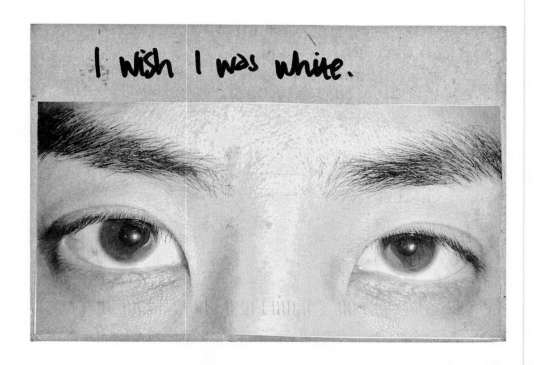

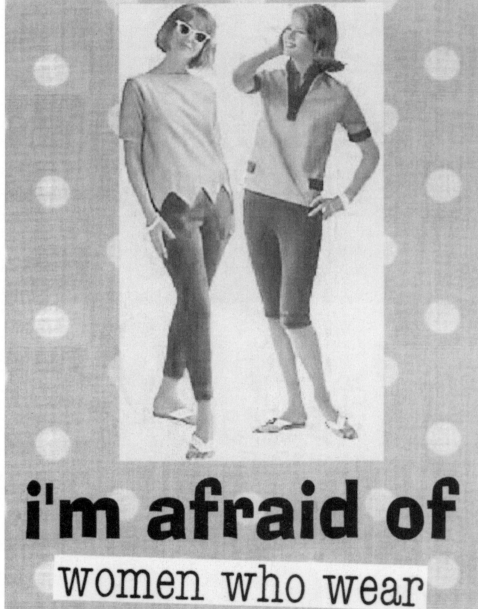

i'm afraid of women who wear capri pants

> I know that sending in a stupid postcard to share a secret
> with a bunch of strangers won't do a damn thing to change
> the daily loneliness and unhappiness in my life.
>
> And I sent this anyway.

Exploring Context

1. Frank Warren continues to post new additions to this project at postsecret.com. Examine the most recent set of postcards, making note of the kinds of secrets people are both keeping and revealing through PostSecret. Can you notice any trends? Do some of these seem more like things that should be kept a secret? Also look at the e-mail responses to recently posted postcards. Do they seem to be supportive? Shaming? What do they say about the validity of the project?

2. PostSecret is so popular that it has its own community website (postsecretcommunity .com). Explore this site, particularly the forums located under "PostSecret Chat," in order to expand your response to Question 1 of Questions for Critical Reading.

3. PostSecret also has its own Twitter feed (twitter.com/postsecret). How do these tweets function differently from the postcards themselves? Why do you think this stream exists?

Questions for Connecting

1. Several of the postcards here deal with race and ethnic identity. Using ideas from Steve Olson's "The End of Race: Hawaii and the Mixing of Peoples" (p. 334), consider why these secrets exist. What do they say about the persistence of race? Do these secrets support Olson's analysis about race's future?

2. Kenji Yoshino examines social demands to "cover" parts of our identity in "Preface" and "The New Civil Rights" (p. 552). How do these postcards function as an antidote to covering? What are the risks of covering, and what avenues do we have to escape these pressures?

3. Peter Singer's "Visible Man: Ethics in a World without Secrets" (p. 462) explores the complicated notions of privacy in relation to technology. How does PostSecret reflect concerns about privacy? What is the relationship between privacy and anonymity?

Language Matters

1. Editors often use correction symbols; your instructor might use them as well. Design symbols to represent some common errors you make. How are design and meaning related? Would your symbols make immediate sense to someone else?

2. Consider the relationship between form and content using these postcards. Given the limited space of a postcard, how do these authors convey information? Apply your findings to the form of the academic paper. What kind of content does it allow? What kind of content doesn't "fit," given the space of the form?

3. Some of these postcards use ellipses. Using a grammar handbook or other reference resource, review the rules for using ellipses and then apply them to the postcards. Are they used properly? When should you use ellipses in your own writing?

Assignments for Writing

1. Select one of the postcards and write a paper in which you analyze its argument. Refer to the introduction for guidance on how to analyze visual arguments (p. 9). Use as well your work from Questions for Critical Reading.

2. Using the secrets revealed in these postcards, write a paper on the relationship between anonymity and secrecy. Does one rely on the other? How does having anonymity allow one to reveal secrets?

3. Write a paper in which you use the postcards selected here to trace a theme. What kinds of secrets do people tend to reveal? How do they reveal them visually? Why might they feel they need to keep these things secret in the first place?

JENNIFER POZNER

Journalist **Jennifer Pozner** is the founder and executive director of Women in Media & News, an organization devoted to media literacy that also advocates for media reform. She has been published in *Bitch* magazine, the *Chicago Tribune, Newsday*, and the *Huffington Post*. Pozner regularly speaks on college campuses and provides commentary on television and radio shows, as well as in the documentary *Miss Representation* (2011). *Reality Bites Back: The Troubling Truth about Guilty Pleasure TV* (2010) is her first book. In 2011, it was included on *Ms.* magazine's list of the "Top 100 Feminist Non-Fiction Books."

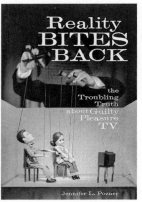

In *Reality Bites Back*, Pozner analyzes reality television's messages through a feminist lens. Pozner locates and analyzes a pattern in the portrayals of race, gender, class, sexuality, romance, and body image in reality television, claiming that most series — from *The Bachelor* to *What Not to Wear* — perpetuate negative and limiting ideals for women. She finds that the images promoted by these shows normalize domestic violence, eating disorders, gossip, and the idea that romance and beauty are the only things that can make women happy.

In "Ghetto Bitches, China Dolls, and Cha Cha Divas," a chapter from *Reality Bites Back*, Pozner examines the mixed messages present in the long-running reality competition series *America's Next Top Model* (*ANTM*). She argues that through selective casting and heavy editing, *ANTM* perpetuates damaging racist stereotypes, while superficially claiming to promote all types of individual beauty and to empower women. Ultimately, Pozner questions the impact that such portrayals of race may have on how women of color view themselves.

▶ TAGS: *stereotypes, reality TV, gender, beauty, identity, sexuality*

Questions for Critical Reading

1. How real do you think reality television is? Jot down notes about your own experiences with these television shows. As you read, pay attention to the ways in which Pozner indicates that these shows are actually highly scripted. Knowing that "reality" shows are mostly scripted, do you think that racial stereotyping on *America's Next Top Model* is as dangerous as Pozner implies?

2. Why do television show producers depict people in racially biased roles? Do you think this is a positive or negative experience for viewers? How so? Look for evidence to support your position as you read Pozner.

3. In this selection, Pozner argues that shows such as *America's Next Top Model* should be taken off the air. Do you agree with her position? Locate passages that support your own position on this issue.

Ghetto Bitches, China Dolls, and Cha Cha Divas

It's my number one passion in my life to stretch the definition of beauty. I listen to many heartbreaking stories of women who thought they would be happier if they looked different. I want every girl to appreciate the skin she's in.

—TYRA BANKS, apologizing for making girls don blackface on *America's Next Top Model*[1]

As executive producer, Tyra Banks claims *America's Next Top Model* aims to expand beauty standards, as she herself did as the first Black solo cover model for *GQ*, *Victoria's Secret*, and *Sports Illustrated*'s swimsuit edition. Chapter 2 [not included here] documented how she fails at this lofty goal regarding weight, size, and eating disorders. Does she do any better at exploding race-based beauty biases?

Sometimes, yes. She exhorts *ANTM* contestants to be confident and love themselves, flaws and all. Her methods may be devised to break most models' spirits for our viewing pleasure, but there's something to be said for casting diverse young women and at least telling them that they're gorgeous. In a TV landscape that has typically depicted girls of color as ugly when not ignoring them entirely, sometimes a slightly positive mixed message is as good as it gets. Better yet, every once in a while a truly subversive, dare I say *feminist*, moment can be found among *ANTM*'s emotional and cultural wreckage. Model Anchal Joseph, who emigrated to the United States from New Delhi when she was six years old, wore blue contacts to her cycle 7 audition. When the judges asked her why, she said she'd always wanted different colored eyes:

> TYRA: Do you think there's something culturally in America or even in your own country that is telling you that a lighter eye is prettier?*
> ANCHAL: In India they do believe that lighter skin and lighter eyes are prettier. I actually want to beat that. Be like, "Hey, I'm dark, I'm beautiful, and I'm Indian, so I don't have to have light skin or have light-colored eyes to be beautiful."

After Anchal's baby browns were photographed au natural, the judges said she was so gorgeous she could be Miss World. Asked how she felt looking at her picture without the contacts, she replied:

> ANCHAL: It makes me feel pretty.
> TYRA: It does? Why's that?

---

* Asking Anchal to discuss beauty standards in the United States versus those from her "own country" is typical of *ANTM*. The show both normalizes and others immigrants, portraying them as an unmistakable part of the beauty that is America, while constantly implying that they are less authentically American than those born here. [All notes are Pozner's.]

ANCHAL: Because in a way I think I was hiding behind them. I'm glad. [At this,
she broke down in tears of self-acceptance—and we got to watch her psychological breakthrough.]

TYRA [to judge Nigel Barker]: Nigel, you being Indian, how do you respond to
that?*

NIGEL: You are beautiful the way you are. We are all unique in our own ways,
and it's that uniqueness that makes people beautiful.

I'll never accuse Tyra Banks of having a tenth of Toni Morrison's wisdom. Still, I
was impressed by the editing of Anchal's initial longing for societal affirmation, à la
The Bluest Eye, followed by her eventual realization that her dark skin and brown eyes
simply make her more authentically stunning.

China Dolls, Dragon Ladies, and Spicy Latinas

Such moments are exceptions on *ANTM*, which [. . .] set many of the templates for ra-   5
cial typecasting on network reality TV.

Of the 170 contestants cast by cycle 13, only five besides Anchal have been East
or South Asian. The first, April Wilkner, half-Japanese and half-white, said that before
she decided to model, "I never really thought about my ethnicity." *ANTM* made sure
viewers could think of little else. They framed her as uncomfortable with her cultural
identity, while confusing that identity by adorning her with symbols from a country
unconnected to her heritage (Chinese lanterns placed on her head, a dragon painted
on her chest).

Cut to the cycle 6 audition of Korean contestant Gina Choe, who said, "I think
there's just not enough Asian models out there. I feel that I can break down that barrier, and I think it's my responsibility." Nice! You'd almost think the casting directors finally sought out an Asian American woman who was proud of her racial background.

Sadly, no. A moment later, she told us, "I'm not into Asian guys." From then until
her elimination five weeks later, Gina was edited as if she was struggling with "an
identity crisis," and stereotyped as an "exotic" fading flower who couldn't stand up for
herself when attacked by her competitors. She was vilified on the show, on fan sites,
and by culture critics as being a poor representative of her race for making statements
such as "As a Korean person and as an American person, I'm just a little bit of both,
and I don't know which one I am more of." What went unexplored was why *Top Model*
thought it appropriate to make Gina feel she had to choose whether she was "more" tied
to her ethnicity or her nationality—the subtext of which implies that a Korean American is not a "real" American, just as Anchal was asked about attitudes in her "own
country."

---

* Close, but no cigar. Fashion photographer and *ANTM* judge Nigel Barker (who passes for white) isn't Indian,
he's British and Sri Lankan. Just another instance of *Top Model* playing the all-Asians-are-alike game, as
many other reality shows do.

Top Model has mixed and matched from various long-held stereotypes about Asian women in American movies, described in *The Asian Mystique* as including the cold and calculating "Dragon Lady" (traits assigned to ambivalent April) and the submissive "Lotus Flower . . . China Doll" (docile Gina).[2] Cycle 11 finally cast a truly proud Asian American woman . . . then promptly reduced her to the clichéd "Vixen/Sex Nymph." When we were first introduced to Sheena Sakai, a half-Japanese, half-Korean go-go dancer with a large rack and an even bigger swagger, she announced, "I'm gonna show you, America. You ain't ready for this yellow fever. One time for the Asians!" Sheena was recruited by a casting director who saw her working as a stuntwoman for the movie *Tropic Thunder*—but as is often the case on reality television, producers revealed only those details that reinforced the frame they'd chosen for her character. Since they wanted her as that season's resident "hootchie," her stunt work wasn't discussed on the show or mentioned on her CW bio. Instead, she was criticized as too sexy in every episode. Early on a judge sneered, "You look like Victoria's Secretions." Later, during a challenge in Amsterdam's red light district, where prostitutes pose in storefronts to entice customers, she was told she looked like she should be selling herself in that window, rather than modeling clothes.

> **She was criticized as too sexy in every episode.**

Latina *Top Model* hopefuls have been consistently typecast as promiscuous sluts, "naturally" good dancers, or bursting with machisma and ready to throw down. Semi-finalist Angelea didn't make cycle 12's final cut after she got into a fight and was written off as hot-tempered, "ghettofied," and easily provoked to violence. 10

Cycle 8 winner Jaslene "Cha Cha Diva" Gonzalez, who spoke Spanish in her Cover-Girl commercial, was called "spicy" and portrayed as a cross between a "drag queen" and Carmen Miranda. High school dropout Felicia "Fo" Porter, half-Mexican and half-Black, was used to reinforce the "Latinos are lazy" trope: The unemployed model said she auditioned for the show to save herself "the busy hassle of putting your pictures out to agencies and hoping to get a call back."

Other Latina models throughout the series have been called "fiery" as a compliment and "hootchie" as an insult. Second-cycle winner Yoanna House, named one of *Latina* magazines "It Girls," notably avoided such typecasting. Since she is fair-skinned enough to pass for white, the show chose to erase her ethnicity, playing into the standard Hollywood convention that positions Caucasians as the "default" American. Most viewers were unaware that she was half-Mexican. Instead, media outlets from NPR and *Time Out Chicago* to *International Cosmetic News* refer to Jaslene as "the first Latina" to win the series, an assumption echoed by *ANTM*'s fans.[3]

Entitled Divas and Ghetto Bitches

African Americans are pigeonholed into similar categories on *ANTM*, which introduced the Angry Black Woman to reality TV before Omarosa was a glint in the eye of *The Apprentice* producer Mark Burnett. Season 1 brought us self-indulgent, catty Camille, the Black model everyone loved to hate. By season 3, Tyra took to pretending she's not an executive producer who casts for type. She warned eventual winner "Eva the Diva" to act sweet, because "I don't want to cast another Black bitch." But of course she did cast and edit Eva as the bitch du jour—until week 8, when two white image consultants instructed her to doff the diva label by "showing your best possible manners."*

The Violent Ghetto Girl (or as one model was described, the "ghetto Black Barbie") also looms large. During her third-season tryout, low-income single mom Tiffany Richardson, who got kicked out of high school for acting like "the Devil," said she wanted to be on *ANTM* to "soften up" because "I don't want to fight no mo." Uh-oh. The semifinalists went out to a bar, where a local "skank" poured a drink over Tiffany's head. She freaked out, yelled, "Bitch poured beer on my weave!" and hurled a glass at her. Bottles started flying, and they hightailed it out of there. A white model condemned violence; Tiffany retorted, "That's great, Martin Luther King. But I'm with Malcolm." Violence is "all I know," she said, because "nobody ever taught me to handle my problems without fighting."

Though she was "trying to change for the better," she got sent home to "the hood" by the end of the episode, calling herself a failure. But because she *always* wants to feature "another Black bitch"—especially of the ratings-generating "ghetto" variety—Banks brought Tiffany back for the fourth season, after she'd been through anger management classes.† She made it to the seventh episode, where she couldn't read from a teleprompter, grumbled, "This is humiliating more and more each week," and was eliminated. This time, instead of calling herself a failure, she smiled, hugged the other models, and told them she'd be okay. This didn't sit well with Tyra, who prefers self-flagellation and depression from rejectees, especially when they're poor and Black. So, she took it upon herself to remind the girl of her place: "This should be serious to you!" Tiffany replied that looks can be deceiving, but she was "sick of crying about stuff that I cannot change. I'm sick of being disappointed, I'm sick of all of it." Now apparently clairvoyant, Tyra yelled that Tiffany wasn't really sick of disappointment, because if she were, "you would stand up and take control of your destiny!"

Tyra continued to criticize her "defeatist attitude" until Tiffany got choked up, saying, "I don't have a bad attitude. Maybe I am angry inside, I've been through stuff, so I'm angry, but—" But she couldn't finish, because Tyra cut her off with a neck-rolling, finger-pointing, top-of-her-lungs tirade:

> Be quiet, Tiffany! BE QUIET! STOP IT! I have never in my life yelled at a girl like this! When my mother yells like this it's because she loves me. I was rooting for you, we were all rooting for you! How dare you! Learn something from this! When you go to bed at night, you lay there and you take responsibility for yourself, because nobody's going to take responsibility for you. You rollin' your eyes and you act like it's because you've heard it all before—you've heard

15

---

* Lighter-skinned African American and biracial girls such as cycle 4 winner Naima Mora and second-season finalist Mercedes Yvette have often escaped this frame. In this way, the show plays to intraracial beauty hierarchies in media, advertising, and political history positing that the darker a woman's complexion, the nastier her personality. Such hierarchies continue to cause pain within communities of color.[4]
† Tiffany never really had a chance of winning *ANTM*, lacking the "girl next door" image demanded by program sponsors CoverGirl and *Seventeen*, which use the winner in their ads. Producers raised her hopes for nothing; they only had her return because they knew she'd be a ratings draw. She was one of the most talked-about contestants on the third season, even though she lasted only one episode. "Bitch poured beer on my weave!" became an iconic quote, repeated on hundreds of fan sites and used as a *Vanity Fair* headline.[5]

it all before—you don't know where the hell I come from, you have no idea what I've been through. But I'm not a victim. I grow from it and I learn. Take responsibility for yourself!*

And with that, Tiffany was turned into *ANTM*'s symbol of the irresponsible ghetto chick who isn't willing to work hard to care for herself or her child. Such pop culture imagery builds on decades of inaccurate, scapegoating news reports dating back to the 1980s, which blamed so-called "welfare queens" (a phrase that became code for poor women of color, often young mothers) for the poverty, educational inequity, and violence that plagued their communities. According to this media mantra, these weren't systemic problems requiring institutional solutions, they simply stemmed from laziness, greed, and lack of discipline inherent among poor youth of color. (Black and Latina girls bore the added burden of being branded promiscuous and immoral, while young men of color were pathologized as "Super Predators.")[†] Tyra's hissy fit about Tiffany's supposed "victim" mentality and "defeatist attitude" was a revival of that sorry script. That she issued this verbal beatdown in the name of "love"—and treated the twenty-two-year-old as "ungrateful" for the chance to be used and shamed on national television—is deeply manipulative. That *Top Model* affects viewers' perceptions of young women of color is even worse. Parroting Tyra's rhetoric, a Television Without Pity commenter wrote, "Tiff *and others like her* can't be bothered to pick up a book? Read. Learn. Get good grades . . . Tyra was right. Get off your ass Tiff and accept responsibility for yourself. Her granmama put a roof over her head and food on the table and yet Tiff can't be bothered to study and get good grades and pull herself out of poverty? Slackers disgust me" (emphasis mine).[7]

Uppity Black Girls Need Humble Pie

Faced with a strong Black woman who couldn't be shoehorned as an ignorant, angry, ghetto bitch, Tyra had only one more card to play: "Bourgie Snob." Meet Yaya DaCosta, cycle 3's Ivy League runner-up. An African Studies and International Relations student

---

* Seems Tyra needed Tiffany's anger management course more than the model did. Faced with the privileged judge screaming in her face, Tiffany remained calm and in control. With an even voice, she told the cameras, "I'm not gonna break down for you or nobody else. You ain't did shit for me but bring me here and put me through hell." As the credits rolled, we heard her say she's glad that Tyra cares about her, and that will inspire her to be a better person. Two years later, Tiffany finally revealed her honest reaction to the incident on an *E! True Hollywood Story* exposé about *ANTM*. "Before, in all of my interviews . . . I would always tell people, 'Oh, Tyra loves me. I feel like the reason that she yelled at me was because she loved me.' That was bull. So let me tell you how I really felt. I feel like if she loved me, she wouldn't have showed it the way she showed it. Like my grandmother said, 'If you love someone, you won't humiliate them.'"

† To convince the public to roll back the social safety net for the poor, 1980s and 1990s conservatives waged a war in the media against poor women. In addition to the derogatory "welfare queen" said to be "popping out babies for checks," African Americans and Latinas in particular were labeled "immoral" "brood mares," and even called "public enemy number one" by ABC's Diane Sawyer. *Newsweek* senior editor Jonathan Alter went further, insisting that "every threat to the fabric of this country—from poverty to crime to homelessness—is connected to out-of-wedlock teen pregnancy." Riddled with inaccuracies, these reports nevertheless helped turn the tide of public opinion, enabling Democratic President Bill Clinton to pass a punitive welfare reform package in 1996 that resulted in hundreds of thousands of women and children falling deeper into poverty.[6]

at Brown University, she spoke Portuguese and French, auditioned with her hair in braids, and intended "to represent a beauty that is Black." She was elegant, intelligent, and poised. Tyra was initially "impressed" with Yaya's education and "her Afro-centric vibe," which may be why she was one of the only girls in *ANTM*'s history to be allowed to wear her hair in a natural 'fro, saying it showed her pride as a strong Black woman.

Alas, the sisterlove was short lived. Yaya looked like a stunning "chocolate Barbarella" in photos, but Tyra said she didn't seem "modelesque" in person. "Think . . . glamour, as opposed to natural," she instructed. A white stylist was brought on to tell her that her "Earth Mother" look would turn off advertisers: "If you go into a toothpaste ad, are you gonna go in a dashiki?" she sneered. "They'll see the big hair and they'll see the African print and it's like, oh my God!" Later, during judging, the stylist disparaged her "intensity to prove your sort of Africanness . . . , it's overbearing. It's just too much. It's sort of a layer on top of a layer." To her credit, the camera caught Tyra glaring, clearly pissed off. In contrast, Yaya wasn't allowed to be upset at this obviously racist swipe.* When she protested being stereotyped and turned into "a cliché," Tyra reprimanded her for "being very defensive, and it's not attractive," and made her apologize to a kente cloth hat. During evaluation, Tyra reiterated that "Yaya brings [a] superiority, condescending attitude" that is "so ugly."

From then on, they had their frame. Through the magic of editing, Yaya's education and elegance became pretentiousness; her eloquence was characterized as showing off. She took dazzling photographs and shined on the catwalk, yet for the rest of the competition Yaya was represented as an arrogant, Blacker-than-thou snob. She was chosen as fashion designers' favorite at client meetings, yet the judges condemned her as so stuck-up and hypersensitive that "no one will want to work with you." She made it to the finale, but lost because the judges didn't consider her "likable" enough.

Viewers tend to believe that the caricatures they've seen on reality TV match (or at least resemble) participants' real-life personalities, regardless of the truth or falseness of that person's portrayal. Yaya is a case in point. The image foisted on her by *ANTM*'s producers clung to her for five years and numerous film and TV jobs later. In 2009, when *Entertainment Weekly* reported that she landed a role on ABC's *Ugly Betty*, readers said they "hate Yaya with a passion," called her "arrogant," "pretentious," and "nasty," and wrote that "she needs a big piece of humble pie!" When a smart, self-possessed African American woman is said to "need humble pie," the message is that this "uppity" Black person just doesn't know her place.[8]

Curious George, Work It Out!

Some of the above tropes, like Tyra's tirade against Tiffany, require some unpacking to realize how they connect to a long history of attacks on women of color in politics and the media. But deep-seated beauty biases were all too clear in the representation of

---

* Banks has regularly encouraged Black models to put up with blatant bigotry she herself would never stand for. For example, on an episode in Spain, a male model disparaged African American contestant Jaeda Young, saying he didn't like Black women and didn't want to kiss her in a commercial they had to film for Secret deodorant. Editing emphasized how shaken she was by his racism, which could have led to a denunciation of bias in the industry by the judges. Instead, they eliminated Jaeda for making "excuses" and having poor chemistry in her ad.

Kelle, an affluent African American gallery owner who called herself "a white girl with a really good tan." She came into the competition exuding confidence to the point of conceit, but a few weeks in Tyra's den of self-doubt changed all that.

Over numerous episodes, viewers were treated to multiple scenes in which Kelle sadly inspected herself in a mirror, pondering newly perceived flaws and telling the camera that she'd grown to believe the judges' appraisal of her. "I just see myself and I'm like, *Oh my God, I'm hideous!*" she sobbed. "I can't look at myself in the mirror anymore. . . . Every time I look in the mirror I'm crying." As one of her competitors explained, "Kelle came in this competition and she was like, 'Oh, oh, I'm beautiful!' and the judges have totally broke her!" After being told repeatedly that her face, and particularly her mouth, were not photogenic, she broke down in a fit of internalized racism. While Tyra made each girl reveal her deepest body insecurity, Kelle complained that she hated her profile. "It's like I have a protruding mouth. You know what I mean? I almost feel like I have a monkey mouth. I guess [it] can look like really, I don't know, primitive."

It's telling that the show chose to air that comment rather than leaving it on the cutting room floor with hundreds of not-ready-for-prime-time hours of tape. Yet such a statement could have been used as a teaching moment, to raise awareness of the historic dehumanization of Black women starting with imagery during slavery and progressing to contemporary ads that depict Black women as exotic, primal animals. So, did Tyra "I'm a proud, beautiful Black woman" Banks break it down for Kelle, and for the millions of young viewers who idolize the former Victoria's Secret supermodel? Did she tell Kelle to do some emotional work to reject the external messages she's gotten from a culture that tells Black women that they are low, ugly creatures? Or did she even spout one of her clichéd "Girl, your mouth is fierce!" Tyra-isms?

Fat chance. Rebuking racist imagery doesn't fly in advertiser-driven reality TV, and Banks's role as producer took precedence over any sense of social responsibility or ethnic solidarity. "We're gonna have to do some profile shots and analyze that . . . I'd be like, 'Go, Curious George, work it out!'" *Top Model*'s diva-in-chief replied. "I'm glad you guys are so honest, you know what I mean? That's what it's about, that everybody understands that you're not perfect. And that this is a business of smoke and mirrors, and fooling people into thinking you look like something else."

Let's unpack, shall we? A Black teenager thinks she's hot until *ANTM*'s judges convince her she's an ugly ape. To make her feel better, Tyra calls her Curious George* but assures her that with the "smoke and mirrors" of makeup, lighting, and camera angles she can "fool people" into thinking she's not so primitive after all. Kelle revealed what *ANTM* taught her in an episode titled, "The Girl Who Cries When She Looks in the Mirror":

> **A Black teenager thinks she's hot until *ANTM*'s judges convince her she's an ugly ape.**

---

* Curious George, the inquisitive monkey of children's book and PBS Kids fame, has been interpreted by literacy and culture scholars as a slave narrative. In the original story, The Man with the Big Yellow Hat kidnaps George from the African jungle and brings him to America, where he gets thrown in jail, escapes, and ends up behind bars in a zoo.[9]

I've realized what it was. It's this part of my mouth. It's like an extra layer of fat or something. So it's like a snout. . . . I was in denial about my snout. And now I know, and so it's just hard to work . . . [it makes me] very limited.

Black Models Gone "Wild"

Here's a phrase I wish I didn't have to say: At least Tyra didn't order Kelle to wear a monkey suit.

Remember the "sexy little animals" ad *ANTM* shot for Lubriderm as soon as they arrived in Cape Town, South Africa, mentioned in chapter 2 [not included here]? That shoot—like Kelle's "Curious George" instruction—fits into a lengthy and shameful history of racist imagery in advertising, media, and American politics.

The depiction of African Americans as animals and/or savages dates back to pre-abolition newspapers and magazines, where political cartoons and crude artwork accompanied editorial copy justifying the ownership of, and denial of basic human rights for, "the Negro race." At the same time, print ads sold all manner of products using such imagery to mock and dehumanize Black men, women, and children. Historically such media images functioned as visual propaganda, working to convince whites that Black people were not quite human—laying the groundwork for rationalizing slavery before abolition, segregation during Jim Crow, and contemporary proeugenics arguments.[10]

Such imagery is no longer considered appropriate in most mainstream news outlets.* But just as modern beauty advertisers discovered more sophisticated ways to package the same messages found in [. . .] early-twentieth-century Camay Soap and skin-whitening ads [. . .], the advertising industry continues to employ these themes, especially with female subjects.

Women's bodies have borne the brunt of this vile ideology in contemporary advertising, which continues to portray Black women as provocatively clothed, snarling-mouthed animals, in jungles, deserts, and safaris. "Tame and timid? That goes against my instincts," says a Black woman smoking a Virginia Slims cigarette in skintight leopard-print pants and matching halter top. "The hunting's always good at Daffy's," reads the caption of an ad featuring a Black model crouched on a beach next to a lion, her leg tucked under her in the same position as the cat's. "Gather your ammunition (cash, check, Mastercard, or Visa) and aim straight for Daffy's. It's the best hunting with the best bargains around." Are we hunting the feline, or the human? The ad draws no distinction—they're both wildcats.[11] In a September 2009 *Harper's Bazaar* spread headlined "Wild Things," supermodel Naomi Campbell skips rope with monkeys, rides an elephant and an alligator, and races a cheetah while her own spotted dress trails like a tail in the wind.†

---

* This is not to say it doesn't exist: During and after the 2008 election, media outlets such as Fox News, along with conservative news sites and blogs, circulated artwork, political cartoons, and protest imagery of President Barack Obama photoshopped as an African witch doctor with a bone through his nose, wearing a tribal headdress.[12]

† According to journalist Claire Sulmers, "The black-woman-in-the-African-wild theme . . . has been in vogue since the press pegged Somalian-born model Iman as a goat herder discovered in the jungle. She was, in fact, a university graduate and the daughter of a gynecologist and a diplomat."[13]

Like *ANTM*'s "sexy little animals" photo shoot, Daffy's ad and *Harper's* spread tread old ground. In 1985, supermodel Iman was photographed next to a cheetah, her head tilted in the same position as the animal, her body turned in a catlike contortion, and her hair wrapped in a cheetah-print scarf. That same year, Iman stalked down a Thierry Mugler runway in safari garb with a live monkey hanging on her shoulder(!), while two buff Black men in loincloths trailed behind her carrying a giant umbrella.

Such images in advertising and fashion code women of color as "primitive," with untamed sexuality both fearful and seductive. Taken to its (il)logical conclusion, this fetishized depiction culminates in images of Black women as dangerous creatures who must be literally deprived of their freedom. Naomi Campbell's "Wild Things" pictorial was shot by world-famous fashion photographer Jean-Paul Goude. Nearly thirty years ago, Goude produced an infamous image of singer Grace Jones on all fours, naked, oiled up, and snarling inside a cage, surrounded by raw meat. Above her head, a zoolike plaque cautioned: Do Not Feed the Animal. (A similar caged photo of Jones graced the cover of Goude's 1981 book, *Jungle Fever*.) Locking her up is the only way to prevent her dangerous sexuality from overwhelming everyone in her wake, the picture suggests. This and several other now-iconic images of Jones posing behind bars, in chains, and with whips were replicated by biracial (Cape Verdian and Italian) model Amber Rose in the September 2009 issue of *Complex* magazine. As journalist Claire Sulmers notes, "Though the photos were taken decades apart, the message is the same. These women are so wild they must be caged—they're sultry, snarling sex beasts."[14]

By dressing a group of models up as "sexy" "native" creatures for a beauty ad as soon as they arrived in South Africa, *ANTM* wasn't engaging in a harmless homage to the land they were visiting. The Lubriderm photo shoot illustrates how the advertising industry's long-held racial essentialism influences the depiction of people of color in product-placement-driven reality TV.

I'm sure some may question whether the episode was actually racist, since white models were also featured as wildlife in the Lubriderm challenge. Yes, it was. The shoot built on a preestablished ad-industry precedent in which the mere *concept* of Africa and Black Africans is conjured to "represent white humans' own more primitive past," writes scholar Lisa Wade, on *Sociological Images*. Wade was describing a 2008–09 ad campaign by "Wild Africa Cream" liqueur, packaged in a leopard-print bottle with *ubuntu* beads around the neck. In the ads, a seductively clothed Black woman has grown a leopard's arm; another sports a cheetah's tail. White women and men in other ads in the series also have nonhuman features. The tagline? "Unleash your wild side." Each ad featured a smoldering male or female model, Black or white, each with a leopard's ear, hand, or arm. In an accompanying radio spot, a man speaks of following a sexy woman, wondering, "Did a leopard escape from the zoo?" while a female voice purrs that the liqueur can help everyone find "a little wild in them."[15]

Since fashion and beauty advertisers have worked with *ANTM*'s producers to build the show's content around their products (and ideas), it's no surprise that *ANTM*'s South African animals shoot shares the "Africa connects us to our animal natures" reasoning of Wild Africa Cream's marketing gambit. It's also why the show would see no problem devoting several episodes to the process of convincing a beautiful (and formerly confident) Black teenager that her "monkey" "snout" makes her ugly.

Dehumanizing African American women in advertising and media carries very real consequences for the self-esteem of Black girls and women, as well as for larger society. When an entire class of people are seen as animals, it becomes harder to prevent violence against them and easier to justify denying them equal social, economic, and political rights. If only Tyra Banks were equipped to realize the impact her programming choices can have.

Tyra Banks: Fashion Victim Turned Fashion Perpetrator

Tyra is a favorite punch line of *The Soup*'s Joel McHale and *The Dish*'s Danielle Fishel, who mock her increasingly cringe-worthy acting and odd insistence on inserting photos of herself into every episode. Culture analysts have wondered why a powerful Black model who seems to really want the best for young women of color would subject them to such demeaning double standards. "On camera, many of the black *ANTM* contestants talk about how thrilled they are to be in Tyra's presence; how her success as a black supermodel inspired them, helping them see themselves as beautiful for the first time," *Slate*'s J. E. Dahl writes, "but how does she repay their adoration? By trying to eradicate ethnic idiosyncrasies in their personality and appearance."[16]

Comics call her crazy, critics dismiss her as an opportunist, and her young fans fiercely defend her as the benevolent granter of young women's dreams. I have a different theory: I believe she has grown up mentally colonized by fashion and beauty advertisers, leaving her with something akin to Stockholm syndrome.*

Tyra Banks is many things. She's someone who believes she's an advocate for girls,   40
especially girls of color. Four years before *ANTM* debuted she founded T-Zone, a summer camp program focused on self-esteem and leadership skills. Yet, she's also the ultimate capitalist beauty industry success story. She grew up without money, but used her nearly naked body, and an incredible parade of wigs, to become a media mogul. In addition to serving as host and executive producer of *ANTM*, she filled both those roles on her daytime chatfest, *The Tyra Banks Show*, for five seasons. This helped her earn an estimated $30 million in 2009 alone, more money than any other woman on prime-time TV. Her increasing fiscal power has drawn comparisons to Oprah Winfrey, despite the intellectual chasm between them.[17]

Most of the rest of us learn to navigate the everyday struggles of adolescence—body image insecurities, emerging sexuality, interpersonal relationships, and personal identity—from our friends, family, and community, at the same time as we are influenced by the media images surrounding us. But those images, and their makers, *were* Tyra's dominant community. From age fifteen on, Banks was raised by the fashion and beauty industry and its advertisers. In loco parentis, they gave her fame and fortune beyond her wildest dreams—but always while pitting her against other women, requiring her to hide her natural hair, and reminding her that her value depended on being young and thin.†

---

* Stockholm syndrome is popularly defined as a psychological condition in which kidnap or abuse victims form attachments to and identify with their captors.

† Banks quit high fashion for Victoria's Secret fame when she realized that curvy adulthood isn't welcome on couture catwalks.

And so the cycle continues. As a curvy Black model who achieved many firsts, Banks fought against unfair race and gender barriers throughout her career. But like so many dysfunctional patterns, Tyra grew up to become the ultimate perpetrator of the ideology of the fashion and beauty advertisers who stunted her intellectual development and shaped her self-image, psychology, and values. In that context, why is anyone surprised that she is simultaneously

- hilariously narcissistic, as well as compassionate;

- wracked with internalized racism and sexism, while renouncing the concept of discrimination; and

- concerned with girls' self-esteem, while profiting from a show that reinforces unhealthy body standards and racial stereotypes?

When she quit *The Tyra Banks Show* in 2010, she announced that her intention was to focus her Bankable Productions company on films that "can promote positive images of women."* I don't doubt Tyra's sincerity. But as *ANTM* illustrates, victims of advertiser-based Stockholm syndrome have an extremely skewed definition of what "positive" media imagery is and what it isn't.

The truth is, the best thing Tyra could do to help "more women and young girls" to "feel as fierce as we truly are" would be to take *ANTM* off the air—or drastically remodel its format.[18]

NOTES

1. "Tyra Banks Apologizes Over Bi-Racial Episode of 'ANTM,'" StyleList.com, Nov. 18, 2009. Oliver, Dana.
2. *The Asian Mystique: Dragon Ladies, Geisha Girls, & Our Fantasies of the Exotic Orient*, (New York: PublicAffairs, 2006). Prasso, Sheridan, p. 87.
3. "Ethnic Magazine Editors Discuss Health, Hollywood Buzz," Sept. 12, 2007. National Public Radio. "Can She Stay on *Top?*" *Time Out Chicago*, no. 163: Apr. 10–16, 2008. Aeh, Kevin; "Hidden Potential; Reaching Consumers," *International Cosmetic News*, Mar. 1, 2008. Guilbault, Laure.
4. *Black Beauty: Aesthetics, Stylization, Politics* (Surrey, UK: Ashgate, 2009). Tate, Shirley Anne.
5. "Bitch Poured Beer on My Weave," *Vanity Fair* contributing editor James Wolcott's blog, Sept. 23, 2004.
6. *Extra!*, the magazine published by media watch organization Fairness & Accuracy in Reporting, produced some of the most well-documented debunking of 1980s and 1990s news coverage scapegoating "welfare queens" and criminalizing youth of color. See: "Five Media Myths about Welfare," *Extra!* May/June 1995; "Public Enemy Number One? Media's Welfare Debate Is a War on Poor Women," *Extra!* May/June l995. Jackson, Janine, and Flanders, Laura; "Wild in Deceit: Why 'Teen Violence' Is Poverty Violence in Disguise," *Extra!* Mar./Apr. 1996. Males, Mike; "Superscapegoating: Teen 'Superpredators' Hype Set Stage for Draconian Legislation," *Extra!* Jan./Feb. 1998.

---

* She also signed a three-book deal to write a YA fantasy series about girls at a magic model school—sort of a *Harry Potter*-meets-*Top Model* franchise—to start being released in the summer of 2011.

Templeton, Robin; "The Smell of Success: After 10 Years of 'Welfare Reform,' Ignoring the Human Impact," *Extra!* Nov./Dec. 2006. deMause, Neil.

7. "Eartha Quake," the avatar of a member of the TelevisionWithoutPity.com fan community, left this comment in the discussion forum devoted to Tiffany during *ANTM*'s fourth season, Apr. 14, 2005.

8. " 'Ugly Betty' Recast: 'Top Model' Is Willi's Daughter!" EW.com, Aug. 11, 2009. Ausiello, Michael.

9. "The Resisting Monkey: 'Curious George,' Slave Captivity Narratives, and the Postcolonial Condition," *Ariel: A Review of International English Literature* 28, no. 1 (Jan. 1997): 69–83. Cummins, June.

10. See: *Ethnic Notions*, 1987, directed by Marlon Riggs; and the Jim Crow Museum of Racist Memorabilia at Ferris State University.

11. The Gender Ads Project. Lukas, Scott A., Ph.D. www.genderads.com/Gender_Ads .com.html.

12. "Obama as Witch Doctor: Racist or Satirical?" CNN.com, Sept. 18, 2009. Fantz, Ashley.

13. "Naomi Campbell in Yet Another 'Out of Africa' Spread," *Black Voices' BV On Style* blog, Aug. 13, 2009.

14. "Caged Black Women: Grace Jones & Amber Rose," FashionBombDaily.com, Aug. 13, 2009. "Iman @ Thierry Mugler in 1985." MakeFetchHappen.blogspot.com, Aug. 22, 2008. Brigitte. "Why Photograph a Black Woman in a Cage?" Jezebel.com, Aug. 14, 2009. Jenna.

15. "Africa Is Wild, and You Can Be Too," SociologicalImages.blogspot.com, July 5, 2009. Wade, Lisa. Also see http://wildafricacream.blogspot.com/search/label/ ADVERTISING.

16. "Is Tyra Banks Racist? The Peculiar Politics of 'America's Next Top Model,' Slate.com, May 18, 2006. Dahl, J. E.

17. "Prime-Time's Top Earning Women," Forbes.com, Oct. 12, 2009. Rose, Lacey; "Who's the Next Oprah?" E! Online, Nov. 27, 2009. Gornstein, Leslie; "Tyra Banks on It," Forbes.com, July 3, 2006. Blakeley, Kiri.

18. "Tyra Banks to Leave Talk Show," Variety.com, Dec. 28, 2009; "Tyra Banks Says Goodbye to Talk Show," People.com, Dec. 28, 2009.

Exploring Context

1. Explore Pozner's tweets at twitter.com/jennpozner. In what ways do they suggest she continues to do the kind of critical work she does in this essay?

2. Visit the website for *America's Next Top Model* (cwtv.com/shows/americas-next-top-model). How do both the design and content of the site engage Pozner's argument?

3. The celebrity news and gossip website TMZ has a category devoted to reality television (tmz.com/category/reality-tv/). Look through recent posts to the site. Are the issues that Pozner explores limited to *America's Next Top Model*? Find evidence that either extends or complicates Pozner's analysis.

Questions for Connecting

1. Steve Olson argues in "The End of Race: Hawaii and the Mixing of Peoples" (p. 334) that although race no longer has any true genetic basis, ethnic divisions continue to per-

sist. Extend Olson's argument by using Pozner's essay. What role do the media play in continuing our understanding of race?

2. Ariel Levy's essay "Female Chauvinist Pigs" (p. 266) examines the ways in which women participate in a raunch culture—a very different setting than the one Pozner examines in her analysis of *America's Next Top Model*. Synthesize these two essays in order to argue for a realistic and holistic understanding of women today. Is it possible to create such an image? Is "women" a category that can be easily described? How broad is it if it can contain both Female Chauvinist Pigs and Cha Cha Divas?

3. In "Paper Tigers" (p. 533), Wesley Yang also examines racial stereotypes. Synthesize his analysis with Pozner's argument. Do racial stereotypes operate in the same ways for men and women? Why or why not?

4. **CONNECTING TO E-PAGES** Extend the synthesis of Levy's and Pozner's views from Question 2 in Questions for Connecting to include Sabrina Rubin Erdely's "Kiki Kannibal: The Girl Who Played with Fire" (bedfordstmartins.com/emerging/epages). How does Kiki Kannibal complicate the descriptions of women in those pieces? How might Pozner and Levy characterize her?

Language Matters

1. Listen to the latest podcast from Grammar Girl at grammar.quickanddirtytips.com. How might you apply what she's talking about in the podcast to this essay? How might you apply it to your writing instead?

2. Sometimes you can get the best feedback from peers by asking them to review a key section of your writing—something you know isn't quite there yet. If you were going to do a targeted peer revision session for Pozner, which section of her essay would you choose, and what feedback would you give?

3. Use a grammar handbook or other reference guide to review the rules for italicizing titles. Should television shows be in quotation marks or italicized? Why?

Assignments for Writing

1. Using Pozner's examples of specific "dehumanizing" racial stereotypes, write a paper in which you argue how shows such as *America's Next Top Model* may affect viewers' perception of race and ethnicity in modern-day America. Incorporate your work from Question 2 of Questions for Critical Reading and Question 2 of Exploring Context.

2. How can racial stereotypes be eradicated from reality TV? Write a paper in which you propose strategies for achieving this goal, using Pozner's essay as support. How might shows' ratings be affected? Use your work from Question 1 of Questions for Critical Reading and Question 1 of Questions for Connecting.

3. Write a paper in which you examine the role media and advertising play in the persistence of racial and ethnic divisions. Working from Pozner's analysis, consider as well the ways in which we support these divisions by viewing shows and participating in popular culture.

RICHARD RESTAK

Richard Restak received his M.D. from Georgetown University School of Medicine. He is a clinical professor of neurology at George Washington Hospital University School of Medicine and Health Sciences and is a former president of the American Neuropsychiatric Association. Known internationally as an expert on the brain, he has written close to twenty books on the human brain and has appeared on *Good Morning America, The Today Show,* and *All Things Considered.* Restak's expertise has led to multiple awards, articles in numerous national newspapers, and invitations to write entries for *Encyclopaedia Britannica, Compton's Encyclopedia,* and *World Book Encyclopedia.* His most recently published books are *Think Smart: A Neuroscientist's Prescription for Improving Your Brain's Performance* (2009) and *The Playful Brain: The Surprising Science of How Puzzles Improve Your Mind* (2012).

Restak's book *The New Brain: How the Modern Age Is Rewiring Your Mind* (2003) details research and technological advances that have provided new insights into the human brain. For example, technologies such as CAT and MRA scans can now prove such things as the harmful effects of television violence, and research on the brain can be leveraged to maximize our capabilities in areas ranging from academics to athletics. Restak suggests that research on the brain has yielded practical applications that we can use every day, from matching drugs to the disorders they can treat to identifying potentially violent individuals before they act out.

"Attention Deficit: The Brain Syndrome of Our Era," a chapter from *The New Brain,* deals with the effects of modern technology on "the plasticity of our brains." Here Restak examines the brain's ability to multitask and the consequences of multitasking—for example, the risks of talking on a cell phone while driving. Our tendency to juggle tasks, Restak warns, may be both unproductive and damaging to our brains. Diagnoses of disorders such as attention deficit disorder (ADD) and attention deficit hyperactivity disorder (ADHD) have become common in recent years, and Restak suggests that one of the reasons for this might be technology's effect on our evolution.

Multitasking forces our brains to process ever-increasing amounts of information at ever-increasing rates, which raises a question: Is the recent social and cultural trend toward multitasking actually rewiring our brains and causing such problems as ADD and ADHD?

▶ TAGS: *technology, multitasking, feedback, creativity, education, medicine*

Questions for Critical Reading

1. Do you think multitasking is possible? How does it function in your own life? According to Restak, what are the problems with multitasking? Locate passages where he discusses the impact of this practice.

2. How does culture affect biology? Perform a critical reading of Restak's text in order to describe the ways in which what we do can change what we are.

3. What are "modern nerves"? Define the term as it is used in Restak's essay and then provide examples from both his text and your own life.

Attention Deficit: The Brain Syndrome of Our Era

The plasticity of our brains, besides responding to the people and training to which we expose it, also responds, for good or for bad, to the technology all around us: television, movies, cell phones, e-mail, laptop computers, and the Internet. And by responding, I mean that our brain literally changes its organization and functioning to accommodate the abundance of stimulation forced on it by the modern world.

This technologically driven change in the brain is the biggest modification in the last 200,000 years (when the brain volume of *Homo sapiens* reached the modern level). But while biological and social factors, such as tool use, group hunting, and language, drove earlier brain changes, exposure to technology seems to be spurring the current alteration. One consequence of this change is that we face constant challenges to our ability to focus our attention.

For example, I was recently watching a televised interview with Laura Bush. While the interview progressed, the bottom of the screen was active with a "crawler" composed of a line of moving type that provided information on other news items.

Until recently, crawlers were used to provide early warning signs for hurricanes, tornados, and other impending threats. Because of their rarity and implied seriousness, crawlers grabbed our immediate attention no matter how engrossed we were in the television program playing out before our eyes. Crawlers, in short, were intended to capture our attention and forewarn us of the possible need for prompt action. But now, the crawler has become ubiquitous, forcing an ongoing split in our attention, a constant state of distraction and divided focus.

During the First Lady's interview I found my attention shifting back and forth from her remarks to the active stream of short phrases running below. From the crawler I learned that National Airport was expected to be opened in two days since its closure in the wake of the September 11 terrorist attacks; that this season's Super Bowl would be played in New Orleans one week later than usual; and that a home run record was about to be broken by Barry Bonds.

Despite my best efforts to concentrate on Laura Bush's words, I kept looking down at the crawler to find out what else might be happening that was perhaps even more interesting. As a result, at several points I lost the thread of the conversation between the

5

First Lady and the interviewer. Usually, I missed the question and was therefore forced to remain in the dark during the first sentence or so of her response.

On other occasions I've watched split-screen interviews, with each half of the screen displaying images or text of the topic under discussion while the crawler continues with short snippets about subjects totally divorced from the interview and accompanying video or text. In these instances I am being asked to split my visual attention into three components.

One can readily imagine future developments when attention must be divided into four or more components—perhaps an interview done entirely in the form of a voice-over, with the split-screen video illustrating two subjects unrelated to the subject of the interview and accompanied all the while by a crawler at the bottom of the screen dealing with a fourth topic.

Yet we shouldn't think of such developments as unanticipated or surprising. In 1916, prophets of the Futurist Cinema* lauded "cinematic simultaneity and interpenetrations of different times and places" and predicted "we shall project two or three different visual episodes at the same time, one next to the other." Yesterday's predictions have become today's reality. And in the course of that makeover we have become more frenetic, more distracted, more fragmented—in a word, more *hyperactive*.

How Many Ways Can Our Attention Be Divided?

Divisions of attention aren't new, of course. People have always been required to do   10
more than one thing at a time or think of more than one thing at a time. But even when engaged in what we now call multitasking, most people maintained a strong sense of unity: They remained fully grounded in terms of what they were doing. Today the sense of unity has been replaced, I believe, by feelings of distraction and difficulty maintaining focus and attention. On a daily basis I encounter otherwise normal people in my neuropsychiatric practice who experience difficulty concentrating. "I no sooner begin thinking of one thing than my mind starts to wander off to another subject and before I know it I'm thinking of yet a third subject," is a typical complaint.

Certainly part of this shift from focus to distraction arises from the many and varied roles we all must now fulfill. But I think the process of personal *dis*-integration is also furthered by our constant exposure to the media, principally television. When watching TV, many of us now routinely flit from one program to another as quickly as our thumb can strike the remote control button. We watch a story for a few minutes and then switch over to a basketball game until we become bored with that, and then move on to Animal Planet. Feeling restless, we may then pick up the phone and talk to a co-worker about topics likely to come up at tomorrow's meeting while simultaneously directing our attention to a weather report on TV or flipping through our mail.

"The demands upon the human brain right now are increasing," according to Todd E. Feinberg, a neurologist at Beth Israel Medical Center in New York City. "For all we know, we're selecting for the capacity to multitask."

---

* Futurist Cinema: Italian Futurism was an influential movement in film in the early twentieth century. Futurism in the arts emphasized and glorified themes associated with contemporary concepts of the future, including youth, noise, new technologies, cities, violence, and speed [Ed.].

Feinberg's comment about "selecting" gets to the meat of the issue. At any given time evolution selects for adaptation and fitness to prevailing environmental conditions. And today the environment demands the capacity to do more than one thing at a time, divide one's attention, and juggle competing, often conflicting, interests. Adolescents have grown up in just such an environment. As a result, some of them can function reasonably efficiently under conditions of distraction. But this ability to multitask often comes at a price—Attention Deficit Disorder (ADD) or Attention Deficit Hyperactivity Disorder (ADHD).

Perhaps the best intuitive understanding of ADD/ADHD comes from the French philosopher Blaise Pascal who said, "Most of the evils in life arise from a man's being unable to sit still in a room." The fourth edition of the *Diagnostic and Statistical Manual of Mental Disorders* (DSM-IV) provides a more contemporary definition. Although ADD/ADHD affects adults as well as children, the DSM-IV describes symptoms as they affect three categories in children: motor control, impulsivity, and difficulties with organization and focus.

The motor patterns include: 15

(a) often fidgets with hands or feet or squirms in seat

(b) often leaves seat in classroom or in other situations in which remaining seated is expected

(c) is often "on the go" or often acts as if driven by a motor

(d) often runs about or expresses a subjective feeling of restlessness

(e) often has difficulty playing or engaging in leisure activities quietly

(f) often talks excessively

The impulsive difficulties include:

(a) often experiences difficulty awaiting turn

(b) interrupts or intrudes on others (e.g., butts into conversation or games)

(c) often blurts out answers before questions have been completed

To earn the diagnosis of the "inattentive subtype" of ADD/ADHD, the child or adolescent shows any six of the following symptoms:

(a) often does not follow through on instructions and fails to finish schoolwork, chores, or duties in the workplace

(b) often fails to give close attention to details or makes careless mistakes in schoolwork, work, or other activities

(c) often has difficulty sustaining attention in tasks or play activities

(d) often does not seem to listen when spoken to directly

(e) often avoids, dislikes, or is reluctant to engage in tasks that require sustained mental effort (such as schoolwork or homework)

(f) often loses things necessary for tasks or activities

(g) is often easily distracted by extraneous stimuli

(h) is often forgetful in daily activities

For years doctors assured the parents of an ADD/ADHD child that the condition would disappear as their child grew older. But such reassurances have turned out to be overly optimistic. In the majority of cases, ADD/ADHD continues into adulthood, although the symptoms change.

In their best-selling book, *Driven to Distraction*, psychiatrists Edward Hallowell and John Ratey developed a list of criteria for the diagnosis of Adult Attention Deficit Disorder. Among the most common manifestations are:

1. A sense of underachievement, of not meeting one's goals

2. Difficulty getting organized

3. Chronic procrastination or trouble getting started

4. Many projects going simultaneously; trouble with follow-through

5. A tendency to say whatever comes to mind without necessarily considering the timing or appropriateness of the remark

6. A frequent search for high stimulation

7. Intolerance of boredom

8. Easy distractibility, trouble in focusing attention, a tendency to tune out or drift away in the middle of a page or conversation

9. Impatience; low frustration tolerance

10. A sense of insecurity

Other experts on adult attention disorder would add:

11. Low self-esteem and

12. Emotional lability: sudden and sometimes dramatic mood shifts

A Distinctive Type of Brain Organization

In many instances childhood and adult ADD/ADHD is inherited. Typically, the parents of a child diagnosed with the disorder will be found upon interview to exhibit many of the criteria for adult ADD/ADHD. But many cases of ADD/ADHD in both children and adults occur without any hereditary disposition, suggesting the probability of culturally induced ADD/ADHD.

As a result of increasing demands on our attention and focus, our brains try to adapt by rapidly shifting attention from one activity to another—a strategy that is now almost a requirement for survival. As a consequence, attention deficit disorder is becoming epidemic in both children and adults. This is unlikely to turn out to be a temporary condition. Indeed, some forms of ADD/ADHD have entered the mainstream of acceptable behavior. Many personality characteristics we formerly labeled as dysfunctional, such as hyperactivity, impulsiveness, and easy distractibility, are now almost the norm.

"With so many distracted people running around, we could be becoming the first society with Attention Deficit Disorder," writes Evan Schartz, a cyberspace critic in *Wired* magazine. In Schartz's opinion, ADHD may be "the official brain syndrome of the information age."

"Civilization is revving itself into a pathologically short attention span. The trend   20 might be coming from the acceleration of technology, the short-horizon perspective of market-driven economies, the next-election perspective of democracies, or the distractions of personal multitasking. All are on the increase," according to Stewart Brand, a noted commentator on technology and social change.

As ADD expert Paul Wender puts it: "The attention span of the average adult is greatly exaggerated."

"It's important to note that neuroscientists and experts within the field are increasingly dissatisfied with ADHD being called a disorder," according to Sam Horn, author of *ConZentrate: Get Focused and Pay Attention—When Life Is Filled with Pressures, Distractions, and Multiple Priorities*, which lists forces in the modern world that "induce" ADD/ADHD. "They prefer to see ADHD as a distinctive type of brain organization."

Such an attitude change toward ADD/ADHD carries practical implications. When creating an optimum environment for learning, for instance, Horn suggests, "blocking out sounds can hurt. Today's younger generation has become accustomed to cacophony. Street sounds, the screeching of brakes, trucks changing gears, and the wails of ambulances are their norm. For these people silence can actually be disconcerting because it's so unusual."

To Horn's list of ADD/ADHD-inducing influences I would add time-compressed speech, which is now routinely used on radio and TV to inject the maximum amount of information per unit of time. As a result we have all become accustomed to rapid-fire motormouth commercials spoken at truly incomprehensible speeds. Think of the last car commercial you saw where all the "fine print" of the latest deal was read with lightning speed, or the pharmaceutical pitch that names a dozen possible side effects in less than five seconds.

> **The attention span of the average adult is greatly exaggerated.**

"The attitude seems to be one of pushing the limits on the listener as far as 'the   25 market will bear' in terms of degrading the auditory signal and increasing the presentation rate of the spoken programming," according to Brandeis University psychologists Patricia A. Tun and Arthur Wingfield in their paper, "Slow But Sure in an Age of 'Make It Quick.'"

As these psychologists point out, laptop computers, cell phones, e-mail, and fax machines keep us in constant touch with the world while simultaneously exerting tremendous pressures on us to respond quickly and accurately. But speed and accuracy often operate at cross-purposes in the human brain.

In study after study both young and older listeners recall less from materials told to them at a rapid rate. A similar situation exists in the visual sphere. A television viewer's memory for information about the weather is actually poorer after viewing weather segments featuring colored charts and moving graphics than after viewing straightforward versions of the same information in which the weather is simply described.

As Tun and Wingfield put it: "The clutter, noise, and constant barrage of information that surround us daily contribute to the hectic pace of our modern lives, in which it is often difficult simply to remain mindful in the moment."

No Time to Listen

As the result of our "make it quick" culture, attention deficit is becoming the paradigmatic disorder of our times. Indeed, ADD/ADHD isn't so much a disorder as it is a cognitive style. In order to be successful in today's workplace you have to incorporate some elements of ADD/ADHD.

You must learn to rapidly process information, function amidst surroundings your parents would have described as "chaotic," always remain prepared to rapidly shift from one activity to another, and redirect your attention among competing tasks without becoming bogged down or losing time. Such facility in rapid information processing requires profound alterations in our brain. And such alterations come at a cost—a devaluation of the depth and quality of our relationships.

For example, a patient of mine who works as a subway driver was once unfortunate enough to witness a man commit suicide by throwing himself in front of her train. Her ensuing anguish and distress convinced her employers that she needed help, and they sent her to me. The hardest part of her ordeal, as she expressed it, was that no one would give her more than a few minutes to tell her story. They either interrupted her or, in her words, "gradually zoned out."

"I can't seem to talk fast enough about what happened to me," she told me. "Nobody has time to listen anymore."

The absence of the "time to listen" isn't simply the result of increased workloads (although this certainly plays a role) but from a reorganization of our brains. Sensory overload is the psychological term for the process, but you don't have to be a psychologist to understand it. Our brain is being forced to manage increasing amounts of information within shorter and shorter time intervals. Since not everyone is capable of making that transition, experiences like my patient's are becoming increasingly common.

"Don't tell me anything that is going to take more than 30 seconds for you to get out," as one of my adult friends with ADD/ADHD told his wife in response to what he considered her rambling. In fact, she was only taking the time required to explain a complicated matter in appropriate detail.

"The blistering pace of life today, driven by technology and the business imperative to improve efficiency, is something to behold," writes David Shenk in his influential book *Data Smog*. "We often feel life going by much, much faster than we wish, as we are carried forward from meeting to meeting, call to call, errand to errand. We have less time to ourselves, and we are expected to improve our performance and output year after year."

Regarding technology's influence on us, Jacques Barzun, in his best-seller, *From Dawn to Decadence*, comments, "The machine makes us its captive servants—by its rhythm, by its convenience, by the cost of stopping it or the drawbacks of not using it. As captives *we come to resemble it in its pace, rigidity, and uniform expectations"* [emphasis added].

Whether you agree that we're beginning to resemble machines, I'm certain you can readily bring to mind examples of the effect of communication technology on identity and behavior. For instance, cinematography provides us with many of our reference points and a vocabulary for describing and even experiencing our personal reality.

While driving to work in the morning we "fast-forward" a half-hour in our mind to the upcoming office meeting. We reenact in our imagination a series of "scenarios" that could potentially take place. A few minutes later, while entering the garage, we experience a "flashback" of the awkward "scene" that took place during last week's meeting and "dub in" a more pleasing "take."

Of course using the vocabulary of the latest technology in conversation isn't new. Soon after their introduction, railways, telegraphs, and telephone switchboards provided useful metaphors for describing everyday experiences: People spoke of someone "telegraphing" their intentions, or of a person being "plugged in" to the latest fashions.

Modern Nerves

In 1891 the Viennese critic Hermann Bahr predicted the arrival of what he called "new human beings," marked by an increased nervous energy. A person with "modern nerves" was "quick-witted, briskly efficient, rigorously scheduled, doing everything on the double," writes social critic Peter Conrad in *Modern Times, Modern Places.* 40

In the 1920s, indications of modern nerves were illustrated by both the silent films of the age, with their accelerated movement, and the change in drug use at the time, from sedating agents like opium to the newly synthesized cocaine—a shift that replaced languid immobility with frenetic hyperactivity and "mobility mania."

Josef Breuer, who coauthored *Studies on Hysteria* with Sigmund Freud, compared the modern nervous system to a telephone line made up of nerves in "tonic excitation." If the nerves were overburdened with too much "current," he claimed, the result would be sparks, frazzled insulation, scorched filaments, short circuits—in essence, a model for hysteria. The mind was thus a machine and could best be understood through the employment of machine metaphors. Athletes picked up on this theme and aimed at transforming their bodies into fine-tuned organisms capable, like machines, of instant responsiveness. "The neural pathways by which will is translated into physical movement are trained until they react to the slightest impulse," wrote a commentator in the 1920s on the "cult" of sports.

The Changing Rhythm of Life

In 1931 the historian James Truslow Adams commented, "As the number of sensations increase, the time which we have for reacting to and digesting them becomes less . . . the rhythm of our life becomes quicker, the wave lengths . . . of our mental life grow shorter. Such a life tends to become a mere search for more and more exciting sensations, undermining yet more our power of concentration in thought. Relief from fatigue and ennui is sought in mere excitation of our nerves, as in speeding cars or emotional movies."

In the 60 years since Adams's observation, speed has become an integral component of our lives. According to media critic Todd Gitlin, writing in *Media Unlimited*, "Speed is not incidental to the modern world—speed of production, speed of innovation, speed of investment, speed in the pace of life and the movement of images—but its essence. . . . Is speed a means or an end? If a means, it is so pervasive as to *become* an end."

In our contemporary society speed is the standard applied to almost everything 45 that we do. Media, especially television, is the most striking example of this acceleration. "It is the limitless media torrent that sharpens the sense that all of life is jetting forward—or through—some ultimate speed barrier," according to Gitlin. "The most widespread, most consequential speed-up of our time is the onrush in images—the speed at which they zip through the world, the speed at which they give way to more of the same, the tempo at which they move."

In response to this media torrent, the brain has had to make fundamental adjustments. The demarcation between here and elsewhere has become blurred. Thanks to technology, each of us exists simultaneously in not just one *here* but in several. While talking with a friend over coffee we're scanning e-mail on our Palm Pilot. At such times where are we *really*? In such instances no less is involved than a fundamental change in our concept of time and place.

> **Thanks to technology, each of us exists simultaneously in not just one *here* but in several.**

Where Is Where?

"Modernity is about the acceleration of time and the dispersal of places. The past is available for instant recall in the present," according to Peter Conrad. For example, I was recently sitting in a restaurant in Washington, D.C., while watching a soccer match take place several time zones away. During an interruption in play, the screen displayed action from another match played more than a decade ago. The commentator made a brief point about similarities and differences in the two matches and then returned to the action of the ongoing match. During all of this I was participating in a "present" comprised of two different time zones along with a "past" drawn from an event that occurred twelve years earlier. Such an experience is no longer unusual. Technology routinely places us in ambiguous time and place relationships.

As another example, while recently sitting on the beach at South Beach in Miami I was amazed at the number of people talking on cell phones while ostensibly spending the afternoon with the person who accompanied them to the beach. In this situation the *here* is at least partly influenced by the technology of the cell phone that both links (the caller and the unseen person on the other end of the cell phone) and isolates (the caller and the temporarily neglected person lying beside him or her on the beach blanket). Such technologies are forcing our brains to restructure themselves and accommodate to a world of multiple identity and presence.

Intellectually we have always known that the "reality" of the here and now before our eyes is only one among many. But we never directly experienced this multilevel reality until technology made it possible to reach from one end of the world to another and wipe out differences in time, space, and place. Starting with telephones we became able to experience the "reality" of people in widely dispersed areas of the world. With the cell phone, that process has become even more intimate. Time, distance, night, and day—the rules of the natural and physical world—cease to be limiting factors.

And while some of us may celebrate such experiences and thrive on constantly being connected, others feel the sensation of a giant electronic tentacle that will ensnare us at any moment. 50

My point here isn't to criticize technology but to emphasize the revolution that technology is causing in our brain's functioning. If, for example, through technology, anyone at any given moment is immediately available, "here" and "there" lose their distinctive meanings. We achieve that "acceleration of time and the dispersal of places" referred to by Peter Conrad.

And yet there is an ironic paradox in all this: As a result of technological advances we participate in many different and disparate "realities," yet as a result of our attention and focus problems we can't fully participate in them. We can shift back and forth from a phone conversation with someone in Hong Kong and someone directly in front of our eyes. Yet thanks to our sense of distraction we're not fully focused on either of them. What to do?

The Plastic on the Cheese

"If I can only learn to efficiently carry out several things simultaneously then my time pressures will disappear," we tell ourselves. And at first sight multitasking seems a sensible response to our compressed, overly committed schedules. Instead of limiting ourselves to only one activity, why not do several simultaneously? If you owe your mother a phone call, why not make that call while in the kitchen waiting for the spaghetti to come to a boil? And if Mom should call you first, why not talk to her while glancing down at today's crossword puzzle?

Actually, multitasking is not nearly as efficient as most of us have been led to believe. In fact, doing more than one thing at once or switching back and forth from one task to another involves time-consuming alterations in brain processing that reduce our effectiveness at accomplishing either one.

Whenever you attempt to do "two things at once," your attention at any given moment is directed to one or the other activity rather than to both at once. And, most important, these shifts decrease rather than increase your efficiency; they are time and energy depleting. 55

With each switch in attention, your frontal lobes—the executive control centers toward the front of your brain—must shift goals and activate new rules of operation. Talking on the phone and doing a crossword puzzle activate different parts of the brain, engage different muscles, and induce different sensory experiences.

In addition, the shift from one activity to another can take up to seven-tenths of a second. We know this because of the research of Joshua Rubinstein, a psychologist at the Federal Aviation Administration's William J. Hughes Technical Center in Atlantic City.

Rubinstein and his colleagues studied patterns of time loss that resulted when volunteers switched from activities of varying complexity and familiarity. Measurements showed that the volunteers lost time during these switches, especially when going from something familiar to something unfamiliar. Further, the time losses increased in direct proportion to the complexity of the tasks. To explain this finding the researchers postulate a "rule-activation" stage, when the prefrontal cortex "disables" or deactivates the rules used for the first activity and then "enables" the rules for the new activity. It's this process of rule deactivation followed by reactivation that takes more than half a second. Under certain circumstances this loss of time due to multitasking can prove not only inefficient but also dangerous.

For example, remember the speculation that cell phone–associated automobile accidents could be eliminated if drivers used hands-free devices? Well, that speculation isn't supported by brain research. The use of cell phones—hands-free or otherwise—divides a driver's attention and increases his or her sense of distraction.

In an important study carried out by psychologist Peter A. Hancock at the University of Central Florida in Orlando and two researchers from the Liberty Mutual Insurance Company, volunteers simulated using a hands-free cell phone while driving. The volunteers were instructed to respond to the ringing of a phone installed on the dashboard of their car. At the instant they heard the ring they had to compare whether the first digit of a number displayed on a computer screen on the dashboard corresponded to the first digit of a number they had previously memorized. If that first digit was the same, the driver was supposed to push a button. In the meantime, they were to obey all traffic rules and, in the test situation, bring the car to a full stop.

While the distracting ring had only a slight effect on the stopping distance of younger drivers (0.61 seconds rather than 0.5 seconds), it had a profound effect on the stopping distance of drivers between 55 and 65 years of age: 0.82 seconds rather than 0.61 seconds, according to the researchers. Distraction, in other words, reduces efficiency.

In another test of the cost of multitasking, volunteers at the Center for Cognitive Brain Imaging at Carnegie Mellon University in Pittsburgh underwent PET scans while simultaneously listening to sentences and mentally rotating pairs of three-dimensional figures. The researchers found a 29 percent reduction in brain activity generated by mental rotation if the subjects were also listening to the test sentences. This decrease in brain activity was linked to an overall decrease in efficiency: It took them longer to do each task.

A reduction in efficiency was also found when the researchers looked at the effect of mental rotation on reading. They discovered that brain activity generated when reading the sentences decreased by 53 percent if the subjects were also trying to mentally rotate the objects.

A similar loss of efficiency occurs when activities are alternated. For instance, David E. Meyer, a professor of mathematical psychology at the University of Michigan in Ann Arbor, recruited young adults to engage in an experiment where they would rapidly switch between working out math problems and identifying shapes. The

60

volunteers took longer for both tasks, and their accuracy took a nosedive compared to their performance when they focused on each task separately.

"Not only the speed of performance, the accuracy of performance, but what I call the fluency of performance, the gracefulness of their performance, was negatively influenced by the overload of multitasking," according to Meyer.   65

All of which leads to this simple rule: Despite our subjective feelings to the contrary, actually our brain can work on only one thing at a time. Rather than allowing us to efficiently do two things at the same time, multitasking actually results in inefficient shifts in our attention. In short, the brain is designed to work most efficiently when it works on a single task and for sustained rather than intermittent and alternating periods of time. This doesn't mean that we can't perform a certain amount of multitasking. But we do so at decreased efficiency and accuracy.

But despite neuroscientific evidence to the contrary, we are being made to feel that we *must* multitask in order to keep our head above the rising flood of daily demands. Instead of "Be Here Now," we're encouraged to split our attention into several fragments and convinced that multitasking improves mental efficiency.

Instead, multitasking comes at a cost. And it's true that sometimes the cost is trivial, or even amusing, as with the following experience of a young mother: "I had to get dressed for my daughter's middle school choral program, get another child started on homework, and feed another who had to be ready to be driven to soccer practice. Of course, the phone kept ringing, too. I thought I had everything under control when the complaints about the grilled cheese started. Without getting too angry, I growled for her to just eat it so that I could finish getting dressed. What else could I do in such a rush? My daughter then said, 'I can't eat it, Mom. You left the plastic on the cheese.'"

Other times, the cost of multitasking can be much less amusing. Imagine yourself driving in light traffic on a clear day while chatting on a cell phone with a friend. You're having no problem handling your vehicle and also keeping up your end of the conversation. But over the next five minutes you encounter heavier traffic and the onset of a torrential rainstorm. Your impulse is to end the conversation and pay more attention to the road, but your friend on the other end of the line keeps talking. After all, he isn't encountering the same hazardous conditions from the comfort of his office or home. You continue to talk a bit longer, shifting your attention between your friend's patter and the rapidly deteriorating road conditions. As a result, you fail to notice that the tractor-trailer to your right is starting to slide in your direction. . . . Your survivors will never know that your divided attention, with its accompanying decrease in brain efficiency, set you up for that fatal accident.

In essence, the brain has certain limits that we must accept. While it's true that we can train our brain to multitask, our overall performance on each of the tasks is going to be less efficient than if we performed one thing at a time.   70

Cerebral Geography

Despite the inefficiency of multitasking, the brain is able to deal with more than one thing at a time. If that weren't true, we wouldn't be able to "walk and chew gum at the same time," as a critic once uncharitably described a former U.S. president. The trick is to avoid activities that interrupt the flow of the main activity.

For example, listening to music can actually enhance the efficiency among those who work with their hands. I first learned of this a year or so ago when a draftsman casually mentioned to me that he felt more relaxed and did better work while listening to background music. Many surgeons make similar claims. In a study aimed at testing such claims, researchers hooked up 50 male surgeons between the ages of 31 and 61 to machines that measured blood pressure and pulse. The surgeons then performed mental arithmetic exercises designed to mimic the stress a surgeon would be expected to experience in the operating room. They then repeated the exercise while the surgeons listened to musical selections of their own choosing. The performances improved when the surgeons were listening to the music.

In another study, listening to music enhanced the surgeons' alertness and concentration. What kind of music worked best? Of 50 instrumental tracks selected, 46 were concertos, with Vivaldi's *Four Seasons* as the top pick, followed by Beethoven's Violin Concerto op. 61, Bach's Brandenburg Concertos, and Wagner's "Ride of the Valkyries"—not exactly your standard "easy listening" repertoire.

But easy listening isn't the purpose, according to one of the surgeons interviewed. "In the O.R. it's very busy with lots of things going on, but if you have the music on you can operate. The music isn't a distraction but a way of blocking out all of the other distractions."

Music undoubtedly exerts its positive effects on surgical performance at least partially through its kinesthetic effects, an observation made by Socrates in Plato's *Republic*:* "More than anything else rhythm and harmony find their way to the inmost soul and take strongest hold upon it." Thanks to music, the surgeon is more concentrated, alert, technically efficient, and—most important—in the frame of mind most conducive to healing. "Take Puccini's *La Bohème*," says Blake Papsin, an ear, nose, and throat surgeon in Toronto. "It's an absolutely beautiful piece of music that compels the human spirit to perform, to care, to love—and that's what surgery is."

Music and skilled manual activities activate different parts of the brain, so interference and competition are avoided. If the surgeon listened to an audiobook instead of a musical composition, however, there would likely be interference. Imagining a scene described by the narrator would interfere with the surgeon's spatial imaging. Listening to the audiobook would activate similar areas of the brain and cause competition between the attention needed to efficiently and accurately operate and to comprehend the images and story in the audiobook. We encounter here an example of the principle of *cerebral geography*: The brain works at its best with the activation of different, rather than identical, brain areas. That's why doodling while talking on the telephone isn't a problem for most people, since speaking and drawing use different brain areas. But writing a thank you note while on the phone results in mental strain because speaking and writing share some of the same brain circuitry.

---

* Socrates in Plato's *Republic*: Socrates was an Athenian Greek philosopher (469–399 BC). He is known chiefly through the writings of his students, notably Plato (c. 428 BC–c. 348 BC). In the *Republic*, one of the foundational texts of Western philosophy, Plato, himself an enormously influential philosopher, recounts dialogues Socrates holds as a means of discovering the truth (the "Socratic method") on such topics as justice [Ed.].

Thanks to new technology, especially procedures like functional MRI scans, neuroscientists will soon be able to compile lists of activities that can be done simultaneously with a minimal lapse in efficiency or accuracy. But, in general, it's wise to keep this in mind: A penalty is almost always paid when two activities are carried out simultaneously rather than separately.

Exploring Context

1. Take the ADD/ADHD test at psychcentral.com/addquiz.htm. How does your score reflect Restak's argument? Connect your response to your work on multitasking from Question 1 of Questions for Critical Reading.

2. Explore the website for Twitter at twitter.com. Is this abbreviated style of blogging a reflection of the problems that Restak explores? Or is staying hyperconnected to your friends a way of combating the demands on attention? Consider the relation between Twitter and your definition of "modern nerves" from Question 3 of Questions for Critical Reading.

3. Play the Multitasking game at itch.com/games/multitasking. How does your performance in the game confirm or complicate Restak's argument? Connect your response to your work on multitasking from Question 1 of Questions for Critical Reading.

Questions for Connecting

1. Kwame Anthony Appiah, in "Making Conversation" and "The Primacy of Practice" (p. 67), explores the persistence of social practices and the possibilities of change. Can we use his ideas to address the problem that Restak describes? Does multitasking, as a practice, have a kind of primacy? Draw on your work in Questions for Critical Reading in making your argument.

2. In "Ethics and the New Genetics" (p. 133), the Dalai Lama asks us to consider the ethical implications of new technologies. But what are the ethical implications of existing technologies? Is multitasking an ethical issue? Synthesize these two texts to make a larger argument about the ethics of technology.

3. How does the biology of the brain shape culture? Consider not only Restak's argument but also Patricia Churchland's ideas in "Networking: Genes, Brains, and Behavior" (p. 113). You may want to draw on your work in Exploring Context in making your argument.

Language Matters

1. Create a series of presentation slides about this essay using PowerPoint or other software. Since such slides are most effective when they contain only a few key points per slide, you will have to locate the most important elements of Restak's argument; in designing the slides, you should also consider how visual elements like color, font, and alignment can enhance an argument.

2. Punctuation marks control the speed of speech: Commas ask us to pause and periods ask us to stop. Given Restak's argument, how can you use punctuation in your writing to guide your reader's attention and combat ADD/ADHD? Which marks might be most helpful, and which might you want to avoid?

3. What are the differences between editing, proofreading, and revising? What would you do to this essay if you were editing it? Revising it? How can you use these different skills in your own writing?

Assignments for Writing

1. Restak examines the way the human brain responds to modern technology, claiming that the changes made in the brain by technology are the biggest changes to that organ in thousands of years. Write an essay that examines the potential benefits of this change in the second decade of the twenty-first century. What is the role of television in the re-wiring of the brain? What other technologies have similar effects? Is this change in brain function for the better? Is it possible that technological advances can move faster than is good for humankind? Consider using your work with Restak's concepts from Questions for Connecting in making your argument.

2. Restak looks closely at the role of modern media and communication devices in our daily lives. Write an essay in which you use Restak and your own experience to assess the ways in which current media has created a culture that demands a high-speed, high-efficiency lifestyle. Does media shape our attention? In what ways are we expected to speed up, and in what ways are we urged to slow down? Restak writes about the "crawler" on TV news. What other media features divide our attention?

3. Write an essay that examines the effectiveness of multitasking in the face of modern technologies, synthesizing Restak's text with your own experience. How does the brain multitask? What impedes our ability to multitask? Why is multitasking not as efficient as we may think? What role does modern technology play in our ability to multitask? Do we multitask more than we think? What demands do we place on ourselves when it comes to multitasking? Draw on your experience and your work with Exploring Context in making your argument.

DAN SAVAGE AND URVASHI VAID

Dan Savage is the cofounder of the It Gets Better Project, which focuses on preventing suicide among adolescents in the LGBT community. He is also the author of a weekly relationship and sex advice column titled "Savage Love" and the editorial director of the *Stranger*, a weekly Seattle newspaper. Savage is a frequent contributor to *This American Life*, *Out* magazine, and HBO's *Real Time with Bill Maher*. He is also the author of *Savage Love: Straight Answers from America's Most Popular Sex Columnist* (1998), *The Kid: What Happened After My Boyfriend and I Decided to Go Get Pregnant* (2000), *Skipping Towards Gomorrah* (2003), and *The Commitment: Love, Sex, Marriage, and My Family* (2006). Most recently, he and his husband, Terry Miller, edited a collection of essays titled *It Gets Better: Coming Out, Overcoming Bullying, and Creating a Life Worth Living* (2011).

Urvashi Vaid received her law degree from Northeastern University School of Law and is now an attorney, community activist, and writer. She directs the Engaging Tradition Project, located at the Center for Gender and Sexuality Law at Columbia University. Vaid is also the author of *Virtual Equality: The Mainstreaming of Gay & Lesbian Liberation* (1996) and *Irresistible Revolution* (2012), and she is coeditor of *Creating Change: Sexuality, Public Policy, and Civil Rights* (2000).

Coming Out, Overcoming Bullying,
and Creating a Life Worth Living

Edited by DAN SAVAGE
and TERRY MILLER

The It Gets Better Project was started in September of 2010 after the suicides of two teenagers who had been bullied because of their sexual orientation. The essays in *It Gets Better: Coming Out, Overcoming Bullying, and Creating a Life Worth Living* are inspired by the project and send messages of hope and encouragement to teenagers within the LGBT community who struggle to overcome bullying. Contributors to the collection include young adults who have overcome this struggle, civil rights activists, and even President Obama.

In his introduction to the book, retitled here "It Gets Better," Savage introduces the tragic deaths that spurred the project. He investigates the heart of the issue of bullying and the difficulties of putting an end to the problem. Perhaps most importantly, he addresses social activism and how it is crucial to making any progress in such a heartbreaking and complex issue. In her contribution to the collection, "Action Makes It Better," Vaid focuses on action and the ways in which advocating for change helps make lives better.

▶ TAGS: *surrogates, community, identity, sexuality, ethics*

Questions for Critical Reading

1. Use both Savage's and Vaid's experiences to explain the claim "it gets better." What gets better? How? Mark passages that support your answer as you read the text.

2. What can be done about bullying? Locate strategies suggested by both Savage and Vaid. Is sending a video message the best response? What other options might we explore?

3. How do Savage's and Vaid's positions differ when it comes to making things better? As you read, locate passages that suggest those differences. Whose position offers a better option? Support your response with quotations from the text.

It Gets Better

One hundred videos.

That was the goal, and it seemed ambitious: one hundred videos — best-case scenario: two hundred videos — made by lesbian, gay, bisexual, and transgender adults for lesbian, gay, bisexual, and transgender youth.

I was sitting in a hotel room in Bloomington, Indiana, when I began to suspect that we were going to see a lot more than one hundred videos. The video that I had made with my husband, Terry, a week earlier, the very first It Gets Better video, had been live on YouTube for just a few hours when e-mails and likes and friend requests started coming in so fast that my computer crashed. The second It Gets Better video arrived within twenty-four hours. Three days later we hit one hundred videos. Before the end of the first week, we hit one thousand videos.

Terry and I were relieved to learn that we weren't the only people out there who wanted to reach out to LGBT kids in crisis.

Justin Aaberg was just fifteen when he killed himself in the summer of 2010. He came   5
out at thirteen, and endured years of bullying at the hands of classmates in a suburban Minnesota high school. Justin hanged himself in his bedroom; his mother found his body.

Billy Lucas, also fifteen, wasn't gay-identified but he was perceived to be gay by his classmates in Greensburg, Indiana. His tormentors threatened him, called him a fag, and urged him to kill himself. Billy hanged himself in a barn on his grandmother's property in early September of 2010. His mother found his body.

Reading about Justin and Billy was emotionally crushing — I was particularly outraged to learn that "Christian" parents were blocking efforts to address the rampant anti-gay bullying at Justin's school, claiming that doing so would somehow infringe upon the "religious freedom" of their straight children — and I began to think about the problem of anti-gay bullying.

I was aware of anti-gay bullying, of course. I had been bullied in the Catholic schools my parents sent me to; my husband endured years of much more intense bullying — it's amazing he survived — at the public high school he attended; I knew that many of my LGBT friends had been bullied. But it wasn't something we talked about or dwelt on.

I was stewing in my anger about what had been done to Justin and Billy when I read this comment, left on a blog post I wrote about Billy: "My heart breaks for the pain and torment you went through, Billy Lucas. I wish I could have told you that things get better."

What a simple and powerful truth. Things get better—things *have* gotten better, things *keep* getting better—for lesbian, gay, bisexual, and transgender people.

I knew that to be true because things had certainly gotten better for me.

I came to fully understand that I was gay—that I had always been gay—when I was a thirteen-year-old boy being bullied at a Catholic school on the north side of Chicago. I became increasingly estranged from my parents at a time when I needed them most because I was working so hard to hide who I was from them. Five years later, I found the courage to start coming out. Coming out is a long process, not a single event, and I tested the waters by telling my eldest brother, Billy, before telling my mom or dad.

> **"My heart breaks for the pain and torment you went through, Billy Lucas. I wish I could have told you that things get better."**

Billy was supportive and it helped me decide to tell my mother, which would be the hardest thing I had yet done in my life. Because coming out in 1982 didn't just mean telling my mother that I was gay. It meant telling her that I would never get married, that I would never be a parent, that my professional life would be forever limited by my sexuality.

Eight years after coming out, I would stumble into a rewarding and unlikely career as a sex-advice columnist, of all things, and somehow leverage that into a side gig as a potty-mouthed political pundit. And fifteen years after coming out, I would adopt a son with the love of my life—the man I would marry—and, with him at my side, present my parents with a new grandchild, my siblings with a new nephew.

Things didn't just get better for me. All of the gay, lesbian, bisexual, and transgender adults I knew were leading rich and rewarding lives. We weren't the same people and we didn't have or want the same things—gay or straight, not everyone wants kids or marriage; people pursue happiness in different ways—but we all had so much to be thankful for, and so much to look forward to. Our lives weren't perfect; there was pain, heartbreak, and struggle. But our lives were better. Our lives were joyful.

What was to be gained by looking backward? Why dwell on the past?

There wasn't anything we could do about the bullying we had endured in school and, for too many of us, at the hands of our families. And it didn't seem like there was anything we could do about or for all the LGBT kids who were currently being bullied.

A bullied gay teenager who ends his life is saying that he can't picture a future with enough joy in it to compensate for the pain he's in now. Justin and Billy—and, as that terrible September ground on, Seth and Asher and Tyler and Raymond and Cody—couldn't see how their own lives might get better. Without gay role models to mentor and support them, without the examples our lives represent, they couldn't see how they might get from bullied gay teenager to safe and happy gay adult. And the people gay teenagers need most—their own parents—often believe that they can somehow prevent their children from growing up to be gay—or from ever coming out—by depriving them of information, resources, support, and positive role models. (Justin Aaberg's parents knew he was gay, and were supportive.)

That fall, as I thought about Justin and Billy, I reflected on how frequently I'm invited to speak at colleges and universities. I address audiences of gay and straight students, and I frequently talk about homophobia and gay rights and tolerance. But I don't get invited to speak at high schools or middle schools, the places where homophobia does the most damage. Gay kids trapped in middle and high schools would benefit from hearing from LGBT adults—lives could be saved—but very few middle or high schools would ever invite gay adults to address their student bodies. Acknowledging the existence of LGBT people, even in sex-ed curriculums, is hugely controversial. A school administrator who invited a gay adult to address an assembly before there was a crisis—before a bullied gay teenager took his own life—would quickly find herself in the crosshairs of homophobic parents and bigoted "Christian" organizations.

It couldn't happen—schools would never invite gay adults to talk to kids; we would never get permission.

I was riding a train to JFK Airport when it occurred to me that I was waiting for   20
permission that I no longer needed. In the era of social media—in a world with You-Tube and Twitter and Facebook—I could speak directly to LGBT kids right now. I didn't need permission from parents or an invitation from a school. I could look into a camera, share my story, and let LGBT kids know that it got better for me and it would get better for them too. I could give 'em hope.

But I didn't want to do it alone. I called Terry from the airport and tentatively explained my idea for a video outreach campaign. I wanted to encourage other LGBT adults to make videos for LGBT kids and post them to YouTube. I wanted to call it: The It Gets Better Project. And I wanted us to make the first video together, to talk about our lives together, to share our joy.

This was a big ask. Terry doesn't do interviews, he doesn't allow cameras in our home, he has no desire to go on television. But he said yes. My husband was the first person to recognize the power of this idea.

The second person to recognize it was our good friend Kelly O, a straight friend and a supremely talented photographer and filmmaker. She had just one question after I explained what we wanted to do: "When can we shoot it?"

We did two takes. The first was a long, depressing video that we shot against a bare wall in our dining room. It looked like a hostage video and we both talked too much about the bullying we'd endured in high school. We watched the video and shook our heads. Kids who are currently being bullied don't need to be told what bullying looks and feels like. Kelly packed up her camera and we went to a friend's bar and tried again. This time Kelly peppered us with questions: Share a happy memory. How did you two meet? What would you tell your teenage self? Are you happy to be alive?

Kelly edited the video, created a YouTube account, and called me when it was live.   25

Four weeks later I got a call from the White House. They wanted me to know that the President's It Gets Better video had just been uploaded to YouTube.

My computer crashed a second time.

The It Gets Better Project didn't just crash my computer. It brought the old order crashing down. By giving ourselves permission to speak directly to LGBT youth, Terry and I gave permission to all LGBT adults everywhere to speak to LGBT youth. It forced straight people—politicians, teachers, preachers, and parents—to decide whose side they were on. Were they going to come to the defense of bullied LGBT teenagers? Or were they going to remain silent and, by so doing, give aid and comfort to the young anti-gay bullies who attack LGBT children in schools and the adult anti-gay bullies at conservative "family" organizations who attack LGBT people for a living?

The culture used to offer this deal to lesbian, gay, bisexual, and transgender people: You're ours to torture until you're eighteen. You will be bullied and tormented at school, at home, at church—until you're eighteen. Then, you can do what you want. You can come out, you can move away, and maybe, if the damage we've done isn't too severe, you can recover and build a life for yourself. There's just one thing you can't do after you turn eighteen: You can't talk to the kids we're still torturing, the LGBT teenagers being assaulted emotionally, physically, and spiritually in the same cities, schools, and churches you escaped from. And, if you do attempt to talk to the kids we're still torturing, we'll impugn your motives, we'll accuse you of being a pedophile or pederast, we'll claim you're trying to recruit children into "the gay lifestyle."

That was the old order and it fell apart when the It Gets Better Project went viral. 30 Suddenly gay, lesbian, bisexual, and transgender adults all over the country—*all over the world*—were speaking to LGBT youth. We weren't waiting for anyone's permission anymore. We found our voices. And LGBT adults who made videos for the project weren't just talking *at* LGBT youth. The kids who watched videos sent e-mails, via YouTube, to the adults posting them. Thousands of LGBT adults who thought they were just going to contribute a video found themselves talking with LGBT youth, offering them not just hope but advice, insight, and something too many LGBT youth lack: the ear of a supportive adult who understands what they're going through.

Soon straight people—politicians and celebrities—were talking to LGBT youth, too, delivering the same message: It gets better, there's nothing wrong with you, and we're working to make it better. LGBT kids could see that the world was full of people like our friend Kelly—loving, supportive, progressive straight people. And as a capstone—living proof—that things were indeed getting better, Don't Ask/Don't Tell was finally repealed. Days later Joe Biden, who also made an It Gets Better video, would go on television and describe marriage equality—marriage rights for lesbian and gay couples—as an inevitability.

Things are getting better before our very eyes.

I do want to acknowledge what the It Gets Better Project can't do, though.

It can't do the impossible. It won't solve the problem of anti-gay bullying, everywhere, all at once, forever, overnight. The point of the project is to give despairing LGBT kids *hope.* The point is to let them know that things *do* get better, using the examples of our own lives. For some people things get better once they get out of high school, for others things get better while they're still in high school. And there are brave, out LGBT kids in high schools and middle schools all over the country who are helping to make things better—for themselves and their peers—in their schools today.

Nothing about letting LGBT kids know that it gets better excuses or precludes us 35 from pressing for the passage of the Student Non-Discrimination Act; demanding anti-bullying programs in all schools; confronting bigots who are making things worse for all kinds of kids; and supporting the work of the Trevor Project, GLSEN, and the American Civil Liberties Union's LGBT Project's Youth & Schools program. (Indeed, the It

Gets Better Project has raised tens of thousands of dollars for these organizations.) But we're not going to get legislation passed this instant and it will be years before we get anti-bullying programs and GSAs (Gay-Straight Alliances) into all public schools, and we may never get them into the private evangelical schools where they're needed most.

In the meantime, while we work to make our schools safer, we can and should use the tools we have at our disposal right now — social media and YouTube and digital video and this book — to get messages of hope to kids who are suffering *right now* in schools that do not have GSAs and to kids whose parents bully and reject them for being lesbian, gay, bisexual, or transgender. There's nothing about the It Gets Better Project — nothing about making a video or sharing one — that prevents people from doing more. Indeed, we've heard from thousands of people who were inspired to do more after making or watching a video.

A few weeks after we launched the It Gets Better Project, this letter arrived for me and my husband:

> Thank you for the It Gets Better Project. My son is 14 and a sophomore in high school in rural Kentucky. He isn't athletic. He isn't religious. He isn't in ROTC. He is constantly being called "gay" or "faggot," oftentimes by the people he thought were his friends. . . . So far, it hasn't gone beyond name-calling, but I worry. I showed him your site the day it went live. He sat down and watched the video that you and Terry put up. Since then, I have seen him checking the site out on his own. I don't know if he is gay, but I do know that your message has touched him. Although he does confide that four years is still a long time to wait for things to get better. I think that seeing so many other people say the same thing holds much more weight than having his mother tell him. So thank you again for sharing.

Four years *is* a long time to wait. So let's all commit to making things better right now, let's all do what we can to create a world where no child, gay or straight, is bullied for being different.

We don't live in that world yet. There are children out there who are being bullied every day, and while gay, lesbian, bisexual, or transgender children aren't the only kids dealing with this harassment, they are often more isolated, more alone, and more at risk.

Nine out of ten LGBT students report experiencing bullying in their schools; LGBT teenagers are four to seven times likelier to attempt suicide. LGBT children who are rejected by their families are eight times likelier to attempt suicide and at much higher risk of winding up homeless and living on the streets.

If you know a child who's being bullied for being gay or perceived to be gay — particularly if you know a child who isn't lucky enough to have a mother like the one who wrote to us — you can help that child find hope by helping them find their way to this book and the It Gets Better Project's website (itgetsbetter.org), with more than ten thousand videos and counting.

Do your part. Give 'em hope.

Action Makes It Better

Despite the title of this book, there is nothing inevitable about change for the better. The only reason big changes happen is when people like you and me decide to fight for things to change, when we take action to make things different.

Gandhi organized for decades in India to get rid of the British. In 1947 (only sixty-four years ago!), the movement he created overthrew one of the biggest colonial empires using nonviolent resistance.

Your grandmothers and great-grandmothers could not vote in the United States—it only changed in 1921 (ninety years ago!).

Black people did not have full voting rights in this country until 1965 (forty-six years ago!).

And lesbian, gay, bisexual, and transgender people did not have the right to have   5
sexual relationships without violating criminal laws until 2003 (only eight years ago!). Or think about India: The LGBT movement just got a court to overturn the laws criminalizing same-sex/same-gender behavior in 2009 (two years ago!).

All of these changes—for women, for African Americans, for LGBT folks—took a massive social movement to make happen.

This is my story of how it's gotten better for me. I'm Indian American, born there, and grew up here since I was eight. Like all Asian kids, my family's expectations—their dreams for me, their demands on me—weighed heavily on me, and never heavier than when I realized I was a lesbian.

But you know what? Activism saved my life. I got involved with a feminist group (of men and women working to really transform gender roles and patriarchy into a more just system). I got involved with a movement trying to end the racist Apartheid system in South Africa (you guys, it only ended in 1994!). I got involved with queer activism, with lefty groups, with all the rabble-rousers and radicals working to end the AIDS epidemic, to create a fairer economy, to win rights for immigrants, to end wars, and make the world more fun and sexy!

What I found in social movements was a whole life that has given me hope, inspiration, friendships, and my lover, Kate (of twenty-three years), whom I met at a queer conference. Social activism is all about optimism, even when you lose. The process of doing something about it all generates lots of adrenaline and serotonin that just make you feel better, like a sweaty dance to music you love.

> **Social activism is all about optimism, even when you lose.**

But truthfully, social change is not always fun—just like life. There's a lot of wacky   10
people, nut-bucket opponents, and powerful forces that want to maintain things just the way they are—so defeat, occasional despair, loss, and discomfort are all part of the process of social action.

What keeps me going, though, is a combination of stubbornness (I'll be damned if they are going to knock me around and get away with it), cold-blooded anger (don't get mad, get even), faith (social-justice activism is an act of belief in the possibility of something you do not know will ever happen), and pleasure (in the people I have met along the way, the incredible change I have been a small part of making, and the massive amounts of fun I have had along the way).

The great news is that there is a global queer movement today. And it is full of young and old people fighting to make space for us to live and love and breathe and be who we are and create the lives we imagine. You can join it; in fact you can lead it. It's all being made right before your eyes.

So make it better — get active.

Exploring Context

1. Savage's and Vaid's essays emerge out of the It Gets Better Project. Visit the project's website at itgetsbetter.org and watch some of the videos there. What are some common themes in these videos? How do they resonate with Savage's and Vaid's discussions?

2. Visit the U.S. government's official anti-bullying website (stopbullying.gov). Given the extent of this problem and its sometimes severe consequences, does the site offer any realistic solutions to the problem?

3. The Trevor Project (thetrevorproject.org) is also focused on helping LGBT youth — specifically in preventing suicide. Explore the site. What can each of us do to help prevent these suicides?

Questions for Connecting

1. In "Preface" and "The New Civil Rights" (p. 552), Kenji Yoshino discusses both "covering" — a way of downplaying aspects of one's identity to fit in — and a new model of civil rights based on basic liberties available to all. How can you use the selections from Savage and Vaid to support Yoshino's claims? Would a liberty paradigm of civil rights solve the kinds of problems that spurred the It Gets Better Project?

2. What effect does bullying have on human dignity? Use Francis Fukuyama's discussion of the concept in "Human Dignity" (p. 185) to analyze the experiences of Savage and Vaid.

3. How do Savage and Vaid function as surrogates? Use Daniel Gilbert's definition of the term from "Reporting Live from Tomorrow" (p. 211) to consider how Savage's and Vaid's essays might offer youth a glimpse of a future that includes happiness.

Language Matters

1. These essays use a number of acronyms, primarily "LGBT." Using the Web or some other reference source, locate the rules for introducing and using acronyms. Examine these rules in the context of these essays. Do the authors introduce acronyms properly? How and when should you use acronyms in your own writing?

2. Review the rules for pronouns and their antecedents using a grammar handbook or other reference resource. In these same sources, review any material on gender-neutral language. How does maintaining gender-neutral language complicate pronoun usage? How do Savage and Vaid handle this problem? How should you handle pronouns in a gender-neutral way in your own writing? Alternating *he* and *she*? Using *he/she*?

3. Vaid's essay is quite short. Outline the essay to trace the argument. How does Vaid manage to make an argument in so little space? What key moves are necessary to make an argument in a short essay? How can you apply these techniques in your own writing?

Assignments for Writing

1. "Action Makes It Better," claims Vaid. Write a paper in which you explore the relationship between social activism and change, using ideas from both Savage and Vaid to support your position.

2. How has technology changed social activism? Consider the It Gets Better Project, using it to form an argument about the ways in which technology and social media facilitate (or hamper) social change.

3. Using your own experience, write a paper about how things get better, addressed to a specific audience — bullied teenagers or LGBT youth. Connect your experiences to Savage and Vaid in making your argument for how things can get better.

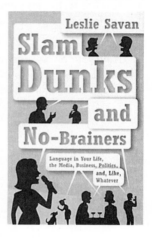

LESLIE SAVAN

Leslie Savan is a former columnist for the *Village Voice* and a three-time Pulitzer Prize finalist. She has written for *Time*, the *New Yorker*, the *New York Times*, the *Los Angeles Times*, and *Salon*. In 1994, she published *The Sponsored Life: Ads, TV, and American Culture*. The following selection, "What's Black, Then White, and Said All Over?" appeared in her book *Slam Dunks and No-Brainers: Language in Your Life, the Media, Business, Politics, and, Like, Whatever* (2005).

In *Slam Dunks and No-Brainers*, Savan examines our everyday language to find out how it originated, what it means, and what it says about our culture. The book explores how a hot new phrase is created and spreads, how media takes advantage of trends in speech, and why we're not sure what pop catchphrases were popular in ancient Rome.

In "What's Black, Then White, and Said All Over?" Savan traces common "pop talk" that has its origins in African American vernacular. "White people," Savan writes, "draw from a black lexicon every day" (p. 435), and in this essay she examines the reasons for and the results of this kind of borrowing. Savan is interested in issues of media appropriation, the "wannabe" phenomenon, the impact of "black talk" on written language, and the idea of "covert prestige" being gained in the process of crossover talk. Ultimately, Savan presents a society that has accepted black vernacular as cool and worthy of imitation yet finds it unacceptable when black students speak it in the classroom.

Language has always been coupled with power. In this piece, Savan helps us to see how language circulates in culture and how its power is used by the media and in advertising.

▶ TAGS: *race, language, creativity, culture, diversity, conversation, collaboration, media*

Questions for Critical Reading

1. What slang terms do you use that derive from other cultural groups? As you read, keep these terms in mind. In particular, consider what Savan says about "covert prestige." Define the term using Savan's text and provide an additional example from your own experience.

2. In this essay, Savan discusses "paying the dues." What do you think that term means? Use Savan's text to develop a definition of the phrase, reading the text critically in order to build your understanding of the term.

3. Savan's primary concern is black talk. Using her text, suggest why other minority or foreign linguistic styles aren't used as prevalently in advertising. You will need to read

her text closely and critically to develop your answer, since she never explicitly addresses this issue.

What's Black, Then White, and Said All Over?

African American vernacular, black English, black talk, Ebonics, hip-hop slang—whatever you want to call it, black-inspired language is all over mainstream pop talk like white on rice.

The talk may be everywhere, but, oddly enough, even during the rabid debate over Ebonics in the late 1990s rarely was there any mention of black English's deep imprint on American English. Yet linguists and other language experts know that America's language wouldn't be what it is—and certainly wouldn't pop as much—without black English.

"In the past, White society has resisted the idea," wrote Robert McCrum, William Cran, and Robert MacNeil in *The Story of English*, "but there is now no escaping the fact that [Blacks' influence] has been one of the most profound contributions to the English language."

"First, one cannot help but be struck by the powerful influence of African American vernacular on the slang of all 20th-century American youth," Tom Dalzell wrote in *Flappers 2 Rappers*. "There were other influences, to be sure, on the slang of America's young, but none as powerful as that of the streets of Harlem and Chicago."

The linguist Connie Eble, author of *Slang and Sociability* and a college and youth   5
slang expert at the University of North Carolina, Chapel Hill, calls the black influence on the American language "overwhelming."

White people (and not just the young) draw from a black lexicon every day, sometimes unaware of the words' origins, sometimes using them because of their origins. Here are just some of the words and phrases—born in different decades and now residing at various levels of popdom—that African Americans either coined or popularized, and, in either case, that they created the catchiest meaning of: *all that, back in the day, bling bling, blues, bogus, boogie, bootie, bro, chick, chill, come again, cook, cool, dawg, dig, dis, do your own thing, don't go there, freak, funky, get-go, get it on, get over, gig, give it up, groovy, heavy, hip, homeboy, hot, in your face, kick back, lame, living large, man, my bad, Micky D's, old school, nitty gritty, player, riff, righteous, rip off, rock 'n' roll, soul, tell it like it is, 24/7, uptight, wannabe, whack, Whassup?/sup?, Whassup with that?, when the shit hits the fan, you know what I'm saying?*

You know what I'm saying. Most of us talk, and all of us hear in the media some of that talk every day. Some phrases are said with an implicit nod to their source (*street cred, chill, You the man*, as well as a fist pound or high five), while others have been so widely adopted that they're beginning to feel sourceless (*24/7, lame, in your face*). *It's a black thang* has become everybody's thing, from *It's a dick thing* to (most offensively, considering who pushed it) "Virginia Slims: It's a Woman Thing."

But black vernacular didn't just add more lively, "colorful" words to the pop vocabulary. Much as marketing has influenced pop language, so black English has changed the American language in more fundamental ways. And that's what we're talking here—not about black talk per se, but about what happens when black talk meets, and transforms, the wider, whiter pop.

First and foremost, this language of outsiders has given us *cool*: the word itself—the preeminent pop word of all time—and quite a sizable chunk of the cool stance that underlies pop culture itself. Pop culture's desire for cool is second only to its desire for money—the two, in fact, are inextricably linked. (Cool may be first and foremost, but more on why it rules later.)

A second way African American vernacular has affected the broader pop is that black talk has operated as a template for what it means to talk pop in the first place. As an often playful, ironic alternative to the official tongue, black slang has prefigured pop language in much the same way that black music has prefigured, and has often become, pop music. While there are important differences, some of the dynamics underlying black talk and pop talk are similar: Like black English, pop language sparks with wordplays and code games; it assumes that certain, often previously unacknowledged experiences deserve their own verbal expression; and it broadcasts the sense that only those who share the experiences can really get the words. For instance, black talk's running commentary on social exclusion is a model for pop talk's running commentary on media experiences.

Why do I say that pop is modeled on black and not the other way around? It's not just because black talk did these things earlier and still does them more intensely than pop, but as the original flipside to the voice of the Man, as the official unofficial speech of America, black talk is the object of pop talk's crush on everything "alternative" and "outsider."

There's an attitude in pop language that it is somehow undermining the stale old ways and sending a wake-up call to anyone who just doesn't get it. You can feel the attitude in everything from advertising's furious but phony rebelliousness to the faintly up-yours, tough-talking phrases like *Get a life* and *Don't even* think *about it*. It's not that these particular phrases are black or black-inspired, or that white people aren't perfectly capable of rebelliousness, anger at authority, and clever put-downs on their own. But the black experience, publicized more widely than ever now through hip-hop and its celebrities, has encouraged everyone else to more vigorously adopt the style of fighting the power—at least with the occasional catchphrase.

> **This language of outsiders has given us *cool*.**

It may seem twisted, given American history, that general pop language draws from the experience of black exclusion at all. But white attempts to *yo* here and *dis* there are an important piece of identity-and-image building for individuals and corporations alike. Today, the language of an excluded people is repeated by the nonexcluded in order to make themselves sound more included. As the mainstream plays the titillating notes of marginalization, we are collectively creating that ideal mass personality mentioned earlier: We can be part black (the part presumed to be cool and soulful, real and down, jazzy or hip-hop, choose your sound) and be part white (the privileged part, the part that has the luxury to easily reference other parts).

Related to all this imitation and referencing is the most noticeable way that pop talk is affected by black talk: Black talk has openly joined the sales force. At white society's major intersection with black language—that is, in entertainment—white society has gone from mocking black talk, as in minstrel shows,* to marketing it, as in hip-hop. In the more than a hundred years between these two forms of entertainment, black language has by and large entered white usage as if it were a sourceless slang or perhaps the latest lingo of some particularly hep white cats, like the fast-talking disc jockeys of the 1950s and 1960s who purveyed black jive to white teenagers. Black language may have been the single most important factor in shaping generations of American slang, primarily through blues, jazz, and rock 'n' roll. But only relatively recently has black talk been used openly, knowingly, and not mockingly to sell products.

This would have been unthinkable once. Even fifteen or twenty years ago, car mak- 15
ers were loath to show black people in commercials for fear that their product would be tainted as inferior or, worse, as "a black car." Although many car companies are still skittish, by 2001 Buick was actually ending its commercials with the rap-popularized phrase "It's all good." (And by 2004, a BMW ad was featuring an interracial couple.) The phrase went from M. C. Hammer's 1994 song "It's All Good" to replacing "I love this game" as the official slogan of the National Basketball Association in 2001. Both Buick and the NBA have since dropped *It's all good*, but with their help the phrase massified, at least for a while. "It's huge" among white "sorority sisters and stoners alike," a twenty-seven-year-old white friend in Chicago told me in 2003.

So it's not all bad, this commercialization of black talk, especially if it can get the auto industry to move from shunning to quoting African Americans. But it comes laden with price tags. To read them, look at MTV, which has to be *the* major force in the sea change from whites-only to black's-da-bomb.

It may be difficult to believe now, but for years MTV wouldn't touch black music videos. The channel relented only under pressure, with videos by Prince and Michael Jackson. Black just wouldn't appeal to its white suburban teen audience, MTV explained. In 1989 with the appearance of the successful *Yo! MTV Raps*, that rationale was turned inside out, and—ka-ching!—black videos began to appear regularly. Since so much of MTV is advertising posing as entertainment (the videos are record company promotions, the parties and other bashes that appear are often visibly sponsored events), MTV has contributed significantly to two marketing trends: To the young, advertising has become an acceptable—nay, desirable—part of the cool life they aspire to; and a black, hip-hop-ish vernacular has become a crucial cog in the youth market machinery.

The outsider style is not solely black or hip-hop, but, at least in the marketing mind, a black package can be the most efficient buy to achieve that style. For corporate purposes, hip-hop in particular is a lucrative formula. Not only does the hip-hop black man represent the ultimate outsider who simultaneously stands at the nexus of cool, but much of hip-hop, created by the kind of people gated communities were meant to exclude, sings the praises of acquiring capitalism's toys. These paradoxes of racism are commercial-ready.

---

* Minstrel shows: American theatrical form popular from the early nineteenth to the early twentieth century, presenting racial stereotypes as humorous entertainment. Early minstrel shows featured white performers in blackface makeup [Ed.].

As the critic Greg Tate wrote on the thirtieth anniversary of hip-hop, "globally speaking, hip-hop is money at this point, a valued form of currency where brothers are offered stock options in exchange for letting some corporate entity stand next to their fire. . . . Oh, the selling power of the Black vernacular."

When Sprite realized that teenagers no longer believed its TV commercials telling them that "Image Is Nothing" and that they shouldn't trust commercials or celebrity endorsements (said only half tongue-in-cheek by celebrities like NBA star Grant Hill), the soft drink's marketing department decided to up the ante. So, when you need outsider verisimilitude, who ya gonna call? Why, black rappers, of course, preferably on the hardcore side. Get *them* to testify to the soft drink's beyond-the-bounds, can't-be-bought spirit at Sprite.com launch parties (to be run later on MTV). Or get real kids, looking and sounding ghetto, to rap their own lyrics in TV spots about, say, "a situation that is not too sweet, which is an attribute of Sprite," as a Sprite publicist said. How else to get kids, usually white kids, to understand that you understand that they're sick of commercials telling them what's cool? 20

And so, while Sprite had long used rappers in its overall "Obey Your Thirst" campaign, now it pumped up the volume. Only by obeying the first commandment that image is everything can you become, as Sprite did by the late nineties, the fastest-growing soft-drink brand in the world. "Sprite has really become an icon," Pina Sciarra, then director of youth brands for Sprite, said on the 2001 PBS documentary *Merchants of Cool.* "It's not just associated with hip-hop, it's really a part of it, as much as baggy jeans and sneakers." Sprite, by the way, is owned by the Coca-Cola Company, the same company that agreed (around the time of the Sprite.com launch in late 2000) to pay $192.5 million to settle a racial discrimination suit by black employees, who accused the company of paying blacks less than whites for the same jobs and of discriminating in promotions and evaluations. (The company denied the allegations, but the settlement was one of the largest of its kind at the time.)

When whites talk black—or, just as commonly, when major corporations do it for them—it makes you wanna shout, *Whassup with that?!*

Terms and Props

Before I address wannabe black talk and other points where black language crosses over into pop, a few words about what "black language" and "black words" are.

I've been using the terms "black English," "black slang," "black talk," and "African American vernacular" rather interchangeably, which, in plain English, seems OK. Yet, at the same time, each term is a bit off the mark.

No one phrase is the perfect vehicle to explain how a people speak, because "a people" don't all speak (or do anything) one way. That's one of the problems with the terms "black English" and "black dialect." "Black English" was more or less booted out of formal linguistic circles, because, as linguist Peter Trudgill wrote in the 1995 revised edition of his book *Sociolinguistics*, "it suggested that all Blacks speak this one variety of English—which is not the case." The newer scholarly term, African American Vernacular English (AAVE), has pros and cons: It "distinguishes those Blacks who do not speak standard American English from those who do," wrote Trudgill, "although it still suggests that only one nonstandard variety, homogeneous through the whole of the USA, is involved, which is hardly likely." The word *Ebonics* was created in 1973 by 25

African American scholars to "define black language from a black perspective," writes Geneva Smitherman, director of the African American Language and Literacy Program at Michigan State University. But the 1997 Ebonics controversy loaded the word with so much baggage (which we'll rummage through later) that, outside of some hip-hop use, it has become nearly immobile.

"Black slang" can't describe black language, because clearly most black language is composed of standard English. However, when referring to actual slang that blacks created (*my bad*, *dis*), "black slang" is the right term. Personally, I like "black talk" (which is also the title of one of Smitherman's books). Although, like any phrase starting with the adjective "black," it might suggest that all black people talk this way all the time, "black talk" (like "pop talk") is colloquial and flexible, encompassing vocabulary and then some.

In mixing up these terms, I take my cue in part from the Stanford University linguistics professor John Russell Rickford. Rickford's not hung up over what black language is called, though he favors "spoken soul," the title of his book (subtitled *The Story of Black English* and written with his son, Russell John Rickford) and a term coined by Claude Brown, the author of *Manchild in the Promised Land*.

In *Spoken Soul*, the Rickfords spell out the dimensions of the language:

> In homes, schools, and churches, on streets, stages, and the airwaves, you can hear soul spoken every day. Most African Americans—including millions who . . . are fluent speakers of Standard English—still invoke Spoken Soul as we have for hundreds of years, to laugh or cry, to preach and praise, to shuck and jive, to sing, to rap, to shout, to style, to express our individual personas and our ethnic identities . . . to create authentic characters and voices in novels, poems, and plays. . . . The fact is that most African Americans *do* talk differently from whites and Americans of other ethnic groups, or at least most of us can when we want to.

If that approximates a definition of black language, what are "black words"? Word origins in general are difficult to trace, but the origins of black words are particularly so. In the dictionary-style *Black Talk: Words and Phrases from the Hood to the Amen Corner*, Smitherman writes that she did not include etymologies because "these are risky propositions at best when dealing with an oral language such as African American Language." Hampton University professor Margaret Lee, who published "Out of the Hood and into the News: Borrowed Black Verbal Expressions in a Mainstream Newspaper" in the linguistic journal *American Speech* and verified the black origins of each phrase with at least two sources, adds, "The approach Smitherman takes and I take is that these expressions and words were created by African Americans or were circulated in the black community before they went mainstream." In order to define black words that have gone pop, I would only add that a pop word is "black" simply if its most popular meaning or nuance was created by black people—for example, *bad* and *girlfriend* are pop when used with black nuance, but not pop when used conventionally.

Origins tend to get lost in the roaring mainstream. Some words that seem white are black, and vice versa. For instance, until I looked into *24/7*, I would have guessed its roots were cyber or maybe something out of the convenience-store industry. But *24/7* arose from a hip-hop fondness for number phrases. Rapdict.org lists some sixty number phrases, many of which are too obscure or gangsta to cross over; *411* is one of the few others that has gone pop. (A recent Mercedes-Benz magazine ad advised, "Get the 411.")

Bogus, which sounds so surfer, dude, dates back at least as far as 1798, when a glossary defined it as a "spurious coin," write David Barnhart and Allan Metcalf in *America in So Many Words*. "Its origins are obscure, but one guess that is as good as any is that it is from *boko*, meaning 'deceit' or 'fake' in the Hausa language of west central Africa. The word then would have been brought over by Africans sold into slavery here." In addition, some nuances that no one doubts are African American may run deeper in black history than most people, black or white, imagine. When *bad* is used to mean good, the meaning (though obviously not the word itself) is derived, Smitherman writes, from a phrase in the Mandinka language in West Africa, "*a ka nyi ko-jugu*, which means, literally, 'it is good badly,' that is, it is very good, or it is so good that it's bad!"

Meanwhile, some words that most people would identify as black, and that black people did indeed popularize, originated among others. Southern phrases in particular jumped races, "from black to white in the case of *bubba* and *big daddy*, from white to black in the case of *grits* and *chitlins*," write the Rickfords. *Cat*, meaning a hip guy, is a dated piece of slang (though often on the verge of a comeback) that most people attribute to black jazz musicians; Ken Burns's television series *Jazz* states that Louis Armstrong was the first person to have said it. But, as Tom Dalzell writes, in "the late 19th century and early 20th century, *cat* in the slang and jargon of hobos meant an itinerant worker . . . possibly because the migratory worker slunk about like a 'homeless cat.'" However, it did take Armstrong, and then other jazz musicians in the 1920s, to introduce the word into broader usage. That old rap word *fly* (stylish, good-looking, smooth) was flying long before rap. "The most well-established slang meaning of *fly* was in the argot of thieves, where *fly* meant sly, cunning, wide-awake, knowing, or smart," writes Dalzell, who notes those uses of *fly* as early as 1724 and in *Bleak House* by Dickens in 1853. But again, *fly* didn't really buzz until black musicians picked up on it, beginning around 1900, well before *Superfly* in the 1970s and rap in the 1980s.

Wannabe Nation

Whether black-born or black-raised, black words are the ones that many white people are wearing like backwards baseball caps. That brings us to a particularly telling term that went from black to pop. *Wannabe* originally referred to people who wanted to be something they weren't; it was often said of a black person who wanted to be white. In Spike Lee's 1988 film *School Daze*, the conflict was between the dark-skinned, activist "Jigaboos" and the light-skinned sorority sister "Wannabes." Beginning around the time of that movie, *wannabe* was used by just about everybody to mean anybody who wanted to be somebody he or she wasn't—there have been surfer wannabes, Madonna wannabes, and dot.com start-up wannabes. But *wannabe* is not just a blast from decades past. More recently, "podcaster wannabes" have developed, and in just one week on TV and radio in late 2004, I heard of "artist wannabes," "geek wannabes," and "wannabe homeland security chief" Bernard Kerik.

Racially speaking, *wannabe* has reversed field. Since at least the early nineties, with hip-hop an entrenched, virtually mainstream hit, *wannabe* has been far more likely to refer to whites, especially teenagers, who want to be black or do the style. Sometimes called *wiggers* or *wiggas* (*white* plus *nigger*/*nigga*), black wannabes try to dance the dance and talk the talk. Even whites who would hate to be black will maintain the right to add the occasional black flourish. Some whites flash a black word or gesture like an honorary badge of cool, to show they're down with black people on certain occasions, usually involving sports or entertainment. Or maybe they do it because some of their best friends and some of the best commercials are flashing it, too. Or maybe they just need to know that black people like them. Take "Johnny and Sally," the fictitious white couple on the very funny Web site BlackPeopleLoveUs.com, which is full of "testimonials" to their racial bigheartedness. As one unnamed black man attested, "Johnny always alters his given name and refers to himself in the third person — for example, 'J-Dog don't play that' or 'J-Dog wants to know wusssaappp.' It comforts me to know that my parlance has such broad appeal."

African Americans aren't the only people whose parlance has broad appeal. Non-Latino blacks dabble in Spanish, Catholics in Yiddish, adults in teenage talk. Cultural skin is always permeable, absorbing any word that has reached a critical mass of usefulness or fun. The human species can't help but borrow — after all, that's how languages develop. [35]

But whether we call it wannabe talk or the less derogatory crossover talk, something about white society's sampling of black speech is more loaded than the usual borrowing. Black vernacular's contributions to English are larger in number and run deeper linguistically and psychologically than do any other ethnic group's. And black English, born in slavery, resounds with our society's senses of guilt, fear, identity, and style.

Black-to-white crossover talk, which also began during slavery, is hardly new. But, like most pop talk today, it radiates a new gloss, a veneer in which you can catch the reflection of its increased market value. Black talk comes from something real — "serious as a heart attack," Smitherman says — but, whoop, there it is, sparking out of TV commercials, out of white politicians, out of anyone who has something to promote, spin, or get over.

"Chill, Orrin," the Democratic senator Patrick Leahy told the Republican senator Orrin Hatch when things got a little testy during a Judiciary Committee hearing in 1998. Behind the *chill* was something more than "relax." One white guy was momentarily able to harness and aim some soulful black power at the other white guy. Saying the black word says, I stake myself closer to black people and their righteous anger than you do. You're more afraid of them and their language than I am — so I win this moment.

"Go on, give it up!" the signs throughout Virgin Records implored. *Give it up*'s "it" referred only obliquely to applause. (Used to introduce about every other musical act these days, the black phrase has long been a verbal welcome mat. "Everybody give it up for my very good friend Marion Barry," someone said on the old comedy series *In Living Color* in 1990.) "It" referred even more obliquely to sex. (*Give it up* originally meant "to agree to engage in copulation," according to the *Random House Historical Dictionary of American Slang* [*RHHDAS*].) No, this "it" meant your money — for "The Sacrifice Sale. Hundreds of titles: 3 for $26."

As recently as 2005, McDonald's, like many a corporation trying to sound more [40] "urban," was getting it all wrong. "DOUBLE CHEESEBURGER? I'D HIT IT," read a

McDonald's banner ad on ESPN.com. As mocking bloggers pointed out, the hip-hop slang actually meant, "I'd have sex with that cheeseburger."

It's not as if there hasn't been enough time to hit it right. Again, black style's market value jumped around the time *Yo! MTV Raps* debuted in 1989. In a TV spot that same year, the pasty white Pillsbury Doughboy performed a mean rap number. By 1994, Dan Rather (a magnet for every catchy, and uncatchy, turn of phrase that comes along) reported that political candidates were "dissing" each other. In 1999, a hip black guy insisted, for Wendy's, "This sandwich is da bomb."

Three years later, *CNN Headline News* asked the writers responsible for the crawl and other graphics that crowd its screen to inject some hip-hop. "In an effort to be sure we are as cutting-edge as possible with our on-screen persona, please refer to this slang dictionary when looking for just the right phrase," read a *Headline News* memo, according to the New York *Daily News*. "Please use this guide to help all you homeys and honeys add a new flava to your tickers and dekos." Among the phrases mentioned were *fly*, *ill*, and *jimmy hat*, for a condom. (A *Headline News* spokeswoman at the time said a mid-level producer sent the memo without top executives knowing about it.)

"You Go, Girl!" ran a 2004 headline in *Today's Christian Woman* for a story about finding supportive friends.

"She said she'd have more gay people in the White House. I'm like, 'You go, Teresa,'" a gay doctor said of Teresa Heinz Kerry at an Ohio campaign rally. "Women to Heinz Kerry: You Go, Girl," an Associated Press headline read. For a brief moment there, Teresa was the nation's "You go, girl" girl.

You go, girl! is democratic and process-oriented — every girl is presumed to have the strength that can propel her forward. But what's a guy to do? When a man needs an equally exciting, gender-saluting pop phrase that expresses personal recognition, he's almost sure to receive the hierarchical, goal-oriented *You da* (or *the*) *man!* Both black and white men scramble to the top of the heap with this winner-take-all phrase. But in the media and off, it's increasingly white men who adorn one another with this verbal king's crown. 45

In the 1998 animated movie *Antz*, the ant voiced-over by Sylvester Stallone says to the Woody Allen ant, who has just saved his species' civilization, "You da ant!" And they exchange high-fives.

"You're the man!" Karl ("Bush's Brain") Rove "bellowed back into his cell phone" to Lloyd Smith, who managed Jim Talent's Missouri Senate campaign in the 2002 mid-term elections, *Time* magazine reported. Smith had just told Rove that it looked as if Talent was going to beat Democratic senator Jean Carnahan, thereby guaranteeing the Senate to Republicans.

You da man! is now so common that when the sports columnist Frank Deford compiled his 2004 Thanksgiving Day list of things "I wish we still had," he included "golf tournaments that were played without idiots screaming 'you da man.'"

But white men still scream *You da man!* because the words (especially *da*, though it's not required) still suggest a wistful tableau of black folks testifying for white folks. Beyond giving a white man props for smiting a foe, *You da man* gives him authenticity clearance, momentary proof that, at the least, he's not the Man, an oppressive white authority figure.

It's better yet if a white guy can get a real black guy to testify for him (just like in   50
all the movies that star a somehow emotionally stunted white hero who's made to see
one light or another by a more soulful black sidekick). An ad campaign awhile back
made this embarrassingly evident. "The Colonel?" asked what intentionally sounded
like a black male voice. "He da man!" The man, of course, was Colonel Sanders of KFC.
He's dead, but in the late nineties the Colonel was not only revived as a cartoon character for TV spots, but he also became black (minus a pigment change). "Go, Colonel!
Go, Colonel!" the voiceover jived. "The Colonel still has a pink face and white suit,"
Mark Schone noted on the radio show *This American Life*, "but these days the erstwhile
Southern gentleman twirls his cane to . . . old school seventies funk. . . . In an ad campaign that began on his 108th birthday, the Colonel has cabbage patched, tap danced,
rapped, and played basketball. . . . What's it mean when a redneck who dressed like a
slaveowner comes back from the dead and gets funky?"

And what's it mean when right-wingers take a catchy phrase that points out racism to express their own sense of victimization? "But to you," "Aaron" wrote to "fazz"
on rightwingnews.com in 2003, "facts don't matter because Abrams committed the
greatest crime of all, he was guilty of BWC (Breathing While Conservative)." (That's El-
liott Abrams, who was indicted for giving false testimony to Congress during the Iran-
Contra affair, pardoned by Bush I, and recently made Bush II's top White House adviser
on global democracy.) "Liberals and their Libertine fellow-travelers accuse Callahan of
the one inexcusable crime in America: BWR ('Breathing While Republican')," "Illbay"
posted on Freerepublic.com in 2002 about a pork barrel project involving Congressman Sonny Callahan of Alabama.

Breathing while Republican (or *conservative*) is based on the phrase *breathing while
black*, the more prominent *voting while black* (which resurfaced during the 2000 and
2004 elections regarding attempts to suppress black votes), and the original *X while
black* pop construction, *driving while black* (police using racial profiling to pull black
people over on the road or to arrest them chiefly because of their race).

Spelling B

Driving while black, itself twisted from *driving while intoxicated*, is simple, classic word-
play. And DWI to DWB to BWR is classic letterplay and codeplay. Coiled in most pop
phrases—and especially in anything compressed further into initials (or numbers,
like *24/7* and *411*)—is a Jack-in-the-box meaning that's just waiting to spring out.
That is, the energy putting the pop in pop language comes from the power of codes. All
language is codes, codes 'R' us and all that,
but coded language is an African American   **Coded language is an African**
art form. The often double meaning of black   **American art form.**
phrases, the way some words may mean
their opposite (*bad, dope, stoopid/stupid*) developed among slaves who needed to talk to
each other in front of the massa without him knowing Jack.

To carry the weight of a twisted meaning not on a word but on a single letter is
to pack the code tighter. Altering a letter in an otherwise ordinary word can alter the
world outlook. When *boys* went to *boyz*, so went Boyz II Men. The title of the 1991 movie

Boyz N the Hood declared it was no suburban frolic. Young black musicians and hip-hop-influenced culture in general wear wayward words like visual rap. Hip-hop and R&B singers and groups have long been seizing the Z (Jay-Z, Outlawz, Limp Bizkit), crossing an X (Xscape, Xzibit), or otherwise kurupting the language (Kurupt, OutKast, Fabolous, Ludacris, Shyne, Mystikal).

Hip-hop didn't invent deliberate misspellings as a mild social subversion (remember the left's *Amerika*, the hippies' *freek?*) or as an attention-getting device (way before hip-hop, marketers were messing with the ABCs, from *Beanz Meanz Heinz* and Kool cigarettes to Kwik Save Foodstores and EZLern driving school). Wacky spelling may in fact serve the status quo quite well. In the late 1800s, a loose group of humorists called the Phunny Phellows "fed their Victorian audiences a bland diet of simple gags, sprinkled liberally with malapropisms, terrible puns, comic misspellings, blatant racism, stock characters, and shopworn topical jokes," wrote Kevin MacDonnell in *Firsts* magazine.

But deliberate misspellings have long been used to declare some form of independence, however deep or shallow it might run. In the 1920s, young people "spelled 'rats' as 'rhatz!' and shortened 'that's too bad' to 'stoo bad,'" Dalzell writes, adding that even the famous *phat*, which seems the epitome of hip-hop spelling, has a surprisingly long history. *Fat* meant "rich" back in the seventeenth century, and examples of *fat* meaning "good," "cool," or "living well" have occurred ever since. As for the "ph," in a list of "Negro argot," *Time* magazine listed *phat* "as one of several 'adjectives of approval'" in 1963. But *phat* predated that. Dalzell found that around the turn of the last century "typesetters referred to type that was easily set as being *phat*. . . . Indeed, in 1885, the Post Express Printing Company in Rochester, New York, published the 'Phat Boy's Birds-Eye Map of the Saint Lawrence River' with a drawing of a corpulent boy."

Despite their varied history, creative misspellings today are mostly associated with hip-hop culture. So much so that in his 2000 movie *Bamboozled*, Spike Lee hilariously spoofed the trend. "I respectfully submit," one rapper tells his gangsta crew, "that we from now on, henceforth and whatnot spell black B-L-A-K, not B-L-A-C-K."

Hip-hop misspellings don't just reject select bits of standard white written style; they also reflect a history, beginning in the 1800s, in which standard writers ridiculed Negro speech with exaggerated misspelling. I'm not referring to the sympathetic, if imperfect, attempts at dialect writing in literature, as in *Uncle Tom's Cabin* and *Huckleberry Finn*, but rather to another, contemporary "trend in comic writing where southern speakers, especially blacks, were portrayed as uneducated or as figures of fun," as David Crystal writes in *The Cambridge Encyclopedia of the English Language*. "Dialect vocabulary and grammar (*hain't, saw* for *seen*, etc.) were used as well as misspelling, though it was the spelling which created the impact." Some of the impact of hip-hop's mangled orthography reflects that dis: Do the disapproved thing first; do it aggressively and obviously intentionally, b4 itz dunn 2 U.

And it's that unorthodox, defiant style that larger, nonblack marketing forces are now sucking image off of. If a company abuses the alphabet today, it's usually doing so to look hip-hop fresh, sometimes to look, dare we say . . . outlaw. Customized spellings that developed in part to subvert the Man's words are now copied by the Man's corporations almost as fast as they'll funnel benjamins to Congress to make them mo' money. (Hey, just like real gangstas!)

In 1999, when Rupert Murdoch's Fox Family Channel launched two new cable   60
channels, it fought the power by naming them the Boyz Channel and the Girlz Channel. (Both were soon zapped.) When it was still running, *Lizzie McGuire* was the most
successful show on the Disney Channel lineup called "Zoog Weekendz." The STARZ!,
BLACK STARZ!, STARZ! Kids, STARZ! Family digital movie channels add all caps and
exclamation marks to convey their over-the-top Zness. *Z* bumped the old-skool *S* in
DreamWorks' *Antz* (the name of Woody's "You da man!" ant, by the way, was "Z"). One
of my favorite stupid attempts of someone to get down is the name of a spammer (apparently now deceased), "BestLoanz.com."

A quick trick to convince children that they're cool and that you, if you're a seller
of stuff, are rad, is to call them "kidz" and otherwise buzz their brains with Zs; hence,
the glitzoid Trollz dolls and cartoons (based on the 1960s cute-ugly Trolls); Bratz dolls
(a massive seller); Nitro Battlerz (cars racing in battle domes and such); Kellogg's Gripz
crackers and cookies; Hershey's Koolerz chewing gum, SnackBarz, and Twizzlers
Sourz. On the health food side of the aisle, Hain's line of children's products is called
Kidz, while EnviroKidz says it makes "The World's First 100% Certified Organic Cereals
for Kidz."

Z—the purple of the alphabet, the last in line shall be first, the snap at the tip of the
whip (Zorro's?)—is the letter that marketing relies on most to represent childlike fun,
diversity, and all things hip-hop.

Z is unconventional, jazzy, but not really dangerous. Like Snoop Dogg's izzle,
fo'shizzle ("for sure") pig-Latin-like lingo, Zs can be damn cuddly. (Snoop Dogg has
dropped his "shizzolating." "I overdosed on it," he told *MTV News* in 2004. "I'm seeing
it everywhere, you know what I'm saying?") For danger, citizens, you gotta get *X*.

X is pornography, the drug ecstasy, a former spouse, the signature of illiteracy,
X out, cross out, the cross, an equation's unknown solution, off the charts, extra, extreme, and (in the exception exposing the rule) kisses. Generation X is the somehow
canceled-out generation. *The X-Files* were stories of the paranormal too threatening for
normals. *X Creatures* was a Discovery Channel show about Loch Ness monsters, giant
squids, and other excessive animals. The *X-Men*—whether the original sixties comic
book or its later incarnations as animated TV shows and live-action movies—is a parable about "the Other," ethnic hatred, and race relations. (The X-Men have a mutant
gene that gives them great powers, but human society reviles them because they're
different.)

But now outsiders are in (Outsider Art, by non-art-world, non-art-schooled, often   65
black, and occasionally psychotic artists, draws big bucks). Exy is sexy—it's hardcore,
outlaw, a black man, Malcolm X, Brand X. And today brands, rather than running
from Xness, practically cut it into their foreheads with razors, probably Schick Xtreme
III blades. *X* is death, like the Slug-X Trap for gardening. In a world of *Survivor*, *The
Sopranos*, and Swift Boat Veterans for Truth, X or be Xed. When NBC and the World
Wrestling Federation (now World Wrestling Entertainment) needed a name for their
newborn, self-designated "outlaw" (and quickly Xed-out) football league, the choice
was obvious: the XFL (and X marked the spot for its teams the Maniax and Xtremes).
When Right Guard decided it needed another market for another deodorant, it created
Right Guard Xtreme Sport. When Kraft's Jell-O sales declined, the company put the
gelatin in push-up packages, named it X-TREME Jell-O Sticks, and took aim at kids:

"They're extreme—yeah!" exclaimed the commercial. And when that foxy Fox needed a name for another cable channel, it chose FX. Yes, the name plays nicely on Fox, and if you happen to know that FX is Hollywood for special effects, you might get a goose bump. But more important, *F* looks cooler slapped up against a bad-ass *X*, the naive, open-mouthed *O* squeezed out all together. "Perpleed?" an ad for FX on a commuter train read. "What would life be like without the X?"

Well, it might not be quite so easy to sell in. In video games, X marks the spot for Microsoft's Xbox. On TV, the letter has done duty for *The X Show* (about relationships, guy talk, and big breasts), *Maximum EXposure* (about extreme activities—man eats live snakes, ex-wife attacks new wife), and, on the relatively staid History Channel, *Extreme History with Roger Daltrey.* "Beyond AM. Beyond FM. XM" went a slogan for XM Satellite Radio. *XXL* is the name of the hip-hop magazine as well as the extra extra large size. *X* is a ride on the wild side that yet another XXL SUV swears it will deliver: A huge sign over Times Square read, "AS NOT SEEN IN THE HAMPTONS—NISSAN XTERRA."

For pure purchased *X*, look at the Jaguar X-Type, Infiniti's QX or FX45, or any vehicular X. X crosses the chrome on cars, says the automotive writer Phil Patton, because of "its connotations of 'experimental' and 'luxury.'" Or, in the case of XTerra, "Gen X and cross-country," he says. "The S in SE or SX is supposed to suggest 'sport,' but the SX also suggests sex."

OK, so *X* brands products. Earth to me: That's what popular symbols *do*. I guess I shouldn't be surprised to see *X* infiltrate newslike missives from media conglomerates, but when I saw the following, I almost had to slip on some Nike Shox to absorb the blow: A CNBC headline for a segment about international reaction to the U.S. invasion of Iraq was succinct, if not right out of the funnies: "World Reax."

So common is *X*, especially when referring to anything "extreme," that *X* has gone from out there to dead center—or, to restate that in pop, *X* is the new *edge*. Back in 2001, when ESPN's X Games (X stands for "extreme sports") were beginning to go global, even ESPN execs paid to propagate *X* were dissing the full *extreme.* "'Extreme' is the old term," Ron Semiao, then in charge of ESPN's Global X division, told *Advertising Age* at the time. "These types of action sports have gone from being an activity of fringe groups to an ingrained part of a generation that influences its fashion, music, entertainment." He helped push for the rather uncatchy term "action sports." (Are there any other kind?) When Heinz's Bagel Bites, which was originally marketed to mothers, revamped to target *X*-attracted "tweens" (kids between childhood and teenhood), a Heinz executive said, "Action sports is a sport that embodies the lifestyle and personality of the Bagel Bites consumer." If true, this proves, finally: Edge is dead, long live the hole in the center.

Obviously, not everything *X* or *Z* is black or black-influenced. Extreme sports, in fact, are pretty darn white. Pornography appears in all colors. *Z* and *X* are mysterious and primal human qualities. But black, according to still-thriving stereotypes, is so often mysterious and primal, so often *Z* and *X*, that the corporate addition of those letters is black pepper for the white sauce. 70

Encouraged by the hip *X* and *Z* hopping around, other letter replacements have gained favor among wannabe companies—that is, they wanna *B*. I'm convinced the whole *B to B* nomenclature (meaning "business to business," the tag of telephone directories and other enterprises in which businesses deal directly with one another rather than with consumers) is a hit because it resonates with the black *B*s: *B-boy*, *B-ball*, and *B* as a form of address, as in "Yo, B, whassup?" (This last *B* was probably reduced from *blood*, "a positive term, noting the genetic kinship and shared bloodlines of African people," Smitherman writes.) Sure, it makes sense in this abbreviation-loving era that *business to business* would be punched down to *B2B*, as in B2BMarketingTrends.com ("to help marketing professionals stay abreast of B2B marketing trends," according to a press release). But *B2B* has become too popular for brevity to be the only explanation. *B2B* has spawned *B2C*, *B2B2C*, *B2G*, *B2E*, and *P2P*—"business to consumer," "business to business to consumer," "business to government," "business to employee," and "peer to peer" (as in electronic file sharing), respectively. All this B-bop can make any business sound less like it consists of a bunch of suits who bore one another at meetings and more like a crew of B-boys doing some def transactions.

   B as short for *be* (along with *U* for *you* and *4* for *for*) has been around for ages (even pre-Prince). But this shading of *B* has been bumped up lately because of its increased use in text messaging as well as in hip-hop. "Now we can b alone," a man writes to a woman on a pager in a noisy concert crowd for a Verizon Wireless spot. A Burger King TV commercial had it both ways, with nods to hip-hop and electronics: "B Real. B Good," voice-overs sang as the lyrics were spelled out on-screen to make sure we C the Bs. "2 Go. BK4U." Bouncy and at the beginning of the alphabet, *B* is on the mild side of businesses that want their bit of blood.

   When corporations misspell, they're trying to spell it out: We refuse to put letters together the way the authorities tell us to!

Covert Operations

Wannabe or crossover talk didn't begin with hip-hop, nor is lingo-lending from one group to another confined to blacks and whites in America. Whites talking some black is part of an apparently universal phenomenon that sociolinguists call covert prestige. This means that speakers of a "standard" language (whatever the language) "have favorable attitudes toward lower-class, nonstandard speech forms," explains the linguist Margaret Lee. "However, these attitudes are not always overtly expressed, and they may be subconscious, because they stray from mainstream—or overt—values about the perceived superior status of the standard forms." This occurs, she adds, "for the most part throughout the world—when new forms enter the mainstream, in fact, they usually come from nonstandard speech."

   Males are more prone than females to imbibing some of that covert prestige. Perhaps that's because, as some studies indicate, males associate standard speech with femininity. "Females tend to use more 'correct' speech forms," Lee says. On the basis of a study in Norwich, England, Peter Trudgill wrote in *Sociolinguistics*, "A large number of male speakers, it seems, are more concerned with acquiring *covert prestige* than with obtaining social status (as this is more usually defined)." This may be, he wrote, "because working-class speech is associated with the 'toughness' traditionally supposed to be characteristic of working-class life—and 'toughness' is quite widely considered to be a desirable masculine characteristic." 75

   Covert or otherwise, black-to-white (and white-to-black) crossover talk in America began during slavery, especially when slave children and white children played together. Most of that language was never recorded, of course, and we have to wait for the development of various media to see how black speech influenced the broader English. "Slavery made its own traditions of speech and vocabulary," McCrum and his coauthors write in *The Story of English.* The entry of black English—an amalgam of Africanisms, the trade English used on slave ships, and plantation English—"into the mainstream of American life began with the Brer Rabbit stories. Later it was to sustain its place there through minstrel shows, vaudeville, music hall, radio, and finally the movies."

By the 1840s, minstrel shows had brought black language to large audiences and in the most overtly covert way possible. White men in blackface sang and told jokes using some variety of black language, often insulting imitations of it, to entertain whites. They were horror shows, "but minstrel shows were also the beginning of influence of African American style on all America," writes Allan Metcalf in *How We Talk: American Regional English Today.*

Black musical forms—spirituals, ragtime, the blues—went on to spread black language to the larger public, but by far the most influential music, until hip-hop, was jazz. Jazz fed generations of slang. Jive, the jokey, mint-cool language that arrived with the swing jazz of the thirties and forties, was slang that went on to become the pop of its time, even spawning a number of dictionaries. Cab Calloway's *Hepster's Dictionary: Language of Jive* (first edition published in 1938) listed jive words like *beat* (exhausted), *chick* (girl), *hip, hype, groovy, in the groove, jam* (improvised swing music), *joint is jumping, mellow, pad, riff, sharp, solid, square, too much,* and *yeah, man.* In *The Original Handbook of Harlem Jive* (1944), Dan Burley wrote: "in the sense that [jive] came into use among Negroes in Chicago about the year 1921, it meant to taunt, scoff, to sneer—an expression of sarcastic comment," and he relates it to the "linguistic procedure which came to be known as 'putting you in the dozens.'"

The whites ("flappers" if they were women) who jammed the Harlem clubs in the 1920s, the jitterbug craze of the 1930s, and influential disc jockeys in the 1940s all contributed to making jive the lingo for black and white youth in the know. Listen, for instance, to this forties DJ: "Hiya cat, wipe ya feet on the mat, let's slap on the fat and dish out some scat. You're a prisoner of wov. W-O-V, 1280 on the dial, New York, and you're picking up the hard spiel and good deal of Fred Robbins, dispensing seven score and ten ticks of ecstatic static and spectacular vernacular from 6:30 to 9."

"A new language has been born," Lou Shelly wrote in 1945 in another jive dictio- 80 nary, *Hepcats Jive Talk Dictionary,* "and with its usual lustiness youth has made jive talk heard from one end of the land to the other." This meant, as always, that corporate interests were moving in—a process then more likely to signal a phenomenon's demise than it does today. "The end of the jive generation," writes Dalzell, "could be measured by the fact that in 1946 Hallmark cards issued a set of 'Solid Sender' cards, 'groovy as the movie MAKE MINE MUSIC,' based on the 'Disney hepcat scene.'"

Though jive began to dive, it kept resurfacing in the slang of later groups. In describing the beat speech of the late-forties hipster, Jack Kerouac called it "a new language, actually spade (Negro) jargon, but you soon learned it." By the 1950s, Kerouac noticed that "even college kids went around hep and cool and using terms I'd heard on Times Square in the early Forties."

Jive, writes Dalzell, "would lay an important foundation for the slang of the hipster/ beat movement of the late 1950s, the hippie movement of the 1960s and early 1970s, and to some extent the hip-hop/rap phenomenon of the 1980s and 1990s. *Cap, fly chick, groovy, homey, hung up, icy, mellow, righteous, sharp, solid*, and *square* all endured quite nicely, playing major roles in the slang of the 1960s and the 1990s."

If the 1960s were the turning point in creating pop language of a different order, that was to a great degree because, simultaneously, black language was undergoing a renaissance and was developing an increased ability to cross over. This black force met up with the big two powers, mass media and marketing, and all three have played with and against one another ever since.

Smitherman describes this blossoming of black language:

> . . . perhaps the richest period of linguistic innovation was the last half of the twentieth century, particularly the 1960s and beyond. The emergence of the Black Freedom Struggle marked a fundamental shift in linguistic conscious-ness as Black intellectuals, scholar-activists, and writer-artists deliberately and consciously engaged in an unprecedented search for a language to ex-press Black identity and the Black condition. This era was in fact the first pe-riod in the history of U.S. slave descendants when there was a critical mass of highly educated Blacks.

White people couldn't help but hear the newly invigorated black talk, she continues. "The 1960s was a defining moment in this cultural diffusion process with Motown, on the one hand, crossing racial boundaries with its music, and the Civil Rights Move-ment, on the other, crossing racial boundaries with its language and rhetoric of protest and moral confrontation, all broadcast live on the eleven o'clock news."

By the 1970s, black was beautiful enough to be in demand in the more liberal cir-cles. As Gerald Boyd, the former managing editor of the *New York Times* and a black man, said in a round-table discussion about race, "When I started out in the early seventies, it was very popular to be black. Every white had to have one." 85

Media Bond

Now, more than a generation later, does every white—or at least every white kid—have to be one?

In the late eighties, the hip-hop movement began to bring black style—music, dance, fashion, language—back harder than anything since the introduction of jive. However, as Dalzell writes, "Unlike the hippie movement where anyone could don a tie-dye shirt and become a weekend hippie, the hip-hop culture did not provide a life-style that most American young people could completely embrace. Simply put, white teenagers could not, as much as they might wish to, become black. They could and did, however, listen to the music, dress the dress . . . mirror the hair cuts, adopt the rap vo-cabulary suitable for their daily lives, mimic the cadence of street speech, and admire from a safe distance the lives of prominent black rappers and athletes."

What made both the mimicking and the distance possible were massive media and marketing, both of which have mushroomed since forties jive. Hip-hop is, for now, the leading culture (followed by various skateboard, drug, and online cultures) that white kids can draw upon to fight the power, be that their parents, their schools, the system, injustice, or the general whateverness of life. Which is why commercial powers want so badly to be associated, however tenuously, with hip-hop. (The truism about "brand loyalty" is, Hook 'em while they're young and you got 'em for life.) For the most part, that rented association is working. If hip-hop weren't commercialized and hadn't hit the pop stage (*stage* in both senses), most of these white kids wouldn't hear or see it enough to wanna be black in the first place.

How easily a word can hop from hep or hippie or hip-hop to shopping pop. In the year 2000, few pop words could compete with *Whassup?!* Perhaps that's because *Whassup?!* (the official Budweiser spelling) was the one phenomenon that most successfully put black style through the marketing processor and coated every particle of implied transgression with a safety seal.

It was advertising, of course, that catapulted the sound into our faces. A Chicago copywriter caught a short movie by filmmaker Charles Stone III in which Stone and some friends, cool black guys all, lay out deep, highly exaggerated *Whassup?!*s for every possible greeting. The ad guy, finding himself mouthing it too, figured, This is exploitable! and signed Stone to transfer his magic word to a client, Budweiser.

Said with tongue hanging out of mouth, the commercial *Whassup?!* was guttural and gross and funny. (Budweiser's spelling was wrong, Stone insisted; since the proper pronunciation is P-less, it should be spelled *Whaazzzaahhh?!* "If you make the P sound, your tongue can't be out," he told me.) After a climactic series of the guys growling *Whaazzzaahhh?!* to one another over phones and intercoms while watching a game on TV, the original spot ended with a sudden calm-down: "What's up, B?" Stone asked one friend over the cordless. "Watching the game. Having a Bud." "True. True," Stone replied. With the spots starring Stone's real-life pals, what emerged through this literally *lingua franca* was a lot of easygoing male bonding among some brotha buds.

(A note on origins: *What's up?* was not originally black. It goes back at least to 1838, Jonathan Lighter, editor of the *RHHDAS*, wrote in a post to the American Dialect Society online discussion group. Nearly a hundred years later, the phrase went mass-pop when Bugs Bunny first uttered a crisp "Eh, what's up, Doc?" in *A Wild Hare* in 1940. But somewhere along the way, African Americans began to unroll *What's up?* into a more all-purpose greeting. By the seventies and eighties, Dalzell writes, long-haired white dudes were saying the blackened *whassup, s'up*, and *z'up*. Stone said he and his pals had been doing the mega *Whaazzzaahhh?!* for sixteen years before selling their shtick to Budweiser. But he feels strongly that it's more of a black thing than Bud's or his own. "Someone suggested to me that I should trademark it," he said. "If it ever came to that, I would hope that someone in the African American community would sue me.")

Whaazzzaahhh?! was just what the nation apparently needed on the eve of a new millennium. The sound instantly became an NBA refrain, a greeting on radio sports shows, the theme of an *SNL* skit (with Brokaw, Koppel, and Shaw *Whaazzzaahhh?!*ing each other), part of another easy question on *Who Wants to Be a Millionaire*, and the basis of numerous Web site parodies.

Largely because of *Whaazzzaahhh?!*, sales for all Anheuser-Busch beers rose by 2.4 million barrels in 2000. Just as important, *Whaazzzaahhh?!* generated at least $20 million worth of free publicity, according to Bud's ad agency, DDB Worldwide in Chicago. (DDB calls this desirable state "talk value" — it means saturation buzz, a phrase that people use almost involuntarily. But since DDB wanted to reap benefits in case *talk value* acquired talk value, it did what Stone said he wouldn't with *Whaazzzaahhh?!* — it trademarked the term.)

Whaazzzaahhh?! clearly filled a catchphrase/catchgesture void. The Arsenio whoop 95
and the high-five, pop as they still are, had already faded into background pop. The
chest bump and the victory dance required actually getting physical. Men, especially
sedentary sports-fan men, were ripe for a word that could reinvigorate their manliness,
update them multiculturally, and refresh their irony.

And the very sound of the earthy, vomity *Whaazzzaahhh?!* was a perfect counter-
point to the entire high-pitched, beeping wired world. *Whaazzzaahhh?!* was disgusting, low-down, and as analogue as it gets—something to make primal *Fight Club* men
out of digital midgets (the 1999 Edward Norton/Brad Pitt movie about wimpy white
guys fleeing office cubicles and regaining testosterone by slapping each other around
in abandoned buildings came out shortly before Bud's campaign), something to add
thick yang to the whiny yin of cell phones and chirping virtuosity and everything
eeeeeeeeeeeeeEEEEEEEE. *Whaazzzaahhh?!* was grit thrown onto the computer screen,
onto the very TV screen the ads ran on. That is—as racial myths still go—*Whaazzzaahhh?!* could make cool black men out of repressed white males.

But it took another spot of the many in Budweiser's campaign to make that perfectly clear. A bunch of preppie white guys—a sweater is draped over one's shoulders
as he watches the "market recap" instead of "the game"—duplicate the plot of the
original spot but instead of gutting out *Whaazzzaahhh?!*, they eke out a clunky *What are
you doooo-ing?!* By the end, their war cry is very loud but very uncool, and the camera
pulls back to show two of Stone's black pals watching these graceless wannabes on
TV and looking at each other in disbelief. The spot, which debuted on the 2001 Super
Bowl, was really funny. But think about what Budweiser was doooo-ing. It was telling its predominantly white customers that they could better identify with these loose,
creative black men than they could with those ghosts-of-men honkies. Pouring on the
covert prestige, it flattered white guys by telling them they shared the cool attitude of
the black men—though, whew, they didn't have to *live* as black men. Drink Bud and
get in touch with your inner black guy.

But not necessarily with an outer one. Because *Whaazzzaahhh?!* was yet another
way for white men, and women, to bond with black people without having to actually
know any. Knowing *media* black people—actors, athletes, any celebrity will do—is so
much easier. If white people can bond with media black people through a phrase or a
gesture, we can all "celebrate" an idyllic racial harmony while ignoring real racial politics—assaults on voting rights, racial profiling, income disparities, leaving no African
American child behind.

But, hey, this ad's for Bud. Budweiser needed a hit of *Whaazzzaahhh?!* as much as
many white people did. Never a big seller to blacks and without an indie bone in its
image, the world's largest-selling beer, made by the world's largest brewer, could now
say: These hops hip hop. Even though it's not true, true.

The Paying Dues Blues

After just a year or so, *Whaazzzaahhh?!* became mere hall-of-fame pop—no longer "top 100
of mind," as ad people say, but hauled out now and then to fill certain mental slots (like
another Budweiser hall-of-famer, "I love you, man"). But within the *Whaazzzaahhh?!*
campaign, particularly the preppie spot, lie the seeds of what's wrong with media-
enabled crossover talk.

Yes, merging languages is great, and we're better off when "standard" English gets goosed firmly and frequently. Anyway, it simply wouldn't be possible for white people not to use black talk—it's part and parcel of American talk. But whether our national experiments in covert prestige are enriching or exploitative depends on the attitude that insiders bring to outsiders' speech. When white people are too tickled with their ability to reference black talk, when they treat it like exotica, when it's too trendy, too knee-jerk, too associated with the selling of something (including oneself) and dissociated from the politics and history that forged it, then you have to ask, What are the hidden costs, and who reaps the profits?

In his show *You Are All Diseased*, George Carlin started in on theme restaurants like the House of Blues: "Burn down the House of Blues!" he said—it has too many white people playing the blues. "White people ought to understand they *give* people the blues. . . . A couple of terms used by lame white people: 'happens to be black,' 'openly gay.' When did 'urban' become synonymous with the word black? I don't think white women should be calling each other girlfriend. . . . 'You go, girl' should probably go along with 'You the man.'"

White people crowing "You the man" does not necessarily flatter black people. "Most black people are not delighted to have aspects of the language borrowed," the linguist John Rickford says. "They think of it as appropriated."

This isn't to say that all imitation of black or hip-hop talk is simply appropriation. Spreading words can spread the word—knowledge, empathy, and certainly the broader hip-hop culture. "It's something to see videos connect white kids in Utah to black kids in South Chicago to Croats and Brazilians," the hip-hop pioneer and former Public Enemy frontman Chuck D. wrote in *Time* magazine's cover story on hip-hop's twentieth anniversary. "This is the sound and style of our young world, the vernacular used in today's speak from scholastics to sports. . . . It's difficult to stop a cultural revolution that bridges people together." Those words began to sound prescient when, five years later, a rousing rap song, "Razom Nas Bahato" ("Together We Are Many"), became the theme music of Ukraine's pro-Yushchenko "Orange revolution."

Hip-hop truly is the young world's vernacular. But borrowing black language 105 alone doesn't bridge people together. The bridges are often not so much between people as they are between people and the media. The college slang expert Connie Eble puts into perspective, for instance, the white use of the black term of address *girl*. "Well, *girl* is just used and that's all there is to it," she says. "It's one black phrase that has been taken over by white females, middle-aged secretaries around campus," as well as students. Eble once believed that the white use of *girl* and other black slang was a sign of hope. "At first I thought, maybe race relations are improving after all. But I have absolutely no evidence that there is more mixing among the races than there ever has been. After researching it, I found that hardly any black slang entered the white vocabulary because a white student has encountered a black student. They've learned it from MTV, the movies, and rap songs."

What's wrong with whites gaining covert prestige through black talk isn't that it fails to bring the races together (that's too much to ask from any one trend or proclivity). What's wrong is that it usually allows whites to feel good about themselves without having to do anything particularly worthwhile. Such easily picked-up prestige encourages the belief that high-fiving or giving it up are the extent of political commitment that an enlightened person needs nowadays. Whites get to blacken up their act "at bargain-basement prices," as Smitherman writes. "They don't have to PAY NO DUES, but reap the psychological, social, and economic benefits of a language and culture born out of enslavement, neo-enslavement, Jim Crow, U.S. apartheid, and twentieth-century hard times."

Dearth of the Cool

The matter of whites reaping benefits from black history brings us to the black-nurtured word and concept that has risen to a status above all others: cool, or rather a dues-free knockoff of it.

Cool is the tent pole of pop culture. Without it, desire flops around; money doesn't know where to put itself. Uttered by folks from two (I've heard it) to seventy, cool is both one of the most expressive concepts of our time and one of the emptiest.

Cool is not just a black thing, by any means. Garbo, Brando, and Eastwood, to name a few obvious cool white symbols, have projected it. Other languages have long had their equivalents—the French royalty displayed *sang-froid*, for instance, on the way to the guillotine. And *cool*, meaning warmer than cold, has been around since the Norman invasion. *Cold, cool, chill, glacier, gelato*, and *Jell-O* all go back to the Latin root *gelare*, meaning to freeze, congeal; by extension, to make rigid, unmoving, with the implication of restraint and control.

Exactly when *cool* jelled into the word we know today is difficult to say. But *cool* as 110
an elixir of composure, detachment, and style is generally thought to have come of age during the era of Count Basie and Duke Ellington. In 1947, Charlie Parker came out with a track called "Cool Blues"; in 1950, Miles Davis, perhaps *the* icon of cool, brought out the album *Birth of the Cool*.

But the cool—the stance, the feeling, the vibe—that early jazz musicians exemplified goes back much further. "Cool is all about trying to make a dollar out of 15 cents. It's about living on the cusp, on the periphery, diving for scraps. Essential to cool is being outside looking in," Donnell Alexander writes in the essay "Are Black People Cooler Than White People?" "So in the days when [slaves] were still literally on the plantation they devised a coping strategy called cool, an elusive mellowing strategy designed to master time and space. Cool, the basic reason blacks remain in the American cultural mix, is an industry of style that everyone in the world can use. It's finding the essential soul while being essentially lost."

To pull off such a strategy, you'd have to at times appear unmoving; you'd have to chill. "A wooden-faced model is aristocratic in its roots," says the classicist Margaret Visser, author of *The Way We Are* and *The Geometry of Love*. "Kings and queens perfected an impassive public face as the look of power. If you have no expression on your face, other people interpret *you*—you are all things to all people." While the keeping of a cool public face by nonroyals is a relatively "modern phenomenon," Visser says, it was "adopted by black culture, people who were the opposite of aristocrats, though they knew how to use that to make themselves powerful."

Sometimes that impassive look can be gotten cheaply, by wearing sunglasses. Or by using other symbols—catchphrases, designer labels, a little something to entice other people to interpret you. The more that millions of people have chased the elusive cool, the more the word's meaning has been diluted. Perhaps the seeds of change were there in the sixties, when cool began to shift from a thing to admire to a thing to idolize. But somewhere along the way, *cool* ceased to be primarily a word denoting composure or detachment and became more an all-purpose murmur of approval (where it's sometimes written and pronounced *kewl*—a blend of *cool* and *cute?*). "That's cool," one might say when a cabby suggests taking Thirteenth Street across town instead of Fourteenth. "Cool," I say instead of listening when my son tells me an amazing fact about his Yu-Gi-Oh! cards.

Perhaps, too, *cool*'s cool dissipated as people used it, as they will any fashion, not to cope with life as an outsider, but to enforce a popular-kids-in-class caste system. I used to say *neat*—until 1991, when I saw Madonna's tour movie, *Truth or Dare.* In it, Kevin Costner visited Madonna backstage and told her that her show was "neat." She acidly repeated the word, withering him on the spot for being an outdated creep and a disingenuous suckup. This was not Madonna at her coolest. Cool, as Alexander further defines it, is "about completing the task of living with enough spontaneity to splurge some of it on bystanders." Ten years after *Truth or Dare,* the caste system *cool* got a comeuppance, of sorts, in another movie, *Save the Last Dance.* In this interracial teenage romance, the white heroine compliments a black friend on her clothes: "Cool outfit." "Slammin'," the friend corrects her, "*slammin'* outfit." I'm not sure, but I doubt that *slammin'* still rules. Such words of praise come and go, but in the grand mall of franchised pop, *cool* has outlasted them all.

As *cool* rose in popularity, it needed a chump. "*Square*, a vital word of the 1950s 115 counterculture," Dalzell writes, "became by the dialectic process of slang a vital word of the 1960s predominant youth culture; it is richly paradoxical that kids whom Beats would have found quite square used the word to vilify those who were out of touch with the latest mainstream fashions, styles, and trends."

Today *cool* has everything to do with mainstream fashions, styles, and trends and very little to do with originality or art, much less with "trying to make a dollar out of 15 cents." And yet repeating the word's sound—its coo, its ooh, its refreshing pool—still gives the faint impression that the speaker is grooving to something the majority just doesn't get, that maybe he's even slyly artistic or, to veer toward another black-cultivated word of complexity, hip. John Leland, author of *Hip: The History,* says *hip* "refers to an awareness or enlightenment. It's the intelligence behind the mask [of cool's composure]." To that I would just add that cool and hip, as words and as forces, intertwine, overlap, and at times are indistinguishable, but that on the whole cool is central to pop culture, while hip influences it more from the sidelines.

Cool's opposite number among the pop superlatives is not *hip*, but *hot*. *Hot* and *cool* both convey the utmost in mass desirability, but *hot* doesn't know from detachment; it's all sex, passion, and hubba hubba. Magazine cover lines have hissed *hot* so often that a women's magazine editor once told me his publication had nixed *hot* as being tepid. "Hot is unusable," he said flatly. The moratorium must have lasted all of three months, because the heavy-breathing *hot* is baaack. "What's Hot?" asks a 2005 print ad for (the co-owned) *In Touch* and *Life & Style* magazines. Citing each mag's sales stats, the ad answers: "That's hot!" The lucre-and-loin-driven *hot* is simpleminded, and has none of the paradoxes of *cool* (much less of the way more subtle *hip*).

No rich concept is without paradoxes, real and apparent. Cool is rife with them. Paradox number one is that beneath the frozen face of real cool, you're actually going with the flow (no paradox at all for Buddhist cool). Paradox number two, touched on earlier, is that borrowing from the excluded can make you feel more included. This is less a paradox than a pragmatic tactic for a market that needs outsiders (and even more so, paradox itself) to sex up its merchandise. Even a few years ago, who'd have imagined that GM and Ford would "trick out" their autos with loads of bling to look like the car makeovers on the MTV show *Pimp My Ride?* ("If you had big chrome rims a few years ago, people thought you were a drug dealer or a pimp," Myles Kovacs, the publisher of the hip-hop car magazine *Dub*, told *Newsweek*. "Now you could be a CEO.") Exuding excluded cool can protect a seller from appearing, God help them, boring. So market researchers, like those featured in Malcolm Gladwell's now classic piece "The Coolhunt," stalk the ghetto for music, garb, and slang to process into product.

If white people have made a fetish out of black cool, that too goes back further than the jazz era, as Greg Tate reminds us. In the introduction to the anthology *Everything But the Burden*, he writes: "Capitalism's original commodity fetish was the Africans auctioned here as slaves, whose reduction from subjects to abstracted objects has made them seem larger than life and less than human at the same time." That paradox reverberates today "in a market-driven world where we continue to find ourselves being sold as hunted outsiders and privileged insiders in the same breath."

Anyone who tries to resist the fruit of the coolhunts is bound to fail frequently. 120 There's almost no way not to respond positively, at least momentarily, to marketed cool, whether in the form of a hip-hop Sprite spot or Nike's latest spectacle. We are really responding to presentations of grace—paid, staged, and third-hand though they may be. But in buying the product, we're not honoring cool, we're merely possessing its congealed representation—while the real thing evaporates from our credit-card-bearing hands.

"Most think cool is something you can put on and take off at will (like a strap-on goatee)," writes Alexander (ESPN once hired him to help hip-hopify its language). "They think it's some shit you go shopping for. And that taints cool, giving the mutant thing it becomes a deservedly bad name." Found in "advertising agencies, record company artist-development departments, and over-art-directed bars," this "ersatz cool," he adds, "fights real cool at every turn."

When Black Talk Goes to School

White society's fetishization of black cool and black talk might go down easier if that society did not react so virulently when black vernacular left the neighborhood of entertainment and moved to more serious areas, like education. I'm talking, of course, about Ebonics.

In December 1996, the Oakland, California, school board approved a resolution to change how it taught African American students who, the board said, spoke not a dialect of English but a separate, African-based language, Ebonics. On the face of it, which was as far as most of the press went, the resolution sounded like identity politics gone mad: calling a bunch of slang a separate language and proposing to teach it. Indeed, at first many blacks, most notably Jesse Jackson, in addition to most of the media and the larger public, trashed the plan.

Ebonics suddenly became the target of a rash of nasty cartoons, Internet jokes, and fuming commentary. Since the controversy arrived during the holiday season, several "Ebonics translations" of "The Night Before Christmas" began to circulate on the Net, like this one:

I looked out thru de bars;
What covered my doe;
'spectin' de sheriff;
Wif a warrent fo sho.

And what did I see;
I said, "Lawd, look at dat!"
Ther' wuz a huge watermellon;
Pulled by giant warf rats!!

The "Ebonics Lectric Library of Classical Literature" Web site (no longer active) [125] introduced itself thus: "Since the recent decision to make Ebonics (Ebony-Phonics) a second language in our schools it has become obvious that e-bliterations of the classics will be required. We will cover here the greater works of world Literature (Litershure) in the hopes of bridging the gap between English and the new Slanguage."

With the general consensus that Ebonics was broken English and teaching it meant the triumph of black special interests, the mockery and stereotypes were suddenly viewed as a healthy dose of politically incorrect humor. "The nationwide roar of laughter over Ebonics is a very good sign," John Leo wrote in *U.S. News Online.*

But most of the outrage against Ebonics was based on the erroneous notion that the Oakland schools had proposed to teach Ebonics and to ignore standard English. Although the resolution was ambiguously and poorly written—a clearer, amended version appeared a few weeks later, partly at the urging of Jackson, who subsequently supported the plan—the idea was never simply to teach Ebonics. Rather it was to compare and contrast the "home language" (Ebonics) of academically failing students with "school English"—that is, to draw on their vernacular to help them master standard English. If teachers ignored the children's home language—or, worse, ridiculed it—the thinking went, the students were less likely to be open to learning the English skills they so desperately needed. The strategy was endorsed by the Linguist Society of America as "linguistically and pedagogically sound."

"The Ebonics controversy confirmed that linguists—whether or not they describe themselves as 'Afrocentric'—are generally united in their respect for the legitimacy and complexity of the language spoken by many African American children," write the Rickfords, who are generally supporters of Ebonics in the classroom. "This perspective clashed with the more widely held public opinion that Ebonics was simply slang and gutter talk, or the product of laziness and carelessness."

Like all languages and dialects, black English follows consistent rules and a system of grammar, most linguists agree. Even vocal opponents of using Ebonics to teach English, like the linguist John McWhorter, say that black English is not simply "bad," "broken," or "inferior" English. Standard English, or the standard version of any language, is but one of many dialects itself. "One of those dialects is chosen as the standard one not because it is somehow 'better' or 'more correct' in the eyes of God, but because it happens to be the one spoken where the center of power coalesces," McWhorter writes in his book *Losing the Race: Self-Sabotage in Black America.* "We have no trouble understanding that a tiger is not a 'degraded version' of a leopard but simply another variation on 'cat'; we do not see house cats' lack of a mane as meaning that they are 'broken' versions of lions. In the same way, Black English is not 'bad standard English' but just another kind of English."

The reason for discussing the Ebonics battle here (in a book that's not about specific dialects themselves) is to look at how conflicts over language and race surface in pop language and the politics that pop can't help but speak of. For whatever you think of Ebonics as an educational tool—and you can find arguments and studies that support or derail it—you have to ask, Why the heat? Why the ridicule at the very mention of Ebonics? 130

Some of the contempt stemmed from ignorance (augmented by the vast majority of the news media, which seemed to willfully ignore the facts, a story the Rickfords detail in *Spoken Soul*). But some of the vehemence was due to a frustrated racism, to prejudices whose outlets of expression had been closing off for years. Condemning Ebonics was a safe way to finally voice anger at and fear of black people and their increasingly confident presence in American culture. Over the last couple of decades, most white people, unless they were outright white supremacists, had been feeling that if they were uncomfortable with black individuals or music or style, they could voice their criticism only gingerly or had to cloak it in disagreements about policies and programs, like affirmative action, welfare, or classroom Ebonics. While I really do believe that you don't have to be racist to oppose any of these programs, if you *are* racist, occasionally have such inclinations, or are just afraid of black people, then mockery of Ebonics can supply convenient cover. (The Ebonics controversy also came, McWhorter reminds us, a few months after the O. J. Simpson verdict in his criminal trial, when white anger at black support for Simpson was at a peak.)

For black opponents of Ebonics, the situation was more complex. For many African Americans the squabble over Ebonics replayed a long-held ambivalence toward their language. The other side of black pride is black shame, something that being treated as subhuman for centuries can engender. "The variously named vernacular of African Americans does have a remarkable capacity to elicit denial and shame from blacks (not to mention others)," write the Rickfords. Arguments among blacks about "talking proper" rise up regularly, they add. "During the Harlem Renaissance of the 1920s," for instance, "debate raged among the black intelligentsia, with Langston Hughes endorsing and exemplifying the use of vernacular, and Alain Locke and others suggesting that African Americans ought to put the quaintness of the idiom behind them and offer the world a more 'refined' view of their culture. These enduring attitudes reflect the attraction-repulsion dynamic, the oscillation between black and white (or mainstream) poles that W. E. B. Du Bois defined a century ago as 'double-consciousness.'"

(If one response to speaking a laughed-at language is to make it bolder and tougher, as hip-hop does, an opposite response might be to brood silently. After the Supreme Court decision against letting Florida recount votes in the 2000 election, during which the Garbo-like Clarence Thomas asked nary a question, the Court's sole black justice discussed his previously unexplained shyness on the bench with a group of high school students. He said his reticence came from fear of being made fun of for speaking his native Gullah, the Creole of the coastal Carolinas, in his otherwise all-white seminary class.)

The attraction-repulsion among blacks toward black English has its parallels among the public at large. "Americans of all types tend to bad-talk soul talk, even though it is the guts of the black music they so relish," write the Rickfords. "Appreciating sung soul is one thing, but appreciating soul as it is spoken is something else entirely. . . . In fact, middle America has quite often jeered those who speak 'jive' in the same breath and with the same enthusiasm that it has grooved to black sounds a la Bessie Smith and Mahalia Jackson and Ray Charles and Lauryn Hill."

There is, however, one other form of black speech as widely grooved to as black ¹³⁵ song lyrics: individual words and phrases that have evolved from black-only slang into everyone-owns-a-piece-of-it pop. Even middle America holds on to these words as if they were talismans of the soul of a people.

None of this is to say that Ebonics itself is pop. The black talk that turns into pop, whether through the avenues of jive, civil rights, or hip-hop, did indeed begin as Ebonics (or whatever you want to call it), but the pop process has stripped that talk of its other dimensions. "The part of black language that is used by the general public is vocabulary," John Rickford says. "But the core elements of Ebonics or black language, which are the distinct grammar, phonology, and pronunciation patterns—that's not being borrowed to any significant extent, because you have to be living it." Since white people gravitate primarily to the vocabulary—with very occasional pronunciation exceptions as in *You da man* and *gangsta*—Rickford doesn't believe that popularization will be the death knell for black talk: "I don't think it has a powerful effect, at least not on black language itself. Anyway, people are always creating new terms—there's a premium on that in black English."

New terms, dwelling on the periphery, tend to have authenticity cred, and some of them, too, will eventually undergo the media glamour treatment that makes them pop. It might be a drag in real life, but marginalization can be marketable—if it's packaged right. Or, as the writer Khephra Burns put it in 1997, speaking of the students who were supposed to be at the center of the Ebonics brawl: "It can't help our children to be told at every utterance that their mode of expression—which is intimately linked to their identity—is wrong, wrong, wrong, when others who plagiarize them are getting paid."

Exploring Context

1. Savan's argument centers on the use of slang in advertising. Visit some websites oriented toward young adults (such as MTV.com, TMZ.com, Vibe.com—even Facebook). What sort of language is used in the online ads? Does it support or complicate Savan's argument?

2. Savan mentions the website Black People Love Us. Visit that website at blackpeopleloveus.com and expand her analysis of the site. You might want to use your

work on "covert prestige" and "paying the dues" from Questions for Critical Reading to build your analysis.

3. Savan discusses Ebonics at the end of this selection. Use the Web to locate any initiatives concerning Ebonics in your area. Has it been an issue locally? In what ways? Why or why not?

Questions for Connecting

1. One way to think of Helen Epstein's essay "AIDS, Inc." (p. 152) is that it's about the triumph of language over advertising. How can we apply Epstein's insights about the fight against HIV infection in Africa to the appropriation of black talk by commercial culture? How might conversation defeat lifestyle branding? Synthesize these two essays to make your argument.

2. Julia Alvarez's exploration of the quinceañera in "Selections from *Once Upon a Quinceañera*" (p. 46) includes a discussion of retroculture. How might this phenomenon influence covert prestige? Is retroculture a form of paying the dues? Use the definition of *paying the dues* that you developed in Questions for Critical Reading in making your response.

3. In "The Dell Theory of Conflict Prevention" (p. 166), Thomas L. Friedman seems to focus primarily on the economic benefits of global supply chains. How does Savan's essay complicate this picture of globalization? What is the price of commercialism in terms of culture?

Language Matters

1. Locate a key sentence from Savan's text and then identify the subject, verb, and object of the sentence. How does the structure of the sentence contribute to Savan's argument? How does it make meaning, and what meaning does it make?

2. How do the headings in Savan's essay contribute to your understanding of it? Devise new headings for this essay. Where would you make the divisions?

3. Select a section of at least four paragraphs in Savan's essay. Find the topic sentence of each paragraph and then copy those sentences together to form a new paragraph. Does the paragraph made out of topic sentences make any sense? Does it reflect the flow of Savan's argument? How can you apply this exercise to your own writing?

Assignments for Writing

1. Savan focuses on the appropriation of black language into pop culture: On the one hand, black talk is fine and acceptable in commercials and ads, but on the other hand, it's seen as unacceptable in education. With this in mind, write a paper in which you evaluate the value of accepted norms for language in education. Should everyone be expected to speak "standard" English? What is the role of education in creating a national

identity? How can we balance cultural uniqueness with such norms? You might want to draw on your work on Ebonics from Question 3 of Exploring Context.

2. Write a paper in which you extend Savan's argument using other specific cultural practices or traits that have been appropriated by American society. To help you complete your essay successfully, you may consider pulling from your own life experiences. You may also want to think about the different kinds of cultural practices and traits that have been appropriated in American culture, including art, language, and ceremonies. Is "paying the dues" an issue? Can you find evidence of "covert prestige"? Use your work on these terms from Questions for Critical Reading to help you make your argument.

3. Using Savan's essay, write a paper in which you determine the possibility of the "melting pot" ideal in America. Is it possible, or will there always be some sort of exploitation of cultures in the process? What gets lost in the melting pot? What do we gain? Can we achieve the goals of such a society without sacrificing the uniqueness of various cultures? How?

PETER SINGER

Peter Singer is the Ira W. DeCamp Professor of Bioethics at Princeton University as well as the Laureate Professor at the Centre for Applied Philosophy and Public Ethics at the University of Melbourne. He founded the Centre for Human Bioethics at Monash University, and the Council of Australian Humanist Societies recognized him as Humanist of the Year in 2004. Singer has published dozens of books and essays, but among the most well-known books are *Animal Liberation: A New Ethics for Our Treatment of Animals* (1975), *Practical Ethics* (1979), *How Are We to Live? Ethics in an Age of Self-Interest* (1993), and *The Life You Can Save: Acting Now to End World Poverty* (2009). Most recently, he has published a third edition of *Practical Ethics* (2011), adding a chapter to address global climate change.

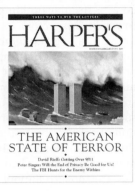

Singer's essay "Visible Man: Ethics in a World without Secrets" was published in the August 2011 edition of *Harper's Magazine*. This issue was published as the country neared the tenth anniversary of the 9/11 tragedy, so accompanying articles were on the FBI's attempt to find internal terrorists as well as the limits of remembrance since the terrorist attacks. The issue also included a series of watercolor images by Steve Mumford, produced while embedded with American troops in Afghanistan (included here on p. 298).

"Visible Man: Ethics in a World without Secrets" focuses on the concepts of transparency and personal privacy. With a focus on the controversial website WikiLeaks (wikileaks .org), Singer discusses the modern-day changes in surveillance technology and how these changes might alter our government as well as our society. While Singer seemingly argues in favor of this transparency, he also makes note of the possibility that information collected by these technologies might be misused. By arguing that surveillance work should both aid and expose government, Singer is encouraging readers to question current views on privacy and examine how new technologies have the ability to affect the future.

▶ TAGS: *technology, privacy, revelations, ethics, secrecy, politics*

Questions for Critical Reading

1. What is privacy? Write your own definition of this term. As you read Singer's essay, mark passages where he explains privacy—especially where he considers how the concept of privacy changes. Can you reconcile your definition with Singer's? What factors cause concepts such as privacy to change meaning?

2. As you read Singer's text, look for the term *sousveillance*. What does this term mean? Does it support or undermine democracy? Locate quotations from Singer that support your position.

3. How can we balance the rights of the individual with the need for security? Consider this question as you read Singer's text. What is his position on this question?

Visible Man: Ethics in a World without Secrets

In 1787, the philosopher Jeremy Bentham proposed the construction of a "Panopticon," a circular building with cells along the outer walls and, at the center, a watchtower or "inspector's lodge" from which all the cells could be seen but no one would know, at any given moment, due to a system of blinds and partitions, whether he was actually being observed. Bentham thought this design would be particularly suited to prisons but suggested it could also be applied to factories, hospitals, mental asylums, and schools. Not only would prisoners, workers, the ill, the insane, and students be subject to observation, but also—if the person in charge of the facility visited the inspector's area—the warders, supervisors, caregivers, and teachers. The gradual adoption of this "inspection principle," would, Bentham predicted, create "a new scene of things," transforming the world into a place with "morals reformed, health preserved, industry invigorated, instruction diffused, public burdens lightened."

The modern Panopticon is not a physical building, and it doesn't require the threat of an inspector's presence to be effective. Technological breakthroughs have made it easy to collect, store, and disseminate data on individuals, corporations, and even the government. With surveillance technology like closed-circuit television cameras and digital cameras now linked to the Internet, we have the means to implement Bentham's inspection principle on a much vaster scale. What's more, we have helped construct this new Panopticon, voluntarily giving up troves of personal information. We blog, tweet, and post what we are doing, thinking, and feeling. We allow friends and contacts, and even strangers, to know where we are at any time. We sign away our privacy in exchange for the conveniences of modern living, giving corporations access to information about our financial circumstances and our spending habits, which will then be used to target us for ads or to analyze our consumer habits.

Then there is the information collected without our consent. Since 2001, the number of U.S. government organizations involved in spying on our own citizens, both at home and abroad, has grown rapidly. Every day, the National Security Agency intercepts 1.7 billion emails, phone calls, instant messages, bulletin-board postings, and other communications. This system houses information on thousands of U.S. citizens, many of them not accused of any wrongdoing. Not long ago, when traffic police stopped a driver they had to radio the station and wait while someone checked records. Now, handheld devices instantly call up a person's Social Security number and license status, records of outstanding warrants, and even mug shots. The FBI can also cross-check your fingerprints against its digital archive of 96 million sets.

Yet the guarded have also struck back, in a sense, against their guardians, using organizations like WikiLeaks, which, according to its founder Julian Assange, has released more classified documents than the rest of the world's media combined, to keep tabs on governments and corporations. When Assange gave the *Guardian* 250,000 confidential cables, he did so on a USB drive the size of your little finger. Efforts to close down the WikiLeaks website have proven futile, because the files are mirrored on hundreds of other sites. And in any case, WikiLeaks isn't the only site revealing private information. An array of groups are able to release information anonymously. Governments, corporations, and other organizations interested in protecting privacy will strive to increase security, but they will also have to reckon with the likelihood that such measures are sometimes going to fail.

New technology has made greater openness possible, but has this openness made us better off? For those who think privacy is an inalienable right, the modern surveillance culture is a means of controlling behavior and stifling dissent. But perhaps the inspection principle, universally applied, could also be the perfection of democracy, the device that allows us to know what our governments are really doing, that keeps tabs on corporate abuses, and that protects our individual freedoms just as it subjects our personal lives to public scrutiny. In other words, will this technology be a form of tyranny or will it free us from tyranny? Will it upend democracy or strengthen it?

> **New technology has made greater openness possible, but has this openness made us better off?**

The standards of what we want to keep private and what we want to make public are constantly evolving. Over the course of Western history, we've developed a desire for more privacy, quite possibly as a status symbol, since an impoverished peasant could not afford a house with separate rooms. Today's affluent Americans display their status not only by having a bedroom for each member of the family, plus one for guests, but also by having a bathroom for every bedroom, plus one for visitors so that they do not have to see the family's personal effects. It wasn't always this way. A seventeenth-century Japanese *shunga* depicts a man making love with his wife while their daughter kneels on the floor nearby, practicing calligraphy. The people of Tikopia, a Pacific island inhabited by Polynesians, "find it good to sleep side by side crowding each other, next to their children or their parents or their brothers and sisters, mixing sexes and generations," according to the anthropologist Dorothy Lee. "[A]nd if a widow finds herself alone in her one-room house, she may adopt a child or a brother to allay her intolerable privacy." The Gebusi people in New Guinea live in communal longhouses and are said to "shun privacy," even showing reluctance to look at photos in which they are on their own.

With some social standards, the more people do something, the less risky it becomes for each individual. The first women to wear dresses that did not reach their knees were no doubt looked upon with disapproval, and may have risked unwanted sexual attention; but once many women were revealing more of their legs, the risks dissipated. So too with privacy: when millions of people are prepared to post personal information, doing so becomes less risky for everyone. And those collective, large-scale forfeitures of personal privacy have other benefits as well, as tens of thousands of Egyptians showed when they openly became fans of the Facebook page "We are all Khaled Said," named after a young man who was beaten to death by police in Alexandria. The page became the online hub for the protests that forced the ouster of President Hosni Mubarak.

Whether Facebook and similar sites are reflecting a change in social norms about privacy or are actually driving that change, that half a billion are now on Facebook suggests that people believe the benefits of connecting with others, sharing information, networking, self-promoting, flirting, and bragging outweigh breaches of privacy that accompany such behavior.

More difficult questions arise when the loss of privacy is not in any sense a choice. Bentham's Panopticon has become a symbol of totalitarian intrusion. Michel Foucault* described it as "the perfection of power." We all know that the police can obtain phone records when seeking evidence of involvement in a crime, but most of us would be surprised by the frequency of such requests. Verizon alone receives 90,000 demands for information from law-enforcement agencies annually. Abuses have undoubtedly accompanied the recent increase in government surveillance. One glaring example is the case of Brandon Mayfield, an Oregon attorney and convert to Islam who was jailed on suspicion of involvement in the 2004 Madrid train bombings. After his arrest, Mayfield sued the government and persuaded a federal judge to declare the provision of the Patriot Act that the FBI used in investigating him unconstitutional. But as with most excesses of state power, the cause is not so much the investigative authority of the state as the state's erroneous interpretation of the information it uncovers and the unwarranted detentions that come about as a result. If those same powers were used to foil another 9/11, most Americans would likely applaud.

There is always a danger that the information collected will be misused—whether by regimes seeking to silence opposition or by corporations seeking to profit from more detailed knowledge of their potential customers. The scale and technological sophistication of this data-gathering enterprise allow the government to intercept and store far more information than was possible for secret police of even the most totalitarian states of an earlier era, and the large number of people who have access to sensitive information increases the potential for misuse.† As with any large-scale human activity, if enough people are involved eventually someone will do something corrupt or malicious. That's a drawback to having more data gathered, but one that may well be outweighed by the benefits. We don't really know how many terrorist plots have been foiled because of all this data-gathering.‡ We have even less idea how many innocent Americans were initially suspected of terrorism but *not* arrested because the enhanced data-gathering permitted under the Patriot Act convinced law-enforcement agents of their innocence.

The degree to which a government is repressive does not turn on the methods by which it acquires information about its citizens, or the amount of data it retains. When regimes want to harass their opponents or suppress opposition, they find ways to do

---

* Michel Foucault: Influential French philosopher and historian (1926–1984), known for his writings on the nature of being, knowledge, and power [Ed.].

† Including those involved in international operations relating to homeland security and intelligence, 854,000 people currently hold top-secret security clearances, according to the *Washington Post*.

‡ In 2003, FBI director Robert Mueller claimed that the number of thwarted plots was more than one hundred.

it, with or without electronic data. Under President Nixon, the administration used tax audits to harass those on his "enemies list." That was mild compared with how "enemies" were handled during the dirty wars in Argentina, Guatemala, and Chile, and by the Stasi in East Germany. These repressive governments "disappeared" tens of thousands of dissidents, and they targeted their political enemies with what now seem impossibly cumbersome methods of collecting, storing, and sorting data. If such forms of abuse are rare in the United States, it is not because we have prevented the state from gathering electronic data about us. The crucial step in preventing a repressive government from misusing information is to have alert and well-informed citizens with a strong sense of right and wrong who work to keep the government democratic, open, just, and under the rule of law. The technological innovations used by governments and corporations to monitor citizens must be harnessed to monitor those very governments and corporations.

One of the first victories for citizen surveillance came in 1991, when George Holliday videotaped Los Angeles police officers beating Rodney King. Without that video, yet another LAPD assault on a black man would have passed unnoticed. Instead, racism and violence in police departments became a national issue, two officers went to prison, and King received $3.8 million in civil damages. Since then, videos and photographs, many of them taken on mobile phones, have captured innumerable crimes and injustices. Inverse surveillance — what Steve Mann, professor of computer engineering and proponent of wearing imaging devices, terms "sousveillance" — has become an effective way of informing the world of abuses of power.

We have seen the usefulness of sousveillance again this year in the Middle East, where the disclosure of thousands of diplomatic cables by WikiLeaks helped encourage the Tunisian and Egyptian revolutions, as well as the protest movements that spread to neighboring countries. Yet most government officials vehemently condemned the disclosure of state secrets. Secretary of State Hillary Clinton claimed that WikiLeaks' revelations "tear at the fabric of the proper function of responsible government." In February of this year, at George Washington University, she went further, saying that WikiLeaks had endangered human rights activists who had been in contact with U.S. diplomats, and rejecting the view that governments should conduct their work in full view of their citizens. As a counterexample, she pointed to U.S. efforts to secure nuclear material in the former Soviet states. Here, she claimed, confidentiality was necessary in order to avoid making it easier for terrorists or criminals to find the materials and steal them.

Clinton is right that it is not a good idea to make public the location of insecurely stored nuclear materials, but how much of diplomacy is like that? There may be some justifiable state secrets, but they certainly are few. For nearly all other dealings between nations, openness should be the norm. In any case, Clinton's claim that WikiLeaks releases documents "without regard for the consequences" is, if not deliberately misleading, woefully ignorant. Assange and his colleagues have consistently stated that they are motivated by a belief that a more transparent government will bring better consequences for all, and that leaking information has an inherent tendency toward greater justice, a view Assange laid out on his blog in December 2006, the month in which WikiLeaks published its first document:

The more secretive or unjust an organization is, the more leaks induce fear and paranoia in its leadership and planning coterie. . . . Since unjust systems, by their nature induce opponents, and in many places barely have the upper hand, leaking leaves them exquisitely vulnerable to those who seek to replace them with more open forms of governance.*

Assange could now claim that WikiLeaks' disclosures have confirmed his theory. For instance, in 2007, months before a national election, WikiLeaks posted a report on corruption commissioned but not released by the Kenyan government. According to Assange, a Kenyan intelligence official found that the leaked report changed the minds of 10 percent of Kenyan voters, enough to shift the outcome of the election.

Two years later, in the aftermath of the global financial crisis, WikiLeaks released documents on dealings by Iceland's Kaupthing Bank, showing that the institution made multibillion-dollar loans, in some cases unsecured, to its major shareholders shortly before it collapsed. Kaupthing's successor, then known as New Kaupthing, obtained an injunction to prevent Iceland's national television network from reporting on the leaked documents but failed to prevent their dissemination. WikiLeaks' revelations stirred an uproar in the Icelandic parliament, which then voted unanimously to strengthen free speech and establish an international prize for freedom of expression. Senior officials of the bank are now facing criminal charges.

And of course, in April 2010, WikiLeaks released thirty-eight minutes of classified cockpit-video footage of two U.S. Army helicopters over a Baghdad suburb. The video showed the helicopter crews engaging in an attack on civilians that killed eighteen people, including two Reuters journalists, and wounded two children. Ever since the attack took place, in 2007, Reuters had unsuccessfully sought a U.S. military inquiry into the deaths of its two employees, as well as access to the cockpit video under the Freedom of Information Act. The United States had claimed that the two journalists were killed during a firefight. Although no action has been taken against the soldiers involved, if the military is ever going to exercise greater restraint when civilian lives are at risk, it will have been compelled to do so through the release of material like this.

Months before the Arab Spring began, Assange was asked whether he would release the trove of secret diplomatic cables that he was rumored to have obtained. Assange said he would, and gave this reason: "These sort of things reveal what the true state of, say, Arab governments are like, the true human rights abuses in those governments." As one young Tunisian wrote to the *Guardian*, his countrymen had known for many years that their leaders were corrupt, but that was not the same as reading the full details of particular incidents, rounded off with statements by American diplomats that corruption was keeping domestic investment low and unemployment high. The success of Tunisia's revolution undoubtedly influenced the rest of the Arab world, putting U.S. diplomats in an uncomfortable predicament. A mere three months after condemning WikiLeaks for releasing stolen documents "without regard to the

---

* Robert Manne, a professor of politics at Australia's La Trobe University and the author of a detailed examination of Assange's writings that appeared recently in *The Monthly*, comments: "There are few original ideas in politics. In the creation of WikiLeaks, Julian Assange was responsible for one."

consequences," Secretary Clinton found herself speaking warmly about one of those outcomes: the movement for reform in the Middle East.

WikiLeaks' revelations have had profound ramifications, but as with any event of this scale, it is not easy to judge whether those consequences are, on the whole, desirable. Assange himself admitted to the *Guardian* that as a result of the leaked corruption report in Kenya, and the violence that swept the country during its elections, 1,300 people were killed and 350,000 displaced; but, he added, 40,000 Kenyan children die every year from malaria, and these and many more are dying because of the role corruption plays in keeping Kenyans poor.* The Kenyan people, Assange believes, had a right to the information in the leaked report because "decision-making that is based upon lies or ignorance can't lead to a good conclusion."

In making that claim, Assange aligned himself with a widely held view in democratic theory, and a standard argument for freedom of speech: elections can express the will of the people only if the people are reasonably well informed about the issues on which they base their votes. That does not mean that decision-making based on the truth always leads to better outcomes than decision-making based on ignorance. There is no reason for Assange to be committed to that claim, any more than a supporter of democracy must be committed to the claim that democratic forms of government always reach better decisions than authoritarian regimes. Nor does a belief in the benefits of transparency imply that people must know the truth about everything; but it does suggest that more information is generally better, and so provides grounds for a presumption against withholding the truth. 20

What of Clinton's claims that the leaks have endangered human rights activists who gave information to American diplomats? When WikiLeaks released 70,000 documents about the war in Afghanistan, in July 2010, Admiral Mike Mullen, chairman of the Joint Chiefs of Staff, said that Assange had blood on his hands, yet no casualties resulting from the leaks have been reported—unless you count the ambassadors forced to step down due to embarrassing revelations. Four months after the documents were released, a senior NATO official told CNN that there had not been a single case of an Afghan needing protection because of the leaks. Of course, that may have been "just pure luck," as Daniel Domscheit-Berg, a WikiLeaks defector, told the *New York Times* in February. Assange himself has admitted that he cannot guarantee that the leaks will not cost lives, but in his view the likelihood that they will save lives justifies the risk.

WikiLeaks has never released the kind of information that Clinton pointed to in defending the need for secrecy. Still, there are other groups out there, such as the Russian anti-corruption site Rospil.info, the European Union site BrusselsLeaks, the Czech PirateLeaks, Anonymous, and so on, that release leaked materials with less scrupulousness. It is entirely possible that there will be leaks that everyone will regret. Yet given that the leaked materials on the wars in Afghanistan and Iraq show tens of thousands of civilian lives lost due to the needless, reckless, and even callous actions of members of the U.S. military, it is impossible to listen to U.S. leaders blame WikiLeaks for endangering innocent lives without hearing the tinkle of shattering glass houses.

---

* The United Nations claimed that as many as 600,000 Kenyans were displaced after the election.

In the Panopticon, of course, transparency would not be limited to governments. Animal rights advocates have long said that if slaughterhouses had glass walls, more people would become vegetarian, and seeing the factory farms in which most of the meat, eggs, and milk we consume are produced would be more shocking even than the slaughterhouses. And why should restaurant customers have to rely on occasional visits by health inspectors? Webcams in food-preparation areas could provide additional opportunities for checking on the sanitary conditions of the food we are about to eat.

Bentham may have been right when he suggested that if we all knew that we were, at any time, liable to be observed, our morals would be reformed. Melissa Bateson and her colleagues at England's Newcastle University tested this theory when they put a poster with a pair of eyes above a canteen honesty box. People taking a hot drink put almost three times as much money in the box with the eyes present as they did when the eyes were replaced by a poster of flowers. The mere suggestion that someone was watching encouraged greater honesty. (Assuming that the eyes did not lead people to overpay, the study also implies a disturbing level of routine dishonesty.)

We might also become more altruistic. Dale Miller, a professor of organizational behavior at Stanford University, has pointed out that Americans assume a "norm of self-interest" that makes acting altruistically seem odd or even irrational. Yet Americans perform altruistic acts all the time, and bringing those acts to light might break down the norm that curtails our generosity. Consistent with that hypothesis, researchers at the University of Pennsylvania found that people are likely to give more to listener-sponsored radio stations when they are told that other callers are giving above-average donations. Similarly, when utility companies send customers a comparison of their energy use with the average in their neighborhood, customers with above-average use reduce their consumption. 25

The world before WikiLeaks and Facebook may have seemed a more secure place, but to say whether it was a better world is much more difficult. Will fewer children ultimately die from poverty in Kenya because WikiLeaks released the report on corruption? Will life in the Middle East improve as a result of the revolutions to which WikiLeaks and social media contributed? As the Chinese communist leader Zhou Enlai responded when asked his opinion of the French Revolution of 1789, it is too soon to say. The way we answer the question will depend on whether we share Assange's belief that decision-making leads to better outcomes when based on the truth than when based on lies and ignorance.

Exploring Context

1. Locate and then review the privacy policy at Facebook or some other site you frequently use. How does the content of that policy relate to Singer's arguments about our willingness to disclose information about ourselves? Given Singer's examples, do you think any privacy policy can protect you? Use your response to Question 1 of Questions for Critical Reading in forming your answer.

2. Explore the website for WikiLeaks (wikileaks.org). Use what you find there to argue whether or not the site threatens or supports democracy. Incorporate your work from Question 3 of Questions for Critical Reading.

3. Some people have been arrested for recording or taking pictures of police on duty — the kind of "sousveillance" that Sanger suggests keeps governments honest. Visit the website Protecting Civil Liberties in the Digital Age, maintained by the American Civil Liberties Union (aclu.org/protecting-civil-liberties-digital-age). How does the information you find there change your understanding of Singer's argument? Does it change your response to Question 2 of Questions for Critical Reading?

Questions for Connecting

1. Kwame Anthony Appiah explores how practices change in societies in his essays "Making Conversation" and "The Primacy of Practice" (p. 67). Apply Appiah's ideas to Singer's analysis of the evolution of privacy. What drives recent changes to our understanding of privacy: values or practices? Incorporate your work from Question 1 of Questions for Critical Reading in making your response.

2. In "Networking: Genes, Brains, and Behavior" (p. 113), Patricia Churchland looks at the relationship between genetics and morality. Use her ideas to expand on Singer's suggestion that our emerging relationship to privacy can affect our sense of altruism. Does that altruism depend on protecting civil liberties in relationship to technology? Draw on your answer to Question 3 of Exploring Context to support your position.

3. In his essays "Preface" and "The New Civil Rights" (p. 552), Kenji Yoshino argues both that we have a tendency to "cover" or downplay parts of our identity and that we need to move to a new model of civil rights, one based on basic rights and freedoms for all individuals. How does the kind of society Singer describes complicate Yoshino's argument? Is it as easy to cover in a society of surveillance with less concern about privacy? Is Yoshino's "liberty paradigm" for civil rights realistic, given social technologies and their impact on privacy?

Language Matters

1. Audience is a primary concern for all writers. Consider the difference between private and public audiences, using Singer's ideas about privacy. How does your writing change based on notions of privacy? What level of privacy, and thus what audience, is reflected in academic writing?

2. Consider how you write for social media — places like Facebook or Twitter. What are the conventions of writing in these arenas, and how do they differ from writing in an academic setting? How important is context to writing?

3. The Swedish furniture maker Ikea uses simplistic pictorial instructions to help people assemble furniture (see, for example, ikea.com/us/en/catalog/products/20085705, and click on the link for "Assembly Instructions" in the Product information tab). Using these instructions as a model, create a pictorial guide to Singer's argument, a set of instructions for understanding his essay.

Assignments for Writing

1. What is the role of privacy in a democracy? Write a paper in which you address this question using ideas from Singer's essay. Should democracies protect privacy? Is transparency necessary for democracy? Use your work from Questions for Critical Reading in making your response.

2. Write a paper in which you determine the ethics of privacy. When, if ever, is it ethical to violate privacy? What ethical standards should we use in determining and protecting privacy? Use Singer's discussion to support your position as well as your work in Questions for Critical Reading. Consider, too, the subtitle of Singer's essay, "Ethics in a World without Secrets."

3. Using Singer's discussion, write a paper in which you trace the evolution and implications of notions of privacy. What forces shape our understanding of privacy? How has privacy changed? What can we do to shape its future?

JAMES SUROWIECKI

James **Surowiecki** writes the business column "The Financial Page" for the *New Yorker* and has contributed to publications such as *Slate*, the *Wall Street Journal*, and *Wired*. Surowiecki was also a writer for the Motley Fool website and editor-in-chief for the Fool's "Rogue" column. Surowiecki edited the anthology *Best Business Crime Fighting of the Year* (2002) before publishing his book *The Wisdom of Crowds: Why the Many Are Smarter Than the Few and How Collective Wisdom Shapes Business, Economies, Societies, and Nations* (2004).

Surowiecki's argument in *The Wisdom of Crowds* is that even when the few are elite, brilliant, or successful, the many are generally smarter. Whether guessing the weight of an ox at a country fair or the answer to a question on *Who Wants to Be a Millionaire*, the crowd tends to be remarkably correct. Though the thought is counterintuitive, a large and largely inexpert group can come up with answers that are often more accurate than those of any of the smartest individuals in the group. Surowiecki shows how group wisdom can predict everything from elections to the location of a lost submarine more accurately than individual experts. This technique, Surowiecki argues, can be as effective in the worlds of business, economics, and science as it is in our daily lives.

In "Committees, Juries, and Teams: The *Columbia* Disaster and How Small Groups Can Be Made to Work," from *The Wisdom of Crowds*, Surowiecki acknowledges that sometimes collective knowledge can fail—with disastrous consequences. However, these exceptions, including "verdict-based" juries and the Mission Management Team of the space shuttle *Columbia* during its final mission, prove the rule while underscoring that it's not sufficient simply to seek the advice of the crowd. Surowiecki suggests that groups are correct only under specific circumstances. Understanding how to foster those circumstances is part of Surowiecki's goal in this excerpt.

Group work is frequently a requirement of college, and it is also a common working practice across an array of professions and careers. Knowing how small groups can fail and, more important, knowing how to make them succeed can offer you valuable insights for your future.

▶ TAGS: *collaboration, groups, education, knowledge, diversity*

Questions for Critical Reading

1. Much of Surowiecki's essay is about the many ways in which small groups can fail. Working from his argument, what are some elements essential to the success of small groups? Use quotations from the text to develop your answer. You will need to read his text critically to compose your response, since it will depend on abstracting those factors essential to the success rather than the failure of small groups.

2. What is "group polarization"? Define the concept using Surowiecki's text and then provide an example from your own experience.

3. Are the benefits of small groups worth the risk? What does Surowiecki think? Begin by critically reading Surowiecki's text and then support your position by using quotations from the text.

Committees, Juries, and Teams: The *Columbia* Disaster and How Small Groups Can Be Made to Work

On the morning of January 21, 2003, the Mission Management Team (MMT) for NASA mission STS-107—the twenty-eighth flight of the space shuttle *Columbia*—held a teleconference, its second since the *Columbia*'s launch on January 16. An hour before the meeting, Don McCormack had been briefed by members of the Debris Assessment Team (DAT), a group of engineers from NASA, Boeing, and Lockheed Martin, who had spent much of the previous five days evaluating the possible consequences of a large-debris strike on the *Columbia*. During the shuttle's ascent into the atmosphere, a large piece of foam had broken off the left bipod area of the shuttle's external fuel tank and had smashed into the ship's left wing. None of the cameras that were tracking the shuttle's launch had provided a clear picture of the impact, so it was difficult to tell how much damage the foam might have caused. And although by January 21 a request had been made for on-orbit pictures of the *Columbia*, they had not been approved. So the DAT had done what it could with the information it had, first estimating the size of the foam and the speed at which it had struck the *Columbia*, and then using an algorithm called Crater to predict how deep a piece of debris that size and traveling at that speed would penetrate into the thermal-protection tiles that covered the shuttle's wings.

The DAT had reached no conclusions, but they made it clear to McCormack that there was reason to be concerned. McCormack did not transmit that sense of concern to the MMT during its teleconference. The foam strike was not mentioned until two-thirds of the way through the meeting, and was brought up only after discussions of, among other things, a jammed camera, the scientific experiments on the shuttle, and a leaky water separator. Then Linda Ham, who was the MMT leader, asked McCormack for an update. He simply said that people were investigating the possible damage and what could potentially be done to fix it, and added that when the *Columbia* had been hit by a similar strike during mission STS-87, five years earlier, it had suffered "fairly significant damage." This is how Ham answered: "And I really don't think there is much we can do so it's not really a factor during the flight because there is not much we can do about it."

Ham, in other words, had already decided that the foam strike was inconsequential. More important, she decided for everyone else in the meeting that it was inconsequential, too. This was the first time the MMT had heard any details about the foam strike. It would have been logical for McCormack to outline the possible consequences and talk about what the evidence from past shuttles that had been struck with debris showed. But instead the meeting moved on.

Hindsight is, of course, twenty-twenty, and just as with the critiques of the U.S. intelligence community after September 11, it's perhaps too easy to fault the MMT at NASA for its failure to see what would happen to the *Columbia* when it reentered the Earth's atmosphere on February 1. Even those who have been exceptionally critical of NASA have suggested that focusing on this one team is a mistake because it obscures the deep institutional and cultural problems that plague the agency (which happen to be many of the same problems that plagued the agency in 1986, when the *Challenger* exploded). But while NASA clearly is an object lesson in organizational dysfunction, that doesn't fully explain just why the MMT handled the *Columbia* crisis so badly. Sifting through the evidence collected by the Columbia Accident Investigation Board (CAIB), there is no way to evade the conclusion that the team had an opportunity to make different choices that could have dramatically improved the chances of the crew surviving. The team members were urged on many different occasions to collect the information they needed to make a reasonable estimate of the shuttle's safety. They were advised that the foam might, in fact, have inflicted enough damage to cause "burn-through"—heat burning through the protective tiles and into the shuttle's fuselage—when the shuttle reentered the Earth's atmosphere. The team's leaders themselves raised the possibility that the debris damage might have been severe. And yet the MMT as a whole never came close to making the right decision on what to do about the *Columbia*.

In fact, the performance of the MMT is an object lesson in how not to run a small group, 5 and a powerful demonstration of the way in which, instead of making people wiser, being in a group can actually make them dumber. This is important for two reasons. First, small groups are ubiquitous in American life, and their decisions are consequential. Juries decide whether or not people will go to prison. Boards of directors shape, at least in theory, corporate strategy. And more and more of our work lives are spent on teams or, at the very least, in meetings. Whether small groups can do a good job of solving complex problems is hardly an academic question.

> **Instead of making people wiser, being in a group can actually make them dumber.**

Second, small groups are different in important ways from groups such as markets or betting pools or television audiences. Those groups are as much statistical realities as experiential ones. Bettors do get feedback from each other in the form of the point spread, and investors get feedback from each other in the stock market, but the nature of the relationship between people in a small group is qualitatively different. Investors do not think of themselves as members of the market. People on the MMT thought of themselves as members of that team. And the collective wisdom that something like the Iowa Electronic Markets produces is, at least when it's working well, the result of many different independent judgments, rather than something that the group as a whole has consciously come up with. In a small group, by contrast, the group—even if it is an ad hoc group formed for the sake of a single project or experiment—has an identity of its own. And the influence of the people in the group on each other's judgment is inescapable.

What we'll see is that this has two consequences. On the one hand, it means small groups can make very bad decisions, because influence is more direct and immediate and small-group judgments tend to be more volatile and extreme. On the other hand, it also means that small groups have the opportunity to be more than just the sum of their parts. A successful face-to-face group is more than just collectively intelligent. It makes everyone work harder, think smarter, and reach better conclusions than they would have on their own. In his 1985 book about Olympic rowing, *The Amateurs*, David Halberstam writes: "When most oarsmen talked about their perfect moments in a boat, they referred not so much to winning a race but to the feel of the boat, all eight oars in the water together, the synchronization almost perfect. In moments like that, the boat seemed to lift right out of the water. Oarsmen called that the moment of *swing*." When a boat has swing, its motion seems almost effortless. Although there are eight oarsmen in the boat, it's as if there's only one person—with perfect timing and perfect strength—rowing. So you might say that a small group which works well has intellectual swing.

Swing, though, is hard to come by. In fact, few organizations have figured out how to make groups work consistently well. For all the lip service paid, particularly in corporate America, to the importance of teams and the need to make meetings more productive, it's still unusual for a small group to be more than just the sum of its parts. Much of the time, far from adding value to their members, groups seem to subtract it. Too often, it's easy to agree with Ralph Cordiner, the former chairman of General Electric, who once said, "If you can name for me one great discovery or decision that was made by a committee, I will find you the one man in that committee who had the lonely insight—while he was shaving or on his way to work, or maybe while the rest of the committee was chattering away—the lonely insight that solved the problem and was the basis for the decision." On this account, groups are nothing but obstacles, cluttering the way of people whose time would be better spent alone.

The performance of the MMT helps explain why. First, the team started not with an open mind but from the assumption that the question of whether a foam strike could seriously damage the shuttle had already been answered. This was, to be fair, partly a matter of bad luck, since one of the team's technical advisers was convinced from the beginning that foam simply could do no serious damage, and kept saying so to anyone who would listen. But there was plenty of evidence to suggest otherwise. Rather than begin with the evidence and work toward a conclusion, the team members worked in the opposite direction. More egregiously, their skepticism about the possibility that something might really be wrong made them dismiss the need to gather more information, especially in the form of pictures, leading to the DAT's requests for on-orbit images being rejected. Even when MMT members dealt with the possibility that there might be a real problem with *Columbia*, their conviction that nothing was wrong limited discussion and made them discount evidence to the contrary. In that sense, the team succumbed to what psychologists call "confirmation bias," which causes decision makers to unconsciously seek those bits of information that confirm their underlying intuitions.

These problems were also exacerbated by the team's belief that it knew more than   10
it did. For instance, when the shuttle managers turned down the request for pictures, one of the justifications they offered was that the resolution of the images would not be good enough to detect the small area where the foam struck. In fact, as the CAIB noted, none of the managers had the necessary security clearances to know how good the resolution of the photos would be, nor did any of them ask the Department of Defense—which would have taken the pictures—about picture quality. In other words, they were "making critical decisions about imagery capabilities based on little or no knowledge," and doing so with an air of complete assurance.

Social scientists who study juries often differentiate between two approaches juries take. Evidence-based juries usually don't even take a vote until after they've spent some time talking over the case, sifting through the evidence, and explicitly contemplating alternative explanations. Verdict-based juries, by contrast, see their mission as reaching a decision as quickly and decisively as possible. They take a vote before any discussion, and the debate after that tends to concentrate on getting those who don't agree to agree. The MMT's approach was practically, though not intentionally, verdict-based. You can see this especially clearly in the way Linda Ham asked questions. On January 22, for instance, the day after the meeting where the foam was first mentioned, Ham e-mailed two members of the team about whether the foam strike might, in fact, pose a threat to the shuttle's safety. "Can we say that for any ET [external tank] foam lost," she wrote, "no 'safety of flight' damage can occur to the Orbiter because of the density?" The answer that Ham wanted was built into the question. It was a way of deflecting genuine inquiry even while seeming to pursue it. As it happens, one of the members of the team did not give Ham the answer she was looking for. Lambert Austin answered her question by writing, "NO," in capital letters, and then went on to explain that there was no way at that point to "PRECLUDE" the possibility that the foam might have seriously damaged the tiles. Yet Austin's cautionary note garnered little attention.

One reason for the team's lack of follow-through may have been its implicit assumption that if something was wrong, there was no possibility of fixing it. At that January 21 meeting, you'll remember, Ham said, "And I really don't think there is much we can do so it's not really a factor during the flight because there is not much we can do about it." Two days later, Calvin Schomburg, the technical expert who insisted throughout that the foam could not seriously damage the tiles, met with Rodney Rocha, a NASA engineer who had become the unofficial representative of the DAT. By this point, the DAT was increasingly concerned that the damage inflicted by the foam could potentially lead to burn-through on reentry, and Rocha and Schomburg argued over the question. At the end of the discussion, Schomburg said that if the tiles had been severely damaged, "Nothing could be done."

The idea that nothing could have been done if the damage to the tiles had been uncovered in time was wrong. In fact, as part of the CAIB investigation, NASA engineers came up with two different strategies that might have brought the *Columbia* crew back to Earth safely (though the shuttle itself was doomed from the moment the foam struck).

There was no reason for the MMT to know what those strategies were, of course. But here again, the team had made a decision before looking at the evidence. And that decision—which roughly amounted to saying, "If there is a problem, we won't be able to find a solution"—undoubtedly shaped the team's approach to figuring out whether there was a problem at all. In fact, the CAIB report includes personal notes from an unnamed NASA source that say that when Ham canceled the DAT's request for pictures of the *Columbia*'s wing, "[she] said it was no longer being pursued since even if we saw something, we couldn't do anything about it." This was not exactly the ethos that brought *Apollo 13** safely back to Earth.

One of the real dangers that small groups face is emphasizing consensus over dissent. The extreme version of this . . . is the kind of groupthink that Irving Janis described in his account of the planning of the Bay of Pigs,† where the members of the group become so identified with the group that the possibility of dissent seems practically unthinkable. But in a more subtle way small groups can exacerbate our tendency to prefer the illusion of certainty to the reality of doubt. On January 24, the DAT engineers met again with Don McCormack, who had become their unofficial liaison to the MMT, to present the findings of their foam-strike study. The briefing room where the presentation took place was so crowded that engineers ended up out in the hallway, which said a lot about how worried people were. In any case, the DAT offered five different scenarios of what might have happened. The team's conclusion was that it was likely that the shuttle was safe. But they qualified their conclusion by saying that their analysis was profoundly limited by their tools and their lack of good information. Because the MMT had refused to authorize on-orbit images, the engineers did not know where exactly the foam had struck. And the Crater algorithm they were using had been designed to measure the impact of pieces of debris hundreds of times smaller than the one that hit *Columbia*, so there was no way to be sure that its results were accurate. The engineers stressed, in other words, how uncertain their analysis was. But NASA management focused instead on their conclusion.

An hour after the briefing, the MMT met, and McCormack summarized what the DAT had said. "They do show obviously there's potential for significant damage here, but thermal analysis does not indicate that there is potential for a burn-through," he said. "Obviously there is a lot of uncertainty in all this in terms of the size of the debris and where it hit and the angle of incidence and it's difficult." This was a relatively obscure way of explaining that the engineers' analysis was built on a lot of untested assumptions, but it was at least an attempt at caution. Ham responded by again asking a question that answered itself: "No burn-through, means no catastrophic damage and the localized heating damage would mean a tile replacement?" McCormack said, "We do not see any kind of safety of flight issue here yet in anything that we've looked at." Ham came back with another nothing-is-wrong question: "No safety of

15

---

* Apollo 13: U.S. spaceflight, launched on April 11, 1970, that suffered an explosion during its aborted voyage to the moon, threatening the lives of the three astronauts on board [Ed.].

† Bay of Pigs: On April 17, 1961, about 1,500 Cuban exiles opposed to Fidel Castro attempted to invade Cuba at the Bahía de Cochinos (Bay of Pigs). The invasion was sponsored by the U.S. government and involved the Central Intelligence Agency. More than 1,100 of the men were captured and imprisoned [Ed.].

flight and no issue for this mission, nothing that we're going to do different, there may be a turnaround?" Then, after a short interchange between Ham and McCormack and Calvin Schomburg, one of the other team members on the conference call said that they hadn't been able to hear what McCormack had said. Ham summarized neatly: "He was just reiterating with Calvin that he doesn't believe that there is any burn-through so no safety of flight kind of issue, it's more of a turnaround issue similar to what we've had on other flights. That's it? Alright, any questions on that?" For all intents and purposes, when that meeting ended, the *Columbia*'s fate had been sealed.

> **When that meeting ended, the *Columbia*'s fate had been sealed.**

What's most striking about that January 24 meeting is the utter absence of debate and minority opinions. As the CAIB noted, when McCormack summarized the DAT's findings, he included none of its supporting analysis nor any discussion of whether there was a division of opinion on the team about its conclusions. More strikingly, not one member of the MMT asked a question. Not one member expressed any interest in seeing the DAT study. One would have thought that when McCormack mentioned the uncertainties in the analysis, someone would have asked him to explain and perhaps even quantify those uncertainties. But no one did. In part, that may have been because Ham was so obviously anxious for the problem to be resolved, and so convinced that there was nothing to talk about. Her attempts to briskly summarize McCormack's conclusions—"No burn-through, means no catastrophic damage"—effectively shut off discussion. And anyone who's ever been in a business meeting knows that "Alright, any questions on that?" really means "There are no questions on that, right?"

The MMT failed to make the right decision in part because of problems that are specific to the culture of NASA. Although we think of NASA as a fundamentally meritocratic, bottom-up culture, it is in fact deeply hierarchical. This meant that even though the DAT engineers had serious qualms from the beginning about the foam strike, their concerns—and, in particular, their insistence that they needed images of the Orbiter's wing before they could make a truly informed analysis—never received a serious hearing from the MMT. At the same time, the MMT violated nearly every rule of good group decision making. To begin with, the team's discussions were simultaneously too structured and not structured enough. They were too structured because most of the discussions—not just about the debris strike, but about everything—consisted of Ham asking a question and someone else answering it. They were not structured enough because no effort was made to ask other team members to comment on particular questions. This is almost always a mistake, because it means that decisions are made based on a very limited supply of analysis and information. One of the consistent findings from decades of small-group research is that group deliberations are more successful when they have a clear agenda and when leaders take an active role in making sure that everyone gets a chance to speak.

The team also, as I've mentioned, started with its conclusion. As a result, every new piece of information that came in was reinterpreted to fit that conclusion. This is a recurring problem with small groups that have a hard time incorporating new information. Social psychologist Garold Stasser, for instance, ran an experiment in which a group of eight people was asked to rate the performance of thirty-two psychology students. Each member of the group was given two relevant pieces of information about the students (say, their grades and their test scores), while two members of the group were given two extra pieces of information (say, their performance in class, etc.), and one member of the group received another two. Although the group as a whole therefore had six pieces of useful information, their ratings were based almost entirely on the two pieces of information that they all shared. The new information was discounted as either unimportant or unreliable. Stasser has also shown that in unstructured, free-flowing discussions, the information that tends to be talked about the most is, paradoxically, the information that everyone already knows. More curiously, information can be presented and listened to and still make little difference, because its contents are misinterpreted. New messages are often modified so that they fit old messages, which is especially dangerous since unusual messages often add the most value. (If people are just saying what you expect them to say, they're hardly likely to change your thinking.) Or they are modified to suit a preexisting picture of the situation.

What was missing most from the MMT, of course, was diversity, by which I mean not sociological diversity but rather cognitive diversity. James Oberg, a former Mission Control operator and now NBC News correspondent, has made the counterintuitive point that the NASA teams that presided over the *Apollo* missions were actually more diverse than the MMT. This seems hard to believe, since every engineer at Mission Control in the late 1960s had the same crew cut and wore the same short-sleeved white shirt. But as Oberg points out, most of those men had worked outside of NASA in many different industries before coming to the agency. NASA employees today are far more likely to have come to the agency directly out of graduate school, which means they are also far less likely to have divergent opinions. That matters because, in small groups, diversity of opinion is the single best guarantee that the group will reap benefits from face-to-face discussion. Berkeley political scientist Chandra Nemeth has shown in a host of studies of mock juries that the presence of a minority viewpoint, all by itself, makes a group's decisions more nuanced and its decision-making process more rigorous. This is true even when the minority viewpoint turns out to be ill conceived. The confrontation with a dissenting view, logically enough, forces the majority to interrogate its own positions more seriously. This doesn't mean that the ideal jury will follow the plot of *Twelve Angry Men*, where a single holdout convinces eleven men who are ready to convict that they're all wrong. But it does mean that having even a single different opinion can make a group wiser. One suspects that, had there been a single devil's advocate pushing the idea that the foam strike might have seriously damaged the wing, the MMT's conclusion would have been very different.

Without the devil's advocate, though, it's likely that the group's meetings actually made its judgment about the possible problem worse. That's because of a phenomenon called "group polarization." Usually, when we think of deliberation, we imagine that it's a kind of recipe for rationality and moderation, and assume that the more people talk about an issue, the less likely they will be to adopt extreme positions. But evidence from juries and three decades of experimental studies suggest that much of the time, the opposite is true. 20

Group polarization is still a phenomenon that is not well understood, and there are clearly cases where it has little or no effect. But since the 1960s, sociologists have documented how, under certain circumstances, deliberation does not moderate but rather radicalizes people's point of view. The first studies of the phenomenon tried to elicit people's attitudes toward risk, by asking them what they would do in specific situations. For instance, they were asked, "If a man with a severe heart illness is told that he must either change his way of life completely or have an operation that will either cure him or kill him, what should he do?" Or, "If an electrical engineer who has a safe job at a small salary is given the chance to take a new job that pays much better but is also less secure, should he move?" Individuals answered these questions privately at first, then gathered into groups to reach collective decisions. At first, researchers thought that group discussions made people more likely to advocate risky positions, and they termed this the "risky shift." But as time went on, it became clear that the shift could be in either direction. If a group was made up of people who were generally risk averse, discussion would make the group even more cautious, while groups of risk takers found themselves advocating riskier positions. Other studies showed that people who had a pessimistic view of the future became even more pessimistic after deliberations. Similarly, civil juries that are inclined to give large awards to plaintiffs generally give even larger awards after talking it over.

More recently, University of Chicago law professor Cass Sunstein has devoted a great deal of attention to polarization, and in his book *Why Societies Need Dissent*, he shows both that the phenomenon is more ubiquitous than was once thought and that it can have major consequences. As a general rule, discussions tend to move both the group as a whole and the individuals within it toward more extreme positions than the ones they entered the discussion with.

Why does polarization occur? One reason is because of people's reliance on "social comparison." This means more than that people are constantly comparing themselves to everyone else (which, of course, they are). It means that people are constantly comparing themselves to everyone else with an eye toward maintaining their relative position within the group. In other words, if you start out in the middle of the group and you believe the group has moved, as it were, to the right, you're inclined to shift your position to the right as well, so that relative to everyone else you're standing still. Of course, by moving to the right you're moving the group to the right, making social comparison something of a self-fulfilling prophecy. What's assumed to be real eventually becomes real.

It's important to see, though, that polarization isn't just the result of people trying to stay in tune with the group. It also results, strangely, from people doing their best to figure out what the right answer is. . . . [P]eople who are uncertain about what they believe will look to other members of the group for help. That's the point of deliberating, after all. But if a majority of the group already supports one position, then most of the arguments that will be made will be in support of that position. So the uncertain people are likely to be swayed in that direction, in part simply because that's more of what they'll hear. Similarly, people who have more extreme positions are more likely to have strong, coherent arguments in favor of their positions and are also more likely to voice them.

This matters because all the evidence suggests that the order in which people 25
speak has a profound effect on the course of a discussion. Earlier comments are more influential, and they tend to provide a framework within which the discussion occurs.

As in an information cascade,* once that framework is in place, it's difficult for a dissenter to break it down. This wouldn't be a problem if the people who spoke earliest were also more likely to know what they were talking about. But the truth is that, especially when it comes to problems where there is no obvious right answer, there's no guarantee that the most-informed speaker will also be the most influential. On juries, for instance, two-thirds of all foremen — who lead and structure deliberations — are men, and during deliberations men talk far more than women do, even though no one has ever suggested that men as a gender have better insight into questions of guilt and innocence. In groups where the members know each other, status tends to shape speaking patterns, with higher-status people talking more and more often than lower-status people. Again, this wouldn't matter as much if the authority of higher-status people was derived from their greater knowledge. But oftentimes it doesn't. Even when higher-status people don't really know what they're talking about, they're more likely to speak. A series of experiments with military fliers who were asked to solve a logic problem, for instance, found that pilots were far more likely to speak convincingly in defense of their solution than navigators were, even when the pilots were wrong and the navigators were right. The navigators deferred to the pilots — even when they had never met the pilots before — because they assumed that their rank meant they were more likely to be right.

That kind of deference is important, because in small groups ideas often do not succeed simply on their own merits. Even when its virtues may seem self-evident, an idea needs a champion in order to be adopted by the group as a whole. That's another reason why a popular position tends to become more popular in the course of deliberations: It has more potential champions to begin with. In a market or even a democracy, champions are far less important because of the sheer number of potential decision makers. But in a small group, having a strong advocate for an idea, no matter how good it is, is essential. And when advocates are chosen, as it were, on the basis of status or talkativeness, rather than perceptiveness or keenness of insight, then the group's chance of making a smart decision shrinks.

Talkativeness may seem like a curious thing to worry about, but in fact talkativeness has a major impact on the kinds of decisions small groups reach. If you talk a lot in a group, people will tend to think of you as influential almost by default. Talkative people are not necessarily well liked by other members of the group, but they are listened to. And talkativeness feeds on itself. Studies of group dynamics almost always show that the more someone talks, the more he is talked to by others in the group. So people at the center of the group tend to become more important over the course of a discussion.

This might be okay if people only spoke when they had expertise in a particular matter. And in many cases, if someone's talking a lot, it's a good sign that they have something valuable to add. But the truth is that there is no clear correlation between talkativeness and expertise. In fact, as the military-flier studies suggest, people who imagine themselves as leaders will often overestimate their own knowledge and

---

* Information cascade: A situation that develops when decisions based on erroneous information are used as examples, leading to further poor choices being made by others based on the earlier bad information [Ed.].

project an air of confidence and expertise that is unjustified. And since, as political scientists Brock Blomberg and Joseph Harrington suggest, extremists tend to be more rigid and more convinced of their own rightness than moderates, discussion tends to pull groups away from the middle. Of course, sometimes truth lies at the extreme. And if the people who spoke first and most often were consistently the people with the best information or the keenest analysis, then polarization might not be much of a problem. But it is.

The obvious temptation is to do away with or at least minimize the role that small groups play in shaping policy or making decisions. Better to entrust one reliable person — who at least we know will not become more extreme in his views — with responsibility than trust a group of ten or twelve people who at any moment, it seems, may suddenly decide to run off a cliff. It would be a mistake to succumb to that temptation. First of all, groups can be, as it were, depolarized. In a study that divided people into groups of six while making sure that each group composed two smaller groups of three who had strongly opposed views, it was found that discussion moved the groups from the extremes and toward each other. That same study found that as groups became less polarized, they also became more accurate when they were tested on matters of fact.

More important, as solid as the evidence demonstrating group polarization is, so too is the evidence demonstrating that nonpolarized groups consistently make better decisions and come up with better answers than most of their members, and surprisingly often the group outperforms even its best member. What makes this surprising is that one would think that in a small group, one or two confused people could skew the group's collective verdict in the wrong direction. (The small group can't, in that sense, rely on errors canceling themselves out.) But there's little evidence of that happening.

One of the more impressive studies of small-group performance was done in 2000 by Princeton economists Alan S. Blinder and John Morgan. Blinder had been vice chairman of the Federal Reserve Board during the mid-1990s, and the experience had made him deeply skeptical of decision making by committee. (Interest-rate changes are set by the Federal Open Market Committee, which consists of twelve members, including the seven members of the Federal Reserve Board and five presidents of regional Federal Reserve banks.) So he and Morgan designed a study that was meant to find out if groups could make intelligent decisions and if they make decisions as a group quickly, since one of the familiar complaints about committees is that they are inefficient.

The study consisted of two experiments that were meant to mimic, crudely, the challenges faced by the Fed. In the first experiment, students were given urns that held equal numbers of blue balls and red balls. They started to draw the balls from the urns, having been told that sometime after the first ten draws, the proportions in the urn would shift, so that 70 percent of the balls would be red and 30 percent blue (or vice versa). The goal was to identify, as soon as possible, which color had become more prevalent. This was roughly analogous to the Fed's job of recognizing when economic conditions have changed and whether a shift in monetary policy is needed. To place a premium on making the right decision quickly, students were penalized for every draw they made after the changeover had happened. The students played the game by themselves first, then played together as a group with free

30

discussion, played as individuals again, and finally once more as a group. (This was to control for the effect of learning.) The group's decisions were both faster and more accurate (the group got the direction right 89 percent of the time, versus 84 percent for individuals), and outperformed even the best individual.

The second experiment demanded more of the students. Essentially, they were asked to play the role of central bankers, and to set interest rates in response to changes in inflation and unemployment. What the experiment was really asking was whether they could detect when the economy had started to slow or was picking up steam, and whether they would move interest rates in the right direction in response. Once again, the group made better decisions than the individuals, who moved interest rates in the wrong direction far more often, and made them as quickly as the individuals. Most strikingly, there was no correlation between the performance of the smartest person in a group and the performance of that group. In other words, the groups were not just piggybacking on really smart individuals. They genuinely were smarter than the smartest people within them. A Bank of England study modeled on Blinder and Morgan's experiment reached identical conclusions: Groups could make intelligent decisions quickly, and could do better than their smartest members.

Given what we've already seen, this is not shocking news. But there are two important things about these studies. The first is that group decisions are not inherently inefficient. This suggests that deliberation can be valuable when done well, even if after a certain point its marginal benefits are outweighed by the costs. The second point is probably obvious, although a surprising number of groups ignore it, and that is that there is no point in making small groups part of a leadership structure if you do not give the group a method of aggregating the opinions of its members. If small groups are included in the decision-making process, then they should be allowed to make decisions. If an organization sets up teams and then uses them for purely advisory purposes, it loses the true advantage that a team has: namely, collective wisdom. One of the more frustrating aspects of the *Columbia* story is the fact that the MMT never voted on anything. The different members of the team would report on different aspects of the mission, but their real opinions were never aggregated. This was a mistake, and it would have been a mistake even had the *Columbia* made it home safely.

Exploring Context

1. At the center of Surowiecki's analysis is the *Columbia* disaster. Visit NASA's website at nasa.gov. Can you find any evidence of change in NASA's culture that might prevent such a disaster from happening again? How are missions handled? Who seems to work there?

2. Visit the website for the Advocates, a jury consulting firm, at theadvocates.com. How might such a service influence the small-group dynamics of a jury? How does this service represent itself in terms of Surowiecki's argument? You may want to draw on your work on group polarization in Question 2 of Questions for Critical Reading.

3. How do small groups work together online? Explore an online collaboration tool such as the online writing tools offered by Google (docs.google.com). How does the interface promote collaboration? How does it open that collaboration to the pitfalls of

small groups documented by Surowiecki? You may want to draw on your work on small groups from Question 1 of Questions for Critical Reading.

Questions for Connecting

1. Can the failure of small groups help explain the challenges of cultivating community and diversity on college campuses? Synthesize Surowiecki's ideas and Rebekah Nathan's analysis in "Community and Diversity" (p. 314).

2. Michael Pollan discusses a different kind of small group in "The Animals: Practicing Complexity" (p. 373). In what ways are organic farming ecosystems like the small groups that Surowiecki discusses? How does the success of organic farming point to strategies for small-group success? Relate your response to your answer to Question 1 of Questions for Critical Reading.

3. What is the economical potential — and risk — of small groups? Synthesize Surowiecki's ideas and Thomas L. Friedman's discussion of global supply chains in "The Dell Theory of Conflict Prevention" (p. 166).

4. **CONNECTING TO E-PAGES** Soldiers in war often work in small groups to reach objectives. Consider Surowiecki's essay in light of Wired.com's "Call of Duty: Afghanistan" video (bedfordstmartins.com/emerging/epages). Based upon your understanding of "Committees, Juries, and Teams: The *Columbia* Disaster and How Small Groups Can Be Made to Work," what important elements, structures, or processes would need to be part of the game in order for it to be used successfully to train soldiers to work in small groups?

Language Matters

1. Indexes help you locate important information quickly. Create a simple index for Surowiecki's essay. What terms or entries would you include? How often do they appear in the text?

2. Surowiecki ultimately believes in the power of small groups. Working in small groups in class, debate a common grammatical issue or error, such as the run-on sentence. Should it be an error? How important is that error or any one type of error? How does your discussion reflect Surowiecki's ideas?

3. Why is "*Columbia*" italicized in this essay? What are the rules for using italics? Develop a system to help you remember when to use them.

Assignments for Writing

1. Surowiecki discusses ways in which group dynamics contributed to the failure of the *Columbia*'s Mission Management Team. Using Surowiecki's observations, write a paper that determines the best practices for organizing and running a small group. In composing your response, consider these questions: What makes a small group more than just the sum of its parts? How can group identity be made to serve the purpose of

the group? What is the ideal structure for a group? How important is cognitive diversity, and why? How can "group polarization" be avoided? In what ways could "talkativeness" be regulated to ensure equal participation?

2. Although the Mission Management Team's decisions were made as a group, Surowiecki pays particular attention to the actions of a few individual members. Using Surowiecki's observations, write a paper that evaluates the influence of an individual person in a group setting. To what extent can an individual voice influence a group? Is a small group more than just the sum of its parts? How does individual identity exist in the larger group identity? How is dissent productive to a group decision? In what ways could an individual voice dissolve group polarization? How do the studies Surowiecki mentions support your evaluation? You may want to use your work from Questions for Critical Reading and from Question 2 of Questions for Connecting.

3. Surowiecki describes the pitfalls of logic that await a small group, paying particular attention to the effects of flawed reasoning on group decisions. Using Surowiecki's observations, write an analysis of the error in reasoning that played the biggest role in the Mission Management Team's failure: Describe all instances of the error, identify its origin in flawed reasoning, and trace its consequences for the group's decision-making process. Consider these questions: Could the Mission Management Team's errors be seen only in hindsight? In what way did the Mission Management Team's small-group dynamics affect its decisions? Does the fundamental error belong to one person, several people, or the group as a whole? Why? Whose influence was most powerful within the group? Whose influence should have been the most powerful within the group?

TOM VANDERBILT

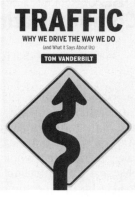

Tom Vanderbilt is a Visiting Scholar at the Rudin Center for Transportation Policy and Management at New York University. Among his many awards are fellowships from the Andy Warhol Foundation for the Visiting Arts, the Canadian Centre for Architecture, and the Design Trust for Public Space. He is a contributing editor to *Artforum* and a contributor to *Design Observer* and *Slate* magazine. His work has been published in many anthologies as well as in *Wired*, *Outside*, the *Financial Times*, the *Wall Street Journal*, *Rolling Stone*, *Travel and Leisure*, and *Popular Science*. Vanderbilt is also the author of *Survival City: Adventures Among the Ruins of Atomic America* (2002), *The Sneaker Book* (1998), and *Traffic: Why We Drive the Way We Do (and What It Says About Us)* (2008), a *New York Times* best-seller.

Traffic is a thorough exploration of driving habits and what they say about us as humans. Throughout the book, Vanderbilt investigates issues such as social interactions on the road, the difficulties of driving, our inability to pay attention, cooperation on the road, gender differences and the psychology of travel, parking, traffic engineering, and traffic in different parts of the world. Vanderbilt explores the complexity of driving in relation to the biological and psychological responses of humans, legal systems and regulations, social engagement, and the connection between driving and who we are as a society.

The chapter from *Traffic* presented here, "Shut Up, I Can't Hear You: Anonymity, Aggression, and the Problems of Communicating While Driving," focuses on human actions and preferences while driving. There are constant decisions and subtle adjustments that have to be made while driving; we base these choices on a limited sense of communication, the ability to identify with other drivers, and sensitivity to loss. Vanderbilt argues, "Traffic messes with our heads in a strangely paradoxical way: We act too human, we do not act human enough." In this chapter, Vanderbilt calls into question not only the ways in which we catch glimpses of humanity while dealing with traffic, but also how driving causes us to question ourselves and those around us.

▶ TAGS: *bias, communication, identity, error, reciprocity, contact, groups*

Questions for Critical Reading

1. In what situations are stereotypes useful? As you read Vanderbilt's essay, pay attention to the ways in which various stereotypes affect driving. In which situations does it feel like stereotypes are necessary?

2. What role does communication play in traffic? Note the various kinds of communication that Vanderbilt explores in his essay. Which kind has the biggest impact on our driving behavior? Locate passages that support your response.

3. What does traffic teach us about human behavior? List key lessons about how we think and act, based on the ideas discussed in Vanderbilt's essay.

Shut Up, I Can't Hear You: Anonymity, Aggression, and the Problems of Communicating While Driving

HORN BROKEN. WATCH FOR FINGER.

— BUMPER STICKER

In *Motor Mania*, a 1950 Walt Disney short, the lovably dim dog Goofy stars as "Mr. Walker," a model pedestrian (on two legs). He is a "good citizen," courteous and honest, the sort who whistles back at birds and wouldn't "step on an ant." Once Mr. Walker gets behind the steering wheel of his car, however, a "strange phenomenon takes place." His "whole personality changes." He becomes "Mr. Wheeler," a power-obsessed "uncontrollable monster" who races other cars at stop lights and views the road as his own personal property (but still "considers himself a good driver"). Then he steps out of his car, and, deprived of his "personal armor," reverts to being Mr. Walker. Every time he gets back into his car, despite the fact that he knows "how the other fellow feels," he is consumed by the personality of Mr. Wheeler.

What Disney was identifying, in his brilliantly simple way, was a commonplace but peculiar fact of life: We are how we move. Like Goofy, I, too, suffer from this multiple personality disorder. When I walk, which as a New Yorker I often do, I view cars as loud, polluting annoyances driven by out-of-town drunks distracted by their cell phones. When I drive, I find that pedestrians are suddenly the menace, whacked-out iPod drones blithely meandering across the street without looking. When I ride a bike, I get the worst of both worlds, buffeted by speeding cars whose drivers resent my superior health and fuel economy, and hounded by oblivious pedestrians who seem to think it's safe to cross against the light if "only a bike" is coming but are then startled and indignant as I whisk past at twenty-five miles per hour.

I am guessing this sort of thing happens to you as well. Let us call it a "modal bias."[1] Some of this has to do with our skewed perceptual senses. . . . Some of it has to do with territoriality, like when bicyclists and pedestrians sharing a path yell at each other or someone pushing a triplet-sized stroller turns into the pedestrian version of the SUV, commandeering the sidewalk through sheer size. But something deeper and more transformative happens when we move from people who walk to people who drive. The "personal armor" described by Disney is perhaps not so far-fetched. One study of pedestrian fatalities by French researchers showed that a significant number were associated with a "change of mode"[2]—for example, moving from car to foot—as if, the authors speculated, drivers leaving their vehicles still felt a certain invulnerability.

Psychologists have struggled to understand the "deviant driver," creating detailed personality profiles to understand who's likely to fall prey to "road rage." An early mantra, originally applied to what was called the "accident-prone driver," has long held sway: "A man drives as he lives."[3] This is why car insurance premiums are tied not only to driving history but, more controversially, to credit scores; risky credit, the thinking goes, correlates with taking risks on the road.[4] The statistical association between lower credit scores and higher insurance losses is just that, however; the reasons why how one lives might be linked to how one drives are less clear. And as inquiries into this question typically involve questionnaires,[5] they're open to various self-reported response biases. How would *you* answer this sample question: Are you a raving psychopath on wheels? (Please check "never," "sometimes," or "always.") Generally, these inquiries come to what hardly seem earth-shattering conclusions: that "sensation-seeking," "risk-seeking," "novelty-seeking," and "aggressive" individuals tend to drive in a riskier, more aggressive manner.[6] You weren't going to bet your paycheck on daredevil drivers being the risk-averse people who crave quiet normalcy and routine, were you?

Even using a phrase like "road rage" lends a clinical legitimacy to what might simply be termed bad or boorish behavior elsewhere. "Traffic tantrums"[7] is a useful alternative, nicely underscoring the raw childishness of aggressive driving. The more interesting question is not whether some of us are more prone to act like homicidal maniacs once we get behind the wheel but why we *all* act differently. What is going on seems to have less to do with a change in personality than with a change in our entire being. In traffic, we struggle to stay human.

Think of language, perhaps the defining human characteristic. Being in a car renders us mostly mute. Instead of complex vocabularies and subtle shifts in facial expression, the language of traffic is reduced — necessarily, for reasons of safety and economy — to a range of basic signals, formal and informal, that convey only the simplest of meanings. Studies have shown that many of these signals, particularly informal ones, are often misunderstood, especially by novice drivers.[8] To take one example, the Reverend David Rowe, who heads a congregation in the wealthy Connecticut suburb of Fairfield and, improbably, is a great fan of the neopunk band Green Day, told me

> **Think of language, perhaps the defining human characteristic. Being in a car renders us mostly mute.**

he was once driving down the road when he spotted a car with a Green Day bumper sticker.[9] He honked to show his solidarity. For his efforts he was rewarded with a finger.

Even formal signals are sometimes hazy: Is that person who keeps driving with their right turn signal on actually going to turn or have they forgotten it's still blinking? Unfortunately, there's no way to ask the driver what they mean. This may lead to a rhetorical outburst: "Are you going to turn or not?" But you can't ask; nor would there be a way to get an answer back. Frustrated by our inability to talk, we gesture violently or honk — a noise the offending driver might misinterpret. At some point you may have been the recipient of an unsolicited honk, to which you immediately responded with defensive anger — *What?!* — only to learn that the honker was trying to convey to you that you left your gas cap open. *Thanks! Have a good one!*

Traffic is riddled with such "asymmetries" in communication, as Jack Katz, a sociologist at the University of California in Los Angeles and the author of *How Emotions*

5

Work, describes them. "You can see but you can't be heard," he told me. "In a very precise way, you're made dumb. You can shout as much as you want but nobody's going to hear you."

Another way to think about this "asymmetry" is that while you can see a lot of other drivers making mistakes, you are less likely to see yourself doing so. (A former mayor of Bogotá, Colombia, had a wonderful solution to this, hiring mimes to people the city's crosswalks and silently mock drivers and pedestrians who violated traffic laws.[10]) Drivers also spend much of their time in traffic looking at the rear ends of other cars, an activity culturally associated with subordination.[11] It also tends to make the communication one-way: You're looking at a bunch of drivers who cannot see you. "It's like trying to talk to someone who's walking in front of you, as opposed to someone who's face-to-face with you," Katz says. "We're looking at everybody's rear, and that's not how human beings were set up to maximize their communicative possibility."

This muteness, Katz argues, makes us mad. We are desperate to say something. In   10
one study, in-car researchers pretended to be measuring the speed and distance perception of drivers. What they were really interested in was how their subjects would react to a honk from another driver. They made this happen by giving subjects instructions as they paused at a stop sign. They then had an accomplice pull up behind the stalled car and honk. More than three-quarters of the drivers reacted verbally, despite the fact they would not be heard by the honker.[12]

When a driver is cut off by another driver, the gesture is read as rude, perhaps hostile. There is no way for the offending driver to indicate that it was anything but rude or hostile.[13] Because of the fleeting nature of traffic, the act is not likely to be witnessed by anyone else. No one, save perhaps your passenger, will shake their heads in unison with you and say, "Can you believe he did that?" There are at least two possible responses. One is to speed ahead and cut the offending driver off in turn, to "teach them a lesson." But there is no guarantee that the person receiving the lesson is aware of what they have done — and so your lesson simply becomes a provocation — or that they will accept your position as the "teacher" in any case. And even if your lesson is successful, you're not likely to receive any future benefit. Another response is to use an "informal" traffic signal, like the middle finger (or, as is gaining currency in Australia, the pinkie, after an ad campaign by the Road and Traffic Authority to suggest that the person speeding or otherwise driving aggressively is overcompensating for deficient male anatomy).[14] This gains power, Katz says, if the person you give the finger to visually registers that you're giving him the finger. But what if that person merely gives the finger back?

Finally, it is often impossible to even send a message to the offending driver in the first place. Yet still we get visibly mad, to an audience of no one. Katz argues that we are engaging in a kind of theatrical storytelling, inside of our cars, angrily "constructing moral dramas"[15] in which we are the wronged victims — and the "avenging hero" — in some traffic epic of larger importance. It is not enough to think bad thoughts about the other driver; we get angry, in essence, to watch ourselves get angry. "The angry driver,"[16] Katz argues, "becomes a magician taken in by his or her own magic." Sometimes, says Katz, as part of this "moral drama," and in an effort to create a "new meaning" for the encounter, we will try to find out something after the fact about the driver who wronged us (perhaps speeding up to see them), meanwhile running down a mental list of potential villains (e.g., women, men, teenagers, senior citizens, truck drivers, Democrats, Republicans, "idiots on cell phones," or, if all else fails, simply "idiots") before finding a suitable resolution to the drama.

This seems an on-road version of what psychologists call the "fundamental attribution error," a commonly observed way in which we ascribe the actions of others to who they are; in what is known as the "actor-observer effect,"[17] meanwhile, we attribute our own actions to how we were forced to act in specific situations. Chances are you have never looked at *yourself* in the rearview mirror and thought, "Stupid #$%&! driver." Psychologists theorize that the actor-observer effect may stem from one's desire to feel more in control[18] of a complex situation, like driving in traffic. It also just might be easier to chastise a "stupid driver" for cutting you off than to fully analyze the circumstances that caused this event to occur.

On a larger scale, it might also help explain, more than actual national or civic chauvinism, why drivers the world around have their own favorite traffic targets: "The Albanians are terrible drivers," say the Greeks. "The Dutch are the worst drivers," say the Germans. It's best not to get New Yorkers started about New Jersey drivers. We even seem to make the fundamental attribution error in the way we travel. When bicyclists violate a traffic law, research has showed it is because, in the eyes of drivers, they are reckless anarchists; drivers, meanwhile, are more likely to view the violation of a traffic law by another driver as somehow being required by the circumstances.[19]

At least some of this anger seems intended to maintain our sense of identity, another human trait that is lost in traffic. The driver is reduced to a brand of vehicle (a rough stereotype at best) and an anonymous license-plate number. We look for glimpses of meaning in this sea of anonymity: Think of the curious joy you get when you see a car that matches your own, or a license plate from your home state or country when you are in another. (Studies with experimental games have shown that people will act more kindly toward someone they have been told shares their birth date.[20]) Some drivers, especially in the United States, try in vain to establish their identities with personalized vanity plates, but this raises the question of whether you really want your life summed up in seven letters—let alone why you want to tell a bunch of people you don't know who you are! Americans seem similarly (and particularly) predisposed to putting cheap bumper stickers on their expensive cars—announcing the academic wizardry of their progeny, jocularly advising that their "other car is a Porsche," or giving subtle hints ("MV") of their exclusive vacation haunts. One never sees a German blazing down the autobahn with a PROUD TO BE GERMAN sticker.

Trying to assert one's identity in traffic is always going to be problematic, in any case, because the driver yields his or her identity to the cars. We become, Katz says, cyborgs.[21] Our vehicle becomes our self. "You project your body way out in front of a vehicle," says Katz. "When somebody's changed lanes a hundred yards ahead, you instantly feel you've been cut off. They haven't touched you physically, they haven't touched your car physically, but in order to adjust the wheel and acceleration and braking, you have projected yourself." We say, "Get out of my way," not "Get out of my and my car's way."

Identity issues seem to trouble the driver alone. Have you ever noticed how passengers rarely seem to get as worked up about these events as you do? Or that they may, in the dreaded case of the "backseat driver," even question your part in the dispute? This

15

may be because the passenger has a more neutral view. They do not feel that their identity is bound up with the car. Studies that have examined the brain activity of drivers and passengers as they engaged in simulated driving have shown that different neural regions are activated in drivers and passengers. They are, in effect, different people.[22] Studies have also shown that solo drivers drive more aggressively, as measured by such indices as speed and following distance.[23] It is as if, lacking that human accompaniment — and thus any sense of shame — they give themselves over to the car.[24]

Like many everyday travails, this whole situation is succinctly illustrated in a hit country song, Chely Wright's "The Bumper of My SUV." The song's protagonist complains that a "lady in a minivan" has given her the finger because of a United States Marine Corps bumper sticker on her SUV. "Does she think she knows what I stand for / Or the things that I believe," sings Wright, just because the narrator has a bumper sticker for the U.S. Marines on the aforementioned bumper of her SUV? The first issue here is the struggle over identity; the narrator is upset that her identity has been defined by someone else. But the narrator may be protesting too much: How *else* would we know the things that you stand for or believe if you did not have a bumper sticker on your SUV? And if you are resentful at having your identity pigeonholed, why put a pigeonholing sticker on your bumper in the first place?

In the absence of any other visible human traits, we do draw a lot of information from bumper stickers. This point was demonstrated by an experiment conducted in 1969 at California State College, a place marked by violent clashes between the Black Panther Party* and the police. In the trial, fifteen subjects of varying appearance and type of car affixed a bright BLACK PANTHER sticker to their auto's rear bumper. No one in the group had received traffic violations in the past year. After two weeks with the bumper sticker, the group had been given thirty-three citations.[25] (The idea that people with distinguishing marks on their vehicle will be singled out for abuse or cause other disruptions of smooth traffic is just one of the problems with proposals to add scarlet letter–style designations to license plates; suggestions have ranged from identifying sex offenders in Ohio to marking the cars of the reckless drivers known as "hoons" in Australia.)

In being offended, the SUV driver has made several huge assumptions of her own. 20 First, she has presumed that the finger had something to do with the bumper sticker, when in fact it could have been directed at a perceived act of aggressive driving on her part.[26] Or could it have been the fact that this single driver was tooling around in a large SUV, inordinately harming the environment, putting pedestrians and drivers of cars at greater risk,[27] and increasing the country's dependence on foreign oil? Secondly, by invoking a "lady in a minivan," later echoed by references to "private schools," she is perpetuating a preemptive negative stereotype against minivans: that their drivers are somehow more elitist than the drivers of SUVs — which makes no sense as SUVs, on average, cost more than minivans. The narrator is guilty of the same thing she accuses the minivan driver of.

---

*Black Panther Party: American black revolutionary party founded in 1966 in Oakland, California, and lasting until the mid-1980s. It called for the arming of all blacks, the exemption of blacks from the draft, and the release of all blacks from jail [Ed.].

In traffic, first impressions are usually the only impressions. Unlike the bar in *Cheers*, traffic is a place where no one knows your name. Anonymity in traffic acts as a powerful drug, with several curious side effects. On the one hand, because we feel that no one is watching, or that no one we know will see us, the inside of the car itself becomes a useful place for self-expression. This may explain why surveys have shown that most people, given the choice, desire a *minimum* commute of at least twenty minutes. Drivers desire this solitary "me time" — to sing, to feel like a teenager again, to be temporarily free from the constricted roles of work and home. One study found that the car was a favored place for people to cry about something ("grieving while driving").[28] Then there's the "nose-pick factor," a term used by researchers who install cameras inside of cars to study drivers. They report that after only a short time, drivers will "forget the camera" and begin to do all sorts of things, including nasal probing.[29]

The flip side of anonymity, as the classic situationist psychological studies of Philip Zimbardo and Stanley Milgram have shown, is that it encourages aggression. In a well-known 1969 study, Zimbardo found that hooded subjects were willing to administer twice the level of electric shock to others than those not wearing hoods.[30] Similarly, this is why hooded hostages are more likely to be killed than those without hoods, and why firing-squad victims are blindfolded or faced backward — not for their sake, but to make them look less human to the executioners.[31] Take away human identity and human contact and we act inhuman. When the situation changes, we change.

> **The flip side of anonymity . . . is that it encourages aggression.**

This is not so different in traffic. Instead of a hood, we have the climate-controlled enclosure of the car. Why not cut that driver off? You do not know them and will likely never see them again. Why not speed through this neighborhood? You don't live here. In one study, researchers planted a car at an intersection ahead of a series of various convertibles, and had the blocking car intentionally not move after the light changed to green. They then measured how quickly the driver behind the plant vehicle honked, how many times they honked, and how long each honk was. Drivers with the top down took longer to honk, honked fewer times, and honked for shorter durations than did the more anonymous drivers with the tops up.[32] It could have been that the people who put their tops down were in a better mood to begin with, but the results suggest that anonymity increases aggressiveness.

Being in traffic is like being in an online chat room under a pseudonym. Freed from our own identity and surrounded by others known only by their "screen names" (in traffic, license plates), the chat room becomes a place where the normal constraints of life are left behind. Psychologists have called this the "online disinhibition effect."[33] As with being inside the car, we may feel that, cloaked in electronic anonymity, we can at last be ourselves. The playing field has been leveled, all are equal, and the individual swells with exaggerated self-importance. As long as we're not doing anything illegal, all is fair game. This also means, unfortunately, that there is little incentive to engage in normal social pleasantries. And so the language is harsh, rude, and abbreviated. One faces no consequences for one's speech: Chat room visitors aren't speaking face-to-face, and do not even have to linger after making a negative comment. They can "flame" someone and sign off. Or give someone the finger and leave them behind a cloud of exhaust.

NOTES

1. "modal bias": This term was suggested to me in a conversation with Aaron Naparstek.
2. "change of mode": Hélène Fontaine and Yves Gourlet, "Fatal Pedestrian Accidents in France: A Typological Analysis," *Accident Analysis and Prevention*, vol. 39, no. 3 (1997), pp. 303–12.
3. "drives as he lives": W. A. Tillman and G. E. Hobbs, "The Accident-Prone Automobile Driver: A Study of the Psychiatric and Social Background," *American Journal of Psychiatry*, vol. 106 (November 1949), pp. 321–31. Many of us may think of "road rage" as a rather new concept, like "air rage" or "surfing rage," but it is really as old as the automobile itself. The year 1968, for example, might have been marked by violent social upheaval in metropolises from Paris to Mexico City, but there was another form of violence in the air: That year, Mayer H. Parry published *Aggression on the Road*, while the *New York Times* reported on government testimony about "uncontrollable violent behavior" on the nation's roads. (Three years later, F. A. Whitlock followed up with his book *Death on the Road: A Study in Social Violence*.) See John D. Morris, "Driver Violence Tied to Crashes," *New York Times*, March 2, 1968.
4. risks on the road: For a discussion, see Patrick L. Brockett and Linda L. Golden, "Biological and Psychobehavioral Correlates of Credit Scores and Automobile Insurance Losses: Toward an Explication of Why Credit Scoring Works," *Journal of Risk and Insurance*, vol. 1, no. 74 (March 2007), pp. 23–63.
5. typically involve questionnaires: See, for example, David L. Van Rooy, James Rotton, and Tina M. Burns, "Convergent, Discriminant, and Predictive Validity of Aggressive Driving Inventories: They Drive as They Live," *Aggressive Behavior*, vol. 3, no. 2 (February 2006), pp. 89–98.
6. more aggressive manner: This is a virtual consensus in the field, as demonstrated by a survey of the scholarly literature in B. A. Jonah, "Sensation Seeking and Risky Driving: A Review and Synthesis of the Literature," *Accident Analysis and Prevention*, vol. 29, no. 5 (1997), pp. 651–65.
7. "Traffic tantrums": Thanks to Ian Walker for this phrase.
8. especially by novice drivers: Kazumi Renge, "Effect of Driving Experience on Drivers' Decoding Process of Roadway Interpersonal Communication," *Ergonomics*, vol. 43, no. 1(1 January 2000), pp. 27–39.
9. Green Day bumper sticker: This brings up the point of whether there should really be any nonessential communication in traffic at all. As the German sociologist Norbert Schmidt-Relenberg has observed, "It could be said that cooperation in traffic is not a means to attain something positive, but to avoid something negative: every participant in the system attempts to attain his destination without friction. Hence traffic is a system all its own; the less its participants come into contact with each other and are compelled to interaction, the better it works: a system defined and approved in the reality by a principle of minimized contact." In other words, not only should we not honk at people with Green Day stickers, we should not put the sticker there in the first place. Norbert Schmidt-Relenberg, "On the Sociology of Car Traffic in Towns," in *Transport Sociology: Social Aspects of Transport Planning*, ed. Enne de Boer (Oxford, New York: Pergamon Press, 1986), p. 122.
10. violated traffic laws: María Cristina Caballero, "Academic Turns City into a Social Experiment," *Harvard University Gazette*, March 11, 2004.
11. associated with subordination: Katz suggests this may be why we so often call other drivers "assholes" and give the "up yours" finger.

12. by the honker: Andrew R. McGarva and Michelle Steiner, "Provoked Driver Aggression and Status: A Field Study," *Transportation Research F: Psychology and Behavior*, vol. 167 (2000), pp. 167–79.

13. anything but rude or hostile: What if our signals were more meaningful? A few years ago, before the Tokyo Motor Show, Simon Humphries, a designer for Lexus in Japan, told me in an e-mail exchange that the Toyota Motor Company had proposed a car — nicknamed POD — that would contain a "vehicle expression operation control system." Accompanying the usual lights and arrows would be a new range of signals. The headlights would be "anthropomorphized" with "eyes" and "eyebrows," the antenna would "wag," and different colors would be used to show emotion. "As traffic grows heavier and vehicle use increases," reads the U.S. patent application, "vehicles having expression functions, such as crying or laughing, like people and other animals do, could create a joyful, organic atmosphere rather than the simple comings and goings of inorganic vehicles." Indeed, a German company even released an aftermarket version of this system, called Flashbox, that uses a series of blinks to signify things like "apology," "annoyed," and "stop for more?" Adding signals, however, creates many new problems. Everyone has to learn the new signals. More information in traffic means more time to process. The receiver of a "smile," moreover, may not understand why they have received it any more so than a honk. And flashing "angry" signals may provoke rather than defuse violence.

14. deficient male anatomy: One male Australian driver was actually fined because when a woman wagged her pinkie at him, he responded by hurling a plastic bottle at her windshield. The man claimed that the gesture was akin to a "sexual assault," a worse insult than the traditional finger. "The 'finger,' it's so common now, that we're over it, but this finger is a whole new thing and it's been promoted so much everybody knows it and you just get offended," he said. David Brouithwaite, "Driver Points to Ad Campaign for His Digitally Enhanced Road Rage," *Sydney Morning Herald*, November 1, 2007.

15. "constructing moral dramas": For a more detailed discussion of Katz's investigation of anger in traffic, see Jack Katz, *How Emotions Work* (Chicago: University of Chicago Press, 1999), in particular the first chapter, "Pissed Off in L.A."

16. "the angry driver": Jack Katz, *How Emotions Work*, p. 48.

17. "actor-observer effect": See L. D. Ross, "The Intuitive Psychologist and His Shortcomings: Distortions in the Attribution Process," in *Advances in Experimental Social Psychology*, vol. 10, ed. L. Berkowitz (New York: Random House, 1977), pp. 173–220.

18. feel more in control: As Thomas Britt and Michael Garrity write, "individuals will probably err in the direction of assuming an internal locus of causality for the offending driver's behavior in order to feel some sense of control over events when driving." "Attributions and Personality as Predictors of the Road Rage Response," *British Journal of Social Psychology*, vol. 45 (2006), pp. 127–47.

19. required by the circumstances: This was the finding arrived at when a group of researchers for England's Transport Research Laboratory conducted a series of interviews with drivers, part of which included assessments of cyclist and driver behavior in traffic scenarios. They concluded, "The underlying unpredictability of cyclists' behavior was seen by drivers as stemming from the attitudes and limited competence of the cyclists themselves, rather than from the difficulty of the situations that cyclists are often forced to face on the road (i.e., drivers made a dispositional rather than a situational attribution). Despite their own evident difficulties in knowing how to respond, drivers never attributed these difficulties to their own attitudes or competencies, nor did they do so in relation to other drivers (i.e., they made a situational attribution about

their own and other drivers' behavior). This pattern of assignment of responsibility is characteristic of how people perceive the behavior of those they consider to be part of the same social group as themselves, versus those seen as part of a different social group." L. Basford, D. Davies, J. A. Thomson, and A. K. Tolmie, "Drivers' Perception of Cyclists," in *TRL Report 549: Phase I — A Qualitative Study* (Crowthorne: Transport Research Laboratory, 2002).

20. shares their birth date: See D. T. Miller, J. S. Downs, and D. A. Prentice, "Minimal Conditions for the Creation of a Unit Relationship: The Social Bond Between Birthday Mates," *European Journal of Social Psychology*, vol. 28 (1998), pp. 475–81. This idea was raised in an interesting paper by James W. Jenness, "Supporting Highway Safety Culture by Addressing Anonymity," *AAA Foundation for Traffic Safety*, 2007.

21. Katz says, cyborgs: This point was made as early as 1930, by a city planner in California who suggested that "Southern Californians have added wheels to their anatomy." The quote comes from J. Flink, *The Automobile Age* (Cambridge, Mass.: MIT Press, 1988), p. 143, via an excellent article by John Urry, a sociologist at Lancaster University. See John Urry, "Inhabiting the Car," published by the Department of Sociology, Lancaster University, Lancaster, United Kingdom, available at http://www.comp.lancs.ac.uk /sociology/papers/Urry-Inhabiting-the-Car.pdf.

22. different people: See Henrik Walter, Sandra C. Vetter, Jo Grothe, Arthur P. Wunderlich, Stefan Hahn, and Manfred Spitzer, "The Neural Correlates of Driving," *Brain Imaging*, vol. 12, no. 8 (June 13, 2001), pp. 1763–67.

23. and following distance: See David Shinar and Richard Compton, "Aggressive Driving: An Observational Study of Driver, Vehicle and Situational Variables," *Accident Analysis & Prevention*, vol. 36 (2004), pp. 429–37.

24. give themselves over to the car: Research also suggests that single drivers are more susceptible to fatigue and being involved in crashes, and it is not difficult to speculate why. Passengers provide another "set of eyes" to warn of potential hazards and can aid in keeping the driver engaged. For the increased risk factors to single drivers, see, for example, Vicki L. Neale, Thomas A. Dingus, Jeremy Sudweeks, and Michael Goodman, "An Overview of the 100-Car Naturalistic Study and Findings," National Highway Traffic Safety Administration, Paper Number 05-0400.

25. thirty-three citations: See F. K. Heussenstamm, "Bumper Stickers and the Cops," *Trans-Action (Society)*, vol. 8 (February 1971), pp. 32 and 33. The author acknowledged that the subjects' driving may have been affected by the experiment itself but argued that "it is statistically unlikely that this number of previously 'safe' drivers could amass such a collection of tickets without assuming real bias by police against drivers with Black Panther bumper stickers." The information about specially designated license plates comes from "New 'Scarlet Letter' for Predators in Ohio," Associated Press, March 1, 2007. The license plates raise, ironically, a problem similar to "Children at Play" signs: They signify that a car without such plates is somehow safe for children to approach, just as the "Children at Play" signs suggest that drivers can act less cautiously in areas *without* the signs.

26. aggressive driving on her part: Women driving SUVs, as at least one set of very limited observational studies found, drove faster in 20-mile-per-hour school zones, parked more often in restricted shopping mall fire zones, came to a stop less frequently at stop signs, and were slower to move through an intersection when the light turned green, as compared to other drivers in other types of vehicles. As the author himself admits, the sample sizes were small, and the higher rates of women SUV drivers may simply have reflected the fact that the study took place in a setting where there happened to be a higher than average number of women driving SUVs. See John Trinkaus, "Shopping

Center Fire Zone Parking Violators: An Informal Look," *Perceptual and Motor Skills*, vol. 95 (2002), pp. 1215–16; John Trinkaus, "School Zone Speed Limit Dissenters: An Informal Look," *Perceptual and Motor Skills*, vol. 88 (1999), pp. 1057–58.

27. at greater risk: See, for example, Devon E. Lefler and Hampton C. Gabler, "The Fatality and Injury Risk of Light Truck Impacts with Pedestrians in the United States," *Accident Analysis & Prevention*, vol. 36 (2004), pp. 295–304.

28. "grieving while driving": Paul C. Rosenblatt, "Grieving While Driving," *Death Studies*, vol. 28 (2004), pp. 679–86.

29. including nasal probing: Thanks to Daniel McGehee for this story.

30. not wearing hoods: Philip Zimbardo, "The Human Choice: Individuation, Reason, and Order vs. Deindividuation, Impulse, and Chaos," In *Nebraska Symposium on Motivation*, ed. W. J. Arnold and D. Levine (Lincoln: University of Nebraska Press, 1970). Zimbardo's description of the conditions that contribute to the sense of "deindividuation" are worth noting in light of traffic. He writes: "Anonymity, diffused responsibility, group activity, altered temporal perspective, emotional arousal, and sensory overload are some of the input variables that can generate deindividuated reactions." Arguably, *all* of Zimbardo's "input variables" can routinely be found in traffic situations. The quote comes from Zimbardo's "Depersonalization" entry in *International Encyclopedia of Psychiatry, Psychology, Psychoanalysis, and Neurology*, vol. 4, ed. B. B. Wolman (New York: Human Sciences Press, 1978), p. 52.

31. to the executioners: The hostage and firing squad information comes from David Grossman, *On Killing: The Psychological Cost of Learning to Kill in War and Society* (Boston: Back Bay Books, 1996), p. 128.

32. with the tops up: Patricia A. Ellison, John M. Govern, Herbert L. Petri, Michael H. Figler, "Anonymity and Aggressive Driving Behavior: A Field Study," *Journal of Social Behavior and Personality*, vol. 10, no. 1 (1995), pp. 265–72.

33. "online disinhibition effect": See J. Suler, "The Online Disinhibition Effect," *CyberPsychology and Behavior*, vol. 7 (2004), pp. 321–26.

Exploring Context

1. Analyze your potential for road rage at RoadRagers.com (roadragers.com/test). Use Vanderbilt's discussion to analyze both the results and the questions asked in the test.

2. Visit Traffic.com. How does knowing about traffic affect driving behavior? Use ideas from Vanderbilt's essay to support your conclusion.

3. Use the Web to locate any laws in your area for bicyclists in traffic. How do these laws reflect the studies concerning the interaction between bicyclists and drivers discussed by Vanderbilt?

Questions for Connecting

1. Although their perspectives on the subject are quite different, both Vanderbilt and Jennifer Pozner, in "Ghetto Bitches, China Dolls, and Cha Cha Divas" (p. 397), discuss the impact of stereotypes. Synthesize their arguments to determine the function of stereotypes in culture. Are they ever useful? Harmful? In which situations?

2. James Surowiecki looks at the risks of small groups in "Committees, Juries, and Teams: The *Columbia* Disaster and How Small Groups Can Be Made to Work" (p. 472). Apply his ideas to Vanderbilt's discussion. How do traffic and small groups function similarly?

3. In "Authenticating" (p. 95), Brian Christian discusses the concept of "nexting" in the context of customer service calls. Connect his discussion to Vanderbilt's ideas about lines and queues.

Language Matters

1. Select a section of the essay and then locate and remove the topic sentence of each paragraph in that section. What strategies did you use to find the topic sentences? How does removing a paragraph's topic sentence affect the meaning of the paragraph?

2. Introductions do a lot of important work in your papers: They introduce the authors, the essays, and, most important, your position or argument. How does Vanderbilt introduce this chapter? How effective is his introduction? Why would you want (or not want) to open your paper that way?

3. Photocopy a couple of pages from Vanderbilt's essay and then cut out each individual paragraph with a pair of scissors. Trade these in small groups. Can everyone put the paragraphs back in the right order? How strong is Vanderbilt's organization? What elements of the paragraphs indicate their order within the piece?

Assignments for Writing

1. Using Vanderbilt's ideas about how we function in traffic, write a paper in which you examine the relationship between identity and anonymity. What role does anonymity play in shaping our identity? How does it threaten our identity? How does it protect identity?

2. What are the risks and advantages of using stereotypes to make everyday decisions? Use Vanderbilt's discussion to write a paper that argues for the proper role of stereotypes in decision making. Use your work from Question 1 of Questions for Critical Reading and Question 1 of Questions for Connecting in making your argument.

3. Write a paper in which you explain the role that communication plays in behavior, using the ideas and examples from Vanderbilt's essay. Incorporate your work from Question 2 of Questions for Critical Reading.

DAVID FOSTER WALLACE

Novelist and essayist **David Foster Wallace** was the Roy E. Disney Professor of Creative Writing at Pomona College until his death in 2008. Highly respected during his lifetime, he was a recipient of the MacArthur fellowship (colloquially known as the "genius grant") from 1997 to 2002, as well as a winner of the Salon Book Award and the Lannan Literary Award for fiction. His significant publications include the novels *The Broom of the System* (1987) and *Infinite Jest* (1996) as well as *Brief Interviews with Hideous Men* (1999), a collection of short stories. Wallace was also a noted essayist, writing for publications such as *Rolling Stone*, *Harper's Magazine*, and the *Atlantic*. Wallace's *The Pale King* (2011), an unfinished novel, was published three years after his death.

CONSIDER
THE
LOBSTER

And Other Essays

David Foster Wallace

Author of *Infinite Jest*

In *Consider the Lobster and Other Essays* (2005), the collection from which this selection is taken, Wallace explores a broad range of topics, including the adult film industry's Adult Video News Awards, the criticisms of novelist John Updike, Kafka's wit, the political underbelly of dictionary publications, Senator John McCain, and the seductive and disappointing paradox of sports athlete memoirs. While these topics appear to be unrelated, Wallace's versatility exemplifies his common concern with current concepts of morality. This notion of morality is strikingly clear in the title essay "Consider the Lobster," originally published in *Gourmet* magazine.

Wallace finds it curious that lobster is the one creature that is usually cooked while still alive. Though many people find this practice unproblematic, believing that lobsters cannot feel pain, Wallace observes that lobsters can at least exhibit a preference for not being lowered into a pot of boiling water. This observation leads Wallace to question our justifications for eating lobster, and indeed, our eating of animals altogether. Ultimately, "Consider the Lobster" raises many questions about the practices we engage in as a species, our definitions of pain and suffering, and our understanding of the world around us.

▶ TAGS: *food, sentience, animals, moral duty, ethics, suffering*

Questions for Critical Reading

1. How does Wallace feel about eating lobsters? As you read, mark passages that reveal his position on the issue. Does it shift through the essay?

2. Wallace asks, "Is it all right to boil a sentient creature alive just for our gustatory pleasure?" (p. 503). Answer this question for yourself, and then as you read Wallace's essay, locate quotations that support your position.

3. Near the end of his essay, Wallace turns to a discussion of "preference." Read this section closely. What does Wallace mean by "preference"? What role does it play in his overall argument?

Consider the Lobster

The enormous, pungent, and extremely well-marketed Maine Lobster Festival is held every late July in the state's midcoast region, meaning the western side of Penobscot Bay, the nerve stem of Maine's lobster industry. What's called the midcoast runs from Owl's Head and Thomaston in the south to Belfast in the north. (Actually, it might extend all the way up to Bucksport, but we were never able to get farther north than Belfast on Route 1, whose summer traffic is, as you can imagine, unimaginable.) The region's two main communities are Camden, with its very old money and yachty harbor and five-star restaurants and phenomenal B&Bs, and Rockland, a serious old fishing town that hosts the festival every summer in historic Harbor Park, right along the water.[1]

Tourism and lobster are the midcoast region's two main industries, and they're both warm-weather enterprises, and the Maine Lobster Festival represents less an intersection of the industries than a deliberate collision, joyful and lucrative and loud. The assigned subject of this *Gourmet* article is the 56th Annual MLF, 30 July–3 August 2003, whose official theme this year was "Lighthouses, Laughter, and Lobster." Total paid attendance was over 100,000, due partly to a national CNN spot in June during which a senior editor of *Food & Wine* magazine hailed the MLF as one of the best food-themed galas in the world. 2003 festival highlights: concerts by Lee Ann Womack and Orleans, annual Maine Sea Goddess beauty pageant, Saturday's big parade, Sunday's William G. Atwood Memorial Crate Race, annual Amateur Cooking Competition, carnival rides and midway attractions and food booths, and the MLF's Main Eating Tent, where something over 25,000 pounds of fresh-caught Maine lobster is consumed after preparation in the World's Largest Lobster Cooker near the grounds' north entrance. Also available are lobster rolls, lobster turnovers, lobster sauté, Down East lobster salad, lobster bisque, lobster ravioli, and deep-fried lobster dumplings. Lobster thermidor is obtainable at a sit-down restaurant called the Black Pearl on Harbor Park's northwest wharf. A large all-pine booth sponsored by the Maine Lobster Promotion Council has free pamphlets with recipes, eating tips, and Lobster Fun Facts. The winner of Friday's Amateur Cooking Competition prepares Saffron Lobster Ramekins, the recipe for which is now available for public downloading at www.mainelobster festival.com. There are lobster T-shirts and lobster bobblehead dolls and inflatable lobster pool toys and clamp-on lobster hats with big scarlet claws that wobble on springs. Your assigned correspondent saw it all, accompanied by one girlfriend and both his own parents — one of which parents was actually born and raised in Maine, albeit in

---

[1] There's a comprehensive native apothegm: "Camden by the sea, Rockland by the smell." [All notes are Wallace's.]

the extreme northern inland part, which is potato country and a world away from the touristic midcoast.[2]

For practical purposes, everyone knows what a lobster is. As usual, though, there's much more to know than most of us care about — it's all a matter of what your interests are. Taxonomically speaking, a lobster is a marine crustacean of the family Homaridae, characterized by five pairs of jointed legs, the first pair terminating in large pincerish claws used for subduing prey. Like many other species of benthic carnivore, lobsters are both hunters and scavengers. They have stalked eyes, gills on their legs, and antennae. There are a dozen or so different kinds worldwide, of which the relevant species here is the Maine lobster, *Homarus americanus*. The name "lobster" comes from the Old English *loppestre*, which is thought to be a corrupt form of the Latin word for locust combined with the Old English *loppe*, which meant spider.

Moreover, a crustacean is an aquatic arthropod of the class Crustacea, which comprises crabs, shrimp, barnacles, lobsters, and freshwater crayfish. All this is right there in the encyclopedia. And arthropods are members of the phylum Arthropoda, which phylum covers insects, spiders, crustaceans, and centipedes/millipedes, all of whose main commonality, besides the absence of a centralized brain-spine assembly, is a chitinous exoskeleton composed of segments, to which appendages are articulated in pairs.

The point is that lobsters are basically giant sea insects.[3] Like most arthropods, they date from the Jurassic period, biologically so much older than mammalia that they might as well be from another planet. And they are — particularly in their natural brown-green state, brandishing their claws like weapons and with thick antennae awhip — not nice to look at. And it's true that they are garbagemen of the sea, eaters of dead stuff,[4] although they'll also eat some live shellfish, certain kinds of injured fish, and sometimes one another.

> **The point is that lobsters are basically giant sea insects.**

But they are themselves good eating. Or so we think now. Up until sometime in the 1800s, though, lobster was literally low-class food, eaten only by the poor and institutionalized. Even in the harsh penal environment of early America, some colonies had laws against feeding lobsters to inmates more than once a week because it was thought to be cruel and unusual, like making people eat rats. One reason for their low status was how plentiful lobsters were in old New England. "Unbelievable abundance" is how one source describes the situation, including accounts of Plymouth Pilgrims wading out and capturing all they wanted by hand, and of early Boston's seashore being littered with lobsters after hard storms — these latter were treated as a smelly nuisance and ground up for fertilizer. There is also the fact that premodern lobster was cooked dead and then preserved, usually packed in salt or crude hermetic containers. Maine's earliest lobster industry was based around a dozen such seaside canneries in

---

[2] N.B. All personally connected parties have made it clear from the start that they do not want to be talked about in this article.

[3] Midcoasters' native term for a lobster is, in fact, "bug," as in "Come around on Sunday and we'll cook up some bugs."

[4] Factoid: Lobster traps are usually baited with dead herring.

the 1840s, from which lobster was shipped as far away as California, in demand only because it was cheap and high in protein, basically chewable fuel.

Now, of course, lobster is posh, a delicacy, only a step or two down from caviar. The meat is richer and more substantial than most fish, its taste subtle compared to the marine-gaminess of mussels and clams. In the U.S. pop-food imagination, lobster is now the seafood analog to steak, with which it's so often twinned as Surf 'n' Turf on the really expensive part of the chain steakhouse menu.

In fact, one obvious project of the MLF, and of its omnipresently sponsorial Maine Lobster Promotion Council, is to counter the idea that lobster is unusually luxe or unhealthy or expensive, suitable only for effete palates or the occasional blow-the-diet treat. It is emphasized over and over in presentations and pamphlets at the festival that lobster meat has fewer calories, less cholesterol, and less saturated fat than chicken.[5] And in the Main Eating Tent, you can get a "quarter" (industry shorthand for a 1¼-pound lobster), a four-ounce cup of melted butter, a bag of chips, and a soft roll w/ butter-pat for around $12.00, which is only slightly more expensive than supper at McDonald's.

Be apprised, though, that the Maine Lobster Festival's democratization of lobster comes with all the massed inconvenience and aesthetic compromise of real democracy. See, for example, the aforementioned Main Eating Tent, for which there is a constant Disneyland-grade queue, and which turns out to be a square quarter mile of awning-shaded cafeteria lines and rows of long institutional tables at which friend and stranger alike sit cheek by jowl, cracking and chewing and dribbling. It's hot, and the sagged roof traps the steam and the smells, which latter are strong and only partly food-related. It is also loud, and a good percentage of the total noise is masticatory. The suppers come in styrofoam trays, and the soft drinks are iceless and flat, and the coffee is convenience-store coffee in more styrofoam, and the utensils are plastic (there are none of the special long skinny forks for pushing out the tail meat, though a few savvy diners bring their own). Nor do they give you near enough napkins considering how messy lobster is to eat, especially when you're squeezed onto benches alongside children of various ages and vastly different levels of fine-motor development — not to mention the people who've somehow smuggled in their own beer in enormous aisle-blocking coolers, or who all of a sudden produce their own plastic tablecloths and spread them over large portions of tables to try to reserve them (the tables) for their own little groups. And so on. Any one example is no more than a petty inconvenience, of course, but the MLF turns out to be full of irksome little downers like this — see for instance the Main Stage's headliner shows, where it turns out that you have to pay $20 extra for a folding chair if you want to sit down; or the North Tent's mad scramble for the Nyquil-cup-sized samples of finalists' entries handed out after the Cooking Competition; or the much-touted Maine Sea Goddess pageant finals, which turn out to be excruciatingly long and to consist mainly of endless thanks and tributes to local sponsors. Let's not even talk about the grossly inadequate Port-A-San facilities or the fact that there's nowhere to wash your hands before or after eating. What the Maine Lobster Festival really is is a midlevel county fair with a culinary hook, and in this respect it's not

---

[5] Of course, the common practice of dipping the lobster meat in melted butter torpedoes all these happy fat-specs, which none of the council's promotional stuff ever mentions, any more than potato industry PR talks about sour cream and bacon bits.

unlike Tidewater crab festivals, Midwest corn festivals, Texas chili festivals, etc., and shares with these venues the core paradox of all teeming commercial demotic events: It's not for everyone.[6] Nothing against the euphoric senior editor of *Food & Wine*, but I'd be surprised if she'd ever actually been here in Harbor Park, amid crowds of people slapping canal-zone mosquitoes as they eat deep-fried Twinkies and watch Professor Paddywhack, on six-foot stilts in a raincoat with plastic lobsters protruding from all directions on springs, terrify their children.

Lobster is essentially a summer food. This is because we now prefer our lobsters fresh, which means they have to be recently caught, which for both tactical and economic reasons takes place at depths less than 25 fathoms. Lobsters tend to be hungriest and most active (i.e., most trappable) at summer water temperatures of 45–50 degrees. In the autumn, most Maine lobsters migrate out into deeper water, either for warmth or to avoid the heavy waves that pound New England's coast all winter. Some burrow into the bottom. They might hibernate; nobody's sure. Summer is also lobsters' molting season — specifically early- to mid-July. Chitinous arthropods grow by molting, rather the way people have to buy bigger clothes as they age and gain weight. Since lobsters can live to be over 100, they can also get to be quite large, as in 30 pounds or more — though truly senior lobsters are rare now because New England's waters are so heavily trapped.[7] Anyway, hence the culinary distinction between hard- and soft-shell lobsters, the latter sometimes a.k.a. shedders. A soft-shell lobster is one that has recently molted. In midcoast restaurants, the summer menu often offers both kinds, with shedders being slightly cheaper even though they're easier to dismantle and the

10

---

[6] In truth, there's a great deal to be said about the differences between working-class Rockland and the heavily populist flavor of its festival versus comfortable and elitist Camden with its expensive view and shops given entirely over to $200 sweaters and great rows of Victorian homes converted to upscale B&Bs. And about these differences as two sides of the great coin that is U.S. tourism. Very little of which will be said here, except to amplify the above-mentioned paradox and to reveal your assigned correspondent's own preferences. I confess that I have never understood why so many people's idea of a fun vacation is to don flip-flops and sunglasses and crawl through maddening traffic to loud, hot, crowded tourist venues in order to sample a "local flavor" that is by definition ruined by the presence of tourists. This may (as my festival companions keep pointing out) all be a matter of personality and hardwired taste: the fact that I do not like tourist venues means that I'll never understand their appeal and so am probably not the one to talk about it (the supposed appeal). But, since this FN will almost surely not survive magazine-editing anyway, here goes:
   As I see it, it probably really is good for the soul to be a tourist, even if it's only once in a while. Not good for the soul in a refreshing or enlivening way, though, but rather in a grim, steely-eyed, let's-look-honestly-at-the-facts-and-find-some-way-to-deal-with-them way. My personal experience has not been that traveling around the country is broadening or relaxing, or that radical changes in place and context have a salutary effect, but rather that intranational tourism is radically constricting, and humbling in the hardest way — hostile to my fantasy of being a true individual, of living somehow outside and above it all. (Coming up is the part that my companions find especially unhappy and repellent, a sure way to spoil the fun of vacation travel.) To be a mass tourist, for me, is to become a pure late-date American: alien, ignorant, greedy for something you cannot ever have, disappointed in a way you can never admit. It is to spoil, by way of sheer ontology, the very unspoiledness you are there to experience. It is to impose yourself on places that in all non-economic ways would be better, realer, without you. It is, in lines and gridlock and transaction after transaction, to confront a dimension of yourself that is as inescapable as it is painful: As a tourist, you become economically significant but existentially loathsome, an insect on a dead thing.
[7] Datum: In a good year, the U.S. industry produces around 80,000,000 pounds of lobster, and Maine accounts for more than half that total.

meat is allegedly sweeter. The reason for the discount is that a molting lobster uses a layer of seawater for insulation while its new shell is hardening, so there's slightly less actual meat when you crack open a shedder, plus a redolent gout of water that gets all over everything and can sometimes jet out lemonlike and catch a tablemate right in the eye. If it's winter or you're buying lobster someplace far from New England, on the other hand, you can almost bet that the lobster is a hard-shell, which for obvious reasons travel better.

As an à la carte entrée, lobster can be baked, broiled, steamed, grilled, sautéed, stir-fried, or microwaved. The most common method, though, is boiling. If you're someone who enjoys having lobster at home, this is probably the way you do it, since boiling is so easy. You need a large kettle w/ cover, which you fill about half full with water (the standard advice is that you want 2.5 quarts of water per lobster). Seawater is optimal, or you can add two tbsp salt per quart from the tap. It also helps to know how much your lobsters weigh. You get the water boiling, put in the lobsters one at a time, cover the kettle, and bring it back up to a boil. Then you bank the heat and let the kettle simmer — ten minutes for the first pound of lobster, then three minutes for each pound after that. (This is assuming you've got hard-shell lobsters, which, again, if you don't live between Boston and Halifax is probably what you've got. For shedders, you're supposed to subtract three minutes from the total.) The reason the kettle's lobsters turn scarlet is that boiling somehow suppresses every pigment in their chitin but one. If you want an easy test of whether the lobsters are done, you try pulling on one of their antennae — if it comes out of the head with minimal effort, you're ready to eat.

A detail so obvious that most recipes don't even bother to mention it is that each lobster is supposed to be alive when you put it in the kettle. This is part of lobster's modern appeal — it's the freshest food there is. There's no decomposition between harvesting and eating. And not only do lobsters require no cleaning or dressing or plucking, they're relatively easy for vendors to keep alive. They come up alive in the traps, are placed in containers of seawater, and can — so long as the water's aerated and the animals' claws are pegged or banded to keep them from tearing one another up under the stresses of captivity[8] — survive right up until they're boiled. Most of us have been in supermarkets or restaurants that feature tanks of live lobsters, from which you can pick out your supper while it watches you point. And part of the overall spectacle of the Maine Lobster Festival is that you can see actual lobstermen's vessels docking at the wharves along the northeast grounds and unloading fresh-caught product, which is transferred by hand or cart 150 yards to the great clear tanks stacked up around the festival's cooker — which is, as mentioned, billed as the World's Largest Lobster Cooker and can process over 100 lobsters at a time for the Main Eating Tent.

---

[8] N.B. Similar reasoning underlies the practice of what's termed "debeaking" broiler chickens and brood hens in modern factory farms. Maximum commercial efficiency requires that enormous poultry populations be confined in unnaturally close quarters, under which conditions many birds go crazy and peck one another to death. As a purely observational side-note, be apprised that debeaking is usually an automated process and that the chickens receive no anesthetic. It's not clear to me whether most *Gourmet* readers know about debeaking, or about related practices like dehorning cattle in commercial feed lots, cropping swine's tails in factory hog farms to keep psychotically bored neighbors from chewing them off, and so forth. It so happens that your assigned correspondent knew almost nothing about standard meat-industry operations before starting work on this article.

So then here is a question that's all but unavoidable at the World's Largest Lobster Cooker, and may arise in kitchens across the U.S.: Is it all right to boil a sentient creature alive just for our gustatory pleasure? A related set of concerns: Is the previous question irksomely PC or sentimental? What does "all right" even mean in this context? Is the whole thing just a matter of personal choice?

As you may or may not know, a certain well-known group called People for the Ethical Treatment of Animals thinks that the morality of lobster-boiling is not just a matter of individual conscience. In fact, one of the very first things we hear about the MLF . . . well, to set the scene: We're coming in by cab from the almost indescribably odd and rustic Knox County Airport[9] very late on the night before the festival opens, sharing the cab with a wealthy political consultant who lives on Vinalhaven Island in the bay half the year (he's headed for the island ferry in Rockland). The consultant and cabdriver are responding to informal journalistic probes about how people who live in the midcoast region actually view the MLF, as in is the festival just a big-dollar tourist thing or is it something local residents look forward to attending, take genuine civic pride in, etc. The cabdriver (who's in his seventies, one of apparently a whole platoon of retirees the cab company puts on to help with the summer rush, and wears a U.S.-flag lapel pin, and drives in what can only be called a very *deliberate* way) assures us that locals do endorse and enjoy the MLF, although he himself hasn't gone in years, and now come to think of it no one he and his wife know has, either. However, the demilocal consultant's been to recent festivals a couple times (one gets the impression it was at his wife's behest), of which his most vivid impression was that "you have to line up for an ungodly long time to get your lobsters, and meanwhile there are all these ex-flower children coming up and down along the line handing out pamphlets that say the lobsters die in terrible pain and you shouldn't eat them."

And it turns out that the post-hippies of the consultant's recollection were activists from PETA. There were no PETA people in obvious view at the 2003 MLF,[10] but they've been conspicuous at many of the recent festivals. Since at least the mid-1990s, articles in everything from the *Camden Herald* to the *New York Times* have described PETA urging boycotts of the Maine Lobster Festival, often deploying celebrity spokesmen like Mary Tyler Moore for open letters and ads saying stuff like "Lobsters are

15

---

[9] The terminal used to be somebody's house, for example, and the lost-luggage-reporting room was clearly once a pantry.

[10] It turned out that one Mr. William R. Rivas-Rivas, a high-ranking PETA official out of the group's Virginia headquarters, was indeed there this year, albeit solo, working the festival's main and side entrances on Saturday, 2 August, handing out pamphlets and adhesive stickers emblazoned with "Being Boiled Hurts," which is the tagline in most of PETA's published material about lobsters. I learned that he'd been there only later, when speaking with Mr. Rivas-Rivas on the phone. I'm not sure how we missed seeing him *in situ* at the festival, and I can't see much to do except apologize for the oversight—although it's also true that Saturday was the day of the big MLF parade through Rockland, which basic journalistic responsibility seemed to require going to (and which, with all due respect, meant that Saturday was maybe not the best day for PETA to work the Harbor Park grounds, especially if it was going to be just one person for one day, since a lot of diehard MLF partisans were off-site watching the parade [which, again with no offense intended, was in truth kind of cheesy and boring, consisting mostly of slow homemade floats and various midcoast people waving at one another, and with an extremely annoying man dressed as Blackbeard ranging up and down the length of the crowd saying, "Arrr" over and over and brandishing a plastic sword at people, etc.; plus it rained]).

extraordinarily sensitive" and "To me, eating a lobster is out of the question." More concrete is the oral testimony of Dick, our florid and extremely gregarious rental-car liaison,[11] to the effect that PETA's been around so much during recent years that a kind of brittlely tolerant homeostasis now obtains between the activists and the festival's locals, e.g.: "We had some incidents a couple years ago. One lady took most of her clothes off and painted herself like a lobster, almost got herself arrested. But for the most part they're let alone. [Rapid series of small ambiguous laughs, which with Dick happens a lot.] They do their thing and we do our thing."

This whole interchange takes place on Route 1, 30 July, during a four-mile, 50-minute ride from the airport[12] to the dealership to sign car-rental papers. Several irreproducible segues down the road from the PETA anecdotes, Dick —whose son-in-law happens to be a professional lobsterman and one of the Main Eating Tent's regular suppliers —explains what he and his family feel is the crucial mitigating factor in the whole morality-of-boiling-lobsters-alive issue: "There's a part of the brain in people and animals that lets us feel pain, and lobsters' brains don't have this part."

Besides the fact that it's incorrect in about nine different ways, the main reason Dick's statement is interesting is that its thesis is more or less echoed by the festival's own pronouncement on lobsters and pain, which is part of a Test Your Lobster IQ quiz that appears in the 2003 MLF program courtesy of the Maine Lobster Promotion Council:

> The nervous system of a lobster is very simple, and is in fact most similar to the nervous system of the grasshopper. It is decentralized with no brain. There is no cerebral cortex, which in humans is the area of the brain that gives the experience of pain.

Though it sounds more sophisticated, a lot of the neurology in this latter claim is still either false or fuzzy. The human cerebral cortex is the brain-part that deals with higher faculties like reason, metaphysical self-awareness, language, etc. Pain reception is known to be part of a much older and more primitive system of nociceptors and prostaglandins that are managed by the brain stem and thalamus.[13] On the other hand, it is true that the cerebral cortex is involved in what's variously called suffering, distress, or the emotional experience of pain —i.e., experiencing painful stimuli as unpleasant, very unpleasant, unbearable, and so on.

---

[11] By profession, Dick is actually a car salesman; the midcoast region's National Car Rental franchise operates out of a Chevy dealership in Thomaston.

[12] The short version regarding why we were back at the airport after already arriving the previous night involves lost luggage and a miscommunication about where and what the midcoast's National franchise was —Dick came out personally to the airport and got us, out of no evident motive but kindness. (He also talked nonstop the entire way, with a very distinctive speaking style that can be described only as manically laconic; the truth is that I now know more about this man than I do about some members of my own family.)

[13] To elaborate by way of example: The common experience of accidentally touching a hot stove and yanking your hand back before you're even aware that anything's going on is explained by the fact that many of the processes by which we detect and avoid painful stimuli do not involve the cortex. In the case of the hand and stove, the brain is bypassed altogether; all the important neurochemical action takes place in the spine.

Before we go any further, let's acknowledge that the questions of whether and how different kinds of animals feel pain, and of whether and why it might be justifiable to inflict pain on them in order to eat them, turn out to be extremely complex and difficult. And comparative neuroanatomy is only part of the problem. Since pain is a totally subjective mental experience, we do not have direct access to anyone or anything's pain but our own; and even just the principles by which we can infer that other human beings experience pain and have a legitimate interest in not feeling pain involve hardcore philosophy — metaphysics, epistemology, value theory, ethics. The fact that even the most highly evolved nonhuman mammals can't use language to communicate with us about their subjective mental experience is only the first layer of additional complication in trying to extend our reasoning about pain and morality to animals. And everything gets progressively more abstract and convoluted as we move farther and farther out from the higher-type mammals into cattle and swine and dogs and cats and rodents, and then birds and fish, and finally invertebrates like lobsters.

The more important point here, though, is that the whole animal-cruelty-and-eating issue is not just complex, it's also uncomfortable. It is, at any rate, uncomfortable for me, and for just about everyone I know who enjoys a variety of foods and yet does not want to see herself as cruel or unfeeling. As far as I can tell, my own main way of dealing with this conflict has been to avoid thinking about the whole unpleasant thing. I should add that it appears to me unlikely that many readers of *Gourmet* wish to think about it, either, or to be queried about the morality of their eating habits in the pages of a culinary monthly. Since, however, the assigned subject of this article is what it was like to attend the 2003 MLF, and thus to spend several days in the midst of a great mass of Americans all eating lobster, and thus to be more or less impelled to think hard about lobster and the experience of buying and eating lobster, it turns out that there is no honest way to avoid certain moral questions.

There are several reasons for this. For one thing, it's not just that lobsters get boiled alive, it's that you do it yourself — or at least it's done specifically for you, on-site.[14] As mentioned, the World's Largest Lobster Cooker, which is highlighted as an attraction in the festival's program, is right out there on the MLF's north grounds for everyone to see. Try to imagine a Nebraska Beef Festival[15] at which part of the festivities is

20

---

[14] Morality-wise, let's concede that this cuts both ways. Lobster-eating is at least not abetted by the system of corporate factory farms that produces most beef, pork, and chicken. Because, if nothing else, of the way they're marketed and packaged for sale, we eat these latter meats without having to consider that they were once conscious, sentient creatures to whom horrible things were done. (N.B. "Horrible" here meaning really, really horrible. Write off to PETA or peta.org for their free "Meet Your Meat" video, narrated by Mr. Alec Baldwin, if you want to see just about everything meat-related you don't want to see or think about. [N.B.2 Not that PETA's any sort of font of unspun truth. Like many partisans in complex moral disputes, the PETA people are fanatics, and a lot of their rhetoric seems simplistic and self-righteous. But this particular video, replete with actual factory-farm and corporate-slaughterhouse footage, is both credible and traumatizing.])

[15] Is it significant that "lobster," "fish," and "chicken" are our culture's words for both the animal and the meat, whereas most mammals seem to require euphemisms like "beef" and "pork" that help us separate the meat we eat from the living creature the meat once was? Is this evidence that some kind of deep unease about eating higher animals is endemic enough to show up in English usage, but that the unease diminishes as we move out of the mammalian order? (And is "lamb"/"lamb" the counterexample that sinks the whole theory, or are there special, biblico-historical reasons for that equivalence?)

watching trucks pull up and the live cattle get driven down the ramp and slaughtered right there on the World's Largest Killing Floor or something — there's no way.

The intimacy of the whole thing is maximized at home, which of course is where most lobster gets prepared and eaten (although note already the semiconscious euphemism "prepared," which in the case of lobsters really means killing them right there in our kitchens). The basic scenario is that we come in from the store and make our little preparations like getting the kettle filled and boiling, and then we lift the lobsters out of the bag or whatever retail container they came home in . . . whereupon some uncomfortable things start to happen. However stuporous a lobster is from the trip home, for instance, it tends to come alarmingly to life when placed in boiling water. If you're tilting it from a container into the steaming kettle, the lobster will sometimes try to cling to the container's sides or even to hook its claws over the kettle's rim like a person trying to keep from going over the edge of a roof. And worse is when the lobster's fully immersed. Even if you cover the kettle and turn away, you can usually hear the cover rattling and clanking as the lobster tries to push it off. Or the creature's claws scraping the sides of the kettle as it thrashes around. The lobster, in other words, behaves very much as you or I would behave if we were plunged into boiling water (with the obvious exception of screaming[16]). A blunter way to say this is that the lobster acts as if it's in terrible pain, causing some cooks to leave the kitchen altogether and to take one of those little lightweight plastic oven-timers with them into another room and wait until the whole process is over.

> **The lobster . . . behaves very much as you or I would behave if we were plunged into boiling water (with the obvious exception of screaming).**

There happen to be two main criteria that most ethicists agree on for determining whether a living creature has the capacity to suffer and so has genuine interests that it may or may not be our moral duty to consider.[17] One is how much of the neurological hardware required for pain-experience the animal comes equipped with — nociceptors, prostaglandins, neuronal opioid receptors, etc. The other criterion is whether the animal demonstrates behavior associated with pain. And it takes a lot of intellectual gymnastics and behaviorist hairsplitting not to see struggling, thrashing, and lid-clattering as just such pain-behavior. According to marine zoologists, it usually takes

---

[16] There's a relevant populist myth about the high-pitched whistling sound that sometimes issues from a pot of boiling lobster. The sound is really vented steam from the layer of seawater between the lobster's flesh and its carapace (this is why shedders whistle more than hard-shells), but the pop version has it that the sound is the lobster's rabbit-like death-scream. Lobsters communicate via pheromones in their urine and don't have anything close to the vocal equipment for screaming, but the myth's very persistent — which might, once again, point to a low-level cultural unease about the boiling thing.

[17] "Interests" basically means strong and legitimate preferences, which obviously require some degree of consciousness, responsiveness to stimuli, etc. See, for instance, the utilitarian philosopher Peter Singer, whose 1974 *Animal Liberation* is more or less the bible of the modern animal-rights movement:

> It would be nonsense to say that it was not in the interests of a stone to be kicked along the road by a schoolboy. A stone does not have interests because it cannot suffer. Nothing that we can do to it could possibly make any difference to its welfare. A mouse, on the other hand, does have an interest in not being kicked along the road, because it will suffer if it is.

lobsters between 35 and 45 seconds to die in boiling water. (No source I could find talks about how long it takes them to die in superheated steam; one rather hopes it's faster.)

There are, of course, other ways to kill your lobster on-site and so achieve maximum freshness. Some cooks' practice is to drive a sharp heavy knife point-first into a spot just above the midpoint between the lobster's eyestalks (more or less where the Third Eye is in human foreheads). This is alleged either to kill the lobster instantly or to render it insensate, and is said at least to eliminate some of the cowardice involved in throwing a creature into boiling water and then fleeing the room. As far as I can tell from talking to proponents of the knife-in-head method, the idea is that it's more violent but ultimately more merciful, plus that a willingness to exert personal agency and accept responsibility for stabbing the lobster's head honors the lobster somehow and entitles one to eat it (there's often a vague sort of Native American spirituality-of-the-hunt flavor to pro-knife arguments). But the problem with the knife method is basic biology: Lobsters' nervous systems operate off not one but several ganglia, a.k.a. nerve bundles, which are sort of wired in series and distributed all along the lobster's underside, from stem to stern. And disabling only the frontal ganglion does not normally result in quick death or unconsciousness.

Another alternative is to put the lobster in cold saltwater and then very slowly bring it up to a full boil. Cooks who advocate this method are going on the analogy to a frog, which can supposedly be kept from jumping out of a boiling pot by heating the water incrementally. In order to save a lot of research-summarizing, I'll simply assure you that the analogy between frogs and lobsters turns out not to hold — plus, if the kettle's water isn't aerated seawater, the immersed lobster suffers from slow suffocation, although usually not decisive enough suffocation to keep it from still thrashing and clattering when the water gets hot enough to kill it. In fact, lobsters boiled incrementally often display a whole bonus set of gruesome, convulsionlike reactions that you don't see in regular boiling.

Ultimately, the only certain virtues of the home-lobotomy and slow-heating methods are comparative, because there are even worse/crueler ways people prepare lobster. Time-thrifty cooks sometimes microwave them alive (usually after poking several vent-holes in the carapace, which is a precaution most shellfish-microwavers learn about the hard way). Live dismemberment, on the other hand, is big in Europe — some chefs cut the lobster in half before cooking; others like to tear off the claws and tail and toss only these parts into the pot.   25

And there's more unhappy news respecting suffering-criterion number one. Lobsters don't have much in the way of eyesight or hearing, but they do have an exquisite tactile sense, one facilitated by hundreds of thousands of tiny hairs that protrude through their carapace. "Thus it is," in the words of T. M. Prudden's industry classic *About Lobster*, "that although encased in what seems a solid, impenetrable armor, the lobster can receive stimuli and impressions from without as readily as if it possessed a soft and delicate skin." And lobsters do have nociceptors,[18] as well as invertebrate

---

[18] This is the neurological term for special pain-receptors that are "sensitive to potentially damaging extremes of temperature, to mechanical forces, and to chemical substances which are released when body tissues are damaged."

versions of the prostaglandins and major neurotransmitters via which our own brains register pain.

Lobsters do not, on the other hand, appear to have the equipment for making or absorbing natural opioids like endorphins and enkephalins, which are what more advanced nervous systems use to try to handle intense pain. From this fact, though, one could conclude either that lobsters are maybe even *more* vulnerable to pain, since they lack mammalian nervous systems' built-in analgesia, or, instead, that the absence of natural opioids implies an absence of the really intense pain-sensations that natural opioids are designed to mitigate. I for one can detect a marked upswing in mood as I contemplate this latter possibility. It could be that their lack of endorphin/enkephalin hardware means that lobsters' raw subjective experience of pain is so radically different from mammals' that it may not even deserve the term "pain." Perhaps lobsters are more like those frontal-lobotomy patients one reads about who report experiencing pain in a totally different way than you and I. These patients evidently do feel physical pain, neurologically speaking, but don't dislike it—though neither do they like it; it's more that they feel it but don't feel anything *about* it—the point being that the pain is not distressing to them or something they want to get away from. Maybe lobsters, who are also without frontal lobes, are detached from the neurological-registration-of-injury-or-hazard we call pain in just the same way. There is, after all, a difference between (1) pain as a purely neurological event, and (2) actual suffering, which seems crucially to involve an emotional component, an awareness of pain as unpleasant, as something to fear/dislike/want to avoid.

Still, after all the abstract intellection, there remain the facts of the frantically clanking lid, the pathetic clinging to the edge of the pot. Standing at the stove, it is hard to deny in any meaningful way that this is a living creature experiencing pain and wishing to avoid/escape the painful experience. To my lay mind, the lobster's behavior in the kettle appears to be the expression of a *preference*; and it may well be that an ability to form preferences is the decisive criterion for real suffering.[19] The logic of this (preference → suffering) relation may be easiest to see in the negative case. If you cut certain kinds of worms in half, the halves will often keep crawling around and going about their vermiform business as if nothing had happened. When we assert, based on their post-op behavior, that these worms appear not to be suffering, what we're really saying is that there's no sign the worms know anything bad has happened or would *prefer* not to have gotten cut in half.

Lobsters, though, are known to exhibit preferences. Experiments have shown that they can detect changes of only a degree or two in water temperature; one reason for their complex migratory cycles (which can often cover 100-plus miles a year) is to pur-

---

[19] "Preference" is maybe roughly synonymous with "interests," but it is a better term for our purposes because it's less abstractly philosophical—"preference" seems more personal, and it's the whole idea of a living creature's personal experience that's at issue.

sue the temperatures they like best.[20] And, as mentioned, they're bottom-dwellers and do not like bright light—if a tank of food-lobsters is out in the sunlight or a store's fluorescence, the lobsters will always congregate in whatever part is darkest. Fairly solitary in the ocean, they also clearly dislike the crowding that's part of their captivity in tanks, since (as also mentioned) one reason why lobsters' claws are banded on capture is to keep them from attacking one another under the stress of close-quarter storage.

In any event, at the MLF, standing by the bubbling tanks outside the World's Largest Lobster Cooker, watching the fresh-caught lobsters pile over one another, wave their hobbled claws impotently, huddle in the rear corners, or scrabble frantically back from the glass as you approach, it is difficult not to sense that they're unhappy, or frightened, even if it's some rudimentary version of these feelings . . . and, again, why does rudimentariness even enter into it? Why is a primitive, inarticulate form of suffering less urgent or uncomfortable for the person who's helping to inflict it by paying for the food it results in? I'm not trying to give you a PETA-like screed here—at least I don't think so. I'm trying, rather, to work out and articulate some of the troubling questions that arise amid all the laughter and saltation and community pride of the Maine Lobster Festival. The truth is that if you, the festival attendee, permit yourself to think that lobsters can suffer and would rather not, the MLF begins to take on the aspect of something like a Roman circus or medieval torture-fest.

Does that comparison seem a bit much? If so, exactly why? Or what about this one: Is it possible that future generations will regard our present agribusiness and eating practices in much the same way we now view Nero's entertainments or Mengele's experiments? My own initial reaction is that such a comparison is hysterical, extreme—and yet the reason it seems extreme to me appears to be that I believe animals are less morally important than human beings;[21] and when it comes to defending such a belief, even to myself, I have to acknowledge that (a) I have an obvious selfish

---

[20] Of course, the most common sort of counterargument here would begin by objecting that "like best" is really just a metaphor, and a misleadingly anthropomorphic one at that. The counterarguer would posit that the lobster seeks to maintain a certain optimal ambient temperature out of nothing but unconscious instinct (with a similar explanation for the low-light affinities upcoming in the main text). The thrust of such a counterargument will be that the lobster's thrashings and clankings in the kettle express not unpreferred pain but involuntary reflexes, like your leg shooting out when the doctor hits your knee. Be advised that there are professional scientists, including many researchers who use animals in experiments, who hold to the view that nonhuman creatures have no real feelings at all, merely "behaviors." Be further advised that this view has a long history that goes all the way back to Descartes, although its modern support comes mostly from behaviorist psychology.

To these what-looks-like-pain-is-really-just-reflexes counterarguments, however, there happen to be all sorts of scientific and pro-animal rights counter-counterarguments. And then further attempted rebuttals and redirects, and so on. Suffice it to say that both the scientific and the philosophical arguments on either side of the animal-suffering issue are involved, abstruse, technical, often informed by self-interest or ideology, and in the end so totally inconclusive that as a practical matter, in the kitchen or restaurant, it all still seems to come down to individual conscience, going with (no pun) your gut.

[21] Meaning *a lot* less important, apparently, since the moral comparison here is not the value of one human's life vs. the value of one animal's life, but rather the value of one animal's life vs. the value of one human's taste for a particular kind of protein. Even the most diehard carniphile will acknowledge that it's possible to live and eat well without consuming animals.

interest in this belief, since I like to eat certain kinds of animals and want to be able to keep doing it, and (b) I haven't succeeded in working out any sort of personal ethical system in which the belief is truly defensible instead of just selfishly convenient.

Given this article's venue and my own lack of culinary sophistication, I'm curious about whether the reader can identify with any of these reactions and acknowledgments and discomforts. I'm also concerned not to come off as shrill or preachy when what I really am is more like confused. For those *Gourmet* readers who enjoy well-prepared and -presented meals involving beef, veal, lamb, pork, chicken, lobster, etc.: Do you think much about the (possible) moral status and (probable) suffering of the animals involved? If you do, what ethical convictions have you worked out that permit you not just to eat but to savor and enjoy flesh-based viands (since of course refined *enjoyment*, rather than mere ingestion, is the whole point of gastronomy)? If, on the other hand, you'll have no truck with confusions or convictions and regard stuff like the previous paragraph as just so much fatuous navel-gazing, what makes it feel truly okay, inside, to just dismiss the whole thing out of hand? That is, is your refusal to think about any of this the product of actual thought, or is it just that you don't want to think about it? And if the latter, then why not? Do you ever think, even idly, about the possible reasons for your reluctance to think about it? I am not trying to bait anyone here — I'm genuinely curious. After all, isn't being extra aware and attentive and thoughtful about one's food and its overall context part of what distinguishes a real gourmet? Or is all the gourmet's extra attention and sensibility just supposed to be sensuous? Is it really all just a matter of taste and presentation?

These last few queries, though, while sincere, obviously involve much larger and more abstract questions about the connections (if any) between aesthetics and morality — about what the adjective in a phrase like "The Magazine of Good Living" is really supposed to mean — and these questions lead straightaway into such deep and treacherous waters that it's probably best to stop the public discussion right here. There are limits to what even interested persons can ask of each other.

Exploring Context

1. Explore the website for the Maine Lobster Festival (mainelobsterfestival.com). How do both the design and content of the site reflect Wallace's experience attending the festival? Is there anything on the site that addresses the ethical concerns that Wallace raises? Why would the organizers of the festival include or omit such information? Why do you think Wallace raises these concerns?

2. Watch the YouTube video "How to Boil a Live Maine Lobster" by Dan "The Lobster Man" of Lobster Gram. How does Wallace's essay change your reaction to this video? In what ways does the video address Wallace's points about lobsters? Incorporate your response to Question 2 of Questions for Critical Reading.

3. Wallace's essay was originally published in *Gourmet* magazine. Visit Epicurious (epicurious.com), a website with a similar audience. Based on what you find there, how do you think Wallace's original audience reacted to his essay? Why might have he written the essay this way for such a magazine?

Questions for Connecting

1. In "Ethics and the New Genetics" (p. 133), the Dalai Lama calls for a "moral compass" to guide us through the rapid advances of science and technology. How can you synthesize the Dalai Lama's position on ethics with Wallace's discussion of lobsters? Pay particular attention to Wallace's suggestion that lobsters have clear "preferences." Is preference sufficient for a moral compass? Use your analysis of "preference" from Question 3 of Questions for Critical Reading.

2. Considering the information that Elizabeth Dickinson presents in "The Future of Food" (p. 144), to what extent are Wallace's musings a moral luxury? That is, given the complex issues involved in feeding a hungry world, can we afford to consider the kinds of ethical questions Wallace raises about lobsters?

3. Both Wallace and Hal Herzog, in "Animals Like Us" (p. 242), are concerned with the relationships between humans and animals. Synthesize their positions to articulate an ethical standard for these relationships. Is there a way to escape the "troubled middle" that Herzog discusses?

Language Matters

1. Wallace's writing makes frequent use of footnotes. How do they function in his text? When should you use footnotes in your own writing? In considering your response, also review the proper format for footnotes using a grammar handbook or other reliable reference resource.

2. Narrowing one's topic can be a challenge, even for writers like Wallace. Imagine a "research pyramid" for this essay, with the broadest category at the bottom and the most ridiculously specific one at the top point of the pyramid. How many different levels can you find for this essay? Would the essay have been as strong if it were less or more specific? Why did Wallace choose this level of the pyramid for his work?

3. Imagine you could invite Wallace into the discussion in your classroom. What questions would you want to ask him about this essay? Use that experience to think about larger issues. What are the limits of written discourse? How might you anticipate your audience's questions when you write?

Assignments for Writing

1. Wallace asks, "Is it possible that future generations will regard our present agribusiness and eating practices in much the same way we now view Nero's entertainments or Mengele's experiments?" (p. 509). Write a paper in which you address Wallace's query. Rather than answering Wallace's admittedly extreme future with a yes or no, consider instead the implications of his scenario as you build an argument that articulates how we might define an ethics of creature-based food.

2. Using Wallace for support, take the point of view of either a committed meat eater or a committed vegetarian, arguing your position by drawing on food-related issues such as

health, hunger, and treatment of animals. Locate support for your position in Wallace's essay.

3. Wallace suggests an ethics built on "preference"—lobsters, that is, clearly would prefer not to be boiled alive. Evaluate the possibility of a preference-based ethics by locating your own example and connecting it to Wallace's discussion of suffering in animals. Is preference sufficient to make moral and ethical decisions? Can it be expanded to other ethical situations or is it limited to questions of food? You may also want to draw on your work in Question 1 of Questions for Connecting.

BILL WASIK

Bill Wasik is a senior editor at *Wired* magazine. Prior to his work there, he was an editor at *Harper's Magazine* and the *Weekly Week*. Wasik is the author of *And Then There's This: How Stories Live and Die in Viral Culture* (2009), coauthor of *Rabid: A Cultural History of the World's Most Diabolical Virus* (2012), as well as the editor of *Submersion Journalism: Reporting in the Radical First Person from Harper's Magazine* (2008), a collection of essays from *Harper's*. Wasik is perhaps best known for inventing the flash mob, which he created as a social experiment in 2003.

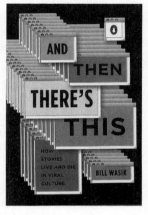

The book from which this selection is taken, *And Then There's This*, investigates our current media culture and the surges of interest that spread throughout our society. He defines these moments of intense, short-lived interest in an event or a person as a "nanostory." Throughout the book, Wasik investigates the people, the culture, the media, and the politics that create our current interest in these nanostories.

In the chapter titled "My Crowd Experiment: The Mob Project," Wasik describes the beginning of the flash mob as a social experiment to satiate his thirst for something new and interesting; simply, he was bored. Yet while the flash mob began as a prank Wasik initiated for the sake of entertainment and curiosity, it quickly took on a life of its own, becoming a "meme" (p. 519) and coming to hold a recognized place in our culture. In looking at the flash mob as a meme, Wasik explores the social forces that enabled the spread of this idea as well as the biological reasoning for our desire to jump on the bandwagon and be part of something big.

Have you ever participated in a flash mob? What memes have you helped spread through e-mail or social media like Facebook?

▶ TAGS: *flash mobs, bandwagon effect, memes, boredom, influence, groups, multitasking*

Questions for Critical Reading

1. Write your own definition of a "flash mob." As you read, mark those places in the text where Wasik defines the term. What makes a flash mob? What are its essential components?

2. You may have heard of Internet memes. Find an example of one from your own experience or by researching online. How does Wasik define "meme"? What role do memes play in our culture today?

3. What purpose, if any, do flash mobs serve? Are they useful forms of social organization, disruptive gatherings, or nothing more than entertainment? As you read Wasik's text, look for passages that support your position.

My Crowd Experiment: The Mob Project

Boredom

I started the Mob Project because I was bored . . . and perhaps that explanation seems simple enough. But before we proceed to the rise and fall of my peculiar social experiment, I think that boredom is worth interrogating in some detail. The first recorded use of the term, per the *OED*, did not take place until 1852, in Charles Dickens's *Bleak House*, Chapter 12. It is deployed by way of describing Lady Dedlock, a woman with whose habits of mind I often find myself in sympathy:

> Concert, assembly, opera, theatre, drive, nothing is new to my Lady, under the worn-out heavens. Only last Sunday, when poor wretches were gay — . . . encompassing Paris with dancing, lovemaking, wine-drinking, tobacco-smoking, tomb-visiting, billiard, card and domino playing, quack-doctoring, and much murderous refuse, animate and inanimate — only last Sunday, my Lady, in the desolation of Boredom and the clutch of Giant Despair, almost hated her own maid for being in spirits.

Psychologists have been trying to elucidate the nature of boredom since at least Sigmund Freud, who identified a "lassitude" in young women that he attributed to penis envy. In 1951, Otto Fenichel described boredom as a state where the "drive-tension" is present but the "drive-aim" is absent, a state of mind that he said could be "schematically formulated" in this enigmatic but undeniably evocative way: "I am excited. If I allow this excitation to continue I shall get anxious. Therefore I tell myself, I am not at all excited, I don't want to do anything. Simultaneously, however, I feel I do want to do something; but I have forgotten my original goal and do not know what I want to do. The external world must do something to relieve me of my tension without making me anxious."

In the 1970s, researchers developed various tests designed, in part to assess the boredom-plagued, from the Imaginal Processes Inventor (Singer and Antrobus, 1970) to the Sensation Seeking Scale (Zuckerman, Eysenck & Eysenck, 1978). But it was not until 1986, with the unveiling of the Boredom Proneness Scale (BPS), that the propensity toward boredom in the individual could be comprehensively measured and reckoned with. The test was created by Richard Farmer and Norman Sundberg, both of the University of Oregon, and it has allowed researchers in the two decades since to tally up boredom's grim wages. The boredom-prone, we have discovered, display higher rates of procrastination, inattention, narcissism, poor work performance, and "solitary/sexual behaviors" including both onanism and the resort to pornography.

The BPS test consists of twenty-eight statements to which respondents answer true or false, with a point assessed for each boredom-aligned choice, e.g.:

1. *It is easy for me to concentrate on my activities.* [*+1 for False.*]

5. *I am often trapped in situations where I have to do meaningless things.* [*+1 for True.*]

25. *Unless I am doing something exciting, even dangerous, I feel half-dead and dull.* [*+1 for True.*]

Farmer and Sundberg found the average score to be roughly 10. My own score is 16, and indeed when I peruse the list of correct answers I feel as if I am scanning a psychological diagnosis of myself. I *do* find it hard to concentrate; I *do* find myself constantly trapped doing meaningless things; and half-dead or dull does not begin to describe how I feel when I lack a project that is adequately transgressive or, worse, find myself exiled somewhere among the slow-witted. I worry about other matters while I work (#2), and I find that time passes slowly (#3). I am bad at waiting patiently (#15), and in fact when I am forced to wait in line, I get restless (#17). Even for those questions to which I give the allegedly nonbored answer, I tend to feel I am forfeiting the points on some technicality. Yes, I do have "projects in mind, all the time" (#7)—so many that few of them ever get acted upon, precisely because my desperate craving for variety means that I am rarely satisfied for very long with even projects that are hypothetical. Yes, others do tend to say that I am a "creative or imaginative person" (#22), but honestly I think this is due to declining standards.

And no, I do not often find myself "at loose ends" (#4), sitting around doing nothing (#14), with "time on my hands" (#16), without "something to do or see to keep me interested" (#13). But such has been true for me only since the start of this viral decade, when my idle stretches have been erased by the grace of the Internet, with its soothingly fast and infinitely available distractions, engaging me for hours on end without assuaging my fundamental boredom in any way. In fact, I would advance the prediction that answers to these latter four questions have become meaningless in recent years, when all of our interactive technologies—video games and mobile devices as well as the web—have kept those of us most boredom-prone from generally thinking, as we might while watching TV, that we are "doing nothing," even if in every practical sense we are doing precisely that. I fear I am ahead of the science, however, because I have been unable to find any study that either supports or undercuts this conjecture. I put the question to Richard Farmer, the lead author of the Boredom Proneness Scale, only to find that he had not done boredom research in many years. He had moved on to other topics. I did not ask him why, though I have the glimmer of a notion.

Experiment: The Mob Project

That May my boredom was especially acute, but none of the projects crowding around in my mind seemed feasible. I wanted to use e-mail to get people to come to some sort of show, where something surprising would happen, perhaps involving a fight; or an entire fake arts scene, maybe, some tight-knit band of fictitious young artists and writers who all lived together in a loft, and we would reel in journalists and would-be admirers eager to congratulate themselves for having discovered the next big thing. Both of these ideas seemed far too difficult. It was while ruminating on these two ideas, in the shower, that I realized I needed to make my idea *lazier*. I could use e-mail to gather an audience for a show, yes, but the point of the show should be no show at all: the e-mail would be straightforward about exactly what people would see, namely nothing but *themselves*, coming together for no reason at all. Such a project would work, I reflected, because it was *meta*, i.e., it was a self-conscious idea for a self-conscious culture, a promise to create something out of nothing. It was the perfect project for me.

During the week between the first MOB e-mail and the appointed day, I found myself anxious, not knowing what to expect. MOB's only goal was to attract a crowd, but as an event it had none of the typical draws: no name of any artist or performer, no endorsement by any noted tastemaker. All it had was its own ironically wild, unsupportable claims — that "tons" of people would be there, that they would constitute a "mob." The subject heading of the e-mail had read *MOB #1*, so as to imply that it was the first in what would be an ongoing series of gatherings. (In fact, I was unsure whether there would be a MOB #2.) As I was gathering my things to head north the seven blocks from my office to the mob site, I received a call from my friend Eugene, a stand-up comedian whose attitude toward daily living I have long admired. Once, on a slow day while he was working at an ice-cream store, he slid a shovel through the inside handles

> **The point of the show would be no show at all.**

of the store's plate-glass front doors, along with a note that read CLOSED DUE TO SHOVEL.

"Is the mob supposed to be at Claire's Accessories?" Eugene asked.

Yes, I said.

"There's six cops standing guard in front of it," he said. "And a paddywagon."

This was not the mob I had been anticipating. If anyone was to land in that paddywagon, I thought, it ought to be me, and so I hastened to the site. The cops, thankfully, did not seem to be in an arresting mood. But they would not allow anyone to enter the store, even when we told them (not unpersuasively, I thought) that we were desperate accessories shoppers. I scanned the faces of passersby, hoping to divine how many had come to mob — quite a few, I judged, based on their excited yet wry expressions, but seeing the police they understandably hurried past. Still others lingered around, filming with handheld video cameras or snapping digital pictures. A radio crew lurked with a boom mike. Despite the police, my single e-mail had generated enough steam to power a respectable spectacle.

The underlying science of the Mob Project seemed sound, and so I readied plans for MOB #2, which would be held two weeks later, on June 17. I found four ill-frequented bars near the intended site and had the participants gather at those beforehand, again split by the month of their birth. Ten minutes before the appointed time of 7:27 PM, slips of paper bearing the final destination were distributed at the bars. The site was the Macy's rugs department, which in that tremendous store is a mysterious and inaccessible kingdom, the farthest reach of the ninth and uppermost floor, accessed by a seemingly endless series of ancient escalators that grind past women's apparel and outerwear and furs and fine china and the in-store Starbucks and Au Bon Pain. By quarter past seven waves of mobbers were sweeping through the dimly illuminated furniture department, glancing sidelong toward the rugs room as they pretended to shop for loveseats and bureaus; but all at once, in a giant rush, two hundred people wandered over to the carpet in the back left corner and, as instructed, informed clerks that they all lived together in a Long Island City commune and were looking for a "love rug."

"E-mail Mob Takes Manhattan" read the headline two days later on *Wired News*, an online technology-news site. More media took note, and interview requests began to filter in to my anonymous webmail account: on June 18, from *New York* magazine;

10

on June 20, from the *New York Observer*, NPR's *All Things Considered*, the BBC World Service, the Italian daily *Corriere della Serra*. By MOB #3, which was held two weeks after the previous one, I had gotten fifteen requests in total. Would-be mobbers in other cities had heard the call as well, and soon I received e-mails from San Francisco, Minneapolis, Boston, Austin, announcing their own local chapters. Some asked for advice, which I very gladly gave. ("Before you send out the instructions, visit the spot at the same time and on the same day of the week, and figure out how long it will take people to get to the mob spot, etc.," I wrote to Minneapolis.)

Perhaps most important, the Mob Project was almost immediately taken up by 15 blogs. A blog called Cheesebikini, run by a thirty-one-year-old graduate student in Berkeley named Sean Savage, gave the concept its name — "flash mobs" — as an homage to a 1973 science-fiction short story called "Flash Crowd," by Larry Niven. The story is a warning about the unexpected downside of cheap teleportation technology: packs of thrill seekers can beam themselves in whenever something exciting is going down. The protagonist, Jerryberry Jensen, is a TV journalist who broadcasts a fight in a shopping mall, which soon, thanks to teleportation booths, grows into a multiday riot, with miscreants beaming in from around the world. Jensen is blamed, and his bosses threaten to fire him, but eventually he clears his name by showing how the technology was to blame. Since the mid-1990s, the term "flash crowd" had been invoked from time to time as a metaphor for the sudden and debilitating traffic surges that can occur when a small website is linked to by a very popular one. This is more commonly known as the "Slashdot effect," after the popular tech-head site Slashdot.org, which was — and still is — known to choke the sites on which it bestows links.

With its meteorological resonance, its evocation of a "flash flood" of people mobbing a place or a site or a thing all at once and then dispersing, the term "flash mob" was utterly perfect. The phenomenon it described, now properly named, could venture out into the universe and begin swiftly, stylishly, assuredly to multiply.

Hypothesis

The logic behind the Mob Project ran, roughly, as follows.

1. At any given time in New York — or in any other city where culture is actively made — the vast majority of events (concerts, plays, readings, comedy nights, and gallery shows, but also protests, charities, association meetings) are summarily ignored, while a small subset of events attracts enormous audiences and, soon, media attention.

2. For most of these latter events, the beneficiaries of that ineffable boon known as *buzz*, one can, after the fact, point out nominal reasons for their sudden popularity: high quality, for example; or perception of high quality due to general acclamation, or at least an assumption of general acclamation, or the participation of some well-liked figure, or the presence, or rumored presence, of same; etc.

3. *But*: so often does popularity, even among the highest of brow, bear no relationship to merit, that an experiment might be devised to determine just how far one might take the former while neglecting the latter entirely; that is, how much buzz one could create about an event whose only point was buzz, a show whose audience

was itself the only show. Given all culture in New York was demonstrably com-
mingled with *scenesterism*, my thinking ran, it should theoretically be possible to
create an art project consisting of *pure scene*—meaning the scene would be the
entire point of the work, and indeed would itself constitute the work.

At its best, the Mob Project brought to this task a sort of formal unity, as can be
illustrated in MOB #3, which took place fifteen days after #2. To get the slips with the
destination, invitees were required to roam the downstairs food court of Grand Central Station, looking for Mob Project representatives reading the *New York Review of
Books*. The secret location was a hotel adjacent to the station on Forty-second Street,
the Grand Hyatt, which has a block-long lobby with fixtures in the high '80s style:
gold-chrome railings and sepia-mirror walls and a fountain in marblish stone and a
mezzanine overhead, ringed around. Mob time was set for 7:07 PM, the tail end of the
evening rush hour; the train station next door was thick with commuters and so (visible through the hotel's tinted-glass facade) was the sidewalk outside, but the lobby
was nearly empty: only a few besuited types, guests presumably, sunk here and there
into armchairs.

Starting five minutes beforehand the mob members slipped in, in twos and threes
and tens, milling around in the lobby and making stylish small talk. Then all at once,
they rode the elevators and escalators up to the mezzanine and wordlessly lined the
banister, like so:

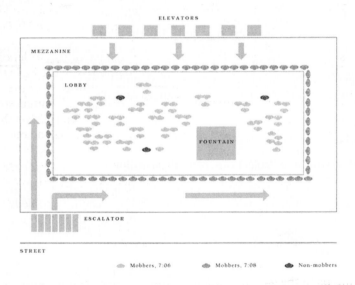

The handful of hotel guests were still there, alone again, except now they were   20
confronted with a hundreds-strong armada of mobbers overhead, arrayed shoulder
to shoulder, staring silently down. Intimidation was not the point; we were staring
down at *where we had just been*, and also across at one another, two hundred artist-
spectators commandeering an atrium on Forty-second Street as a coliseum-style theater of self-regard. After five minutes of staring, the ring erupted into precisely fifteen
seconds of tumultuous applause—for itself—after which it scattered back downstairs
and out the door, just as the police cruisers were rolling up, flashers on.

The Meme, Supreme

From the moment flash mobs first began to spread, there was a term applied to them by both boosters and detractors, and that term was *meme*. "The Flash Mob meme is #1 with a bullet," wrote the author Howard Rheingold on his blog. Three days later, on MetaFilter, one commenter wrote, "I was going to take the time to savage this wretched warmed-over meme, but am delighted to see that so many of you have already done so"; countered the next commenter, "I happen to think the meme is a bit silly, but the backlash even more so." In September, when the comic strip *Doonesbury* had one of its characters create flash mobs for Howard Dean, one blogger named Eric enthused, "Trust Gary [*sic*] Trudeau to combine the hottest memes of the summer," adding as an aside: "Yes, I fully realize that [I] just called Dr Dean a meme."

Readers will be excused for their ignorance of this term, though in 1998 it did enter the Merriam-Webster dictionary, which defines it as "an idea, behavior, style, or usage that spreads from person to person within a culture." The operative word here is "spreads," for this simple monosyllabic noun has buried within it a particular vision of culture and how it evolves. In a meme's-eye view of the world, any idea—from a religious belief or a political affiliation to a new style of jeans or a catchy tune—can be seen as a sort of independent agent loosed into the population, where it travels from mind to mind, burrowing into each, colonizing all as widely and ruthlessly as it can. Some brains are more susceptible than others to certain memes, but by and large memes spread by virtue of their own inherent contagiousness. The meme idea, that is, sees cultural entities as being similar to genes, or better, to *viruses*, and in fact the term "viral" is often used to express the same idea.

If we consider the meme idea itself as a meme, we see that its virulence in the Internet era has been impressive. The term was coined in 1976 by the biologist Richard Dawkins in his first book, *The Selfish Gene*, in which he persuasively argues that genes are the operative subjects of evolutionary selection: that is, individuals struggle first and foremost to perpetuate their genes, and insofar as evolution is driven by the "survival of the fittest," it is the fitness of our genes, not of us, that is the relevant factor. He puts forward a unified vision of history in which replication is king: in Dawkins's view, from that very first day when, somewhere in the murk, there emerged the first genes—molecules with the ability to create copies of themselves—these selfish replicators have been orchestrating the whole shebang. After extending out this argument to explain the evolution of species, Dawkins turns to the question of human culture. If replication, over long periods of time, explains why we exist, then might it not serve also to explain what inhabits our minds? Dawkins writes, with characteristic flourish,

> I think that a new kind of replicator has recently emerged on this very planet. It is staring us in the face. It is still in its infancy, still drifting clumsily about in its primeval soup. . . . The new soup is the soup of human culture. We need a name for the new replicator, a noun that conveys the idea of a unit of cultural transmission, or a unit of imitation. "Mimeme" [Greek for "that which is imitated"] comes from a suitable Greek root, but I want a monosyllable that sounds a bit like gene. I hope my classicist friends will forgive me if I abbreviate mimeme to *meme*.

Although Dawkins clearly intends the meme to be analogous first and foremost to the gene—which spreads itself only through successive generations, through the reproduction of its host—on the very same page he invokes the more apt biological metaphor of the virus. "When you plant a fertile meme in my mind you literally parasitize my brain," he wrote, "turning it into a vehicle for the meme's propagation in just the way that a virus may parasitize the genetic mechanism of a host cell."

Why has the meme meme spread? Why has the viral become so viral? *The Selfish Gene* was a bestselling book thirty years ago, but it was not until the mid-1990s that the meme and viral ideas became epidemics of their own. I would hazard two reasons for this chronology, one psychological and one technological. The psychological reason is the rise of market consciousness, in a culture where stock ownership increased during the 1990s from just under a quarter to more than half. After all, the meme vision of culture—where ideas compete for brain space, unburdened by history or context— really resembles nothing so much as an economist's dream of the free market. We are asked to admire the marvelous theoretical efficiencies (no barriers to entry, unfettered competition, persistence of the fittest) but to ignore the factual inequalities: the fact, for example, that so many of our most persistent memes succeed only through elaborate sponsorship (what would be a genetic analogy here? factory-farm breeding, perhaps?), while other, fitter memes wither.

The other, technological reason for the rise of the meme/viral idea is perhaps more obvious: the Internet. But it is worth teasing out just *what* about the Internet has conjured up these memes all around us. Yes, the Internet allows us to communicate instantaneously with others around the world, but that has been possible since the telegraph. Yes, the Internet allows us to find others with similar interests and chat among ourselves; but this is just an online analogue of what we always have been able to do in person, even if perhaps not on such a large scale. What the Internet has done to change culture—to create a new, viral culture—is to *archive* trillions of our communications, to make them linkable, trackable, searchable, quantifiable, so they can serve as ready grist for yet more conversation. In an offline age, we might have had a vague notion that a slang phrase or a song or a perception of a product or an enthusiasm for a candidate was spreading through social groups; but lacking any hard data about *how* it was spreading, why would any of us (aside from marketers and sundry social scientists) really care? Today, though, in the Internet, we have a trillion-terabyte answer that in turn has influenced our questions. We can see how we are embedded in numerical currents, how we precede or lag curves, how we are enmeshed in so-called social networks, and how our networks compare to the networks of others. The Internet has given us not just new ways of communicating but new ways of measuring ourselves.

Propagation

To spread the Mob Project, I endeavored to devise a *media strategy* on the project's own terms. The mob was all about the herd instinct, I reasoned, about the desire not to be left out of the latest fad; logically, then, it should grow as quickly as possible, and eventually—this seemed obvious—to buckle under the weight of its own popularity. I developed a simple maxim for myself, as custodian of the mob: "Anything that grows the mob is pro-mob." And in accordance with this principle, I gave interviews to all reporters who asked. In the six weeks following MOB #3 I did perhaps thirty different interviews, not only with local newspapers (the *Post* and the *Daily News*, though not yet the *Times*—more on that later) but also with *Time*, *Time Out New York*, the *Christian*

Science Monitor, the *San Francisco Chronicle*, the *Chicago Tribune*, the Associated Press, Reuters, Agence France-Presse, and countless websites.

There was also the matter of how I would be identified. My original preference had been to remain entirely anonymous, but I had only half succeeded; at the first, aborted mob, a radio reporter had discovered my first name and broadcast it, and so I was forced to be Bill—or, more often, "Bill"—in my dealings with the media thereafter. "[L]ike Cher and Madonna, prefers to use only his first name," wrote the *Chicago Daily Herald*. (To those who asked my occupation, I replied simply that I worked in the "culture industry.") Usually a flash-mob story would invoke me roughly three quarters of the way down, as the "shadowy figure" at the center of the project. There were dark questions as to my intentions. "Bill, who denies he is on a power-trip, declined to be identified," intoned Britain's *Daily Mirror*. Here is an exchange from Fox News's *On the Record with Greta Van Susteren*:

> **There were dark questions as to my intentions.**

ANCHOR: Now, the guy who came up with the Mob Project is a mystery man named Bill. Do either of you know who he is?

MOBBER ONE: Nope.

MOBBER TWO: Well, I've—I've e-mailed him. That's about it.

MOBBER ONE: Oh, you have . . . ?

ANCHOR: What—what—who is this Bill? Do you know anything about him?

MOBBER TWO: Well, from what I've read, he's a—he works in the culture industry, and that's—that's about as specific as we've gotten with him.

As the media frenzy over the mobs grew, so did the mobs themselves. For MOB #4, I sent the mob to a shoe store in SoHo, a spacious plate-glassed corner boutique whose high ceilings and walls made of undulating mosaic gave it an almost aquatic feel, and I was astonished to see the mob assemble: as I marched with one strand streaming down Lafayette, we saw another mounting a pincers movement around Prince Street from the east, pouring in through the glass doors past the agape mouths of the attendants, perhaps three hundred bodies, packing the space and then, once no one else could enter, crowding around the sidewalk, everyone gawking, taking pictures with cameras, calling friends on cell phones (as the instructions for this mob had ordered), each pretending to be a tourist, all feigning awe—an awe I myself truly felt—to be not merely in New York but so close to the center of something so big.

Outside New York, too, the mob was multiplying in dizzying ways, far past the point that I could correspond with the leaders or even keep up with all the different new cities: not only all across the United States but London, Vienna, twenty-one different municipalities in Germany. In July, soon after New York's MOB #4, Rome held its first two flash mobs; in the first, three hundred mobbers strode into a bookstore and demanded nonexistent titles (e.g., *Pinocchio 2: The Revenge*), while the second (which, based on descriptions I read later, is perhaps my favorite flash mob of any ever assembled) was held right in the Piazza dell'Esquilino, in a crosswalk just in front of the glorious Basilica di Santa Maria Maggiore, where the crowd broke into two and balletically crossed back and forth and met each other multiple times, first hugging, then fighting, and then asking for the time: *"CHE ORE SONO?"* yelled one semi-mob, and the other replied, *"LE SETTE E QUARANTA,"*—"It's 7:40"—which, in fact, it was exactly.

Up: The Bandwagon Effect

When a British art magazine asked me who, among artists past or present, had most influenced the flash-mob project, I named Stanley Milgram—i.e., the social psychologist best known for his authority experiments in which he induced average Americans to give seemingly fatal shocks to strangers. As it happens, I later discovered that Milgram also did a project much like a flash mob, in which a "stimulus crowd" of his confederates, varying in number from one to fifteen, stopped on a busy Manhattan sidewalk and all at once looked up to the same sixth-floor window. The results, in a chart from his paper "Notes on the Drawing Power of Crowds of Different Size":

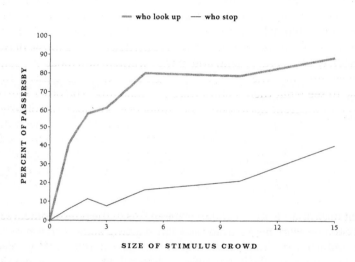

In this single chart, Milgram elegantly documented the essence of herd behavior, what economists call a "bandwagon effect": the instinctive tendency of the human animal to rely on the actions of others in choosing its own course of action. We get interested in the things we see others getting interested in. *Homo sapiens* has been jumping on bandwagons, as the expression goes, since long before the vogue for such vehicles in the late nineteenth century (when less popular American politicians would clamor to be seen aboard the bandwagon of a more popular candidate for another office, hence the meaning we have today); since long before, even, the invention of the wheel.

The bandwagon effect is especially pronounced in Internet culture-making, however, because popularity can immediately be factored into how choices are presented to us. If in our nonwired lives we jump on a bandwagon once a day, in our postwired existence we hop whole fleets of them—often without even knowing it. Start, for example, where most of us start online, with Google: when we search for a phrase, Google's sophisticated engine delivers our results in an order determined (at least in part) by how many searchers before us eventually clicked on the pages in question. Whenever we click on a top-ten Google result, we are jumping on an invisible bandwagon. Similarly with retailers such as Amazon, whose front-page offerings, tailored to each customer, are based on what other customers have bought: another invisible bandwagon. Then there are the countless visible bandwagons, in the form of the ubiquitous lists: most bought, most downloaded, most e-mailed, most linked-to. Even the august *New York Times*, through its "most e-mailed" list, has turned the news into a popularity contest, whose winners in turn get more attention among Internet readers who have only a limited amount of attention to give. Thus do the attention-rich invariably get richer.

In some cases, our bandwagons—online or off—do us a service, by weeding out extraneous or undesirable information through the "wisdom of crowds" (as a bestselling book by James Surowiecki put it). Moreover, in the case of culture, what is already popular in some respect has more intrinsic value: we read news, or watch television, or listen to music in part so we can have discussions with other people who have done the same. But it is a severe mistake to assume, as the economically minded often do, that the bandwagon effect manages to select for intrinsic worth, or even to give individuals what they actually want. This was demonstrated ingeniously a few years ago in an experiment run by Matthew Salganik, a sociologist who was then at Columbia University. Fourteen thousand participants were invited to join a music network where they could listen to songs, rate them, and, if they wanted, download the songs for free. A fifth of the volunteers—the "independent" group—were left entirely to their own tastes, unable to see what their fellows were downloading. The other four-fifths were split up into eight different networks—the "influence" groups—all of which saw the same songs, but listed in rank order based on how often they had been downloaded in that particular group. The songs were by almost entirely unknown bands, to avoid having songs get popular based on preexisting associations with the band's name.

What Salganik and his colleagues found was that the "independent" group chose songs that differed significantly from those chosen in the "influence" groups, which in turn differed significantly from one another. In their paper, the sociologists call the eight different networks "worlds," and they mean this in the philosophical sense of possible worlds: each network began from the same starting point with the same universe of songs, but each of these independent evolutionary environments yielded very different outcomes. A band called 52metro, for example, was #1 in one world but didn't even rate the top ten in five of the other seven worlds. Similarly, a band called Silent Film topped one chart but was #3, #4, #7, or #8 (twice) on five of the charts, and was entirely left off the other two. "Quality"—if we define that to mean the independent group's choices—did not seem to be entirely irrelevant: the top-rated song on their list, by a group called Parker Theory, made all eight of the "influence" lists and topped five of them. But of the other nine acts on the independent list, one was entirely shut out of the influence lists, and three made only two lists. On average, the top ten bands for the independent group made only four of the eight influence lists. Apparently they were drowned out, in the other worlds, by noise from the bandwagons.

The Mob Project was a *self-conscious* bandwagon—advertised itself as a bandwagon, as a joke about conformity, and it lampooned bandwagons in doing so. But curiously, this seemed not to diminish its actual bandwagonesque properties. Indeed, if anything, the self-consciousness made it even more viral. The e-mails poured in: "I WANT IN." "Request to mob, sir." "Girls can keep secrets!" "Want to get my mob on." In Boston's first flash mob, entitled "Ode to Bill," hundreds packed the greeting-card aisles of a Harvard Square department store, telling bystanders who inquired that they were looking for a card for their "friend Bill in New York." By making a halfhearted, jesting attempt to elevate me to celebrity status, Boston had given the flash-mob genre an appropriately sly turn.

Peak and Backlash

The best attended of all the New York gatherings was MOB #6, which for a few beautiful minutes stifled what has to be the most ostentatious chain store in the entire city: the Times Square Toys "Я" Us, whose excesses are too many to catalog here but include, in the store's foyer, an actual operational Ferris wheel some sixty feet in diameter. Up until the appointed time of 7:18 PM, the mobbers loitered on the upper level, among the GI Joes and the Nintendos and up inside the glittering pink of the two-floor Barbie palace. But then all at once the mob,

> **"Fill in all around it," the mob slip had instructed. "It is like a terrible god to you."**

five hundred strong, crowded around the floor's centerpiece, a life-size animatronic Tyrannosaurus rex that growls and feints with a Hollywood-class lifelikeness. "Fill in all around it," the mob slip had instructed. "It is like a terrible god to you."

Two minutes later, the mob dropped to its knees, moaning and cowering at the beast behind outstretched hands; in doing so we repaid this spectacle, which clearly was the product of not only untold expenditure but many man-months of *imagineering*, with an en masse enactment of the very emotions—visceral fright and infantile fealty—that it obviously had been designed to evoke. MOB #6 was, as many bloggers pointed out pejoratively, "cute," but the cuteness had been massed, refracted, and focused to such a bright point that it became a physical menace. For six minutes the upper level was paralyzed; the cash registers were cocooned behind the moaning, kneeling bodies pressed together; customers were trapped; business could not be done. The terror-stricken personnel tried in vain to force the crowd out. "Is anyone making a purchase?" one was heard to call out weakly. As the mob dispersed down the escalators and out into the street, the police were downstairs, telling us to leave, but we had already accomplished the task, had delivered what was in effect a warning.

Almost unanimously, though, the bloggers panned MOB #6. "Another Mob Botched" was the verdict on the blog Fancy Robot: "[I]nstead of setting the Flash Mob out in public on Times Square itself, as everyone had hoped, The Flash Master decided to set it in Toys "Я" Us, with apparently dismal results." SatansLaundromat.com (a photo-blog that contains the most complete visual record of the New York project) concurred—"not public enough," the blogger wrote, without enough "spectators to bewilder"—as did Chris from the CCE Blog: "I think the common feeling among these blogger reviews is: where does the idea go from here? . . . After seeing hundreds of people show up for no good reason, it's obvious that there's some kind of potential for artistic or political expression here."

The idea seemed to be that flash mobs could be made to convey a message, but for a number of reasons this dream was destined to run aground. First, as outlined above, flash mobs were gatherings of *insiders*, and as such could hardly communicate to those who did not already belong. They were intramural play; they drew their energies not from impressing outsiders or freaking them out but from showing them utter disregard, from using the outside world as merely a terrain for private games. Second, in terms of time, flash mobs were by definition *transitory*, ten minutes or fewer, and thereby not exactly suited to standing their ground and testifying. Third, in terms of physical space, flash mobs relied on *constraints* to create an illusion of superior strength. I never held mobs in the open, the bloggers complained, in view of enough onlookers, but this was entirely purposeful on my part, for like Colin Powell I hewed to a doctrine of overwhelming force. Only in enclosed spaces could the mob generate the necessary self-awe; to allow the mob to feel small would have been to destroy it.

The following week, the interview request from the *New York Times* finally arrived. On the phone the reporter, Amy Harmon, made it clear to me that the *Times* knew it was behind on the story. The paper would be remedying this, she told me, by running a prominent piece on flash mobs in its Sunday Week in Review section. What the *Times* did, in fascinating fashion, was not just to run the backlash story (which I had been expecting in three to five more weeks) but to do so preemptively — i.e., before there was actually a backlash. Harmon's piece bore the headline "Guess Some People Don't Have Anything Better to Do," and its nut sentence ran: "[T]he flash mob juggernaut has now run into a flash mob backlash that may be spreading faster than the fad itself." As evidence, she mustered the following:

> E-mail lists like "antimob" and "slashmob" have sprung up, as did a Web site warning that "flashmuggers" are bound to show up "wherever there's groups of young, naïve, wealthy, bored fashionistas to be found." And a new definition was circulated last week on several Web sites: "flash mob, noun: An impromptu gathering, organized by means of electronic communication, of the unemployed."

Two e-mail lists, a website, and a forwarded definition hardly constituted a "backlash" against this still-growing, intercontinental fad, but what I think Harmon and the *Times* rightly understood was that a backlash was the only avenue by which they could advance the story, i.e., find a new narrative. Whether through direct causation or mere journalistic intuition, the *Times* timed its backlash story (8/17/03) with remarkable accuracy:

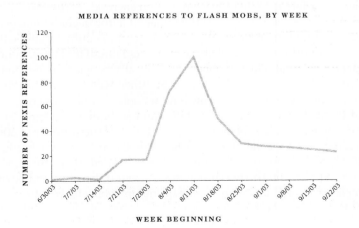

MEDIA REFERENCES TO FLASH MOBS, BY WEEK

Permutations

Whether the backlash was real or not, it almost didn't matter: there was no way for the flash mob to keep growing, and since the entire logic of the mob was to grow, the mob was destined to die. It couldn't become political, or even make any statement at all, within the prescribed confines of a ten-minute burst. After six mobs, even conceiving of new enough crowd permutations started to feel like a challenge. We had done consumers collaborating (MOB #2) and consumers not collaborating (MOB #4). We had done an ecstatic, moaning throng (MOB #6) and a more sedate, absurdist one (MOB #5, in which the mob hid in some Central Park woods and simulated animal noises). In MOB #3, we had formed an inward-facing ring, and the idea of another geometrical mob appealed to me. I decided that MOB #7, set for late August, should be a queue.

Scouting locations had become in many ways the most pleasant task of the experiment. Roughly a week before each appointed day, having chosen the neighborhood in advance, I would stroll nonchalantly around the streets, looking at parks and stairways and stores, imagining a few hundred people descending at once upon each: How would such a mob arrive? How would it array itself? What would it do? Could it be beautiful? For MOB #7 I had picked Midtown, the commercial heart of the city, and so one Thursday in the late afternoon I took the subway uptown from my office to envision a crowd. I started on Fiftieth Street at Eighth Avenue and walked east, slipping through the milling Broadway tourists: too much real crowd for a fake crowd to stand out successfully. At Sixth Avenue I eyed Radio City Music Hall—an inviting target, to be sure, but the sidewalk in front was too narrow, too trafficked, for a mob comfortably to do its work. At Rockefeller Center, I eyed the Christmas tree spot, which was empty that August; but there was far too much security lurking about.

When I arrived at Fifth Avenue, though, and looked up at the spires of Saint Patrick's Cathedral, I realized I had found just the place. A paramount Manhattan landmark with not much milling out front (since tourists were generally allowed inside); a sacred site, moreover, all the better for profaning with a disposable crowd. Crossing Fifth, I started around the structure from the north, following it to Madison and coming around the south side back to Fifth Avenue. I wanted a line, but it would be too risky to have it start at the front doors, since the cathedral staff that stood near the door might disperse it before it could fully form. But on each side of the cathedral, I noticed, was a small wooden door, not open to the public. If a line began at one of these doors, it could wind around the grand structure but keep staff confused long enough to last for the allotted five minutes. I stood at the corner of Fiftieth and Fifth, pondering what should happen after that. Flash mobbers were mostly people like me, downtown and Brooklyn kids, a demographic seldom seen in either Midtown or church. I loved the idea that Saint Patrick's might somehow have inexplicably become cool, a place where if one lined up at the side door, one might stand a chance of getting in for—*what?* Tickets to see some stupidly cool band, I thought; and in the summer of 2003 the right band to make fun of was the Strokes, a band that had been clearly manufactured, Monkees-like, precisely for our delectation. It was settled, then: the mob would line up from the small door on the north side, wind around the front and down the south side. When passersby asked why they were lining up, mobbers were to say they "heard they're selling Strokes tickets."

45

Having settled the script that Thursday afternoon, I started back down Fiftieth, only to see a man walk out of the side door. He was a short man with curly hair tight to his head, and he wore a knit blue tie over a white patterned button-down shirt. Without acknowledging me in any way, he walked to the curb and then stood still, staring up at the sky. Back at Madison, I saw that since I last was at the corner, the stoplight had gone dark: an uncommon city sight. As I headed south down Madison, weaving through accumulating traffic crowding crosswalks, more people began to trickle out of the office buildings, looking dazed, rubbing their eyes in the sunlight. A woman dressed as Nefertiti was fanning herself. Customers lined up at bodegas to buy bottles of water. I thought I would walk south until I got out of the blackout zone; by Union Square I realized that the blackout zone was very large indeed, though it was not until I got back to work, walking the eleven flights up, that I was told the zone was not just all of New York City but most of the northeastern United States. Having spent my last half hour envisioning my own absurdist mob, I had suddenly stepped into a citywide flash mob planned by no one, born not of a will to metaspectacle but of basic human need. The power returned within the week, and MOB #7 went on exactly as planned; but to gather a crowd on New York's streets never felt quite the same, and I knew my days making mobs were dwindling fast.

Down: Boredom Redux

I wrote of boredom as inspiring the mob's birth; but I suspect that boredom helped to hasten its death, as well—the boredom, that is, of the constantly distracted mind. This paradoxical relationship between boredom and distraction was demonstrated elegantly in 1989, by psychologists at Clark University in Worcester, Massachusetts. Ninety-one undergraduates, broken up into small groups, were played a tape-recorded reading of fifteen minutes in length, but during the playback for some of the students a modest distraction was introduced: the sound of a TV soap opera, playing at a "just noticeable" level. Afterward, when the students were asked if their minds had wandered during the recording, the results were as to be expected. Seventy percent of the intentionally distracted listeners said their minds had wandered, as opposed to 55 percent of the control group. What was far more surprising, however, were the reasons they gave: among those whose minds wandered, 76 percent of the distracted listeners said this was because the tape was "boring," versus only 41 percent of their nondistracted counterparts. We tend to think of boredom as a response to having too few external stimuli, but here boredom was perceived more keenly at the precise time that more stimuli were present.

The experiment's authors, Robin Damrad-Frye and James Laird, argue that the results make sense in the context of "self-perception theory": the notion that we determine our internal states in large part by observing our own behavior. Other studies have supported this general idea. Subjects asked to mimic a certain emotion will then report feeling that emotion. Subjects made to argue in favor of a statement, either through a speech or an essay, will afterward attest to believing it. Subjects forced to gaze into each other's eyes will later profess sexual attraction for each other. In the case of boredom, the authors write, "The reason people know they are bored is, at least in part, that they find they cannot keep their attention focused where it should be." That is, they ascribe their own inattention to a deficiency not in themselves, or in their surroundings, but in that to which they are supposed to be attending.

Today, in the advanced stages of our information age, with our e-mail in-boxes and phones and instant messages all chirping for our attention, it is as if we are conducting Damrad-Frye and Laird's experiment on a society-wide scale. Gloria Mark, a professor at the University of California at Irvine, has found that white-collar officeworkers can work for only eleven minutes, on average, without being interrupted. Among the young, permanent distraction is a way of life: the majority of seventh- to twelfth-graders in the United States say that they "multitask" — using other media — some or even most of the time they are reading or using the computer. The writer and software expert Linda Stone has called this lifestyle one of "continuous partial attention," an elegant phrase to describe the endless wave of electronic distraction that so many of us ride. There is ample evidence that all this distraction impairs our ability to do things well: a psychologist at the University of Michigan found that multitasking subjects made more errors in each task and took from 50 to 100 percent more time to finish. But far more intriguing, I think, is how our constant distraction may be feeding back into our perception of the world — the effect observed among those Clark undergraduates, writ large; the sense, that is, that nothing we attend to is adequate, precisely because nothing can escape the roiling scorn of our distraction.

This, finally, is what kills nanostories, I think, and what surely killed the flash mob,   50 not only in the media but in my own mind: this always-encroaching boredom, this need to tell ever *new stories* about our society and ourselves, even when there are no new stories to be told. This impulse itself is far from new, of course; it is a species of what Neil Postman meant in 1984 when he decried the culture of news as entertainment, and indeed of what Daniel Boorstin meant in 1961 when he railed against our "extravagant expectations" for the world of human events. What viral culture adds is, in part, just pure acceleration — the speed born of more data sources, more frequent updates, more churn — but far more crucially it adds interactivity, and with it a perverse kind of market democracy. As more of us take on the media mantle ourselves, telling our own stories rather than allowing others to tell them for us, it is we who can act to assuage our own boredom, our inadequacy, our despair by projecting them out through how we describe the world.

Dispersal

I announced that MOB #8, in early September, would be the last. The invitation e-mail's subject was *MOB #8: The end*, and the text began with a FAQ:

Q. The end?
A. Yes.

Q. Why?
A. It can't be explained. Like the individual mobs, the Mob Project appeared for
  no reason, and like the mobs it must disperse.

Q. Will the Mob Project ever reappear?
A. It might. But don't expect it.

The site was a concrete alcove right on Forty-second Street, just across from the Condé Nast building. Participants had been told to follow the instructions blaring from a cheap boom box I had set up beforehand atop a brick ledge. I had prerecorded a tape of myself, barking out commands. I envisioned my hundreds of mobbers, following the dictates of what was effectively a loudspeaker on a pole. It was hard to get more straightforward than that, I thought.

But the cheering of the hundreds grew so great that it drowned out the speakers. The mob soon became unmoored. All of a sudden a man in a toque, apparently some sort of opportunistic art shaman, opened his briefcase to reveal a glowing neon sign, and the crowd bent to his will. He held up two fingers, and to my horror the mob began chanting "Peace!" In retrospect, I saw it as a fitting end for an experiment about bandwagons and conformity, about inattention and media hype. My crowd had ultimately been hijacked by a figure more mysterious, more enigmatic than even the semianonymous "Bill"—by a better story, that is, than me.

Of all my experiments in viral culture, the Mob Project was by far the most impressive in its spread; and indeed this spread spurred much of my ensuing interest in the subject. In starting the project, my major interest had been in the intersection of the virtual and the physical—I had seen the mob as a way for online connections to manifest themselves visually, corporeally, disruptively in the sidewalks and spaces of urban life. But as the mob grew beyond my most optimistic projections, and then collapsed, I became less fixated on the mobs themselves and more focused on the *storytelling* about them. The arc of a mob, of the Mob Project, of flash mobs as a general phenomenon, of the media narrative *about* the phenomenon—all were strangely congruent in the rapid rise and fall, and I desperately wanted to understand the storytelling that made these spikes operate.

Chapter 2 [not included here] is an exploration of the most basic breeding ground for spikes, and the stories—i.e., the nanostories—that fuel them: the *niche*, or *subculture*, which the Internet as a medium has both invigorated and transformed. 55

Exploring Context

1. Explore the website for Improv Everywhere (improveverywhere.com), "a New York City–based prank collective that causes scenes of chaos and joy in public places." How does this group use flash mobs? While exploring the site, look for additional evidence to support your answer to Question 3 of Questions for Critical Reading.

2. Flash Mob America (flashmobamerica.com) claims to be the "#1 Flash Mob Company in the World." Explore its site, paying special attention to the section on how to hire this company. Does the meaning of a flash mob change when it's commercialized? Use your findings to extend your answer to Question 1 of Questions for Critical Reading.

3. Visit the Internet Meme Database (knowyourmeme.com). Working with the information on the site, can you determine how memes are created? How does the site confirm or complicate your work from Question 2 of Questions for Critical Reading?

Questions for Connecting

1. What is the relationship between viral culture and media advertising? Use Wasik's experience with flash mobs and his discussion of memes to examine the appropriation of black talk by pop culture as explained by Leslie Savan in "What's Black, Then White, and Said All Over?" (p. 435). Is covert prestige a response to boredom? How do advertisers use black talk as a meme? You might want to draw on your work from Question 3 of Exploring Context.

2. Both Wasik and James Surowiecki are interested in the behavior of groups. Synthesize Wasik's experience with flash mobs and Surowiecki's analysis of the failure of small groups in "Committees, Juries, and Teams: The *Columbia* Disaster and How Small Groups Can Be Made to Work" (p. 472). In what ways did the Mission Management Team function like a flash mob? What strategies can be used to promote successful groups? Incorporate your work from Question 3 of Questions for Critical Reading.

3. Wasik ends by discussing the death of the "nanostory" and the return of boredom. Use Richard Restak's discussion of technology's impact on brain biology in "Attention Deficit: The Brain Syndrome of Our Era" (p. 411) to extend Wasik's discussion. Does multitasking necessarily result in an increase of boredom? What is the best way to address this problem?

Language Matters

1. Ellipses and brackets are useful punctuation marks when using quotations. Select a long quotation from Wasik that represents an important part of his essay. How would you use these punctuation marks to incorporate the quotation into your own writing? How might they be instead used, even unintentionally, to misrepresent the meaning of the quotation? How can you be sure you're using these punctuation marks correctly?

2. The most solid transitions come from a statement that directly ties together two paragraphs. Select two paragraphs from Wasik's essay. Write a one-sentence summary of the first paragraph and then another one-sentence summary of the second paragraph. Then combine these two sentences into one to form a new transition between the paragraphs. How does your sentence differ from Wasik's transition? How can you use this skill in your own writing?

3. Section headings can help a reader understand the organization of your writing. Make a list of Wasik's headings. How do they provide insight into the structure of his essay? In what situations might you use headings in your own writing?

Assignments for Writing

1. Wasik begins his flash mob project out of boredom. Write a paper in which you assess the role of boredom in our culture today. Does technology produce boredom? Does choice? How do we cope with boredom? Is there a boredom "epidemic"? How might Wasik's essay offer strategies to deal with boredom? Consider using your work from Question 3 of Questions for Critical Reading or Question 3 of Questions for Connecting.

2. How do memes function? Write a paper in which you determine the role that memes play in digital society. Use your work from Questions for Critical Reading, Exploring Context, and Questions for Connecting. Why do memes spread so quickly in our culture? Are memes harmless? Can they be used for social change? Locate your own example of a meme and analyze it using Wasik's ideas.

3. Although Wasik ended his own flash mob experiment, the phenomenon continues to be a part of our culture today. Write a paper in which you trace the continuing role that flash mobs play in our culture. Use your work from Questions for Critical Reading, Exploring Context, and Questions for Connecting. Do flash mobs function as remedies to boredom? Are they simply driven by memes? Are they a kind of performance art? Locate another example of a flash mob and use it to extend or complicate Wasik's observations.

WESLEY YANG

Wesley Yang is a contributing editor at both *Tablet* and *New York* magazines, with more than ten of his essays appearing in both the print and online editions of the latter. His varied articles on race, sexuality, and politics have also been published in noted magazines such as *Salon*, the *New York Observer*, and the *National*.

The May 16, 2011, issue of *New York* magazine, from which this selection was taken, was enveloped in the then-recent killing of Osama bin Laden, which took place just over two weeks prior, with blurbs about the event on the cover alongside feature pieces on Lady Gaga. But the cover image, one of Wesley Yang himself in stark closeup fading to white with his own words superimposed over the photo, signified that "Paper Tigers" was indeed the centerpiece of the issue.

In "Paper Tigers," Wesley Yang discusses his own experiences as an Asian American, tying them into the larger picture of Asians functioning in American society. Yang argues that while Asian Americans are indeed the most "successful" ethnic group in the country in terms of education and accumulation of wealth (often trumping the majority demographic—whites), there is a perception in popular culture that Asian Americans are "the products of a timid culture, easily pushed around by more assertive people" (p. 534). Yang asks us to consider the implications of stereotypes—even positive ones—and how they affect not only the viewing of other peoples, but the way those very people being stereotyped integrate into society.

What stereotypes have been applied to you? Is it possible for us to discard stereotypes altogether, especially in the face of continual evidence of their tendency toward misrepresentation?

▶ TAGS: *race, tiger children, Bamboo Ceiling, social hierarchy, unconscious bias, education*

Questions for Critical Reading

1. We've all heard about the "American Dream." Before you read this essay, write a brief definition of what this term means to you. As you read, pay attention to how Yang defines the term. What does it mean to him, and how does he apply it to minorities? Is the "American Dream" the same for all Americans?

2. Look up the meaning of the word *estrangement*. How does Yang define this term? While reading, take note of places where he discusses estrangement. How does it relate to the argument he wants to make?

3. Yang discusses the "Bamboo Ceiling" (p. 539). Do you agree with his analysis and use of the concept? What other "ceilings" might there be for other classes of people? You might begin your response by looking into the "glass ceiling" faced by women in the workplace.

Paper Tigers

Sometimes I'll glimpse my reflection in a window and feel astonished by what I see. Jet-black hair. Slanted eyes. A pancake-flat surface of yellow-and-green-toned skin. An expression that is nearly reptilian in its impassivity. I've contrived to think of this face as the equal in beauty to any other. But what I feel in these moments is its strangeness to me. It's my face. I can't disclaim it. But what does it have to do with me?

Millions of Americans must feel estranged from their own faces. But every self-estranged individual is estranged in his own way. I, for instance, am the child of Korean immigrants, but I do not speak my parents' native tongue. I have never called my elders by the proper honorific, "big brother" or "big sister." I have never dated a Korean woman. I don't have a Korean friend. Though I am an immigrant, I have never wanted to strive like one.

You could say that I am, in the gently derisive parlance of Asian-Americans, a banana or a Twinkie (yellow on the outside, white on the inside). But while I don't believe our roots necessarily define us, I do believe there are racially inflected assumptions wired into our neural circuitry that we use to sort through the sea of faces we confront. And although I am in most respects devoid of Asian characteristics, I do have an Asian face.

Here is what I sometimes suspect my face signifies to other Americans: an invisible person, barely distinguishable from a mass of faces that resemble it. A conspicuous person standing apart from the crowd and yet devoid of any individuality. An icon of so much that the culture pretends to honor but that it in fact patronizes and exploits. Not just people "who are good at math" and play the violin, but a mass of stifled, repressed, abused, conformist quasi-robots who simply do not matter, socially or culturally.

I've always been of two minds about this sequence of stereotypes. On the one hand, it offends me greatly that anyone would think to apply them to me, or to anyone else, simply on the basis of facial characteristics. On the other hand, it also seems to me that there are a lot of Asian people to whom they apply. 5

Let me summarize my feelings toward Asian values: Fuck filial piety. Fuck grade-grubbing. Fuck Ivy League mania. Fuck deference to authority. Fuck humility and hard work. Fuck harmonious relations. Fuck sacrificing for the future. Fuck earnest, striving middle-class servility.

I understand the reasons Asian parents have raised a generation of children this way. Doctor, lawyer, accountant, engineer: These are good jobs open to whoever works hard enough. What could be wrong with that pursuit? Asians graduate from college at a rate higher than any other ethnic group in America, including whites. They earn a higher median family income than any other ethnic group in America, including whites. This is a stage in a triumphal narrative, and it is a narrative that is much shorter than many remember. Two thirds of the roughly 14 million Asian-Americans are foreign-born. There were less than 39,000 people of Korean descent living in America in 1970, when my elder brother was born. There are around 1 million today.

Asian-American success is typically taken to ratify the American Dream and to prove that minorities can make it in this country without handouts. Still, an undercurrent of racial panic always accompanies the consideration of Asians, and all the more so as China becomes the destination for our industrial base and the banker controlling our burgeoning debt. But if the armies of Chinese factory workers who make our fast fashion and iPads terrify us, and if the collective mass of high-achieving Asian-American students arouse an anxiety about the laxity of American parenting, what of the Asian-American who obeyed everything his parents told him? Does this person really scare anyone?

Earlier this year, the publication of Amy Chua's *Battle Hymn of the Tiger Mother* incited a collective airing out of many varieties of race-based hysteria. But absent from the millions of words written in response to the book was any serious consideration of whether Asian-Americans were in fact taking over this country. If it is true that they are collectively dominating in elite high schools and universities, is it also true that Asian-Americans are dominating in the real world? My strong suspicion was that this was not so, and that the reasons would not be hard to find. If we are a collective juggernaut that inspires such awe and fear, why does it seem that so many Asians are so readily perceived to be, as I myself have felt most of my life, the products of a timid culture, easily pushed around by more assertive people, and thus basically invisible?

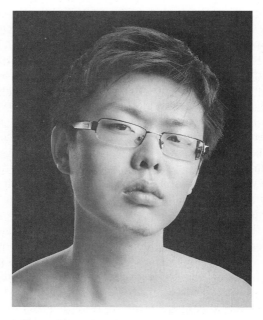

Jefferson Mao

A few months ago, I received an e-mail from a young man named Jefferson Mao, who   10
after attending Stuyvesant High School had recently graduated from the University of
Chicago. He wanted my advice about "being an Asian writer." This is how he described
himself: "I got good grades and I love literature and I want to be a writer and an intellectual; at the same time, I'm the first person in my family to go to college, my parents
don't speak English very well, and we don't own the apartment in Flushing that we live
in. I mean, I'm proud of my parents and my neighborhood and what I perceive to be my
artistic potential or whatever, but sometimes I feel like I'm jumping the gun a generation or two too early."

One bright, cold Sunday afternoon, I ride the 7 train to its last stop in Flushing,
where the storefront signs are all written in Chinese and the sidewalks are a slow-
moving river of impassive faces. Mao is waiting for me at the entrance of the Main
Street subway station, and together we walk to a nearby Vietnamese restaurant.

Mao has a round face, with eyes behind rectangular wire-frame glasses. Since
graduating, he has been living with his parents, who emigrated from China when Mao
was 8 years old. His mother is a manicurist; his father is a physical therapist's aide.
Lately, Mao has been making the familiar hour-and-a-half ride from Flushing to downtown Manhattan to tutor a white Stuyvesant freshman who lives in Tribeca. And what
he feels, sometimes, in the presence of that amiable young man is a pang of regret. Now
he understands better what he ought to have done back when he was a Stuyvesant
freshman: "Worked half as hard and been twenty times more successful."

Entrance to Stuyvesant, one of the most competitive public high schools in the
country, is determined solely by performance on a test: The top 3.7 percent of all New
York City students who take the Specialized High Schools Admissions Test hoping to
go to Stuyvesant are accepted. There are no set-asides for the underprivileged or, conversely, for alumni or other privileged groups. There is no formula to encourage "diversity" or any nebulous concept of "well-roundedness" or "character." Here we have
something like pure meritocracy. This is what it looks like: Asian-Americans, who
make up 12.6 percent of New York City, make up 72 percent of the high school.

This year, 569 Asian-Americans scored high enough to earn a slot at Stuyvesant, along with 179 whites, 13 Hispanics, and 12 blacks. Such dramatic overrepre-
sentation, and what it may be read to imply about the intelligence of different groups of
New Yorkers, has a way of making people uneasy. But intrinsic intelligence, of course,
is precisely what Asians don't believe in. They believe—and have proved—that the
constant practice of test-taking will improve the scores of whoever commits to it. All
throughout Flushing, as well as in Bayside, one can find "cram schools," or storefront
academies, that drill students in test preparation after school, on weekends, and during summer break. "Learning math is not about learning math," an instructor at one
called Ivy Prep was quoted in the *New York Times* as saying. "It's about weightlifting.
You are pumping the iron of math." Mao puts it more specifically: "You learn quite
simply to nail any standardized test you take."

And so there is an additional concern accompanying the rise of the Tiger Chil-   15
dren, one focused more on the narrowness of the educational experience a non-Asian
child might receive in the company of fanatically preprofessional Asian students. Jenny
Tsai, a student who was elected president of her class at the equally competitive New
York public school Hunter College High School, remembers frequently hearing that

"the school was becoming too Asian, that they would be the downfall of our school." A couple of years ago, she revisited this issue in her senior thesis at Harvard, where she interviewed graduates of elite public schools and found that the white students regarded the Asian students with wariness. (She quotes a music teacher at Stuyvesant describing the dominance of Asians: "They were mediocre kids, but they got in because they were coached.") In 2005, the *Wall Street Journal* reported on "white flight" from a high school in Cupertino, California, that began soon after the children of Asian software engineers had made the place so brutally competitive that a B average could place you in the bottom third of the class.

Colleges have a way of correcting for this imbalance: The Princeton sociologist Thomas Espenshade has calculated that an Asian applicant must, in practice, score 140 points higher on the SAT than a comparable white applicant to have the same chance of admission. This is obviously unfair to the many qualified Asian individuals who are punished for the success of others with similar faces. Upper-middle-class white kids, after all, have their own elite private schools, and their own private tutors, far more expensive than the cram schools, to help them game the education system.

You could frame it, as some aggrieved Asian-Americans do, as a simple issue of equality and press for race-blind quantitative admissions standards. In 2006, a decade after California passed a voter initiative outlawing any racial engineering at the public universities, Asians composed 46 percent of UC–Berkeley's entering class; one could

Eddie Huang

imagine a similar demographic reshuffling in the Ivy League, where Asian-Americans currently make up about 17 percent of undergraduates. But the Ivies, as we all know, have their own private institutional interests at stake in their admissions choices, including some that are arguably defensible. Who can seriously claim that a Harvard University that was 72 percent Asian would deliver the same grooming for elite status its students had gone there to receive?

Somewhere near the middle of his time at Stuyvesant, a vague sense of discontent started to emerge within Mao. He had always felt himself a part of a mob of "nameless, faceless Asian kids," who were "like a part of the décor of the place." He had been content to keep his head down and work toward the goal shared by everyone at Stuyvesant: Harvard. But around the beginning of his senior year, he began to wonder whether this march toward academic success was the only, or best, path.

"You can't help but feel like there must be another way," he explains over a bowl of phô. "It's like, we're being pitted against each other while there are kids out there in the Midwest who can do way less work and be in a garage band or something—and if they're decently intelligent and work decently hard in school . . ."

Mao began to study the racially inflected social hierarchies at Stuyvesant, where, in a survey undertaken by the student newspaper this year, slightly more than half of the respondents reported that their friends came from within their own ethnic group. His attention focused on the mostly white (and Manhattan-dwelling) group whose members seemed able to manage the crushing workload while still remaining socially active. "The general gist of most high-school movies is that the pretty cheerleader gets with the big dumb jock, and the nerd is left to bide his time in loneliness. But at some point in the future," he says, "the nerd is going to rule the world, and the dumb jock is going to work in a carwash.

"At Stuy, it's completely different: If you looked at the pinnacle, the girls and the guys are not only good-looking and socially affable, they also get the best grades and star in the school plays and win election to student government. It all converges at the top. It's like training for high society. It was jarring for us Chinese kids. You got the sense that you had to study hard, but it wasn't enough."

Mao was becoming clued in to the fact that there was another hierarchy behind the official one that explained why others were getting what he never had—"a high-school sweetheart" figured prominently on this list—and that this mysterious hierarchy was going to determine what happened to him in life. "You realize there are things you really don't understand about courtship or just acting in a certain way. Things that somehow come naturally to people who go to school in the suburbs and have parents who are culturally assimilated." I pressed him for specifics, and he mentioned that he had visited his white girlfriend's parents' house the past Christmas, where the family had "sat around cooking together and playing Scrabble." This ordinary vision of suburban-American domesticity lingered with Mao: Here, at last, was the setting in which all that implicit knowledge "about social norms and propriety" had been transmitted. There was no cram school that taught these lessons.

Before having heard from Mao, I had considered myself at worst lightly singed by the last embers of Asian alienation. Indeed, given all the incredibly hip Asian artists and fashion designers and so forth you can find in New York, it seemed that this feeling was destined to die out altogether. And yet here it was in a New Yorker more than a

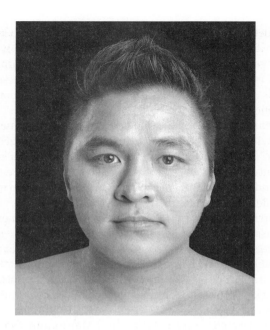

J. T. Tran

dozen years my junior. While it may be true that sections of the Asian-American world are devoid of alienation, there are large swaths where it is as alive as it has ever been.

A few weeks after we meet, Mao puts me in touch with Daniel Chu, his close friend from Stuyvesant. Chu graduated from Williams College last year, having won a creative-writing award for his poetry. He had spent a portion of the $18,000 prize on a trip to China, but now he is back living with his parents in Brooklyn Chinatown.

Chu remembers that during his first semester at Williams, his junior adviser would   25 periodically take him aside. Was he feeling all right? Was something the matter? "I was acclimating myself to the place," he says. "I wasn't totally happy, but I wasn't depressed." But then his new white friends made similar remarks. "They would say, 'Dan, it's kind of hard, sometimes, to tell what you're thinking.'"

Chu has a pleasant face, but it would not be wrong to characterize his demeanor as reserved. He speaks in a quiet, unemphatic voice. He doesn't move his features much. He attributes these traits to the atmosphere in his household. "When you grow up in a Chinese home," he says, "you don't talk. You shut up and listen to what your parents tell you to do."

At Stuyvesant, he had hung out in an exclusively Asian world in which friends were determined by which subway lines you traveled. But when he arrived at Williams, Chu slowly became aware of something strange: The white people in the New England wilderness walked around smiling at each other. "When you're in a place like that, everyone is friendly."

He made a point to start smiling more. "It was something that I had to actively practice," he says. "Like, when you have a transaction at a business, you hand over the money — and then you smile." He says that he's made some progress but that there's still plenty of work that remains. "I'm trying to undo eighteen years of a Chinese upbringing. Four years at Williams helps, but only so much." He is conscious of how his father, an IT manager, is treated at work. "He's the best programmer at his office," he says, "but because he doesn't speak English well, he is always passed over."

Though Chu is not merely fluent in English but is officially the most distinguished poet of his class at Williams, he still worries that other aspects of his demeanor might attract the same kind of treatment his father received. "I'm really glad we're having this conversation," he says at one point — it is helpful to be remembering these lessons in self-presentation just as he prepares for job interviews.

"I guess what I would like is to become so good at something that my social deficiencies no longer matter," he tells me. Chu is a bright, diligent, impeccably credentialed young man born in the United States. He is optimistic about his ability to earn respect in the world. But he doubts he will ever feel the same comfort in his skin that he glimpsed in the people he met at Williams. That kind of comfort, he says — "I think it's generations away." 30

While he was still an electrical-engineering student at Berkeley in the nineties, James Hong visited the IBM campus for a series of interviews. An older Asian researcher looked over Hong's résumé and asked him some standard questions. Then he got up without saying a word and closed the door to his office.

"Listen," he told Hong, "I'm going to be honest with you. My generation came to this country because we wanted better for you kids. We did the best we could, leaving our homes and going to graduate school not speaking much English. If you take this job, you are just going to hit the same ceiling we did. They just see me as an Asian Ph.D., never management potential. You are going to get a job offer, but don't take it. Your generation has to go farther than we did, otherwise we did everything for nothing."

It is a part of the bitter undercurrent of Asian-American life that so many graduates of elite universities find that meritocracy as they have understood it comes to an abrupt end after graduation.

The researcher was talking about what some refer to as the "Bamboo Ceiling" — an invisible barrier that maintains a pyramidal racial structure throughout corporate America, with lots of Asians at junior levels, quite a few in middle management, and virtually none in the higher reaches of leadership.

The failure of Asian-Americans to become leaders in the white-collar workplace does not qualify as one of the burning social issues of our time. But it is a part of the bitter undercurrent of Asian-American life that so many Asian graduates of elite universities find that meritocracy as they have understood it comes to an abrupt end after graduation. If between 15 and 20 percent of every Ivy League class is Asian, and if the Ivy Leagues are incubators for the country's leaders, it would stand to reason that Asians would make up some corresponding portion of the leadership class.

And yet the numbers tell a different story. According to a recent study, Asian-   35
Americans represent roughly 5 percent of the population but only 0.3 percent of corporate officers, less than 1 percent of corporate board members, and around 2 percent of
college presidents. There are nine Asian-American CEOs in the Fortune 500. In specific
fields where Asian-Americans are heavily represented, there is a similar asymmetry.
A third of all software engineers in Silicon Valley are Asian, and yet they make up
only 6 percent of board members and about 10 percent of corporate officers of the Bay
Area's 25 largest companies. At the National Institutes of Health, where 21.5 percent
of tenure-track scientists are Asians, only 4.7 percent of the lab or branch directors are,
according to a study conducted in 2005. One succinct evocation of the situation appeared in the comments section of a website called Yellowworld: "If you're East Asian,
you need to attend a top-tier university to land a good high-paying gig. Even if you
land that good high-paying gig, the white guy with the pedigree from a mediocre state
university will somehow move ahead of you in the ranks simply because he's white."

Jennifer W. Allyn, a managing director for diversity at PricewaterhouseCoopers,
works to ensure that "all of the groups feel welcomed and supported and able to thrive
and to go as far as their talents will take them." I posed to her the following definition of
parity in the corporate workforce: If the current crop of associates is 17 percent Asian,
then in fourteen years, when they have all been up for partner review, 17 percent of
those who are offered partner will be Asian. Allyn conceded that Pricewaterhouse-
Coopers was not close to reaching that benchmark anytime soon—and that "nobody
else is either."

Part of the insidious nature of the Bamboo Ceiling is that it does not seem to be
caused by overt racism. A survey of Asian-Pacific-American employees of Fortune 500
companies found that 80 percent reported they were judged not as Asians but as individuals. But only 51 percent reported the existence of Asians in key positions, and only
55 percent agreed that their firms were fully capitalizing on the talents and perspectives of Asians.

More likely, the discrepancy in these numbers is a matter of unconscious bias.
Nobody would affirm the proposition that tall men are intrinsically better leaders, for
instance. And yet while only 15 percent of the male population is at least six feet tall,
58 percent of all corporate CEOs are. Similarly, nobody would say that Asian people
are unfit to be leaders. But subjects in a recently published psychological experiment
consistently rated hypothetical employees with Caucasian-sounding names higher in
leadership potential than identical ones with Asian names.

Maybe it is simply the case that a traditionally Asian upbringing is the problem. As
Allyn points out, in order to be a leader, you must have followers. Associates at PricewaterhouseCoopers are initially judged on how well they do the work they are assigned.
"You have to be a doer," as she puts it. They are expected to distinguish themselves with
their diligence, at which point they become "super-doers." But being a leader requires
different skill sets. "The traits that got you to where you are won't necessarily take you
to the next level," says the diversity consultant Jane Hyun, who wrote a book called
Breaking the Bamboo Ceiling. To become a leader requires taking personal initiative and
thinking about how an organization can work differently. It also requires networking,
self-promotion, and self-assertion. It's racist to think that any given Asian individual
is unlikely to be creative or risk-taking. It's simple cultural observation to say that a

group whose education has historically focused on rote memorization and "pumping the iron of math" is, on aggregate, unlikely to yield many people inclined to challenge authority or break with inherited ways of doing things.

Sach Takayasu had been one of the fastest-rising members of her cohort in the marketing department at IBM in New York. But about seven years ago, she felt her progress begin to slow. "I had gotten to the point where I was overdelivering, working really long hours, and where doing more of the same wasn't getting me anywhere," she says. It was around this time that she attended a seminar being offered by an organization called Leadership Education for Asian Pacifics. 40

LEAP has parsed the complicated social dynamics responsible for the dearth of Asian-American leaders and has designed training programs that flatter Asian people even as it teaches them to change their behavior to suit white-American expectations. Asians who enter a LEAP program are constantly assured that they will be able to "keep your values, while acquiring new skills," along the way to becoming "culturally competent leaders."

In a presentation to 1,500 Asian-American employees of Microsoft, LEAP president and CEO J. D. Hokoyama laid out his grand synthesis of the Asian predicament in the workplace. "Sometimes people have perceptions about us and our communities which may or may not be true," Hokoyama told the audience. "But they put those perceptions onto us, and then they do something that can be very devastating: They make decisions about us not based on the truth but based on those perceptions." Hokoyama argued that it was not sufficient to rail at these unjust perceptions. In the end, Asian people themselves would have to assume responsibility for unmaking them. This was both a practical matter, he argued, and, in its own way, fair.

Aspiring Asian leaders had to become aware of "the relationship between values, behaviors, and perceptions." He offered the example of Asians who don't speak up at meetings. "So let's say I go to meetings with you and I notice you never say anything. And I ask myself, 'Hmm, I wonder why you're not saying anything. Maybe it's because you don't know what we're talking about. That would be a good reason for not saying anything. Or maybe it's because you're not even interested in the subject matter. Or maybe you think the conversation is beneath you.' So here I'm thinking, because you never say anything at meetings, that you're either dumb, you don't care, or you're arrogant. When maybe it's because you were taught when you were growing up that when the boss is talking, what are you supposed to be doing? Listening."

Takayasu took the weeklong course in 2006. One of the first exercises she encountered involved the group instructor asking for a list of some qualities that they identify with Asians. The students responded: upholding family honor, filial piety, self-restraint. Then the instructor solicited a list of the qualities the members identify with leadership, and invited the students to notice how little overlap there is between the two lists.

At first, Takayasu didn't relate to the others in attendance, who were listing typical Asian values their parents had taught them. "They were all saying things like 'Study hard,' 'Become a doctor or lawyer,' blah, blah, blah. That's not how my parents were. They would worry if they saw me working too hard." Takayasu had spent her childhood shuttling between New York and Tokyo. Her father was an executive at Mitsubishi; her mother was a concert pianist. She was highly assimilated into American culture, fluent in English, poised and confident. "But the more we got into it, as we 45 moved away from the obvious things to the deeper, more fundamental values, I began to see that my upbringing had been very Asian after all. My parents would say, 'Don't create problems. Don't trouble other people.' How Asian is that? It helped to explain why I don't reach out to other people for help." It occurred to Takayasu that she was a little bit "heads down" after all. She was willing to take on difficult assignments without seeking credit for herself. She was reluctant to "toot her own horn."

Takayasu has put her new self-awareness to work at IBM, and she now exhibits a newfound ability for horn tooting. "The things I could write on my résumé as my team's accomplishments: They're really impressive," she says.

The law professor and writer Tim Wu grew up in Canada with a white mother and a Taiwanese father, which allows him an interesting perspective on how whites and Asians perceive each other. After graduating from law school, he took a series of clerk-ships, and he remembers the subtle ways in which hierarchies were developed among the other young lawyers. "There is this automatic assumption in any legal environment that Asians will have a particular talent for bitter labor," he says, and then goes on to define the word *coolie*, a Chinese term for "bitter labor." "There was this weird self-selection where the Asians would migrate toward the most brutal part of the labor."

By contrast, the white lawyers he encountered had a knack for portraying themselves as above all that. "White people have this instinct that is really important: to give off the impression that they're only going to do the really important work. You're a quarterback. It's a kind of arrogance that Asians are trained not to have. Someone told me not long after I moved to New York that in order to succeed, you have to understand which rules you're supposed to break. If you break the wrong rules, you're finished. And so the easiest thing to do is follow all the rules. But then you consign yourself to a lower status. The real trick is understanding what rules are not meant for you."

This idea of a kind of rule-governed rule-breaking—where the rule book was un-written but passed along in an innate cultural sense—is perhaps the best explanation I have heard of how the Bamboo Ceiling functions in practice. LEAP appears to be very good at helping Asian workers who are already culturally competent become more self-aware of how their culture and appearance impose barriers to advancement. But I am not sure that a LEAP course is going to be enough to get Jefferson Mao or Daniel Chu the respect and success they crave. The issue is more fundamental, the social dynamics at work more deeply embedded, and the remedial work required may be at a more basic level of comportment.

What if you missed out on the lessons in masculinity taught in the gyms and locker rooms of America's high schools? What if life has failed to make you a socially domi-nant alpha male who runs the American boardroom and prevails in the American bedroom? What if no one ever taught you how to greet white people and make them comfortable? What if, despite these deficiencies, you no longer possess an immigrant's dutiful forbearance for a secondary position in the American narrative and want to be a player in the scrimmage of American appetite right now, in the present? 50

How do you undo eighteen years of a Chinese upbringing?

This is the implicit question that J. T. Tran has posed to a roomful of Yale under-graduates at a master's tea at Silliman College. His answer is typically Asian: practice. Tran is a pickup artist who goes by the handle Asian Playboy. He travels the globe running "boot camps," mostly for Asian male students, in the art of attraction. Today, he has been invited to Yale by the Asian-American Students Alliance.

"Creepy can be fixed," Tran explains to the standing-room-only crowd. "Many guys just don't realize how to project themselves." These are the people whom Tran spends his days with, a new batch in a new city every week: nice guys, intelligent guys, motivated guys, who never figured out how to be successful with women. Their mothers had kept them at home to study rather than let them date or socialize. Now Tran's company, ABCs of Attraction, offers a remedial education that consists of three four-hour seminars, followed by a supervised night out "in the field," in which J. T., his assistant Gareth Jones, and a tall blonde wing-girl named Sarah force them to approach women. Tuition costs $1,450.

"One of the big things I see with Asian students is what I call the Asian poker face—the lack of range when it comes to facial expressions," Tran says. "How many times has this happened to you?" he asks the crowd. "You'll be out at a party with your white friends, and they will be like—'Dude, are you angry?'" Laughter fills the room. Part of it is psychological, he explains. He recalls one Korean-American student he was teaching. The student was a very dedicated schoolteacher who cared a lot about his students. But none of this was visible. "Sarah was trying to help him, and she was like, 'C'mon, smile, smile,' and he was like . . ." And here Tran mimes the unbearable tension of a face trying to contort itself into a simulacrum of mirth. "He was so completely unpracticed at smiling that he literally could not do it." Eventually, though, the student fought through it, "and when he finally got to smiling he was, like, really cool."

Tran continues to lay out a story of Asian-American male distress that must be   55
relevant to the lives of at least some of those who have packed Master Krauss's living room. The story he tells is one of Asian-American disadvantage in the sexual marketplace, a disadvantage that he has devoted his life to overturning. Yes, it is about picking up women. Yes, it is about picking up white women. Yes, it is about attracting those women whose hair is the color of the midday sun and eyes are the color of the ocean, and it is about having sex with them. He is not going to apologize for the images of blonde women plastered all over his website. This is what he prefers, what he stands for, and what he is selling: the courage to pursue anyone you want, and the skills to make the person you desire desire you back. White guys do what they want; he is going to do the same.

But it is about much more than this, too. It is about altering the perceptions of Asian men—perceptions that are rooted in the way they behave, which are in turn rooted in the way they were raised—through a course of behavior modification intended to teach them how to be the socially dominant figures that they are not perceived to be. It is a program of, as he puts it to me later, "social change through pickup."

Tran offers his own story as an exemplary Asian underdog. Short, not good-looking, socially inept, sexually null. "If I got a B, I would be whipped," he remembers of his childhood. After college, he worked as an aerospace engineer at Boeing and

Raytheon, but internal politics disfavored him. Five years into his career, his entire white cohort had been promoted above him. "I knew I needed to learn about social dynamics, because just working hard wasn't cutting it."

His efforts at dating were likewise "a miserable failure." It was then that he turned to "the seduction community," a group of men on Internet message boards like alt .seduction.fast. It began as a "support group for losers" and later turned into a program of self-improvement. Was charisma something you could teach? Could confidence be reduced to a formula? Was it merely something that you either possessed or did not possess, as a function of the experiences you had been through in life, or did it emerge from specific forms of behavior? The members of the group turned their computer-science and engineering brains to the question. They wrote long accounts of their dates and subjected them to collective scrutiny. They searched for patterns in the raw material and filtered these experiences through social-psychological research. They eventually built a model.

This past Valentine's Day, during a weekend boot camp in New York City sponsored by ABCs of Attraction, the model is being played out. Tran and Jones are teaching their students how an alpha male stands (shoulders thrown back, neck fully extended, legs planted slightly wider than the shoulders). "This is going to feel very strange to you if you're used to slouching, but this is actually right," Jones says. They explain how an alpha male walks (no shuffling; pick your feet up entirely off the ground; a slight sway in the shoulders). They identify the proper distance to stand from "targets" (a slightly bent arm's length). They explain the importance of "kino escalation." (You must touch her. You must not be afraid to do this.) They are teaching the importance of sub-communication: what you convey about yourself before a single word has been spoken. They explain the importance of intonation. They explain what intonation is. "Your voice moves up and down in pitch to convey a variety of different emotions."

All of this is taught through a series of exercises. "This is going to feel completely artificial," says Jones on the first day of training. "But I need you to do the biggest shit-eating grin you've ever made in your life." Sarah is standing in the corner with her back to the students—three Indian guys, including one in a turban, three Chinese guys, and one Cambodian. The students have to cross the room, walking as an alpha male walks, and then place their hands on her shoulder—firmly but gently—and turn her around. Big smile. Bigger than you've ever smiled before. Raise your glass in a toast. Make eye contact and hold it. Speak loudly and clearly. Take up space without apology. This is what an alpha male does.

Before each student crosses the floor of that bare white cubicle in midtown, Tran asks him a question. "What is good in life?" Tran shouts.

The student then replies, in the loudest, most emphatic voice he can muster: "To crush my enemies, see them driven before me, and to hear the lamentation of their women—in my bed!"

For the intonation exercise, students repeat the phrase "I do what I want" with a variety of different moods.

"Say it like you're happy!" Jones shouts. ("I do what I want.") Say it like you're sad! ("I do what I want." The intonation utterly unchanged.) Like you're sad! ("I . . . do what I want.") Say it like you've just won $5 million! ("I do what I want.")

Raj, a 26-year-old Indian virgin, can barely get his voice to alter during intonation exercise. But on Sunday night, on the last evening of the boot camp, I watch him cold-approach a set of women at the Hotel Gansevoort and engage them in conversation for a half-hour. He does not manage to "number close" or "kiss close." But he had done something that not very many people can do.

Of the dozens of Asian-Americans I spoke with for this story, many were successful artists and scientists; or good-looking and socially integrated leaders; or tough, brassy, risk-taking, street-smart entrepreneurs. Of course, there are lots of such people around—do I even have to point that out? They are no more morally worthy than any other kind of Asian person. But they have figured out some useful things.

The lesson about the Bamboo Ceiling that James Hong learned from his interviewer at IBM stuck, and after working for a few years at Hewlett-Packard, he decided to strike off on his own. His first attempts at entrepreneurialism failed, but he finally struck pay dirt with a simple, not terribly refined idea that had a strong primal appeal: hotornot .com. Hong and his co-founder eventually sold the site for roughly $20 million.

Hong ran hotornot.com partly as a kind of incubator to seed in his employees the habits that had served him well. "We used to hire engineers from Berkeley—almost all Asian—who were on the cusp of being entrepreneurial but were instead headed toward jobs at big companies," he says. "We would train them in how to take risk, how to run things themselves. I remember encouraging one employee to read *The Game*— the infamous pickup-artist textbook—"because I figured growing the *cojones* to take risk was applicable to being an entrepreneur."

If the Bamboo Ceiling is ever going to break, it's probably going to have less to do with any form of behavior assimilation than with the emergence of risk-takers whose success obviates the need for Asians to meet someone else's behavioral standard. People like Steve Chen, who was one of the creators of YouTube, or Kai and Charles Huang, who created Guitar Hero. Or Tony Hsieh, the founder of Zappos.com, the online shoe retailer that he sold to Amazon for about a billion dollars in 2009. Hsieh is a short Asian man who speaks tersely and is devoid of obvious charisma. One cannot imagine him being promoted in an American corporation. And yet he has proved that an awkward Asian guy can be a formidable CEO and the unlikeliest of management gurus.

Hsieh didn't have to conform to Western standards of comportment because he 70
adopted early on the Western value of risk-taking. Growing up, he would play recordings of himself in the morning practicing the violin, in lieu of actually practicing. He credits the experience he had running a pizza business at Harvard as more important than anything he learned in class. He had an instinctive sense of what the real world would require of him, and he knew that nothing his parents were teaching him would get him there.

You don't, by the way, have to be a Silicon Valley hotshot to break through the Bamboo Ceiling. You can also be a chef like Eddie Huang, whose little restaurant on the Lower East Side, BaoHaus, sells delicious pork buns. Huang grew up in Orlando with a hard-core Tiger Mom and a disciplinarian father. "As a kid, psychologically, my day was all about not getting my ass kicked," he says. He gravitated toward the black kids at school, who also knew something about corporal punishment. He was the smallest member of his football team, but his coach named him MVP in the seventh grade. "I was defensive tackle and right guard because I was just mean. I was nasty. I had this mentality where I was like, 'You're going to accept me or I'm going to fuck you up.'"

Huang had a rough twenties, bumping repeatedly against the Bamboo Ceiling. In college, editors at the Orlando *Sentinel* invited him to write about sports for the paper. But when he visited the offices, "the editor came in and goes, 'Oh, no.' And his exact words: 'You can't write with that face.'" Later, in film class at Columbia, he wrote a script about an Asian-American hot-dog vendor obsessed with his small penis. "The screenwriting teacher was like, 'I love this. You have a lot of Woody Allen in you. But do you think you could change it to Jewish characters?'" Still later, after graduating from Cardozo School of Law, he took a corporate job, where other associates would frequently say, "You have a lot of opinions for an Asian guy."

Finally, Huang decided to open a restaurant. Selling food was precisely the fate his parents wanted their son to avoid, and they didn't talk to him for months after he quit lawyering. But Huang understood instinctively that he couldn't make it work in the professional world his parents wanted him to join. "I've realized that food is one of the only places in America where we are the top dogs," he says. "Guys like David Chang or me—we can hang. There's a younger generation that grew up eating Chinese fast food. They respect our food. They may not respect anything else, but they respect our food."

Rather than strive to make himself acceptable to the world, Huang has chosen to buy his way back in, on his own terms. "What I've learned is that America is about money, and if you can make your culture commodifiable, then you're relevant," he says. "I don't believe anybody agrees with what I say or supports what I do because they truly want to love Asian people. They like my fucking pork buns, and I don't get it twisted."

Sometime during the hundreds of hours he spent among the mostly untouched English-language novels at the Flushing branch of the public library, Jefferson Mao discovered literature's special power of transcendence, a freedom of imagination that can send you beyond the world's hierarchies. He had written to me seeking permission to swerve off the traditional path of professional striving—to devote himself to becoming an artist—but he was unsure of what risks he was willing to take. My answer was highly ambivalent. I recognized in him something of my own youthful ambition. And I knew where that had taken me.

Unlike Mao, I was not a poor, first-generation immigrant. I finished school alienated both from Asian culture (which, in my hometown, was barely visible) and the manners and mores of my white peers. But like Mao, I wanted to be an individual. I had refused both cultures as an act of self-assertion. An education spent dutifully acquiring credentials through relentless drilling seemed to me an obscenity. So did adopting the manipulative cheeriness that seemed to secure the popularity of white Americans.

Instead, I set about contriving to live beyond both poles. I wanted what James Baldwin sought as a writer—"a power which outlasts kingdoms." Anything short of that seemed a humiliating compromise. I would become an aristocrat of the spirit, who prides himself on his incompetence in the middling tasks that are the world's business. Who does not seek after material gain. Who is his own law.

This, of course, was madness. A child of Asian immigrants born into the suburbs of New Jersey and educated at Rutgers cannot be a law unto himself. The only way to approximate this is to refuse employment, because you will not be bossed around by people beneath you, and shave your expenses to the bone, because you cannot afford more, and move into a decaying Victorian mansion in Jersey City, so that your sense of eccentric distinction can be preserved in the midst of poverty, and cut yourself free of every form of bourgeois discipline, because these are precisely the habits that will keep you chained to the mediocre fate you consider worse than death.

Throughout my twenties, I proudly turned away from one institution of American life after another (for instance, a steady job), though they had already long since turned away from me. Academe seemed another kind of death—but then again, I had a transcript marred by as many F's as A's. I had come from a culture that was the middle path incarnate. And yet for some people, there can be no middle path, only transcendence or descent into the abyss.

I was descending into the abyss. 80

All this was well deserved. No one had any reason to think I was anything or anyone. And yet I felt entitled to demand this recognition. I knew this was wrong and impermissible; therefore I had to double down on it. The world brings low such people. It brought me low. I haven't had health insurance in ten years. I didn't earn more than $12,000 for eight consecutive years. I went three years in the prime of my adulthood without touching a woman. I did not produce a masterpiece.

I recall one of the strangest conversations I had in the city. A woman came up to me at a party and said she had been moved by a piece of writing I had published. She confessed that prior to reading it, she had never wanted to talk to me, and had always been sure, on the basis of what she could see from across the room that I was nobody worth talking to, that I was in fact someone to avoid.

But she had been wrong about this, she told me: It was now plain to her that I was a person with great reserves of feeling and insight. She did not ask my forgiveness for this brutal misjudgment. Instead, what she wanted to know was—why had I kept that person she had glimpsed in my essay so well hidden? She confessed something of her own hidden sorrow: She had never been beautiful and had decided, early on, that it therefore fell to her to "love the world twice as hard." Why hadn't I done that?

Here was a drunk white lady speaking what so many others over the years must have been insufficiently drunk to tell me. It was the key to many things that had, and had not, happened. I understood this encounter better after learning about LEAP, and visiting Asian Playboy's boot camp. If you are a woman who isn't beautiful, it is a social reality that you will have to work twice as hard to hold anyone's attention. You can either linger on the unfairness of this or you can get with the program. If you are an Asian person who holds himself proudly aloof, nobody will respect that, or find it intriguing, or wonder if that challenging façade hides someone worth getting to know. They will simply write you off as someone not worth the trouble of talking to.

Having glimpsed just how unacceptable the world judges my demeanor, could I 85 too strive to make up for my shortcomings? Practice a shit-eating grin until it becomes natural? Love the world twice as hard?

I see the appeal of getting with the program. But this is not my choice. Striving to meet others' expectations may be a necessary cost of assimilation, but I am not going to do it.

Often I think my defiance is just delusional, self-glorifying bullshit that artists have always told themselves to compensate for their poverty and powerlessness. But sometimes I think it's the only thing that has preserved me intact, and that what has been preserved is not just haughty caprice but in fact the meaning of my life. So this is what I told Mao: In lieu of loving the world twice as hard, I care, in the end, about expressing my obdurate singularity at any cost. I love this hard and unyielding part of myself more than any other reward the world has to offer a newly brightened and ingratiating demeanor, and I will bear any costs associated with it.

The first step toward self-reform is to admit your deficiencies. Though my early adulthood has been a protracted education in them, I do not admit mine. I'm fine. It's the rest of you who have a problem. Fuck all y'all.

Amy Chua returned to Yale from a long, exhausting book tour in which one television interviewer had led off by noting that Internet commenters were calling her a monster. By that point, she had become practiced at the special kind of self-presentation required of a person under public siege. "I do not think that Chinese parents are superior," she declared at the annual gathering of the Asian-American Students Alliance. "I think there are many ways to be a good parent."

Much of her talk to the students, and indeed much of the conversation surround- 90 ing the book, was focused on her own parenting decisions. But just as interesting is how her parents parented her. Chua was plainly the product of a brute-force Chinese education. *Battle Hymn of the Tiger Mother* includes many lessons she was taught by her parents—lessons any LEAP student would recognize. "Be modest, be humble, be simple," her mother told her. "Never complain or make excuses," her father instructed. "If something seems unfair at school, just prove yourself by working twice as hard and being twice as good."

In the book, Chua portrays her distaste for corporate law, which she practiced before going into academe. "My entire three years at the firm, I always felt like I was playacting, ridiculous in my suit," she writes. This malaise extended even earlier, to her time as a student. "I didn't care about the rights of criminals the way others did, and I froze whenever a professor called on me. I also wasn't naturally skeptical and questioning; I just wanted to write down everything the professor said and memorize it."

At the AASA gathering at Yale, Chua made the connection between her upbringing and her adult dissatisfaction. "My parents didn't sit around talking about politics and philosophy at the dinner table," she told the students. Even after she had escaped from corporate law and made it onto a law faculty, "I was kind of lost. I just didn't feel the passion." Eventually, she made a name for herself as the author of popular books about foreign policy and became an award-winning teacher. But it's plain that she was no better prepared for legal scholarship than she had been for corporate law. "It took me a long, long time," she said. "And I went through lots and lots of rejection." She recalled her extended search for an academic post, in which she was "just not able to do a good interview, just not able to present myself well."

In other words, *Battle Hymn* provides all the material needed to refute the very cultural polemic for which it was made to stand. Chua's Chinese education had gotten her through an elite schooling, but it left her unprepared for the real world. She does not hide any of this. She had set out, she explained, to write a memoir that was "defiantly self-incriminating"—and the result was a messy jumble of conflicting impulses, part provocation, part self-critique. Western readers rode roughshod over this paradox and made of Chua a kind of Asian minstrel figure. But more than anything else, *Battle Hymn* is a very American project—one no traditional Chinese person would think to undertake. "Even if you hate the book," Chua pointed out, "the one thing it is not is meek."

"The loudest duck gets shot" is a Chinese proverb. "The nail that sticks out gets hammered down" is a Japanese one. Its Western correlative: "The squeaky wheel gets the grease." Chua had told her story and been hammered down. Yet here she was, fresh from her hammering, completely unbowed.

There is something salutary in that proud defiance. And though the debate she sparked about Asian-American life has been of questionable value, we will need more people with the same kind of defiance, willing to push themselves into the spotlight and to make some noise, to beat people up, to seduce women, to make mistakes, to become entrepreneurs, to stop doggedly pursuing official paper emblems attesting to their worthiness, to stop thinking those scraps of paper will secure anyone's happiness, and to dare to be interesting. 95

Exploring Context

1. The popular TV show *Glee* had an episode called "Asian F." Watch a clip of this episode on YouTube and read the comments left in response. How does this clip and viewer reactions reflect the issues that Yang discusses in his essay?

2. In some ways, Yang's essay is a response to Amy Chua's book *Battle Hymn of the Tiger Mother*, in which she discusses a set of culturally inflected parenting techniques that are packed into the term "Tiger Mom." Visit Tiger Mom Says (tigermomsays.tumblr.com). How do the images there reflect the themes of Yang's essay?

3. Review the Ivy League college acceptance rates as represented by Bradshaw College Consulting, a company that specializes in helping students get into universities (bradshawcollegeconsulting.com/college_acceptance_rate.html). How do these acceptance rates confirm or complicate Yang's argument? What does the existence of companies such as Bradshaw College Consulting suggest about the claims Yang makes?

Questions for Connecting

1. In "The End of Race: Hawaii and the Mixing of Peoples" (p. 334), Steve Olson suggests that race no longer has any genetic basis even though the notion of race (and the ramifications of it) continues to exist. How does Yang contribute to Olson's argument? Synthesize both authors to consider why race is persistent. Can it ever be possible for us to move beyond the idea of race? Use both authors to support your position.

2. Kenji Yoshino, an Asian American himself, talks about the ways we tend to downplay part of our identity—a process he calls "covering" in "Preface" and "The New Civil Rights" (p. 552). What response does Yang offer to Yoshino's concept of covering? Given Yang's argument, what are the possibilities of achieving Yoshino's goals for civil rights?

3. In part, Yang is concerned with exploring the realities behind the stereotypes of Asian Americans. Jennifer Pozner's "Ghetto Bitches, China Dolls, and Cha Cha Divas" (p. 397) examines how racial stereotypes play out in popular media, specifically the television show *America's Next Top Model*. In what ways does Yang confirm Pozner's argument? Synthesize the arguments of both authors to form a statement about the impact of racial stereotypes on individuals and on society.

Language Matters

1. At the start of this selection, Yang uses several sentence fragments (see if you can find them). Why does Yang use these? In what situations might a sentence fragment be acceptable? In what ways does intentional use of sentence fragments rely on an understanding of context and audience? When, if ever, should fragments be used in academic writing?

2. Quotations in academic writing must be of appropriate length. Find a significant passage from the essay and choose the shortest and longest useful quotations from the passage. How short is too short? How long is too long? How might you use quotations of different lengths for different ends?

3. The classic rhetorical triangle is composed of receiver, sender, and message. Using this essay, design a new shape to explain its rhetorical situation: What additional elements should be considered? Would the inclusion of style make a rhetorical square? What elements would be included in a rhetorical hexagon?

Assignments for Writing

1. Yang's essay is centrally concerned with the relationship between stereotypes and the realities behind them. Write a paper on the impact of stereotypes on individuals. In what ways are stereotypes enabling? Can there be positive stereotypes? Is it possible to get rid of stereotypes?

2. How can Asian Americans break through the "Bamboo Ceiling"? Write a paper in which you propose strategies for overcoming this limitation, building on the strategies discussed in Yang's essay and incorporating your work from Question 3 of Questions for Critical Reading.

3. Both education and upbringing play important roles in the lives of the people Yang discusses in his essay. How do these factors interact to shape a person's future? Write a paper in which you discuss the roles of education and parenting in the shaping of an individual. Is it possible to escape these influences? To what end? How does Yang challenge either or both?

KENJI YOSHINO

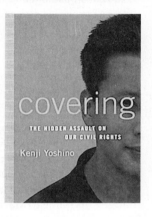

Kenji Yoshino is the Chief Justice Earl Warren Professor of Constitutional Law at New York University. Previously, Yoshino was a professor of law and the deputy dean of intellectual life at Yale Law School, where he earned a J.D. after graduating from Harvard and Oxford universities. His articles have appeared in various law journals as well as the *New York Times*, the *Village Voice*, the *Boston Globe*, and the *Nation*. He is the author of *Covering: The Hidden Assault on Our Civil Rights* (2006) and *A Thousand Times More Fair: What Shakespeare's Plays Teach Us About Justice* (2011).

Covering offers a unique perspective on the familiar concepts of assimilation and passing, utilizing Yoshino's background experience as both a law scholar and a gay Asian American. Yoshino combines personal narrative and legal argument to lay out a new definition of civil rights. The term *covering*, as Yoshino uses it, means "to tone down a disfavored identity to fit into the mainstream" (p. 552), and Yoshino argues that though Americans value the idea of the melting pot as a model for our culture, that ideal can have unintended negative consequences. Despite our avowed appreciation for multiculturalism, the unstated public expectation is still for people of all genders, sexual orientations, and races to conform to rigid expectations.

The selections here, "Preface" and "The New Civil Rights," form something close to a set of bookends for Yoshino's argument in *Covering*. After defining the concept of covering and the problems caused by it in the "Preface" and investigating the issue of a distinct "True Self" and "False Self" in the second excerpt, Yoshino moves on to propose a new paradigm for civil rights. Questioning the idea of legislating civil rights, Yoshino suggests that the next step may have to occur in bars, restaurants, and Internet chat rooms; he also suggests that in order to accommodate an increasingly diverse population, the model of civil rights itself must change. Yoshino points the way by helping us to rethink our model of civil rights and the mechanisms used to bring those rights into existence.

The United States is more diverse than ever. How can we balance the rights of diverse groups with the demands of individuals and the nation?

▶ TAGS: *civil rights, social change, identity, human dignity, community, diversity, sexuality*

Questions for Critical Reading

1. What does Yoshino mean by the "new" civil rights? Define the term as you read by locating passages from his text. What makes it new? How does it differ from "old" civil rights? Use Yoshino's text to define "liberty" and "equality" paradigms as part of your response.

2. What is "covering"? Define the concept using Yoshino's text and then offer your own example.

3. How does Yoshino think we can achieve the new civil rights? Identify passages that show his position, and then respond to it. Do you think his vision is possible? Is it something we should strive for? To prepare for your response, read Yoshino's text critically to locate points of connection between his position and yours.

Preface

Everyone covers. To cover is to tone down a disfavored identity to fit into the mainstream. In our increasingly diverse society, all of us are outside the mainstream in some way. Nonetheless, being deemed mainstream is still often a necessity of social life. For this reason, every reader of this book has covered, whether consciously or not, and sometimes at significant personal cost.

Famous examples of covering abound. Ramón Estévez covered his ethnicity when he changed his name to Martin Sheen, as did Krishna Bhanji when he changed his name to Ben Kingsley. Margaret Thatcher covered her status as a woman when she trained with a voice coach to lower the timbre of her voice. Long after they came out as lesbians, Rosie O'Donnell and Mary Cheney still covered, keeping their same-sex partners out of the public eye. Issur Danielovitch Demsky covered his Judaism when he became Kirk Douglas, as did Joseph Levitch when he became Jerry Lewis. Franklin Delano Roosevelt covered his disability by ensuring his wheelchair was always hidden behind a desk before his Cabinet entered.

I doubt any of these people covered willingly. I suspect they were all bowing to an unjust reality that required them to tone down their stigmatized identities to get along in life. Sheen says he needed to "get a name people could pronounce and connect with" if he "wanted to work commercially." Yet he now regrets having done so, and has exhorted his sons—Emilio and Charlie—to use the family name. One of them has not done so, signaling the enduring force of the covering demand.

In a supposedly enlightened age, the persistence of the covering demand presents a puzzle. Today, race, national origin, sex, religion, and disability are all protected by federal civil rights laws. An increasing number of states and localities include sexual orientation in civil rights laws as well. Albeit with varying degrees of conviction, Americans have come to a consensus that people should not be penalized for being different along these dimensions. That consensus, however, does not protect individuals against demands that they mute those differences. We need an explanation for why the civil rights revolution has stalled on covering.

Covering has enjoyed such a robust and stubborn life because it is a form of assimilation. At least since Hector St. John de Crèvecoeur's 1782 *Letters from an American*

5

Farmer, this country has touted assimilation as the way Americans of different backgrounds would be "melted into a new race of men." By the time Israel Zangwill's play of that name was performed in 1908, the "melting pot" had acquired the burnish of an American ideal. Only with the civil rights movement of the 1960s was this ideal challenged in any systematic way, with calls to move "beyond the melting pot" and to "celebrate diversity." And not withstanding that challenge, assimilation has never lost its hold on the American imagination. Indeed, as our country grows more pluralistic, we have seen a renaissance of the melting pot ideal. Fearful that we are spinning apart into balkanized groups, even liberals like Arthur Schlesinger have called for a recommitment to that ethic. In the United States, as in other industrialized democracies, we are seeing the "return of assimilation."

I recognize the value of assimilation, which is often necessary to fluid social interaction, to peaceful coexistence, and even to the dialogue through which difference is valued. For that reason, this is no simple screed against conformity. What I urge here is that we approach the renaissance of assimilation in this country critically. We must be willing to see the dark side of assimilation, and specifically of covering, which is the most widespread form of assimilation required of us today.

Covering is a hidden assault on our civil rights. We have not been able to see it as such because it has swaddled itself in the benign language of assimilation. But if we look closely, we will see that covering is the way many groups are being held back today. The reason racial minorities are pressured to "act white" is because of white supremacy. The reason women are told to downplay their child-care responsibilities in the workplace is because of patriarchy. And the reason gays are asked not to "flaunt" is because of homophobia. So long as such covering demands persist, American civil rights will not have completed its work.

Unfortunately, the law has yet to perceive covering as a threat. Contemporary civil rights law generally only protects traits that individuals cannot change, like their skin color, chromosomes, or innate sexual orientations. This means that current law will not protect us against most covering demands, because such demands direct themselves at the behavioral aspects of our personhood. This is so despite the fact that covering imposes costs on us all.

The universality of the covering demand, however, is also a potential boon for civil rights advocates. I, too, worry about our current practice of fracturing into groups, each clamoring for state and social solicitude. For this reason, I do not think we can move forward by focusing on old-fashioned group-based identity politics. We must instead build a new civil rights paradigm on what draws us together rather than on what drives us apart. Because covering applies to us all, it provides an issue around which we can make common cause. This is the desire for authenticity, our common human wish to express ourselves without being impeded by unreasoning demands for conformity.

I thought I would make this argument in purely political terms. As a law professor, I have become accustomed to the tones of legal impersonality. But I came to see that I could not compose an argument about the importance of human authenticity without risking such authenticity myself. So I have written this . . . in a more intimate voice, blending memoir with argument. In trying to make the stakes of assimilation vivid, I draw on my attempts to elaborate my identity as a gay man, and, to a lesser extent, my identity as an Asian-American.

Yet this is not a standard "coming out" narrative or racial memoir. I follow the Romantics here in their belief that if a human life is described with enough particularity, the universal will begin to speak through it. What interests me about my story, and the stories of others, is how similar they are in revealing the bones of our common human endeavor, the yearning for human emancipation that stirs within us all.

The New Civil Rights

To describe the new civil rights, I return to the source of my argument. What most excited me about gay civil rights was its universal resonance. Unlike other civil rights groups, gays must articulate invisible selves without the initial support of our immediate communities. That makes the gay project of self-elaboration emblematic of the search for authenticity all of us engage in as human beings. It is work each of us must do for ourselves, and it is the most important work we can do.

In looking for a vocabulary for this quest for authenticity, I found psychoanalysts more helpful than lawyers. The object-relations theorist D. W. Winnicott makes a distinction between a True Self and a False Self that usefully tracks the distinction between the uncovered and covered selves. The True Self is the self that gives an individual the feeling of being real, which is "more than existing; it is finding a way to exist as oneself, and to relate to objects as oneself, and to have a self into which to retreat for relaxation." The True Self is associated with human spontaneity and authenticity: "Only the True Self can be creative and only the True Self can feel real." The False Self, in contrast, gives an individual a sense of being unreal, a sense of futility. It mediates the relationship between the True Self and the world.

What I love about Winnicott is that he does not demonize the False Self. To the contrary, Winnicott believes the False Self protects the True Self: "The False Self has one positive and very important function: to hide the True Self, which it does by compliance with environmental demands." Like a king castling behind a rook in chess, the more valuable but less powerful piece retreats behind the less valuable but more powerful one. Because the relationship between the True Self and the False Self is symbiotic, Winnicott believes both selves will exist even in the healthy individual.

Nonetheless, Winnicott defines health according to the degree of ascendancy the True Self gains over the False one. At the negative extreme, the False Self completely obscures the True Self, perhaps even from the individual herself. In a less extreme case, the False Self permits the True Self "a secret life." The individual approaches health only when the False Self has "as its main concern a search for conditions which will make it possible for the True Self to come into its own." Finally, in the healthy individual, the False Self is reduced to a "polite and mannered social attitude," a tool available to the fully realized True Self.

This paradigm captures my coming-out experience. My gay self, the True Self, was hidden behind an ostensibly straight False Self. Yet it would be wrong to cast the closeted self as purely inimical to the gay one. In my adolescence, this False Self protected the True Self until its survival was assured. Only at this point did the False

Self switch from being a help to being a hindrance. And even after I came out, the False Self never disappeared. It was reduced to the minimum necessary to regulate relations between the True Self and the world.

I could slot other civil rights identities into Winnicott's paradigm. The importance of the paradigm, however, lies in its self-conscious universality. Winnicott posits that each of us has a True Self that must be expressed for us to have the feeling of being switched on, of being alive. And if the True Self embodies the importance of authenticity, the False Self embodies our ambivalence about assimilation, which is both necessary to survival and obstructive of life. The goal is not to eliminate assimilation altogether, but to reduce it to the necessary minimum. This is what the reason-forcing conversation seeks to do.

When I describe the uncovered self in Winnicott's terms, many people respond immediately with stories that attest to the concept's universality. Most of these have little to do with conventional civil rights categories. They often pertain to choices about people's careers or personal lives, like the woman who left a career in law to write plays, or the man who left his fiancée at the altar to pursue his first childhood love. I nonetheless hear the same themes threading through these stories as I do through the traditional civil rights cases. These individuals cannot articulate what authenticity is, but know an existence lived outside its imperative would be a substitute for life.

Parents often respond to the concept of the True Self by speaking of their children. Based on extensive clinical research, psychologist Carol Gilligan argues that children have an authentic voice they lose as they mature, with girls retaining it longer than boys. (The breaking of this emotional voice mirrors the breaking of the physical voice, as the voices of boys break earlier and more dramatically than those of girls.) Gilligan's work is replete with instances of parents awed by the directness and realness of their children. These parents suggest that one of the most agonizing dilemmas of parenting is how much they should require their children to cover in the world.

This psychological discourse about authentic selves sounds distant from current civil rights discourse. We must close that gap. The new civil rights must harness this universal impulse toward authenticity. That impulse should press us toward thinking of civil rights less in terms of groups than in terms of our common humanity. 20

Two recent cases show that the Supreme Court is sympathetic to that shift. In the 2003 case of *Lawrence v. Texas* . . . the Supreme Court struck down a Texas statute that criminalized same-sex sodomy. Many assumed the Court would use this case to decide whether to give gays the judicial protections currently accorded to racial minorities and women. But while the Court struck down the statute (and overruled *Bowers v. Hardwick* in the process), it did not do so based on the equality rights of gays. Rather, it held that the statute violated the fundamental right of all persons—straight, gay, or otherwise—to control our intimate sexual relations.

Similarly, in the 2004 case of *Tennessee v. Lane*, the Supreme Court considered the question of whether two paraplegic individuals could sue Tennessee for failing to make its courthouses wheelchair accessible. (One plaintiff was forced to crawl up the courthouse steps to answer criminal charges against him; the other, a certified court reporter, alleged she had lost job opportunities because some county courthouses were inaccessible.) Again, the Court ruled in favor of the minority group without framing its ruling in group-based equality rhetoric. Rather, it held that all persons—disabled or otherwise—have a "right of access to the courts," which had been denied in this case.

In an era when the Supreme Court has closed many civil rights doors, it has left this one wide open. It is much more sympathetic to "liberty" claims about freedoms we all hold than to "equality" claims asserted by a subset of the population. It is easy to see why. Equality claims—such as group-based accommodation claims—inevitably involve the Court in picking favorites among groups. In an increasingly pluralistic society, the Court understandably wishes to steer clear of that enterprise. Liberty claims, on the other hand, emphasize what all Americans (or more precisely, all persons within the jurisdiction of the United States) have in common. The claim that we all have a right to sexual intimacy, or that we all have a right to access the courts, will hold no matter how many new groups proliferate in this country.

The Supreme Court's shift toward a more universal register can also be seen in its nascent acceptance of human rights. I worked on a friend-of-the-court brief in the *Lawrence* case produced by a team centered at Yale Law School. With the former President of Ireland and U.N. High Commissioner Mary Robinson as our client, we argued that decisions by international tribunals and courts in other Western democracies had recognized the fundamentality of the right to adult consensual sexual intimacy. We knew this argument would be resisted by some justices on the Court, who do not take kindly to arguments that decisions outside the United States should guide their jurisprudence. But to our surprise, the majority opinion cited our brief for the proposition that *Bowers* violated "values we share with a wider civilization."

At the end of their lives, both Martin Luther King Jr. and Malcolm X argued for this transition from civil rights to human rights. Both believed that civil rights unduly focused on what distinguished individuals from one another, rather than emphasizing what they had in common. As Stewart Burns, one of the editors of the King papers at Stanford, observes, King "grasped that 'civil rights' carried too much baggage of the dominant tradition of American individualism and not enough counterweight from a tradition of communitarian impulses, collective striving, and common good." Similarly, Malcolm X exhorted Americans to "expand the civil-rights struggle to the level of human rights," so that the "jurisdiction of Uncle Sam" would not prevent us from allying with our "brothers" of other nations.

The universal rights of persons will probably be the way the Court will protect difference in the future. I predict that if the Court ever recognizes language rights, it will protect them as a liberty to which we are all entitled, rather than as an equality right attached to a particular national-origin group. And if the Court recognizes rights to grooming, such as the right to wear cornrows or not to wear makeup, I believe it will do so under something more akin to the German Constitution's right to personality rather than as a right attached to groups like racial minorities or women.

One of the great benefits of analyzing civil rights in terms of universal liberty rather than in terms of group-based equality is that it avoids making assumptions about group cultures. I've touched on the problem that the covering concept might assume too quickly that individuals behaving in "mainstream" ways are hiding some true identity, when in fact they might just be "being themselves." A female colleague of mine gave me a powerful version of this critique: "Here is what I dislike about your project. When I do something stereotypically masculine—like fixing my bike—your project makes it more likely people will think I'm putting on a gender performance rather than accepting the most straightforward explanation for what I'm doing. I don't fix my bike because I'm trying to downplay the fact that I'm a woman. I fix it because it's broken."

She gave another example: "When I was in graduate school, there was an African-American man who studied German Romantic poetry. Under your model, I could easily see someone saying he was 'covering' his African-American identity by studying something so esoteric and highbrow. But it was clear to me he was studying Romantic poetry because he was seized by it. And if someone had assumed he was studying it to 'act white,' they would have diminished him as a human being."

The coup de grâce: "Your commitment is to help people 'be themselves' — to resist demands to conform that take away their ability to be the individuals they are. But the covering idea could perpetuate the stereotypes you want to eliminate. One way minorities break stereotypes is by acting against them. If every time they do so, people assume they are 'covering' some essential stereotypical identity, the stereotypes will never go away."

I have literally lost sleep over this criticism. But in my waking hours, I take it more   30 as a caution than as a wholesale indictment. I agree that we must not assume that individuals behaving in "mainstream" ways are necessarily covering. My ultimate commitment is to autonomy as a means of achieving authenticity, rather than to a fixed conception of what authenticity might be. (Here I follow Winnicott, who observes the

I have literally lost sleep over this criticism.

True Self is not susceptible to specific definition, as its nature differs for each of us.) In talking about classic civil rights groups, I have focused on the demand to conform to the mainstream because I think that for most groups (except women) these are the demands that most threaten our authenticity. But I am equally opposed to demands that individuals reverse cover, because such demands are also impingements on our autonomy, and therefore on our authenticity.

In practice, I expect the liberty paradigm to protect the authentic self better than the equality paradigm. While it need not do so, the equality paradigm is prone to essentializing the identities it protects. Under an equality paradigm, if a woman who wore a lot of makeup were protected by a court because makeup is an "essential" part of being a woman, this could reinforce the stereotype that women wear makeup. But if the same woman were given the liberty right to elaborate her own gender identity in ways that did not impinge on her job performance, she would be protected from demands to be either more "masculine" or more "feminine." Marsha Wislocki-Goin would be protected for wearing "too much makeup" and Darlene Jespersen would be protected for not wearing it at all. Each woman would then have the full panoply of options from which she could fashion her gender identity. And in protecting that range, the law would not articulate any presupposition about what an "authentic" or "essential" woman would look like. Authenticity would be something these women, and not the state or employer, would find for themselves.

Group-based identity politics is not dead. As I have argued, I still believe in a group-based accommodation model for existing civil rights groups. This is in part because I believe we have made a commitment to those groups to protect them from such covering demands. The statutory language of the Civil Rights Act and the Americans with Disabilities Act already protects racial minorities, religious minorities, women, and individuals with disabilities *as groups* against covering demands. It has been the courts that have erroneously limited the ambit of those protections. Such a group-based equality paradigm is completely consistent with the individual liberty paradigm. In fact, the equality and liberty strands of antidiscrimination law are inextricably intertwined.

Moreover, even if we shift the focus of civil rights law away from equality to liberty, identity politics will still be crucial. If it weren't for the gay rights movement, or the disability rights movement, cases like *Lawrence* or *Lane* would never have made it to the Court. But I'm sympathetic to the Court's desire to frame these cases not as "gay" or "disability" cases, but as cases touching on rights that, like a rising tide, will lift the boat of every person in America. Ironically, it may be the explosion of diversity in this country that will finally make us realize what we have in common. Multiculturalism has forced us to vary and vary the human being in the imagination until we discover what is invariable about her.

While I have great hopes for this new legal paradigm, I also believe law will be a relatively trivial part of the new civil rights. A doctor friend told me that in his first year of medical school, his dean described how doctors were powerless to cure the vast majority of human ills. People would get better, or they would not, but it would not be doctors who would cure them. Part of becoming a doctor, the dean said, was to surrender a layperson's awe for medical authority. I wished then that someone would give an analogous lecture to law students, and to Americans at large. My education in law has been in part an education in its limitations.

For starters, many covering demands are made by actors the law does not—and 35 in my view should not—hold accountable, such as friends, family, neighbors, or people themselves. When I hesitate before engaging in a public display of same-sex affection, I am not thinking of the state or my employer, but of the strangers around me and my own internal censor. And while I am often tempted to sue myself, this is not my healthiest impulse.

Law is also an incomplete solution to coerced assimilation because it has yet to recognize the myriad groups subjected to covering demands outside traditional civil rights classifications like race, sex, orientation, religion, and disability. Whenever I speak about covering, I receive new instances of identities that can be covered. This is Winnicott's point—each one of us has a False Self that hides a True one. The law may someday move to protect some of these identities. But it will never protect them all.

Most important, law is incomplete in the qualitative remedies it provides. I confronted this recently when I became a plaintiff in a lawsuit against the Department of Defense. Under a congressional statute called the Solomon Amendment, the department threatened to cut off $350 million of federal funding from Yale University if the law school did not exempt the military from the law school's policy of protecting gays against discrimination by employers. Our suit argues that the statute is unconstitutional. I believe in this lawsuit, and was heartened that the vast majority of my law school colleagues signed on as plaintiffs. I was also elated when the district court judge, Judge Janet Hall, granted summary judgment in our favor. (As the government has taken an appeal, the case is still pending.) But there is nothing like being a plaintiff to realize that lawsuits occur between people who have no better way of talking to each other.

When I think about the elaboration of my gay identity, I am grateful to see litigation has had little to do with it. The department is the only entity I have ever wanted to sue. Even when I encountered demands for assimilation, my best response was to draw my interlocutor into a conversation. Just as important, framing the project of self-elaboration in purely legal—and therefore adversarial—terms would fail to honor all those who were not adversaries. I have described in these pages many individuals who helped me toward myself. But there were many more. I think here of my law professor Charles Reich, who wrote a memoir about coming out in 1976, when it was an act of real courage to do so, and who let me write the essay that begins this book in his class, though its relationship to the law was then entirely unclear. I think of the chair of my midtenure review committee, who sat me down when I was the only untenured member of the faculty and, unsurprisingly, a mass of nerves, to give me the verdict of the committee. He told me his only advice for the coming years was that I should be more myself, that instead of reasoning within the law as it existed, I should speak my truth and make the law shape itself around me. And I think of my parents, whose response to this manuscript was to say, with calm and conviction, that they were proud of the man I have become.

For these reasons, I am troubled that Americans seem increasingly to turn toward the law to do the work of civil rights precisely when they should be turning away from it. The real solution lies in all of us as citizens, not in the tiny subset of us who are lawyers. People who are not lawyers should have reason-forcing conversations outside the law. They should pull Goffman's term "covering" out of academic obscurity and press it into the popular lexicon, so that it has the same currency as terms like "passing" or "the closet." People confronted with demands to cover should feel emboldened to seek a reason for that demand, even if the law does not reach the actors making the demand, or recognize the group burdened by it. These reason-forcing conversations should happen outside courtrooms—in workplaces and restaurants, schools and playgrounds, chat rooms and living rooms, public squares and bars. They should occur informally and intimately, where tolerance is made and unmade.

What will constitute a good enough reason to justify assimilation will obviously 40 be controversial. But I want to underscore that we have come to some consensus that certain reasons are illegitimate—like white supremacy, patriarchy, homophobia, religious intolerance, and animus toward the disabled. I ask us to be true to the commitments we have made by never accepting such biases as legitimate grounds for covering demands. Beyond that, I have sought to engender a series of conversations, rather than a series of results—what reasons count, and for what purposes, will be for us to decide by facing one another as individuals. My personal inclination is always to privilege the claims of the individual against countervailing interests like "neatness" or "workplace harmony." But we should have that conversation.

Such conversations are the best—and perhaps the only—way to give both assimilation and authenticity their proper due. These conversations will help us chart and stay the course between the monocultural America suggested by conservative alarmists and the balkanized America suggested by the radical multiculturalists. They will reveal the true dimension of civil rights. The aspiration of civil rights has always been to permit people to pursue their human flourishing without limitations based on bias. Focusing on law prevents us from seeing the revolutionary breadth of that aspiration, as law has limited civil rights to particular groups. I am not faulting that limitation, as I think prioritization is necessary, and that the law's priorities are correct. But civil rights, which has always extended far beyond the law, may now need to do so more than ever. It is only when we leave the law that civil rights suddenly stops being about particular groups and starts to become a project of human flourishing in which we all have a stake.

We must use the relative freedom of adulthood to integrate the many selves we hold. This includes uncovering the selves we buried long ago because they were inconvenient, impractical, or even hated. Because they must pass the test of survival, most of the selves we hold, like most of our lives, are ordinary. Yet sometimes, what is consequential in us begins to shine.

Exploring Context

1. Explore the website for the U.S. Commission on Civil Rights (usccr.gov). Which paradigm does it reflect, "liberty" or "equality"? Use your definition of these terms from Question 1 of Questions for Critical Reading.

2. Yoshino uses recent Supreme Court decisions to make his argument. Visit the website for the Supreme Court at supremecourtus.gov. What recent cases have concerned civil rights? What impact do these cases (or the lack of such cases) have on Yoshino's argument?

3. According to Yoshino, changes in civil rights should come not from legislation but through conversation. Search Internet blogs and forums for "civil rights" and related terms. Are people talking about these issues online? What does this say about Yoshino's argument? Connect your exploration to your response to Question 3 of Questions for Critical Reading.

Questions for Connecting

1. Kwame Anthony Appiah also extols the power of conversation in "Making Conversation" and "The Primacy of Practice" (p. 67). Place his ideas in conversation with Yoshino's essay, synthesizing the authors' ideas about the power of conversation. Is Yoshino also calling for cosmopolitanism? How do civil rights function like other social practices?

2. Though explicitly concerned with the quinceañera, Julia Alvarez's "Selections from *Once Upon a Quinceañera*" (p. 46) might also be considered as an essay on social demands to cover in relation to cultural assimilation. How does Alvarez's essay extend Yoshino's understanding of the term *covering*? Does the quinceañera represent a way to resist covering or have elements of it acceded to such social demands? Use your definition of covering from Question 2 of Questions for Critical Reading in your response.

3. Francis Fukuyama argues for the necessity of a concept of human dignity in his essay of the same name (p. 185). What role might human dignity play in civil rights? Is Factor X an essential component of a new civil rights? Synthesize the ideas of Fukuyama and Yoshino into an argument about human rights.

Language Matters

1. Every part of speech and every punctuation mark has certain "rights"; for example, the period has the right to end a sentence and the comma does not. How can we describe the rules of grammar using Yoshino's ideas of liberty and equality paradigms?

2. Defining terms is an important part of academic writing. Locate a passage where Yoshino defines a term. What strategies does he use? Does he offer a dictionary definition? An example? An authority? How should you define terms in your own text?

3. Is there a form of covering that takes place in peer revision? Are people tempted to tone down unfavorable comments? How does Yoshino's discussion of covering offer advice for more effective peer revision?

Assignments for Writing

1. Yoshino discusses the concept of groups and individuals covering in order to conform to the mainstream. Locate your own example of covering and then write an essay that extends or complicates Yoshino's argument through your example. Does your example reinforce or refute Yoshino's ideas about covering? Are any civil rights at stake in your example? What relation is there between covering and civil rights? You will want to use your definition of the term *covering* from Question 2 of Questions for Critical Reading.

2. Yoshino discusses the challenges to civil rights posed by the proliferation of groups engendered by a diverse society; he offers his own vision of how to transform civil rights to account for these groups. Write a paper in which you suggest what changes we should make to civil rights and how we might achieve those changes. Draw on your work in Questions for Critical Reading and Questions for Connecting in making your argument. Consider, too: Should we use a liberty paradigm or an equality paradigm? Would you propose a different paradigm of your own? Is legislation the best way to achieve your vision for civil rights? Is conversation?

3. In response to Question 3 of Exploring Context, you examined current online conversations about civil rights. Yoshino suggests that such conversations are the best means of achieving a new civil rights. Write a paper in which you argue for the role of conversation in social change. Is talking about an issue enough to engender change? Does it matter who is doing the talking? How does change happen in society?

ASSIGNMENT SEQUENCES

SEQUENCE 1

Identity: Rites/Rights of Passage

JULIA ALVAREZ

MADELEINE ALBRIGHT

SABRINA RUBIN ERDELY **e**

JAYME POISSON

POSTSECRET

MARA HVISTENDAHL

ARIEL LEVY

In this sequence you will examine the connection between rites that help us form our identities and the larger rights of our communities. You'll begin by using Julia Alvarez to consider the role of quinceañeras in the development of self-identity. Building on that analysis, you will use Madeleine Albright to explore the ways in which national as well as personal identities can be shaped by forces such as religion. Then you'll explore the extent with which identity is linked to gender, using Jayme Poisson. The final assignments of this sequence deal with the relationship between anonymity and rites of passage, and whether it is possible to have both, by synthesizing the ideas of Poisson and Albright, as well as the anonymous images in PostSecret. Alternative assignments include a further discussion of the emerging connection between gender and rites of passage with Sabrina Rubin Erdely, Mara Hvistendahl, and Ariel Levy.

▶ TAGS: *kinship, family, change, rituals, tradition, religion, gender, community, anonymity, culture, identity*

Assignment 1. Analyze: ALVAREZ

How do quinceañeras help to define self-identity in the Hispanic community? Write a paper in which you define the relationship between these rituals and self-identity. In making your argument you may want to use the other rituals you explored in Question 3 of Exploring Context (p. 63) or some of the concepts you synthesized in Questions for Connecting, such as super-replicators or cultural performance.

    To help you begin your critical thinking on this assignment, consider these questions: How do traditions, both native and acquired, contribute to the development of identity? How does gender determine self-identity in the Hispanic community? Why do only girls receive quinceañeras? What part does retroculturation play in the establishing of self-identity? Is this rite of passage similar to or different from rites of passage in other cultures? Does the commercialization of the quinceañera affect its overall value in establishing a girl's self-worth and self-identity? If so, how?

Assignment 2. Connect: ALVAREZ AND ALBRIGHT

Quinceañeras often have a religious component. And, as Madeleine Albright's essay makes clear, religion is often a significant force in shaping identities, both personal and national. Write a paper in which you explore the ways in which personal and national identities are shaped by faith. You might begin by revisiting your work on the relationship between religion and diplomacy in Question 1 of Questions for Critical Reading for Albright (p. 34).

To help you begin your critical thinking on this assignment, reflect on these questions: What role does religion play in shaping personal and national identities? Can retroculturation assist in creating a faith-based diplomacy? How do quinceañeras transcend national borders? In what sense are they a kind of international diplomacy? Do girls have a right to a quinceañera or to other rites of passage?

Alternative Assignment 2. Connect: ALVAREZ AND ERDELY

One way of thinking about Sabrina Rubin Erdely's "Kiki Kannibal: The Girl Who Played with Fire" is that it is the story of a teenage girl coming of age through technology without any rite of passage. Write a paper in which you analyze Kiki Kannibal's experience using Julia Alvarez's discussion of the quinceañera.

What role does technology play today in coming of age? How does technology challenge tradition? In what ways does Kiki's experience reinforce Alvarez's insights about gender? Does Kiki Kannibal represent what happens when a girl doesn't have some sort of coming-of-age ritual?

Assignment 3. Synthesize: ALVAREZ AND POISSON

Both Julia Alvarez's and Jayme Poisson's essays are centrally concerned with families. Both, too, consider the ways in which families, whether immediate or extended, influence who and what we are. Using both Alvarez and Poisson to support your argument, write a paper in which you examine the role that family plays in shaping self-identity.

To help you begin your critical thinking on this assignment, ask yourself these questions: Does a sense of gender identity come from the home or the culture as a whole? How do families change when gender is not a focus? Is gender assignment an important part of rites of passage? Is it an important rite of passage itself? Where is the boundary between an individual and the family?

Alternative Assignment 3. Synthesize: ALVAREZ AND HVISTENDAHL

Both Julia Alvarez's and Mara Hvistendahl's essays are centrally concerned with families. Both, too, consider the ways in which families, whether present or absent, influence who and what we are. Using both Alvarez and Hvistendahl to support your argument, write a paper in which you examine the role that the absence of family plays in shaping self-identity.

To help you begin your critical thinking on this assignment, ask yourself these questions: Does a sense of identity come from the home or the culture as a whole? How important is the gender gap to rites of passage? What happens if rites of passage are missed because of social or economic concerns? What happens if a rite of passage is forced upon an individual?

Assignment 4. Emerge: POSTSECRET AND ONE OTHER

Using the images from PostSecret and one of the other authors you've worked with, write a paper in which you identify and analyze the challenges that emerge when rites of passage are documented anonymously. Consider starting with your analysis of the role identity plays in rites of passage.

Also think about these questions: Do anonymous rites of passage have the same level of importance as rites that are more inclusive? Is it possible for identity to be built anonymously? Does family have the responsibility to an individual within it to facilitate rites of passage? Is it the responsibility of the individual to include the family in rites of passage?

Alternative Assignment 4. Emerge: LEVY AND ONE OTHER

Write a paper in which you identify and analyze whether or not being a "loophole woman" is a modern rite of passage. Utilize the ideas of Ariel Levy and one other author in this sequence to make your argument. Consider starting with your analysis of the role gender plays in rites of passage and the building of individual identity.

Also think about these questions: Does a sense of gender identity come from the home or the culture as a whole? How integral is gender to rites of passage? To identity as a whole? Is gender identity an important rite of passage in itself?

SEQUENCE 2

Cosmopolitanism: Ethical Conflict in a Global Economy

KWAME ANTHONY APPIAH

HELEN EPSTEIN

THOMAS L. FRIEDMAN

CHARLES DUHIGG AND DAVID BARBOZA **e**

MALCOLM GLADWELL

PATRICIA CHURCHLAND

ANDREW MARANTZ

This sequence asks you to examine how we can survive and indeed thrive in an inter-connected and diverse world. The first assignment, with Kwame Anthony Appiah, asks you to develop a set of conceptual tools for creating social change. In the second assignment, you will extend these tools using the work of Helen Epstein, considering how they can be used to create change on a global scale. The third assignment more specifically asks you to apply that work to the global fight against terrorism, drawing additionally from Thomas L. Friedman's work on mutant supply chains. In the final assignment, you will use Malcolm Gladwell to consider the limits of global cooperation and the boundaries between surviving together and surviving alone. Alternative as-signments include a further discussion of the limits of global cooperation using Charles Duhigg and David Barboza, Patricia Churchland, and Andrew Marantz.

▶ TAGS: *international policy, globalization, ethics, terrorism, community, social change*

Assignment 1. Analyze: APPIAH

Kwame Anthony Appiah discusses his choice of cosmopolitanism as a rubric for mov-ing forward. At the same time, he also discusses the problems of realizing social change. Based on his discussion of the primacy of practice, how can we advocate for change in social practices? Write a paper in which you identify the best tools for achieving social change. You may wish to build on the cultural practice you explored in Question 2 of Exploring Context (p. 83) in constructing and supporting your argument.

e bedfordstmartins.com/emerging/epages

Assignment 2. Connect: APPIAH AND EPSTEIN

Helen Epstein describes two very different approaches to HIV/AIDS prevention in Africa. She points out that in South Africa, where open discussion of the epidemic is taboo, prevention programs that avoid the harsh realities of the AIDS epidemic are popular but less successful than their counterparts in Uganda, where the realities of the disease are openly acknowledged. To what extent can Appiah's primacy of practice be applied to AIDS prevention in countries with stringent social taboos? Drawing on Epstein's and Appiah's ideas, write a paper in which you determine how individuals acting locally can create global change. You may want to draw from your definition of *social cohesion* from Question 2 of Questions for Critical Reading for Epstein (p. 152).

Ask yourself these questions: How can we overcome the primacy of practice when such practices put lives at risk from disease? What role does conversation have in creating change locally or globally? How can we take action to solve problems like HIV/AIDS even when we hold different values? Is social cohesion an effect of cosmopolitanism, or do these two concepts work against each other? What role might global companies and advertising play in social change?

Assignment 3. Synthesize: EPSTEIN AND FRIEDMAN

Thomas L. Friedman argues that countries participating in global supply chains become economically interdependent and are thus less likely to be involved in political conflicts. At the same time he warns that terrorists are using similar supply chains to spread violence around the world. Given that both terrorism and HIV/AIDS threaten lives without respect for borders, how can we mitigate terrorist supply chains? Write an essay in which you use Epstein's insights about HIV/AIDS prevention in Africa to propose strategies for fighting terrorism globally. Use your work on the role of collaboration as well as your analysis of mutant supply chains from Question 3 of Questions for Critical Reading for Friedman (pp. 165–66).

Also think about: How can we promote collaboration while minimizing its destructive potential? How can social cohesion play a role in the fight against terrorism? What about lifestyle brands? What role do supply chains play in the transmission of and fight against HIV/AIDS in Africa?

Alternative Assignment 3. Synthesize: APPIAH, FRIEDMAN, AND DUHIGG/BARBOZA

Both Thomas L. Friedman and Kwame Anthony Appiah suggest that cooperation and collaboration can lead to peace and security in a global and globally connected world. However, in exposing the human cost involved in manufacturing Apple's iPad, Charles Duhigg and David Barboza bring to light the darker side of global cooperation. Write a paper in which you synthesize the ideas of these authors to propose practices we can promote to maximize the benefits of globalization while minimizing its costs.

Do global supply chains sometimes behave like mutant supply chains? What are the implications of cosmopolitanism for human and labor rights? Given the primacy of practice, how can countries reshape global economic practices to maintain collaboration while preventing downsides like terrorist supply chains and labor exploitation?

Alternative Assignment 3. Synthesize: EPSTEIN AND CHURCHLAND

Patricia Churchland argues that there is no simple biological basis for cooperation. She presents alternatives to a biological model for collaboration, including learned social behaviors. Given that HIV/AIDS threatens lives without respect for borders, how can we collaborate on a global level to address the problem? Write an essay in which you synthesize Churchland's ideas and Epstein's insights about HIV/AIDS prevention in Africa to propose further strategies for global collaboration.

Also think about: How does morality affect collaboration? How can social cohesion play a role in long-term cooperation? What role can morality play in the fight against HIV/AIDS?

Assignment 4. Emerge: GLADWELL AND ONE OTHER

Malcolm Gladwell focuses on the influence surrounding social networking and "weak ties." Using Gladwell and one of the other authors in this sequence, write a paper in which you determine the limits of "weak ties" and the implications of your findings on the global economy.

Should social networking be considered an integral part of international communication? Are social networking sites a part of a global supply chain? How important are social networks to global activism? How can we extend the use of social networks to create "strong ties"?

Alternative Assignment 4. Emerge: MARANTZ AND ONE OTHER

Andrew Marantz focuses on the interdependent nature of call centers and the services their workers provide across the globe. However, many times callers depend on the help of these workers yet resent receiving help from outsiders. Using Marantz and one of the other authors in this sequence, write a paper in which you determine the limits of human cooperation in a supply chain.

Should individuals be trained to adopt other cultural ideals in order to be part of a global supply chain? When health is at stake, as with HIV/AIDS, does that make a difference? Should governments mandate individual behavior? How do we work together while retaining our rights as individuals?

SEQUENCE 3

Ethics: Yes We Can, But Should We?
The Politics of Science

THE DALAI LAMA

KENJI YOSHINO

FRANCIS FUKUYAMA

MADELEINE ALBRIGHT

PETER SINGER

HAL HERZOG

How can we develop an ethical system to guide us in scientific and technological progress? In this sequence of assignments, you will begin to answer that question by first working with the Dalai Lama's examination of genetic technologies, considering the ramifications of these technologies for economic and political stability. Then you will turn to Kenji Yoshino's discussion of civil rights, synthesizing his ideas with the Dalai Lama's to argue for the best balance between progress and rights. In the third assignment, you will discuss all of these issues specifically in the context of stem cell research, folding Francis Fukuyama's ideas about biotechnology and human dignity into your analysis. Finally, you will use Madeleine Albright to look at the role of religion in science. If our ethics are not based in faith, then what system can we develop to guide us in the search for new knowledge? Alternative assignments include a further discussion of privacy and technology using Peter Singer, as well as a look at broader ethical concerns involving technology and animals using Hal Herzog.

▶ TAGS: *diplomacy, morality, biotechnology, knowledge and responsibility, human dignity, ethics, civil rights*

Assignment 1. Analyze: THE DALAI LAMA

The possible consequences of genetic manipulation reach far beyond the sphere of science. Consider, for example, the role of national and global politics in relation to scientific breakthroughs that have the potential to literally change the face of humanity but will almost certainly not be available to everyone. Write a paper in which you examine the consequences of technology in terms of social and economic stability. How does the Dalai Lama characterize the relationship between knowledge and responsibility? In what ways does genetic engineering have the potential to perpetuate our disparities on social, political, and ethical levels? Should new technologies be available to everyone?

Assignment 2. Connect: THE DALAI LAMA AND YOSHINO

According to the Dalai Lama, rapid advances in technology demand new ethical standards. Kenji Yoshino makes a similar argument in claiming that the proliferation of groups in a diverse society necessitates a new civil rights. Connecting the positions of these two authors, write an essay in which you determine the best means of balancing political rights and technological progress. You might want to use the understanding of Yoshino's concept of civil rights that you developed in Questions for Critical Reading (p. 552) in making your argument.

And consider: Are scientists just another group demanding rights? Should we use a liberty paradigm or an equality paradigm in considering the ethical quandaries raised by biotechnology? Are reason-forcing conversations the best means of achieving the Dalai Lama's vision for ethics, or is legislation? What role does a moral compass play in both science and civil rights?

Assignment 3. Synthesize: THE DALAI LAMA, YOSHINO, AND FUKUYAMA

In the first two assignments of this sequence you were asked to consider the impact of science and technology on social and economic stability as well as on political rights. Francis Fukuyama addresses some of the same concerns in his discussion of biotechnology and human dignity. Synthesize the ideas of these three authors to write a paper in which you determine the ethics of stem cell research. Your goal in writing this paper is not to argue for or against this particular field of scientific inquiry. Instead, you will want to propose how we can make decisions about such difficult matters.

Reflect on the Dalai Lama's moral compass. Does human dignity help us find that moral compass? Is human dignity part of the True Self or the False Self? How do the needs for both a moral compass and human dignity limit any claims to a liberty paradigm for civil rights?

Alternative Assignment 3. Synthesize: THE DALAI LAMA, YOSHINO, AND SINGER

In the first two assignments of this sequence you were asked to consider the impact of science and technology on social and economic stability as well as on political rights. Peter Singer addresses some of the same concerns in his discussion of technology and secrecy. Synthesize the ideas of these three authors to write a paper in which you determine the ethics of online privacy. Your goal in writing this paper is not to argue for or against this particular area of technological advancement. Instead, you will want to propose how we can make decisions about such difficult matters.

Reflect on the Dalai Lama's moral compass. Can the dissemination of private information actually help people? Is the greater good worth sacrificing the privacy of a few? Of many? How do the needs for both a moral compass and civil rights complicate the need for both privacy and information?

Assignment 4. Emerge: ALBRIGHT AND ONE OTHER

The authors you've examined so far have largely separated ethics from the question of religion, even though faith serves as the foundation for many people's ethical systems. Madeleine Albright suggests that we should take faith into consideration when it comes to foreign policy. Should we do the same for science? Working with Albright and one of the authors from this sequence, write an essay in which you determine the role faith should play in science. You might want to begin by revisiting your response to Question 1 of Questions for Critical Reading for Albright (p. 34), in which you explored whether faith was ultimately a help or a hindrance to diplomacy.

Also consider: How can we create an ethical system apart from religion? Should faith play a role in determining research agendas? How can we accommodate religious concerns while still pursuing technological and scientific progress?

Alternative Assignment 4. Emerge: HERZOG AND ONE OTHER

The authors you've examined so far have largely separated ethics from the question of animal rights, even though animals are used to test many of the products and technologies we use every day. Hal Herzog suggests that humans have a complicated relationship with animals, which extends to moral and social implications. Morality surrounding animal research is currently ambiguous, but should it remain so? Working with Herzog and one of the authors from this sequence, write an essay in which you determine the role ethics should play in animal research.

To get started, think about these questions: Do animals have "Factor X"? Does a moral compass play a role in animal research? How can we accommodate the ethical treatment of animals while still pursuing technological and scientific progress?

....

Communication: The Talking Cure

DANIEL GILBERT

HELEN EPSTEIN

JAMES SUROWIECKI

BRIAN CHRISTIAN

DAN SAVAGE AND URVASHI VAID

ELIZABETH DICKINSON

In this sequence you will analyze the role conversations can play in creating social change. To start, you will explore Daniel Gilbert's concept of a surrogate, a way of predicting your own future happiness through conversations with someone experiencing the future you would like to have. Then you will extend Gilbert's idea using Helen Epstein's analysis of HIV/AIDS prevention in Africa in order to consider the potential for conversation to create social and not just personal change. Yet conversation is not without its risks, and so you will turn to James Surowiecki's analysis of the failure of small groups in order to determine the limits of conversation as a social medicine. Finally, with Brian Christian, you will synthesize these positions to consider technologies that can harness conversation as social medicine. Alternative assignments that include further analysis of technology and conversation focus on the work of Dan Savage and Urvashi Vaid as well as Elizabeth Dickinson.

▶ TAGS: *conversation, social change, technology, surrogates*
....

Assignment 1. Analyze: GILBERT

According to Daniel Gilbert, surrogates can offer us an accurate sense of our future happiness. Write a paper in which you assess the potential of the kind of surrogates that Gilbert describes. You will want to extend, complicate, or refute Gilbert's argument for surrogates and their reliability in predicting the future. Consider these questions: What role does individuality have in determining our future happiness? Is Gilbert correct in claiming that we are not as unique as we believe? Can surrogates be used to examine all future events? How can surrogates be used to control social processes? If we are not unique, why do we see ourselves as individuals? Use your definition of *surrogate* from Question 2 of Questions for Critical Reading (p. 210) as well as your work with Yahoo! Answers from Question 3 of Exploring Context (p. 228).

Assignment 2. Connect: GILBERT AND EPSTEIN

In the last assignment you considered the power of conversation—specifically conversations with surrogates—to help people shape their futures. Helen Epstein, however, is concerned with the future of more than just individuals. Her analysis of HIV/AIDS prevention programs pertains to the future of that disease on the African continent. Using Gilbert's and Epstein's ideas, write a paper in which you determine the power of conversation to change people's behavior. Consider drawing on your work with Epstein, particularly your analysis of how social networking sites like Facebook can facilitate conversations around HIV/AIDS, from Question 3 of Exploring Context (p. 163).

   Contemplate these questions to help you in formulating your argument: Could surrogates play a role in the fight against HIV/AIDS? What role does imagination play in social cohesion? How might Gilbert explain the failure of the loveLife campaign? Can conversation about the disease function as a kind of super-replicator?

Assignment 3. Synthesize: SUROWIECKI AND ONE OTHER

To some extent, James Surowiecki's essay is centrally concerned with the failure of conversations—for example, the conversation of the Mission Management Team regarding *Columbia*. You've already explored the potential of conversation to create change, but what are the risks of conversation in group or social settings? Write a paper in which you explore the failures of conversation using the work of Surowiecki and one or more of the other authors you've read. Recall your determination of whether or not small groups are worth the risk from Question 3 of Questions for Critical Reading for Surowiecki (p. 472).

   Consider, too: What are the risks involved when conversation fails? Given those risks, is conversation a good choice as social medicine? Given Surowiecki's analysis, how might surrogates fail to predict your future? Does group polarization threaten social cohesion?

Assignment 4. Emerge: CHRISTIAN AND TWO OTHERS

Brian Christian explores the authenticity of identity in a technologically advanced society. These ideas can be extended into the discussion of authenticity and communication. Is authentic communication across a digital network possible? Using the work of Christian and two of the other authors you've read in this sequence, write a paper in which you determine how technology can harness the power of conversation in creating social change. What other technologies can enable this transformative power of conversation?

   Ask yourself: How does technology enable the spread of super-replicators? How does it enable greater access to surrogates? What role might technology play in the prevention of HIV/AIDS? How can it be used to expand Uganda's success at that task? Does "concinnity" play a role? Can technology mitigate the factors that cause small groups to fail? Is technology inherently "stateless"?

Alternative Assignment 4. Emerge: SAVAGE/VAID, DICKINSON, AND ONE OTHER

Dan Savage and Urvashi Vaid provide working examples of technology as social medicine in their discussion of anti-bullying videos. Similarly, Dickinson also changes the way we think about conversation through her infographic essay discussing the future of global sustainability. Considering such media as YouTube and other digital arguments, is face-to-face communication enough to create social change? Using the work of Savage and Vaid, Dickinson, and one of the other authors you've read in this sequence, write a paper in which you determine how technology can harness the power of conversation in creating social change. What other technologies can enable this transformative power of conversation?

Ask yourself: How does technology enable the spread of super-replicators? How does it enable greater access to surrogates? What role might technology play in the prevention of HIV/AIDS? How can it be used to expand Uganda's success at that task? To what extent do the "It Gets Better" videos function as effective surrogates? Can technology mitigate the factors that cause small groups to fail?

SEQUENCE 5

Art: Revelations, Displays, and Cultures

RACHEL KADISH

ARWA ABURAWA

PORTFOLIO 🄴

RICHARD RESTAK

DAN SAVAGE AND URVASHI VAID

STEVE MUMFORD

In this sequence you will evaluate the role that art plays in shaping culture as well as the boundaries for creative expression. First you will explore Rachel Kadish's argument by locating your own example of representative art. Then you will explore the opposite role that cultural objects play when transformed into art through Aburawa's discussion of veils as guerrilla art. In the final assignments of the sequence, you will use Richard Restak as well as Dan Savage and Urvashi Vaid to think about the future of art and aesthetics in a technological culture. Alternative assignments include thinking about the nature of art using infographics and utilizing the images of Steve Mumford to supplement the connection between art and representation.

▶ TAGS: *culture, art, performance, aesthetic boundaries, censorship, creativity, technology*

Assignment 1. Analyze: KADISH

Rachel Kadish explores the idea of appropriating an anonymous image and using it to represent a social or political cause. Locate your own example of an image representing a group and write an essay in which you discuss its effect. Is your example used to support a specific group? Multiple groups at once? Is your example anonymous? Consider the photographs of Noam Galai screaming when discussing the ability of art to express opinions or desires.

🄴 bedfordstmartins.com/emerging/epages

Assignment 2. Connect: KADISH AND ABURAWA

Rachel Kadish and Arwa Aburawa are both concerned with the role of art representing a culture. Aburawa, however, specifically considers the role of appropriating objects that already represent cultural ideals. Connecting these essays, what is the effect of using subversive tactics on the original image or object? Is some of the original importance of the image or object lost in the appropriation of it? Is the final representative product worth more than an original image or object? Drawing on these ideas, write a paper in which you argue how best to balance the rights of the community and those of the individual in terms of art and aesthetics.

What role should artistic creativity have in a community? What is expressive freedom? Is advertising oppressive? Can graffiti also be oppressive? Why or why not?

Assignment 3. Synthesize: RESTAK AND ONE OTHER

Richard Restak examines how technology affects the way we perform everyday tasks. On the one hand, technology enables us to perform many tasks at once; on the other hand, none of these tasks are done well because of the competing demands on our brains. Using Restak and one of the other authors from this sequence, write a paper in which you determine the impact of technology on creative expression.

Also ask yourself these questions: Is multitasking a form of subversion? Are we moving so fast that we are unable to appreciate art? Are we moving into a future that will make the arts unnecessary in culture? How might the rewiring of our brains change our understanding of art and aesthetics?

Alternative Assignment 3. Synthesize: KADISH, ABURAWA, AND PORTFOLIO

Both Rachel Kadish and Arwa Aburawa, in some ways, examine how art is being challenged and redefined in the digital age. Synthesize their arguments by extending this conversation to infographics. Write a paper in which you consider the role of art in the digital age.

Is art only about pleasure and aesthetics? How do politics and economics function in art? Who owns art? Does art carry a message? What happens when the function of visual images is to convey a message? Does it cease to be art? Are infographics an art?

Assignment 4. Emerge: RESTAK, SAVAGE/VAID, AND ONE OTHER

While technology is responsible for multitasking and competing demands on our brains, it may also be responsible for increased activism and social change. Dan Savage and Urvashi Vaid show us another example of art, in this case YouTube videos, representing a specific group and its demands. Using Restak, Savage and Vaid, and one of the other authors from this sequence, write a paper in which you determine the impact of art on social change.

How does technology affect social activism? How might videos be more effective than other visual images? Do videos better engage our lapsing attention spans?

Alternative Assignment 4. Emerge: MUMFORD AND TWO OTHERS

As you have learned in this sequence, images can be powerful enough to represent an entire group. However, our interpretations of art are ultimately subjective. Consider the various appropriations of Noam Galai's image, for example. Mumford's images are similarly problematic. Should a single image be representative of an entire culture? Use Mumford and two others from this sequence in your analysis.

Consider these questions in your discussion: How does perspective affect art? Can someone outside of a culture literally paint a clear picture of what is going on inside of it? How effective is art if only one side of a culture is represented?

· ·

SEQUENCE 6

Communities: Trouble with a Capital "C"

REBEKAH NATHAN

KWAME ANTHONY APPIAH

THOMAS L. FRIEDMAN

MARSHALL POE

MANUEL MUÑOZ

WESLEY YANG

In this sequence you will explore the role of diversity in forming successful communities. You'll begin by using Rebekah Nathan's work to consider the possibility of a fully integrated community. You will then expand that analysis using Kwame Anthony Appiah's work, identifying the tools we can use to form successful and diverse communities. Such communities are not without risk, and so you will turn to an analysis of Thomas L. Friedman to examine the dangers of community both in general and, more specifically, through an analysis of ethnic conflicts in the world today. Finally, you will use Marshall Poe's examination of Wikipedia's success to imagine an open, collaborative world. In completing these assignments, you will gain an understanding of the challenges facing community formation, the risks of diversity, and the possibilities of integration in the world today. Alternative assignments include an exploration of the ways community affects cultural identity by synthesizing the ideas of Manuel Muñoz and Wesley Yang.

▶ TAGS: *community, globalization, diversity, education, supply chains, ethnic conflict, integration, cosmopolitanism*

· ·

Assignment 1. Analyze: NATHAN

Rebekah Nathan notes that despite AnyU's best efforts to unite the university's population, students who make up the different communities within the school would rather bond within their own social groups than venture outside of them. Assess the situation Nathan talks about in her essay. Thinking beyond Nathan's findings, write a paper in which you examine the possibilities of communities becoming fully integrated. Is such integration even possible in a world made up of so many diverse and differing communities? The purpose of this essay is for you to apply the concepts in Nathan's essay to your own specific observations and experiences. Rather than simply writing a story about your own opinions, you should instead use your experiences among and observations of diverse communities, on an academic campus or elsewhere, to explore the possibilities of a truly integrated community. You may also want to use your responses to Questions for Critical Reading (pp. 313–14) and Exploring Context (p. 330) in supporting your argument.

Assignment 2. Connect: NATHAN AND APPIAH

In the last assignment you considered the possibility of integrating communities and the challenges inherent in such a task. Kwame Anthony Appiah's ideas about cosmopolitanism and the processes of changes in practice offer additional insight on this topic. Using both Appiah and Nathan, write a paper in which you determine the key tools necessary for successfully forming diverse communities. You might build your argument from the work you did in Question 2 of Questions for Critical Reading for Appiah (p. 67), in which you explored the tools needed to enact cosmopolitanism.

Also consider: Can we form diverse communities in practice without agreeing on the values behind such communities? How does the challenge of accomplishing diversity on college campuses reflect the challenge of embracing community on a global scale? Can conversation overcome ego-centered networks?

Assignment 3. Synthesize: FRIEDMAN AND APPIAH

Kwame Anthony Appiah argues for the need for cosmopolitanism among world citizens; in Thomas L. Friedman's essay we see how companies and nations also benefit from "world citizen" attitudes. Yet Friedman also illustrates how such networks can have undesirable effects and consequences. Use Friedman's examination of global networks and mutant supply chains to complicate Appiah's discussion about the importance of interconnected social networks, writing a paper in which you explore the dangers of a connected, flattened world. In the end, is a completely interconnected world really the ideal world? You might begin your critical thinking by revisiting your discussion of collaboration and mutant supply chains from Questions for Critical Reading for Friedman (pp. 165–66).

Also contemplate: Can cosmopolitanism mitigate mutant supply chains? Is terrorism a consequence of the lack of diversity? How can we agree on practices for global peace while holding different values? Can businesses contribute to cosmopolitanism?

Assignment 4. Emerge: POE AND ONE OTHER

Marshall Poe explores how the collaborative construction of knowledge plays out on the Internet, but the ideas and problems he touches on have much wider implications. Using Poe's work and at least one other reading from this sequence, consider the possibility of a world that is completely "open," without any rules aside from those agreed upon by a majority. Examine the lessons that could be learned from entities like Wikipedia and use these lessons to write a paper in which you argue how our world would differ if it were left completely "open."

In making your argument, respond to these questions: What would happen to minority groups in such a society? Would groups form more diverse connections between each other, or would there be greater segregation? What chance would cosmopolitanism have in such a world? Would global supply chains be possible? Would they be necessary? Is such a world possible or even desirable?

Alternative Assignment 4. Emerge: MUÑOZ, YANG, AND ONE OTHER

Both Manuel Muñoz and Wesley Yang explore how a new community can affect cultural identity through the adopting of new cultural norms. In both cases, complete assimilation into a new culture is not possible because of the host culture's perception of cultural identities outside its own. Using Muñoz, Yang, and one other author from this sequence, write a paper in which you argue how our world would be different if cultural norms were not preserved.

In making your argument, respond to these questions: What would happen to minority groups in such a society? Would groups form more diverse connections between each other, or would there be greater segregation? What chance would cosmopolitanism have in such a world? Would global supply chains be possible? Would they be necessary? Is such a world possible or even desirable?

SEQUENCE 7

Deep Impact: Technology and Our World

MARSHALL POE

THOMAS L. FRIEDMAN

ALEXANDRA SAMUEL

RICHARD RESTAK

FRANCIS FUKUYAMA

BILL WASIK

In this sequence you will explore the impact of technology on ourselves, on our world, and on what it means to be human. You'll begin by looking at the ways in which technology has changed our understanding of "experts," specifically using Marshall Poe's analysis of Wikipedia and the collaborative creation of knowledge. In the next assignment, you will turn to Thomas L. Friedman's examination of the globalized, "flattened" world to determine the economic and political effects of technology. In the final assignments of this sequence, you will use first Richard Restak's work and then Francis Fukuyama's to assess technology's impact on biology and our concepts of the human race. In performing these analyses, you will gain a new understanding of the ways in which technology permeates our lives. You will also gain conceptual tools for assessing and perhaps mitigating technology's impact on humanity. Alternative assignments include using Alexandra Samuel to consider the risks and rewards of being online and Bill Wasik to further discuss the impact of technology on our culture through memes and the bandwagon effect.

▶ TAGS: *politics, technology, knowledge, human dignity, multitasking, collaboration, economics*

Assignment 1. Analyze: POE

What is the power of experts? Does a consensus determine the truth? Marshall Poe's essay asks us to consider these questions, since the collaborative authorship of Wikipedia suggests that experts are not vital in the creation of knowledge. Write a paper in which you suggest the proper boundaries between experts and nonexperts in relation to knowledge.

bedfordstmartins.com/emerging/epages

Also think about what role technology plays in this process. Should experts be granted special status in relation to knowledge? What makes an expert "expert" anyway?

Assignment 2. Connect: POE AND FRIEDMAN

In the first assignment of this sequence, you were asked to consider the impact technology has had on our concept of what an "expert" is. Thomas L. Friedman is also concerned with how technology has changed our world, addressing this topic both directly, through his opening narrative about the construction of his laptop, and more generally, through a discussion of the complex networks of supply chains around the world. Write a paper in which you consider the ways in which technology has influenced both economics and politics.

Consider: How did social networking sites affect the 2008 presidential election? How did television determine the outcome of the 1960 election? How do supply chains determine international or domestic politics? How did the economic crisis or "financiapocalypse" of 2008 reflect the dangers of a technologically interconnected world? In what specific ways has technology connected economics and politics?

Alternative Assignment 2. Connect: POE AND SAMUEL

Marshall Poe explores the risks and rewards of working together online in "The Hive." In her manifesto, Alexandra Samuel also examines what we gain and what we lose through technology. Write a paper in which you connect the ideas of both authors to determine whether, in the end, we gain or lose by spending time online.

Is Wikipedia one way to "plug in better"? How does the conflict between Sanger and Cunc represent some of the risks of being online? How might you adapt Samuel's strategies to Wikipedia?

Assignment 3. Synthesize: RESTAK AND ONE OTHER

Through your analyses of Marshall Poe and Thomas L. Friedman, you've considered the impact of technology on knowledge, economics, and politics. But Richard Restak raises a far more fundamental question: How is technology rewiring our brains? Do you think that the strategies described by Poe or Friedman can mitigate these effects? Write a paper in which you use the work of Restak and one of the other authors from this sequence to explore the ways in which collaboration can counteract the detrimental effects of multitasking. You might want to begin with your examination of multitasking from Question 1 of Questions for Critical Reading for Restak (p. 411).

In thinking critically about this assignment, ask: How does Wikipedia represent the benefits of collaborative attention to a subject? Does it represent a kind of antidote to "modern nerves"? Do mutant supply chains represent the potential for a kind of hyperfocus? Does global interconnection through supply chains minimize the effects of ADHD?

Assignment 4. Emerge: FUKUYAMA AND ONE OTHER

Francis Fukuyama is centrally concerned with what it means to be human, particularly in relation to emerging genetic technologies. Throughout this sequence you've considered the impact of technology on ourselves and on our world. Now, using the work of Fukuyama and one of the other authors from this sequence, write a paper in which you determine the point at which science, financial wealth, and access to technology will be, or is already, intrinsic to the development of the human race. Your definition of "Factor X" from Question 1 of Questions for Critical Reading for Fukuyama (p. 185) will be a critical starting point for thinking about your argument.

Ask yourself: What makes us human? Are we overreaching the ethical boundaries of science? What are the benefits of genetic manipulation to our development, and what are the possible pitfalls? Will genetic engineering level the playing field between people, or will it merely reinforce the economic stratification present today?

Alternative Assignment 4. Emerge: WASIK AND ONE OTHER

You have already written about countering the negative effects of multitasking, but perhaps the effects of multitasking aren't completely bad for society. In some ways multitasking might represent our culture. Bill Wasik examines the origin of the meme and how flash mobs have the potential to evolve in a technologically aware society. Write a paper in which you use the work of Wasik and one of the other authors from this sequence to explore the ways in which memes are representative of our culture.

In thinking critically about this assignment, ask: What is the effect of boredom and procrastination on our culture? On a global culture? Can memes lead to social change? Is a flash mob powerful?

Assimilation: The Melting Not

LESLIE SAVAN

STEVE OLSON

REBEKAH NATHAN

MADELEINE ALBRIGHT

JENNIFER POZNER

NAMIT ARORA

In this sequence you will explore the problems and potential of community and diversity. You will begin by using Leslie Savan's analysis of the appropriation of black talk by pop talk to consider the possibility of achieving a melting pot ideal in America. Then you will turn to Steve Olson's argument about genetics and race to further explore why ethnicity persists in society, despite the lack of any genetic basis for conceptions of race. Rebekah Nathan's exploration of these issues on college campuses will provide you with an opportunity to ground them in very specific and very local examples. Finally, with Madeleine Albright's essay, you will explore the role that faith might have in achieving the goal of a melting pot society. At the end of this sequence, you will have a greater understanding of the challenges of community and diversity. But you will also have a set of conceptual tools for describing and perhaps solving this challenge. Alternative assignments include a further analysis of the media's representation of other cultures using Jennifer Pozner, and a discussion of the value of skills by Namit Arora.

▶ TAGS: *melting pot, diversity, religion, faith, diplomacy, community of descent, ethnicity, race, education*

Assignment 1. Analyze: SAVAN

Using Leslie Savan's essay, write a paper in which you determine the possibility of actualizing the melting pot ideal in America. Is it possible to achieve that ideal, or will there always be some sort of exploitation of cultures in the process? What gets lost in the melting pot? What do we gain? Can we achieve the goals of such a society without sacrificing the uniqueness of various cultures? How?

Alternative Assignment 1. Analyze: POZNER

Using Jennifer Pozner's essay, write a paper in which you determine the possibility of actualizing the melting pot ideal in America. Is it possible to achieve that ideal, or will there always be some sort of exploitation of cultures in the process? Can we achieve the goals of such a society without sacrificing the uniqueness of various cultures? How? How does television contribute to the melting pot? Is it possible to accurately portray another culture on American television?

Assignment 2. Connect: SAVAN AND OLSON

According to Steve Olson, there is no longer any genetic basis for race, yet he also makes it clear that concepts of race and ethnicity in Hawaii and elsewhere continue to persist. Connecting Olson's and Savan's arguments, write a paper in which you explain the reasons for the persistence of ethnic divisions in America and in which you consider the possibility of a solution to these divisions. Begin with your response to Question 3 of Questions for Critical Reading for Olson (p. 334), in which you located reasons for the persistence of race. Incorporate Savan's ideas in making your argument.

Ask yourself: What role do the media and advertising play in the persistence of race and ethnicity? Does covert prestige promote the end of race, or does it further entrench racial divisions? Does one need to "pay the dues" in order to join a community of descent? What role does education play in the persistence of race and ethnicity, according to both authors?

Assignment 3. Synthesize: NATHAN AND ONE OTHER

Rebekah Nathan examines the challenges to achieving community and diversity on college campuses, bringing issues from the essays you've read so far down to a specific and local level. Using the work of Nathan and one other author from this sequence, write a paper in which you propose strategies for achieving community on college campuses. You might want to use your experience at your school as an example to support your argument. You could also draw from your work in Question 3 of Questions for Critical Reading for Nathan (p. 314), in which you identified the tools needed to reach this goal; synthesize these tools with the concepts from the second author you've chosen to work with.

To further help you think critically about your argument, consider these questions: How does Savan's discussion of the controversy over Ebonics suggest the challenges of forming community on college campuses? How might "paying the dues" suggest a solution? Does covert prestige contribute to the problem? How might communities of descent function on campus? How does Olson's discussion of schools in Hawaii also emphasize the challenges of such a project?

Assignment 4. Emerge: ALBRIGHT AND ONE OTHER

So far in this sequence you've examined some of the challenges of achieving an integrated community. And though Madeleine Albright's explicit concern is the role of faith in diplomacy, she does have a lot to say about the role of religion in integrating communities. For this last assignment, use ideas from Albright and one other author from this sequence to write a paper in which you propose what role religion and faith might play in achieving the vision of a melting pot in the United States. You might decide that such a vision is impossible, in which case your argument should work with Albright and another author in order to argue that point.

In crafting your argument, reflect: Could faith play a role in mediating appropriations of ethnic languages? Could religion provide a neutral language through which groups might communicate? Does faith function as a community of descent? Can it transcend race? What role might religion play on college campuses? Could it enhance community, or would it be divisive?

Alternative Assignment 4. Emerge: ARORA AND ONE OTHER

So far in this sequence you've examined some of the challenges of achieving an integrated community. Though Namit Arora's explicit concern lies in economic equality, this idea directly relates to the melting pot ideal. For this last assignment, use ideas from Arora and one other author from this sequence to write a paper in which you propose what role the economy might play in achieving the vision of a melting pot in the United States.

In crafting your argument, reflect: Are lower-class citizens truly assimilated into American society? Is it possible for Americans to not conform to the ideals of their own culture? What role does the economy play in assimilation? How can we determine the value of skills? How can we determine fair rewards across cultures?

Putting the "I" in Team: The Practices of Collaboration

JAMES SUROWIECKI

MARSHALL POE

WIRED.COM e

THOMAS L. FRIEDMAN

MICHAEL POLLAN

DAVID FOSTER WALLACE

TOM VANDERBILT

In this sequence you will explore the practices of collaboration. You will begin by using James Surowiecki's exploration of the failure of small groups in order to deduce the best practices for making such groups successful. Then you will extend those ideas by using Marshall Poe's analysis of Wikipedia to determine what role the size of a group has in its success. In the third assignment of this sequence, you will use your understanding of collaborative practices to propose strategies for minimizing their dangers, as represented in the mutant supply chains examined by Thomas L. Friedman. In the last assignment of this sequence, you will use Michael Pollan's idea of the holon to argue for the role of the individual in collaboration. At the end of this sequence you will have an understanding of what makes groups succeed or fail. You will also understand the dangers of collaborative processes and the strategies you can use to avoid those dangers, all the while preserving the individual within the group. Alternative assignments include a further analysis of the role of small groups in hierarchical environments, of ethics in the supply chain using David Foster Wallace, and of the addition of anonymity in cooperation using Tom Vanderbilt.

▶ TAGS: *holons, technology, groups, Wikipedia, knowledge, collaboration, supply chains*

Assignment 1. Analyze: SUROWIECKI

James Surowiecki discusses ways in which group dynamics contributed to the failure of the *Columbia*'s Mission Management Team. Using Surowiecki's observations, write a paper that determines the best practices for organizing and running a small group. In composing your response, consider these questions: What makes a small group more

e bedfordstmartins.com/emerging/epages

than just the sum of its parts? How can group identity be made to serve the purpose of the group? What is the ideal structure for a group? How important is cognitive diversity, and why? How can group polarization be avoided? In what ways could "talkativeness" be regulated to ensure equal participation by all members of the group?

Assignment 2. Connect: SUROWIECKI AND POE

While James Surowiecki explores the failure of groups, Marshall Poe focuses on the success of the group effort behind Wikipedia. One way to account for the vastly different results of the collaborative efforts in these two essays is to consider the size of each group. Write a paper in which you use both Surowiecki and Poe to explore how the dangers, advantages, and strategies change as the size of a group collaboration increases.

In composing your response, ask yourself these questions: Would the small-group practices you identified in the first assignment of this sequence work for Wikipedia? Would a bottom-up organization work for a small group? Does the cathedral model or the bazaar model have an optimal size? Could the "Cunctator" have succeeded as a member of the Mission Management Team? Could group polarization and talkativeness plague Wikipedia? How is the sense of community altered by the size of the community?

Alternative Assignment 2. Connect: SUROWIECKI AND WIRED.COM

As "Call of Duty: Afghanistan" makes clear, small groups are essential to military success. Connect Surowiecki's ideas about the risks and rewards of small groups to military training by writing a paper in which you determine the value of small groups in hierarchical settings like the military.

How does using video games to train troops tap into the processes of group dynamics that Surowiecki explores? Does this approach to training avoid the pitfalls of small groups? Given Surowiecki's analysis of the rigid hierarchy at NASA, how might using video games to train troops increase the risk of failure in small groups?

Assignment 3. Synthesize: FRIEDMAN AND POE

Thomas L. Friedman's essay is largely concerned with the benefits of collaboration represented by global supply chains. But in turning to mutant supply chains, he reveals the dangers that collaboration can pose as well. Using Friedman and Poe, write a paper in which you propose a solution to mitigate these dangers that incorporates Wikipedia's strategies of collaborative knowledge. You might want to begin with your discussion of collaboration in Question 1 of Questions for Critical Reading for Friedman (pp. 165–66).

In formulating your argument you might also think about these questions: How could Nupedia's neutral point of view work for the Internet at large? How could it mitigate terrorist propaganda? What significance does the aphorism "Given enough eyeballs, all bugs are shallow" have for this situation? How can your solution avoid the fear of centralized authority that the Cunctator worried about?

Alternative Assignment 3. Synthesize: VANDERBILT AND POE

Tom Vanderbilt introduces the idea of collaborating anonymously, with both positive and negative results. He also reveals the dangers of collaborating in some cases, highlighting the effects of people collaborating anonymously when on the road. Using Vanderbilt and Poe, write a paper in which you propose a solution to mitigate these dangers that incorporates Wikipedia's strategies of collaborative knowledge.

In formulating your argument you might also think about these questions: What are the negative effects of a person deviating from normal collaboration? How must others adapt to compensate? How does anonymity factor into collaboration on Wikipedia?

Assignment 4. Emerge: POLLAN AND ONE OTHER

So far in this sequence you've considered practices of collaboration, practices that are also at work on Polyface Farm, as Michael Pollan makes clear. Yet in introducing the concept of the holon, Pollan also suggests the role that individuals play in group processes. For this final assignment, use the work of Pollan and one other author from this sequence to write a paper in which you determine the importance of the individual in collaboration. You might draw on the definition of *holon* that you developed for Question 2 of Questions for Critical Reading for Pollan (p. 373).

Also consider: Does the individual hurt or hinder the small-group processes that Surowiecki describes? Could an individual have made a difference on the Mission Management Team? Are Wikipedia's contributors holons? How are supply chains similar to Polyface?

Alternative Assignment 4. Emerge: POLLAN, WALLACE, AND ONE OTHER

So far in this sequence you've considered practices of collaboration, practices that are also at work on Polyface Farm, as Michael Pollan makes clear. Yet in introducing the concept of the holon, Pollan also suggests the role that individuals play in group processes. In addition to this, David Foster Wallace introduces ethical concerns. For this final assignment, use the work of Pollan, Wallace, and one other author in this sequence to write a paper in which you discuss the importance of ethics in collaboration.

Also contemplate these questions: Does the consideration of individual rights hurt or hinder the small-group processes that Surowiecki describes? Should animal rights also be taken into consideration when discussing a supply chain? How might we determine a set of standards by which to treat members of the supply chain, human or animal?

Acknowledgments (continued from page iv)

Madeleine Albright, "Faith and Diplomacy," from *The Mighty and the Almighty: Reflections on America, God, and World Affairs*, Chapter Five, pp. 65–78, by Madeleine Albright. Copyright © 2006 by Madeleine Albright. Reprinted by permission of HarperCollins Publishers.

Julia Alvarez, selections from *Once Upon a Quinceañera: Coming of Age in the USA*, by Julia Alvarez. Copyright © 2007 by Julia Alvarez. Published by Plume, a member of the Penguin Group (USA), Inc., and originally in hardcover by Viking. By permission of Susan Bergholz Literary Services, New York, NY, and Lamy, NM. All rights reserved.

Kwame Anthony Appiah, "Making Conversation" and "The Primacy of Practice," from *Cosmopolitanism: Ethics in a World of Strangers* by Kwame Anthony Appiah. Copyright © 2006 by Kwame Anthony Appiah. Used by permission of W. W. Norton & Company, Inc.

Namit Arora, "What Do We Deserve?" from *The Humanist* magazine, May/June 2011, is reprinted by permission of the author.

Brian Christian, from *The Most Human Human: What Talking with Computers Teaches Us About What It Means to Be Alive*. Copyright © 2011 by Brian Christian. Used by permission of Doubleday, a division of Random House, Inc.

Patricia Churchland, "Networking: Genes, Brains, and Behavior," from *Braintrust: What Neuroscience Tells Us about Morality*. Copyright © 2011 by Princeton University Press. Reprinted by permission of Princeton University Press.

The Dalai Lama, "Ethics and the New Genetics," from *The Universe in a Single Atom: The Convergence of Science and Spirituality by His Holiness The Dalai Lama*. Copyright © 2005 The Dalai Lama. Used by permission of an imprint of the Doubleday Broadway Publishing, a division of Random House, Inc.

Elizabeth Dickinson, "The Future of Food," courtesy of *Foreign Policy*.

Charles Duhigg and David Barboza, "In China, Human Costs Are Built Into an iPad" [e-Pages], from the *New York Times*, January 25, 2012: the *New York Times*. All rights reserved. Used by permission and protected by the Copyright Laws of the United States. The printing, copying, redistribution, or retransmission of this Content without express written permission is prohibited.

Helen Epstein, "AIDS, Inc.," from *The Invisible Cure: Africa, the West, and the Fight against AIDS* by Helen Epstein. Copyright © 2007 by Helen Epstein. Reprinted by permission of Farrar, Straus and Giroux, LLC.

Sarah Rubin Erdely, "Kiki Kannibal: The Girl Who Played with Fire" [e-Pages], first published in *Rolling Stone Magazine*, April 28, 2011.

Thomas L. Friedman, "The Dell Theory of Conflict Prevention," from *The World Is Flat: A Brief History of the Twenty-First Century* (updated and expanded; further updated and expanded) by Thomas L. Friedman. Copyright © 2005, 2006, 2007 by Thomas L. Friedman. Reprinted by permission of Farrar, Straus and Giroux, LLC.

Francis Fukuyama, "Human Dignity," from *Our Posthuman Future: Consequences of the Biotechnology Revolution* by Francis Fukuyama. Copyright © 2002 by Francis Fukuyama. Reprinted by permission of Farrar, Straus and Giroux, LLC.

Daniel Gilbert, "Reporting Live from Tomorrow," from *Stumbling on Happiness* by Daniel Gilbert. Copyright © 2006 by Daniel Gilbert. Used by permission of Alfred A. Knopf, a division of Random House, Inc.

Malcolm Gladwell, "Small Change: Why the Revolution Will Not Be Tweeted." Copyright © 2010 by Malcolm Gladwell. Originally published in the *New Yorker*. Reprinted by permission of the author.

Hal Herzog, from *Some We Love, Some We Hate, Some We Eat*, pp. 1–11. Copyright © 2010 by Hal Herzog. Reprinted by permission of HarperCollins Publishers.

Peter Singer, "Visible Man: Ethics in a World without Secrets." Copyright © 2011 by *Harper's Magazine*. All rights reserved. Reproduced from the August issue by special permission.

James Surowiecki, "Committees, Juries, and Teams: The *Columbia* Disaster and How Small Groups Can Be Made to Work" from *The Wisdom of Crowds: Why the Many Are Smarter Than the Few and How Collective Wisdom Shapes Business, Economies, Societies, and Nations* by James Surowiecki. Copyright © 2004 by James Surowiecki. Used by permission of Doubleday, a division of Random House, Inc.

Urvashi Vaid, "Action Makes It Better" from *It Gets Better*, ed. by Dan Savage and Terry Miller (Dutton 2011) is reprinted by permission of Urvashi Vaid.

Tom Vanderbilt, from *Traffic: Why We Drive the Way We Do (and What It Says about Us)*. Copyright © 2008 by Tom Vanderbilt. Used by permission of Alfred A. Knopf, a division of Random House, Inc.

David Foster Wallace, from *Consider the Lobster* by David Foster Wallace. Copyright © 2005 by David Foster Wallace. By permission of Little, Brown and Company. All rights reserved.

Bill Wasik, "My Crowd Experiment: The Mob Project" from *And Then There's This* by Bill Wasik. Copyright © 2009 by Bill Wasik. Used by permission of Viking Penguin, a division of Penguin Group (USA), Inc.

Wired.com, "Call of Duty: Afghanistan" [e-Pages], courtesy of Video Department, *Wired*, Condé Nast.

Wesley Yang, "Paper Tigers" from *New York* magazine, May 16, 2011, is reprinted by permission of the publisher.

Kenji Yoshino, from *Covering* by Kenji Yoshino. Copyright © 2006 by Kenji Yoshino. Used by permission of Random House, Inc.

Art Credits

Author Photos

Aburawa: Ikem Nzeribe
Alvarez: Ramon Espinosa/AP Photo
Appiah: Corbis News/Corbis
Arora: Namit Arora
Barboza [e-Pages]: Naum Kazhdan/The *New York Times*/Redux
Christian: Michael Langan
Churchland: Niines Minguez
Dickinson: Element One Studio. Courtesy of Elizabeth Dickinson
Duhigg [e-Pages]: Earl Wilson/The *New York Times*/Redux
Epstein: Peter Peter
Erdely [e-Pages]: Karen Rubin
Friedman: Greg Martin
Fukuyama: Eric Feferberg/Getty Images
Gilbert: Rich Friedman/Corbis
Gladwell: Brooke Williams
Herzog: Western Carolina University
Hvistendahl: Courtesy of Public Affairs
Kadish: Andrew Kelly
Levy: Courtesy of Ariel Levy
Marantz: Sarah Lustbader
Martinet [e-Pages]: Drake Martinet. @withdrake, Instagram
Mumford: Steve Mumford
Muñoz: Stuart Bernstein
Olson: Haraz N. Ghanbari/AP Photo
Poisson: David Cooper/*Toronto Star*

Pollan: Corbis News/Corbis
Pozner: Thomas Lascher
Restak: Courtesy of Rodale Press
Samuel [e-Pages]: Kris Klüg
Savage: Marius Bugge
Savan: Jerry Bauer
Singer: Princeton University, Office of Communications
Surowiecki: David Surowiecki/Getty Images
Vaid: Photography © Jurek Wajdowicz
Vanderbilt: Kate Burton
Wallace: Corbis
Wasik: *Wired Magazine*
Yang: Marco Grob/Trunk Archive
Yoshino: Julia Lovallo

Cover Images

Aburawa: Courtesy of Bitch Media. www.bitchmedia.org.
Albright: Book cover from *The Mighty and the Almighty: Reflections on America, God, and World Affairs* by
    Madeleine Albright. Copyright © 2006 by Madeleine Albright.
Alvarez: Cover design by Roseanne J. Serra; cover photo by Trujillo-Paumier/Getty Images. Courtesy of
    Penguin Group.
Appiah: From *Cosmopolitanism: Ethics in a World of Strangers* by Kwame Anthony Appiah. Used by
    permission of W. W. Norton and Company, Inc.
Arora: *Humanist Magazine.* Reprinted with permission. Dreamstime.com.
Christian: Jacket cover copyright © 2011 by Doubleday, a division of Random House, Inc., from *The Most
    Human Human: What Talking with Computers Teaches Us About What It Means to Be Alive,* by Brian
    Christian. Used by permission of Doubleday, a division of Random House, Inc.
Churchland: *Braintrust* © 2011 Princeton University Press. Reprinted with permission.
The Dalai Lama: Jacket cover from *The Universe in a Single Atom: The Convergence of Science and Spiritual-
    ity* by His Holiness The Dalai Lama. Used by permission of an imprint of the Doubleday Broadway, a
    division of Random House, Inc.
Dickinson: Courtesy of *Foreign Policy.*
Epstein: Courtesy of Picador Press.
Friedman: Courtesy of Picador Press.
Fukuyama: Courtesy of Picador Press.
Gilbert: Book cover copyright © 2006 by Alfred A. Knopf, from *Stumbling on Happiness* by Daniel Gilbert.
    Used by permission of Alfred A. Knopf, a division of Random House, Inc.
Gladwell: David Hockney Cover for the *New Yorker* October 4, 2010 issue. "The Breakfast Plate," 2010 iPad
    Drawing © David Hockney.
Herzog: Permission granted by HarperCollins.
Hvistendahl: Courtesy of Public Affairs.
Kadish: Courtesy of *Utne Reader.*
Levy: Courtesy of Simon & Schuster–Free Press.
Marantz: Courtesy of *Mother Jones.*
Mumford: Courtesy of *Harper's Magazine.* Cover designed by Roger Black and Scott MacNeil.
Muñoz: From the *New York Times*, August 1, 2007. © 2007 the *New York Times*. All rights reserved.
        Used by permission and protected by the Copyright Laws of the United States. The printing, copying,
        redistribution, or retransmission of this Content without express written permission is prohibited.
Nathan: *My Freshman Year* by Rebekah Nathan, 2005 Penguin edition.
Olson: Cover of *Mapping Human History* by Steve Olson (Boston: Mariner Books, 2003).
Poe: Courtesy of the *Atlantic Monthly.*
Pollan: *The Omnivore's Dilemma* by Michael Pollan, 2006 Penguin Press edition.
PostSecret: HarperCollins.
Pozner: Courtesy of the Perseus Books Group.
Restak: Courtesy of Rodale Press.

Savage/Vaid: From *It Gets Better Project*.

Savan: Book cover copyright © 2005 by Alfred A. Knopf, from *Slam Dunks and No-Brainers* by Leslie Savan. Used by permission of Alfred A. Knopf, a division of Random House, Inc.

Singer: Courtesy of *Harper's Magazine*. Cover designed by Roger Black and Scott MacNeil.

Surowiecki: Jacket cover from *The Wisdom of Crowds: Why the Many Are Smarter Than the Few and How Collective Wisdom Shapes Business, Economies, Societies, and Nations* by James Surowiecki. Used by permission of Doubleday, a division of Random House, Inc.

Vanderbilt: Book cover copyright © 2008 by Alfred A. Knopf, a division of Random House, Inc., from *Traffic: Why We Drive the Way We Do (and What It Says about Us)* by Tom Vanderbilt. Used by permission of Alfred A. Knopf, a division of Random House, Inc.

Wallace: *Consider the Lobster* by David Foster Wallace. Little Brown and Company, a division of Hachette Book Group, Inc.

Wasik: From *And Then There's This* by Bill Wasik, copyright © 2009 by Bill Wasik. Used by permission of Viking Penguin, a division of Penguin Group (USA) Inc.

Yang: Photograph by Marco Grob for *New York Magazine*.

Yoshino: Book cover, copyright © 2006 by Random House, Inc., from *Covering* by Kenji Yoshino. Used by permission of Random House, Inc.

Interior Illustrations

Aburawa: All images courtesy of Bitch Media. www.bitchmedia.org.

Arora: "Average Income per U.S. Family" pie chart graphic copyright *Humanist Magazine*. Reprinted with permission.

Dickinson: All graphics courtesy of *Foreign Policy*. Photos: p. 145, ChinaFotoPress/Getty Images (t), Scott Barbour/Getty Images (b); p. 146, Behrouz Mehri/AFP/Getty Images; p. 147, Ashraf Shazly/AFP/Getty Images.

Duhigg/Barboza [e-Pages]: Photos: nurses at explosion site, Color China Photo/Associated Press; Foxconn dormitory, Ym Yik/European Pressphoto Agency; Xiaodong shrine and Foxconn plant, Ryan Pyle for the *New York Times*. "Made in China" video and "Compliance by the Numbers" graphic: from the *New York Times*, January 25, 2012: the *New York Times*. All rights reserved. Used by permission and protected by the Copyright Laws of the United States. The printing, copying, redistribution, or retransmission of this Content without express written permission is prohibited.

Erdely [e-Pages]: "Kiki's Real World" photo: Danielle Levitt/August. All other photos: Kirsten Leigh Ostrenga.

Gilbert: Graphics are copyright © 2006 by Alfred A. Knopf, from *Stumbling on Happiness* by Daniel Gilbert. Used by permission of Alfred A. Knopf, a division of Random House, Inc.

Kadish: Photos: p. 256, Noam Galai; p. 257, Gino DePinto (t), Tseela Cohen (m), Shani Zach (b); p. 258, Noam Galai (tl), Laura Kasakoff (tr), Onofrei Julian (m), Samuel Joubert (b).

Marantz: All photos by Sanjit Das/Panos. Graph courtesy of *Mother Jones*.

Mumford: All paintings used by permission of Steve Mumford.

Olson: Hawaiian migration map from *Mapping Human History* by Steve Olson. Copyright © 2002 by Steve Olson. Reprinted by permission of Houghton Mifflin Harcourt Publishing Company. All rights reserved.

Poisson: Photo by Steve Russell/*Toronto Star*.

PostSecret: All postcards from *PostSecret: Extraordinary Confessions from Ordinary Lives* by Frank Warren. Copyright © 2005 by Frank Warren. Reprinted by permissions of HarperCollins Publisher.

Samuel [e-Pages]: Illustration from VLADGRIN/Shutterstock.

Wasik: Graphics from *And Then There's This* by Bill Wasik. Copyright © 2009 by Bill Wasik. Used by permission of Viking Penguin, a division of Penguin Group (USA) Inc.

Yang: All photos by Marco Grob/Trunk Archive.